THE WILLIAM STALLINGS BOOKS ON COMPUTER AND DATA COMMUNICATIONS TECHNOLOGY

COMPUTER ORGANIZATION AND ARCHITECTURE, THIRD EDITION

A unified view of this broad field. Covers fundamentals such as CPU, control unit, microprogramming, instruction set, I/O, and memory. Also covers advanced topics such as RISC, superscalar, and parallel organization.

BUSINESS DATA COMMUNICATIONS, SECOND EDITION

A comprehensive presentation of data communications and telecommunications from a business perspective. Covers voice, data, image, and video communications and applications technology and includes a number of case studies.

OPERATING SYSTEMS, SECOND EDITION

A state-of-the art survey of operating system principles. Covers fundamental technology as well as contemporary design issues, such as threads, real-time systems, multiprocessor scheduling, distributed systems, and security.

HANDBOOK OF COMPUTER-COMMUNICATIONS STANDARDS
VOLUME I: THE OPEN SYSTEMS INTERCONNECTION (OSI) MODEL AND OSI-RELATED STANDARDS, SECOND EDITION
VOLUME 2: LOCAL AREA NETWORK STANDARDS, SECOND EDITION
VOLUME 3: THE TCP/IP PROTOCOL SUITE, SECOND EDITION

These three volumes provide comprehensive coverage of computer-communications standards. The books provide a clear tutorial exposition, a discussion of the relevance and value of each standard, an analysis of options within each standard, and an explanation of underlying technology.

NETWORK AND INTERNETWORK SECURITY PRINCIPLES AND PRACTICE

NETWORK AND INTERNETWORK SECURITY PRINCIPLES AND PRACTICE

William Stallings, Ph.D.

PRENTICE HALL, Englewood Cliffs, New Jersey 07632

  IEEE PRESS

The Institute of Electrical and Electronics Engineers, Inc., New York

LIBRARY OF CONGRESS CATALOGING-IN-PUBLICATION DATA

Stallings, William.
    Network and internetwork security : principles and practice /
William Stallings.
        p.   cm.
    Includes index.
    ISBN 0-02-415483-0
    1. Computer networks—Security measures.   2. Computer security.
I. Title.
TK5105.5.S728   1995
005.8—dc20   94-6003
                                                          CIP

Production Supervisor: John Travis
Production Manager: Francesca Drago
Cover Designer: Robert Freese

 © 1995 by Prentice-Hall, Inc.
A Division of Simon & Schuster, Inc.
Englewood Cliffs, New Jersey 07632

Printed in the United States of America

10 9 8 7 6 5 4 3 2 1

Prentice-Hall International (UK) Limited, *London*
Prentice-Hall of Australia Pty. Limited, *Sydney*
Prentice-Hall Canada, Inc., *Toronto*
Prentice-Hall Hispanoamericana, S. A., *Mexico*
Prentice-Hall of India Private Limited, *New Delhi*
Prentice-Hall of Japan, Inc., *Tokyo*
Simon & Schuster Asia Pte. Ltd., *Singapore*
Editora Prentice-Hall do Brasil, Ltda., *Rio de Janeiro*

IEEE Order Number:–PC04614
IEEE ISBN:–0-7803-1107-8

To Tricia, as always my loving wife,
and Geoffroi, Chartreux nonpareil

Preface

"The tie, if I might suggest it, sir, a shade more tightly knotted. One aims at the perfect butterfly effect. If you will permit me . . ."

"What does it matter, Jeeves, at a time like this? Do you realize that Mr. Little's domestic happiness is hanging in the scale?"

"There is no time, sir, at which ties do not matter."

> — *Very Good, Jeeves!*
>   P. G. Wodehouse

In this age of universal electronic connectivity, of viruses and hackers, of electronic eavesdropping and electronic fraud, there is indeed no time at which security does not matter. Two trends have come together to make the topic of this book of vital interest. First, the explosive growth in computer systems and their interconnections via networks has increased the dependence of both organizations and individuals on the information stored and communicated using these systems. This in turn has led to a heightened awareness of the need to protect data and resources from disclosure, to guarantee the authenticity of data and messages, and to protect systems from network-based attacks. Second, the disciplines of cryptography and network security have matured, leading to the development of practical, readily available applications to enforce network security.

Objectives

It is the purpose of this book to provide a practical survey of both the principles and practice of network and internetwork security. In the first part of the book, the basic issues to be addressed by a network security capability are explored. This part is therefore a tutorial and survey of network security technology. The second part of the book deals with the practice of network security: practical applications that have been implemented and are in use to provide network security.

The subject, and therefore this book, draws on a variety of disciplines. In particular, it is impossible to appreciate the significance of some of the techniques discussed in this book without a basic understanding of number theory and some results from probability theory. Nevertheless, an attempt has been made to make the book self-contained. The book presents not only the basic mathematical results that are needed but provides the reader with an intuitive understanding of those results. Such background material is introduced as needed, generally in the form of chapter appendices. This approach helps to motivate the material that is introduced, and the author considers this preferable to simply presenting all of the mathematical material in a lump at the beginning of the book.

Intended Audience

This book is intended for a broad range of readers interested in network security, including:

- Students and professionals in data processing and data communications: This book is designed to be both a tutorial/textbook for study and a reference volume for this exciting field.
- Designers and implementers: The book discusses the critical design issues and explores alternative approaches to meeting security requirements.
- Computer and communication system customers and managers: This book helps readers understand what features and architectures are needed in a network security facility and provides information about current and evolving standardized applications. This information provides a means of assessing specific implementations and vendor offerings.

Plan of the Book

The book is organized to clarify the unifying and differentiating concepts underlying the field of network security. The organization of chapters is as follows:

1. Overview: An introduction to the book, as well as a discussion of security threats, mechanisms, and services.

Following the overview chapter, the next five chapters provide a survey of the principles of network security.

2. Conventional Encryption: Introduces cryptography, then examines issues relating to conventional, or symmetric, encryption. The focus of the chapter is the Data Encryption Standard (DES).
3. Confidentiality Using Conventional Encryption: Discusses design issues relating to the use of conventional encryption to provide confidentiality, including the location of the encryption function, key management issues, and requirements for random number generation.
4. Public-Key Cryptology: Analyzes the principles of public-key cryptography and uses RSA as an example. The issue of key management is revisited.
5. Authentication and Digital Signatures: Provides a detailed, systematic analysis of approaches to authentication and digital signature, including a discussion of hash functions and authentication protocols.
6. Intruders, Viruses, and Worms: Discusses the various network-based threats to computer security, focusing on intruders and viruses. The chapter describes the nature of the threats and analyzes countermeasures.

The final four chapters describe network security practice, presenting algorithms and applications that are either already in widespread use or are likely to enjoy widespread use in the near future.

7. Cryptographic Algorithms: Describes important encryption and hash function algorithms, including MD5, SHA, and IDEA.
8. Authentication and Key Exchange: Describes and analyzes the most important authentication-related tools and applications, including Kerberos, X.409, the Digital Signature Standard (DSS), and the Diffie-Hellman key exchange protocol.
9. Electronic Mail Security: Provides a detailed description of the two most important security packages for electronic mail: Pretty Good Privacy (PGP) and Privacy Enhanced Mail (PEM).
10. Network Management Security: Describes and analyzes the security features in the most widely used network management standard, the Simple Network Management Protocol (SNMP).

In addition, the book includes an extensive glossary, a list of frequently used acronyms, and a bibliography. There are also end-of-chapter problems and suggestions for further reading.

This book is intended for both a professional and an academic audience. The book serves as a tutorial and basic reference volume and is suitable for self-study. As a textbook, it can be used for a one-semester course. Part I covers topics listed for two courses in the Computing Curricula 1991, developed by the ACM/IEEE Joint Curriculum Task Force: OS8 Security and Protection and the advanced course on Computer Security. The material is enhanced by the inclusion of real-world algorithms and applications in Part II.

Internet Mailing List

An internet mailing list has been set up so that instructors using this book can exchange information, suggestions, and questions with each other and with the author. To subscribe, send a message to stallings@ACM.org, giving your name, affiliation, and e-mail address. To post a message, send to ws-security@ACM.org.

Acknowledgments

This book has benefited from review by numerous experts in the field, who gave generously of their time and expertise. The following people reviewed all or a large part of the manuscript: Steve Kent , Chief Scientist, Security Technology, Bolt Beranek and Newman, M. E. Kabay, Director of Education at the National Computer Security Association, Luke O'Connor of the Information Security Research Centre at the Queensland University of Technology, Donald Henderson, Professor Emeritus, Mankato State University, T.C. Ting, Associate Dean, School of Engineering, University of Connecticut, Richard Schott, Professor at Wayne State University, Vernon Eubanks of MITRE.

In addition, I was extremely fortunate to have reviews of each of the applications in Part II by "subject-area gurus," including Ron Rivest at M.I.T. (MD5), Michael Markowitz of Information Security Corporation (SHA and DSA), Xuejia Lai of R3 Security Engineering AG (IDEA), Dorothy Denning of Georgetown University (SKIPJACK), Christopher Skinner of Cybanim Pty Ltd (LUC), Don Davis of Openvision Technologies (Kerberos), Steve Kent (X.509, PEM), and Phil Zimmermann of Boulder Software Engineering (PGP).

Also, I would like to acknowledge those who contributed homework problems: Luke O'Connor, Joseph Kusmiss of MITRE, Carl Ellison of Stratus, Shunmugavel Rajarathinam, and Jozef Vyskoc, who contributed those marvelous Sherlock Holmes problems.

With all this assistance, little remains for which I can take full credit. However, I am proud to say that, with no help whatsoever, I selected all of the quotations.

W. S.

CONTENTS

CHAPTER 1

OVERVIEW

*The combination of space, time, and strength that must be considered as the basic
elements of this theory of defense makes this a fairly complicated matter. Consequently,
it is not easy to find a fixed point of departure.*

> — *On War*
> Carl Von Clausewitz

*With the end of the Cold War and the resulting shift in focus from military to economic
power, there is evidence that economic espionage has become a growing problem for
U.S. companies at home and abroad.*

> — *Communications Privacy: Federal Policy and Actions*
> General Accounting Office Report GAO/OSI-94-2
> November 1993

*Security is a concern of organizations with assets that are controlled by computer
systems. By accessing or altering data, an attacker can steal tangible assets or lead an
organization to take actions it would not otherwise take. By merely examining data, an
attacker can gain a competitive advantage, without the owner of the data being any the
wiser.*

> — *Computers at Risk: Safe Computing in the Information Age*
> National Research Council, 1991

The requirements of **information security** within an organization have undergone
two major changes in the last several decades. Before the widespread use of data
processing equipment, the security of information felt to be valuable to an organization was provided primarily by physical and administrative means. An example
of the former is the use of rugged filing cabinets with a combination lock for stor-
ing sensitive documents. An example of the latter is personnel screening procedures used during the hiring process.

With the introduction of the computer, the need for automated tools for protecting files and other information stored on the computer became evident. This is
especially the case for a shared system, such as a time-sharing system, and the
need is even more acute for systems that can be accessed over a public telephone
or data network. The generic name for the collection of tools designed to protect
data and to thwart hackers is **computer security.**

The second major change that affected security is the introduction of distributed systems and the use of networks and communications facilities for carrying data between terminal user and computer and between computer and computer. **Network security** measures are needed to protect data during their transmission. In fact, the term *network security* is somewhat misleading, because virtually all business, government, and academic organizations interconnect their data processing equipment with a collection of interconnected networks. Such a collection is often referred to as an *internetwork*.[1] Hence, the title of this book refers to **internetwork security.**

There are no clear boundaries between these three forms of security. For example, one of the most publicized types of attack on information systems is the computer virus. A virus may be introduced into a system physically when it arrives on a diskette and is subsequently loaded onto a computer. Viruses may also arrive over an internetwork. In either case, once the virus is resident on a computer system, internal computer security tools are needed to detect and recover from the virus.

This book focuses on internetwork security, which consists of measures to deter, prevent, detect, and correct security violations that involve the transmission of information. Now, that is a broad statement that covers a host of possibilities. To give you a feel for the areas covered in this book, consider the following examples of security violations:

1. User A transmits a file to user B. The file contains sensitive information (e.g., payroll records) that are to be protected from disclosure. User C, who is not authorized to read the file, is able to monitor the transmission and capture a copy of the file during its transmission.

2. A network manager, D, transmits a message to a computer, E, under its management. The message instructs computer E to update an authorization file to include the identities of a number of new users who are to be given access to that computer. User F intercepts the message, alters its contents to add or delete entries, and then forwards the message to E, which accepts the message as coming from manager D and updates its authorization file accordingly.

3. Rather than intercept a message, user F constructs its own message with the desired entries and transmits that message to E *as if it had come from manager D.* Computer E accepts the message as coming from manager D and updates its authorization file accordingly.

4. An employee is fired without warning. The personnel manager sends a message to a server system to invalidate the employee's account. When the invalidation is accomplished, the server is to post a notice to the employee's file as confirmation of the action. The employee is able to intercept the message and delay it long enough to make a final access to the server to retrieve sensitive in-

---

[1]Not to be confused with the term *Internet*. The term *Internet*, with a capital *I*, refers to a specific collection of networks that has become something of a global public networking utility. Thousands of networks and hundreds of thousands of hosts constitute the Internet, which supports millions of users. The Internet may be one of the facilities used by an organization to construct its internetwork.

formation. The message is then forwarded, the action taken, and the confirmation posted. The employee's action may go·unnoticed for some considerable time.

5. A message is sent from a customer to a stock broker with instructions for various transactions. Subsequently, the investments lose value and the customer denies sending the message.

Although this list by no means exhausts the possible types of security violations, it illustrates the range of concerns of internetwork security.

Internetwork security is both fascinating and complex. Some of the reasons follow:

1. Security involving communications and networks is not as simple as it might first appear to the novice. The requirements seem to be straightforward; indeed, most of the major requirements for security services can be given self-explanatory one-word labels: confidentiality, authentication, nonrepudiation, integrity. But the mechanisms used to meet those requirements can be quite complex, and understanding them may involve rather subtle reasoning.

2. In developing a particular security mechanism or algorithm, one must always consider potential countermeasures. In many cases, countermeasures are designed by looking at the problem in a completely different way, thereby exploiting an unexpected weakness in the mechanism.

3. Because of point (2), the procedures used to provide particular services are often counterintuitive: It is not obvious from the statement of a particular requirement that such elaborate measures are needed. It is only when the various countermeasures are considered that the measures used make sense.

4. Having designed various security mechanisms, it is necessary to decide where to use them. This is true both in terms of physical placement (e.g., at what points in a network are certain security mechanisms needed) and in a logical sense (e.g., at what layer or layers of an architecture such as TCP/IP should mechanisms be placed).

5. Security mechanisms usually involve more than a particular algorithm or protocol. They usually also require that participants be in possession of some secret information (e.g., an encryption key), which raises questions about the creation, distribution, and protection of that secret information. There is also a reliance on communications protocols whose behavior may complicate the task of developing the security mechanism. For example, if the proper functioning of the security mechanism requires setting time limits on the transit time of a message from sender to receiver, then any protocol or network that introduces variable, unpredictable delays may render such time limits meaningless.

Thus, there is much to consider. This chapter provides a general overview of the subject matter that structures the material in the remainder of the book. We begin with a discussion of the types of attacks that create the need for internetwork security services and mechanisms. Then we develop a very general overall model within which the security services and mechanisms can be viewed.

ATTACKS, SERVICES, AND MECHANISMS

To assess the security needs of an organization effectively and to evaluate and choose various security products and policies, the manager responsible for security needs some systematic way of defining the requirements for security and characterizing the approaches to satisfying those requirements. One approach is to consider three aspects of information security:

- *Security attack:* Any action that compromises the security of information owned by an organization.
- *Security mechanism:* A mechanism that is designed to detect, prevent, or recover from a security attack.
- *Security service:* A service that enhances the security of the data processing systems and the information transfers of an organization. The service counters security attacks and makes use of one or more security mechanisms to provide the service.

Services

Let us consider these topics briefly, in reverse order. We can think of information security services as replicating the types of functions normally associated with physical documents. Much of the activity of humankind, in areas as diverse as commerce, foreign policy, military action, and personal interactions, depends on the use of documents and on both parties to a transaction having confidence in the integrity of those documents. Documents typically have signatures and dates; they may need to be protected from disclosure, tampering, or destruction; they may be notarized or witnessed; they may be recorded or licensed; and so on.

As information systems become ever more pervasive and essential to the conduct of our affairs, electronic information takes on many of the roles traditionally performed by paper documents. Accordingly, the types of functions traditionally associated with paper documents must be performed on documents that exist in electronic form. Several aspects of electronic documents make the provision of such functions or services challenging:

1. It is usually possible to discriminate between an original paper document and a xerographic copy. However, an electronic document is merely a sequence of bits; there is no difference whatsoever between the "original" and any number of copies.
2. An alteration to a paper document may leave some sort of physical evidence of the alteration. For example, an erasure can result in a thin spot or a roughness in the surface. Altering bits in a computer memory or in a signal leaves no physical trace.
3. Any "proof" process associated with a physical document typically depends on the physical characteristics of that document (e.g., the shape of a handwritten

TABLE 1.1   A Partial List of Common Information Integrity Functions[a]

Identification	Endorsement
Authorization	Access (egress)
License and/or certification	Validation
Signature	Time of occurrence
Witnessing (notarization)	Authenticity—software and/or files
Concurrence	Vote
Liability	Ownership
Receipts	Registration
Certification of origination and/or receipt	Approval/disapproval
	Privacy (secrecy)

[a]From [SIMM92b].

signature or an embossed notary seal). Any such proof of the authenticity of an electronic document must be based on internal evidence present in the information itself.

Table 1.1 lists some of the common functions traditionally associated with documents and for which some analogous function for electronic documents and messages is required. We can think of these functions as requirements to be met by a security facility.

The list of Table 1.1 is lengthy and is not by itself a useful guide to organizing a security facility. Computer and network security research and development have instead focused on three or four general security services that encompass the various functions required of an information security facility. One useful classification[2] of security services is the following:

- *Confidentiality:* Requires that the information in a computer system and transmitted information be accessible only for reading by authorized parties. This type of access includes printing, displaying, and other forms of disclosure, including simply revealing the existence of an object.
- *Authentication:* Requires that the origin of a message be correctly identified, with an assurance that the identity is not false.
- *Integrity:* Requires that computer system assets and transmitted information be capable of modification only by authorized parties. Modification includes writing, changing, changing status, deleting, creating, and the delaying or replaying of transmitted messages.
- *Nonrepudiation:* Requires that neither the sender nor the receiver of a message be able to deny the transmission.
- *Access control:* Requires that access to information resources be controlled by or for the target system.

---

[2]There is no universal agreement about many of the terms used in the security literature. For example, the term *integrity* is sometimes used to refer to all aspects of information security. The term *authenticity* is sometimes used to refer both to verification of identity and to the various functions listed under integrity in the following list.

- *Availability:* Requires that computer system assets be available to authorized parties when needed.

Mechanisms

There is no single mechanism that will provide all the services just listed or perform all the functions listed in Table 1.1. As the book proceeds, we will see a variety of mechanisms that come into play. However, we can note at this point that there is one particular element that underlies most of the security mechanisms in use: cryptographic techniques. Encryption or encryption-like transformations of information are the most common means of providing security. Thus, this book focuses on the development, use, and management of such techniques.

TABLE 1.2   Reasons for Cheating[a]

1. Gain unauthorized access to information (i.e., violate secrecy or privacy).
2. Impersonate another user either to shift responsibility (i.e., liability) or else to use the other's license for the purpose of:
   a. originating fraudulent information,
   b. modifying legitimate information,
   c. using fraudulent identity to gain unauthorized access,
   d. fraudulently authorizing transactions or endorsing them.
3. Disavow responsibility or liability for information that the cheater did originate.
4. Claim to have received from some other user information that the cheater created (i.e., fraudulent attribution of responsibility or liability).
5. Claim to have sent to a receiver (at a specified time) information that was not sent (or was sent at a different time).
6. Either disavow receipt of information that was in fact received, or claim a false time of receipt.
7. Enlarge cheater's legitimate license (for access, origination, distribution, etc.).
8. Modify (without authority to do so) the license of others (fraudulently enroll others, restrict or enlarge existing licenses, etc.).
9. Conceal the presence of some information (a covert communication) in other information (the overt communication).
10. Insert self into a communications link between other users as an active (undetected) relay point.
11. Learn who accesses which information (sources, files, etc.) and when the accesses are made (even if the information itself remains concealed) (e.g., a generalization of traffic analysis from communications channels to data bases, software, etc.).
12. Impeach an information integrity protocol by revealing information that the cheater is supposed to (by the terms of the protocol) keep secret.
13. Pervert the function of software, typically by adding a covert function.
14. Cause others to violate a protocol by means of introducing incorrect information.
15. Undermine confidence in a protocol by causing apparent failures in the system.
16. Prevent communication among other users, in particular surreptitious interference to cause authentic communications to be rejected as unauthentic.

[a]From [SIMM92b].

Attacks

As G. J. Simmons perceptively points out, information security is about how to prevent cheating, or failing that, to detect cheating in information-based systems wherein the information itself has no meaningful physical existence [SIMM92a].

Table 1.2 lists some of the more obvious examples of cheating, each of which has arisen in a number of real-world cases. These are examples of specific attacks that an organization or an individual (or an organization on behalf of its employees) may need to counter. The nature of the attack that concerns an organization varies greatly from one set of circumstances to another. Fortunately, we can approach the problem from a different angle by looking at the generic types of attack that might be encountered. That is the subject of the next section.

1.2

SECURITY ATTACKS

The types of attacks on the security of a computer system or network are best characterized by viewing the function of the computer system as providing information. In general, there is a flow of information from a source, such as a file or a region of main memory, to a destination, such as another file or a user. This normal flow is depicted in Figure 1.1(a). The remaining parts of the figure show the following four general categories of attack:

- *Interruption:* An asset of the system is destroyed or becomes unavailable or unusable. This is an attack on **availability.** Examples include destruction of a piece of hardware, such as a hard disk, the cutting of a communication line, or the disabling of the file management system.
- *Interception:* An unauthorized party gains access to an asset. This is an attack on **confidentiality.** The unauthorized party could be a person, a program, or a computer. Examples include wiretapping to capture data in a network, and the illicit copying of files or programs.
- *Modification:* An unauthorized party not only gains access to but tampers with an asset. This is an attack on **integrity.** Examples include changing values in a data file, altering a program so that it performs differently, and modifying the content of messages being transmitted in a network.
- *Fabrication:* An unauthorized party inserts counterfeit objects into the system. This is an attack on **authenticity.** Examples include the insertion of spurious messages in a network or the addition of records to a file.

A useful categorization of these attacks is in terms of passive attacks and active attacks (Figure 1.2).[3]

---

[3]The categorization of attacks in this section is based on one initially proposed by Steve Kent [KENT77]. This breakdown is still valid today and is the basis for most descriptions of security attacks.

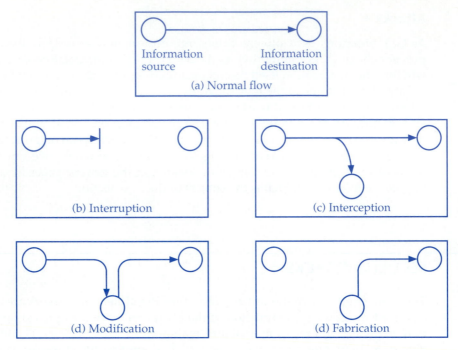

FIGURE 1.1.   Security Threats

Passive Attacks

Passive attacks are in the nature of eavesdropping on, or monitoring of, transmissions. The goal of the opponent is to obtain information that is being transmitted. Two types of attacks are involved here: release of message contents and traffic analysis.

The **release of message contents** is easily understood. A telephone conversation, an electronic mail message, a transferred file may contain sensitive or confidential information. We would like to prevent the opponent from learning the contents of these transmissions.

The second passive attack, **traffic analysis,** is more subtle. Suppose that we had a way of masking the contents of messages or other information traffic so that opponents, even if they captured the message, could not extract the information from the message. The common technique for masking contents is encryption. If we had encryption protection in place, an opponent might still be able to observe the pattern of these messages. The opponent could determine the location and identity of communicating hosts and could observe the frequency and length of messages being exchanged. This information might be useful in guessing the nature of the communication that was taking place.

Passive attacks are very difficult to detect since they do not involve any alteration of the data. However, it is feasible to prevent the success of these attacks.

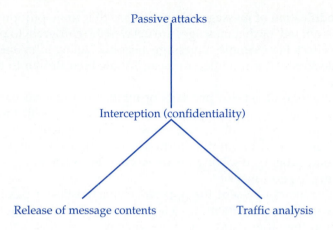

FIGURE 1.2.   **Active and Passive Network Threats to Security**

Thus, the emphasis in dealing with passive attacks is on prevention rather than detection.

Active Attacks

The second major category of attack is **active attacks.** These attacks involve some modification of the data stream or the creation of a false stream and can be subdivided into four categories: masquerade, replay, modification of messages, and denial of service.

A **masquerade** takes place when one entity pretends to be a different entity. A masquerade attack usually includes one of the other forms of active attack. For example, authentication sequences can be captured and replayed after a valid authentication sequence has taken place, thus enabling an authorized entity with few privileges to obtain extra privileges by impersonating an entity that has those privileges.

Replay involves the passive capture of a data unit and its subsequent retransmission to produce an unauthorized effect.

Modification of messages simply means that some portion of a legitimate message is altered, or that messages are delayed or reordered, to produce an unauthorized effect. For example, a message meaning "Allow John Smith to read confidential file *accounts*" is modified to mean "Allow Fred Brown to read confidential file *accounts.*"

The **denial of service** prevents or inhibits the normal use or management of communications facilities. This attack may have a specific target; for example, an entity may suppress all messages directed to a particular destination (e.g., the security audit service). Another form of service denial is the disruption of an entire network, either by disabling the network or by overloading it with messages so as to degrade performance.

Active attacks present the opposite characteristics of passive attacks. Whereas passive attacks are difficult to detect, measures are available to prevent their success. On the other hand, it is quite difficult to prevent active attacks absolutely, since to do so would require physical protection of all communications facilities and paths at all times. Instead, the goal is to detect them and to recover from any disruption or delays caused by them. Because the detection has a deterrent effect, it may also contribute to prevention.

1.3

SECURITY SERVICES

Confidentiality

Confidentiality is the protection of transmitted data from passive attacks. With respect to the release of message contents, several levels of protection can be identified. The broadest service protects all user data transmitted between two users over a period of time. For example, if a virtual circuit is set up between two systems, this broad protection would prevent the release of any user data transmitted over the virtual circuit. Narrower forms of this service can also be defined, including the protection of a single message or even specific fields within a message. These refinements are less useful than the broad approach and may even be more complex and expensive to implement.

The other aspect of confidentiality is the protection of traffic flow from analysis. This requires that an attacker not be able to observe the source and destination, frequency, length, or other characteristics of the traffic on a communications facility.

Authentication

The authentication service is concerned with assuring that a communication is authentic. In the case of a single message, such as a warning or alarm signal, the function of the authentication service is to assure the recipient that the message is from the source that it claims to be from. In the case of an ongoing interaction, such as the connection of a terminal to a host, two aspects are involved. First, at the time of connection initiation, the service assures that the two entities are authentic, that is, that each is the entity that it claims to be. Second, the service must assure that the connection is not interfered with in such a way that a third party can masquerade as one of the two legitimate parties for the purposes of unauthorized transmission or reception.

Integrity

As with confidentiality, integrity can apply to a stream of messages, a single message, or selected fields within a message. Again, the most useful and straightforward approach is total stream protection.

A connection-oriented integrity service, one that deals with a stream of messages, assures that messages are received as sent, with no duplication, insertion, modification, reordering, or replays. The destruction of data is also covered under this service. Thus, the connection-oriented integrity service addresses both message stream modification and denial of service. On the other hand, a connectionless integrity service, one that deals with individual messages only without regard to any larger context, generally provides protection against message modification only. Kent points out that a hybrid service can be offered for applications that require some protection against replay and reordering but that do not require strict sequencing [KENT93a]. One example of such an application is SNMPv2, discussed in Chapter 10.

We can make a distinction between the service with and without recovery. Because the integrity service relates to active attacks, we are concerned with detection rather than prevention. If a violation of integrity is detected, then the service may simply report this violation, and some other portion of software or human intervention is required to recover from the violation. Alternatively, there are mechanisms available to recover from the loss of integrity of data. We will review them subsequently. The incorporation of automated recovery mechanisms is in general the more attractive alternative.

Nonrepudiation

Nonrepudiation prevents either sender or receiver from denying a transmitted message. Thus, when a message is sent, the receiver can prove that the message was in fact sent by the alleged sender. Similarly, when a message is received, the sender can prove that the message was in fact received by the alleged receiver.

Access Control

In the context of network security, access control is the ability to limit and control the access to host systems and applications via communications links. To achieve this control, each entity trying to gain access must first be identified, or authenticated, so that access rights can be tailored to the individual.

Availability

A variety of attacks can result in the loss of or reduction in availability. Some of these attacks are amenable to automated countermeasures, such as authentication and encryption, whereas others require some sort of physical action to prevent or recover from loss of availability of elements of a distributed system.

1.4

A MODEL FOR INTERNETWORK SECURITY

A model for much of what we will be discussing is captured, in very general terms, in Figure 1.3. A message is to be transferred from one party to another across some sort of internetwork. The two parties, who are the *principals* in this transaction, must cooperate for the exchange to take place. A logical information channel is established by defining a route through the internetwork from source to destination and by the cooperative use of communication protocols (e.g., TCP/IP) by the two principals.

Security aspects come into play when it is necessary or desirable to protect the information transmission from an opponent who may present a threat to confidentiality, authenticity, and so on. All the techniques for providing security have two components:

- A security-related transformation on the information to be sent. Examples include the encryption of the message, which scrambles it so that it is unreadable by the opponent, and the addition of a code based on the contents of the message, which can be used to verify the identity of the sender.
- Some secret information shared by the two principals and, it is hoped, unknown to the opponent. An example is an encryption key used in conjunction with the transformation to scramble the message before transmission and unscramble it on reception.[4]

A trusted third party may be needed to achieve secure transmission. For example, a third party may be responsible for distributing the secret information to the two principals while keeping it from any opponent. Or a third party may be needed to arbitrate disputes between the two principals concerning the authenticity of a message transmission.

This general model shows us that there are four basic tasks in designing a particular security service:

---

[4]Chapter 4 discusses a form of encryption, known as public-key encryption, in which only one of the two principals needs to have the secret information.

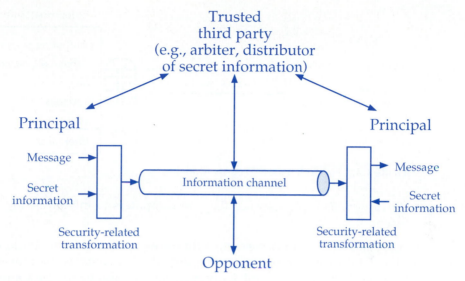

FIGURE 1.3. Model for Network Security

1. Design an algorithm for performing the security-related transformation. The algorithm should be such that an opponent cannot defeat its purpose.
2. Generate the secret information to be used with the algorithm.
3. Develop methods for the distribution and sharing of the secret information.
4. Specify a protocol to be used by the two principals that makes use of the security algorithm and the secret information to achieve a particular security service.

This book concentrates on the types of security mechanisms and services that fit into the model shown in Figure 1.3. However, there are other security-related situations of interest that do not neatly fit this model but that are considered in this book. A general model of these other situations is illustrated by Figure 1.4, which reflects a concern for protecting an information system from unwanted access. Most readers are familiar with the concerns caused by the existence of hackers who attempt to penetrate systems that can be accessed over a network. The hacker can be someone who with no malign intent simply gets satisfaction from breaking and entering a computer system. Or, the intruder can be a disgruntled employee who wishes to do damage, or a criminal who seeks to exploit computer assets for financial gain (e.g., obtaining credit card numbers or performing illegal money transfers).

Another type of unwanted access is the placement in a computer system of logic that exploits vulnerabilities in the system and that can affect application programs as well as utility programs such as editors and compilers. Two kinds of threats can be presented by programs:

- *Information access threats* intercept or modify data on behalf of users who should not have access to those data.

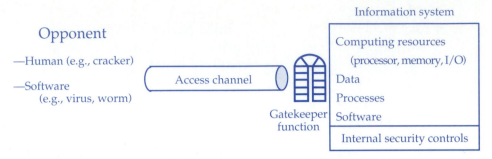

FIGURE 1.4.   Network Access Security Model

- *Service threats* exploit service flaws in computers to inhibit use by legitimate users.

Viruses and worms are two examples of software attacks. Such attacks can be introduced into a system by means of a diskette that contains the unwanted logic concealed in otherwise useful software. They can also be inserted into a system across a network; this latter mechanism is of more concern in internetwork security.

The security mechanisms needed to cope with unwanted access fall into two broad categories (see Figure 1.4). The first category might be termed a gatekeeper function. It includes password-based log-in procedures that are designed to deny access to all but authorized users and screening logic that is designed to detect and reject worms, viruses, and other similar attacks. Once access is gained, by either an unwanted user or unwanted software, the second line of defense consists of a variety of internal controls that monitor activity and analyze stored information in an attempt to detect the presence of unwanted intruders.

1.5

OUTLINE OF THE BOOK

Chapter Summary

This chapter serves as an introduction to the entire book. A brief synopsis of the remaining chapters follows.

Conventional Encryption

By far the most important automated tool for network and communications security is encryption. Two forms of encryption are in common use: conventional, or symmetric, encryption and public-key, or asymmetric, encryption. Chapter 2 describes conventional encryption techniques, with an emphasis on the most widely used encryption technique, the data encryption standard (DES). The chapter includes a discussion of design considerations and cryptanalysis.

Confidentiality Using Conventional Encryption

Beyond questions dealing with the actual construction of a conventional encryption algorithm, a number of design issues relate to the use of conventional encryption to provide confidentiality. Chapter 3 surveys the most important of these issues. The chapter includes a discussion of end-to-end versus link encryption, techniques for achieving traffic confidentiality, and key distribution techniques. An important related topic, random number generation, is also addressed.

Public-Key Encryption

After conventional encryption, the other major form of encryption is public-key encryption, which has revolutionized communications security. Chapter 4 introduces public-key encryption and concentrates on its use to provide confidentiality. The Rivest–Shamir–Adleman (RSA) algorithm is examined in detail, and the issue of key management is reconsidered. Many public-key schemes are based on number theory; an appendix to the chapter provides a basic introduction to the subject.

Authentication and Digital Signatures

Of equal importance to confidentiality as a security measure is authentication. At a minimum, message authentication assures that a message comes from the alleged source. In addition, authentication can include protection against modification, delay, replay, and reordering. Chapter 5 begins with an analysis of the requirements for authentication and then provides a systematic presentation of approaches to authentication. A key element of authentication schemes is the use of an authenticator, usually either a cryptographic checksum or a hash function. Both of these types of algorithms are examined. An important type of authentication is the digital signature. The chapter examines the techniques used to construct digital signatures.

The various authentication techniques are building blocks in putting together authentication algorithms. The design of such algorithms involves the analysis of subtle attacks that can defeat many apparently secure protocols. This issue is also addressed in Chapter 5.

Intruders, Viruses, and Worms

Chapter 6 examines a variety of information access and service threats presented by hackers and programs that exploit vulnerabilities in network-based computing systems. The chapter begins with a discussion of the types of attacks that can be made by unauthorized users, or intruders, and analyzes various approaches to prevention and detection. Programmed threats, including viruses and worms, are then discussed. In addition to analyzing specific countermeasures, the chapter describes a general approach to meeting all these threats: trusted system technology.

Cryptographic Algorithms

Chapter 7 describes a number of specific cryptographic algorithms that, in addition to DES and RSA (described in Chapters 2 and 4, respectively), are important components of contemporary applications or have significant promise for future use. Two hash functions are described:

- MD5 message digest algorithm: This important hash function is perhaps the most popular algorithm for providing authentication and digital signatures in a variety of applications.
- Secure Hash Algorithm (SHA): SHA is similar to MD5 and has been issued by the U.S. National Institute of Standards and Technology (NIST) as a federal standard.

Three encryption algorithms are also discussed:

- International Data Encryption Algorithm (IDEA): Proposed as an international encryption standard, IDEA has received widespread support as a successor to DES and is already widely used.
- SKIPJACK: This algorithm was developed by the National Security Agency (NSA) to provide a tool for secure voice and data communications and at the same time provide access to authorized law enforcement agencies for wiretapping.
- LUC: LUC is a public-key algorithm of comparable strength and efficiency to RSA.

Authentication Applications

Chapter 8 is a survey of some of the most important authentication algorithms in current use. Kerberos is an authentication protocol based on conventional encryption that has received widespread support and is used in a variety of systems. X.509 specifies an authentication algorithm and defines a certificate facility. The latter enables users to obtain certificates of public keys so that a community of users can have confidence in the validity of the public keys. This facility can be used in the context of the X.500 Directory service but is also employed as a building block in other applications. The Digital Signature Standard (DSS) has been proposed by NIST as a federal standard. The Diffie-Hellman key exchange protocol is one of the oldest public-key schemes and is a popular means of exchanging temporary keys.

Electronic Mail Security

The most heavily used distributed application is electronic mail, and there is a growing interest in providing authentication and confidentiality services as part of an electronic mail facility. Chapter 9 looks at the two approaches likely to dominate electronic mail security in the near future. Pretty Good Privacy (PGP) is a widely used scheme that does not depend on any organization or authority. Thus, it is as well suited to individual, personal use as it is to incorporation in network configurations operated by organizations. Privacy Enhanced Mail (PEM) was developed specifically to be an Internet Standard.

Network Management Security

With the increasing use of network management systems to control multivendor networks, there is increasing demand for security capabilities. Chapter 10 focuses on the most widely used multivendor network management scheme, the Simple Network Management Protocol (SNMP). Version 1 of SNMP has only a rudimentary password-based authentication facility. Version 2 has a full-blown facility for confidentiality and authentication.

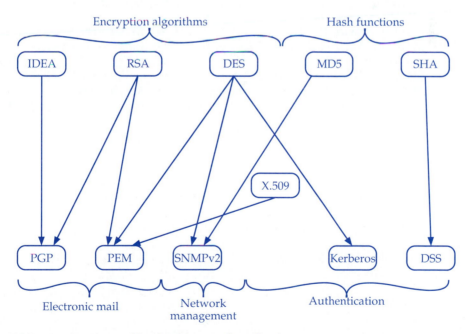

FIGURE 1.5.   Cryptographic Algorithms and Applications

Relationship Among Algorithms and Applications

Figure 1.5 illustrates the relationships among the major algorithms and applications discussed in this book. Along the top of the figure are the most widely used encryption algorithms and hash functions. The applications described in this book are arrayed along the bottom of the figure. The arrowed lines indicate which algorithms are incorporated into which applications.

1.6

RECOMMENDED READING

[PFLE89] provides a good introduction to both computer and network security. A more in-depth treatment of network security issues is found in [DAVI89]. A somewhat less technical but very broad treatment of both computer and network security is to be found in [RUSS91]. [ABRA87] contains reprints of a number of important articles and papers on computer and network security, some of which would otherwise be hard to find.

[MADR92] and [COOP89] treat the subject from a management point of view.

ABRA87   Abrams, M., and Podell, H. *Computer and Network Security.* Los Alamitos, CA:
   IEEE Computer Society Press, 1987.
COOP89   Cooper, J. *Computer and Communications Security: Strategies for the 1990s.* New
   York: McGraw-Hill, 1989.
DAVI89   Davies, D., and Price, W. *Security for Computer Networks.* New York: Wiley, 1989.
MADR92   Madron, T. *Network Security in the '90s: Issues and Solutions for Managers.* New
   York: Wiley, 1992.
PFLE89   Pfleeger, C. *Security in Computing.* Englewood Cliffs, NJ: Prentice-Hall, 1989.
PURS93   Purser, M. *Secure Data Networking.* Boston: Artech House, 1993.
RUSS91   Russel, D., and Gangemi, G. *Computer Security Basics.* Sebastopol, CA: O'Reilly &
   Associates, 1991.

PART I

INTERNETWORK SECURITY PRINCIPLES

The committee believes it is possible to enunciate a basic set of security-related principles that are so broadly applicable and effective for the design and use of systems that they ought to be a part of any system with significant operational requirements.

— *Computers at Risk: Safe Computing in the Information Age*
National Research Council, 1991

Security in an internetwork environment depends on the practical application of a number of fundamental security principles. The basic tools of internetwork security deal with protecting the content of information during transmission across a network, assuring the authenticity of network interactions, and thwarting attempts to subvert systems by means of network access capabilities. Part I provides a survey of these principles.

Chapter 2 surveys perhaps the most fundamental and widespread tool used in providing for internetwork security: conventional encryption. The chapter looks at some of the classic approaches to conventional encryption and then examines the most widely used algorithm, DES. Chapter 3 then examines how conventional encryption algorithms can be used to provide a confidentiality service. Issues addressed include the protection of messages from eavesdropping, the use of conventional encryption to distribute keys, and techniques for random number generation, the latter being an important tool in many encryption schemes.

Chapter 4 presents an overview of public-key encryption, which has transformed the way in which communications security is implemented. The chapter examines the basic principles of public-key encryption and then examines the most widely used algorithm, RSA. The chapter also discusses the issue of key management.

Of equal importance to confidentiality in communications is authenticity. Chapter 5 systematically analyzes the various approaches to authenticating messages and users, including a description of digital signatures.

Finally, Chapter 6 examines network-based threats to attached systems, including intruders, viruses, and worms.

CHAPTER 2

CONVENTIONAL ENCRYPTION

Cryptography is probably the most important aspect of communications security and is becoming increasingly important as a basic building block for computer security.

> — *Computers at Risk: Safe Computing in the Information Age*
> National Research Council, 1991

Many savages at the present day regard their names as vital parts of themselves, and therefore take great pains to conceal their real names, lest these should give to evil-disposed persons a handle by which to injure their owners.

> — *The Golden Bough*
> Sir James George Frazer

All the afternoon Mungo had been working on Stern's code, principally with the aid of the latest messages which he had copied down at the Nevin Square drop. Stern was very confident. He must be well aware London Central knew about that drop. It was obvious that they didn't care how often Mungo read their messages, so confident were they in the impenetrability of the code.

> — *Talking to Strange Men*
> Ruth Rendell

Conventional encryption, also referred to as symmetric encryption or single-key encryption, was the only type of encryption in use prior to the development of public-key encryption.[1] It remains by far the more widely used of the two types of encryption. This chapter studies a variety of conventional encryption algorithms; some of the issues surrounding the use of keys are discussed in Chapter 3.

We begin with a look at a general model for the conventional encryption process; this will enable us to understand the context within which the algorithms are used. Next, we examine a variety of algorithms in use before the computer era. We followed this with an examination of the most widely used contemporary encryption algorithm: DES.

[1]Public-key encryption was first described in the open literature in 1976; the National Security Agency (NSA) claims to have discovered it some years earlier.

CONVENTIONAL ENCRYPTION MODEL

Figure 2.1 illustrates the conventional encryption process. The original intelligible message, referred to as *plaintext,* is converted into apparently random nonsense, referred to as *ciphertext.* The encryption process consists of an algorithm and a key. The key is a value independent of the plaintext that controls the algorithm. The algorithm will produce a different output depending on the specific key being used at the time. Changing the key changes the output of the algorithm.

Once the ciphertext is produced, it is transmitted. Upon reception, the ciphertext can be transformed back to the original plaintext by using a decryption algorithm and the same key that was used for encryption.

The security of conventional encryption depends on several factors. First, the encryption algorithm must be powerful enough so that it is impractical to decrypt a message on the basis of the ciphertext alone. Beyond that, the security of conventional encryption depends on the secrecy of the key, not the secrecy of the algorithm. That is, it is assumed that it is impractical to decrypt a message on the basis of the ciphertext *plus* knowledge of the encryption/decryption algorithm. In other words, we don't need to keep the algorithm secret; we need to keep only the key secret.

This feature of conventional encryption is what makes it feasible for widespread use. The fact that the algorithm need not be kept secret means that manufacturers can and have developed low-cost chip implementations of data encryption algorithms. These chips are widely available and incorporated into a number of products. With the use of conventional encryption, the principal security problem is maintaining the secrecy of the key.

Let us take a closer look at the essential elements of a conventional encryption scheme, using Figure 2.2. There is some source for a message, which produces a message in plaintext; $X = [X_1, X_2, \ldots, X_M]$. The M elements of X are letters in some finite alphabet. Traditionally, the alphabet usually consisted of the 26 capital let-

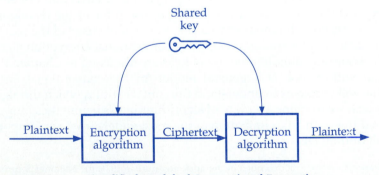

Shared
key

Plaintext → Encryption algorithm → Ciphertext → Decryption algorithm → Plaintext

FIGURE 2.1.   Simplified Model of Conventional Encryption

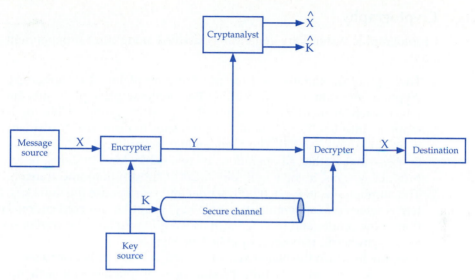

FIGURE 2.2.   Model of Conventional Cryptosystem

ters. Nowadays, the binary alphabet $\{0, 1\}$ is typically used. For encryption, a key of the form $K = [K_1, K_2, \ldots, K_J]$ is generated. If the key is generated at the message source, then it must also be provided to the destination by means of some secure channel. Alternatively, a third party could generate the key and securely deliver it to both source and destination.

With the message X and the encryption key K as input, the encryption algorithm, or encrypter, forms the ciphertext $Y = [Y_1, Y_2, \ldots, Y_N]$. We can write this as

$$Y = E_K(X)$$

This notation indicates that Y is produced by using encryption algorithm E as a function of the plaintext X, with the specific function determined by the value of the key K.

The intended receiver, in possession of the key, is able to invert the transformation:

$$X = D_K(Y)$$

An opponent, observing Y but not having access to K or X, must attempt to recover X or K or both. It is assumed that the opponent does have knowledge of the encryption (E) and decryption (D) algorithms. If the opponent is interested in only this particular message, then the focus of effort is to recover X by generating a plaintext estimate $\hat{X}$. Often, however, the opponent is interested in being able to read future messages as well, in which case an attempt is made to recover K by generating an estimate $\hat{K}$.

Cryptography

Cryptographic systems are generically classified along three independent dimensions:

1. The type of operations used for transforming plaintext to ciphertext. All encryption algorithms are based on two general principles: substitution, in which each element in the plaintext (bit, letter, group of bits or letters) is mapped into another element, and transposition, in which elements in the plaintext are rearranged. The fundamental requirement is that no information be lost—that is, that all operations be reversible. Most systems, referred to as product systems, involve multiple stages of substitutions and transpositions.
2. The number of keys used. If both sender and receiver use the same key, the system is referred to as symmetric, single-key, secret-key, or conventional encryption. If the sender and receiver each uses a different key, the system is referred to as asymmetric, two-key, or public-key encryption.
3. The way in which the plaintext is processed. A block cipher processes the input one block of elements at a time, producing an output block for each input block. A stream cipher processes the input elements continuously, producing output as it goes along.

Cryptanalysis

The process of attempting to discover X or K or both is known as *cryptanalysis*. The strategy used by the cryptanalyst depends on the nature of the encryption scheme and the information available to the cryptanalyst.

Table 2.1 summarizes the various types of cryptanalytic attacks, based on the amount of information known to the cryptanalyst. The most difficult problem is presented when all that is available is the ciphertext itself. In some cases, not even the encryption algorithm is known, but in general we can assume that the opponent does know the algorithm used for encryption. One possible attack under these circumstances is the brute-force approach of trying all possible keys. If the key space is very large, this becomes impractical. Thus, the opponent must rely on an analysis of the ciphertext itself, generally applying various statistical tests to it. To use this approach, the opponent must have some general idea of the type of plaintext that is concealed, such as English or French text, a PC-DOS EXE file, a Pascal source listing, an accounting file, and so on.

The ciphertext-only attack is the easiest to defend against, because the opponent has the least amount of information to work with. In many cases, however, the analyst has more information. The analyst may be able to capture one or more plaintext messages as well as their encryptions. Or the analyst may know that certain plaintext patterns will appear in a message. For example, a file that is encoded in the Postscript format always begins with the same pattern, or there may be a standardized header or banner to an electronic funds transfer message, and so on. All these are examples of known plaintext. With this knowledge, the analyst may be able to deduce the key on the basis of the way in which the known plaintext is transformed.

TABLE 2.1   Types of Attacks on Encrypted Message

Type of Attack	Known to Cryptanalyst
Ciphertext only	Encryption algorithm
	Ciphertext to be decoded
Known plaintext	Encryption algorithm
	Ciphertext to be decoded
	One or more plaintext-ciphertext pairs formed with the secret key
Chosen plaintext	Encryption algorithm
	Ciphertext to be decoded
	Plaintext message chosen by cryptanalyst, together with its corresponding ciphertext generated with the secret key
Chosen ciphertext	Encryption algorithm
	Ciphertext to be decoded
	Purported ciphertext chosen by cryptanalyst, together with its corresponding decrypted plaintext generated with the secret key
Chosen text	Encryption algorithm
	Ciphertext to be decoded
	Plaintext message chosen by cryptanalyst, together with its corresponding ciphertext generated with the secret key
	Purported ciphertext chosen by cryptanalyst, together with its corresponding decrypted plaintext generated with the secret key

Closely related to the known-plaintext attack is what might be referred to as a probable-word attack. If the opponent is working with the encryption of some general prose message, he or she may have little knowledge of what is in the message. However, if the opponent is after some very specific information, then parts of the message may be known. For example, if an entire accounting file is being transmitted, the opponent may know the placement of certain key words in the header of the file. As another example, the source code for a program developed by Corporation X might include a copyright statement in some standardized position.

If the analyst is able somehow to get the source system to insert into the system a message chosen by the analyst, then a chosen-plaintext attack is possible. An example of this strategy is differential cryptanalysis, explored later in this chapter. In general, if the analyst is able to choose the messages to encrypt, the analyst may deliberately pick patterns that can be expected to reveal the structure of the key.

Table 2.1 lists two other types of attack: chosen ciphertext and chosen text. These are less commonly employed as cryptanalytic techniques but are nevertheless possible avenues of attack.

Only relatively weak algorithms fail to withstand a ciphertext-only attack. Generally, an encryption algorithm is designed to withstand a known-plaintext attack.

Two more definitions are worthy of note. An encryption scheme is **unconditionally secure** if the ciphertext generated by the scheme does not contain enough information to uniquely determine the corresponding plaintext, no matter how much ciphertext is available. That is, no matter how much time an opponent has, it is impossible for him or her to decrypt the ciphertext, simply because the required information is not there. With the exception of a scheme known as the one-time pad, there is no encryption algorithm that is unconditionally secure. Therefore, all that the users of an encryption algorithm can strive for is an algorithm that meets one or both of the following criteria:

- The cost of breaking the cipher exceeds the value of the encrypted information.
- The time required to break the cipher exceeds the useful lifetime of the information.

An encryption scheme is said to be **computationally secure** if the foregoing two criteria are met. The rub is that it is very difficult to estimate the amount of effort to successfully cryptanalyze ciphertext.

As a first cut, we can consider the time required to use a brute-force approach, which simply involves trying every possible key until an intelligible translation of the ciphertext into plaintext is obtained. On average, half of all possible keys must be tried to achieve success. Table 2.2 shows how much time is involved for various key spaces. Results are shown for three binary key sizes. The 56-bit key size is used with the DES (data encryption standard) algorithm. Results are also shown for what are called substitution codes that use a 26-character key (discussed later), in which all possible permutations of the 26 characters serve as keys. For each key size, the results are shown assuming that it takes 1 μs to perform a single decryption, which is a reasonable order of magnitude for today's machines. With the use of massively parallel organizations of microprocessors, it may be possible to achieve processing rates many orders of magnitude greater. The final column of the table considers the results for a system that can process 1 million keys per microsecond. As you can see, at this performance level, DES can no longer be considered computationally secure.

All forms of cryptanalysis for conventional encryption schemes are designed to exploit the fact that traces of structure or pattern in the plaintext may survive encryption and be discernible in the ciphertext. This will become clear as we examine various conventional encryption schemes in this chapter. We will see in Chapter 4 that cryptanalysis for public-key schemes proceeds from a fundamentally different premise, namely, that the mathematical properties of the pair of keys may make it possible for one of the two keys to be deduced from the other.

TABLE 2.2 Time Required for Exhaustive Key Search

Key Size	Number of Alternative Keys	One Encryption per μs	10^6 Encryptions per μs
32 bits	2^{32} = 4.3×10^9	2^{31} μs = 35.8 minutes	2.15 ms
56 bits	2^{56} = 7.2×10^{16}	2^{55} μs = 1142 years	10.01 h
128 bits	2^{128} = 3.4×10^{38}	2^{127} μs = 5.4×10^{24} years	5.4×10^{18} years
26 characters (permutation)	26! = 4.03×10^{26}	2×10^{26} μs = 6.4×10^{12} years	6.4×10^6 years

2.2

CLASSICAL ENCRYPTION TECHNIQUES

In this section, we examine a sampling of what might be called classical encryption techniques. Although these techniques are of no direct interest for modern network security applications, a study of them enables us to illustrate the basic approaches to encryption used even today and the types of cryptanalytic attacks that must be anticipated.

We begin with a discussion of a technique that is, strictly speaking, not encryption, namely, steganography. Then we examine the two basic building blocks of all encryption techniques: substitution and transposition. Finally, systems that combine both substitution and transposition are discussed.

Steganography

A plaintext message may be hidden in one of two ways. The methods of steganography conceal the very existence of the message, whereas the methods of cryptography render the message unintelligible to outsiders by various transformations of the text.[2]

A simple form of steganography, but one that is time-consuming to construct, is one in which an arrangement of words or letters within an apparently innocuous text spells out the real message. For example, the sequence of first letters of each word of the overall message spells out the hidden message. Figure 2.3 shows an example in which a subset of the words of the overall message are used to convey the hidden message.

Various other techniques have been used historically. Some examples are the following [MYER91]:

- *Character marking:* Selected letters of printed or typewritten text are overwritten in pencil. The marks are ordinarily not visible unless the paper is held at an angle to bright light.
- *Invisible ink:* A number of substances can be used for writing but leave no visible trace until heat or some chemical is applied to the paper.
- *Pin punctures:* Small pin punctures on selected letters are ordinarily not visible unless the paper is held up in front of a light.
- *Typewriter correction ribbon:* Used between lines typed with a black ribbon, the results of typing with the correction tape are visible only under a strong light.

Although these techniques may seem archaic, they have contemporary equivalents. [WAYN93] proposes hiding a message by using the least significant bits of frames on a CD. For example, the Kodak Photo CD format's maximum resolution is 2048 by 3072 pixels, with each pixel containing 24 bits of RGB information. The least significant bit of each 24-bit pixel can be changed without greatly affecting the quality of the image. The result: You can hide a 2.3-megabyte message in a single digital snapshot.

---

[2]*Steganography* was an obsolete word that was revived by David Kahn and given the meaning it has today [KAHN67].

3rd March

Dear George,

*Greetings to all at Oxford. Many thanks for your
letter and for the Summer examination package.
All Entry Forms and Fees Forms should be ready
for final despatch to the Syndicate by Friday
20th or at the very latest, I'm told, by the 21st.
Admin has improved here, though there's room
for improvement still; just give us all two or three
more years and we'll really show you! Please
don't let these wretched 16+ proposals destroy
your basic O and A pattern. Certainly this
sort of change, if implemented immediately,
would bring chaos.*

Sincerely yours,

FIGURE 2.3.   A Puzzle for Inspector Morse (From *The Silent World of Nicholas Quinn,* **by Colin Dexter)**

Steganography has a number of drawbacks when compared to encryption. It requires a lot of overhead to hide a relatively few bits of information, although using some scheme like that proposed in the preceding paragraph may make it more effective. Also, once the system is discovered, it becomes virtually worthless. This problem, too, can be overcome if the insertion method depends on some sort of key (e.g., see Problem 2.2).

The advantage of steganography is that it can be employed by parties who have something to lose should the fact of their secret communication (not necessarily the content) be discovered. Encryption flags traffic as important or secret, or it may identify the sender or receiver as someone with something to hide.

Substitution Techniques

A substitution technique is one in which the letters of plaintext are replaced by other letters or by numbers or symbols.[3] If the plaintext is viewed as a sequence of

---

[3]When letters are involved, the following conventions are used in this book. Plaintext is always in lowercase; ciphertext is in uppercase; key values are in italicized lowercase.

bits, then substitution involves replacing plaintext bit patterns with ciphertext bit patterns.

Caesar Cipher

The earliest known use of a substitution cipher, and the simplest, was by Julius Caesar. The Caesar cipher involves replacing each letter of the alphabet with the letter standing three places further down the alphabet. For example:

```
plain:   meet me after the toga party
cipher:  PHHW PH DIWHU WKH WRJD SDUWB
```

Note that the alphabet is wrapped around, so that the letter following Z is A. We can define the transformation by exhaustively listing all possibilities, as follows:

```
plain:   a b c d e f g h i j k l m n o p q r s u v w x y z
cipher:  D E F G H I J K L M N O P Q R S U V W X Y Z A B C
```

If we assign a numerical equivalent to each letter (a = 1, b = 2, etc.), then the algorithm can be expressed as follows. For each plaintext letter p, substitute the ciphertext letter C:

$$C = E(p) = (p + 3) \bmod (26)$$

A shift may be of any amount, so that the general Caesar algorithm is:

$$C = E(p) = (p + k) \bmod (26)$$

where k takes on a value in the range 1 to 25. The decryption algorithm is simply:

$$p = D(C) = (C - k) \bmod (26)$$

If it is known that a given ciphertext is a Caesar cipher, then a brute-force cryptanalysis is easily performed: simply try all the 25 possible keys. Figure 2.4 shows the results of applying this strategy to the example ciphertext. In this case, the plaintext leaps out as occupying the third line.

Three important characteristics of this problem enabled us to use a brute-force cryptanalysis:

1. The encryption and decryption algorithms are known.
2. There are only 25 keys to try.
3. The language of the plaintext is known and easily recognizable.

In most networking situations, we can assume that the algorithms are known. What generally makes brute-force cryptanalysis impractical is the use of an algorithm that employs a large number of keys. For example, the DES algorithm, examined later in this chapter, makes use of a 56-bit key, giving a key space of 2^{56} or greater than 7×10^{16} possible keys.

The third characteristic is also significant. If the language of the plaintext is unknown, then plaintext output may not be recognizable. Furthermore, the input may be abbreviated or compressed in some fashion, again making recognition

	PHHW PH DIWHU WKH WRJD SDUWB
KEY	
1	oggv og chvgt vjg vqic rctva
2	nffu nf bgufs uif uphb qbsuz
3	meet me after the toga party
4	ldds ld zesdq sgd snfz ozqsx
5	kccr kc ydrcp rfc rmey nyprw
6	jbbq jb xcqbo qeb qldx mxoqv
7	iaap ia wbpan pda pkcw lwnpu
8	hzzo hz vaozm ocz ojbv kvmot
9	gyyn gy uznyl nby niau julns
10	fxxm fx tymxk max mhzt itkmr
11	ewwl ew sxlwj lzw lgys hsjlq
12	dvvk dv rwkvi kyv kfxr grikp
13	cuuj cu qvjuh jxu jewq fqhjo
14	btti bt puitg iwt idvp epgin
15	assh as othsf hvs hcuo dofhm
16	zrrg zr nsgre gur gbtn cnegl
17	yqqf yq mrfqd ftq fasm bmdfk
18	xppe xp lqepc esp ezrl alcej
19	wood wo kpdob dro dyqk zkbdi
20	vnnc vn jocna cqn cxpj yjach
21	ummb um inbmz bpm bwoi xizbg
22	tlla tl hmaly aol avnh whyaf
23	skkz sk glzkx znk zumg vgxze
24	rjjy rj fkyjw ymj ytlf ufwyd
25	qiix qi ejxiv xli xske tevxc

FIGURE 2.4.   Brute-Force Cryptanalysis of the Caesar Cipher

difficult. For example, Figure 2.5 shows a portion of a text file compressed by using an algorithm called ZIP. If this file is then encrypted with a simple substitution cipher (expanded to include more than just 26 alphabetic characters), then the plaintext may not be recognized when it is uncovered in the brute-force cryptanalysis.

```
~+W̄µ"— Ω–O)≤4{∞‡ , ë~Ω%ràu· ̄í ◊ ̄z–
Ú≠2Ò#Åæ∂ œ«q7 ̦Ωn·®3N◊Ú Œz'Y–ƒ∞í[±Û_ èΩ,<NO¬±«ˇxã  Åäƒèü3Å
x}ö§kºÂ
_yÍ ˆΔÉ] ̦¤ J/˙iTê&1 'c<uΩ–
 ÄD(G WÄC~y_ĩõÄW PÔ1«ÎÜ†ç],¤¡ˇÌˆüÑπˇ≈ˇLˇ9OgflOˇ&Œ≤ ¬≤ ØÔ§ˇ:
 ˇŒ!SGqèvoˆ ú\ ̦S>h<–*6ø‡%x'" ̸|fiÓ#≈~my%ˇ≥ñP<,fi Áj Å◊¿"Zù–
Ω ̈õ ̄6Œÿ{% „ΩÊó ̦i π+Áî˙úO2çSÿ´O–
2Äflßi /@ˆ"∏Kºª PŒπ ̦úéˆ´3∑ˇö ̌ÔZÌ"Y–ŸΩœY> Ω+eô/˙<K£¿*÷~"≤û~
B ZøK~QßÿÜƒ ̦!ÒflÎzsS/]>ÈQ ü
```

FIGURE 2.5.   Sample of Compressed Text

Monoalphabetic Ciphers

With only 25 possible keys, the Caesar cipher is far from secure. A dramatic increase in the key space can be achieved by allowing an arbitrary substitution. Recall the assignment for the Caesar cipher:

```
plain:   a b c d e f g h i j k l m n o p q r s t u v w x y z
cipher:  D E F G H I J K L M N O P Q R S T U V W X Y Z A B C
```

If instead, the "cipher" line can be any permutation of the 26 alphabetic characters, then there are 26! or greater than 4×10^{26} possible keys. This is 10 orders of magnitude greater than the key space for DES and would seem to effectively eliminate brute-force techniques for cryptanalysis.

There is, however, another line of attack. If the cryptanalyst knows the nature of the plaintext (e.g., noncompressed English text), then the analyst can exploit the regularities of the language. To see how such a cryptanalysis might proceed, we give a partial example here that is adapted from one in [SINK66]. The ciphertext to be solved is:

```
UZQSOVUOHXMOPVGPOZPEVSGZWSZOPFPESXUDBMETSXAIZ
VUEPHZHMDZSHZOWSFPAPPDTSVPQUZWYMXUZUHSX
EPYEPOPDZSZUFPOMBZWPFUPZHMDJUDTMOHMQ
```

As a first step, the relative frequency of the letters can be determined and compared to a standard frequency distribution for English, such as is shown in Table 2.3. If the message were long enough, this technique alone might be sufficient, but since this is a relatively short message, we cannot expect an exact match. In any case, the relative frequency of the letters in the ciphertext (in percentages) are as follows:

P	13.13	H	5.83	F	3.33	B	1.67	C	0.00
Z	11.67	D	5.00	W	3.33	G	1.67	K	0.00
S	8.33	E	5.00	Q	2.50	Y	1.67	L	0.00
U	8.33	V	4.17	T	2.50	I	0.83	N	0.00
O	7.50	X	4.17	A	1.67	J	0.83	R	0.00
M	6.67								

Comparing this breakdown with Table 2.3, it seems likely that cipher letters P and Z are the equivalents of plain letters e and t, but it is not certain which is which. The letters S, U, O, M, and H are all of relatively high frequency and prob-

TABLE 2.3   Relative Frequency of Letters in English Text[a]

Letter	Relative Frequency (%)	Letter	Relative Frequency (%)	Letter	Relative Frequency (%)
E	12.75	L	3.75	W	1.50
T	9.25	H	3.50	V	1.50
R	8.50	C	3.50	B	1.25
N	7.75	F	3.00	K	0.50
I	7.75	U	3.00	X	0.50
O	7.50	M	2.75	Q	0.50
A	7.25	P	2.75	J	0.25
S	6.00	Y	2.25	Z	0.25
D	4.25	G	2.00		

[a]From [SEBE89].

ably correspond to plain letters from the set {r, n, i, o, a, s}. The letters with the lowest frequencies, namely, A, B, G, Y, I, J, are likely included in the set {w, v, b, k, x, q, j, z}.

There are a number of ways to proceed at this point. We could make some tentative assignments and start to fill in the plaintext to see if it looked like a reasonable "skeleton" of a message. A more systematic approach is to look for other regularities. For example, certain words may be known to be in the text. Or we could look for repeating sequences of cipher letters and try to deduce their plaintext equivalents.

A powerful tool is to look at the frequency of two-letter combinations, known as digraphs. A table similar to Table 2.3 could be drawn up showing the relative frequency of digraphs. The most common such digraph is th. In our ciphertext, the most common digraph is ZW, which appears three times. So, we make the correspondence of Z with t and W with h. Then, by our earlier hypothesis, we can equate P with e. Now notice that the sequence ZWP appears in the ciphertext, and we can now translate that sequence as "the." This is the most frequent trigraph (three-letter combination) in English, which seems to indicate that we are on the right track.

Next, notice the sequence ZWSZ in the first line. We don't know that these four letters form a complete word, but if they do, it is of the form th_t. Therefore, S equates with a.

So far, then, we have:

```
UZQSOVUOHXMOPVGPOZPEVSGZWSZOPFPESXUDBMETSXAIZ
  t a        e  e te  a that e e a             a
VUEPHZHMDZSHZOWSFPAPPDTSVPQUZWYMXUZUHSX
   e   t  ta  t ha ee  a e  th     t   a
EPYEPOPDZSZUFPOMBZWPFUPZHMDJUDTMOHMQ
   e  e e tat  e   the    t
```

Only four letters have been identified, but already we have quite a bit of the message. Continued analysis of frequencies plus trial and error should easily yield a solution from this point. The complete plaintext, with spaces added between words, follows:

```
it was disclosed yesterday that several informal but
direct contacts have been made with political
representatives of the viet cong in moscow
```

Monoalphabetic ciphers are easy to break because they reflect the frequency data of the original alphabet. A countermeasure is to provide multiple substitutes for a single letter, known as homophones. For example, the letter e could be assigned a number of different cipher symbols, such as 16, 74, 35, and 21, with each homophone used in rotation, or randomly. If the number of symbols assigned to each letter is proportional to the relative frequency of that letter, then single-letter frequency information is completely obliterated. The great mathematician Carl Friedrich Gauss believed that he had devised an unbreakable cipher using homophones. However, even with homophones, each element of plaintext affects only one element of ciphertext, and multiple-letter patterns (e.g., digraph frequencies) still survive in the ciphertext, making cryptanalysis relatively straightforward.

Two main methods are used in substitution ciphers to lessen the extent to which the structure of the plaintext survives in the ciphertext: One approach is to encrypt multiple letters of plaintext, and the other is to use multiple cipher alphabets. We briefly examine each.

Multiple-Letter Encryption

The best-known multiple-letter encryption cipher is the Playfair, which treats digraphs in the plaintext as single units and translates these units into ciphertext digraphs.[4] The Playfair algorithm is based on the use of a 5×5 matrix of letters constructed by using a keyword. Here is an example, solved by Lord Peter Wimsey[5] in Dorothy Sayers's *Have His Carcase:*

M	O	N	A	R
C	H	Y	B	D
E	F	G	I/J	K
L	P	Q	S	T
U	V	W	X	Z

[4]This cipher was actually invented by British scientist Sir Charles Wheatstone in 1854, but it bears the name of his friend Baron Playfair of St. Andrews, who championed the cipher at the British foreign office.

[5]The book provides an absorbing account of a probable-word attack.

In this case, the keyword is *monarchy*. The matrix is constructed by filling in the letters of the keyword (minus duplicates) from left to right and from top to bottom, and then filling in the remainder of the matrix with the remaining letters in alphabetic order. The letters I and J count as one letter. Plaintext is encrypted two letters at a time, according to the following rules:

1. Repeating plaintext letters are separated with a filler letter, such as X, so that balloon would be enciphered as ba lx lo on.
2. Plaintext letters that fall in the same row of the matrix are each replaced by the letter to the right, with the first element of the row circularly following the last. For example, ar is encrypted as RM.
3. Plaintext letters that fall in the same column are each replaced by the letter beneath, with the top element of the row circularly following the last. For example, mu is encrypted as CM.
4. Otherwise, each plaintext letter is replaced by the letter that lies in its own row and the column occupied by the other plaintext letter. Thus, hs becomes BP and ea becomes IM (or JM as the encipherer wishes).

The Playfair cipher is a great advance over simple monoalphabetic ciphers. For one thing, whereas there are only 26 letters, there are $26 \times 26 = 676$ digraphs, so that identification of individual digraphs is more difficult. Furthermore, the relative frequencies of individual letters exhibit a much greater range than that of digraphs, making frequency analysis much more difficult. For these reasons, the Playfair cipher was for a long time considered unbreakable. It was used as the standard field system by the British Army in World War I and still enjoyed considerable use by the U.S. Army and other allied forces during World War II.

Despite this level of confidence in its security, the Playfair cipher is in fact relatively easy to break because it still leaves much of the structure of the plaintext language intact. A few hundred letters of ciphertext are generally sufficient.

One way of revealing the effectiveness of the Playfair and other ciphers is shown in Figure 2.6. The line labeled *plaintext* plots the frequency distribution of the more than 70,000 alphabetic characters in the Encyclopaedia Brittanica article on cryptology.[6] This is also the frequency distribution of any monoalphabetic substitution cipher. The plot was developed in the following way: The number of occurrences of each letter in the text was counted and divided by the number of occurrences of the letter e (the most frequently used letter). As a result, e has a relative frequency of 1, t of about 0.76, and so on. The points on the horizontal axis corespond to the letters in order of decreasing frequency.

The figure also shows the frequency distribution that results when the text is encrypted by using the Playfair cipher. To normalize the plot, the number of occurrences of each letter in the ciphertext was again divided by the number of occurrences of e in the plaintext. The resulting plot therefore shows the extent to which the frequency distribution of letters, which makes it trivial to solve substitution ci-

---

[6]I am indebted to Gustavus Simmons for providing the plots and explaining their method of construction.

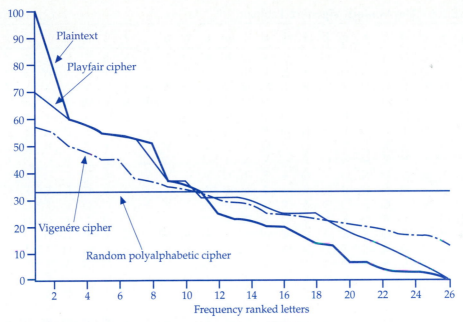

FIGURE 2.6.   Relative Frequency of Occurrence of Letters

phers, is masked by encryption. If the frequency distribution information were to-tally concealed in the encryption process, the ciphertext plot of frequencies would be flat, and cryptanalysis using ciphertext only would be effectively impossible. As the figure shows, the Playfair cipher has a flatter distribution than does plaintext; nevertheless it reveals plenty of structure for a cryptanalyst to work with.

Polyalphabetic Ciphers

Another way to improve on the simple monoalphabetic technique is to use differ-ent monoalphabetic substitutions as one proceeds through the plaintext message. The general name for this approach is polyalphabetic cipher. All these techniques have the following features in common:

1. A set of related monoalphabetic substitution rules is used.
2. A key determines which particular rule is chosen for a given transformation.

The best-known, and one of the simplest, such algorithms is referred to as the Vigenère cipher. In this scheme, the set of related monoalphabetic substitution rules consists of the 26 Caesar ciphers, with shifts of 0 through 25. Each cipher is denoted by a key letter, which is the ciphertext letter that substitutes for the plain-text letter a. Thus, a Caesar cipher with a shift of 3 is denoted by the key value *d*.

To aid in understanding the scheme and also to aid in its use, a matrix known as the Vigenère tableau is constructed (Table 2.4). Each of the 26 ciphers is laid out

TABLE 2.4 The Modern Vigenère Tableau

	a	b	c	d	e	f	g	h	i	j	k	l	m	n	o	p	q	r	s	t	u	v	w	x	y	z
a	A	B	C	D	E	F	G	H	I	J	K	L	M	N	O	P	Q	R	S	T	U	V	W	X	Y	Z
b	B	C	D	E	F	G	H	I	J	K	L	M	N	O	P	Q	R	S	T	U	V	W	X	Y	Z	A
c	C	D	E	F	G	H	I	J	K	L	M	N	O	P	Q	R	S	T	U	V	W	X	Y	Z	A	B
d	D	E	F	G	H	I	J	K	L	M	N	O	P	Q	R	S	T	U	V	W	X	Y	Z	A	B	C
e	E	F	G	H	I	J	K	L	M	N	O	P	Q	R	S	T	U	V	W	X	Y	Z	A	B	C	D
f	F	G	H	I	J	K	L	M	N	O	P	Q	R	S	T	U	V	W	X	Y	Z	A	B	C	D	E
g	G	H	I	J	K	L	M	N	O	P	Q	R	S	T	U	V	W	X	Y	Z	A	B	C	D	E	F
h	H	I	J	K	L	M	N	O	P	Q	R	S	T	U	V	W	X	Y	Z	A	B	C	D	E	F	G
i	I	J	K	L	M	N	O	P	Q	R	S	T	U	V	W	X	Y	Z	A	B	C	D	E	F	G	H
j	J	K	L	M	N	O	P	Q	R	S	T	U	V	W	X	Y	Z	A	B	C	D	E	F	G	H	I
k	K	L	M	N	O	P	Q	R	S	T	U	V	W	X	Y	Z	A	B	C	D	E	F	G	H	I	J
l	L	M	N	O	P	Q	R	S	T	U	V	W	X	Y	Z	A	B	C	D	E	F	G	H	I	J	K
m	M	N	O	P	Q	R	S	T	U	V	W	X	Y	Z	A	B	C	D	E	F	G	H	I	J	K	L
n	N	O	P	Q	R	S	T	U	V	W	X	Y	Z	A	B	C	D	E	F	G	H	I	J	K	L	M
o	O	P	Q	R	S	T	U	V	W	X	Y	Z	A	B	C	D	E	F	G	H	I	J	K	L	M	N
p	P	Q	R	S	T	U	V	W	X	Y	Z	A	B	C	D	E	F	G	H	I	J	K	L	M	N	O
q	Q	R	S	T	U	V	W	X	Y	Z	A	B	C	D	E	F	G	H	I	J	K	L	M	N	O	P
r	R	S	T	U	V	W	X	Y	Z	A	B	C	D	E	F	G	H	I	J	K	L	M	N	O	P	Q
s	S	T	U	V	W	X	Y	Z	A	B	C	D	E	F	G	H	I	J	K	L	M	N	O	P	Q	R
t	T	U	V	W	X	Y	Z	A	B	C	D	E	F	G	H	I	J	K	L	M	N	O	P	Q	R	S
u	U	V	W	X	Y	Z	A	B	C	D	E	F	G	H	I	J	K	L	M	N	O	P	Q	R	S	T
v	V	W	X	Y	Z	A	B	C	D	E	F	G	H	I	J	K	L	M	N	O	P	Q	R	S	T	U
w	W	X	Y	Z	A	B	C	D	E	F	G	H	I	J	K	L	M	N	O	P	Q	R	S	T	U	V
x	X	Y	Z	A	B	C	D	E	F	G	H	I	J	K	L	M	N	O	P	Q	R	S	T	U	V	W
y	Y	Z	A	B	C	D	E	F	G	H	I	J	K	L	M	N	O	P	Q	R	S	T	U	V	W	X
z	Z	A	B	C	D	E	F	G	H	I	J	K	L	M	N	O	P	Q	R	S	T	U	V	W	X	Y

horizontally, with the key letter for each cipher to its left. A normal alphabet for the plaintext runs across the top. The process of encryption is quite simple: Given a key letter x and a plaintext letter y, the ciphertext letter is at the intersection of the row labeled x and the column labeled y.

Now, to encrypt a message, a key is needed that is as long as the message. Usually, the key is a repeating keyword. For example if the keyword is *deceptive,* the message "we are discovered save yourself" is encrypted as follows:

```
key:          deceptivedeceptivedeceptive
plaintext:    wearediscoveredsaveyourself
ciphertext:   ZICVTWQNGRZGVTWAVZHCQYGLMGJ
```

Decryption is equally simple. The key letter again identifies the row. The position of the ciphertext letter in that row determines the column, and the plaintext letter is at the top of that column.

The strength of this cipher is that there are multiple ciphertext letters for each plaintext letter, one for each unique letter of the keyword. Thus, the letter frequency information is obscured. However, not all knowledge of the plaintext structure is lost. For example, Figure 2.6 shows the frequency distribution for a Vigenère cipher with a keyword of length 9. An improvement is achieved over the Playfair cipher, but considerable frequency information remains.

It is instructive to sketch a method of breaking this cipher, since it reveals some of the mathematical principles that apply in cryptanalysis.

First, suppose that the opponent believes that the ciphertext was encrypted using either monoalphabetic substitution or a Vigenère cipher. A simple test can be made to make a determination. If a monoalphabetic substitution is used, then the statistical properties of the ciphertext should be the same as that of the language of the plaintext. Thus, referring to Table 2.3, there should be one cipher letter with a relative frequency of occurrence of about 12.75%, one with about 9.25%, and so on. If only a single message is available for analysis, we would not expect an exact match of this small sample with the statistical profile of the plaintext language. Nevertheless, if the correspondence is close, we can assume a monoalphabetic substitution.

If, on the other hand, a Vigenère cipher is suspected, then progress depends on determining the length of the keyword, as will be seen in a moment. For now, let us concentrate on how the keyword length can be determined. The important insight that leads to a solution is the following: If two identical sequences of plaintext letters occur at a distance that is an integer multiple of the keyword length, they will generate identical ciphertext sequences. In the foregoing example, two instances of the sequence "red" are separated by 9 character positions. Consequently, in both cases, r is encrypted using key letter *e*, e is encrypted using key letter *p*, and d is encrypted using key letter *t*. Thus, in both cases the ciphertext sequence is VTW.

An analyst looking at only the ciphertext would detect the repeated sequences VTW at a displacement of 9, and make the assumption that the keyword is either 3 or 9 letters in length. The appearance of VTW twice could be by chance and not reflect identical plaintext letters encrypted with identical key letters. However, if the message is long enough, there will be a number of such repeated ciphertext sequences. By looking for common factors in the displacements of the various sequences, the analyst should be able to make a good guess of the keyword length.

Solution of the cipher now depends on the following observation. If the keyword length is N, then the cipher, in effect, consists of N monoalphabetic substitution ciphers. For example, with the keyword DECEPTIVE, the letters in positions 1, 10, 19, and so on are all encrypted with the same monoalphabetic cipher. Thus, we can use the known frequency characteristics of the plaintext language to attack each of the monoalphabetic ciphers separately.

The periodic nature of the keyword can be eliminated by using a nonrepeating keyword that is as long as the message itself. Vigenère proposed what is referred to as an autokey system, in which a keyword is concatenated with the plaintext itself to provide a running key. For our example:

```
key:         deceptivewearediscoveredsav
plaintext:   wearediscoveredsaveyourself
ciphertext:  ZICVTWQNGKZEIIGASXSTSLVVWLA
```

Even this scheme is vulnerable to cryptanalysis. Because the key and the plaintext share the same frequency distribution of letters, statistical technique can be applied. For example, E enciphered with E, by Table 2.3, can be expected to occur with a frequency of $(0.1275)^2 \approx 0.0163$, whereas T enciphered by T would occur only about half as often. These regularities can be exploited to achieve successful cryptanalysis.[7]

The ultimate defense against such a cryptanalysis is to choose a keyword that is as long as the plaintext and has no statistical relationship to it. Such a system was introduced by an AT&T engineer named Gilbert Vernam in 1918. His system works on binary data rather than letters. The system can be expressed succinctly as follows:

$$c_i = p_i \oplus k_i$$

where

p_i = ith binary digit of plaintext
k_i = ith binary digit of key
c_i = ith binary digit of ciphertext
$\oplus$ = exclusive–or (XOR) operation

Thus, the ciphertext is generated by performing the bitwise XOR of the plaintext and the key. Because of the properties of the XOR, decryption simply involves the same bitwise operation:

$$p_i = c_i \oplus k_i$$

The essence of this technique is the means of construction of the key. Vernam proposed the use of a running loop of tape that eventually repeated the key, so that in fact the system worked with a very long but repeating keyword. Although such a scheme, with a long key, presents formidable cryptanalytic difficulties, it can be broken with sufficient ciphertext, the use of known or probable plaintext sequences, or both.

An Army Signal Corp officer, Joseph Mauborgne, proposed an improvement to the Vernam cipher that yields the ultimate in security. Mauborgne suggested using a random key that was truly as long as the message, with no repetitions. Such a scheme, known as a one-time pad, is unbreakable. It produces random output that bears no statistical relationship to the plaintext. Because the ciphertext contains no information whatsoever about the plaintext, there is simply no way to break the code. The practical difficulty with this method is that sender and receiver must be in possession of, and protect, the random key. Thus, the Vernam cipher, despite its preeminence among ciphers, is rarely used.

---

[7]Although the techniques for breaking a Vigenère cipher are by no means complex, a 1917 issue of *Scientific American* characterized this system as "impossible of translation." This is a point worth remembering when similar claims are made for modern algorithms!

Transposition Techniques

All the techniques examined so far involve the substitution of a ciphertext symbol for a plaintext symbol. A very different kind of mapping is achieved by performing some sort of permutation on the plaintext letters. This technique is referred to as a transposition cipher.

The simplest such cipher is the rail fence technique, in which the plaintext is written down a sequence of columns and then read off as a sequence of rows. For example, to encipher the message "meet me after the toga party" with a rail fence of depth 2, we write the following:

```
mematrhtgpry
etefeteoaat
```

The encrypted message is:

```
MEMATRHTGPRYETEFETEOAAT
```

This sort of thing would be trivial to cryptanalyze. A more complex scheme is to write the message in a rectangle, row by row, and read the message off, column by column, but permute the order of the columns. The order of the columns then becomes the key to the algorithm. For example:

```
Key:          4 3 1 2 5 6 7
Plaintext:    a t t a c k p
              o s t p o n e
              d u n t i l t
              w o a m x y z


Ciphertext:   TTNAAPTMTSUOAODWCOIXKNLYPETZ
```

A pure transposition cipher is easily recognized because it has the same letter frequencies as the original plaintext. For the type of columnar transposition just shown, cryptanalysis is fairly straightforward and involves laying out the ciphertext in a matrix and playing around with column positions. Digraph and trigraph frequency tables can be useful.

The transposition cipher can be made significantly more secure by performing more than one stage of transposition. The result is a more complex permutation that is not easily reconstructed. Thus, if the foregoing message is re-encrypted using the same algorithm:

```
Key:       4 3 1 2 5 6 7
Input:     t t n a a p t
           m t s u o a o
           d w c o i x k
           n l y p e t z


Output:    NSCYAUOPTTWLTMDNAOIEPAXTTOKZ
```

To visualize the result of this double transposition, designate the letters in the original plaintext message by the numbers designating their position. Thus, with 28 letters in the message, the original sequence of letters is:

```
1  2  3  4  5  6  7  8  9  10  11  12  13  14  15  16  17  18  19  20  21  22  23
                        24  25  26  27  28
```

After the first transposition we have:

```
3  10  17  24  4  11  18  25  2  9  16  23  1  8  15  22  5  12  19  26  6  13
                        20  27  7  14  21  28
```

which has a somewhat regular structure. But after the second transposition, we have:

```
17  9  5  27  24  16  12  7  10  2  22  20  3  25  15  13  4  23  19  14  11  1
                        26  21  18  8  6  28
```

This is a much less structured permutation and is much more difficult to cryptanalyze.

Rotor Machines

The example just given suggests that multiple stages of encryption can produce an algorithm that is significantly more difficult to cryptanalyze. This is as true of substitution ciphers as it is of transposition ciphers. Before the introduction of the data encryption standard (DES), the most important application of the principle of multiple stages of encryption was a class of systems known as rotor machines.[8]

The basic principle of the rotor machine is illustrated in Figure 2.7. The machine consists of a set of independently rotating cylinders through which electrical pulses can flow. Each cylinder has 26 input pins and 26 output pins, with internal wiring that connects each input pin to a unique output pin. For simplicity, only three of the internal connections in each cylinder are shown.

If we associate each input and output pin with a letter of the alphabet, then a single cylinder defines a monoalphabetic substitution. For example, in the figure, if an operator depresses the key for the letter A, an electric signal is applied to the first pin of the first cylinder and flows through the internal connection to the 25th output pin.

Now, consider a machine with a single cylinder. After each input key is depressed, the cylinder rotates one position, so that the internal connections are accordingly shifted. Thus, a different monoalphabetic substitution cipher is defined. After 26 letters of plaintext, the cylinder would be back to the initial position. Thus, we have a polyalphabetic substitution algorithm with a period of 26.

A single-cylinder system is trivial and does not present a formidable cryptanalytic task. The power of the rotor machine is in the use of multiple cylinders, in

---

[8]Machines based on the rotor principle were used by both Germany (Enigma) and Japan (Purple) in World War II. The breaking of both codes by the Allies was a significant factor in the war's outcome.

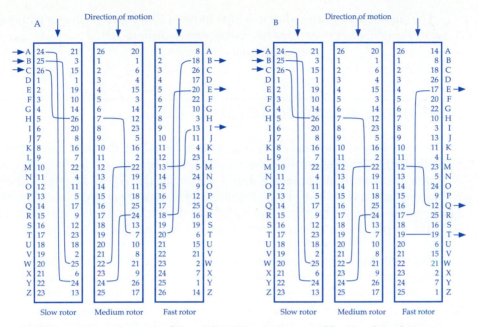

FIGURE 2.7. Three-Rotor Machine with Wiring Represented by Numbered Contacts

which the output pins of one cylinder are connected to the input pins of the next. Figure 2.7 shows a three-cylinder system. The left half of the figure shows a position in which the input from the operator to the first pin (plaintext letter a) is routed through the three cylinders to appear at the output of the second pin (ciphertext letter B).

With multiple cylinders, the one farthest from the operator input rotates one pin position with each keystroke. For every complete rotation of the outer cylinder, the middle cylinder rotates one pin position. Finally, for every complete rotation of the middle cylinder, the inner cylinder rotates one pin position. This is the same type of operation seen with an odometer. The result is that there are $26 \times 26 \times 26$ = 17,576 different substitution alphabets used before the system repeats. The addition of fourth and fifth rotors results in periods of 456,976 and 11,881,376 letters, respectively. As David Kahn eloquently put it, referring to a five-rotor machine [KAHN67, page 413]:

> A period of that length thwarts any practical possibility of a straightforward solution on the basis of letter frequency. This general solution would need about 50 letters per cipher alphabet, meaning that all five rotors would have to go through their combined cycle 50 times. The ciphertext would have to be as long as all the speeches made on the floor of the Senate and the House of Representatives in three successive sessions of Congress. No cryptanalyst is likely to bag that kind of trophy in his lifetime; even diplomats, who can be as verbose as politicians, rarely scale those heights of loquacity.

The significance of the rotor machine today is that it points the way to the most widely used cipher ever: the Data Encryption Standard (DES).

THE DATA ENCRYPTION STANDARD (DES)

The most widely used encryption scheme is based on the data encryption standard (DES) adopted in 1977 by the National Bureau of Standards, now the National Institute of Standards and Technology (NIST), as Federal Information Processing Standard 46 (FIPS PUB 46). For DES, data are encrypted in 64-bit blocks using a 56-bit key. The algorithm transforms 64-bit input in a series of steps into a 64-bit output. The same steps, with the same key, are used to reverse the encryption.

The DES has enjoyed increasingly widespread use. Unfortunately, it has also been the subject of much controversy as to how secure the DES is. To appreciate the nature of the controversy, let us quickly review the history of the DES.

In the late 1960s, IBM set up a research project in computer cryptography led by Horst Feistel. The project concluded in 1971 with the development of an algorithm with the designation LUCIFER [FEIS73], which was sold to Lloyd's of London for use in a cash-dispensing system, also developed by IBM. LUCIFER was a block cipher that operated on blocks of 64 bits, using a key size of 128 bits. Because of the promising results produced by the LUCIFER project, IBM embarked on an effort to develop a marketable commercial encryption product that ideally could be implemented on a single chip. The effort was headed by Walter Tuchman and Carl Meyer, and it involved not only IBM researchers but also outside consultants and technical advice from NSA. The outcome of this effort was a refined version of LUCIFER that was more resistant to cryptanalysis but that had a reduced key size of 56 bits, so as to fit on a single chip.

Meanwhile, the National Bureau of Standards (NBS) in 1973 issued a request for proposals for a national cipher standard. IBM submitted the results of its Tuchman-Meyer project. This was by far the best algorithm proposed and was adopted in 1977 as the Data Encryption Standard.

Before its adoption as a standard, the proposed DES was subjected to intense criticism that has not subsided to this day. Two areas drew the critics' fire. First, the key length in IBM's original LUCIFER algorithm was 128 bits, but that of the proposed system was only 56 bits, an enormous reduction in key size of 72 bits. Critics feared (and still fear) that this key length is too short to withstand brute-force attacks. The second area of concern was that the design criteria for the internal structure of DES, the S-boxes, were and still are classified. Thus, users cannot be sure that the internal structure of DES is free of any hidden weak points that would enable NSA to decipher messages without benefit of the key. Subsequent events, particularly the recent work on differential cryptanalysis, seem to indicate that DES has a very strong internal structure. Furthermore, according to IBM participants, the only changes that were made to the proposal were changes to the S-boxes, suggested by NSA, that removed vulnerabilities identified in the course of the evaluation process. We return to these areas of concern at the end of this section.

Whatever the merits of the case, DES has flourished in recent years and is widely used, especially in financial applications. In 1994, NIST "reaffirmed" DES for federal use for another 5 years; NIST recommends the use of DES for applications other than the protection of classified information. The author feels that, except in areas of extreme sensitivity, the use of DES in commercial applications should not be a cause for concern by the responsible managers.

DES Encryption

The overall scheme for DES encryption is illustrated in Figure 2.8. As with any encryption scheme, there are two inputs to the encryption function: the plaintext to

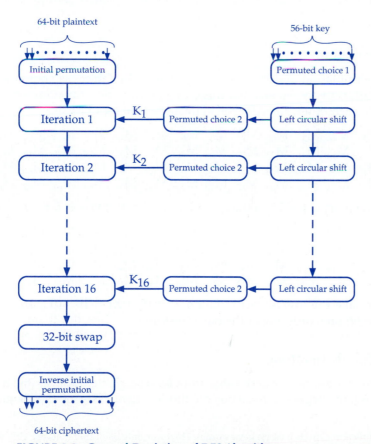

FIGURE 2.8. General Depiction of DES Algorithm

be encrypted and the key. In this case, the plaintext must be 64 bits in length and the key is 56 bits in length.[9]

Looking at the left-hand side of the figure, we can see that the processing of the plaintext proceeds in three phases. First, the 64-bit plaintext passes through an initial permutation (IP) that rearranges the bits to produce the *permuted input*. This is followed by a phase consisting of 16 iterations of the same function, which involves both permutation and substitution functions. The output of the last (16th) iteration consists of 64 bits that are a function of the input plaintext and the key. The left and right halves of the output are swapped to produce the **preoutput.** Finally, the preoutput is passed through a permutation (IP^{-1}) that is the inverse of the initial permutation function, to produce the 64-bit ciphertext.

The right-hand portion of Figure 2.8 shows the way in which the 56-bit key is used. Initially, the key is passed through a permutation function. Then, for each of the 16 iterations, a *subkey* (K_i) is produced by the combination of a left circular shift and a permutation. The permutation function is the same for each iteration, but a different subkey is produced because of the repeated shifting of the key bits.

Initial Permutation

The initial permutation and its inverse are defined by tables, as shown in Table 2.5a and b, respectively. To see that these two permutation functions are indeed the inverse of each other, consider the following 64-bit input M:

M_1 M_2 M_3 M_4 M_5 M_6 M_7 M_8 M_9 M_{10} M_{11} M_{12} M_{13} M_{14} M_{15} M_{16}
M_{17} M_{18} M_{19} M_{20} M_{21} M_{22} M_{23} M_{24} M_{25} M_{26} M_{27} M_{28} M_{29} M_{30} M_{31} M_{32}
M_{33} M_{34} M_{35} M_{36} M_{37} M_{38} M_{39} M_{40} M_{41} M_{42} M_{43} M_{44} M_{45} M_{46} M_{47} M_{48}
M_{49} M_{50} M_{51} M_{52} M_{53} M_{54} M_{55} M_{56} M_{57} M_{58} M_{59} M_{60} M_{61} M_{62} M_{63} M_{64}

where M_i is a binary digit. Then the permutation X = IP(M) is as follows:

M_{58} M_{50} M_{42} M_{34} M_{26} M_{18} M_{10} M_2 M_{60} M_{52} M_{44} M_{36} M_{28} M_{20} M_{12} M_4
M_{62} M_{54} M_{46} M_{38} M_{30} M_{22} M_{14} M_6 M_{64} M_{56} M_{48} M_{40} M_{32} M_{24} M_{16} M_8
M_{57} M_{49} M_{41} M_{33} M_{25} M_{17} M_9 M_1 M_{59} M_{51} M_{43} M_{35} M_{27} M_{19} M_{11} M_3
M_{61} M_{53} M_{45} M_{37} M_{29} M_{21} M_{13} M_5 M_{63} M_{55} M_{47} M_{39} M_{31} M_{23} M_{15} M_7

If we then take the inverse permutation Y = IP^{-1}(X) = IP^{-1}(IP(M)), it can be seen that the original ordering of the bits is restored.

Details of Single Iteration

Now let us look more closely at the algorithm for a single iteration, as illustrated in Figure 2.9. Again, begin by focusing on the left-hand side of the diagram. In

[9]Actually, the function expects a 64-bit key as input. However only 56 of these bits are ever used; the other 8 bits can be used as parity bits or simply set arbitrarily.

TABLE 2.5　Permutation Tables for DES

(a) Initial Permutation (IP)

Output bit	1	2	3	4	5	6	7	8	9	10	11	12	13	14	15	16
From input bit	58	50	42	34	26	18	10	2	60	52	44	36	28	20	12	4
Output bit	17	18	19	20	21	22	23	24	25	26	27	28	29	30	31	32
From input bit	62	54	46	38	30	22	14	6	64	56	48	40	32	24	16	8
Output bit	33	34	35	36	37	38	39	40	41	42	43	44	45	46	47	48
From input bit	57	49	41	33	25	17	9	1	59	51	43	35	27	19	11	3
Output bit	49	50	51	52	53	54	55	56	57	58	59	60	61	62	63	64
From input bit	61	53	45	37	29	21	13	5	63	55	47	39	31	23	15	7

(b) Inverse Initial Permutation (IP^{-1})

Output bit	1	2	3	4	5	6	7	8	9	10	11	12	13	14	15	16
From input bit	40	8	48	16	56	24	64	32	39	7	47	15	55	23	63	31
Output bit	17	18	19	20	21	22	23	24	25	26	27	28	29	30	31	32
From input bit	38	6	46	14	54	22	62	30	37	5	45	13	53	21	61	29
Output bit	33	34	35	36	37	38	39	40	41	42	43	44	45	46	47	48
From input bit	36	4	44	12	52	20	60	28	35	3	43	11	51	19	59	27
Output bit	49	50	51	52	53	54	55	56	57	58	59	60	61	62	63	64
From input bit	34	2	42	10	50	18	58	26	33	1	41	9	49	17	57	25

(c) Expansion Permutation (E)

Output bit	1	2	3	4	5	6	7	8	9	10	11	12
From input bit	32	1	2	3	4	5	4	5	6	7	8	9
Output bit	13	14	15	16	17	18	19	20	21	22	23	24
From input bit	8	9	10	11	12	13	12	13	14	15	16	17
Output bit	25	26	27	28	29	30	31	32	33	34	35	36
From input bit	16	17	18	19	20	21	20	21	22	23	24	25
Output bit	37	38	39	40	41	42	43	44	45	46	47	48
From input bit	24	25	26	27	28	29	28	29	30	31	32	1

(d) Permutation Function (P)

Output bit	1	2	3	4	5	6	7	8	9	10	11	12	13	14	15	16
From input bit	16	7	20	21	29	12	28	17	1	15	23	26	5	18	31	10
Output bit	17	18	19	20	21	22	23	24	25	26	27	28	29	30	31	32
From input bit	2	8	24	14	32	27	3	9	19	13	30	6	22	11	4	25

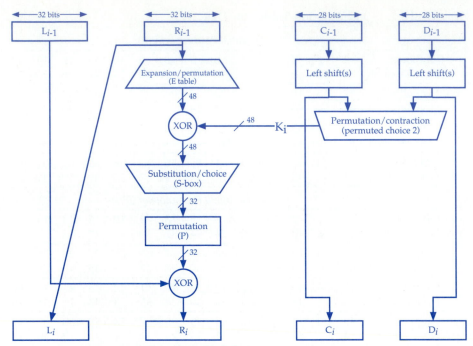

FIGURE 2.9. Single Iteration of DES Algorithm

essence, the 64-bit permuted input passes through 16 iterations, producing an intermediate 64-bit value at the conclusion of each iteration. The left and right half of each 64-bit intermediate value are treated as separate 32-bit quantities, labeled L (left) and R (right). The overall processing at each iteration can be summarized in the following formulas:

$$L_i = R_{i-1}$$
$$R_i = L_{i-1} \oplus f(R_{i-1}, K_i)$$

where $\oplus$ denotes the bitwise XOR function.

Thus, the left-hand output of an iteration (L_i) is simply equal to the right-hand input to that iteration (R_{i-1}). The right-hand output (R_i) is the exclusive-or *(XOR)* of L_{i-1} and a complex function f of R_{i-1} and K_i.

The function f is illustrated in Figure 2.10. The iteration key K_i is 48 bits. The R input is 32 bits. This R input is first expanded to 48 bits by using a table that defines a permutation plus an expansion that involves duplication of 16 of the R bits (Table 2.5c). The resulting 48 bits are XORed with K_i. This 48-bit result passes through a substitution function that produces a 32-bit output, which is permuted as defined by Table 2.5d.

The substitution consists of a set of eight S-boxes, each of which accepts 6 bits as input and produces 4 bits as output. These transformations are defined in Table

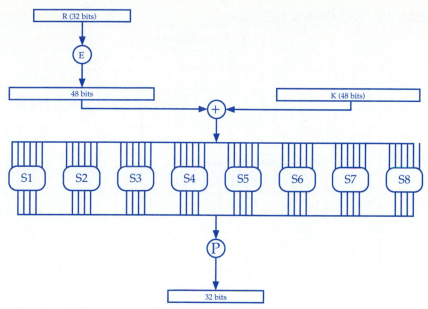

FIGURE 2.10. Calculation of f(R,K)

2.6, which is interpreted as follows: The first and last bits of the input to box S_i form a 2-bit binary number to select a particular row in the table for S_i. The middle 4 bits select a particular column. The decimal value in the cell selected by the row and column is then converted to its 4-bit representation to produce the output. For example in S_1, for input 011011, the row is 01 (row 1) and the column is 1101 (column 13). The value in row 1, column 13 is 5, so the output is 0101.

Figure 2.11 provides a detail for S-box operation that may be useful in understanding the mapping. The first and last bits of the input select one of four permutations defined by the rows of the S-box table. The figure shows the permutation for row 0 of box S_1.

The structure of the S-boxes is worth further comment. Ignore for the moment the contribution of the key (K_i). Now, if you examine the expansion table, you see that the 32 bits of input are split into groups of 4 bits, and then become groups of 6 bits by taking the outer bits from the two adjacent groups. For example, if part of the input word is:

```
. . . efgh ijkl mnop . . .
```

this becomes

```
. . . defghi   hijklm lmnopq . . .
```

The outer two bits of each group select one of four possible substitution tables. Then, a 4-bit output value is substituted for the particular 4-bit input (the middle four input bits). The 32-bit output from the eight S-boxes is then permuted, so that

TABLE 2.6   Definition of DES S-Boxes

							Column Number									
Row	0	1	2	3	4	5	6	7	8	9	10	11	12	13	14	15	Box
0	14	4	13	1	2	15	11	8	3	10	6	12	5	9	0	7	
1	0	15	7	4	14	2	13	1	10	6	12	11	9	5	3	8	S_1
2	4	1	14	8	13	6	2	11	15	12	9	7	3	10	5	0	
3	15	12	8	2	4	9	1	7	5	11	3	14	10	0	6	13	
0	15	1	8	14	6	11	3	4	9	7	2	13	12	0	5	10	
1	3	13	4	7	15	2	8	14	12	0	1	10	6	9	11	5	S_2
2	0	14	7	11	10	4	13	1	5	8	12	6	9	3	2	15	
3	13	8	10	1	3	15	4	2	11	6	7	12	0	5	14	9	
0	10	0	9	14	6	3	15	5	1	13	12	7	11	4	2	8	
1	13	7	0	9	3	4	6	10	2	8	5	14	12	11	15	1	S_3
2	13	6	4	9	8	15	3	0	11	1	2	12	5	10	14	7	
3	1	10	13	0	6	9	8	7	4	15	14	3	11	5	2	12	
0	7	13	14	3	0	6	9	10	1	2	8	5	11	12	4	15	
1	13	8	11	5	6	15	0	3	4	7	2	12	1	10	14	9	S_4
2	10	6	9	0	12	11	7	13	15	1	3	14	5	2	8	4	
3	3	15	0	6	10	1	13	8	9	4	5	11	12	7	2	14	
0	2	12	4	1	7	10	11	6	8	5	3	15	13	0	14	9	
1	14	11	2	12	4	7	13	1	5	0	15	10	3	9	8	6	S_5
2	4	2	1	11	10	13	7	8	15	9	12	5	6	3	0	14	
3	11	8	12	7	1	14	2	13	6	15	0	9	10	4	5	3	
0	12	1	10	15	9	2	6	8	0	13	3	4	14	7	5	11	
1	10	15	4	2	7	12	9	5	6	1	13	14	0	11	3	8	S_6
2	9	14	15	5	2	8	12	3	7	0	4	10	1	13	11	6	
3	4	3	2	12	9	5	15	10	11	14	1	7	6	0	8	13	
0	4	11	2	14	15	0	8	13	3	12	9	7	5	10	6	1	
1	13	0	11	7	4	9	1	10	14	3	5	12	2	15	8	6	S_7
2	1	4	11	13	12	3	7	14	10	15	6	8	0	5	9	2	
3	6	11	13	8	1	4	10	7	9	5	0	15	14	2	3	12	
0	13	2	8	4	6	15	11	1	10	9	3	14	5	0	12	7	
1	1	15	13	8	10	3	7	4	12	5	6	11	0	14	9	2	S_8
2	7	11	4	1	9	12	14	2	0	6	10	13	15	3	5	8	
3	2	1	14	7	4	10	8	13	15	12	9	0	3	5	6	11	

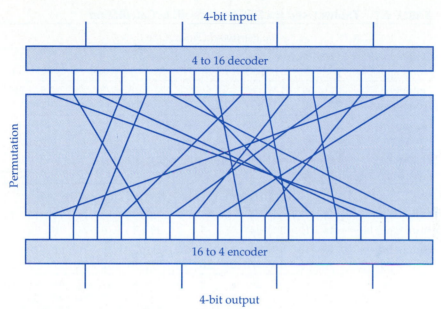

4-bit input

4 to 16 decoder

Permutation

16 to 4 encoder

4-bit output

FIGURE 2.11. S-Box Detail (Row 0 of S_1)

on the next iteration the output from each S-box immediately affects as many others as possible.

Key Generation

Returning to Figure 2.9, we see that the 56-bit key used as input to the algorithm is first subjected to a permutation governed by a table labeled Permuted Choice One (Table 2.7a). The resulting 56-bit key is then treated as two 28-bit quantities, labeled C_0 and D_0. At each iteration, C and D are separately subjected to a circular left shift, or rotation, of 1 or 2 bits, as governed by Table 2.7c. These shifted values serve as input to the next iteration. They also serve as input to Permuted Choice Two (Table 2.7b), which produces a 48-bit output that serves as input to the function $f(R_{i-1}, K_i)$.

DES Decryption

The process of decryption with DES is essentially the same as the encryption process. The rule is as follows: Use the ciphertext as input to the DES algorithm, but use the keys K_i in reverse order. That is, use K_{16} on the first iteration, K_{15} on the second iteration, and so on until K_1 is used on the 16th and last iteration.

To see that the same algorithm with a reversed key order produces the correct result, consider Figure 2.12, which shows the encryption process going down the left-hand side and the decryption process going up the right-hand side. The

TABLE 2.7   Tables Used for DES Key Schedule Calculation

(a) Permuted Choice One (PC-1)

Output bit	1	2	3	4	5	6	7	8	9	10	11	12	13	14
From input bit	57	49	41	33	25	17	9	1	58	50	42	34	26	18
Output bit	15	16	17	18	19	20	21	22	23	24	25	26	27	28
From input bit	10	2	59	51	43	35	27	19	11	3	60	52	44	36
Output bit	29	30	31	32	33	34	35	36	37	38	39	40	41	42
From input bit	63	55	47	39	31	23	15	7	62	54	46	38	30	22
Output bit	43	44	45	46	47	48	49	50	51	52	53	54	55	56
From input bit	14	6	61	53	45	37	29	21	13	5	28	20	12	4

(b) Permuted Choice Two (PC-2)

Output bit	1	2	3	4	5	6	7	8	9	10	11	12	13	14	15	16
From input bit	14	17	11	24	1	5	3	28	15	6	21	10	23	19	12	4
Output bit	17	18	19	20	21	22	23	24	25	26	27	28	29	30	31	32
From input bit	26	8	16	7	27	20	13	2	41	52	31	37	47	55	30	40
Output bit	33	34	35	36	37	38	39	40	41	42	43	44	45	46	47	48
From input bit	51	45	33	48	44	49	39	56	34	53	46	42	50	36	29	32

(c) Schedule of Left Shifts

Iteration number	1	2	3	4	5	6	7	8	9	10	11	12	13	14	15	16
Bits rotated	1	1	2	2	2	2	2	2	1	2	2	2	2	2	2	1

diagram indicates that, at every stage, the intermediate value of the decryption process is equal to the corresponding value of the encryption process with the two halves of the value swapped. To put this another way, let the output of the ith encryption stage be $L_i||R_i$ (L_i concatenated with R_i). Then the corresponding input to the $(16-i)$th decryption stage is $R_i||L_i$.

Let us walk through Figure 2.12 to demonstrate the validity of the preceding assertions.[10] After the last iteration of the encryption process, the two halves of the output are swapped, so that the input to the final IP^{-1} stage is $R_{16}||L_{16}$. The output of that stage is the ciphertext. Now, take the ciphertext and use it as input to the DES algorithm. The first step is to pass the ciphertext through the IP stage, producing the 64-bit quantity $L^d_0||R^d_0$. But we have already seen that IP is the inverse of IP^{-1}. Therefore

$$L^d_0||R^d_0 = IP(\text{ciphertext})$$
$$\text{ciphertext} = IP^{-1}(R_{16}||L_{16})$$
$$L^d_0||R^d_0 = IP(IP^{-1}(R_{16}||L_{16})) = R_{16}||L_{16}$$

Thus, the input to the first stage of the decryption process is equal to the 32-bit swap of the output of the 16th stage of the encryption process.

---

[10]To simplify the diagram, it is unwrapped, not showing the crossover that occurs at the end of each iteration. But please note that the intermediate result at the end of the ith stage of the encryption process is the 64-bit quantity formed by concatenating L_i and R_i, and that the intermediate result at the end of the ith stage of the decryption process is the 64-bit quantity formed by concatenating L^d_i and R^d_i.

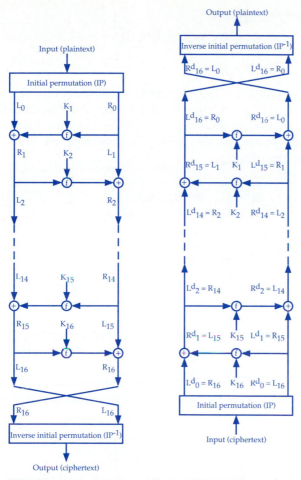

FIGURE 2.12.   DES Encryption and Decryption

Now, we would like to show that the output of the first stage of the decryption process is equal to the 32-bit swap of the input to the 16th stage of the encryption process. First, consider the encryption process. We see that:

$$L_{16} = R_{15}$$
$$R_{16} = L_{15} \oplus f(R_{15}, K_{16})$$

On the decryption side:

$$L^d{}_1 = R^d{}_0 = L_{16} = R_{15}$$
$$R^d{}_1 = L^d{}_0 \oplus f(R^d{}_0, K_{16})$$
$$= R_{16} \oplus f(R_{15}, K_{16})$$
$$= [L_{15} \oplus f(R_{15}, K_{16})] \oplus f(R_{15}, K_{16})$$

The XOR has the following properties:

$$[A \oplus B] \oplus C = A \oplus [B \oplus C]$$
$$D \oplus D = 0$$
$$E \oplus 0 = E$$

Thus, we have $L^d_1 = R_{15}$ and $R^d_1 = L_{15}$. Therefore, the output of the first stage of the decryption process is $L_{15}||R_{15}$, which is the 32-bit swap of the input to the 16th stage of the encryption. This correspondence holds all the way through the 16 iterations, as is easily shown. We can cast this process in general terms. For the ith iteration of the encryption algorithm:

$$L_i = R_{i-1}$$
$$R_i = L_{i-1} \oplus f(R_{i-1}, K_i)$$

Rearranging terms:

$$R_{i-1} = L_i$$
$$L_{i-1} = R_i \oplus f(R_{i-1}, K_i) = R_i \oplus f(L_i, K_i)$$

Thus, we have described the inputs to the ith iteration as a function of the outputs, and these equations confirm the assignments shown in the right-hand side of Figure 2.12.

Finally, we see that the output of the last stage of the decryption process is $R_0||L_0$. A 32-bit swap is performed so that the input to the IP^{-1} stage is $L_0||R_0$. But

$$IP^{-1}(L_0||R_0) = IP^{-1}(IP(plaintext)) = plaintext$$

So the original plaintext is recovered, demonstrating the validity of the DES decryption process.

The Avalanche Effect

A desirable property of any encryption algorithm is that a small change in either the plaintext or the key should produce a significant change in the ciphertext. In particular a change in one bit of the plaintext or one bit of the key should produce a change in many bits of the ciphertext. If the change were small, this might provide a way to reduce the size of the plaintext or key space to be searched.

DES exhibits a strong avalanche effect. Table 2.8 shows some results taken from [KONH81]. In the first table, these two plaintexts were used:

00000000 00000000 00000000 00000000 00000000 00000000 00000000 00000000
10000000 00000000 00000000 00000000 00000000 00000000 00000000 00000000

with the key

0000001 1001011 0100100 1100010 0011100 0011000 0011100 0110010

The table shows that after just two rounds, 21 bits differ between the two encryptions. On completion, the two ciphertexts differ in 34 bit positions.

Table 2.8b shows a similar test in which a single plaintext is input:

TABLE 2.8   Avalanche Effect in DES

(a) Change in Plaintext		(b)Change in Key	
Round	Number of bits that differ	Round	Number of bits that differ
0	1	0	0
1	6	1	2
2	21	2	14
3	35	3	28
4	39	4	32
5	34	5	30
6	32	6	32
7	31	7	35
8	29	8	34
9	42	9	40
10	44	10	38
11	32	11	31
12	30	12	33
13	30	13	28
14	26	14	26
15	29	15	34
16	34	16	35

01101000 10000101 0010111 01111010 00010011 01110110 11101011 10100100

with two keys that differ in only one bit position:

1110010 1111011 1101111 0011000 0011101 0000100 0110001 11011100
0110010 1111011 1101111 0011000 0011101 0000100 0110001 11011100

Again, the results show that about half of the bits in the ciphertext differ and that the avalanche effect is pronounced after just a few rounds.

Concerns About DES

Since its adoption as a federal standard, there have been lingering concerns about the level of security provided by DES. These concerns, by and large, fall into two areas: key size and the nature of the algorithm.

The Use of 56-Bit Keys

With a key length of 56 bits, there are 2^{56} possible keys, which is approximately 7.2×10^{16} keys. Thus, on the face of it, a brute-force attack appears impractical. Assuming that on average half the key space has to be searched, a single machine performing one DES encryption per microsecond would take more than 1,000 years (see Table 2.2) to break the cipher.

However, the assumption of one encryption per microsecond is overly conservative. As far back as 1977, Diffie and Hellman postulated that the technology existed to build a parallel machine with 1 million encryption devices, each of which could perform one encryption per microsecond [DIFF77]. The authors estimated that the cost would be about $20 million in 1977 dollars.

The most rigorous recent analysis of the problem was done by Wiener [WIEN93] and is based on a known plaintext attack. That is, it is assumed that the attacker has at least one (plaintext, ciphertext) pair. Wiener takes care to provide the details of his design. To quote his paper:

> There have been numerous unverifiable claims about how fast the DES key space can be searched. To avoid adding to this list of questionable claims, a great deal of detail in the design of a key search machine is included in the appendices. This detailed work was done to obtain an accurate assessment of the cost of the machine and the time required to find a DES key. There are no plans to actually build such a machine.

Wiener reports on the design of a chip that uses pipelined techniques to achieve a key search rate of 50 million keys per second. Using 1993 costs, he designed a module that costs $100,000 and contains 5,760 key search chips. With this design, the following results are obtained:

Key Search Machine Unit Cost	Expected Search Time
$100,000	35 hours
$1,000,000	3.5 hours
$10,000,000	21 minutes

In addition, Wiener estimates a one-time development cost of about $500,000.

However, there is more to a key-search attack than simply running through all possible keys. Unless known plaintext is provided, the analyst must be able to recognize plaintext as plaintext. If the message is just plain text in English, then the result pops out immediately, although the task of recognizing English would have to be automated. If the text message has been compressed before encryption, then recognition is more difficult. And if the message is some more general type of data, such as a numerical file, and this has been compressed, the problem becomes even more difficult to automate. Thus, to supplement the brute-force approach, some degree of knowledge about the expected plaintext is needed, and some means of automatically distinguishing plaintext from garble is also needed.

The Wiener design represents the culmination of years of concern about the security of DES and may in retrospect have been a turning point. As of the time of this writing, it still seems reasonable to rely on DES for personal and commercial applications. But the time has come to investigate alternatives for conventional encryption. The two most promising candidates for replacing DES are triple DES, described later in this chapter, and IDEA, discussed in Chapter 7.

The Nature of the DES Algorithm

Perhaps of more concern is the possibility that cryptanalysis is possible by exploiting the characteristics of the DES algorithm. The focus of concern has been on the eight substitution tables, or S-boxes, that are used in each iteration. Because the design criteria for these boxes, and indeed for the entire algorithm, have never been made public, there is a suspicion that the boxes were constructed in such a way that cryptanalysis is possible for an opponent who knows the weaknesses in the S-boxes. This assertion is tantalizing, and over the years a number of regularities and unexpected behaviors of the S-boxes have been discovered. Despite this, no one has so far succeeded in discovering the supposed fatal weaknesses in the S-boxes.[11]

Differential Cryptanalysis

One of the most significant advances in cryptanalysis in recent years is differential cryptanalysis. In this section, we provide a brief overview of the technique and its applicability to DES.

History

Differential cryptanalysis was not reported in the open literature until 1990. The first published effort appears to have been the cryptanalysis of a block cipher called FEAL by Murphy [MURP90]. This was followed by a number of papers by Biham and Shamir, who demonstrated this form of attack on a variety of encryption algorithms and hash functions; their results are summarized in [BIHA93].

The most publicized results for this approach have been those that have application to DES. Differential cryptanalysis is the first published attack that is capable of breaking DES in less than 2^{55} complexity. The scheme, as reported in [BIHA93], can successfully cryptanalyze DES with an effort on the order of 2^{47}, requiring 2^{47} chosen plaintexts. Although 2^{47} is certainly significantly less than 2^{55}, the need to find 2^{47} chosen plaintexts makes this attack of only theoretical interest.

Although differential cryptanalysis is a powerful tool, it does not do very well against DES. The reason, according to a member of the IBM team that designed DES [COPP92], is that differential cryptanalysis was known to the team as early as 1974. The need to strengthen DES against attacks using differential cryptanalysis played a large part in the design of the S-boxes and the permutation P. As evidence of the impact of these changes, consider these comparable results reported in [BIHA93]. Differential cryptanalysis of an 8-round LUCIFER algorithm requires only 256 chosen plaintexts, whereas an attack on an 8-round version of DES requires 2^{14} chosen plaintexts.

Differential cryptanalysis also influenced the design of IDEA, perhaps the most important conventional encryption algorithm since DES (described in Chapter 7). The designers of IDEA were unaware of differential cryptanalysis when they published their original design, known as the Proposed Encryption Standard (PES)

[11]At least, no one has publicly acknowledged such a discovery.

[LAI90]. PES uses a 128-bit key yet is vulnerable to differential cryptanalysis with a level of effort of only 264. The authors made minor modifications to PES to produce the IDEA design [LAI91] and they claim that IDEA is invulnerable to differential cryptanalysis.

Differential Cryptanalysis Attack

The differential cryptanalysis attack is quite complex, and you are referred to [BIHA93] for a complete description. Here, we provide a brief overview so that you can get the flavor of the attack.

We begin with a change in notation for DES. Consider the original plaintext block m to consist of two halves m_0, m_1. Each round of DES maps the right-hand input into the left-hand output, and sets the right-hand output to be a function of the left-hand input and the subkey for this round. So, at each round, only one new 32-bit block is created. If we label each new block m_i ($2 \leq i \leq 17$), then the intermediate message halves are related as follows:

$$m_{i+1} = m_{i-1} \oplus f(m_i, K_i), \qquad\qquad i = 1, 2, \ldots, 16$$

In differential cryptanalysis, one starts with two messages m, m' with a known XOR difference $\Delta m = m \oplus m'$, and considers the difference between the intermediate message halves: $\Delta m_i = m_i \oplus m'_i$. Then we have:

$$\begin{aligned} \Delta m_{i+1} &= m_{i+1} \oplus m'_{i+1} \\ &= [(m_{i-1} \oplus f(m_i, K_i)] \oplus [m'_{i-1} \oplus f(m'_i, K_i)] \\ &= \Delta m_{i-1} \oplus [f(m_i, K_i) \oplus f(m'_i, K_i)] \end{aligned}$$

Now, suppose that many pairs of inputs to f with the same difference yield the same output difference if the same subkey is used. To put this more precisely, let us say that *X may cause Y with probability p*, if for a fraction p of the pairs in which the input XOR is X, the output XOR equals Y. We want to suppose that there are a number of values of X that have high probability of causing a particular output difference. Therefore, if we know Δm_{i-1} and Δm_i with high probability, then we know Δm_{i+1} with high probability. Furthermore, if a number of such differences are determined, it is feasible to determine the subkey used in the function f.

The overall strategy of differential cryptanalysis is based on these considerations of a single round. The procedure is to begin with two plaintext messages m and m' with a given difference and trace through a probable pattern of differences after each round to yield a probable difference for the ciphertext. Actually, there are two probable differences for the two 32-bit halves: ($\Delta m_{17} \,||\, \Delta m_{16}$). Next, we submit m and m' for encryption to determine the actual difference under the unknown key, and compare the result to the probable difference. If there is a match,

$$E_k(m) \oplus E_k(m') = (\Delta m_{17} \,||\, \Delta m_{16})$$

then we suspect that all the probable patterns at all the intermediate rounds are correct. With that assumption, we can make some deductions about the key bits. This procedure must be repeated many times to actually determine all the key bits.

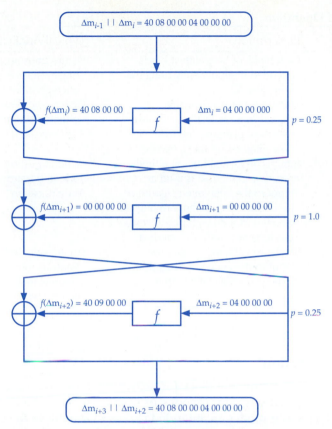

$\Delta m_{i-1} \; || \; \Delta m_i = 40\ 08\ 00\ 00\ 04\ 00\ 00\ 00$

$f(\Delta m_i) = 40\ 08\ 00\ 00$　　f　　$\Delta m_i = 04\ 00\ 00\ 000$　　$p = 0.25$

$f(\Delta m_{i+1}) = 00\ 00\ 00\ 00$　　f　　$\Delta m_{i+1} = 00\ 00\ 00\ 00$　　$p = 1.0$

$f(\Delta m_{i+2}) = 40\ 09\ 00\ 00$　　f　　$\Delta m_{i+2} = 04\ 00\ 00\ 00$　　$p = 0.25$

$\Delta m_{i+3} \; || \; \Delta m_{i+2} = 40\ 08\ 00\ 00\ 04\ 00\ 00\ 00$

FIGURE 2.13. Differential Propagation Through Three Rounds of DES (numbers in hexa-decimal)

Figure 2.13, based on one in [BIHA93], illustrates the propagation of differences through three rounds of DES. The probabilities shown on the right refer to the probability that a given set of intermediate differences will appear as a function of the input differences. Overall, after three rounds the probability that the output difference is as shown is equal to $0.25 \times 1 \times 0.25 = 0.0625$.

Linear Cryptanalysis

A more recent development is linear cryptanalysis, described in [MATS93]. This method can find a DES key given 2^{47} known plaintexts, as compared to 2^{47} chosen plaintexts for differential cryptanalysis. Although this is a minor improvement, since it may be easier to acquire known plaintext rather than chosen plaintext, it still leaves linear cryptanalysis infeasible as an attack on DES. So far, little work has been done by other groups to validate the linear cryptanalytic approach.

TABLE 2.9   DES Modes Of Operation

Mode	Description	Typical Application
Electronic Codebook (EBC)	Each block of 64 plaintext bits is encoded independently using the same key.	Secure transmission of single values (e.g., an encryption key)
Cipher Block Chaining (CBC)	The input to the encryption algorithm is the XOR of the next 64 bits of plaintext and the preceding 64 bits of ciphertext.	General-purpose block-oriented transmission Authentication
Cipher Feedback(CFB)	Input is processed J bits at a time. Preceding ciphertext is used as input to the encryption algorithm to produce pseudorandom output, which is XORed with plaintext to produce next unit of ciphertext.	General-purpose stream-oriented transmission Authentication
Output Feedback (OFB)	Similar to CFB, except that the input to the encryption algorithm is the preceding DES output.	Stream-oriented transmission over noisy channel (e.g., satellite communication)

DES Modes of Operation

The DES algorithm is a basic building block for providing data security. To apply DES in a variety of applications, four "modes of operation" have been defined (FIPS PUB 74, 81). These four modes are intended to cover virtually all the possible applications of encryption for which DES could be used. The modes are summarized in Table 2.9 and described briefly in the remainder of this section.

Electronic Codebook (ECB) Mode

The simplest mode is the electronic codebook mode, in which plaintext is handled 64 bits at a time and each block of plaintext is encrypted using the same key (Figure 2.14). The term codebook is used because, for a given key, there is a unique ciphertext for every 64-bit block of plaintext. Therefore, one can imagine a gigantic codebook in which there is an entry for every possible 64-bit plaintext pattern showing its corresponding ciphertext.

For a message longer than 64 bits, the procedure is to simply break the message up into 64-bit blocks, padding the last block if necessary. Decryption is performed one block at a time, always using the same key. In the figure, the plaintext (padded as necessary) consists of a sequence of 64-bit blocks, $P_1, P_2, \ldots, P_N$; the corresponding sequence of ciphertext blocks is $C_1, C_2, \ldots, C_N$.

The ECB method is ideal for a short amount of data, such as an encryption key. Thus, if you want to securely transmit a DES key, ECB is the appropriate mode to use.

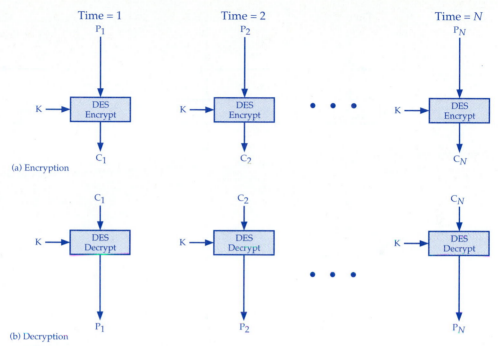

FIGURE 2.14.   Electronic Codebook (ECB) Mode

The most significant characteristic of ECB is that the same 64-bit block of plaintext, if it appears more than once in the message, always produces the same ciphertext.

For lengthy messages, the ECB mode may not be secure. If the message is highly structured, it may be possible for a cryptanalyst to exploit these regularities. For example, if it is known that the message always starts out with certain predefined fields, then the cryptanalyst may have a number of known plaintext/ciphertext pairs to work with. If the message has repetitive elements, with a period of repetition a multiple of 64 bits, then these elements can be identified by the analyst. This may help in the analysis or may provide opportunity for substituting or rearranging blocks.

Cipher Block Chaining (CBC) Mode

To overcome the security deficiencies of ECB, we would like a technique in which the same plaintext block, if repeated, produces different ciphertext blocks. A quite simple way to satisfy this requirement is the CBC mode (Figure 2.15). In this scheme, the input to the encryption algorithm is the XOR of the current plaintext block and the preceding ciphertext block; the same key is used for each block. In effect, we have chained together the processing of the sequence of plaintext

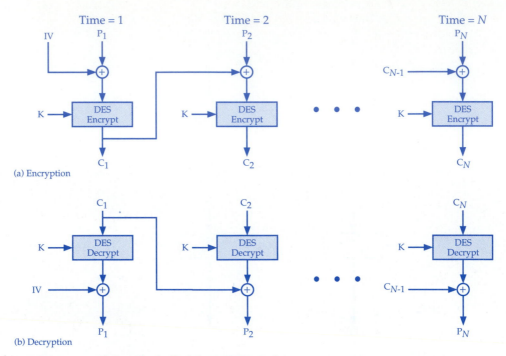

(a) Encryption

(b) Decryption

FIGURE 2.15.   Cipher Block Chaining (CBC) Mode

blocks. The input to the encryption function for each plaintext block bears no fixed relationship to the plaintext block. Therefore, repeating patterns of 64 bits are not exposed.

For decryption, each cipher block is passed through the decryption algorithm. The result is XORed with the preceding ciphertext block to produce the plaintext block. To see that this works, we can write:

$$C_n = E_K[C_{n-1} \oplus P_n]$$

Then,

$$
\begin{aligned}
D_K[C_n] &= D_K[E_K(C_{n-1} \oplus P_n)] \\
D_K[C_n] &= C_{n-1} \oplus P_n \\
C_{n-1} \oplus D_K[C_n] &= C_{n-1} \oplus C_{n-1} \oplus P_n = P_n
\end{aligned}
$$

To produce the first block of ciphertext, an initialization vector (IV) is XORed with the first block of plaintext. On decryption, the IV is XORed with the output of the decryption algorithm to recover the first block of plaintext.

The IV must be known to both the sender and receiver. For maximum security, the IV should be protected as well as the key. This could be done by sending the IV using ECB encryption. One reason for protecting the IV is as follows: If an opponent is able to fool the receiver into using a different value for IV, then the opponent is able to invert selected bits in the first block of plaintext. To see this, consider the following:

$$C_1 = E_K(IV \oplus P_1)$$
$$P_1 = IV \oplus D_K(C_1)$$

Now, use the notation that $X[i]$ denotes the ith bit of the 64-bit quantity X. Then,

$$P_1[i] = IV[i] \oplus D_K(C_1)[i]$$

Then, using the properties of XOR, we can state

$$P_1[i]' = IV[i]' \oplus D_K(C_1)[i]$$

where the prime notation denotes bit complementation. This means that if an opponent can predictably change bits in IV, the corresponding bits of the received value of P_1 can be changed.

For other possible attacks based on knowledge of IV, see [VOYD83].

In conclusion, because of the chaining mechanism of CBC, it is an appropriate mode for encrypting messages of length greater than 64 bits.

In addition to its use to achieve confidentiality, the CBC mode can be used for authentication. This use is described in Chapter 5.

Cipher Feedback (CFB) Mode

The DES scheme is essentially a block cipher technique that uses 64-bit blocks. However, it is possible to convert DES into a stream cipher, using either the cipher feedback or the output feedback mode. A stream cipher eliminates the need to pad a message to be an integral number of blocks. It also can operate in real time. Thus, if a character stream is being transmitted, each character can be encrypted and transmitted immediately using a character-oriented stream cipher.

One desirable property of a stream cipher is that the ciphertext be of the same length as the plaintext. Thus, if 8-bit characters are being transmitted, each character should be encrypted using 8 bits. If more than 8 bits are used, transmission capacity is wasted.

Figure 2.16 depicts the CFB scheme. In the figure, it is assumed that the unit of transmission is j bits; a common value is $j = 8$. As with CBC, the units of plaintext are chained together, so that the ciphertext of any plaintext unit is a function of all the preceding plaintext.

First, consider encryption. The input to the encryption function is a 64-bit shift register that is initially set to some initialization vector (IV). The leftmost (most significant) j bits of the output of the encryption function are XORed with the first unit of plaintext P_1 to produce the first unit of ciphertext C_1, which is then transmitted. In addition, the contents of the shift register are shifted left by j bits, and C_1 is placed in the rightmost (least significant) j bits of the shift register. This process continues until all plaintext units have been encrypted.

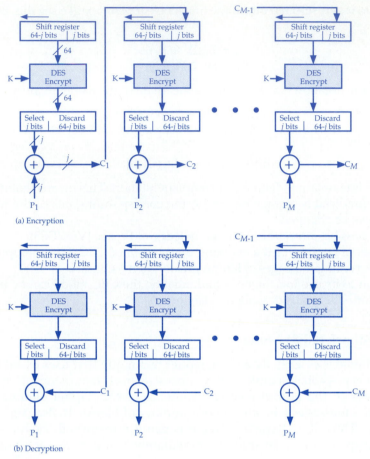

FIGURE 2.16.   J-Bit Cipher Feedback (CFB) Mode

For decryption, the same scheme is used, except that the received ciphertext unit is XORed with the output of the encryption function to produce the plaintext unit. Note that it is the *encryption* function that is used, not the decryption function. This is easily explained. Let $Sj(X)$ be defined as the most significant j bits of X. Then

$$C_1 = P_1 \oplus SjE(IV)$$

Therefore

$$P_1 = C_1 \oplus S_jE(IV)$$

The same reasoning holds for subsequent steps in the process.

In addition to its use to achieve confidentiality, the CFB mode can be used for authentication. This procedure is described in Chapter 5.

Output Feedback (OFB) Mode

The output feedback mode is similar in structure to that of CFB, as illustrated in Figure 2.17. As can be seen, it is the output of the encryption function that is fed back to the shift register in OFB, whereas in CFB the ciphertext unit is fed back to the shift register.

One advantage of the OFB method is that bit errors in transmission do not propagate. For example, if a bit error occurs in C_1, only the recovered value of P_1 is affected; subsequent plaintext units are not corrupted. With CFB, C_1 also serves as input to the shift register and therefore causes additional corruption downstream.

The disadvantage of OFB is that it is more vulnerable to a message-stream modification attack than is CFB. Consider that complementing a bit in the ciphertext complements the corresponding bit in the recovered plaintext. Thus, controlled

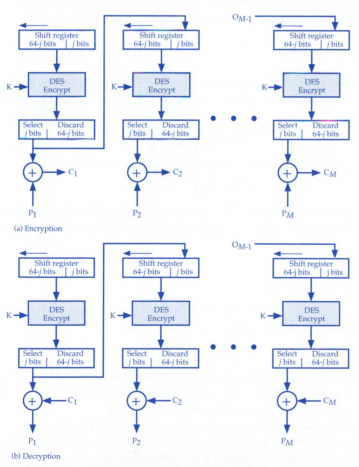

(a) Encryption

(b) Decryption

FIGURE 2.17.   J-Bit Output Feedback (OFB) Mode

changes to the recovered plaintext can be made. This may make it possible for an opponent, by making the necessary changes to the checksum portion of the message as well as to the data portion, to alter the ciphertext in such a way that it is not detected by an error-correcting code. For a further discussion, see [VOYD83].

2.4

TRIPLE DES

Given the potential vulnerability of DES to a brute-force attack, there has been considerable interest in finding an alternative. One approach is to design a completely new algorithm. An apparently successful example of this is IDEA, described in Chapter 7. Another alternative, which would preserve the existing investment in software and equipment, is to use multiple encryption with DES and multiple keys. We begin by examining the simplest example of this second alternative. We then look at the widely-accepted triple DES approach.

Double DES

The simplest form of multiple encryption has two encryption stages and two keys (Figure 2.18a). Given a plaintext P and two encryption keys K_1 and K_2, ciphertext C is generated as:

$$C = E_{K_2}\left[E_{K_1}[P]\right]$$

Decryption requires that the keys be applied in reverse order:

$$P = D_{K_1}\left[D_{K_2}[C]\right]$$

For DES, this scheme apparently involves a key length of $56 \times 2 = 112$ bits, resulting in a dramatic increase in cryptographic strength. But we need to examine the algorithm more closely.

Reduction to a Single Stage

Suppose it were true for DES, for all 56-bit key values, that given any two keys K_1 and K_2, it would be possible to find a key K_3 such that:

$$E_{K_2}\left[E_{K_1}[P]\right] = E_{K_3}[P] \tag{2.1}$$

If this were the case, then double encryption, and indeed any number of stages of multiple encryption with DES, would be useless because the result would be equivalent to a single encryption with a single 56-bit key.

On the face of it, it does not appear that Equation (2.1) is likely to hold. Consider that encryption with DES is a mapping of 64-bit blocks to 64-bit blocks. In fact, the mapping is a permutation. That is, if we consider all 2^{64} possible input blocks, DES encryption with a specific key will map each block into a unique 64-bit block.

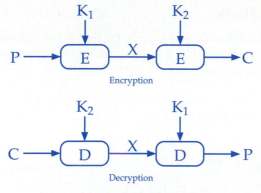

(a) Double encryption

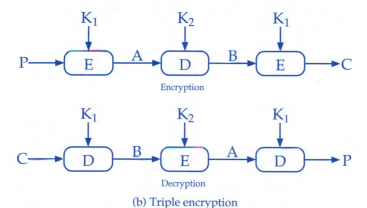

(b) Triple encryption

FIGURE 2.18.   Multiple Encryption

Otherwise, if, say, two given input blocks mapped to the same output block, then decryption to recover the original plaintext would be impossible. Now, with 2^{64} possible inputs, how many different mappings are there that generate a permutation of the input blocks? The value is easily seen to be:

$$(2^{64})! > 10^{347380000000000000000} > (10^{10^{20}})$$

On the other hand, DES defines one mapping for each different key, for a total number of mappings:

$$2^{56} < 10^{17}$$

Therefore, it is reasonable to assume that if DES is used twice with different keys, it will produce one of the many mappings that is not defined by a single application of DES. Although there was much supporting evidence for this assumption, it was not until 1992 that the assumption was proved [CAMP92].

Meet-in-the-Middle Attack

Thus, the use of double DES results in a mapping that is not equivalent to a single DES encryption. But there is another way to attack this scheme, one that does not depend on any particular property of DES but that will work against any block encryption cipher.

The algorithm, known as a meet-in-the-middle attack, was first described in [DIFF77]. It is based on the observation that, if we have

$$C = E_{K_2}\Big[E_{K_1}[P]\Big]$$

Then (see Figure 2.18a):

$$X = E_{K_1}[P] = D_{K_2}[C]$$

Given a known pair, (P, C), the attack proceeds as follows. First, encrypt P for all 2^{56} possible values of K_1. Store these results in a table and then sort the table by the values of X. Next, decrypt C using all 2^{56} possible values of K_2. As each decryption is produced, check the result against the table for a match. If a match occurs, then test the two resulting keys against a new known plaintext-ciphertext pair. If the two keys produce the correct ciphertext, accept them as the correct keys.

For any given plaintext P, there are 2^{64} possible ciphertext values that could be produced by double DES. Double DES uses in effect a 112-bit key, so that there are 2^{112} possible keys. Therefore, on average, for a given plaintext P, the number of different 112-bit keys that will produce a given ciphertext C is $2^{112}/2^{64} = 2^{48}$. Thus, the foregoing procedure will produce about 2^{48} false alarms on the first (P, C) pair. A similar argument indicates that with an additional 64 bits of known plaintext and ciphertext, the false alarm rate is reduced to $2^{48-64} = 2^{-16}$. Put another way, if the meet-in-the-middle attack is performed on two blocks of known plaintext-ciphertext, the probability that the correct keys are determined is $1 - 2^{-16}$. The result is that a known plaintext attack will succeed against double DES, which has a key size of 112 bits, with an effort on the order of 2^{56}.

Triple DES with Two Keys

An obvious counter to the meet-in-the-middle attack is to use three stages of encryption with three different keys. This raises the cost of the known-plaintext attack to 2^{112}, which is beyond what is practical now and far into the future. However, it has the drawback of requiring a key length of $56 \times 3 = 168$ bits, which is somewhat unwieldy.

As an alternative, Tuchman proposed a triple encryption method that uses only two keys [TUCH79]. The function follows an encrypt-decrypt-encrypt (EDE) sequence (Figure 2.18b):

$$C = E_{K_1}\Big[D_{K_2}\Big[E_{K_1}[P]\Big]\Big]$$

There is no cryptographic significance to the use of decryption for the second stage. Its only advantage is that it allows users of triple DES to decrypt data encrypted by users of the older single DES:

$$C = E_{K_1}\left[D_{K_1}\left[E_{K_1}[P]\right]\right] = E_{K_1}[P]$$

Triple DES is a relatively popular alternative to DES and has been adopted for use in the key management standards ANS X9.17 and ISO 8732, and for Privacy-Enhanced Mail (PEM), described in Chapter 9.[12]

Currently, there are no practical cryptanalytic attacks on triple DES. Coppersmith [COPP92] notes that the cost of a brute force key search on triple DES is on the order of $2^{112} \approx 5 \times 10^{35}$ and estimates that the cost of differential cryptanalysis suffers an exponential growth, compared to single DES, exceeding 10^{52}.

It is worth looking at several proposed attacks on triple DES that, although not practical, give a flavor for the types of attacks that have been considered and that could form the basis for more successful future attacks.

The first serious proposal came from Merkle and Hellman [MERK81]. Their plan involves finding plaintext values that produce a first intermediate value of $A = 0$ (Figure 2.18b) and then using the meet-in-the-middle attack to determine the two keys. The level of effort is 2^{56}, but the technique requires 2^{56} chosen plaintext-ciphertext pairs, a number unlikely to be provided by the holder of the keys.

A known-plaintext attack is outlined in [OORS90]. This method is an improvement over the chosen-plaintext approach but requires more effort. The attack is based on the observation that if we know A and C (Figure 2.18b), then the problem reduces to that of an attack on double DES. Of course, the attacker does not know A, even if P and C are known, so long as the two keys are unknown. However, the attacker can choose a potential value of A and then try to find a known (P, C) pair that produces A. The attack proceeds as follows:

1. Obtain n (P, C) pairs. This is the known plaintext. Place these in a table (Table 1) sorted on the values of P (Figure 2.19b).
2. Pick an arbitrary value a for A, and create a second table (Figure 2.19c) with entries defined in the following fashion. For each of the 2^{56} possible keys $K_1 = i$, calculate the plaintext value P_i that produces a:

$$P_i = D_i\,[a]$$

For each P_i that matches an entry in Table 1, create an entry in Table 2 consisting of the K_1 value and the value of B that is produced for the (P, C) pair from Table 1, assuming that value of K_1:

$$B = D_i\,[C]$$

At the end of this step, sort Table 2 on the values of B.

---

[12](ANS X9.17) American National Standard: Financial Institution Key Management (Wholesale). From its title, X9.17 appears to be a somewhat obscure standard. Yet a number of techniques specified in this standard have been adopted for use in other standards and applications, as we shall see throughout this book.

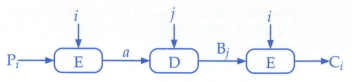

(a) Two-key triple encryption with candidate pair of keys

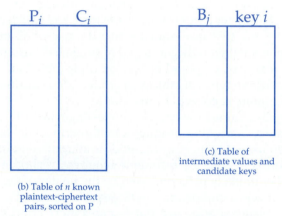

(b) Table of n known
plaintext-ciphertext
pairs, sorted on P

(c) Table of
intermediate values and
candidate keys

FIGURE 2.19.   Known-Plaintext Attack on Triple DES

3. We now have a number of candidate values of K_1 in Table 2 and are in a position to search for a value of K_2. For each of the 2^{56} possible keys $K_2 = j$, calculate the second intermediate value for our chosen value of a:

$$B_j = D_j[a]$$

At each step, look up B_j in Table 2. If there is a match, then the corresponding key i from Table 2 plus this value of j are candidate values for the unknown keys (K_1, K_2). Why? Because we have found a pair of keys (i, j) that produce a known (P, C) pair (Figure 2.19a).

4. Test each candidate pair of keys (i, j) on a few other plaintext-ciphertext pairs. If a pair of keys produce the desired ciphertext, the task is complete. If no pair succeeds, repeat from step 1 with a new value of a.

For a given known (P, C), the probability of selecting the unique value of a that leads to success is $1/64$. Thus, given n (P, C) pairs, the probability of success for a single selected value of a is $n/64$. A basic result from probability theory is that the expected number of draws required to draw one red ball out of a bin containing n red balls and $N - n$ green balls is $(N + 1)/(n + 1)$ if the balls are not replaced. So, the expected number of values of a that must be tried is, for large n,

$$\frac{2^{64}+1}{n+1} \approx \frac{2^{64}}{n}$$

Thus, the expected running time of the attack is on the order of:

$$(2^{56})\frac{2^{64}}{\mathbf{n}} = 2^{120-\log_2 n}$$

2.5

RECOMMENDED READING

There is a wealth of information on conventional encryption. Some of the more worthwhile references are listed here.

[SIMM93] is a model of clarity and conciseness; its 14 pages contain a perceptive history of cryptology and a good overview of cryptographic techniques.

Anyone interested in the history of code-making and code-breaking simply must read [KAHN67]. Although it is concerned more with the impact of cryptology than its technical development, it is an excellent introduction and makes for exciting reading.

An essential reference work is [SCHN94]. This remarkable work contains descriptions of virtually every cryptographic algorithm and protocol published in the last 15 years. The author pulls together results from journals, conference proceedings, government publications, and standards documents, and organizes these into a comprehensive and comprehensible survey.

For coverage of contemporary cryptology, Simmons's book of that same name is unexcelled [SIMM92a]. This is actually a collection of papers, some original and some of which are revised from earlier versions that appeared in the May 1988 issue of the *Proceedings of the IEEE*. The book provides an in-depth survey of the field.

Two rather mathematical treatments of the subject are [DENN82] and [PATT87]. Both are reasonably self-contained, providing the necessary mathematical background.

The foregoing references provide coverage of public-key as well as conventional encryption.

A detailed mathematical treatment of rotor machines is contained in [KOHN81]

For a discussion of the potential weaknesses of DES, see [RHEE94] and [DAVI89]. [BARK91] provides a readable and interesting analysis of the structure of DES and of potential cryptanalytic approaches to DES. [MEYE82], written by two of the designers of DES, provides a detailed mathematical treatment of DES.

BARK91   Barker, W. *Introduction to the Analysis of the Data Encryption Standard (DES)*. Laguna Hills, CA: Aegean Park Press, 1991.

DAVI89   Davies, D., and Price, W. *Security for Computer Networks*. New York: Wiley, 1989.

DENN82   Denning, D. *Cryptography and Data Security*. Reading, MA: Addison-Wesley, 1982.

KAHN67   Kahn, D. *The Codebreakers: The Story of Secret Writing.* New York: Macmillan, 1967 (abridged edition, New York: New American Library, 1974).

KOHN81   Konheim, A. *Cryptography: A Primer.* New York: Wiley, 1981.

MEYE82   Meyer, C, and Matyas, S. *Cryptography: A New Dimension in Computer Data Security.* New York: Wiley, 1982.

PATT87   Patterson, W. *Mathematical Cryptology for Computer Scientists and Mathematicians.* Totowa, NJ: Rowman & Littlefield, 1987.

RHEE94   Rhee, M. *Cryptography and Secure Communications.* New York: McGraw-Hill, 1994.

SCHN94   Schneier, B. *Applied Cryptography.* New York: Wiley, 1994.

SIMM92a Simmons, G., ed. *Contemporary Cryptology: The Science of Information Integrity.* Piscataway, NJ: IEEE Press, 1992.

SIMM93   Simmons, G. "Cryptology." *Encyclopaedia Britannica,* 1993.

2.6

PROBLEMS

2.1 What is the message embedded in Figure 2.3?

2.2 The purpose of this problem is to show the unbreakability of the one-time pad. Suppose that we are using a Vigenére scheme with 27 characters in which the 27th character is the space character, but with a one-time key that is as long as the message. Given the ciphertext

> ANKYODKYUREPFJBYOJDSPLREYIUNOFDOIUERFPLUYTS

Find the key that yields the following plaintext:

> MR MUSTARD WITH THE CANDLESTICK IN THE HALL

and find another key that yields the following plaintext:

> MISS SCARLET WITH THE KNIFE IN THE LIBRARY

Comment on the result.

2.3 In one of Dorothy Sayers's mysteries, Lord Peter is confronted with the message shown in Figure 2.20. He also discovers the key to the message, which is a sequence of integers:

> 7876565434321123434565678788787656543432112343456567878887 87
> 65654433211234

    a. Decrypt the message. Hint: What is the largest integer value?

    b. If the algorithm is known but not the key, how secure is the scheme?

    c. If the key is known but not the algorithm, how secure is the scheme?

2.4 The following ciphertext was generated using a simple substitution algorithm:

> 53‡‡†305))6*;4826)4‡.)4‡);806*;48†8¶60))85;;]8*;:‡*8†83
> (88)5*†;46(;88*96*?;8)*‡(;485);5*†2:*‡(;4956*2(5*—4)8¶8*

I thought to see the fairies in the fields, but I saw only the evil elephants with their black backs. Woe! how that sight awed me! The elves danced all around and about while I heard voices calling clearly. Ah! how I tried to see—throw off the ugly cloud—but no blind eye of a mortal was permitted to spy them. So then came minstrels, having gold trumpets, harps and drums. These played very loudly beside me, breaking that spell. So the dream vanished, whereat I thanked Heaven. I shed many tears before the thin moon rose up, frail and faint as a sickle of straw. Now though the Enchanter gnash his teeth vainly, yet shall he return as the Spring returns. Oh, wretched man! Hell gapes, Erebus now lies open. The mouths of Death wait on thy end.

FIGURE 2.20. A Puzzle for Lord Peter

```
;4069285);)6†8)4‡‡;1(‡9;48081;8;8‡1;48†85;4)485†528806*81
(‡9;48;(88;4(‡?34;48)4‡;161;:188;‡?;
```

Decrypt this message. Hints:

1. As you know, the most frequently occurring letter in English is e. Therefore, the first or second (or perhaps third?) most common character in the message is likely to stand for e. Also, e is often seen in pairs (e.g., meet, fleet, speed, seen, been, agree, etc.). Try to find a character in the ciphertext that decodes to e.
2. The most common word in English is "the." Use this fact to guess the characters that stand for t and h.
3. Decipher the rest of the message by deducing additional words.

Warning: the resulting message is in English but may not make much sense on a first reading.

2.5 One way to solve the key distribution problem is to use a line from a book that both the sender and the receiver possess. Typically, at least in spy novels, the first sentence of a book serves as the key. The particular scheme discussed in this problem is from one of the best suspense novels involving secret codes, *Talking to Strange Men,* by Ruth Rendell. Work this problem without consulting that book!

Consider the following message:

```
SIDKHKDM AF HCRKIABIE SHIMC KD LFEAILA
```

This ciphertext was produced using the first sentence of *The Other Side of Silence* (a book about the spy Kim Philby):

> The snow lay thick on the steps and the snowflakes driven by the wind looked black in the headlights of the cars.

A simple substitution cipher was used.

  a. What is the encryption algorithm?
  b. How secure is it?
  c. To make the key distribution problem simple, both parties can agree to use the first or last sentence of a book as the key. To change the key, they simply need to agree on a new book. The use of the first sentence would be preferable to the use of the last. Why?

2.6 In one of his cases, Sherlock Holmes was confronted with the following message.

```
534 C2 13 127 36 31 4 17 21 41
DOUGLAS 109 293 5 37 BIRLSTONE
     26 BIRLSTONE 9 127 171
```

Although Watson was puzzled, Holmes was able to immediately deduce the type of cipher. Can you?

2.7 A disadvantage of the general monoalphabetic cipher is that both sender and receiver must commit the permuted cipher sequence to memory. A common technique for avoiding this is to use a keyword from which the cipher sequence can be generated. For example, using the keyword *CIPHER,* write out the keyword followed by unused letters in normal order and match this against the plaintext letters:

```
plain:   a b c d e f g h i j k l m n o p q r s t u v w x y z
cipher:  C I P H E R A B D F G J K L M N O Q S T U V W X Y Z
```

If it is felt that this process does not produce sufficient mixing, write the remaining letters on successive lines and then generate the sequence by reading down the columns:

```
C I P H E R
A B D F G J
K L M N O Q
S T U V W X
Y Z
```

This yields the sequence:

```
C A K S Y I B L T Z P D M U H F N V E G O W R J Q X
```

Such a system is used in the example in Section 2.2. Determine the keyword.

2.8 Decrypt the following:

```
UFMDHQAQTMGRGBXGRAZTWPWMUFMDHBGMGHWOGVWDW
AVGBABAWGRODTWXQUHAQOWTMHCQHHFQUWGBXGHFIU
```

HIFWBFDQHHWFARAHCWDTQRAHWLHOQMGIFJRJWWAUF
MDHRBAQAVSWVRGUWFARSTWRAHCWURDCWFHWLH

2.9 Let π be a permutation of the integers $1, 2, \ldots 2^n - 1$, such that $\pi(m)$ gives the permuted value of m, $0 \le m \le 2^n$. Put another way, π maps the set of n-bit integers into itself and no two integers map into the same integer. DES is such a permutation for 64-bit integers. We say that π has a fixed point at m if $\pi(m) = m$. That is, if π is an encryption mapping, then a fixed point corresponds to a message that encrypts to itself. We are interested in the probability that π has no fixed points. Show the somewhat unexpected result that over 60 percent of mappings will have at least one fixed point.

2.10 Consider a block encryption algorithm that encrypts blocks of length $N = 2^n$. Say we have t plaintext/ciphertext pairs $P_i, C_i = E_K[P_i]$ where we assume that the key K selects one of the $N!$ possible mappings. Imagine that we wish to find K by exhaustive search. We could generate key K′ and test whether $C_i = E_{K'}(P_i)$ for $1 \le i \le t$. If K′ encrypts each P_i to its proper C_i then we have evidence that K = K′. However, it may be the case that the mappings $E_K(\bullet)$ and $E_{K'}(\bullet)$ exactly agree on the t plaintext/ciphertext pairs P_i, C_i and agree on no other pairs.

  a. What is the probability that $E_K(\bullet)$ and $E_{K'}(\bullet)$ are in fact distinct mappings?
  b. What is the probability that $E_K(\bullet)$ and $E_{K'}(\bullet)$ agree on another t' plaintext/ciphertext pairs where $0 \le t' \le N - k$?

2.11 The 32-bit swap after the 16th iteration of the DES algorithm is needed to make the encryption process invertible by simply running the ciphertext back through the algorithm with the key order reversed. This was demonstrated in Figure 2.12. However, it still may not be entirely clear why the 32-bit swap is needed. To demonstrate why, solve the following exercises. First, some notation:

A||B	=	the concatenation of bit strings A and B
$T_i(R\|\|L)$	=	the transformation defined by the ith iteration of the encryption algorithm, for $1 \le i \le 16$
$TD_i(R\|\|L)$	=	the transformation defined by the ith iteration of the decryption algorithm, for $1 \le i \le 16$
$T_{17}(R\|\|L)$	=	L||R. This transformation occurs after the 16th iteration of the encryption algorithm.

  a. Show that the composition $TD_1(IP(IP^{-1}(T_{17}(T_{16}(L_{15}\|\|R_{15})))))$ is equivalent to the transformation that interchanges the 32-bit halves, L_{15} and R_{15}. That is, show that

$$TD_1(IP(IP^{-1}(T_{17}(T_{16}(L_{15}\|\|R_{15}))))) = R_{15}\|\|L_{15}$$

  b. Now suppose that we did away with the final 32-bit swap in the encryption algorithm. Then we would want the following equality to hold:

$$TD_1(IP(IP^{-1}(T_{16}(L_{15}\|\|R_{15})))) = L_{15}\|\|R_{15}$$

Does it?

2.12 Compare the Initial Permutation table (Table 2.5a) with the Permuted Choice One table (Table 2.7a). Are the structures similar? If so, describe the similarities. What conclusions can you draw from this?

2.13 When using the DES algorithm for decryption, the 16 keys (K_1, K_2, . . . , K_{16}) are used in reverse order. Therefore, the right hand side of Figure 2.9 is no longer valid. Design a key-generation scheme with the appropriate shift schedule (analogous to Table 2.7c) for the decryption process.

2.14 **a.** Let M′ be the bitwise complement of M. Prove that if the complement of the plaintext block is taken and the complement of an encryption key is taken, then the result of encryption with these values is the complement of the original ciphertext. That is:

$$\text{If} \quad Y = DES_K(X)$$
$$\text{Then } Y' = DES_{K'}(X')$$

Hint: Begin by showing that for any two bit strings of equal length, A and B, $(A \oplus B)' = A' \oplus B$.

b. It has been said that a brute-force attack on DES requires searching a key space of 2^{56} keys. Does the result of part (a) change that?

2.15 Show that in DES the first 24 bits of each subkey come from the same subset of 28 bits of the initial key and that the second 24 bits of each subkey come from a disjoint subset of 28 bits of the initial key.

2.16 With the ECB mode of DES, if there is an error in a block of the transmitted ciphertext, only the corresponding plaintext block is affected. However, in the CBC mode, this error propagates. For example, an error in the transmitted C_1 (Figure 2.15) obviously corrupts P_1 and P_2.

a. Are any blocks beyond P_2 affected?

b. Suppose that there is a bit error in the source version of P1. Through how many ciphertext blocks is this error propagated? What is the effect at the receiver?

2.17 If a bit error occurs in the transmission of a ciphertext character in 8-bit CFB mode, how far does the error propagate?

2.18 A brute-force key search as the basis for a known-plaintext attack on the DES ECB mode is straightforward: given the 64-bit plaintext and the 64-bit ciphertext, try all of the 2^{56} possible keys until one is found that generates the known ciphertext from the known plaintext. The situation is more complex for the other three modes, which include the use of a 64-bit initialization vector (IV). This seems to introduce an additional 64 bits of uncertainty.

a. Suggest strategies for known-plaintext attacks on the other three modes of DES that are of the same order of magnitude of effort as the ECB attack.

b. Now consider a ciphertext-only attack. For ECB mode, the strategy is to try to decrypt the given ciphertext with all 2^{56} keys and test each result to see if it appears to be syntactically legal plaintext. Will this strategy work for the other three modes? If so, explain. If not, describe attack strategies for these modes and estimate the level of effort.

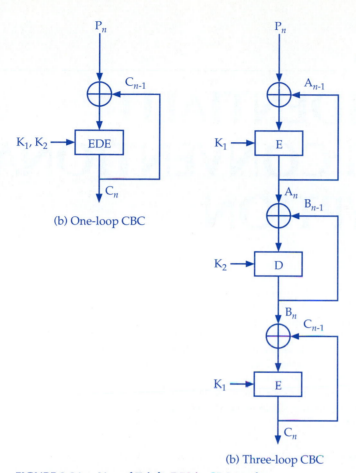

(b) One-loop CBC

(b) Three-loop CBC

FIGURE 2.21.   Use of Triple DES in CBC Mode

2.19 You want to build a hardware device to do block encryption in the cipher block chaining (CBC) mode using an algorithm stronger than DES. Triple DES is a good candidate but it is defined only in ECB mode. Although there is no established standard for CBC mode for triple DES, Figure 2.21 shows two contenders, both of which follow from the definition of CBC. Which of the two would you choose:
a. For security?
b. For performance?

2.20 Can you suggest a security improvement to either option in Figure 2.21, using only three DES chips and some number of XOR functions? Assume you are still limited to two keys.

2.21 The Merkle-Hellman attack on triple DES begins by assuming a value of $A = 0$ (Figure 2.18b). Then, for each of the 2^{56} possible values of K_1, the plaintext P which produces $A = 0$ is determined. Describe the rest of the algorithm.

CHAPTER 3

CONFIDENTIALITY USING CONVENTIONAL ENCRYPTION

Amongst the tribes of Central Australia every man, woman, and child has a secret or sacred name which is bestowed by the older men upon him or her soon after birth, and which is known to none but the fully initiated members of the group. This secret name is never mentioned except upon the most solemn occasions; to utter it in the hearing of men of another group would be a most serious breach of tribal custom. When mentioned at all, the name is spoken only in a whisper, and not until the most elaborate precautions have been taken that it shall be heard by no one but members of the group. The native thinks that a stranger knowing his secret name would have special power to work him ill by means of magic.

> — *The Golden Bough*
> Sir James George Frazer

Increased use of computer and communications networks, computer literacy, and dependence on information technology heighten U.S. industry's risk of losing proprietary information to economic espionage. In part to reduce the risk, industry is more frequently using hardware and software with encryption capabilities.

> — *Communications Privacy: Federal Policy and Actions*
> General Accounting Office Report GAO/OSI-94-2
> November 1993

If a secret piece of news is divulged by a spy before the time is ripe, he must be put to death, together with the man to whom the secret was told.

> — *The Art of War*
> Sun Tzu

John wrote the letters of the alphabet under the letters in its first lines and tried it against the message. Immediately he knew that once more he had broken the code. It was extraordinary the feeling of triumph he had. He felt on top of the world. For not only had he done it, had he broken the July code, but he now had the key to every future coded message, since instructions as to the source of the next one must of necessity appear in the current one at the end of each month.

— *Talking to Strange Men*
Ruth Rendell

Historically, the focus of cryptology has been the use of conventional encryption to provide confidentiality. It is only in the last several decades that other considerations, such as authentication, integrity, digital signatures, and the use of public-key encryption, have been included in the theory and practice of cryptology.

Before examining some of these more recent topics, we concentrate in this chapter on the use of conventional encryption to provide confidentiality. This topic remains important in itself. In addition, an understanding of the issues involved here helps to motivate the development of public-key encryption and clarifies the issues involved in other applications of encryption, such as authentication.

We begin with a discussion of the location of encryption logic; the main choice here is between what are known as link and end-to-end encryption. Next, we look at the use of encryption to counter traffic analysis attacks. This is followed by a discussion of the difficult problem of key distribution. Finally, this chapter discusses the principles underlying an important tool in providing a confidentiality facility: random number generation.

3.1

PLACEMENT OF ENCRYPTION FUNCTION

If encryption is to be used to counter attacks on confidentiality, we need to decide what to encrypt and where the encryption function should be located. To begin, this section examines the potential locations of a security attack and then looks at the two major approaches to encryption placement: link and end-to-end.

Potential Locations for Confidentiality Attacks

As an example, consider a user workstation in a typical business organization. Figure 3.1 suggests the types of communications facilities that might be employed by such a workstation and therefore gives an indication of the points of vulnerability.

In most organizations, workstations are attached to local area networks (LANs). Typically, the user can reach other workstations, hosts, and servers directly on the LAN or on other LANs in the same building that are interconnected with bridges and routers. Here, then, is the first point of vulnerability. In this case, the main concern is eavesdropping by another employee. Typically, a LAN is a broadcast network: A transmission from any station to any other station is visible on the LAN medium to all stations. Data are transmitted in the form of frames, with each frame

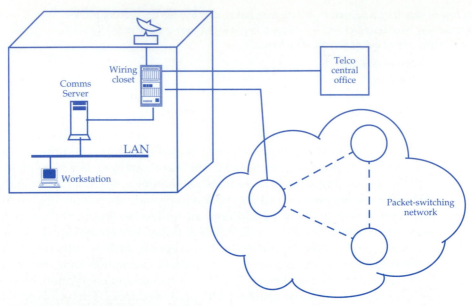

FIGURE 3.1.   Points of Vulnerability

containing the source and destination address. An eavesdropper can monitor the traffic on the LAN and capture any traffic desired on the basis of source and destination addresses.

Furthermore, the eavesdropper need not necessarily be an employee in the building. If the LAN, through a communications server or one of the hosts on the LAN, offers a dial-in capability, then it is possible for an intruder to gain access to the LAN and monitor traffic.

Access to the outside world from the LAN is almost always available in the form of a router, a bank of dial-out modems, or some other type of communications server. From the communications server, there is a line leading to a wiring closet. The wiring closet serves as a patch panel for interconnecting internal data and phone lines and for providing a staging point for external communications.

The wiring closet itself is vulnerable. If an intruder can penetrate to the closet, he or she can tap into each wire to determine which are used for data transmission. After isolating one or more lines, the intruder can attach a low-power radio transmitter. The resulting signals can be picked up from a nearby location (e.g., a parked van or a nearby building).

Several routes out of the wiring closet are possible. A standard configuration provides access to the nearest central office of the local telephone company. Wires in the closet are gathered into a cable, which is usually consolidated with other cables in the basement of the building. From there, a larger cable runs underground to the central office.

In addition, the wiring closet may provide a link to a microwave antenna, either an earth station for a satellite link or a point-to-point terrestrial microwave link. The antenna link can be part of a private network, or it can be a local bypass to hook in to a long-distance carrier, such as AT&T or MCI.

The wiring closet may also provide a link to a node of a packet-switching network. This link can be a leased line, a direct private line, or a switched connection through a public telecommunications network such as ISDN. Inside the network, data pass through a number of nodes and links between nodes until arriving at the node to which the destination end system is connected.

An attack can take place at any of the communications links. For active attacks, the attacker needs to gain physical control of a portion of the link and be able to insert and capture transmissions. For a passive attack, the attacker merely needs to be able to observe transmissions. The communications links involved can be cable (telephone twisted pair, coaxial cable, or optical fiber), microwave links, or satellite channels. Twisted pair and coaxial cable can be attacked using either invasive taps or inductive devices that monitor electromagnetic emanation. Invasive taps allow both active and passive attacks, whereas inductive taps are useful for passive attacks. Neither type of tap is particularly useful with optical fiber, which is one of the advantages of this medium. The fiber does not generate electromagnetic emanations and hence is not vulnerable to inductive taps. Physically breaking the cable seriously degrades signal quality and is therefore detectable. Microwave and satellite transmissions can be intercepted with little risk to the attacker. This is especially true of satellite transmissions, which cover a broad geographic area. Active attacks on microwave and satellite transmissions are also possible, although they are more difficult technically and can be quite expensive.

In addition to the potential vulnerability of the various communications links, the various processors along the path are themselves subject to attack. An attack can take the form of attempts to modify the hardware or software, to gain access to the memory of the processor, or to monitor the electromagnetic emanations. These attacks are less likely than those involving communications links but are nevertheless a source of risk.

Thus, there are a large number of locations at which an attack can occur. Furthermore, for wide-area communications, many of these locations are not under the physical control of the end user. Even in the case of local area networks, in which physical security measures are possible, there is always the threat of the disgruntled employee.

Link Versus End-to-End Encryption

The most powerful and most common approach to securing the points of vulnerability highlighted in the preceding section is encryption. If encryption is to be used to counter these attacks, then we need to decide what to encrypt and where the encryption gear should be located. As Figure 3.2 indicates, there are two fundamental alternatives: link encryption and end-to-end encryption.

Basic Approaches

With link encryption, each vulnerable communications link is equipped on both ends with an encryption device. Thus, all traffic over all communications links is secured. Although this recourse requires a lot of encryption devices in a large network, its value is clear. One of its disadvantages is that the message must be decrypted each time it enters a packet switch because the switch must read the address (virtual circuit number) in the packet header in order to route the packet. Thus, the message is vulnerable at each switch. If working with a public packet-switching network, the user has no control over the security of the nodes.

Several implications of link encryption should be noted. For this strategy to be effective, all the potential links in a path from source to destination must use link encryption. Each pair of nodes that share a link should share a unique key, with a different key used on each link. Thus, many keys must be provided. However, each key must be distributed to only two nodes.

With end-to-end encryption, the encryption process is carried out at the two end systems. The source host or terminal encrypts the data. The data in encrypted form are then transmitted unaltered across the network to the destination terminal or host. The destination shares a key with the source and so is able to decrypt the data. This plan seems to secure the transmission against attacks on the network links or switches. Thus, end-to-end encryption relieves the end user of concerns about the degree of security of networks and links that support the communication. There is, however, still a weak spot.

Consider the following situation. A host connects to an X.25 packet-switching network, sets up a virtual circuit to another host, and is prepared to transfer data to that other host by using end-to-end encryption. Data are transmitted over such a network in the form of packets that consist of a header and some user data. What part of each packet will the host encrypt? Suppose that the host encrypts the entire packet, including the header. This will not work because, remember, only the other host can perform the decryption. The packet-switching node will receive an encrypted packet and be unable to read the header. Therefore, it will not be able to route the packet! It follows that the host may encrypt only the user data portion of the packet and must leave the header in the clear so that it can be read by the network.

Thus, with end-to-end encryption, the user data are secure. However, the traffic pattern is not, because packet headers are transmitted in the clear. On the other hand, end-to-end encryption does provide a degree of authentication. If two end systems share an encryption key, then a recipient is assured that any message that it receives comes from the alleged sender, since only that sender shares the relevant key. Such authentication is not inherent in a link encryption scheme.

To achieve greater security, both link and end-to-end encryption are needed, as is shown in Figure 3.2. Figure 3.3 illustrates the separate and joint effects of the two forms of encryption. In this simplified illustration, only a single packet-switching node is shown. When both forms of encryption are employed, the host encrypts the user data portion of a packet using an end-to-end encryption key. The entire

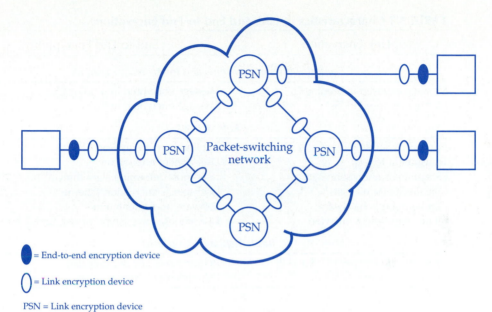

● = End-to-end encryption device

◖◗ = Link encryption device

PSN = Link encryption device

FIGURE 3.2.   Encryption Across A Packet-Switching Network

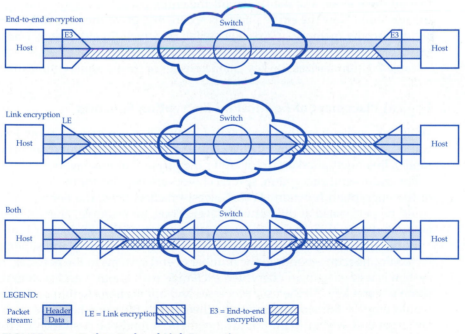

FIGURE 3.3.   End-to-End and Link Encryption

TABLE 3.1 Characteristics of Link and End-to-End Encryption[a]

Link Encryption	End-to-End Encryption
Security within end systems and intermediate systems	
Message exposed in sending ES	Message encrypted in sending ES
Message exposed in ISs	Message encrypted in ISs
Role of User	
Applied by sending ES	Applied by sending process
Transparent to user	User applies encryption
ES maintains encryption facility	User must determine algorithm
One facility for all users	User selects encryption scheme
Can be done in hardware	Software implementation
All or no messages encryted	User chooses to encrypt, or not, for each message
Implementation Concerns	
Requires one key per ES–IS and IS–IS pair	Requires one key per user pair
Provides ES authentication	Provides user authentication

[a]From [PFLE89].

packet is then encrypted by using a link encryption key. As the packet traverses the network, each switch decrypts the packet, using a link encryption key in order to read the header, and then encrypts the entire packet again for sending it out on the next link. Now the entire packet is secure except for the time that the packet is actually in the memory of a packet switch, at which time the packet header is in the clear.

Table 3.1 summarizes the key characteristics of the two encryption strategies.

Logical Placement of End-to-End Encryption Function

With link encryption, the encryption function is performed at a low level of the communications hierarchy. In terms of the open systems interconnection (OSI) model, link encryption occurs at either the physical or link layers.

For end-to-end encryption, several choices are possible for the logical placement of the encryption function. At the lowest practical level, the encryption function could be performed at the network layer. Thus, for example, encryption could be associated with X.25, so that the user data portion of all X.25 packets is encrypted.

With network-layer encryption, the number of identifiable and separately protected entities corresponds to the number of end systems in the network. Each end system can engage in an encrypted exchange with another end system if the two share a secret key. All the user processes and applications within each end system would employ the same encryption scheme with the same key to reach a particular target end system. With this arrangement, it might be desirable to off-load the encryption function to some sort of front-end processor (typically a communications board in the end system).

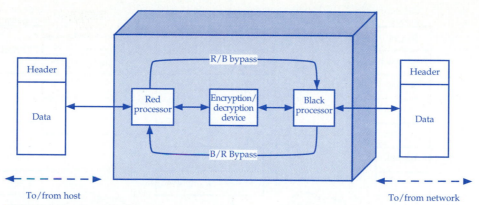

FIGURE 3.4.   Front-End Processor Function

Figure 3.4 shows the encryption function of the front-end processor (FEP). On the host side, the FEP accepts packets. The user-data portion of the packet is encrypted, while the packet header bypasses the encryption process.[1] The resulting packet is delivered to the network. In the opposite direction, for packets arriving from the network, the user data portion is decrypted and the entire packet is delivered to the host. If the transport layer functionality (e.g., the ISO transport protocol or TCP) is implemented in the front end, then the transport-layer header is also left in the clear and the user data portion of the transport protocol data unit is encrypted.

Deployment of encryption services on end-to-end protocols, such as a network-layer X.25 or TCP, provides end-to-end security for traffic within a fully integrated internetwork. However, such a scheme cannot deliver the necessary service for traffic that crosses internetwork boundaries, such as electronic mail, electronic data interchange (EDI), and file transfers that cross such boundaries.

Figure 3.5 illustrates the issues involved. In this example, an electronic mail gateway is used to interconnect an internetwork that uses an OSI-based architecture with one that uses a TCP/IP-based architecture. In such a configuration, there is no end-to-end protocol below the application layer. The transport and network connections from each end system terminate at the mail gateway, which sets up new transport and network connections to link to the other end system. Furthermore, such a scenario is not limited to the case of a gateway between two different architectures. Even if both end systems use TCP/IP or OSI, there are plenty of instances in actual configurations in which mail gateways sit between otherwise isolated internetworks. Thus, for applications like electronic mail that have a store-and-forward capability, the only place to achieve end-to-end encryption is at the application layer.

[1]The terms *red* and *black* are frequently used. Red data are sensitive or classified data in the clear. Black data are encrypted data.

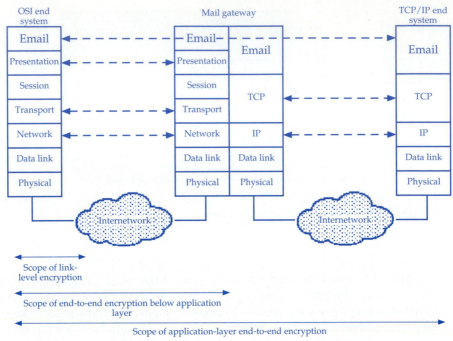

FIGURE 3.5.   Encryption Coverage Implications of Store-and Forward Applications

A drawback of application-layer encryption is that the number of entities to consider increases dramatically. A network that supports hundreds of hosts may support thousands of users and processes. Thus, many more secret keys need to be generated and distributed.

An interesting way of viewing the alternatives is to note that as we move up the communications hierarchy, less information is encrypted but it is more secure. Figure 3.6 highlights this point, using the TCP/IP architecture as an example. In the figure, an intermediate system (IS) refers to an IP-level router or a bridge, and an application-level gateway refers to a store-and-forward device that operates at the application level.[2]

With application-level encryption (Figure 3.6a), only the user data portion of a TCP segment is encrypted. The TCP, IP, network-level, and link-level headers and link-level trailer are in the clear. By contrast, if encryption is performed at the TCP level (Figure 3.6b), then, on a single end-to-end connection, the user data and the TCP header are encrypted. The IP header remains in the clear since it is needed by routers to route the IP datagram from source to destination. Note, however, that if a message passes through a gateway, the TCP

---

[2]Unfortunately, most TCP/IP documents use the term *gateway* to refer to what is more commonly referred to as a *router* or a *layer-3 IS*.

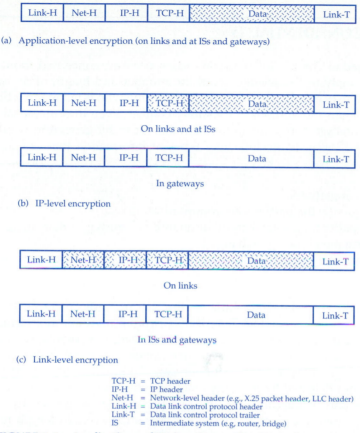

(a)   Application-level encryption (on links and at ISs and gateways)

On links and at ISs

In gateways

(b)   IP-level encryption

On links

In ISs and gateways

(c)   Link-level encryption

TCP-H = TCP header
IP-H   = IP header
Net-H = Network-level header (e.g., X.25 packet header, LLC header)
Link-H = Data link control protocol header
Link-T = Data link control protocol trailer
IS   = Intermediate system (e.g, router, bridge)

FIGURE 3.6.   Implications of Various Encryption Strategies

connection is terminated and a new transport connection is opened for the
next hop. Furthermore, the gateway is treated as a destination by the underlying IP. Thus, the encrypted portions of the data unit are decrypted at the gateway. If the next hop is over a TCP/IP network, then the user data and TCP
header are encrypted again before transmission. However, in the gateway itself the data unit is buffered entirely in the clear. Finally, for link level encryption (Figure 3.6c), the entire data unit except for the link header and trailer is
encrypted on each link, but the entire data unit is in the clear at each IS and
gateway.[3]

[3]The figure actually shows but one alternative. It is also possible to encrypt part or even all of the link
header and trailer except for the starting and ending frame flags.

TRAFFIC CONFIDENTIALITY

We mentioned in Chapter 1 that, in some cases, users are concerned about security from traffic analysis. Knowledge about the number and length of messages between nodes may enable an opponent to determine who is talking to whom. This can have obvious implications in a military conflict. Even in commercial applications, traffic analysis may yield information that the traffic generators would like to conceal. [MUFT89] lists the following types of information that can be derived from a traffic analysis attack:

- Identities of partners
- How frequently the partners are communicating
- Message pattern, message length, or quantity of messages that suggest important information is being exchanged
- The events that correlate with special conversations between particular partners

Another concern related to traffic is the use of traffic patterns to create a *covert channel*. A covert channel is a means of communication in a fashion unintended by the designers of the communications facility. Typically, the channel is used to transfer information in a way that violates a security policy. For example, an employee may wish to communicate information to an outsider in a way that is not detected by management and which requires simple eavesdropping on the part of the outsider. The two participants could set up a code in which an apparently legitimate message of a less than certain length represents binary zero, whereas a longer message represents a binary 1. Other such schemes are possible.

Link Encryption Approach

With the use of link encryption, packet headers are encrypted, reducing the opportunity for traffic analysis. However, it is still possible in those circumstances for an attacker to assess the amount of traffic on a network and to observe the amount of traffic entering and leaving each end system. An effective countermeasure to this attack is traffic padding, illustrated in Figure 3.7.

Traffic padding produces ciphertext output continuously, even in the absence of plaintext. A continuous random data stream is generated. When plaintext is available, it is encrypted and transmitted. When input plaintext is not present, random data are encrypted and transmitted. This makes it impossible for an attacker to distinguish between true data flow and padding and therefore impossible to deduce the amount of traffic.

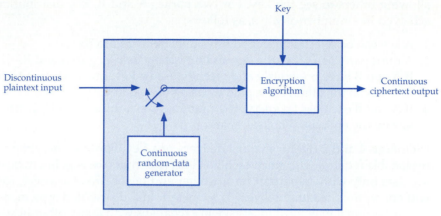

FIGURE 3.7.   Traffic-Padding Encryption Device

End-to-End Encryption Approach

Traffic padding is essentially a link encryption function. If only end-to-end encryption is employed, then the measures available to the defender are more
limited. For example, if encryption is implemented at the application layer, then
an opponent can determine which transport entities   engaged in dialogue. If
encryption techniques are housed at the transport layer, then network-layer
addresses and traffic patterns remain accessible.

   One technique that might prove useful is to pad out data units to a uniform
length at either the transport or application level. In addition, null messages can be
inserted randomly into the stream. These tactics deny an opponent knowledge
about the amount of data exchanged between end users and obscure the underlying traffic pattern.

3.3

KEY DISTRIBUTION

For conventional encryption to work, the two parties to an exchange must
have the same key, and that key must be protected from access by others.
Furthermore, frequent key changes are usually desirable to limit the amount of
data compromised if an attacker learns the key. Therefore, the strength of any
cryptographic system rests with the *key distribution technique,* a term that refers to
the means of delivering a key to two parties who wish to exchange data, without

allowing others to see the key. For two parties A and B, key distribution can be achieved in a number of ways, as follows:

1. A key can be selected by A and physically delivered to B.
2. A third party can select the key and physically deliver it to A and B.
3. If A and B have previously and recently used a key, one party can transmit the new key to the other, encrypted by using the old key.
4. If A and B each has an encrypted connection to a third party C, C can deliver a key on the encrypted links to A and B.

Options 1 and 2 call for manual delivery of a key. For link encryption, this is a reasonable requirement, since each link encryption device is going to be exchanging data only with its partner on the other end of the link. However, for end-to-end encryption, manual delivery is awkward. In a distributed system, any given host or terminal may need to engage in exchanges with many other hosts and terminals over time. Thus, each device needs a number of keys supplied dynamically. The problem is especially difficult in a wide-area distributed system.

The scale of the problem depends on the number of communicating pairs that must be supported. If end-to-end encryption is done at a network or IP level, then

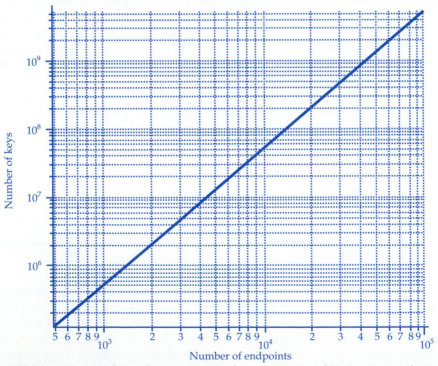

FIGURE 3.8. Number of Keys Required to Support Arbitrary Connections Between Endpoints

a key is needed for each pair of hosts on the network that wish to communicate. Thus, if there are N hosts then the number of required keys is $[N(N - 1)]/2$. If encryption is done at the application level, then a key is needed for every pair of users or processes that require communication. Thus, a network may have hundreds of hosts but thousands of users, or processes. Figure 3.8 illustrates the magnitude of the key distribution task for end-to-end encryption. A network using node-level encryption with 1,000 nodes would conceivably need to distribute as many as half a million keys. If that same network supported 10,000 applications, then as many as 50 million keys may be required for application-level encryption!

Returning to our list, option 3 is a possibility for either link encryption or end-to-end encryption, but if an attacker ever succeeds in gaining access to one key, then all subsequent keys will be revealed. Furthermore, the initial distribution of potentially millions of keys must still be made.

For end-to-end encryption, some variation on option 4 has been widely adopted. In this scheme, a key distribution center is responsible for distributing keys to pairs of users (hosts, processes, applications) as needed. Each user must share a unique key with the key distribution center for purposes of key distribution.

The use of a key distribution center is based on the use of a hierarchy of keys. At a minimum, two levels of keys are used (Figure 3.9). Communication between end systems is encrypted using a temporary key, often referred to as a *session key*. Typically, the session key is used for the duration of a logical connection, such as a virtual circuit or transport connection, and then discarded. Each session key is obtained from the key distribution center over the same networking facilities used

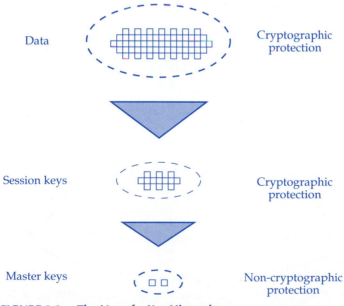

Data		Cryptographic protection
Session keys		Cryptographic protection
Master keys		Non-cryptographic protection

FIGURE 3.9.   The Use of a Key Hierarchy

for end-user communication. Accordingly, session keys are transmitted in en-crypted form, using a *master key* that is shared by the key distribution center and an end system or user.

For each end system or user, there is a unique master key that it shares with the key distribution center. Of course, these master keys must be distributed in some fashion. However, the scale of the problem is vastly reduced. If there are N entities that wish to communicate in pairs, then, as was mentioned, as many as $[N(N-1)]/2$ session keys are needed at any one time. However, only N master keys are required, one for each entity. Thus, master keys can be distributed in some noncryptographic way, such as physical delivery.

A Key Distribution Scenario

The key distribution concept can be deployed in a number of ways. A typical sce-nario is illustrated in Figure 3.10, which is based on a figure in [POPE79]. The sce-nario assumes that each user shares a unique master key with the key distribution center (KDC).

Let us assume that user A wishes to establish a logical connection with B and re-quires a one-time session key to protect the data transmitted over the connection. A has a secret key, K_a, known only to itself and the KDC; similarly, B shares the master key K_b with the KDC. The following steps occur:

1. A issues a request to the KDC for a session key to protect a logical connection to B. The message includes the identity of A and B and a unique identifier for this transaction, which we refer to as a *nonce*. The nonce may be a timestamp, a

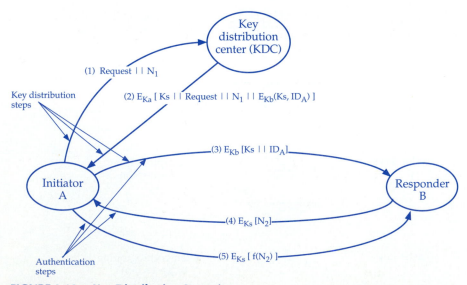

FIGURE 3.10.   Key Distribution Scenario

counter, or a random number; the minimum requirement is that it differ with each request. Also, to prevent masquerade, it is desirable for it to be difficult for an opponent to guess the nonce. Thus, a random number is a good choice for a nonce.

2. The KDC responds with a message encrypted by using K_a. Thus, A is the only one who can successfully receive the message, and A knows that it originated at the KDC. The message includes two items intended for A:
   - The one-time session key, K_s, to be used for the session
   - The original request message, including the nonce, to enable A to match this response with the appropriate request

   Thus, A can verify that its original request was not altered before reception by the KDC, and because of the nonce, that this is not a replay of some previous request. In addition, the message includes two items intended for B:
   - The one-time session key, K_s, to be used for the session
   - An identifier of A (e.g., its network address): ID_A

   These last two items are encrypted with the master key that the KDC shares with B. They are to be sent to B to establish the connection and prove A's identity.

3. A stores the session key for use in the upcoming session and forwards to B the information that originated at the KDC for B, namely, $E_{Kb}[K_s \mid\mid ID_A]$. Because this information is encrypted with K_b, it is protected from eavesdropping. B now knows the session key (K_s), knows that the other party is A (from ID_A), and that the information originated at the KDC (because it is encrypted using E_{Kb}).

At this point, a session key has been securely delivered to A and B, and they may begin their protected exchange. However, two additional steps are desirable:

4. Using the newly minted session key for encryption, B sends a nonce, N_2, to A.
5. Also using K_s, A responds with $f(N_2)$, where f is a function that performs some transformation on N_2 (e.g., adding one).

These steps assure B that the original message it received (step 3) was not a replay.

Note that the actual key distribution involves only steps 1 through 3 but that steps 4 and 5, as well as 3, perform an authentication function.

Hierarchical Key Control

It is not necessary to limit the key distribution function to a single KDC. Indeed, for very large networks, it may not be practical to do so. As an alternative, a hierarchy of KDCs can be established. For example, there can be local KDCs, each responsible for a small domain of the overall internetwork, such as a single LAN or a single building. For communication among entities within the same local domain, the local KDC is responsible for key distribution. If two entities in different domains desire a shared key, then the corresponding local KDCs can communicate through a global KDC. In this case, any one of the three KDCs involved can actually select the key. The hierarchical concept can be extended to three or even more layers, depending on the size of the user population and the geographic scope of the internetwork.

A hierarchical scheme minimizes the effort involved in master key distribution, because most master keys are those shared by a local KDC with its local entities. Furthermore, such a scheme limits the damage of a faulty or subverted KDC to its local area only.

Session Key Lifetime

The more frequently session keys are exchanged, the more secure they are, since the opponent has less ciphertext to work with for any given session key. On the other hand, the distribution of session keys delays the start of any exchange and places a burden on network capacity. A security manager must try to balance these competing considerations in determining the lifetime of a particular session key.

For connection-oriented protocols, one obvious choice is to use the same session key for the length of time that the connection is open, using a new session key for each new session. If a logical connection has a very long lifetime, then it would be prudent to change the session key periodically, perhaps every time the PDU sequence number cycles.

For a connectionless protocol, such as a transaction-oriented protocol, there is no explicit connection initiation or termination. Thus, it is not obvious how often one needs to change the session key. The most secure approach is to use a new session key for each exchange. However, this negates one of the principal benefits of connectionless protocols, which is minimum overhead and delay for each transaction. A better strategy is to use a given session key for a certain fixed period only or for a certain number of transactions.

A Transparent Key Control Scheme

The approach suggested in Figure 3.10 has many variations, one of which is now described. The scheme (Figure 3.11) is useful for providing end-to-end encryption at a network or transport level in a way that is transparent to the end users. The approach assumes that communication makes use of a connection-oriented end-to-end protocol, such as X.25 or TCP. The noteworthy element of this approach is a front-end processor (such as shown in Figure 3.4) that performs end-to-end encryption and obtains session keys on behalf of its host or terminal.

Figure 3.11 shows the steps involved in establishing a connection. When one host wishes to set up a connection to another host, it transmits a connection-request packet (step 1). The front-end processor saves that packet and applies to the KDC for permission to establish the connection (step 2). The communication between the FEP and the KDC is encrypted by using a master key shared only by

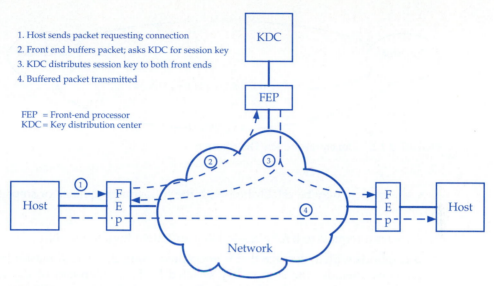

1. Host sends packet requesting connection
2. Front end buffers packet; asks KDC for session key
3. KDC distributes session key to both front ends
4. Buffered packet transmitted

FEP = Front-end processor
KDC = Key distribution center

FIGURE 3.11. Automatic Key Distribution for Connection-Oriented Protocol

the FEP and the KDC. If the KDC approves the connection request, it generates the session key and delivers it to the two appropriate front-end processors, using a unique permanent key for each front end (step 3). The requesting front-end processor can now release the connection request packet, and a connection is set up between the two end systems (step 4). All user data exchanged between the two end systems are encrypted by their respective front-end processors by using the one-time session key.

The advantage of this approach is that it minimizes the impact on the end systems. From the host's point of view, the FEP appears to be a packet-switching node, and the host interface to the network is unchanged. From the network's point of view, the FEP appears to be a host, and the packet-switch interface to the host is unchanged.

Decentralized Key Control

The use of a key distribution center imposes the requirement that the KDC be trusted and be protected from subversion. This requirement can be avoided if key distribution is fully decentralized. Although full decentralization is not practical for larger networks, it may be useful within a local context.

A decentralized approach requires that each end system be able to communicate in a secure manner with all potential partner end systems for purposes of session key distribution. Thus, there may need to be as many as $[N(N-1)]/2$ master keys for a configuration with n end systems.

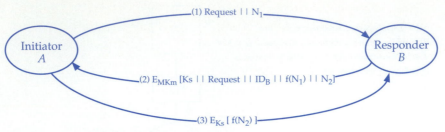

FIGURE 3.12.　Decentralized Key Distribution

A session key may be established with the following sequence of steps (Figure 3.12):

1. A issues a request to B for a session key and includes a nonce, N_1.
2. B responds with a message that is encrypted using the shared master key. The response includes the session key selected by B, an identifier of B, the value $f(N_1)$, and another nonce, N_2.
3. Using the new session key, A returns $f(N_2)$ to B.

Thus, although each node must maintain at most $(n - 1)$ master keys, as many session keys as required may be generated and used. Since the messages transferred using the master key are short, cryptanalysis is difficult. As before, session keys are used for only a limited time to protect them.

Controlling Key Usage

The concept of a key hierarchy, and the use of automated key distribution techniques, greatly reduce the number of keys that must be manually managed and distributed. It may also be desirable to impose some control on the way in which automatically distributed keys are used. For example, in addition to separating master keys from session keys, we may wish to define different types of session keys on the basis of use, such as:

- Data-encrypting key, for general communication across a network
- PIN-encrypting key, for personal identification numbers (PINs) used in electronic funds transfer and point-of-sale applications
- File-encrypting key, for encrypting files stored in publicly accessible locations

To illustrate the value of separating keys by type, consider the risk that a master key is imported as a data-encrypting key into a device. Normally, the master key is physically secured within the cryptographic hardware of the key distribution center and of the end systems. Session keys encrypted with this master key are available to application programs, as are the data encrypted with such session keys. However, if a master key is treated as a session key, it may be possible for an unauthorized application to obtain plaintext of session keys encrypted with that master key.

Thus, it may be desirable to institute controls in systems that limit the ways in which keys are used, based on characteristics associated with those keys. One simple plan is to associate a tag with each key ([JONE82]; see also [DAVI89]). The proposed technique is for use with DES, and makes use of the extra 8 bits in each 64-bit DES key. That is, the 8 nonkey bits ordinarily reserved for parity checking form the key tag. The bits have the following interpretation:

- One bit indicates whether the key is a session key or a master key.
- One bit indicates whether the key can be used for encryption.
- One bit indicates whether the key can be used for decryption.
- The remaining bits are spares for future use.

Because the tag is embedded in the key, it is encrypted along with the key when that key is distributed, providing protection. The drawbacks of this scheme are (1) the tag length is limited to 8 bits, limiting its flexibility and functionality, and (2) because the tag is not transmitted in clear form, it can be used only at the point of decryption, limiting the ways in which key use can be controlled.

A more flexible scheme, referred to as the control vector, is described in [MATY91a and b]. In this scheme, each session key has an associated control vector consisting of a number of fields that specify the uses and restrictions for that session key. The length of the control vector may vary.

The control vector is cryptographically coupled with the key at the time of key generation at the KDC. The coupling and decoupling processes are illustrated in Figure 3.13 As a first step, the control vector is passed through a hash function that produces a value whose length is equal to the encryption key length. Hash

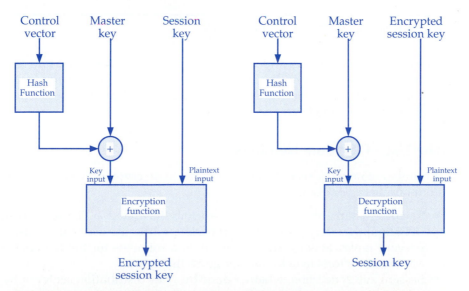

FIGURE 3.13.   Control Vector Encryption and Decryption

tions are discussed in detail in Chapter 5. In essence a hash function maps values from a larger range into a smaller range, with a reasonably uniform spread. Thus, for example, if numbers in the range 1 to 100 are hashed into numbers in the range 1 to 10, approximately 10% of the source values should map into each of the target values.

The hash value is then XORed with the master key to produce an output that is used as the key input for encrypting the session key. Thus,

$$\text{Hash value} = H = h(CV)$$
$$\text{Key input} = K_m \oplus H$$
$$\text{Ciphertext} = E_{Km \oplus H}[Ks]$$

where K_m is the master key and K_s is the session key. The session key is recovered in plaintext by the reverse operation:

$$K_s = D_{Km \oplus H}[E_{Km \oplus H}[K_s]]$$

When a session key is delivered to a user from the KDC, it is accompanied by the control vector in clear form. The session key can be recovered only by using both the master key that the user shares with the KDC and the control vector. Thus, the linkage between the session key and its control vector is maintained.

Using the control vector has two advantages over the use of an 8-bit tag. First, there is no restriction on length of the control vector, which enables arbitrarily complex controls to be imposed on key use. Second, the control vector is available in clear form at all stages of operation. Thus control of key use can be exercised in multiple locations.

3.4

RANDOM NUMBER GENERATION

Random numbers play an important role in the use of encryption for various network security applications. In this section, we provide a brief overview of the use of random numbers in network security and then look at two approaches to generating random numbers.

The Use of Random Numbers

A number of network security algorithms based on cryptography make use of random numbers. For example:

- Reciprocal authentication schemes, such as illustrated in Figures 3.10 and 3.12. In both of these key distribution scenarios, nonces are used for handshaking to prevent replay attacks. The use of random numbers for the nonces frustrates opponents' efforts to determine or guess the nonce.
- Session key generation, whether done by a key distribution center or by one of the principals.

- Generation of keys for the RSA public-key encryption algorithm (described in Chapter 4).

These applications give rise to two distinct and not necessarily compatible requirements for a sequence of random numbers, randomness and unpredictability.

Randomness

Traditionally, the concern in the generation of a sequence of allegedly random numbers has been that the sequence of numbers be random in some well-defined statistical sense. The following two criteria are used to validate that a sequence of numbers is random:

- *Uniform distribution:* The distribution of numbers in the sequence should be uniform; that is, the frequency of occurrence of each of the numbers should be approximately the same.
- *Independence:* No one value in the sequence can be inferred from the others.

Although there are well-defined tests for determining that a sequence of numbers matches a particular distribution such as the uniform distribution, there is no such test to "prove" independence. Rather, a number of tests can be applied to demonstrate that a sequence does not exhibit independence. The general strategy is to apply a number of such tests until the confidence that independence exists is sufficiently strong.

In the context of our discussion, the use of a sequence of numbers that appear statistically random often occurs in the design of algorithms related to cryptography. For example, a fundamental requirement of the RSA public-key encryption scheme discussed in Chapter 4 is the ability to generate prime numbers. In general, it is difficult to determine if a given large number N is prime. A brute-force approach would be to divide N by every integer less than $\sqrt{N}$. If it is on the order, say, of 10^{150}, a not uncommon occurrence in public-key cryptography, such a brute-force approach is beyond the reach of human analysts and their computers. However, a number of effective algorithms exist that test the primality of a number by using a sequence of randomly chosen integers as input to relatively simple computations. If the sequence is sufficiently long (but far, far less than 10^{150}), the primality of a number can be determined with near certainty. This type of approach, known as randomization, crops up frequently in the design of algorithms. In essence, if a problem is too hard or time-consuming to solve exactly, a simpler, shorter approach based on randomization is used to provide an answer with any desired level of confidence.

Unpredictability

In applications such as reciprocal authentication and session key generation, the requirement is not so much that the sequence of numbers be statistically random but that the successive members of the sequence are unpredictable. With "true" random sequences, each number is statistically independent of other numbers in the sequence and therefore unpredictable. However, as is discussed shortly, true random numbers are rarely used; rather, sequences of numbers that appear to be random are generated by some algorithm. In this latter case, care must be taken that an opponent not be able to predict future elements of the sequence on the basis of earlier elements.

Sources of Random Numbers

Sources of true random number are hard to come by. Physical noise generators, such as pulse detectors of ionizing radiation events, gas discharge tubes, and leaky capacitors, are one potential source. However, such devices are of limited utility in network security applications. There are problems both with the randomness and the precision of such numbers [BRIG79], to say nothing of the clumsy requirement of attaching one of these devices to every system in an internetwork. Another alternative is to dip into a collection of good-quality random numbers that have been published (e.g., [RAND55] [TIPP27]). However, these collections provide a very limited source of numbers compared to the potential requirements of a sizable network security application. Furthermore, although the numbers in these books do indeed exhibit statistical randomness, they are predictable, since an opponent who knows that the book is in use can obtain a copy.

Thus, cryptographic applications universally make use of algorithmic techniques for random number generation. These algorithms are deterministic and therefore produce sequences of numbers that are not statistically random. However, if the algorithm is good, the resulting sequences will pass many reasonable tests of randomness. Such numbers are often referred to as "pseudorandom" numbers.

You may be somewhat uneasy about the concept of using numbers generated by a deterministic algorithm as if they were random numbers. Despite what might be called philosophical objections to such a maneuver, it in fact generally works. As one expert on probability theory puts it [HAMM91]:

> For practical purposes we are forced to accept the awkward concept of "relatively random" meaning that with regard to the proposed use we can see no reason why they will not perform as if they were random (as the theory usually requires). This is highly subjective and is not very palatable to purists, but it is what statisticians regularly appeal to when they take "a random sample"—they hope that any results they use will have approximately the same properties as a complete counting of the whole sample space that occurs in their theory.

We examine the two most popular algorithmic approaches to random number generation in the remainder of this section.

Pseudorandom Number Generators

By far the most widely used technique for random number generation is an algorithm first proposed by Lehmer [LEHM51], which is known as the linear congruential method. The algorithm is parameterized with four numbers, as follows:

$$
\begin{array}{lll}
m & \text{the modulus} & m > 0 \\
a & \text{the multiplier} & 0 \le a < m \\
c & \text{the increment} & 0 \le c < m \\
X_0 & \text{the starting value, or seed} & 0 \le X_0 < m
\end{array}
$$

The sequence of random numbers $\{X_n\}$ is obtained via the following iterative equation:

$$X_{n+1} = (aX_n + c) \bmod m$$

If m, a, c, and X_0 are integers, then this technique will produce a sequence of integers with each integer in the range $0 \le X_n < m$.

The selection of values for a, c, and m is critical in developing a good random number generator. For example, consider $a = c = 1$. The sequence produced is obviously not satisfactory. Now consider the values $a = 7$, $b = 0$, $m = 32$ and $X_0 = 1$. This generates the sequence $\{7, 17, 23, 1, 7, \text{etc.}\}$, which is also clearly unsatisfactory. Of the 32 possible values, only 4 are used; thus the sequence is said to have a period of 4. If instead, we change the value of a to 5, then the sequence is $\{1, 5, 35, 39, 27, 21, 9, 13, 1, \text{etc.})$, which increases the period to 8.

We would like m to be very large, so that there is the potential for producing a long series of distinct random numbers. A common criterion is that m be nearly equal to the maximum representable nonnegative integer for a given computer. Thus, a value of m near to or equal to 2^{31} is typically chosen.

[PARK88] proposes three criteria to be used in evaluating a random number generator:

T_1: The function should be a full-period generating function. That is, the function should generate all the numbers between 0 and m before repeating.

T_2: The generated sequence should appear random. The sequence is not random because it is generated deterministically, but there is a variety of statistical tests that can be used to assess the degree to which a sequence exhibits randomness.

T_3: The function should implement efficiently with 32-bit arithmetic.

With appropriate values of a, c, and m, these three tests can be passed. With respect to T_1, it can be shown that if m is prime and $c = 0$, then for certain values of a, the period of the generating function is $m - 1$, with only the value 0 missing. For 32-bit arithmetic, a convenient prime value of m is $2^{31} - 1$. Thus, the generating function becomes:

$$X_{n+1} = (aX_n) \bmod (2^{31} - 1)$$

Of the more than 2 billion possible choices for a, only a handful of multipliers pass all three tests. One such value is $a = 7^5 = 16807$, which was originally designed for use in the IBM 360 family of computers [LEWI69]. This generator is widely used, and has been subjected to a more thorough testing than any other pseudorandom number generator. It is frequently recommended for statistical and simulation work (e.g., [KOBA78], [PARK88], [SAUE81]).

The strength of the linear congruential algorithm is that if the multiplier and modulus are properly chosen, the resulting sequence of numbers will be statistically indistinguishable from a sequence drawn at random (but without replacement) from the set $1, 2, \ldots, m-1$. But there is nothing random at all about the algorithm, apart from the choice of the initial value X_0. Once that value is chosen, the remaining numbers in the sequence follow deterministically. This has implications for cryptanalysis.

If an opponent knows that the linear congruential algorithm is being used and if the parameters are known (e.g., $a = 7^5, c = 0, m = 2^{31} - 1$), then once a single number is discovered, all subsequent numbers are known. Even if the opponent knows only that a linear congruential algorithm is being used, knowledge of a small part of the sequence is sufficient to determine the parameters of the algorithm. Suppose that the opponent is able to determine values for $X_0, X_1, X_2,$ and X_3. Then:

$$X_1 = (aX_0 + c) \bmod m$$
$$X_2 = (aX_1 + c) \bmod m$$
$$X_3 = (aX_2 + c) \bmod m$$

These equations can be solved for $a, c,$ and m.

Thus, although it is nice to be able to use a good pseudo-random number generator, it is desirable to make the actual sequence used nonreproducible, so that knowledge of part of the sequence on the part of an opponent is insufficient to determine future elements of the sequence. This goal can be achieved in a number of ways. For example, [BRIG79] suggests using an internal system clock to modify the random number stream. One way to use the clock would be to restart the sequence after every N numbers, using the current clock value (mod m) as the new seed. Another way would be to simply add the current clock value to each random number (mod m).

Cryptographically Generated Random Numbers

For cryptographic applications, it makes some sense to take advantage of the encryption logic available to produce random numbers. A number of means have been used, and we look here at three representative examples.

Cyclic Encryption

Figure 3.14 illustrates an approach suggested in [MEYE82]. In this case, the procedure is used to generate session keys from a master key. A counter with period N provides input to the encryption logic. For example, if 56-bit DES

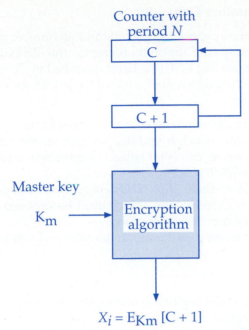

Counter with
period N

C

$C + 1$

Master key

K_m → Encryption
algorithm

$$X_i = E_{K_m}[C + 1]$$

FIGURE 3.14.   Pseudorandom Number Generation from a Counter

keys are to be produced, then a counter with period 2^{56} can be used. After each key is produced, the counter is incremented by one. Thus, the pseudorandom numbers produced by this scheme cycle through a full period: Each of the outputs $X_0, X_1, \ldots X_{N-1}$ is based on a different counter value, and therefore $X_0 \neq X_1 \neq \ldots \neq X_{N-1}$. Since the master key is protected, it is not computationally feasible to deduce any of the secret keys through knowledge of one or more earlier keys.

To further strengthen the algorithm, the input could be the output of a full-period pseudorandom number generator, rather than a simple counter.

DES Output Feedback Mode

The output feedback (OFB) mode of DES, illustrated in Figure 2.17, can be used for key generation as well as for stream encryption. Notice that the output of each stage of operation is a 64-bit value, of which the j leftmost bits are fed back for encryption. Successive 64-bit outputs constitute a sequence of pseudorandom numbers with good statistical properties. Again, as with the approach suggested in the preceding subsection, the use of a protected master key protects the generated session keys.

ANSI X9.17 Pseudorandom Number Generator

One of the strongest (cryptographically speaking) pseudorandom number generators is specified in ANSI X9.17. A number of applications employ this technique, including financial security applications and PGP (the latter described in Chapter 9).

Figure 3.15 illustrates the algorithm, which makes use of triple DES for encryption. The ingredients are as follows:

- *Input:* Two pseudorandom inputs drive the generator. One is a 64-bit representation of the current date and time, which is updated on each number generation. The other is a 64-bit seed value; this is initialized to some arbitrary value and is updated during the generation process.
- *Keys:* The generator makes use of three triple DES encryption modules. All three make use of the same pair of 56-bit keys, which must be kept secret and are used only for pseudorandom number generation.
- *Output:* The output consists of a 64-bit pseudorandom number and a 64-bit seed value.

Define the following quantities:

DT_i Date and time value at the beginning of ith generation stage
V_i Seed value at the beginning of ith generation stage
R_i Pseudorandom number produced by the ith generation stage
K_1, K_2 DES keys used for each stage

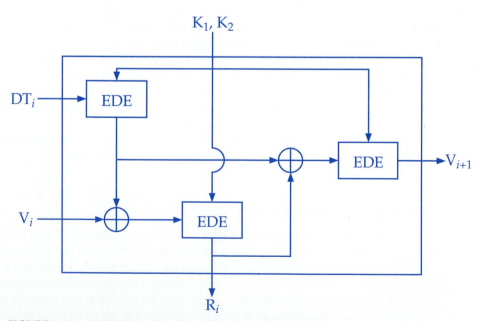

FIGURE 3.15. ANSI X9.17 Pseudorandom Number Generator

Then:

$$R_i = \mathrm{EDE}_{K_1,K_2}\Big[\mathrm{EDE}_{K_1,K_2}[\mathrm{DT}_i] \oplus V_i\Big]$$

$$V_{i+1} = \mathrm{EDE}_{K_1,K_2}\Big[\mathrm{EDE}_{K_1,K_2}[\mathrm{DT}_i] \oplus R_i\Big]$$

Several factors contribute to the cryptographic strength of this method. The technique involves a 112-bit key and 3 EDE encryptions for a total of 9 DES encryptions. The scheme is driven by two pseudorandom inputs, the date and time value, and a seed produced by the generator that is distinct from the pseudorandom number produced by the generator. Thus, the amount of material that must be compromised by an opponent is overwhelming. Even if a pseudorandom number R_i were compromised, it would be impossible to deduce the V_{i+1} from the R_i since an additional EDE operation is used to produce the V_{i+1}.

3.5

RECOMMENDED READING

[FUMY93] is a good survey of key management principles.

[MEYE82] contains a very detailed description of a key distribution and key management facility.

Perhaps the best treatment of pseudo-random number generators is to be found in [KNUT81]. An alternative to the standard linear congruential algorithm, known as the linear recurrence algorithm, is explained in some detail in [BRIG79]. [ZENG91] assesses various pseudorandom generation algorithms for use in generating variable-length keys for Vernam types of ciphers.

BRIG79   Bright, H., and Enison, R. "Quasi-Random Number Sequences from Long-Period TLP Generator with Remarks on Application to Cryptography." *Computing Surveys,* December 1979.

FUMY93   Fumy, S., and Landrock, P. "Principles of Key Management." *IEEE Journal on Selected Areas in Communications,* June 1993.

KNUT81   Knuth, D. *The Art of Computer Programming, Volume 2: Seminumerical Algorithms.* Reading, MA: Addison-Wesley, 1981.

MEYE82   Meyer, C., and Matyas, S. *Cryptography: A New Dimension in Computer Data Security.* New York: Wiley, 1982.

ZENG91   Zeng., K.; Yang, C.; Wei, D.; and Rao, T. "Pseudorandom Bit Generators in Stream-Cipher Cryptography." *Computer,* February 1991.

3.6

PROBLEMS

3.1 Electronic mail systems differ in the manner in which multiple recipients are handled. In some systems, the originating mail-handler makes all the necessary copies, and these are sent out independently. An alternative approach is to determine the route for each destination first. Then a single message is sent out on a common portion of the route, and copies are made only when the routes diverge; this process is referred to as *mail-bagging*.

a. Leaving aside considerations of security, discuss the relative advantages and disadvantages of the two methods.

b. Discuss the security requirements and implications of the two methods.

3.2 Section 3.2 describes the use of message length as a means of constructing a covert channel. Describe three additional schemes for using traffic patterns to construct a covert channel.

3.3 One local area network vendor provides a key distribution facility as illustrated in the following diagram:

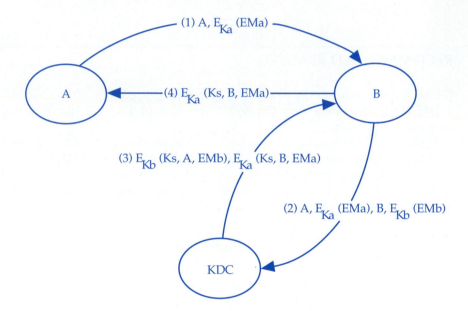

a. Describe the scheme.

b. Compare this scheme to that of Figure 3.10. What are the pros and cons?

3.4 If we take the linear congruential algorithm with an additive component of 0:

$$X_{n+1} = (aX_n) \bmod m$$

then it can be shown that if m is prime, and if a given value of a produces the maximum period of $m - 1$, then a^k will also produce the maximum period, provided that k is less than m and that $m - 1$ is not divisible by k. Demonstrate this by using $X_0 = 1$ and $m = 31$, and producing the sequences for $a = 3, 3^2, 3^3$, and 3^4.

3.5 You may wonder why the modulus $m = 2^{31} - 1$ was chosen for the linear congruential method instead of simply 2^{31}, since this latter number can be represented with no additional bits, and the mod operation should be easier to perform. In general, the modulus $2^k - 1$ is preferable to 2^k. Why is this so?

3.6 With the linear congruential algorithm, a choice of parameters that provides a full period does not necessarily provide a good randomization. For example, consider the two generators:

$$X_{n+1} = (6X_n) \bmod 13$$
$$X_{n+1} = (7X_n) \bmod 13$$

Write out the two sequences to show that both are full period. Which one appears more random to you?

3.7 In any use of pseudorandom numbers, whether for encryption, simulation, or statistical design, it is dangerous to blindly trust the random number generator that happens to be available in your computer's system library. [PARK88] found that many contemporary textbooks and programming packages make use of flawed algorithms for pseudorandom number generation. This exercise will enable you to test your system.

The test is based on a theorem attributed to Ernesto Cesaro (see [KNUT81] for a proof), which states that the probability that the greatest common divisor of two randomly chosen integers is 1 is equal to $6/\pi^2$. Use this theorem in a program to determine statistically the value of π. The main program should call three subprograms: the random number generator from the system library to generate the random integers; a subprogram to calculate the greatest common divisor of two integers using Euclid's Algorithm, and a subprogram that calculates square roots. If these latter two programs are not available, you will have to write them as well. The main program should loop through a large number of random numbers to give an estimate of the probability referenced above. From this, it is a simple matter to solve for your estimate of π.

If the result is close to 3.14, congratulations! If not, then the result is probably low, usually a value of around 2.7. Why would such an inferior result be obtained?

3.8 Suppose that someone suggests the following way to confirm that the two of you are both in possession of the same secret key. You create a random bit string the length of the key, XOR it with the key, and send the result over the channel. Your partner XORs the incoming block with the key (which should be the same as your key) and sends it back. You check and if what you receive is your original random string, you have verified that your partner has the same secret key, yet neither of you has ever transmitted the key. Is there a flaw in this scheme?

3.9 "We are under great pressure, Holmes." Detective Lestrade looked nervous. "We positively know that copies of a bunch of sensitive governmental documents are stored in computers of one foreign embassy here in London. Normally these documents exist in electronic form only on a selected few of governmental computers that satisfy the most stringent security requirements. However, sometimes they must be sent through the network connecting all governmental computers. But all messages in this network are encrypted using top secret encryption algorithms certified by our best crypto experts. We positively know that even NSA and the KGB are unable to break it. And now these documents have appeared in the hands of diplomats of a small, otherwise insignificant, country. And we have no idea how it could happen."

"But you do have some suspicion who did it, do you?" asked Holmes.

"Yes, we did some routine investigation. It turned out that there is a man having legal access to one of the governmental computers, and having frequent contacts with diplomats from the embassy. But the computer he has access to doesn't belong to the trusted ones where these documents are normally stored. He is the suspect, but we have no idea how he could obtain copies of the documents. Even if he could obtain a copy of encrypted documents, he couldn't decrypt it."

"Hmm, could you please describe the communication protocol used in the network of governmental computers?" Holmes opened his eyes, thus proving that he had followed Lestrade's talk with an attention that contrasted with his sleepy look.

"Well, the protocol is as follows. Each node of the network has been assigned a unique secret key K_n. This key is used to secure communication between the node and a trusted server. That is, all the keys are stored also on the server. User A wishing to send a secret message M to user B initiates the following protocol:

1. A generates a random number R and sends to server his name A, destination B, and $EK_a[R]$
2. Server responds by sending $EK_b[R]$ to A
3. A sends $E_R[M]$ together with $EK_b[R]$ to B
4. B knows K_b, thus decrypts $EK_b[R]$ to get R and will subsequently use R to decrypt $E_R[M]$ to get M

I have already stated that the encryption algorithm used is in fact unbreakable, and you see that a random key is generated every time a message has to be sent. You know that the use of a random one-time key belongs to proper procedures that contribute to the strength of cryptosystems. I admit the man could intercept messages sent between the top secret trusted nodes, but I see no way he could decrypt them."

"Well, I think you have your man, Lestrade. The protocol isn't secure because the server doesn't authenticate users who send him a request. Apparently designers of the protocol have believed that sending $EK_x[R]$ implicitly authenticates user X as the sender, as only X (and the server) knows K_x. But you know that $EK_x[R]$ can be intercepted and later replayed. Once you understand where the hole is, you will be able to obtain enough evidence by monitoring the man's use of the computer he has access to. Most likely he works as follows. After intercepting $EK_a[R]$ and $E_R[M]$ (see steps 1 and 3 of the protocol) the man, let's denote him as Z, will continue by pretending to be A and . . .

CHAPTER 4

PUBLIC-KEY CRYPTOLOGY

For practical reasons, it is desirable to use different encryption and decryption keys in a crypto-system. Such asymmetric systems allow the encryption key to be made available to anyone while preserving confidence that only people who hold the decryption key can decipher the information.

— *Computers at Risk: Safe Computing in the Information Age*
   National Research Council, 1991

Every Egyptian received two names, which were known respectively as the true name and the good name, or the great name and the little name; and while the good or little name was made public, the true or great name appears to have been carefully concealed.

— *The Golden Bough*
   Sir James George Frazer

The development of public-key cryptography is the greatest and perhaps the only true revolution in the entire history of cryptography (Table 4.1). From its earliest beginnings, right down to modern times, virtually all cryptographic systems have been based on the elementary tools of substitution and permutation. After millennia of working with algorithms that could essentially be calculated by hand, a major advance in conventional cryptography occurred with the development of the rotor encryption/decryption machine. The electromechanical rotor enabled the development of fiendishly complex cipher systems. With the availability of computers, even more complex systems were devised, the most prominent of which was the Lucifer effort at IBM that culminated in the Data Encryption Standard (DES). But both rotor machines and DES, although representing significant advances, still relied on the bread-and-butter tools of substitution and permutation.

Public-key cryptography provides a radical departure from all that has gone before. For one thing, public-key algorithms are based on mathematical functions rather than on substitution and permutation. But more important, public-key cryptography is asymmetric, involving the use of two separate keys, in contrast to the symmetric conventional encryption, which uses only one key. The use of two

TABLE 4.1   Milestones in Cryptology

~1900 B.C.	Beginnings of the use of cryptographic transformations on tomb inscriptions; first known use of cryptography.
~475 B.C.	Sparta develops the first use of cryptography for communications and the first encryption device: the skytale, which produced a transposition cipher.
~350 B.C	Aeneas the Tactician publishes the first text on communications security and cryptography.
~60 B.C.	Julius Ceasar becomes the first known user of a substitution cipher in military affairs.
1412	Oldest known treatise on cryptanalysis published by Egyptian scholar al-Kalkashandi.
1917	Edward Hugh Hebern develops the first rotor machine.
1971	IBM develops the Lucifer encryption scheme.
1975	Data Encryption Standard (DES) announced (approved in 1977).
1976	First public presentation of public-key concept, by Diffie and Hellman [DIFF76a, b].
1978	Merkle develops knapsack algorithm [MERK78], and offers $100 reward to anyone who can break the single-iteration version.
	Rivest–Shamir–Adelman (RSA) algorithm published [RIVE78].
1982	Shamir announces a solution to the cryptanalysis of the single-iteration knapsack problem; collects $100 [SHAM82].
	Merkle offers $1000 reward to anyone who can break the multiple-iteration knapsack problem.
1984	Brickell announces a solution to the cryptanalysis of the multiple-iteration knapsack problem; collects $1000 [BRIC84].

keys has profound consequences in the areas of confidentiality, key distribution, and authentication, as we shall see in this chapter and the next.

Before proceeding, we should mention several common misconceptions concerning public-key encryption. One such misconception is that public-key encryption is more secure from cryptanalysis than conventional encryption. Such a claim was made, for example, in a famous article in *Scientific American* by Gardner [GARD77]. In fact, the security of any encryption scheme depends on the length of the key and the computational work involved in breaking a cipher. There is nothing in principle about either conventional or public-key encryption that makes one superior to another from the point of view of resisting cryptanalysis.

A second misconception is that public-key encryption is a general-purpose technique that has made conventional encryption obsolete. On the contrary, because of the computational overhead of current public-key encryption schemes, there seems no foreseeable likelihood that conventional encryption will be abandoned. As one of the inventors of public-key encryption has put it [DIFF88]: "The restriction of public-key cryptography to key management and signature applications is almost universally accepted."

Finally, there is a feeling that key distribution is trivial when using public-key encryption, compared to the rather cumbersome handshaking involved with key distribution centers for conventional encryption. In fact, some form of protocol is needed, generally involving a central agent, and the procedures involved are no simpler nor any more efficient than those required for conventional encryption (e.g., see analysis in [NEED78]).

This chapter provides an overview of public-key encryption. First, we look at the conceptual framework of public-key encryption. Interestingly, the concept for this technique was developed and published before it was shown to be practical to adopt it. Next, we examine the RSA algorithm, which is the most important encryption/decryption algorithm that has been shown to be feasible for public-key encryption. Finally, we examine key distribution and management for public-key systems.

4.1

PRINCIPLES OF PUBLIC-KEY CRYPTOSYSTEMS

The concept of public-key cryptography evolved from an attempt to attack two of the most difficult problems associated with conventional encryption. The first problem is that of key distribution, which was examined in some detail in Chapter 3.

As we have seen, key distribution under conventional encryption requires either (a) that two communicants already share a key, which somehow has been distributed to them, or (b) the use of a key distribution center. Whitfield Diffie, one of the discoverers of public-key encryption (along with Martin Hellman, both at Stanford University at the time), reasoned that this requirement negated the very essence of cryptography: the ability to maintain total secrecy over your own communication. As Diffie put it [DIFF88]: "What good would it do after all to develop impenetrable cryptosystems, if their users were forced to share their keys with a KDC that could be compromised by either burglary or subpoena?"

The second problem that Diffie pondered, and one that was apparently unrelated to the first, was that of "digital signatures." If the use of cryptography was to become widespread, not just in military situations but for commercial and private purposes, then electronic messages and documents would need the equivalent of signatures used in paper documents. That is, could a method be devised that would stipulate, to the satisfaction of all parties, that a digital message had been sent by a particular person? This is a somewhat broader requirement than that of authentication, and its characteristics and ramifications are explored in Chapter 5.

Diffie and Hellman achieved an astounding breakthrough in 1976 [DIFF76 a, b] by coming up with a method that addressed both problems and that was radically different from all previous approaches to cryptography, going back over four millennia.

In the next subsection, we look at the overall framework for public-key cryptography. Then we examine the requirements for the encryption/decryption algorithm that is at the heart of the scheme. The final subsection provides a brief overview of suggested algorithms.

Public-Key Cryptosystems

For conventional encryption schemes, the keys used for encryption and decryption of a given message are the same. This is not a necessary condition. Instead, it is possible to develop a cryptographic algorithm that relies on one key for encryption and a different but related key for decryption. Furthermore, these algorithms have the following important characteristic:

- It is computationally infeasible to determine the decryption key given only knowledge of the cryptographic algorithm and the encryption key.

In addition, some algorithms, such as RSA, also exhibit the following characteristic:

- Either of the two related keys can be used for encryption, with the other used for decryption.

In this chapter, we assume that both characteristics are present; in Chapter 8 we examine some public-key algorithms that do not enjoy the second characteristic.

Figure 4.1 illustrates the public-key encryption process (compare with Figure 2.1). The essential steps are the following:

1. Each end system in a network generates a pair of keys to be used for encryption and decryption of messages that it will receive.
2. Each system publishes its encryption key by placing it in a public register or file. This is the public key. The companion key is kept private.
3. If A wishes to send a message to B, it encrypts the message using B's public key.
4. When B receives the message, it decrypts it using B's private key. No other recipient can decrypt the message because only B knows B's private key.

With this approach, all participants have access to public keys, and private keys are generated locally by each participant and therefore need never be distributed.

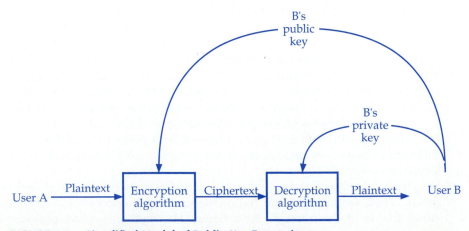

FIGURE 4.1.   Simplified Model of Public-Key Encryption

TABLE 4.2   Conventional and Public-Key Encryption

Conventional Encryption	Public-key Encryption
Needed to Work	*Needed to Work*
1. The same algorithm with the same key is used for encryption and decryption.	1. One algorithm is used for encryption and decryption with a pair of keys, one for encryption and one for decryption.
2. The sender and receiver must share the algorithm and the key.	2. The sender and receiver must each have one of the matched pair of keys.
Needed for Security	*Needed for Security*
1. The key must be kept secret.	1. One of the two keys must be kept secret.
2. It must be impossible or at least impractical to decipher a message if no other information is available.	2. It must be impossible or a least impractical to decipher a message if no other information is available.
3. Knowledge of the algorithm plus samples of ciphertext must be insufficient to determine the key.	3. Knowledge of the algorithm plus one of the keys plus samples of ciphertext must be insufficient to determine the other key.

As long as a system controls its private key, its incoming communication is secure. At any time, a system can change its private key and publish the companion public key to replace its old public key.

Table 4.2 summarizes some of the important aspects of conventional and public-key encryption. To discriminate between the two, we will generally refer to the key used in conventional encryption as a **secret key.** The two keys used for public-key encryption are referred to as the **public key** and the **private key.**[1] Invariably, the private key is kept secret, but it is referred to as a private key rather than a secret key to avoid confusion with conventional encryption.

Let us take a closer look at the essential elements of a public-key encryption scheme, using Figure 4.2 (compare with Figure 2.2). There is some source A for a message, which produces a message in plaintext, $X = [X_1, X_2, \ldots, X_M]$. The M elements of X are letters in some finite alphabet. The message is intended for destination B. B generates a related pair of keys: a public key KU_b, and a private key, KR_b. KR_b is secret, known only to B, whereas KU_b is publicly available, and therefore accessible by A.

With the message X and the encryption key KU_b as input, A forms the ciphertext $Y = [Y_1, Y_2, \ldots, Y_N]$:

$$Y = E_{KUb}(X)$$

---

[1]The following notation is used consistently throughout. A secret key is represented by K_m, where m is some modifier; for example, K_s is a session key. A public key is represented by KU_a, for user A, and the corresponding private key is KR_a. Encryption of plaintext P can be performed with a secret key, a public key, or a private key, denoted by $E_{Km}[P]$, $E_{KUa}[P]$, and $E_{KRa}[P]$, respectively. Similarly, decryption of ciphertext C can be performed with a secret key, a public key, or a private key, denoted by $D_{Km}[C]$, $D_{KUa}[C]$, and $D_{KRa}[C]$, respectively.

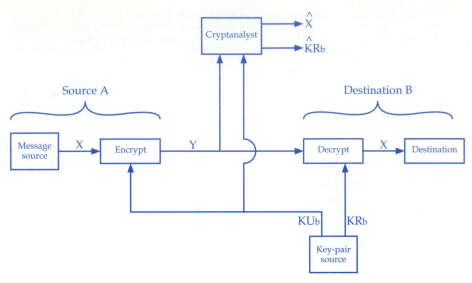

FIGURE 4.2.   Public-Key Cryptosystem: Secrecy

The intended receiver, in possession of the matching private key, is able to invert the transformation:

$$X = D_{KRb}(Y)$$

An opponent, observing Y and having access to KU_b, but not having access to KR_b or X, must attempt to recover X and/or KR_b. It is assumed that the opponent does have knowledge of the encryption (E) and decryption (D) algorithms. If the opponent is interested in only this particular message, then the focus of effort is to recover X by generating a plaintext estimate $\hat{X}$. Often, however, the opponent is interested in being able to read future messages as well, in which case an attempt is made to recover KR_b by generating a plaintext estimate $\hat{KR}_b$.

We mentioned earlier that either of the two related keys can be used for encryption, with the other being used for decryption. This enables a rather different cryptographic scheme to be implemented. Whereas the scheme illustrated in Figure 4.2 provides confidentiality, Figure 4.3 shows the use of public-key encryption to provide authentication:

$$Y = E_{KRa}(X)$$
$$X = D_{KUa}(Y)$$

In this case, A prepares a message to B and encrypts it using A's private key before transmitting it. B can decrypt the message using A's public key. Because the message was encrypted using A's private key, only A could have prepared the message. Therefore, the entire encrypted message serves as a *digital signature*. In addition, it is impossible to alter the message without access to A's private key, so the message is authenticated both in terms of source and in terms of data integrity.

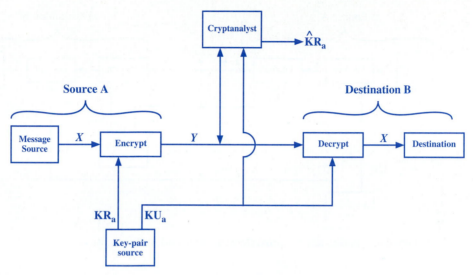

FIGURE 4.3.   Public-Key Cryptosystem: Authentication

In the preceding scheme, the entire message is encrypted, which although validating both author and contents, requires a great deal of storage. Each document must be kept in plaintext to be used for practical purposes. A copy also must be stored in ciphertext so that the origin and contents can be verified in case of a dispute. A more efficient way of achieving the same results is to encrypt a small block of bits that is a function of the document. Such a block, called an authenticator, must have the property that it is infeasible to change the document without changing the authenticator. If the authenticator is encrypted with the sender's private key, it serves as a signature that verifies origin, content, and sequencing. Chapter 5 examines this technique in detail.

It is important to emphasize that the encryption process just described does not provide confidentiality. That is, the message being sent is safe from alteration but not safe from eavesdropping. This is obvious in the case of a signature based on a portion of the message, since the rest of the message is transmitted in the clear. Even in the case of complete encryption, as shown in Figure 4.3, there is no protection of confidentiality because any observer can decrypt the message by using the sender's public key.

It is, however, possible to provide both the authentication function and confidentiality by a double use of the public-key scheme (Figure 4.4):

$$Z = E_{KUb}[E_{KRa}(X)]$$
$$X = D_{KUa}[D_{KRb}(Z)]$$

In this case, we begin as before by encrypting a message, using the sender's private key. This provides the digital signature. Next, we encrypt again, using the receiver's public key. The final ciphertext can be decrypted only by the

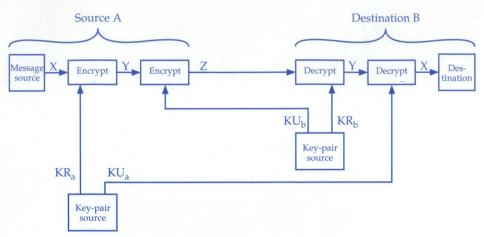

FIGURE 4.4.   Public-Key Cryptosystem: Secrecy and Authentication

intended receiver, who alone has the matching private key. Thus confidentiality is provided. The disadvantage of this approach is that the public-key algorithm, which is complex, must be exercised four times rather than two in each communication.

Applications for Public-Key Cryptosystems

Before proceeding, we need to clarify one aspect of public-key cryptosystems that is otherwise likely to lead to confusion. Public-key systems are characterized by the use of a cryptographic type of algorithm with two keys, one held private and one available publicly. Depending on the application, the sender uses either the sender's private key or the receiver's public key, or both, to perform some type of cryptographic function. In broad terms, we can classify the use of public-key cryptosystems into three categories:

- *Encryption/decryption:* The sender encrypts a message with the recipient's public key.
- *Digital signature:* The sender "signs" a message with its private key. Signing is achieved by a cryptographic algorithm applied to the message or to a small block of data that is bound in some way to the message.
- *Key exchange:* Two sides cooperate to exchange a session key. Several quite different approaches are possible, involving the private key(s) of one or both parties.

Some algorithms are suitable for all three applications, whereas others can only be used for one or two of these applications. Table 4.3 indicates the applications supported by the algorithms discussed in this book. In this chapter we focus on algorithms such as RSA that can be used for all three applications.

TABLE 4.3   Applications for Public-Key Cryptosystems

Algorithm	Encryption/Decryption	Digital Signature	Key Exchange
RSA	Yes; impractical for large blocks	Yes	Yes
LUC	Yes; impractical for large blocks	Yes	Yes
DSS	No	Yes	No
Diffie–Hellman	No	No	Yes

Requirements for Public-Key Cryptography

The cryptosystem illustrated in Figures 4.2 through 4.4 depends on a cryptographic algorithm based on two related keys. Diffie and Hellman postulated this system without demonstrating that such algorithms exist. However, they did lay out the conditions that such algorithms must fulfill [DIFF76b]:

1. It is computationally easy for a party B to generate a pair (public key KU, private key KR).
2. It is computationally easy for a sender A, knowing the public key and the message to be encrypted, M, to generate the corresponding ciphertext:

$$C = E_{KUb}(M)$$

3. It is computationally easy for the receiver B to decrypt the resulting ciphertext using the private key to recover the original message:

$$M = D_{KRb}(C) = D_{KRb}[E_{KUb}(M)]$$

4. It is computationally infeasible for an opponent, knowing the public key, KU_b, to determine the private key, KR_b.
5. It is computationally infeasible for an opponent, knowing the public key, KU_b, and a ciphertext, C, to recover the original message, M.

We can add a sixth requirement that, although useful, is not necessary for all public-key applications:

6. The encryption and decryption functions can be applied in either order:

$$M = E_{KUb}[D_{KRb}(M)]$$

These are formidable requirements, as evidenced by the fact that only one such algorithm has received widespread acceptance in over a quarter-century since the concept of public-key cryptography was proposed.

Before elaborating on why the requirements are so formidable, let us first recast them. The requirements boil down to the need for a trapdoor one-way function. A *one-way function*[2] is one that maps a domain into a range such that every function value has a unique inverse, with the condition that the calculation of the function is easy whereas the calculation of the inverse is infeasible:

$$Y = f(X) \quad \text{easy}$$
$$X = f^{-1}(Y) \quad \text{infeasible}$$

Generally, *easy* is defined to mean a problem that can be solved in polynomial time as a function of input length. Thus, if the length of the input is n bits, then the time to compute the function is proportional to n^a, where a is a fixed constant. Such algorithms are said to belong to the class **P**. The term *infeasible* is a much fuzzier concept. In general, we can say a problem is infeasible if the effort to solve it grows faster than polynomial time as a function of input size. For example, if the length of the input is n bits and the time to compute the function is proportional to 2^n, it is considered infeasible. Unfortunately, it is difficult to determine if a particular algorithm exhibits this complexity. Furthermore, traditional notions of computational complexity focus on the worst-case or average-case complexity of an algorithm. These measures are worthless for cryptography, which requires that it be infeasible to invert a function for virtually all inputs, not for the worst case or even average case. A brief introduction to some of these concepts is in Appendix 4B.

We now turn to the definition of a *trapdoor one-way function,* which, like the one-way function, is easy to calculate in one direction and infeasible to calculate in the other direction unless certain additional information is known. With the additional information the inverse can be calculated in polynomial time. We can summarize as follows: A trapdoor one-way function is a family of invertible functions f_k, such that,

$$Y = f_k(X) \quad \text{easy, if k and X are known}$$
$$X = f_k^{-1}(Y) \quad \text{easy, if k and Y are known}$$
$$X = f_k^{-1}(Y) \quad \text{infeasible, if Y is known but k is not known}$$

Thus, the development of a practical public-key scheme depends on discovery of a suitable trapdoor one-way function.

Public-Key Cryptanalysis

As with conventional encryption, a public-key encryption scheme is vulnerable to a brute-force attack. The countermeasure is the same: Use large keys. However, there is a trade-off to be considered. Public-key systems depend on the use of some sort of invertible mathematical function. The complexity of calculating these functions may not scale linearly with the number of bits in the key but grow more rapidly than that. Thus, the key size must be large enough to make brute-force attack impractical but small enough for practical encryption and decryption. In practice, the key sizes that have been proposed do make brute-force attack impractical

---

[2]Not to be confused with a one-way hash function that takes an arbitrarily large data field as its argument and maps it to a fixed output. Such functions are used for authentication (see Chapter 5).

but result in encryption/decryption speeds that are too slow for general purpose use. Instead, as was mentioned earlier, public-key encryption is currently confined to key management and signature applications.

Another form of attack is to find some way to compute the private key, given the public key. To date, it has not been mathematically proven that this form of attack is infeasible for a particular public-key algorithm. Thus, any given algorithm, including the widely used RSA algorithm, is suspect. The history of cryptanalysis shows that a problem that seems insoluble from one perspective can be found to have a solution if looked at in an entirely different way.

Finally, there is a form of attack that is peculiar to public-key systems. This is, in essence, a probable-message attack. Suppose, for example, that a message were to be sent that consisted solely of a 56-bit DES key. An opponent could encrypt all possible keys using the public key and could decipher any message by matching the transmitted ciphertext. Thus, no matter how large the key size of the public-key scheme, the attack is reduced to a brute-force attack on a 56-bit key. This attack can be thwarted by appending some random bits to such simple messages.

The Knapsack Algorithm

A number of algorithms have been proposed for the public-key scheme. A number of these, though initially promising, turned out to be breakable. It is instructive to review the most important such scheme.

By far, the most famous of the fallen contenders is the trapdoor knapsack proposed by Ralph Merkle [MERK78]. The knapsack problem deals with determining which objects are in a container, such as a knapsack. A simple example is shown in Figure 4.5 [HELL78]. The knapsack is filled with a subset of the items shown, whose weights in grams are indicated. Given the weight of the filled knapsack, 1156 grams, the problem is to determine which of the items are contained in the knapsack.

The problem shown here is relatively simple but generally becomes computationally infeasible when there are, say, 100 items rather than the 10 of this example. Merkle's contribution was to show (1) how to turn the knapsack problem into a scheme for encryption and decryption, and (2) how to incorporate "trapdoor" information that would enable a person to quickly solve a knapsack problem.

First, let us state the general approach for encryption/decryption using the knapsack problem. Suppose we wish to send messages in blocks of n bits. Then, define:

$$\text{cargo vector} \qquad \mathbf{a} = (a_1, a_2, \ldots, a_n) \qquad a_i \text{ integer}$$
$$\text{plaintext message block} \quad \mathbf{x} = (x_1, x_2, \ldots, x_n) \qquad x_i \text{ binary}$$

$$\text{corresponding ciphertext} \quad S = \mathbf{a} \bullet \mathbf{x} = \sum_{i=1}^{n} (a_i \times x_i)$$

Consider the cargo vector $\mathbf{a}$ to be a list of potential elements to be put in the knapsack, with each vector element equal to the weight of the corresponding

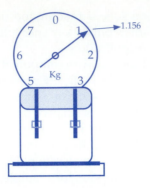

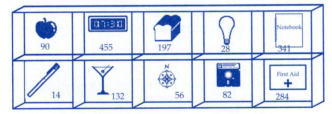

FIGURE 4.5.   Illustration of the Knapsack Problem

cargo element. And consider **x** to be a selection of elements from the cargo vector, with $x_i = 1$ for each cargo element a_i that is selected for inclusion in the knapsack. Then the vector product S is simply the sum of the selected items, which is the weight in the knapsack.

For encryption, **a** is used as the public key. A party wishing to send message **x** performs $S = $ **a** $\bullet$ **x** and transmits S. For decryption, the receiving party must recover **x**, given S and **a**.

The first requirement is that there be a unique inverse for each value of S. For example, consider the following:

$$\mathbf{a} = (1, 3, 2, 5)$$
$$S = 3$$

This problem has two solutions: **x** = 1010 and **x** = 0100. Thus, the elements of **a** must be chosen such that each combination of elements yields a unique value.

The second requirement is that decryption is hard in general but easy if special knowledge is available. Certainly, for large values of n, the knapsack problem is hard in general. But, under special circumstances, the problem is easy to solve. Suppose we impose the condition that each element of **a** is larger than the sum of the preceding elements:

$$a_i > \sum_{j=1}^{i-1} a_j \quad 1 < i \leq n$$

This is known as a *superincreasing vector*. In this case, the solution is easy. For example, consider the vector

$$\mathbf{a'} = (171, 197, 459, 1191, 2410)$$

which satisfies the condition. Suppose we have S' = $\mathbf{a'} \cdot \mathbf{x'}$ = 3798. Because 3798 > 2410, a_5 must be included ($x_5 = 1$), because without a_5 the other elements cannot contribute enough to add up to 3798. Now consider 3798 − 2410 = 1388. Because this number is greater than 1191, a_4 must also be included ($x_4 = 1$). Continuing in this fashion, we find that $x_3 = 0$, $x_2 = 1$, and $x_1 = 0$.

What Merkle did was find a way to tie an easy superincreasing knapsack problem to a difficult general knapsack problem.[3] Suppose we choose at random an easy knapsack vector, $\mathbf{a'}$, with n elements. Also select two integers, m and w, such that m is greater than the sum of the elements of $\mathbf{a'}$ and w is relatively prime to m. That is:

$$m > \sum_{i=1}^{n} a_i$$

$$\gcd(w, m) = 1$$

Now, we construct a hard knapsack vector $\mathbf{a}$ by multiplying the easy vector $\mathbf{a'}$ by w, modulo m.

$$\mathbf{a} = w\mathbf{a'} \bmod m$$

The vector $\mathbf{a}$ will, in general, not be superincreasing and can therefore be used to construct hard knapsack problems. However, knowledge of w and m enables the conversion of this hard knapsack problem to an easy one. To see this, first observe that since w and m are relatively prime, there exists a unique multiplicative inverse w^{-1}, modulo m. Therefore,

$$w^{-1}\mathbf{a} = \mathbf{a'} \bmod m$$

We are now ready to state the knapsack scheme. The ingredients are the following:

$\mathbf{a'}$, a superincreasing vector   (private, chosen)

m, an integer larger than $\displaystyle\sum_{i=1}^{n} a_i$ (private, chosen)

---

[3]For the discussion that follows, you should be familiar with the concepts of prime numbers and modular arithmetic, both of which are discussed briefly in Appendix 4A. Also, the notation gcd(w, m) is used to mean the greatest common divisor of w and m.

w, an integer relatively prime to m (private, chosen)
w^{-1}, the inverse of w, modulo m (private, calculated)
$\mathbf{a}$, equal to $w\mathbf{a'}$ mod m (public, calculated)

The private key consists of the triple $\{w^{-1}, m, \mathbf{a'}\}$ and the public key consists of the value of $\mathbf{a}$. Suppose that user A has published its public key $\mathbf{a}$ and that user B wishes to send the message $\mathbf{x}$ to A. Then, B calculates the sum

$$S = \mathbf{a} \bullet \mathbf{x}$$

The determination of $\mathbf{x}$ given S and $\mathbf{a}$ is difficult, so this is a secure transmission. However, on receipt, user A is able to decrypt easily. Define $S' = w^{-1}S$ mod m. We have

Key generation

Easy knapsack, $\mathbf{a'}$

1	3	7	13	26	65	119	267

Multiplier $w = 467$ Modulus $m = 523$ $w^{-1} = 28$ (mod 523)

Hard knapsack, $\mathbf{a}$

467	355	131	318	113	21	135	215

Public key, KU = $\mathbf{a}$ Private key, KR = $\{w^{-1}, m, \mathbf{a'}\}$

Encryption

Plaintext   =   01001011

Ciphertext   = $0\times467+1\times355+0\times131+0\times318+1\times113+0\times21+1\times135+1\times215$
            =   818

Decryption

$818\times w^{-1} = 818\times28 = 415$ (mod 523)

$415\geq267$	=>	$x_8=1$
$415-267=148 \geq119$	=>	$x_7=1$
$148-119=29 <65$	=>	$x_6=0$
$29\geq26$	=>	$x_5=1$
$29-26=3 <13$	=>	$x_4=0$
$3<7$	=>	$x_3=0$
$3\geq3$	=>	$x_2=1$
$3-3=0 < 1$	=>	$x_1=0$

Plaintext = $x_1x_2x_3x_4x_5x_6x_7x_8$ = 01001011

FIGURE 4.6. Example of Trapdoor Encryption/Decryption

$$S = a \bullet x = wa' \bullet x$$
$$S' = w^{-1}S \bmod m$$
$$= w^{-1}wa' \bullet x \bmod m$$
$$= a' \bullet x$$

Thus we have converted the hard problem of finding **x** given S and **a** to the easy problem of finding **x** given S' and **a**′.

Figure 4.6 shows an example. Given the plaintext message **x** = 01001011, user B computes **a** • **x** = 818. User A first computes $S' = w^{-1}S \bmod m$ = 415, and then solves the easy knapsack to recover 01001011.

The knapsack algorithm was hailed as an unbreakable system. Merkle, confident though not rich, offered a reward of $100 to anyone who could break it. It took four years, but Adi Shamir, one of the inventors of RSA, broke the system and collected the $100.

But Merkle was not through. He observed that the hard knapsack problem could be made even harder by using multiple transformations (w_1, m_1), (w_2, m_2), and so on. The overall transformation that results is not equivalent to any single (w, m) transformation. With this in mind, Merkle upped the ante to $1000 for anyone who could break the multiple-iteration problem. This time he had only two years to wait before paying up. This ended serious consideration of knapsacks as a basis for public-key cryptography.[4]

4.2

THE RSA ALGORITHM

The pioneering paper by Diffie and Hellman [DIFF76b] introduced a new approach to cryptography and, in effect, challenged cryptologists to come up with a cryptographic algorithm that met the requirements for public-key systems. One of the first of the responses to the challenge was developed in 1977 by Ron Rivest, Adi Shamir, and Len Adleman at MIT, and first published in 1978 [RIVE78]. The Rivest-Shamir-Adleman (RSA) scheme has since that time reigned supreme as the only widely accepted and implemented approach to public-key encryption.

The RSA scheme is a block cipher in which the plaintext and ciphertext are integers between 0 and $n - 1$ for some n. Because this is the only widely accepted approach to public-key cryptography, we examine it in this section in some detail, beginning with an explanation of the algorithm.[5] Then we examine some of the computational and cryptanalytical implications of RSA.

---

[4]A number of other knapsack or knapsack-like cryptosystems have been proposed. All of these have either been broken or require an excessive amount of computation. See [SCNH94] for pointers to the literature.

[5]If you are unfamiliar with number theory, you should at this point review Appendix 4A.

Description of the Algorithm

The scheme developed by Rivest, Shamir, and Adleman makes use of an expression with exponentials. Plaintext is encrypted in blocks, with each block having a binary value less than some number n. Encryption and decryption are of the following form, for some plaintext block M and ciphertext block C:

$$C = M^e \bmod n$$
$$M = C^d \bmod n = (M^e)^d \bmod n = M^{ed} \bmod n$$

Both sender and receiver must know the value of n. The sender knows the value of e, and only the receiver knows the value of d. Thus, this is a public-key encryption algorithm with a public key of KU = $\{e, n\}$ and a private key of KR = $\{d, n\}$. For this algorithm to be satisfactory for public-key encryption, the following requirements must be met:

1. Is it possible to find values of e, d, n such that $M^{ed} = M \bmod n$ for all $M < n$?
2. Is it relatively easy to calculate M^e and C^d for all values of $M < n$?
3. Is it infeasible to determine d given e and n?

For now, we focus on the first question and consider the other questions later. We need to find a relationship of the form:

$$M^{ed} = M \bmod n$$

The corollary to Euler's theorem, presented in Appendix 4A (Equation 4.7), fits the bill: Given two prime numbers, p and q, and two integers n and m, such that $n = pq$ and $0 < m < n$, and arbitrary integer k, the following relationship holds:

$$m^{k\phi(n)+1} = m^{k(p-1)(q-1)+1} \equiv m \bmod n$$

where $\phi(n)$ is the Euler totient function, which is the number of positive integers less than n and relatively prime to n. It is shown in Appendix 4A that for p, q prime, $\phi(pq) = (p - 1)(q - 1)$. Thus, we can achieve the desired relationship if:

$$ed = k\phi(n) + 1$$

This is equivalent to saying:

$$ed \equiv 1 \bmod \phi(n)$$
$$e \equiv d^{-1} \bmod \phi(n)$$

That is, e and d are multiplicative inverses mod $\phi(n)$. Note that, according to the rules of modular arithmetic, this is true only if d (and therefore e) is relatively prime to $\phi(n)$. Equivalently, $\gcd(\phi(n), d) = 1$.

We are now ready to state the RSA scheme. The ingredients are the following:

p, q, two prime numbers	(private, chosen)
$n = pq$	(public, calculated)
d, with $\gcd(\phi(n), d) = 1$; $1 < d < \phi(n)$	(private, calculated)
$e \equiv d^{-1} \bmod \phi(n)$	(public, chosen)

The private key consists of {d, n} and the public key consists of {e, n}. Suppose that user A has published its public key and that user B wishes to send the message M to A. Then, B calculates $C = M^e$ (mod n) and transmits C. On receipt of this ciphertext, user A decrypts by calculating $M = C^d$ (mod n).

It is worthwhile to summarize the justification for this algorithm. We have chosen e and d such that

$$e \equiv d^{-1} \bmod \phi(n)$$

Therefore

$$ed \equiv 1 \bmod \phi(n)$$

Therefore ed is of the form $k\phi(n) + 1$. But by the corollary to Euler's theorem, provided in Appendix 4A, given two prime numbers, p and q, and integers $n = pq$ and M, with $0 < M < n$:

$$M^{k\phi(n)+1} = M^{k(p-1)(q-1)+1} \equiv M \bmod n$$

So $M^{ed} \equiv M \bmod n$. Now

$$C = M^e \bmod n$$
$$M = C^d \bmod n \equiv (M^e)^d \bmod n \equiv M^{ed} \bmod n \equiv M \bmod n$$

Figure 4.7 summarizes the RSA algorithm. An example is shown in Figure 4.8. For this example, the keys were generated as follows:

1. Select two prime numbers, $p = 7$ and $q = 17$.
2. Calculate $n = pq = 7 \times 17 = 119$.
3. Calculate $\phi(n) = (p - 1)(q - 1) = 96$.
4. Select e such that e is relatively prime to $\phi(n) = 96$ and less than $\phi(n)$; in this case, $e = 5$.
5. Determine d such that $de = 1 \bmod 96$ and $d < 96$. The correct value is $d = 77$, because $77 \times 5 = 385 = 4 \times 96 + 1$.

The resulting keys are public key KU = {5, 119} and private key KR = {77, 119}. The example shows the use of these keys for a plaintext input of M = 19. For encryption, 19 is raised to the 5th power, yielding 2476099. Upon division by 119, the remainder is determined to be 66. Hence $19^5 \equiv 66 \bmod 119$, and the ciphertext is 66. For decryption, it is determined that $66^{77} \equiv 19 \bmod 119$.

Computational Aspects

We now turn to the issue of the complexity of the computation required to use RSA. There are actually two issues to consider: key generation and encryption/decryption. Let us look first at the process of encryption and decryption, and then return to the issue of key generation.

Key Generation

Select p, q p and q both prime

Calculate $n = p \times q$

Select integer d $\gcd(\phi(n), d) = 1; 1 < d < \phi(n)$

Calculate e $e = d^{-1} \bmod \phi(n)$

Public key $KU = \{e,n\}$

Private key $KR = \{d,n\}$

Encryption

Plaintext: $M < n$

Ciphertext: $C = M^e \,(\bmod\ n)$

Decryption

Ciphertext: C

Plaintext: $M = C^d \,(\bmod\ n)$

FIGURE 4.7.   The RSA Algorithm

Encryption and Decryption

Both encryption and decryption in RSA involve raising an integer to an integer power, mod n. If the exponentiation is done over the integers and then reduced modulo n, the intermediate values would be gargantuan. Fortunately, we can make use of a property of modular arithmetic:

$$[(a \bmod n) \times (b \bmod n)] \bmod n = (a \times b) \bmod n$$

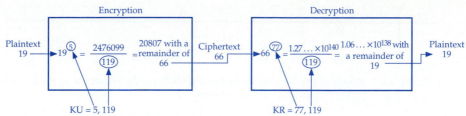

FIGURE 4.8.   Example of RSA Algorithm

Thus, we can reduce intermediate results modulo n. This makes the calculation practical.

Another consideration is the efficiency of exponentiation, since with RSA we are dealing with potentially quite large exponents. To see how efficiency might be increased, consider that we wish to compute x^{16}. A straightforward approach requires 15 multiplications:

$$x^{16} = x \times x \times x \times x \times x \times x \times x \times x \times x \times x \times x \times x \times x \times x \times x \times x$$

However, we can achieve the same final result with only four multiplications if we repeatedly take the square of each partial result, successively forming x^2, x^4, x^8, x^{16}.

More generally, suppose we wish to find the value a^m, with a and m positive integers. If we express m as a binary number $b_k b_{k-1} \ldots b_0$, then we have

$$m = \sum_{b_i \neq 0} 2^i$$

Therefore,

$$a^m = a^{\left(\sum_{b_i \neq 0} 2^i\right)} = \prod_{b_i \neq 0} a^{(2^i)}$$

$$a^m \bmod n = \left[\prod_{b_i \neq 0} a^{(2^i)}\right] \bmod n = \prod_{b_i \neq 0}\left[a^{(2^i)} \bmod n\right]$$

We can therefore develop the following algorithm[6] for computing $a^b \bmod n$:

```
c ← 0; d ← 1
for i ← k downto 0
    do c ← 2 × c
       d ← (d × d) mod n
       if   b_i = 1
            then   c ← c + 1
                   d ← (d × a) mod n
return d
```

[6]The algorithm has a long history; this particular pseudocode expression is from [CORM90].

i	9	8	7	6	5	4	3	2	1	0
b_i	1	0	0	0	1	1	0	0	0	0
c	1	2	4	8	17	35	70	140	280	560
d	7	49	157	526	160	241	298	166	67	1

FIGURE 4.9.   Result of the Fast Modular Exponentiation Algorithm for a_b mod n, where $a = 7$, $b = 560 = 1000110000$, $n = 561$ [CORM90]

Figure 4.9 [CORM90] shows an example of the execution of this algorithm. Note that the variable c is not needed; it is included for explanatory purposes. The final value of c is the value of the exponent.

Key Generation

Before the application of the public-key cryptosystem, each participant must generate a pair of keys. This involves the following tasks:

- Determining two prime numbers, p and q
- Selecting either e or d and calculating the other

First, consider the selection of p and q. Because the value of $n = pq$ will be known to any potential opponent, to prevent the discovery of p and q by exhaustive methods, these primes must be chosen from a sufficiently large set (i.e., p and q must be large numbers). On the other hand, the method used for finding large primes must be reasonably efficient.

At present, there are no useful techniques that yield arbitrarily large primes, so some other means of tackling the problem is needed. The procedure that is generally used is to pick at random an odd number of the desired order of magnitude and test whether that number is prime. If not, pick successive random numbers until one is found that tests prime.

A variety of tests for primality have been developed (e.g., see [KNUT81] for a description of a number of such tests). Almost invariably, the tests are probabilistic. That is, the test will merely determine that a given integer is *probably* prime. Despite this lack of certainty, these tests can be run in such a way as to make the probability as close to 1.0 as desired. As an example, one of the more efficient and effective algorithms, the Miller–Rabin algorithm, is described in Appendix 4A. With this algorithm and most such algorithms, the procedure for testing whether a given integer n is prime is to perform some calculation that involves n and a randomly chosen integer a. If n "fails" the test, then n is not prime. If n "passes" the test, then n may be prime or nonprime. If n passes many such tests with many different randomly chosen values for a, then we can have high confidence that n is in fact prime.

In summary, the procedure for picking a prime number is as follows:

1. Pick an odd integer n at random (e.g., using a pseudorandom number generator).

2. Pick an integer $a < n$ at random.
3. Perform the probabilistic primality test, such as Miller-Rabin. If n fails the test, reject the value n and go to step 1.
4. If n has passed a sufficient number of tests, accept n; otherwise, go to step 2.

This is a somewhat tedious procedure. However, remember that this process is performed relatively infrequently: only when a new pair (KU, KR) is needed.

It is worth noting how many numbers are likely to be rejected before a prime number is found. A result from number theory, known as the prime number theorem, states that the primes near N are spaced on the average one every (ln N) integers. Thus, on average, one would have to test on the order of ln(N) integers before a prime is found. Actually, since all even integers can be immediately rejected, the correct figure is ln(N)/2. For example, if a prime on the order of magnitude of 2^{200} were sought, then about ln(2^{200})/2 = 70 trials would be needed to find a prime.

Having determined prime numbers p and q, the process of key generation is completed by selecting a value of d and calculating e or, alternatively, selecting a value of e and calculating d. Assuming the former, then we need to select a d such that $gcd(\phi(n), d) = 1$ and then calculate $e = d^{-1} \bmod \phi(n)$. Fortunately, there is a single algorithm that will at the same time calculate the greatest common divisor of two integers and, if the gcd is 1, determine the inverse of one of the integers modulo the other. The algorithm, referred to as the extended Euclid's algorithm, is explained in Appendix 4A. Thus, the procedure is to generate a series of random numbers, testing each against $\phi(n)$ until a number relatively prime to $\phi(n)$ is found. Again, we can ask the question: How many random numbers must we test to find a usable number, that is, a number relatively prime to $\phi(n)$? It can be easily shown that the probability that two random numbers are relatively prime is about 0.6; thus, very few tests would be needed to find a suitable integer (see Problem 4.8).

Cryptanalytic Considerations

Four possible approaches to cryptanalysis of the RSA algorithm can be identified:

*   Brute force: try all possible private keys.
*   Factor p into its two prime factors. This enables calculation of $\phi(n) = (p - 1) \times (q - 1)$, which in turn enables determination of $d = e^{-1} \pmod{\phi(n)}$.
*   Determine $\phi(n)$ directly, without first determining p and q. Again, this enables determination of $d = e^{-1} \pmod{\phi(n)}$.
*   Determine d directly, without first determining $\phi(n)$.

The defense against the brute-force approach is the same for RSA as for other cryptosystems, namely, use a large key space. Thus, the larger the number of bits in e and d, the better. However, because the calculations involved, both in key generation and in encryption/decryption, are complex, the larger the size of the key, the slower the system will run.

Most discussions of the cryptanalysis of RSA have focused on the task of factoring p into its two prime factors. Currently, no reasonable algorithm is known that can factor the product of two primes for very large values (e.g., several hundred decimal digits). The best of known algorithms factor an integer n in a time proportional to:

$$L(n) = e^{\sqrt{\ln n \times \ln (\ln n)}}$$

Figure 4.10 indicates the scale of the problem facing the cryptanalyst. Unless some better algorithm is discovered, the foregoing result suggests that a magnitude of n on the order of 100 to 200 digits is secure for the present time [DIFF88]. Considerations of current computer technology suggest that a 100-digit number could be factored at modest cost in about two weeks. For an expensive configuration (e.g., on the order of $10 million), a 150-digit number could be factored in about a year. A 200-digit number appears beyond reach for a very long time, barring a mathematical breakthrough. For example, even if a performance level of 10^{12} operations per second were reached, which is beyond current technology and would cost billions of dollars to develop, then it would take on the order of 1000 years to factor a 200-digit number using existing algorithms [NECH92]. For efficient implementation of RSA, a magnitude of 154 digits, which could be handled in 512 bits is attractive, whereas a 200-digit number would require around 660 bits and would be awkward to implement.

With presently known algorithms, the tasks of determining $\phi(n)$ given n or of determining d given e and n, appear to be at least as time-consuming as the factor-

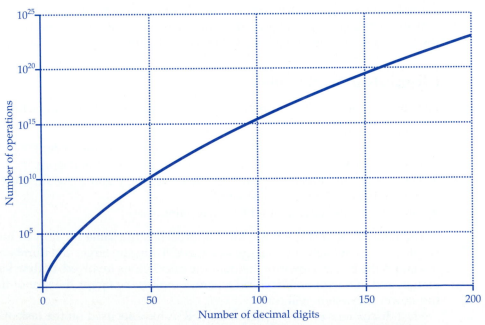

FIGURE 4.10. Number of Operations Required to Factor Integer with N Digits

ing problem. Hence, we can use factoring performance as a benchmark against which to evaluate the security of RSA.

In addition to specifying that n should be on the order of 10^{150} to 10^{200}, a number of other constraints have been suggested by researchers. To avoid values of n that may be more easily factored, the algorithm's inventors suggest the following constraints on p and q:

1. p and q should differ in length by only a few digits. Thus, both p and q should be on the order of 10^{75} to 10^{100}.
2. Both $(p - 1)$ and $(q - 1)$ should contain a large prime factor.
3. $\gcd(p - 1, q - 1)$ should be small.

In addition, it has been demonstrated that if $e < n$ and $d < n^{1/4}$, then d can be easily determined [WIEN90].

4.3

KEY MANAGEMENT

In Chapter 3, we examined the problem of the distribution of secret keys. One of the major roles of public-key encryption has been to address the problem of key distribution. There are actually two distinct aspects to the use of public-key encryption in this regard:

- The distribution of public keys
- The use of public-key encryption to distribute secret keys

We examine each of these areas in turn.

Distribution of Public Keys

Several techniques have been proposed for the distribution of public keys. Virtually all these proposals can be grouped into the following general schemes:

- Public announcement
- Publicly available directory
- Public-key authority
- Public-key certificates

Public Announcement of Public Keys

On the face of it, the point of public-key encryption is that the public key is public. Thus, if there is some broadly accepted public-key algorithm, such as RSA, any participant can send his or her public key to any other participant or broadcast the key to the community at large (Figure 4.11). For example, because of the growing popularity of PGP (pretty good privacy, discussed in Part II), which makes use of RSA, many PGP users have adopted the practice of appending their public key to

FIGURE 4.11.   Uncontrolled Public Key Distribution

messages that they send to public forums, such as USENET newsgroups and Internet mailing lists.

Although this approach is convenient, it has a major weakness. Anyone can forge such a public announcement. That is, some user could pretend to be user A and send a public key to another participant or broadcast such a public key. Until such time as user A discovers the forgery and alerts other participants, the forger is able to read all encrypted messages intended for A and can use the forged keys for authentication (see Figure 4.3).

Publicly Available Directory

A greater degree of security can be achieved by maintaining a publicly available dynamic directory of public keys. Maintenance and distribution of the public directory would have to be the responsibility of some trusted entity or organization (Figure 4.12). Such a scheme would include the following elements:

1. The authority maintains a directory with a {name, public key} entry for each participant.
2. Each participant registers a public key with the directory authority. Registration would have to be in person or by some form of secure authenticated communication.
3. A participant may replace the existing key with a new one at any time, either because of the desire to replace a public key that has already been used for a large amount of data, or because the corresponding private key has been compromised in some way.
4. Periodically, the authority publishes the entire directory or updates to the directory. For example, a hard-copy version much like a telephone book could be published, or updates could be listed in a widely circulated newspaper.
5. Participants could also access the directory electronically. For this purpose, secure, authenticated communication from the authority to the participant is mandatory.

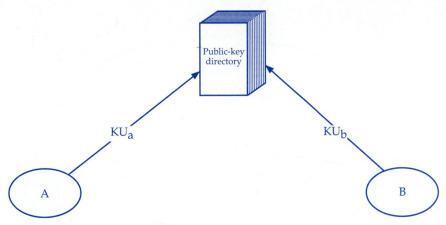

FIGURE 4.12.   Public-Key Publication

This scheme is clearly more secure than individual public announcements, but still has vulnerabilities. If an opponent succeeds in obtaining or computing the private key of the directory authority, the opponent could authoritatively pass out counterfeit public keys and subsequently impersonate any participant and eavesdrop on messages sent to any participant. Another way to achieve the same end is for the opponent to tamper with the records kept by the authority.

Public-Key Authority

Stronger security for public-key distribution can be achieved by providing tighter control over the distribution of public keys from the directory. A typical scenario is illustrated in Figure 4.13, which is based on a figure in [POPE79]. As before, the scenario assumes that a central authority maintains a dynamic directory of public keys of all participants. In addition, each participant reliably knows a public key for the authority, with only the authority knowing the corresponding private key. The following steps (matched by number to Figure 4.13) occur:

1. A sends a time-stamped message to the public-key authority containing a request for the current public key of B.
2. The authority responds with a message that is encrypted using the authority's private key, KR_{auth}. Thus, A is able to decrypt the message using the authority's public key. Therefore, A is assured that the message originated with the authority. The message includes the following:
    *   B's public key, KU_b, which A can use to encrypt messages destined for B.
    *   The original request, to enable A to match this response with the corresponding earlier request and to verify that the original request was not altered before reception by the authority.
    *   The original timestamp, so A can determine that this is not an old message from the authority containing a key other than B's current public key.

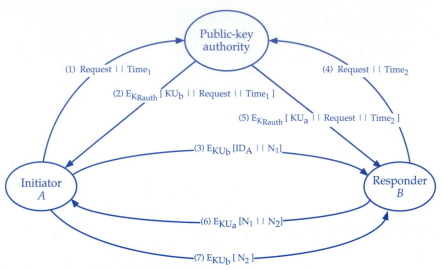

FIGURE 4.13.   Public-Key Distribution Scenario

3. A stores B's public key and also uses it to encrypt a message to B containing an identifier of A (ID_A) and a nonce (N_1), which is used to uniquely identify this transaction.

4, 5. B retrieves A's public key from the authority in the same manner as A retrieved B's public key.

At this point, public keys have been securely delivered to A and B, and they may begin their protected exchange. However, two additional steps are desirable:

6. B sends a message to A encrypted with KU_a and containing A's nonce (N_1) as well as a new nonce generated by B (N_2). Since only B could have decrypted message (3), the presence of N_1 in message (6) assures A that the correspondent is B.

7. A returns N_2, encrypted using B's public key, to assure B that its correspondent is A.

Thus, a total of seven messages are required. However, the initial four messages need be used only infrequently because both A and B can save the other's public key for future use, a technique known as caching. Periodically, a user should request fresh copies of the public keys of its correspondents to ensure currency.

Public-Key Certificates

The scenario of Figure 4.13 is attractive, yet it still has some drawbacks. The public-key authority could be somewhat of a bottleneck in the system, for a user must appeal to the authority for a public key for every other user that it wishes to contact. As before, the directory of names and public keys maintained by the authority is vulnerable to tampering.

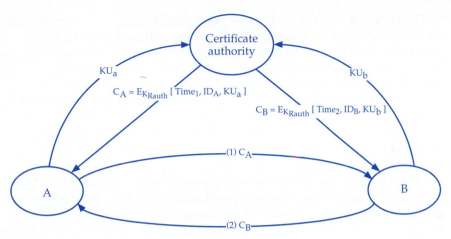

FIGURE 4.14.   Exchange of Public-Key Certificates

An alternative approach, first suggested by Kohnfelder [KOHN78], is to create certificates that can be used by participants to exchange keys without contacting a public-key authority, in a way that is as reliable as if the keys were obtained directly from a public-key authority. Each certificate contains a public key and other information, is created by a certificate authority, and is given to the participant with the matching private key. A participant conveys its key information to another by transmitting its certificate. Other participants can verify that the certificate was created by the authority. We can place the following requirements on this scheme:

1. Any participant can read a certificate to determine the name and public key of the certificate's owner.
2. Any participant can verify that the certificate originated from the certificate authority and is not counterfeit.
3. Only the certificate authority can create and update certificates.

These requirements are satisfied by the original proposal in [KOHN78]. Denning [DENN83] added the following additional requirement:

4. Any participant can verify the currency of the certificate.

A certificate scheme is illustrated in Figure 4.14. Each participant applies to the certificate authority, supplying a public key and requesting a certificate. Application must be in person or by some form of secure authenticated communication. For participant A, the authority provides a certificate of the form:

$$C_A = E_{KR_{auth}}[T, ID_A, KU_A]$$

where KR_{auth} is the private key used by the authority. A may then pass this certificate on to any other participant, who reads and verifies the certificate as follows:

$$D_{KU_{auth}}[C_A] = D_{KU_{auth}}\left[E_{KR_{auth}}[T, ID_A, KU_A]\right] = (T, ID_A, KU_A)$$

The recipient uses the authority's public key, KU_{auth}, to decrypt the certificate. Since the certificate is readable only using the authority's public key, this verifies that the certificate came from the certificate authority. The elements ID_A and KU_A provide the recipient with the name and public key of the certificate's holder. Finally, the timestamp T validates the currency of the certificate. The timestamp counters the following scenario. A's private key is learned by an opponent. A generates a new private/public key pair and applies to the certificate authority for a new certificate. Meanwhile, the opponent replays the old certificate to B. If B then encrypts messages using the compromised old public key, the opponent can read those messages.

In this context, the compromise of a private key is comparable to the loss of a credit card. The owner cancels the credit card number but is at risk until all possible communicants are aware that the old credit card is obsolete. Thus, the timestamp serves as something like an expiration date. If a certificate is sufficiently old, it is assumed to be expired.

Public-Key Distribution of Secret Keys

Once public keys have been distributed or have become accessible, secure communication that thwarts eavesdropping (Figure 4.3), tampering (Figure 4.4), or both (Figure 4.5) is possible. However, few users will wish to make exclusive use of public-key encryption for communication because of the relatively slow data rates that can be achieved. Accordingly, public-key encryption is more reasonably viewed as a vehicle for the distribution of secret keys to be used for conventional encryption.

Simple Secret Key Distribution

An extremely simple scheme was put forward by Merkle [MERK79], as illustrated in Figure 4.15. If A wishes to communicate with B, the following procedure is employed:

1. A generates a public/private key pair $\{KU_a, KR_a\}$ and transmits a message to B consisting of KU_a and an identifier of A, IDA.
2. B generates a secret key, K_s, and transmits it to A, encrypted with A's public key.
3. A computes $D_{KRa}[E_{KUa}[K_s]]$ to recover the secret key. Since only A can decrypt the message, only A and B will know the identity of K_s.
4. A discards KU_a and KR_a and B discards KU_a.

A and B can now securely communicate using conventional encryption and the session key Ks. At the completion of the exchange, both A and B discard Ks. Despite its simplicity, this is an attractive protocol. No ys exist before the start of the communication and none exist after the completion of communication. Thus, the risk of compromise of the keys is minimal. At the same time, the communication is secure from eavesdropping.

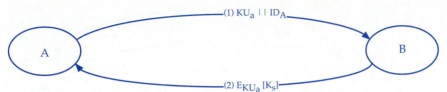

FIGURE 4.15. Simple Use of Public-Key Encryption to Establish a Session Key

This protocol is vulnerable to an active attack. If an opponent, E, has control of the intervening communication channel, then E can compromise the communication in the following fashion without being detected:

1. A generates a public/private key pair $\{KU_a, KR_a\}$ and transmits a message intended for B consisting of KU_a and an identifier of A, ID_A.
2. E intercepts the message, creates its own public/private key pair $\{KU_e, KR_e\}$ and transmits $KU_e \,||\, ID_A$ to B.
3. B generates a secret key, K_s, and transmits $E_{KUe}[K_s]$.
4. E intercepts the message, and learns Ks by computing $D_{KRe}[E_{KUe}[K_s]]$.
5. E transmits $E_{KUa}[K_s]$ to A.

The result is that both A and B know K_s and are unaware that K_s has also been revealed to E. A and B can now exchange messages using K_s. E no longer actively interferes with the communications channel but simply eavesdrops. Knowing, K_s, E can decrypt all messages, and both A and B are unaware of the problem. Thus, this simple protocol is only useful in an environment where the only threat is eavesdropping.

Secret Key Distribution with Confidentiality and Authentication

Figure 4.16, based on an approach suggested in [NEED78], provides protection against both active and passive attacks. We begin when it is assumed that A and B have exchanged public keys by one of the schemes described earlier in this section. Then, the following steps occur:

1. A uses B's public key to encrypt a message to B containing an identifier of A (ID_A) and a nonce (N_1), which is used to uniquely identify this transaction.
2. B sends a message to A encrypted with KU_a and containing A's nonce (N_1) as well as a new nonce generated by B (N_2). Since only B could have decrypted message (1), the presence of N_1 in message (2) assures A that the correspondent is B.
3. A returns N_2, encrypted using B's public key, to assure B that its correspondent is A.
4. A selects a secret key K_s and sends $M = E_{KUb}[E_{KRa}[K_s]]$ to B. Encryption of this message with B's public key ensures that only B can read it; encryption with A's private key ensures that only A could have sent it.
5. B computes $D_{KUa}[D_{KRb}[M]]$ to recover the secret key.

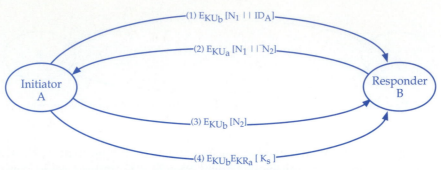

FIGURE 4.16.   Public-Key Distribution of Secret Keys

Notice that the first three steps of this scheme are the same as the last three steps of Figure 4.13. The result is that this scheme ensures both confidentiality and authentication in the exchange of a secret key.

A Hybrid Scheme

Yet another way to use public-key encryption to distribute secret keys is a hybrid approach in use on IBM mainframes [LE93]. This scheme retains the use of a key distribution center (KDC) that shares a secret master key with each user and distributes secret session keys encrypted with the master key. A public key scheme is used to distribute the master keys. The following rationale is provided for using this three-level approach:

- *Performance:* There are many applications, especially transaction-oriented applications, in which the session keys change frequently. Distribution of session keys by public-key encryption could degrade overall system performance because of the relatively high computational load of public-key encryption and decryption. With a three-level hierarchy, public-key encryption is used only occasionally to update the master key between a user and the KDC.
- *Backward Compatibility:* The hybrid scheme is easily overlaid on an existing KDC scheme, with minimal disruption or software changes.

The addition of a public-key layer provides a secure, efficient means of distributing master keys. This is an advantage in a configuration in which a single KDC serves a widely distributed set of users.

4.4
_____

RECOMMENDED READING

The recommended treatments of encryption provided in Chapter 2 cover public-key as well as conventional encryption.

[DIFF88] describes in detail the several attempts to devise secure two-key cryptoalgorithms and the gradual evolution of a variety of protocols based on them. A comprehensive treatment of contemporary public-key cryptology is given in [NECH92]. [CORM90] provides a concise but complete and readable summary of all of the algorithms relevant to the verification, computation, and cryptanalysis of RSA.

There are many basic texts on the subject of number theory that provide far more detail than most readers of this book will desire. An elementary but nevertheless useful short introduction is [ORE67]. For the reader interested in a more in-depth treatment, [ORE76] and [LEVE90] are highly recommended. [KOBL87] is a more advanced treatment and concentrates on those aspects of number theory relevant to cryptology.

CORM90   Cormen, T.; Leiserson, C.; and Rivest, R. *Introduction to Algorithms*. Cambridge, MA: MIT Press, 1990.

DIFF88   Diffie, W. "The First Ten Years of Public-Key Cryptography." *Proceedings of the IEEE,* May 1988. Reprinted in [SIMM92a].

KOBL87   Koblitz, N. *A Course in Number Theory and Cryptography*. New York: Springer-Verlag, 1987.

LEVE90   Leveque, W. *Elementary Theory of Numbers*. New York: Dover, 1990.

NECH92   Nechvatal, J. "Public Key Cryptography." in [SIMM92a].

ORE67   Ore, O. *Invitation to Number Theory*. Washington, DC: The Mathematical Association of America, 1967,

ORE76   Ore, O. *Number Theory and Its History*. New York: Dover 1976.

SIMM92a   Simmons, G., editor. *Contemporary Cryptology: The Science of Information Integrity*. Piscataway, NJ: IEEE Press, 1992.

4.5

PROBLEMS

4.1 What items are in the knapsack of Figure 4.5?

4.2 Perform encryption and decryption using the knapsack algorithm, as in Figure 4.6, for the following:

  a. $\mathbf{a}' = (1, 3, 5, 10)$; $w = 7$; $m = 20$; $\mathbf{x} = 1101$

  b. $\mathbf{a}' = (1, 3, 5, 11, 23, 46, 136, 263)$; $w = 203$; $m = 491$; $\mathbf{x} = 11101000$

  c. $\mathbf{a}' = (2, 3, 6, 12, 25)$; $w = 46$; $m = 53$; $\mathbf{x} = 11101$

  d. $\mathbf{a}' = (15, 92, 108, 279, 563, 1172, 2243, 4468)$; $w = 2393$; $m = 9291$; $\mathbf{x} = 10110001$

4.3 **a.** For the knapsack algorithm, why is it a requirement that $m > \sum a_i$?

  b. Why is it a requirement that $m > w$?

4.4 Consider the following scheme.

  1. Pick an odd number, E.

  2. Pick two prime numbers, P and Q, where $(P - 1)(Q - 1) - 1$ is evenly divisible by E.

  3. Multiply P and Q to get N.

4. Calculate

$$D = \frac{(P-1)(Q-1)(E-1)+1}{E}$$

Is this scheme equivalent to RSA? Show why or why not.

4.5 Perform encryption and decryption using the RSA algorithm, as in Figure 4.8, for the following:

   a. $p = 3; q = 11, d = 7; M = 5$
   b. $p = 5; q = 11, e = 3; M = 9$
   c. $p = 7; q = 11, e = 17; M = 8$
   d. $p = 11; q = 13, e = 11; M = 7$
   e. $p = 17; q = 31, e = 7; M = 2$. Hint: decryption is not as hard as you think; use some finesse.

4.6 In using the RSA algorithm, if a small number of repeated encodings give back the plaintext, what is the likely cause?

4.7 Suppose we have a set of blocks encoded with the RSA algorithm and we don't have the private key. Assume $n = pq$, e is the public key. Suppose also someone tells us they know one of the plaintext blocks has a common factor with n. Does this help us in any way?

4.8 In the RSA public-key encryption scheme, each user has a public key, e, and a private key, d. Suppose Bob leaks his private key. Rather than generating a new modulus, he decides to generate a new public and a new private key. Is this safe?

4.9 "I want to tell you, Holmes," Dr. Watson's voice was enthusiastic, "that your recent activities in network security have increased my interest in cryptography. And just yesterday I found a way to make one-time pad encryption really practical."

"Oh, really?" Holmes' face lost its sleepy look. "So you have found a way to generate cryptographically strong sequences in a deterministic fashion, have you?"

"Yes, Holmes. The idea is really simple. For a given one-way function F, I suggest to generate a long pseudorandom sequence of elements by applying F to some standard sequence of arguments. The cryptanalyst is assumed to know F and the general nature of the sequence, which may be as simple as $S, S + 1, S + 2, \ldots$, but not secret S. And due to the one-way nature of F no one is able to extract S given $F(S + i)$ for some i, thus even if he somehow obtains a certain segment of the sequence, he will not be able to determine the rest."

"I am afraid, Watson, that your proposal isn't without flaws and at least it needs some additional conditions to be satisfied by F. Let's consider, for instance, RSA encryption function, that is $F(M) = M^K \bmod N$, K is secret. This function is believed to be one-way, but I wouldn't recommend its use, for example, to the sequence $M = 2, 3, 4, 5, 6, \ldots$"

"But why, Holmes?" Dr. Watson apparently didn't understand. "Why do you think that the resulting sequence $2^K \bmod N$, $3^K \bmod N$, $4^K \bmod N$, $\ldots$ is not appropriate for one-time pad encryption if K is kept secret?"

"Because it is—at least partially—predictable, dear Watson, even if K is kept secret. You have said that the cryptanalyst is assumed to know F and the general nature of the sequence. Now let's assume that he will obtain somehow a short segment of the output sequence. In crypto circles this assumption is generally considered to be a viable one. And for this output sequence, knowledge of just the first two elements will allow him to predict quite a lot of the next elements of the sequence, even if not all of them, thus this sequence can't be considered to be cryptographically strong. And with the knowledge of a longer segment he could predict even more of the next elements of the sequence. Look, knowing the general nature of the sequence and its first two elements $2^K \bmod N$ and $3^K \bmod N$, you can easily compute its following elements . . . ."

4.10 "This is a very interesting case, Watson," Holmes said to Dr. Watson, who met Holmes's client just on the leave. "The young man loves a girl and she loves him too. However, her father is a strange fellow who insists that his would-be son in law must design a simple and secure protocol for an appropriate public-key cryptosystem he could use in his company's computer network. The young man came up with the following protocol for communication between two parties, for example, user A wishing to send message M to user B: (messages exchanged are in the format (sender's name, text, receiver's name)

1. A sends B (A, E_{KUb}[M, A], B)
2. B acknowledges receipt by sending to A (B, E_{KUa}[M, B], A)

"You can see that the protocol is really simple. But the girl's father claims that the young man has not satisfied his call for a simple protocol, because the proposal contains a certain redundancy and can be further simplified to the following:

1. A sends B (A, E_{KUb}[M], B)
2. B acknowledges receipt by sending to A (B, E_{KUa}[M], A)

"On the basis of that, the girl's father refuses to allow his daughter to marry the young man, thus making them both unhappy. The young man was just here to ask me for help."

"Hmm, I don't see how you can help him," Watson was visibly unhappy with the idea that the sympathetic young man has to lose his love.

"Well, I think I could help. You know, Watson, redundancy is sometimes good to ensure the security of protocol. Thus, the simplification the girl's father has proposed could make the new protocol vulnerable to an attack the original protocol was able to resist," mused Holmes. "Yes, it is so, Watson! Look, all an adversary needs is to be one of the users of the network and to be able to intercept messages exchanged between A and B. Being a user of the network, he has his own public encryption key and is able to send his own messages to A or to B and to receive theirs. With the help of the simplified protocol, he could then obtain message M user A has previously sent to B using the following procedure . . ."

4.11 Here is another realization of the fast exponentiation algorithm. Demonstrate that it is equivalent to the one in Section 4.2.
  1. $d \leftarrow 1; T \leftarrow a; E \leftarrow b$
  2. **if** odd(E) **then** $d \leftarrow d \times T$
  3. $E \leftarrow \lfloor E \div 2 \rfloor$
  4. $T \leftarrow T \times T \bmod n$
  5. **if** $E > 0$ **then goto** 2
  6. **output** d

4.12 Determine gcd(24140, 16762)

4.13 The purpose of this problem is to justify the assertion, made in Section 4.2, that the probability that two random numbers are relatively prime is about 0.6.
  a. Let $P = \Pr[\gcd(a, b) = 1]$. Show that $\Pr[\gcd(a, b) = d] = P/d^2$. Hint: Consider the quantity $\gcd\left[\dfrac{a}{d}, \dfrac{b}{d}\right]$
  b. The sum of the result of part (a) over all possible values of d is 1. That is:
$$\sum_{d \geq 1} \Pr[\gcd(a, b) = d] = 1$$
  Use this equality to determine the value of P. Hint: Use the identity
$$\sum_{i=1}^{\infty} \frac{1}{i^2} = \frac{\pi^2}{6}$$

4.14 Why is $\gcd(n, n + 1) = 1$ for two consecutive integers n and $n + 1$?

4.15 In Appendix 4A, we define the congruence relationship as follows: Two integers a and b are said to be congruent modulo n, if $(a \bmod n) = (b \bmod n)$. We then prove that $a \equiv b \bmod n$ if $n|(a - b)$. Some texts on number theory use this latter relationship as the definition of congruence: Two integers a and b are said to be congruent modulo n, if $n|(a - b)$. Using this latter definition as the starting point, prove that $(a \bmod n) = (b \bmod n)$ implies $a \equiv b \bmod n$.

4.16 Prove the following:
  a. $(a \bmod n) = (b \bmod n)$ implies $a \equiv b \bmod n$
  b. $a \equiv b \bmod n$ implies $b \equiv a \bmod n$
  c. $a \equiv b \bmod n$ and $b \equiv c \bmod n$ imply $a \equiv c \bmod n$

4.17 Prove the following:
  a. $[(a \bmod n) - (b \bmod n)] \bmod n = (a - b) \bmod n$
  b. $[(a \bmod n) \times (b \bmod n)] \bmod n = (a \times b) \bmod n$

4.18 Improve on algorithm P1 in Appendix 4B.
  a. Develop an algorithm that requires $2n$ multiplications and $n + 1$ additions. Hint: $x^{i+1} = x^i \times x$.
  b. Develop an algorithm that requires only $n + 1$ multiplications and $n + 1$ additions. Hint: $P(x) = a_0 + x \times q(x)$, where $q(x)$ is a polynomial of degree $(n - 1)$.

APPENDIX 4A

INTRODUCTION TO NUMBER THEORY

In this appendix, we provide a brief overview of some of the mathematical principles used in this chapter.

Prime and Relatively Prime Numbers

In this section, unless otherwise noted, we deal only with the nonnegative integers. The use of negative integers would introduce no essential differences.

Divisors

We say that $b \neq 0$ divides a if $a = mb$ for some m. That is, b divides a if there is no remainder on division. The notation $b|a$ is commonly used to mean b divides a. Also, if $b|a$, we say that b is a *divisor* of a. For example, the divisors of 24 are 1, 2, 3, 4, 6, 8, 12, and 24.

The following relations hold:

If $a|1$, then $a = \pm 1$
If $a|b$ and $b|a$, then $a = \pm b$
Any $b \neq 0$ divides 0
If $b|g$ and $b|h$, then $b|(mg + nh)$ for arbitrary integers m and n

To see this last point, note that

if $b|g$ then g is of the form $g = b \times g_1$ for some integer g_1
if $b|h$ then h is of the form $h = b \times h_1$ for some integer h_1

So

$$mg + nh = mbg_1 + nbh_1 = b \times (mg_1 + nh_1)$$

and therefore b divides $mg + nh$.

Prime Numbers

An integer $p > 1$ is a prime number if its only divisors are ± 1 and $\pm p$. Prime numbers play a critical role in number theory and in the techniques discussed in this chapter. Table 4.4 shows the primes under 2000.

Any positive integer $a > 1$ can be factored in a unique way as

$$a = p_1^{\alpha_1} p_2^{\alpha_2} \dots p_t^{\alpha_t}$$

where $p_1 > p_2 > \dots > p_t$ are prime numbers and where each $\alpha_i > 0$. For example, $91 = 7 \times 13$, and $11011 = 7 \times 11^2 \times 13$.

TABLE 4.4 Primes Under 2000

2	3	5	7	11	13	17	19	23	29	31	37	41	43	47	53	59	61	67	71	73	79	83	89	97
101	103	107	109	113	127	131	137	139	149	151	157	163	167	173	179	181	191	193	197	199				
211	223	227	229	233	239	241	250	257	263	269	271	277	281	283	293									
307	311	313	317	331	337	347	349	353	359	367	373	379	383	389	397									
401	409	419	421	431	433	439	443	449	457	461	463	467	479	487	491	499								
503	509	521	523	541	547	558	563	569	571	577	587	593	599											
601	607	613	617	619	631	641	643	647	653	659	661	673	677	683	691									
701	709	719	727	733	739	743	751	757	761	769	773	787	797											
809	811	821	823	827	829	839	853	857	859	863	877	881	883	887										
917	911	919	929	937	941	947	953	967	971	977	983	991	997											
1009	1013	1019	1021	1031	1033	1039	1049	1051	1061	1063	1069	1087	1091	1093	1097									
1103	1109	1117	1123	1129	1151	1153	1163	1171	1181	1187	1193													
1201	1213	1217	1223	1229	1231	1237	1249	1259	1277	1279	1283	1289	1291	1297										
1301	1303	1307	1319	1321	1327	1361	1367	1373	1381	1399														
1409	1423	1427	1429	1433	1439	1447	1451	1453	1459	1471	1481	1483	1487	1489	1493	1499								
1511	1523	1531	1543	1549	1553	1559	1567	1571	1579	1583	1597													
1604	1607	1609	1613	1619	1621	1627	1637	1657	1663	1667	1669	1693	1697	1699										
1709	1721	1723	1733	1741	1747	1753	1759	1777	1783	1787	1789													
1801	1811	1823	1831	1847	1861	1867	1871	1873	1877	1879	1889													
1901	1907	1913	1931	1933	1949	1950	1973	1979	1987	1993	1997	1999												

It is useful for what follows to cast this another way. If P is the set of all prime numbers, then any positive integer can be written uniquely in the following form:

$$a = \prod_P p^{a_p} \text{ where each } a_p \geq 0$$

The right-hand side is the product over all possible prime numbers p; for any particular value of a, most of the exponents a_p will be 0.

The value of any given positive integer can be specified by simply listing all the nonzero exponents in the foregoing formulation. Thus, the integer 12 is represented by $\{a_2 = 2, a_3 = 1\}$ and the integer 18 is represented by $\{a_2 = 1, a_3 = 2\}$. Multiplication of two numbers is equivalent to adding the corresponding exponents:

$$k = mn \quad => \quad k_p = m_p + n_p \quad \text{for all } p$$

Now, what does it mean, in terms of these prime factors, to say that $a|b$? Well, any integer of the form p^k can be divided only by an integer that is of a lesser or equal power of the same prime number, p^j with $j \leq k$. Thus, we can say

$$a|b \quad => \quad a_p \leq b_p \quad \text{for all } p$$

Relatively Prime Numbers

We will use the notation $\gcd(a, b)$ to mean the greatest common divisor of a and b. The positive integer c is said to be the greatest common divisor of a and b if:

1. c is a divisor of a and of b;
2. any divisor of a and b is a divisor of c.

An equivalent definition is the following:

$$\gcd(a, b) = \max [k, \text{ such that } k|a \text{ and } k|b]$$

Because we require that the greatest common divisor be positive, $\gcd(a, b) = \gcd(a, -b) = \gcd(-a, b) = \gcd(-a, -b)$. For example, $\gcd(60, 24) = \gcd(60, -24) = 12$. Also, because all nonzero integers divide 0, we have $\gcd(a, 0) = |a|$

It is easy to determine the greatest common divisor of two positive integers if we express each integer as the product of primes. For example

$$192 \qquad = 2^2 \times 3^1 \times 4^2$$
$$18 \qquad = 2^1 \times 3^2$$
$$\gcd(18, 192) = 2^1 \times 3^1 \times 4^0 = 6$$

In general,

$$k = \gcd(a, b) \quad =>k_p = \min(a_p, b_p) \quad \text{for all } p$$

The integers a and b are relatively prime if they have no prime factors in common, that is, if their only common factor is 1. This is equivalent to saying that a and

b are relatively prime if $\gcd(a, b) = 1$. For example, 8 and 15 are relatively prime because the divisors of 8 are 1, 2, 4, and 8 and the divisors of 15 are 1, 3, 5, 15.

Modular Arithmetic

Given any positive integer n and any integer a, if we divide a by n, we get a quotient q and a remainder r that obey the following relationship:

$$a = qn + r \quad 0 \le r < n; q = \lfloor a/n \rfloor$$

Figure 4.17 demonstrates that, given a and positive n, it is always possible to find q and r that satisfy the above relationship. Represent the integers on the number line; a will fall somewhere on that line (positive a is shown, a similar demonstration can be made for negative a). Starting at 0, proceed to n, $2n$, up to qn such that $qn \le a$ and $(q+1)n > a$. The distance from qn to a is r, and we have found the unique values of q and r. The remainder r is often referred to as a **residue.**

If a is an integer and n is a positive integer, we define $a \bmod n$ to be the remainder when a is divided by n. Thus, for any integer a, we can always write:

$$a = \lfloor a/n \rfloor \times n + (a \bmod n)$$

Two integers a and b are said to be **congruent modulo n,** if $(a \bmod n) = (b \bmod n)$. This is written $a \equiv b \bmod n$. For example $73 \equiv 4 \bmod 23$ and $21 \equiv -9 \bmod 10$. Note that if $a \equiv 0 \bmod n$, then $n \mid a$.

The modulo operator has the following properties:

1. $a \equiv b \bmod n$ if $n \mid (a - b)$
2. $(a \bmod n) = (b \bmod n)$ implies $a \equiv b \bmod n$
3. $a \equiv b \bmod n$ implies $b \equiv a \bmod n$
4. $a \equiv b \bmod n$ and $b \equiv c \bmod n$ imply $a \equiv c \bmod n$

To demonstrate the first point, if $n \mid (a - b)$ then $(a - b) = kn$ for some k. So we can write $a = b + kn$. Therefore $(a \bmod n) = ($remainder when $b + kn$ is divided by $n) = ($remainder when b is divided by $n) = (b \bmod n)$. The remaining points are as easily proved.

Note that, by definition (Figure 4.17), the $(\bmod\ n)$ operator maps all integers into the set of integers $\{0, 1, \ldots (n - 1)\}$. This suggests the question: Can we perform arithmetic operations within the confines of this set? It turns out that we can; the technique is known as **modular arithmetic.**

FIGURE 4.17.   The Relationship $a = qn + r; 0 \le r < n$

Modular arithmetic exhibits the following properties:

1. $[(a \bmod n) + (b \bmod n)] \bmod n = (a + b) \bmod n$
2. $[(a \bmod n) - (b \bmod n)] \bmod n = (a - b) \bmod n$
3. $[(a \bmod n) \times (b \bmod n)] \bmod n = (a \times b) \bmod n$

We demonstrate the first point. Define $(a \bmod n) = r_a$ and $(b \bmod n) = r_b$. Then we can write $a = r_a + jn$ for some integers j and $b = r_b + kn$ for some integer k. Then

$$
\begin{aligned}
(a + b) \bmod n &= (r_a + jn + r_b + kn) \bmod n \\
&= (r_a + r_b + (k + j)n) \bmod n \\
&= (r_a + r_b) \bmod n \\
&= [(a \bmod n) + (b \bmod n)] \bmod n
\end{aligned}
$$

The remaining points are as easily proved.

Thus, the rules for ordinary arithmetic involving addition, subtraction, and multiplication carry over into modular arithmetic. Let us examine this more closely. Define the set

$$Z_n = \{0, 1, \ldots, (n - 1)\}$$

This is referred to as the set of residues modulo n. If we perform modular arithmetic within this set, the following properties hold for integers in Z_n:

Property	Expression
Commutative laws	$(w + x) \bmod n = (x + w) \bmod n$
	$(w \times x) \bmod n = (x \times w) \bmod n$
Associative laws	$[(w + x) + y] \bmod n = [w + (x + y)] \bmod n$
	$[(w \times x) \times y] \bmod n = [w \times (x \times y)] \bmod n$
Distributive law	$[w \times (x + y)] \bmod n = [(w \times x) + (w \times y)] \bmod n$
Identities	$(0 + w) \bmod n = w \bmod n$
	$(1 \times w) \bmod n = w \bmod n$
Additive inverse $(-w)$	For each $w \in Z_n$, there exists a z such that $w + z \equiv 0 \bmod n$

There is one peculiarity of modular arithmetic that sets it apart from ordinary arithmetic. The following statement is true:

$$\text{if } (a + b) \equiv (a + c) \bmod n \quad \text{then} \quad b \equiv c \bmod n$$

However, the following statement is true only with the attached condition:

$$\text{if } (a \times b) \equiv (a \times c) \bmod n \text{ then } b \equiv c \bmod n \quad \text{if } a \text{ is relatively prime to } n \quad (4.1)$$

To see this, consider an example in which the condition does not hold:

$$
\begin{aligned}
6 \times 3 &= 18 \equiv 2 \bmod 8 \\
6 \times 7 &= 42 \equiv 2 \bmod 8
\end{aligned}
$$

Yet $3 \not\equiv 7 \bmod 8$. The reason for this strange result is that for any general modulus n, a multiplier a when applied in turn to the numbers 0 through $(n - 1)$ will fail to produce a complete set of residues if a and n have any factors in common. For example, with $a = 6$ and $n = 8$:

Z_8:	0	1	2	3	4	5	6	7
Multiply by 6:	0	6	12	18	24	30	36	42
Residues:	0	6	4	2	0	6	4	2

Since we do not have a complete set of residues when multiplying by 6, more than one number in Z_8 maps into the same residue. Specifically, $6 \times 0 \bmod 8 = 6 \times 4 \bmod 8$; $6 \times 1 \bmod 8 = 6 \times 5 \bmod 8$; and so on. Because this is a many-to-one mapping, there is not a unique inverse to the multiply operation.

However, if we take $a = 5$ and $n = 8$:

Z_8:	0	1	2	3	4	5	6	7
Multiply by 5:	0	5	10	15	20	25	30	35
Residues:	0	5	2	7	4	1	6	3

The line of residues contains all the numbers in Z_8, in a different order.

Finally, we can observe that if p is a prime number, then all the elements of Z_p are relatively prime to p. This enables us to add one additional property to those listed earlier

---

Multiplicative inverse (w^{-1})   For each $w \in Z_p$, there exists a z such that $w \times z \equiv 1 \bmod p$

Since w is relatively prime to p, if we multiply all the elements of Z_p by w, the resulting residues include all of the elements of Z_p permuted. Thus at least one of the residues has the value 1. Therefore, there is some number in Z_p which, when multiplied by w, yields the residue 1. That number is the multiplicative inverse of w, designated w^{-1}.

A final point: Some but not all integers will have a multiplicative inverse even if the modulus is not a prime number. Specifically, if $\gcd(a, n) = 1$, one can find b in Z_n, such that $a \times b \equiv 1 \bmod n$. The reasoning is the same as that of the preceding paragraph. Since a is relatively prime to n, if we multiply all the elements of Z_n by a, the resulting residues include all the elements of Z_n permuted. Therefore, there is some number b in Z_n such that $a \times b \equiv 1 \bmod n$.

Table 4.5 provides an example that illustrates the concepts of this section.

Euler's Totient Function

An important quantity in number theory, referred to as Euler's totient function, and written $\phi(n)$, is the number of positive integers less than n and relatively prime to n. It should be clear that for a prime number p,

$$\phi(p) = p - 1$$

TABLE 4.5 Arithmetic Modulo 7

	0	1	2	3	4	5	6
0	0	1	2	3	4	5	6
1	1	2	3	4	5	6	0
2	2	3	4	5	6	0	1
3	3	4	5	6	0	1	2
4	4	5	6	0	1	2	3
5	5	6	0	1	2	3	4
6	6	0	1	2	3	4	5

(a) Addition modulo 7

	0	1	2	3	4	5	6
0	0	0	0	0	0	0	0
1	0	1	2	3	4	5	6
2	0	2	4	6	1	3	5
3	0	3	6	2	5	1	4
4	0	4	1	5	2	6	3
5	0	5	3	1	6	4	2
6	0	6	5	4	3	2	1

(b) Multiplication modulo 7

w	$-w$	w^{-1}
0	0	—
1	6	1
2	5	4
3	4	5
4	3	2
5	2	3
6	1	6

(c) Additive and multiplicative inverses modulo 7

Now suppose that we have two prime numbers p and q; then for $n = pq$,

$$\phi(n) = \phi(pq) = \phi(p) \times \phi(q) = (p - 1) \times (q - 1)$$

To see this, consider that the set of residues in Z_n is $\{0, 1, \ldots, (pq - 1)\}$. The residues that are not relatively prime to n are the set $\{p, 2p, \ldots, (q - 1)p\}$, the set $\{q, 2q, \ldots, (p - 1)q\}$, and 0. Accordingly

$$\phi(n) = pq - [(q - 1) + (p - 1) + 1]$$
$$= pq - (p + q) + 1$$
$$= (p - 1) \times (q - 1)$$
$$= \phi(p) \times \phi(q)$$

We now develop two important theorems that are relevant to public-key cryptography. The first is **Fermat's theorem,** which states:

$$a^{n-1} \equiv 1 \bmod n \quad \text{if } a, n \text{ relatively prime} \tag{4.2}$$

Proof: From our previous discussion, we know that if all the elements of Z_n are multiplied by a, modulo n, the result consists of the elements of Z_n in some order. Furthermore, $a \times 0 \equiv 0 \bmod n$. Therefore, the $(n - 1)$ numbers $\{a \bmod n, 2a \bmod n, \ldots (n - 1)a \bmod n\}$ are just the numbers $\{1, 2, \ldots, (n - 1)\}$ in some order. Now, multiply these numbers together:

$$a \times 2a \times \ldots \times ((n - 1)a) \equiv [(a \bmod n) \times (2a \bmod n) \times \ldots \times ((n - 1)a \bmod n)] \bmod n$$
$$\equiv (n - 1)! \bmod n$$

But

$$a \times 2a \times \ldots \times ((n - 1)a) = (n - 1)!a^{n-1}$$

Therefore,

$$(n - 1)!a^{n-1} \equiv (n - 1)! \bmod n$$

We can cancel the $(n - 1)!$ term since it is relatively prime to n (see Equation 4.1). An alternative form of the theorem is also useful:

$$a^n \equiv a \bmod n \quad \text{if } a, n \text{ relatively prime} \tag{4.3}$$

Another important theorem is **Euler's theorem,** which states that for every a and n that are relatively prime:

$$a^{\phi(n)} \equiv 1 \bmod n \tag{4.4}$$

Proof: This is true if n is prime, since in that case $\phi(n) = (n-1)$, and Fermat's theorem holds. However, it also holds for any integer n. Recall that $\phi(n)$ is the number of positive integers less than n that are relatively prime to n. Consider the set of such integers, labeled as follows:

$$R = \{x_1, x_2, \ldots, x_{\phi(n)}\}$$

Now multiply each element by a, modulo n:

$$S = \{(ax_1 \bmod n), (ax_2 \bmod n), \ldots, (ax_{\phi(n)} \bmod n)\}$$

This set is a permutation of R, by the following line of reasoning:

1. Because a is relatively prime to n and x_i is relatively prime to n, ax_i must also be relatively prime to n. Thus, all the members of S are integers less than n that are relatively prime to n.
2. There are no duplicates in S. Refer to Equation 4.1. If $ax_i \bmod n = ax_j \bmod n$, then $x_i = x_j$.

Therefore

$$\prod_{i=1}^{\phi(n)} (ax_i \bmod n) = \prod_{i=1}^{\phi(n)} x_i$$

$$\prod_{i=1}^{\phi(n)} ax_i \equiv \prod_{i=1}^{\phi(n)} x_i \quad (\bmod n)$$

$$a^{\phi(n)} \times \left[\prod_{i=1}^{\phi(n)} x_i \right] \equiv \prod_{i=1}^{\phi(n)} x_i \quad (\bmod n)$$

$$a^{\phi(n)} \equiv 1 \quad (\bmod n)$$

An alternative form of the theorem is also useful:

$$a^{\phi(n)+1} \equiv a \;(\bmod n) \tag{4.5}$$

We can develop a corollary to Euler's theorem that is useful in demonstrating the validity of the RSA algorithm. Given two prime numbers, p and q and integers $n = pq$ and m, with $0 < m < n$, the following relationship holds:

$$m^{\phi(n)} = m^{(p-1)(q-1)} \equiv 1 \bmod n \tag{4.6}$$

If $\gcd(m, n) = 1$, that is, if m and n are relatively prime, then the relationship holds by virtue of Euler's theorem (Equation 4.4). Now, suppose $\gcd(m, n) \neq 1$. What does this mean? Well, since $n = pq$, the equality $\gcd(m, n) = 1$ is equivalent to the logical expression: (m is not a multiple of p) AND (m is not a multiple of q).

If m is a multiple of p, then n and m share the prime factor p and are not relatively prime, and if m is a multiple of q, then n and m share the prime factor q and are not relatively prime. Therefore, the expression $\gcd(m, n) \neq 1$ must be equivalent to the negation of the foregoing logical expression. Therefore $\gcd(m, n) \neq 1$ is equivalent to the logical expression: (m is a multiple of p) OR (m is a multiple of q).

Let us look at the case in which m is a multiple of p, so that the relationship $m = cp$ holds for some positive integer c. In this case, we must have $\gcd(m, q) = 1$. Otherwise, we have m a multiple of p and m a multiple of q and yet $m < pq$. Now, if $\gcd(m, q) = 1$, then Euler's theorem holds and:

$$m^{\phi(q)} \equiv 1 \bmod q$$

But then, by the rules of modular arithmetic:

$$[m^{\phi(q)}]^{\phi(p)} \equiv 1 \bmod q$$
$$m^{\phi(n)} \equiv 1 \bmod q$$

Therefore, there is some integer k such that,

$$m^{\phi(n)} = 1 + kq$$

Multiplying each side by $m = cp$:

$$m^{\phi(n)+1} = m + kcpq = m + kcn$$
$$m^{\phi(n)+1} \equiv m \bmod n$$
$$m^{\phi(n)} \equiv 1 \bmod n$$

A similar line of reasoning is used for the case in which m is a multiple of q. Thus Equation 4.6 is proven. An alternative form of this corollary is also useful.

$$[m^{\phi(n)}]^k \equiv 1 \bmod n$$
$$m^{k\phi(n)} \equiv 1 \bmod n$$
$$m^{k\phi(n)+1} = m^{k(p-1)(q-1)+1} \equiv m \bmod n \qquad (4.7)$$

Testing for Primality

There is no simple yet efficient means of determining whether a large number is prime. In this section, we present one attractive approach. First, we need to derive some results. The first of these is as follows:

If p is an odd prime, then the equation

$$x^2 \equiv 1 \ (\bmod \ p)$$

has only two solutions, namely $x \equiv 1$ and $x \equiv -1$.

Proof: We have:

$$x^2 - 1 \equiv 0 \ (\bmod \ p)$$
$$(x + 1)(x - 1) \equiv 0 \ (\bmod \ p)$$

By the rules of modular arithmetic, the latter equality requires that p divide $(x + 1)$ or p divide $(x - 1)$, or both. Suppose that p divides both $(x + 1)$ and $(x - 1)$. Then we can say that $(x + 1) = kp$ and $(x - 1) = jp$ for some integers k and j. Subtracting the two equations yields $2 = (k - j)p$. This equation can be true only for $p = 2$. By the terms of the theorem we are concerned only with odd primes. Therefore, for a given solution x, either $p|(x + 1)$ or $p|(x - 1)$ but not both. Suppose $p|(x - 1)$. Then,

$$x - 1 = kp \quad \text{for some } k$$

Therefore $x \equiv 1 \bmod p$. By similar reasoning we arrive at the other solution of $x \equiv -1 \bmod p$.

The theorem can be stated the opposite way: If there exists solutions to $x^2 \equiv 1$ (mod n) other than ± 1, then n is not a prime number.

We can now state an algorithm, due to Miller and Rabin [MILL75, RABI80], for testing whether a number is prime. The core algorithm, called WITNESS, is defined as follows:

```
        WITNESS (a, n)
 1.     let b_k b_{k-1} . . . b_0 be the binary representation of(n - 1)
 2.     d ← 1
 3.     for i ← k downto 0
 4.          do    x ← d
 5.          d ← (d × d) mod n
 6.          if  d = 1 and x ≠ 1 and x ≠ n - 1
 7.          then return TRUE
 8.          if  b_i = 1
 9.          then d ← (d × a) mod n
10.     if  d ≠ 1
11.     then return TRUE
12.     return FALSE
```

The inputs to WITNESS are the number n, to be tested for primality, and some integer a less than n. The purpose is to test whether n is prime. If WITNESS returns TRUE, then n is definitely not prime; if WITNESS returns FALSE, then n may be prime.

A comparison of WITNESS to the algorithm for computing a power in modular arithmetic, described in Section 4.2, shows that lines 3 to 9 compute d as the value $a^{n-1} \bmod n$. We know from Fermat's theorem (Equation 4.2) that $a^{n-1} \equiv 1 \bmod n$ if n is prime. Thus, if the final result for d is not equal to 1, we know that n is not prime, and return TRUE. Now consider the test at line 6. Because $(n - 1) \equiv -1 \bmod n$, this line tests whether $x^2 \equiv 1 \bmod n$ with a root other than ± 1. By the theorem stated earlier, this condition holds only if x is not prime. Thus, if this test is passed, WITNESS returns TRUE.

As an example, consider again Figure 4.9. In this case, $n = 561$ and $a = 7$. WITNESS discovers a square root other than ± 1 in the last squaring step, because $a^{280} \equiv 67 \bmod 561$ and $a^{560} \equiv 1 \bmod 561$. At this point, WITNESS returns TRUE.

So, if WITNESS returns TRUE, the number n is not prime. It can be shown (e.g., see [CORM90]) that given an odd number n that is not prime, and a randomly chosen integer $a < n$, the probability that WITNESS will return FALSE (i.e., fail to detect that n is not prime) is less than 0.5. This gives us a basis for determining whether an odd integer n is prime with a reasonable degree of confidence. The procedure is as follows: Repeatedly invoke WITNESS (a, n) using randomly chosen values for a. If at any point, WITNESS returns TRUE, then n is determined to be nonprime. If WITNESS returns FALSE s times in succession, then the probability that n is prime is at least $1 - 2^{-s}$ (see [CORM90], p.843). Thus, for a sufficiently large value of s, we can be confident that n is prime.

Euclid's Algorithm

Euclid's algorithm is a simple procedure for determining the greatest common divisor of two positive integers. An extended form of Euclid's algorithm determines the greatest common divisor of two positive integers and, if those numbers are relatively prime, the multiplicative inverse of one with respect to the other.

Finding the Greatest Common Divisor

Euclid's algorithm is based on the following theorem: For any nonnegative integer a and any positive integer b:

$$\gcd(a, b) = \gcd(b, a \bmod b) \tag{4.8}$$

To see this, consider if $d = \gcd(a, b)$. Then, by the definition of gcd, $d|a$ and $d|b$. Now, for any positive integer b, a can be expressed in the form

$$a = kb + r = kb + a \bmod b$$

Therefore, $(a \bmod b) = a - kb$ for some integer k. But, since $d|b$, it also divides kb. We also have $d|a$. Therefore $d|(a \bmod b)$. This shows that d is a common divisor of b and $(a \bmod b)$. Conversely, if d is a common divisor of b and $(a \bmod b)$, then $d|kb$ and thus $d|[kb + (a \bmod b)]$, which is equivalent to $d|a$. Thus the set of common divisors of a and b is equal to the set of common divisors of b and $(a \bmod b)$. Therefore, the gcd of one is the same as the gcd of the other, proving the theorem.

Equation (4.8) can be used repetitively to determine the greatest common divisor. For example, $\gcd(12, 18) = \gcd(18, 6) = \gcd(6, 0) = 6$. Another example: $\gcd(10, 11) = \gcd(11, 1) = \gcd(1, 0) = 1$.

Euclid's algorithm makes repeated use of Equation 4.8 to determine the greatest common divisor, as follows:

```
EUCLID(d, f)
1.  X ← f; Y ← d
2.  if Y = 0     return X = gcd(d,f)
3.  R = X mod Y
4.  X ← Y
5.  Y ← R
6.  goto 2
```

Finding the Multiplicative Inverse

If $\gcd(d, f) = 1$, then d has a multiplicative inverse modulo f. That is, for positive integer $d < f$, there exists a $d^{-1} < f$ such that $dd^{-1} = 1 \bmod f$. Euclid's algorithm can be extended so that, in addition to finding $\gcd(d, f)$, if the gcd is 1, returns the multiplicative inverse of d.

```
EXTENDED-EUCLID(d, f)
1.  (X1, X2, X3) ← (1, 0, f); (Y1, Y2, Y3) ← (0, 1, d)
2.  if Y3 = 0     return X3 = gcd(d,f); no inverse
3.  if Y3 = 1     return Y3 = gcd(d,f); Y2 = d⁻¹ mod f
```

4. $Q = \left\lfloor \dfrac{X3}{Y3} \right\rfloor$

```
5.  (T1, T2, T3) ← (X1 − QY1, X2 − QY2, X3 − QY3)
6.  (X1, X2, X3) ← (Y1, Y2, Y3)
7.  (Y1, Y2, Y3) ← (T1, T2, T3)
8.  goto 2
```

Throughout the computation, the following relationships hold:

$$fT1 + dT2 = T3 \qquad fX1 + dX2 = X3 \qquad fY1 + dY2 = Y3$$

To see that this algorithm correctly returns $\gcd(d, f)$, note that if we equate X and Y in Euclid's algorithm with X3 and Y3 in the extended Euclid's algorithm, then the treatment of the two variables is identical. At each iteration of Euclid's algorithm, X is set equal to the previous value of Y and Y is set equal to the previous value of X mod Y. Similarly, at each step of the extended Euclid's algorithm, X3 is set equal to the previous value of Y3, and Y3 is set equal to the previous value of X3 minus the quotient of X3 divided by Y3. This latter value is simply the remainder of X3 divided by Y3, which is X3 mod Y3.

Note also that if $\gcd(d, f) = 1$, then on the final step, we would have Y3 = 0 and X3 = 1. Therefore on the preceding step, Y3 = 1. But if Y3 = 1, then we can say the following:

TABLE 4.6   Extended—Euclid (550, 1769)

Q	X_1	X_2	X_3	Y_1	Y_2	Y_3
—	1	0	1769	0	1	550
3	0	1	550	1	-3	119
4	1	-3	119	-4	13	74
1	-4	13	74	5	-16	45
1	5	-16	45	-9	29	29
1	-9	29	29	14	-45	16
1	14	-45	16	-23	74	13
1	-23	74	13	37	-119	3
4	37	-119	3	-171	550	1

$$fY1 + dY2 = Y3$$
$$fY1 + dY2 = 1$$
$$dY2 = 1 + (-Y1) \times f$$
$$dY2 \equiv 1 \bmod f$$

And Y2 is the multiplicative inverse of d, modulo f. Table 4.6 is an example of the execution of the algorithm. It shows that gcd(550, 1769) = 1 and that the multiplicative inverse of 550 is itself; that is, $550 \times 550 \equiv 1 \bmod 1769$.

For a more detailed proof of this algorithm, see [KNUT73].

APPENDIX 4B

THE COMPLEXITY OF ALGORITHMS

The central issue in assessing the resistance of an encryption algorithm to crypt-analysis is the amount of time that a given type of attack will take. Typically, one cannot be sure that one has found the most efficient attack algorithm. The most that one can say is that for a particular algorithm, the level of effort for an attack is of a particular order of magnitude. One can then compare that order of magnitude to the speed of current or predicted processors to determine the level of security of a particular algorithm.

A common measure of the efficiency of an algorithm is its time complexity. We define the time complexity of an algorithm to be $f(n)$ if, for all n and all inputs of length n, the execution of the algorithm takes at most $f(n)$ steps. Thus, for a given size of input and a given processor speed, the time complexity is an upper bound on the execution time.

There are several ambiguities here. First, the definition of a step is not precise. A step could be a single operation of a Turing machine, a single processor machine instruction, a single high-level language machine instruction, and so on. However, these various definitions of step should all be related by simple multiplicative constants. For very large values of n, these constants are not important. What is important is how fast the relative execution time is growing. For example, if we are concerned about whether to use 50-digit ($n = 10^{50}$) or 100-digit ($n = 10^{100}$) keys for RSA, it is not necessary (or really possible) to know exactly how long it would take to break each size of key. Rather, we are interested in ballpark figures for level of effort and in knowing how much extra relative effort is required for the larger key size.

A second issue is that generally speaking, we cannot pin down an exact formula for $f(n)$. We can only approximate it. But again, we are primarily interested in the rate of change of $f(n)$ as n becomes very large.

There is a standard mathematical notation, known as the "big-O" notation, for characterizing the time complexity of algorithms that is useful in this context. The definition is as follows: $f(n) = O(g(n))$ if and only if there exist two numbers a and M such that

$$|f(n)| \leq a \times |g(n)|, \quad n \geq M \tag{4.9}$$

An example helps clarify the use of this notation. Suppose we wish to evaluate a general polynomial of the form:

$$P(x) = a_n x^n + a_{n-1} x^{n-1} + \ldots + a_1 x + a_0$$

The following simple algorithm is from [POHL81]:

```
algorithm P1;
    n, i, j: integer; x, polyval: real;
    a, S: array [0..100] of real;
    begin
        read(x, n);
        for i := 0 upto n do
        begin
            S[i] := 1; read(a[i]);
            for j := 1 upto i do S[i] := x × S[i];
            S[i] := a[i] × S[i]
        end;
        polyval := 0;
        for i : = 0 upto n do polyval := polyval + S[i];
        write ('value at', x, 'is', polyval)
    end.
```

In this algorithm, each subexpression is evaluated separately. Each $S[i]$ requires $(i + 1)$ multiplication: i multiplications to compute $S[i]$ and one to multiply by $S[i]$. Computing all n terms requires

$$\sum_{i=0}^{n} (i+1) = \frac{(n+2)(n+1)}{2}$$

multiplications. There are also $(n + 1)$ additions, which we can ignore relative to the much larger number of multiplications. Thus, the time complexity of this algorithm is $f(n) = (n + 2)(n + 1)/2$. We now show that $f(n) = O(n^2)$. From the definition of Equation (4.9), we want to show that for $a = 1$ and $M = 4$, the relationship holds for $g(n) = n^2$. We do this by induction on n. The relationship holds for $n = 4$, since $(4 + 2)(4 + 1)/2 = 15 < 4^2 = 16$. Now assume that it holds for all values of n up to k; that is, $(k + 2)(k + 1)/2 < k^2$. Then, with $n = k + 1$:

$$\frac{(n+2)(n+1)}{2} = \frac{(k+3)(k+2)}{2}$$
$$= \frac{(k+2)(k+1)}{2} + k + 2$$
$$\leq k^2 + k + 2$$
$$\leq k^2 + 2k + 2$$
$$= (k + 1)^2$$
$$= n^2$$

Therefore the result is true for $n = k + 1$.

In general, the big-O notation makes use of the term that grows the fastest. Examples:

1. $O(ax^7 + 3x^3 + \sin(x)) = O(ax^7) = O(x^7)$
2. $O(e^n + an^{10}) = O(e^n)$
3. $O(n! + n^{50}) = O(n!)$

There is much more to the big-O notation, with fascinating ramifications. For the interested reader, one of the best accounts is in [GRAH89].

An algorithm with an input of size n is said to be:

linear, if the running time is $O(n)$
polynomial, if the running time is $O(n^t)$ for some constant t
exponential, if the running time is $(t^{h(n)})$ for some constant t and polynomial $h(n)$

Generally, a problem that can be solved in polynomial time is considered feasible, whereas anything worse than polynomial time, especially exponential time, is considered infeasible. But you must be careful with these terms. First, if the size of the input is small enough, even very complex algorithms become feasible.

TABLE 4.7   Level of Effort for Various Levels of Complexity

Complexity	Size	Operations
$\log_2 n$	$2^{10^{12}} = 10^{3 \times 10^{11}}$	10^{12}
$e^{\sqrt{\ln n \times \ln(\ln n)}}$	$e^{150} = 10^{65}$	10^{12}
n	10^{12}	10^{12}
n^2	10^6	10^{12}
n^6	10^2	10^{12}
2^n	28	10^{12}
$n!$	15	10^{12}

Suppose, for example, that you have a system that can execute 10^{12} operations per hour. Table 4.7 shows the size of input that can be handled in one hour for algorithms of various complexities. For algorithms of exponential or factorial time, only very small inputs can be accommodated.

The second thing to be careful about is the way in which the input is characterized. For example, the complexity of cryptanalysis of an encryption algorithm can equally well be characterized in terms of the number of possible keys or the length of the key. For DES, for example, the number of possible keys is 2^{56}, and the length of the key is 56 bits. If we consider a single encryption to be a "step" and the number of possible keys to be $N = 2^n$, then the time complexity of the algorithm is linear in terms of the number of keys $O(N)$ but exponential in terms of the length of the key $O(2^n)$.

CHAPTER 5

AUTHENTICATION AND DIGITAL SIGNATURES

If one waits until a threat is manifest through a successful attack, then significant damage can be done before an effective countermeasure can be developed and deployed. Therefore countermeasure engineering must be based on speculation. Effort may be expended in countering attacks that are never attempted. The need to speculate and to budget resources for countermeasures also implies a need to understand what it is that should be protected, and why; such understanding should drive the choice of a protection strategy.

    — *Computers at Risk: Safe Computing in the Information Age*
      National Research Council, 1991

To guard against the baneful influence exerted by strangers is therefore an elementary dictate of savage prudence. Hence before strangers are allowed to enter a district, or at least before they are permitted to mingle freely with the inhabitants, certain ceremonies are often performed by the natives of the country for the purpose of disarming the strangers of their magical powers, or of disinfecting, so to speak, the tainted atmosphere by which they are supposed to be surrounded.

    — *The Golden Bough*
      Sir James George Frazer

At cats' green on the Sunday he took the message from the inside of the pillar and added Peter Moran's name to the two names already printed there in the "Brontosaur" code. The message now read: 'Leviathan to Dragon: Martin Hillman, Trevor Allan, Peter Moran: observe and tail.' What was the good of it John hardly knew. He felt better, he felt that at last he had made an attack on Peter Moran instead of waiting passively and effecting no retaliation. Besides, what was the use of being in possession of the key to the codes if he never took advantage of it?

    — *Talking to Strange Men*
      Ruth Rendell

Perhaps the most confusing area of network security is that of message authentication and the related topic of digital signatures. The attacks and countermeasures become so convoluted that practitioners in this area begin to remind one of the astronomers of old, who built epicycles on top of epicycles in an attempt to account for all contingencies. Fortunately, it appears that today's designers of cryptographic protocols, unlike those long-forgotten astronomers, are working from a fundamentally sound model.

It would be impossible, in anything less than book length, to exhaust all the cryptographic functions and protocols that have been proposed or implemented for message authentication and digital signatures. Instead, the purpose of this chapter is to provide a broad overview of the subject and to develop a systematic means of describing the various approaches.

The chapter begins with an introduction that looks at the requirements for authentication and digital signature and the types of attacks to be countered. Then, the basic approaches are surveyed. Next, the two principal functional tools used in authentication and digital signature are described: cryptographic checksums and hash functions. This is followed by a discussion of digital signature techniques. Finally, authentication protocols are examined.

5.1

AUTHENTICATION REQUIREMENTS

In the context of communications across a network, the following attacks can be identified:

1. *Disclosure:* Release of message contents to any person or process not possessing the appropriate cryptographic key.
2. *Traffic analysis:* Discovery of the pattern of traffic between parties. In a connection-oriented application, the frequency and duration of connections could be determined. In either a connection-oriented or connectionless environment, the number and length of messages between parties could be determined.
3. *Masquerade:* Insertion of messages into the network from a fraudulent source. This includes the creation of messages by an opponent that are purported to come from an authorized entity. Also included are fraudulent acknowledgments of message receipt or nonreceipt by someone other than the message recipient.
4. *Content modification:* Changes to the contents of a message, including insertion, deletion, transposition, or modification.
5. *Sequence modification:* Any modification to a sequence of messages between parties, including insertion, deletion, and reordering.
6. *Timing modification:* Delay or replay of messages. In a connection-oriented application, an entire session or sequence of messages could be a replay of some previous valid session, or individual messages in the sequence could be delayed or replayed. In a connectionless application, an individual message (e.g., datagram) could be delayed or replayed.

7. *Repudiation:* Denial of receipt of message by destination or denial of transmission of message by source.

Measures to deal with the first two attacks are in the realm of message confidentiality and are the subject of Chapters 2 through 4. Measures to deal with items 3 through 6 in the foregoing list are generally regarded as message authentication. Mechanisms for dealing specifically with item 7 come under the heading of digital signatures. Generally, a digital signature technique will also counter some or all the attacks listed under items 3 through 6.

In summary, message authentication is a procedure to verify that received messages come from the alleged source and have not been altered. Message authentication may also verify sequencing and timeliness. A digital signature is an authentication technique that also includes measures to counter repudiation by either source or destination.

5.2

AUTHENTICATION FUNCTIONS

Any message authentication or digital signature mechanism can be viewed as having fundamentally two levels. At the lower level, there must be some sort of function that produces an authenticator: a value to be used to authenticate a message. This lower-level function is then used as primitive in a higher-level authentication protocol that enables a receiver to verify the authenticity of a message.

This section is concerned with the types of functions that may be used to produce an authenticator. These functions may be grouped into three classes, as follows:

- *Message encryption:* The ciphertext of the entire message serves as its authenticator.
- *Cryptographic checksum:* A public function of the message and a secret key that produces a fixed-length value that serves as the authenticator.
- *Hash function:* A public function that maps a message of any length into a fixed-length hash value, which serves as the authenticator.

We now briefly examine each of these topics; cryptographic checksums and hash functions are then examined in greater detail in Sections 5.3 and 5.4.

Message Encryption

Message encryption by itself can provide a measure of authentication. The analysis differs for conventional and public-key encryption schemes.

Conventional Encryption

Consider the straightforward use of conventional encryption (Figure 5.1a). A message transmitted from source A to destination B is encrypted using a secret key K shared by A and B. If no other party knows the key, then confidentiality is provided: no other party can recover the plaintext of the message.

In addition, we may say that B is assured that the message was generated by A. Why? The message must have come from A since A is the only other party that possesses K and therefore the only other party with the information necessary to construct ciphertext that can be decrypted with K. Furthermore, if M is recovered, B knows that none of the bits of M have been altered, because an opponent that does not know K would not know how to alter bits in the ciphertext to produce desired changes in the plaintext.

So, we may say that conventional encryption provides authentication as well as confidentiality. However, this flat statement needs to be qualified. Consider

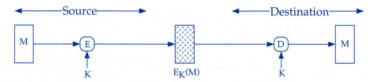

(a) Conventional encryption: confidentiality and authentication

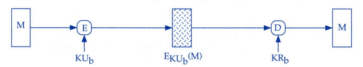

(b) Public-key encryption: confidentiality

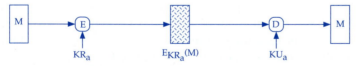

(c) Public-key encryption: authentication and signature

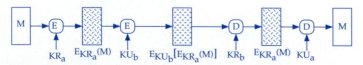

(d) Public-key encryption: confidentiality, authentication, and signature

FIGURE 5.1.   Basic Uses of Message Encryption

exactly what is happening at B. Given a decryption function D and a secret key K, the destination will accept *any* input X and produce output $Y = D_K(X)$. If X is the ciphertext of a legitimate message M produced by the corresponding encryption function, then Y is some plaintext message M. Otherwise, Y will be a meaningless sequence of bits. There must be some automated means of determining at B whether Y is legitimate plaintext and therefore must have come from A.

The implications of the line of reasoning in the preceding paragraph are profound from the point of view of authentication. Suppose the message M can be any arbitrary bit pattern. In that case, there is no way to automatically determine, at the destination, whether an incoming message is the ciphertext of a legitimate message or not! This conclusion is incontrovertible: If M can be any bit pattern, then regardless of the value of X, $Y = D_K(X)$ is *some* bit pattern and therefore must be accepted as authentic plaintext.

Thus, in general, we require that only a small subset of all possible bit patterns is to be considered legitimate plaintext. In that case, any spurious ciphertext is unlikely to produce legitimate plaintext. For example, suppose that only one bit pattern in 10^6 is legitimate plaintext. Then the probability that any randomly chosen bit pattern, treated as ciphertext, will produce a legitimate plaintext message is only 10^{-6}.

For a number of applications and encryption schemes, the desired conditions prevail as a matter of course. For example, suppose that we are transmitting English-language messages using a Caesar cipher with a shift of one (K = 1). A sends the following legitimate ciphertext:

NBSFTFBUPBUTBOEEPFTFBUPBUTBOEMJUUMFMBNCTFBUJWZ

B decrypts to produce the following plaintext:

mareseatoatsanddoeseatoatsandlittlelambseativy

A simple frequency analysis confirms that this message has the profile of ordinary English. On the other hand, if an opponent generates the following random sequence of letters

ZUVRSOEVGQXLZWIGAMDVNMHPMCCXIUUREOSFBCEBTQXSXQ

which decrypts to

ytuqrndufpwkyvhfzlcumlgolbbwhttqdnreabdaspwrwp

which does not fit the profile of ordinary English.

It may be difficult to *automatically* determine if incoming ciphertext decrypts to intelligible plaintext. If the plaintext is a binary object file or digitized x-rays, determination of properly formed and therefore authentic plaintext may be difficult. Thus, an opponent could achieve a certain level of disruption simply by issuing messages with random content purporting to come from a legitimate user.

One solution to this problem is to force the plaintext to have some structure that is easily recognized but that cannot be replicated without recourse to the encryption function. We could for example, append an error-detecting code, also known

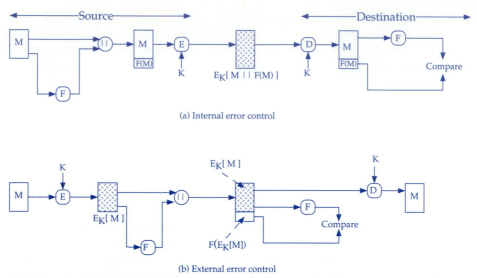

(a) Internal error control

(b) External error control

FIGURE 5.2.   Internal and External Error Control

as a frame check sequence (FCS) or checksum, to each message before encryption, as illustrated in Figure 5.2a. A prepares a plaintext message M and then provides this as input to a function F that produces an FCS. The FCS is appended to M and the entire block is then encrypted. At the destination, B decrypts the incoming block and treats the results as a message with an appended FCS. B applies the same function F to attempt to reproduce the FCS. If the calculated FCS is equal to the incoming FCS, then the message is considered authentic. It is unlikely that any random sequence of bits would exhibit the desired relationship.

Note that the order in which the FCS and encryption functions are performed is critical. The sequence illustrated in Figure 5.2a is referred to in [DIFF79] as internal error control, which the authors contrast with external error control (Figure 5.2b). With internal error control, authentication is provided because an opponent would have difficulty generating ciphertext which, when decrypted, would have valid error control bits. If instead the FCS is the outer code, an opponent can construct messages with valid error-control codes. Although the opponent cannot know what the decrypted plaintext will be, he or she can still hope to create confusion and disrupt operations.

An error-control code is just one example; in fact, any sort of structuring added to the transmitted message serves to strengthen the authentication capability. Such structure is provided by the use of a communications architecture consisting of layered protocols. As an example, consider the structure of messages transmitted using the TCP/IP protocol architecture. Figure 5.3 shows the format of a TCP segment, illustrating the TCP header. Now suppose that each pair of hosts shared a unique secret key, so that all exchanges between a pair of hosts used the same key, regardless of application. Then, one could simply encrypt all of the datagram

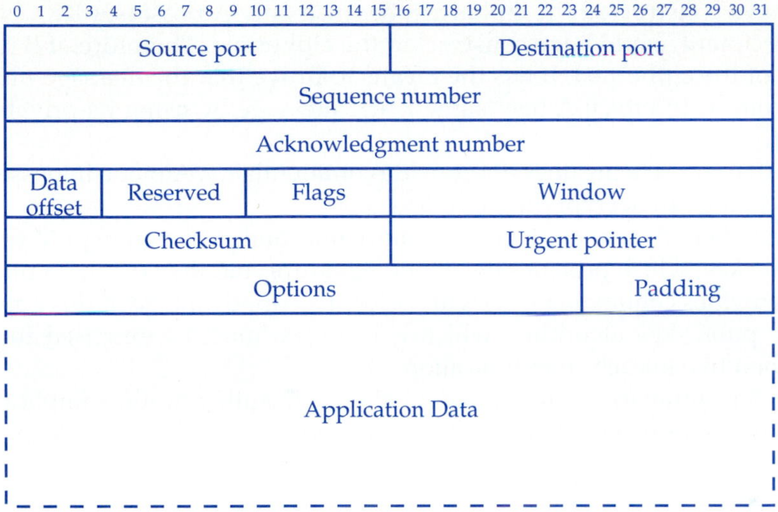

0 1 2 3 4 5 6 7 8 9 10 11 12 13 14 15 16 17 18 19 20 21 22 23 24 25 26 27 28 29 30 31

Source port		Destination port	
Sequence number			
Acknowledgment number			
Data offset	Reserved	Flags	Window
Checksum		Urgent pointer	
Options			Padding

Application Data

FIGURE 5.3.   TCP Segment

except the IP header (see Figure 3.6). Again, if an opponent substituted some arbitrary bit pattern for the encrypted TCP segment, the resulting plaintext would not include a meaningful header. In this case, the header includes not only a checksum (which covers the header) but other useful information, such as the sequence number. Because successive TCP segments on a given connection are numbered sequentially, encryption assures that an opponent does not delay, misorder, or delete any segments.

Public-Key Encryption

The straightforward use of public-key encryption (Figure 5.1b) provides confidentiality but not authentication. The source (A) uses the public key KU_b of the destination (B) to encrypt M. Because only B has the corresponding private key KR_b, only B can decrypt the message. This scheme provides no authentication because any opponent could also use B's public key to encrypt a message, claiming to be A.

To provide authentication, A uses its private key to encrypt the message, and B uses A's public key to decrypt (Figure 5.1c). This provides a measure of authentication using the same type of reasoning as in the conventional encryption case: The message must have come from A because A is the only party that possesses KR_a and therefore the only party with the information necessary to construct ciphertext that can be decrypted with KU_a. Again, the same reasoning as before applies: There must be some internal structure to the plaintext so that the receiver can distinguish between well-formed plaintext and random bits.

Assuming there is such structure, then the scheme of Figure 5.1c does provide authentication. It also provides what is known as digital signature. Only A could have constructed the ciphertext because only A possesses KR_a. Not even B, the recipient, could have constructed the ciphertext. Therefore, if B is in possession of the ciphertext, B has the means to prove that the message must have come from A. In effect, A has "signed" the message by using its private key to encrypt.

Note that this scheme does not provide confidentiality. Anyone in possession of A's public key can decrypt the ciphertext.

To provide both confidentiality and authentication, A can encrypt M first using its private key, which provides the digital signature, and then using B's public key, which provides confidentiality (Figure 5.1d). The disadvantage of this approach is that the public-key algorithm, which is complex, must be exercised four times rather than two in each communication.

Table 5.1 summarizes the confidentiality and authentication implications of these various approaches to message encryption.

TABLE 5.1   Confidentiality and Authentication Implications of Message Encryption

---

Conventional (symmetric) Encryption

$A \rightarrow B: E_K[M]$
- Provides confidentiality
  - Only A and B share K
- Provides a degree of authentication
  - Could come only from A
  - Has not been altered in transit
  - Requires some formatting/redundancy
- Does not provide signature
  - Receiver could forge message
  - Sender could deny message

Public-Key (asymmetric) Encryption

$A \rightarrow B: E_{KUb}[M]$
- Provides confidentiality
  - Only B has KR_b to decrypt
- Provides no authentication
  - Any party could use KU_b to encrypt message and claim to be A

$A \rightarrow B: E_{KRa}[M]$
- Provides authentication and signature
  - Only A has KR_a to encrypt
  - Has not been altered in transit
  - Requires some formatting/redundancy
  - Any party can use KU_b to verify signature

$A \rightarrow B: E_{KUb}[E_{KRa}(M)]$
- Provides confidentiality because of KU_b
- Provides authentication and signature because of KR_a

Cryptographic Checksum

An alternative authentication technique involves the use of a secret key to generate a small fixed-size block of data, known as a cryptographic checksum, or message authentication code (MAC), that is appended to the message. This technique assumes that two communicating parties, say A and B, share a common secret key K. When A has a message to send to B, it calculates the cryptographic checksum as a function of the message and the key: $C_{K}(M)$. The message plus checksum are transmitted to the intended recipient. The recipient performs the same calculation on the received message, using the same secret key, to generate a new cryptographic checksum. The received checksum is compared to the calculated checksum (Figure 5.4a). If we assume that only the receiver and the sender know the identity of the secret key, and if the received checksum matches the calculated checksum, then:

1. The receiver is assured that the message has not been altered. If an attacker alters the message but does not alter the checksum, then the receiver's calculation of the checksum will differ from the received checksum. Because the attacker is assumed not to know the secret key, the attacker cannot alter the checksum to correspond to the alterations in the message.

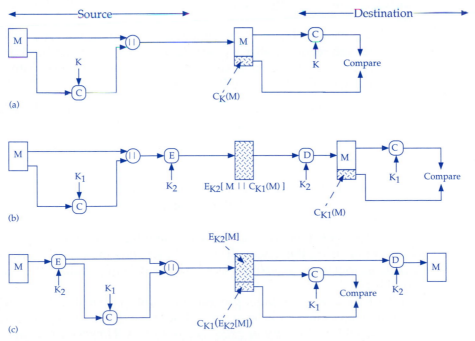

FIGURE 5.4. Basic Uses of Cryptographic Checksum

2. The receiver is assured that the message is from the alleged sender. Because no one else knows the secret key, no one else could prepare a message with a proper checksum.

3. If the message includes a sequence number (such as is used with X.25, HDLC, TCP, and the ISO transport protocol), then the receiver can be assured of the proper sequence, because an attacker cannot successfully alter the sequence number.

A cryptographic checksum function is similar to encryption. One difference is that the checksum algorithm need not be reversible, as it must for decryption. It turns out that because of the mathematical properties of the authentication function, it is less vulnerable to being broken than is encryption.

The process just described provides authentication but not confidentiality, because the message as a whole is transmitted in the clear. Confidentiality can be provided by performing message encryption either after (Figure 5.4b) or before (Figure 5.4c) the cryptographic checksum algorithm. In both these cases, two separate keys are needed, each of which is shared by the sender and the receiver. In the first case, the checksum is calculated with the message as input and is then concatenated to the message. The entire block is then encrypted. In the second case, the message is encrypted first. Then the checksum is calculated using the resulting ciphertext and is concatenated to the ciphertext to form the transmitted block. Typically, it is preferable to tie the authentication directly to the plaintext, so that the method of Figure 5.4b is used.

Because conventional encryption will provide authentication, and because it is widely used with readily available products, why not simply use this instead of a separate message authentication code? [DAVI89] suggests three situations in which a message authentication code is used:

1. There are a number of applications in which the same message is broadcast to a number of destinations. Examples are notification to users that the network is now unavailable or an alarm signal in a military control center. It is cheaper and more reliable to have only one destination responsible for monitoring authenticity. Thus, the message must be broadcast in plaintext with an associated message authentication code. The responsible system has the secret key and performs authentication. If a violation occurs, the other destination systems are alerted by a general alarm.

2. Another possible scenario is an exchange in which one side has a heavy load and cannot afford the time to decrypt all incoming messages. Authentication is carried out on a selective basis, messages being chosen at random for checking.

3. Authentication of a computer program in plaintext is an attractive service. The computer program can be executed without having to decrypt it every time, which would be wasteful of processor resources. However, if a message authentication code were attached to the program, it could be checked whenever assurance was required of the integrity of the program.

Three other rationales may be added, as follows:

4. For some applications, it may not be of concern to keep messages secret, but it is important to authenticate messages. An example is the Simple Network Management Protocol Version 2 (SNMPv2), which separates the functions of confidentiality and authentication. For this application, it is usually important for a managed system to authenticate incoming SNMP messages, particularly if the message contains a command to change parameters at the managed system. On the other hand, it may not be necessary to conceal the SNMP traffic.[1]

5. Separation of authentication and confidentiality functions affords architectural flexibility. For example, it may be desired to perform authentication at the application level but to provide confidentiality at a lower level, such as the transport layer.

6. A user may wish to prolong the period of protection beyond the time of reception and yet allow processing of message contents. With message encryption, the protection is lost when the message is decrypted, so the message is protected against fraudulent modifications only in transit but not within the target system.

Finally, note that the cryptographic checksum does not provide a digital signature because both sender and receiver share the same key.

Table 5.2 summarizes the confidentiality and authentication implications of the approaches illustrated in Figure 5.4.

---

[1]In fact, SNMPv2 makes use of a hash code with a secret value rather than a message authentication code; the reasoning still applies.

TABLE 5.2   Basic Uses of Cryptographic Checksum C

(a) $A \rightarrow B: M \,||\, C_K(M)$
- Provides authentication
  - Only A and B share K

(b) $A \rightarrow B: E_{K_2}\left[M \,||\, C_{K_1}(M)\right]$
- Provides authentication
  - Only A and B share K_1
- Provides confidentiality
  - Only A and B share K_2

(c) $A \rightarrow B: E_{K_2}[M] \,||\, C_{K_1}\left(E_{K_2}[M]\right)$
- Provides authentication
  - Using K_1
- Provides confidentiality
  - Using K_2

Hash Function

A variation on the message authentication code that has received much attention recently is the one-way hash function. As with the message authentication code, a hash function accepts a variable-size message M as input and produces a fixed-size hash code H(M), sometimes called a message digest, as output. The hash code is a function of all the bits of the message and provides an error detection capability: A change to any bit or bits in the message results in a change to the hash code.

Figure 5.5 illustrates a variety of ways in which a hash code can be used to provide message authentication, as follows:

a. The message plus concatenated hash code is encrypted using conventional encryption. This is identical in structure to the internal error control strategy shown in Figure 5.2a. The same line of reasoning applies: because only A and B share the secret key, the message must have come from A and has not been altered. The hash code provides the structure or redundancy required to achieve authentication. Because encryption is applied to the entire message plus hash code, confidentiality is also provided.

b. Only the hash code is encrypted, using conventional encryption. This reduces the processing burden for those applications that do not require confidentiality. Note that the combination of hashing and encryption results in an overall function that is in fact a cryptographic checksum (Figure 5.4a). That is, $E_K[H(M)]$ is a function of a variable-length message M and a secret key K that produces a fixed-size output that is secure against an opponent that does not know the secret key.

c. Only the hash code is encrypted, using public-key encryption and using the sender's private key. As with (b), this provides authentication. It also provides a digital signature, because only the sender could have produced the encrypted hash code.

d. If confidentiality as well as a digital signature is desired, then the message plus the public-key-encrypted hash code can be encrypted using a conventional secret key.

e. This technique uses a hash function but no encryption for message authentication. The technique assumes that the two communicating parties share a common secret value S. A computes the hash value over the concatenation of M and S and appends the resulting hash value to M. Because B possesses S, it can recompute the hash value to verify. Because the secret value itself is not sent, an opponent cannot modify an intercepted message and cannot generate a false message.

f. Confidentiality can be added to the approach of (e) by encrypting the entire message plus the hash code.

When confidentiality is not required, methods (b) and (c) have an advantage over those that encrypt the entire message in that less computation is required. Nevertheless, there has been growing interest in techniques that avoid encryption

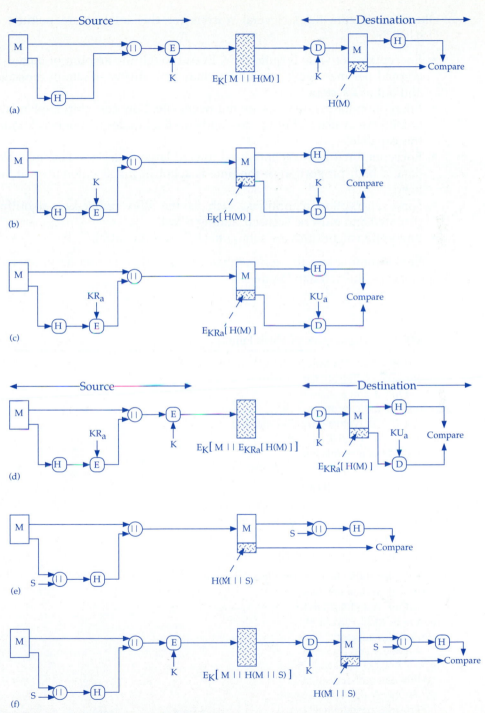

FIGURE 5.5. Basic Uses of Hash Function

altogether (Figure 5.5e). Several reasons for this interest are pointed out in [TSUD92]:

- Encryption software is quite slow. Even though the amount of data to be encrypted per message is small, there may be a steady stream of messages into and out of a system.
- Encryption hardware costs are not negligible. Low-cost chip implementations of DES are available, but the cost adds up if all nodes in a network must have this capability.
- Encryption hardware is optimized toward large data sizes. For small blocks of data, a high proportion of the time is spent in initialization/invocation overhead.
- Some encryption algorithms, such as the RSA public-key algorithm, are patented and must be licensed, adding a cost.
- Encryption algorithms are subject to U. S. export control.

Table 5.3 summarizes the confidentiality and authentication implications of the approaches illustrated in Figure 5.5.

TABLE 5.3   Basic Uses of Hash Function H

(a) $A \rightarrow B$: $E_K[M \mid\mid H(M)]$
- Provides confidentiality
  —Only A and B share K
- Provides authentication
  —H(M) is cryptographically protected

(b) $A \rightarrow B$: $M \mid\mid E_K[H(M)]$
- Provides authentication
  —H(M) is cryptographically protected

(c) $A \rightarrow B$: $M \mid\mid E_{KR_a}\left[H(M)\right]$
- Provides authentication and digital signature
  —H(M) is cryptographically protected
  —Only A could create $E_{KRa}[H(M)]$

(d) $A \rightarrow B$: $E_K\left[M \mid\mid E_{KR_a}\left[H(M)\right]\right]$
- Provides authentication and digital signature
- Provides confidentiality
  —Only A and B share K

(e) $A \rightarrow B$: $M \mid\mid H(M \mid\mid S)$
- Provides authentication
  —Only A and B share S

(f) $A \rightarrow B$: $E_K[M \mid\mid H(M \mid\mid S)]$
- Provides authentication
  —Only A and B share S
- Provides confidentiality
  —Only A and B share K

5.3

CRYPTOGRAPHIC CHECKSUMS

A cryptographic checksum, also known as a message authentication code (MAC), is generated by a function C of the form

$$MAC = C_K(M)$$

where M is a variable-length message, K is a secret key shared only by sender and receiver, and $C_K(M)$ is the fixed-length authenticator. The MAC is appended to the message at the source at a time when the message is assumed or known to be correct. The receiver authenticates that message by recomputing the MAC.

In this section, we review the requirements for the function C and then examine a specific example.

Requirements for Cryptographic Checksums

When an entire message is encrypted for confidentiality, using either symmetric or asymmetric encryption, the security of the scheme generally depends on the bit length of the key. Barring some weakness in the algorithm, the opponent must resort to a brute-force attack using all possible keys. On average, such an attack will require $2^{(k-1)}$ attempts for a k-bit key. In particular, for a ciphertext-only attack, the opponent, given ciphertext C, would perform $P_i = D_{K_i}(C)$ for all possible key values K_i until a P_i was produced that matched the form of acceptable plaintext.

In the case of a cryptographic checksum, the considerations are entirely different. In general, the checksum function is a many-to-one function. The domain of the function consists of messages of some arbitrary length, whereas the range consists of all possible MACs and all possible keys. If an n-bit MAC is used, then there are 2^n possible checksums, whereas there are N possible messages with $N \gg 2^n$. Furthermore, with a k-bit key, there are 2^k possible keys.

Using brute-force methods, how would an opponent attempt to discover a key? If confidentiality is not employed, the opponent has access to plaintext messages and their associated MACs. Suppose $k > n$; that is, suppose that the key size is greater than the MAC size. Then, given a known M_1 and MAC_1, with $M_1 = C_{K_1}(MAC_1)$, the cryptanalyst can perform $M_i = C_{K_i}(MAC_1)$ for all possible key values K_i. At least one key is guaranteed to produce a match of $M_i = M_1$. Note that a total of 2^k checksums will be produced, but there are only $2^n < 2^k$ different checksum values. Thus, a number of keys will produce the correct checksum and the opponent has no way of knowing which is the correct key! On average a total of $2^k/2^n = 2^{(k-n)}$ keys will produce a match. Thus, the opponent must iterate the attack:

> Round 1
> Given: M_1, $MAC_1 = C_K(M_1)$
> Compute $M_i = C_{K_i}(MAC_1)$ for all 2^k keys
> Number of matches $\approx 2^{(k-n)}$

Round 2

Given: M_2, $MAC_2 = C_K(M_2)$

Compute $M_i = C_{K_i}(MAC_2)$ for the remaining $2^{(k-n)}$ keys

Number of matches $\approx 2^{(k-2 \times n)}$

And so on. On average, a rounds will be needed if $k = a \times n$. For example, if an 80-bit key is used and the checksum is 32 bits long, then the first round will produce about 2^{48} possible keys. The second round will narrow the possible keys to about 2^{16} possibilities. The third round should produce only a single key, which must be the one used by the sender.

If the key length is equal to or less than the checksum length, then it is likely that a first round will produce a single match. It is possible that more than one key will produce such a match, in which case the opponent would need to perform the same test on a new (message, checksum) pair.

Thus, a brute-force attempt to discover the authentication key is no less effort, and may be more effort, than that required to discover a decryption key of the same length. However, other attacks that do not require the discovery of the key are possible.

Consider the following cryptographic checksum algorithm. Let $M = (X_1 \;||\; X_2 \;||\; \ldots \;||\; X_m)$ be a message that is treated as a concatenation of 64-bit blocks X_i. Then define:

$$\Delta(M) = X_1 \oplus X_2 \oplus \cdots \oplus X_m$$
$$C_K(M) = E_K[\Delta(M)]$$

where $\oplus$ is the exclusive-OR (XOR) operation and the encryption algorithm is DES in electronic codebook mode. Thus, the key length is 56 bits and the MAC length is 64 bits. Now, if an opponent observes $\{M \;||\; C_K(M)\}$, a brute-force attempt to determine K will require at least 2^{56} encryptions. But the opponent can attack the system by replacing X_1 through X_{m-1} with any desired values Y_1 through Y_{m-1} and replacing X_m with Y_m, where Y_m is calculated as follows:

$$Y_m = Y_1 \oplus Y_2 \oplus \cdots \oplus Y_{m-1} \oplus \Delta(M)$$

The opponent can now concatenate the new message, which consists of Y_1 through Y_m, with the original checksum to form a message that will be accepted as authentic by the receiver. With this tactic, any message of length $64 \times (m-1)$ bits can be fraudulently inserted.

Thus, in assessing the security of a cryptographic checksum function, we need to consider the types of attacks that may be mounted against it. With that in mind, let us state the requirements for the function. Assume that an opponent knows the checksum function C but does not know K. Then the checksum function should have the following properties:

1. If an opponent observes M and $C_K(M)$, it should be computationally infeasible for the opponent to construct a message M′ such that $C_K(M') = C_K(M)$.
2. $C_K(M)$ should be uniformly distributed in the sense that for randomly chosen

messages, M and M′, the probability that $C_K(M) = C_K(M')$ is 2^{-n}, where n is the number of bits in the checksum.

3. Let M′ be equal to some known transformation on M. That is, $M' = f(M)$. For example, f may involve inverting one or more specific bits. In that case, Pr $[C_K(M) = C_K(M')] = 2^{-n}$.

The first requirement speaks to the earlier example, in which an opponent is able to construct a new message to match a given MAC, even though the opponent does not know and does not learn the key. Requirement (2) deals with the need to thwart a brute-force attack based on chosen plaintext. That is, if we assume that the opponent does not know K but does have access to the checksum function and can present messages for checksum generation, then the opponent could try various messages until finding one that matches a given checksum. If the checksum function exhibits uniform distribution, then a brute-force method would require on average $2^{(n-1)}$ attempts before finding a message that fit a given checksum.

The final requirement dictates that the authentication algorithm should not be weaker with respect to certain parts or bits of the message than others. If this were not the case, then an opponent who had M and $C_K(M)$ could attempt variations on M at the known "weak spots" with a likelihood of early success at producing a new message that matched the old checksum.

Cryptographic Checksum Based on DES

One of the most widely used cryptographic checksums, referred to as the Data Authentication Algorithm, is based on DES. The algorithm is both a FIPS publication (FIPS PUB 113) and an ANSI standard (X9.17).

The algorithm can be defined as using the cipher block chaining (CBC) mode of operation of DES with an initialization vector of zero. The data (e.g., message,

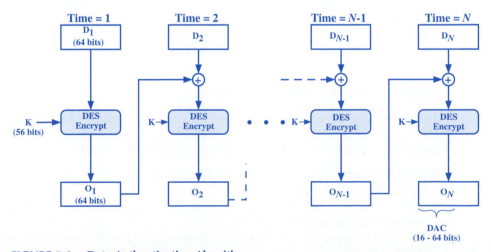

FIGURE 5.6. Data Authentication Algorithm

record, file, or program) to be authenticated is grouped into contiguous 64-bit blocks: $D_1, D_2, \ldots, D_N$. If necessary, the final block is padded on the right with zeroes to form a full 64-bit block. Using the DES encryption algorithm, E, and a secret key, K, a data authentication code (DAC) is calculated as follows (Figure 5.6):

$$O_1 = E_K(D_1)$$
$$O_2 = E_K(D_2 \oplus O_1)$$
$$O_3 = E_K(D_3 \oplus O_2)$$
$$\bullet$$
$$\bullet$$
$$\bullet$$
$$O_N = E_K(D_N \oplus O_{N-1})$$

The DAC consists of either the entire block O_N, or the leftmost M bits of the block, with $16 \leq M \leq 64$.

This algorithm appears to meet the requirements specified earlier.

5.4

HASH FUNCTIONS

A hash value is generated by a function H of the form

$$h = H(M)$$

where M is a variable-length message, and H(M) is the fixed-length hash value. The hash value is appended to the message at the source at a time when the message is assumed or known to be correct. The receiver authenticates that message by recomputing the hash value. Because the hash function itself is not considered to be secret, some means is required to protect the hash value (Figure 5.5).

We begin by examining the requirements for a hash function to be used for message authentication. Because hash functions are, typically, quite complex, it is useful to examine next some very simple hash functions to get a feel for the issues involved. We then look at several approaches to hash function design.

Requirements for a Hash Function

The purpose of a hash function is to produce a "fingerprint" of a file, message, or other block of data. To be useful for message authentication, a hash function H must have the following properties (adapted from a list in [NECH92]):

1. H can be applied to a block of data of any size.
2. H produces a fixed-length output.
3. $H(x)$ is relatively easy to compute for any given x, making both hardware and software implementations practical.
4. For any given code m, it is computationally infeasible to find x such that $H(x) = m$.

5. For any given block x, it is computationally infeasible to find $y \neq x$ with $H(y) = H(x)$.
6. It is computationally infeasible to find any pair (x, y) such that $H(x) = H(y)$.

The first three properties are requirements for the practical application of a hash function to message authentication.

The fourth property is the "one-way" property: It is easy to generate a code given a message but virtually impossible to generate a message given a code. This property is important if the authentication technique involves the use of a secret value (Figure 5.5e). The secret value itself is not sent; however, if the hash function is not one-way, an attacker can easily discover the secret value: If the attacker can observe or intercept a transmission, the attacker obtains the message M and the hash code $C = H(S_{AB}||M)$. The attacker then inverts the hash function to obtain $S_{AB}||M = H^{-1}(C)$. Because the attacker now has both M and $S_{AB}||M$, it is a trivial matter to recover S_{AB}.

The fifth property guarantees that an alternative message hashing to the same value as a given message cannot be found. This prevents forgery when an encrypted hash code is used (Figure 5.5b and c). For these cases, the opponent can read the message and therefore generate its hash code. But, because the opponent does not have the secret key, the opponent should not be able to alter the message without detection. If this property were not true, an attacker would be capable of the following sequence: First, observe or intercept a message plus its encrypted hash code; second, generate an unencrypted hash code from the message; third, generate an alternate message with the same hash code.

A hash function that satisfies the first five properties in the preceding list is referred to as a weak hash function. If the sixth property is also satisfied, then it is referred to as a strong hash function. The sixth property protects against a sophisticated class of attack known as the birthday attack, which we examine shortly.

Simple Hash Functions

All hash functions operate using the following general principles. The input (message, file, etc.) is viewed as a sequence of n-bit blocks. The input is processed one block at a time in an iterative fashion to produce an n-bit hash function.

One of the simplest hash functions is the bit-by-bit exclusive-or (XOR) of every block. This can be expressed as follows:

$$C_i = b_{i1} \oplus b_{i2} \oplus \cdots \oplus b_{im}$$

where

C_i = ith bit of the hash code, $1 \leq i \leq n$
m = number of n-bit blocks in the input
b_{ij} = ith bit in jth block
$\oplus$ = XOR operation

Figure 5.7 illustrates this operation; it produces a simple parity for each bit position and is known as a longitudinal redundancy check. It is reasonably

	bit 1	bit 2	• • •	bit n
Block 1	b_{11}	b_{21}		b_{n1}
Block 2	b_{11}	b_{22}		b_{n2}
	• • •	• • •	• • •	• • •
Block m	b_{1m}	b_{2m}		b_{nm}
Hash code	C_1	C_1		C_n

FIGURE 5.7.   Simple Hash Function Using Bitwise XOR

effective for random data as a data integrity check. Each n-bit hash value is equally likely. Thus, the probability that a data error will result in an unchanged hash value is 2^{-n}. With more predictably formatted data, the function is less effective. For example, in most normal text files, the high-order bit of each octet is always zero. So, if a 128-bit hash value is used, instead of an effectiveness of 2^{-128}, the hash function on this type of data has an effectiveness of 2^{-112}.

A simple way to improve matters is to perform a one-bit circular shift, or rotation, on the hash value after each block is processed. The procedure can be summarized as follows:

1. Initially set the n-bit hash value to zero.
2. Process each successive n-bit block of data as follows:
   (a) Rotate the current hash value to the left by one bit.
   (b) XOR the block into the hash value.

This has the effect of "randomizing" the input more completely and overcoming any regularities that appear in the input. Figure 5.8 illustrates these two types of hash functions for 16-bit hash values.

Although the second procedure provides a good measure of data integrity, it is virtually useless for data security when an encrypted hash code is used with a plaintext message, as in Figure 5.5b and c. Given a message, it is an easy matter to produce a new message that yields that hash code: Simply prepare the desired alternate message and then append an n-bit block that forces the new message plus block to yield the desired hash code.

Although a simple XOR or rotated XOR (RXOR) is insufficient if only the hash code is encrypted, you may still feel that such a simple function could be useful when the message as well as the hash code are encrypted (Figure 5.5a). But one must be careful. A technique originally proposed by the National Bureau of Standards used the simple XOR applied to 64-bit blocks of the message and then an encryption of the entire message that used the cipher block chaining (CBC) mode. We can define the scheme as follows: Given a message consisting of a se-

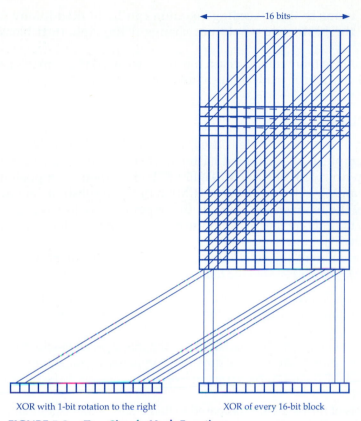

XOR with 1-bit rotation to the right   XOR of every 16-bit block

FIGURE 5.8.   Two Simple Hash Functions

quence of 64-bit blocks $X_1, X_2, \ldots, X_N$, define the hash code C as the block-by-block XOR or all blocks and append the hash code as the final block:

$$C = X_{N+1} = X_1 \oplus X_2 \oplus \cdots \oplus X_N$$

Next, encrypt the entire message plus hash code, using CBC mode to produce the encrypted message $Y_1, Y_2, \ldots, Y_{N+1}$. [JUEN85] points out several ways in which the ciphertext of this message can be manipulated in such a way as to not be detectable by the hash code. For example, by the definition of CBC (Figure 2.14), we have:

$$\begin{aligned} X_1 &= IV \oplus D_K(Y_1) \\ X_i &= Y_{i-1} \oplus D_K(Y_i) \\ X_{N+1} &= Y_N \oplus D_K(Y_{N+1}) \end{aligned}$$

But X_{N+1} is the hash code:

$$\begin{aligned} &X_{N+1} \oplus X_1 \oplus X_2 \oplus \cdots \oplus X_N \\ &\quad = (IV \oplus D_K(Y_1)) \oplus (Y_1 \oplus D_K(Y_2)) \oplus \cdots \oplus (Y_{N-1} \oplus D_K(Y_N)) \end{aligned}$$

Because the terms in the preceding equation can be XORed in any order, it follows that the hash code would not change if the ciphertext blocks were permuted.

Before turning to more complex hash functions, we need to examine a particular type of attack that can be made on such functions.

Birthday Attacks

Suppose that a 64-bit hash code is used. One might think that this is quite secure. For example, if an encrypted hash code C is transmitted with the corresponding unencrypted message M (Figure 5.5b or c), then an opponent would need to find an M' such that H(M') = H(M) in order to substitute another message and fool the receiver. On average, the opponent would have to try about 2^{63} messages to find one that matches the hash code of the intercepted message (see Appendix 5A).

However, a different sort of attack is possible, based on the birthday paradox (Appendix 5A). Yuval proposed the following strategy [YUVA79]:

1. The source, A, is prepared to "sign" a message by appending the appropriate m-bit checksum and encrypting that checksum with A's private key (Figure 5.5c).
2. The opponent generates $2^{m/2}$ variations on the message, all of which convey essentially the same meaning. The opponent prepares an equal number of messages, all of which are variations on the fraudulent message to be substituted for the real one.
3. The two sets of messages are compared to find a pair of messages that produces the same hash code. The probability of success, by the birthday paradox, is greater than 0.5. If no match is found, additional valid and fraudulent messages are generated until a match is made.
4. The opponent offers the valid variation to A for signature. This signature can then be attached to the fraudulent variation for transmission to the intended recipient. Because the two variations have the same hash code, they will produce the same signature; the opponent is assured of success even though the encryption key is not known.

Thus, if a 64-bit hash code is used, the level of effort required is only on the order of 2^{32}.

The generation of many variations that convey the same meaning is not difficult. For example, the opponent could insert a number of "space-space-backspace" character pairs between words throughout the document. Variations could then be generated by substituting "space-backspace-space" in selected instances. Alternatively, the opponent could simply reword the message but retain the meaning. Figure 5.9 [DAVI89] provides an example.

The conclusion to be drawn from this is that the length of the hash code should be substantial. A length of only 64 bits is probably not secure. Something in excess of 100 bits would be preferable.

Dear Anthony,

{This letter is | I am writing} to introduce {you to | to you} {Mr. | —} Alfred {P. | —}

Barton, the {new | newly appointed} {chief | senior} jewellery buyer for {our | the}

Northern {European | Europe} {area | division}. He {will take | has taken} over {the | —}

responsibility for {all | the whole of} our interests in {watches and jewellery | jewellery and watches}

in the {area | region}. Please {afford | give} him {every | all the} help he {may need | needs}

to {seek out | find} the most {modern | up to date} lines for the {top | high} end of the

market. He is {empowered | authorized} to receive on our behalf {samples | specimens} of the

{latest | newest} {watch and jewellery | jewellery and watch} products, {up | subject} to a {limit | maximum}

of ten thousand dollars. He will {carry | hold} a signed copy of this {letter | document}

as proof of identity. An order with his signature, which is {appended | attached}

{authorizes | allows} you to charge the cost to this company at the {above | head office}

address. We {fully | —} expect that our {level | volume} of orders will increase in

the {following | next} year and {trust | hope} that the new appointment will {be | prove}

{advantageous | an advantage} to both our companies.

FIGURE 5.9. A Fraudulent Letter in 2^{37} Variations

Block Chaining Techniques

A number of proposals have been made for hash functions based on using a cipher block chaining technique, but without the secret key. One of the first such proposals was that of Rabin [RABI78]. Divide a message M into fixed-size blocks M_1, $M_2, \ldots, M_N$ and use a conventional encryption system such as DES to compute the hash code G as follows:

$$H_0 = \text{initial value}$$
$$H_i = E_{M_i}[H_{i-1}]$$
$$G = H_N$$

This is similar to the CBC technique, but in this case there is no secret key. As with any hash code, this scheme is subject to the birthday attack, and if the encryption algorithm is DES and only a 64-bit hash code is produced, then the system is vulnerable.

Furthermore, another version of the birthday attack can be used even if the opponent has access to only one message and its valid signature and cannot obtain multiple signings. Here is the scenario; we assume that the opponent intercepts a message with a signature in the form of an encrypted hash code and that the unencrypted hash code is m bits long:

1. Use the algorithm defined at the beginning of this subsection to calculate the unencrypted hash code G.
2. Construct any desired message in the form $Q_1, Q_2, \ldots, Q_{N-2}$.
3. Compute $H_i = E_{Q_i}[H_{i-1}]$ for $1 \le i \le (N - 2)$.
4. Generate $2^{m/2}$ random blocks; for each block X, compute $E_X[H_{N-2}]$. Generate an additional $2^{m/2}$ random blocks; for each block Y, compute $D_Y[G]$, where D is the decryption function corresponding to E.
5. Based on the birthday paradox, with high probability there will be an X and Y such that $E_X[H_{N-2}] = D_Y[G]$.
6. Form the message $Q_1, Q_2, \ldots, Q_{N-2}, X, Y$. This message has the hash code G and therefore can be used with the intercepted encrypted signature.

This form of attack is known as a "meet in the middle" attack. A number of researchers have proposed refinements intended to strengthen the basic block chaining approach. For example, Davies and Price [DAVI89] describe the following variation:

$$H_i = E_{M_i}[H_{i-1}] \oplus H_{i-1}$$

Another variation, proposed in [MEYE88]:

$$H_i = E_{H_{i-1}}[M_i] \oplus M_i$$

However, both of these schemes have been shown to be vulnerable to a variety of attacks [MIYA90]. More generally, it can be shown that some form of birthday attack will succeed against any hash scheme involving the use of cipher block chaining without a secret key provided that either the resulting hash code is small enough (e.g., 64 bits or less) or that a larger hash code can be decomposed into independent subcodes [JUEN87].

Thus, attention has been directed at finding other approaches to hashing. Unfortunately, most of these have also been shown to have weaknesses [MITC92]. In the next subsection, we look at one interesting approach. Several other techniques are examined in Chapter 9.

Snefru

Snefru was developed by Ralph Merkle (he of the $1,000 knapsack fame) with the objectives of providing good security and ease of implementation on 32-bit processors [MERK90].

In general terms, the Snefru scheme can be stated as follows. The hash function, H, produces a k-bit hash code for a message of arbitrary length. The function H involves iteration of a more primitive function H512 that maps a 512-bit input into a

k-bit output. For each iteration, H512 takes as input the output of the preceding iteration (k bits) plus one block of the message ($512 - k$ bits).

As before, we divide a message M into fixed-size blocks $X_1, X_2, \ldots, X_N$. In this case the block size is 384 bits if the output is a 128-bit hash code, and 256 bits if the output is a 256-bit hash code. Let us describe the 128-bit version. Now, compute the hash code G as follows:

$$
\begin{aligned}
H_0 &= \text{128-bit block of all 0s} \\
H_i &= \text{H512}(H_{i-1} \,||\, X_i) \\
H_N &= \text{H512}(H_{n-1} \,||\, X_N) \\
G &= \text{H512}(H_n \,||\, <\text{length of M in bits}>)
\end{aligned}
$$

Figure 5.10 illustrates this logic.

Next, we must define the function H512, which operates on a single block of the message, together with the preceding result. Merkle defines this function in terms of a more primitive function that "looks like" an encryption function. In fact, it is not an encryption function and no encryption key is involved. The function, E512, takes a 512-bit input block and produces a 512-bit output block. The function per-

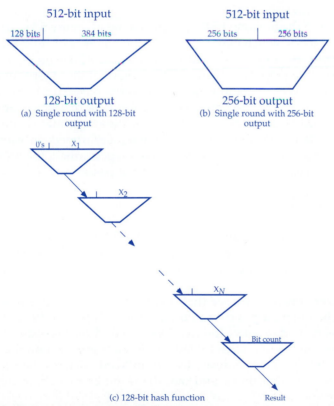

(a) Single round with 128-bit output

(b) Single round with 256-bit output

(c) 128-bit hash function

FIGURE 5.10. **Snefru Hash Function**

forms a series of exclusive-OR (XOR) operations on the block interspersed with rotations.

Before looking at the details of E512, let us see how it fits into the overall hash function. The general form is as follows:

$$h(x) = x \oplus E512[x]$$

That is, we take the output of E512 and do a bit-by-bit XOR with the input. This produces a 512-bit result. However, because of the way the iteration is defined, we need a 128-bit (or 256-bit) result. Accordingly, the leftmost 128 bits (or 256 bits) are taken. With this in mind, we can expand the preceding definition of the hash function as follows:

$$H_0 = \text{128-bit block of all 0s}$$
$$H_i = \text{LEFT128}[[H_{i-1} \mid\mid X_i] \oplus \text{E512}[H_{i-1} \mid\mid X_i]]$$
$$H_N = \text{LEFT128}[[H_{N-1} \mid\mid X_N] \oplus \text{E512}[H_{N-1} \mid\mid X_N]]$$
$$G = \text{LEFT128}[[H_N \mid\mid \text{<length of M in bits>}] \oplus \text{E512}[H_N \mid\mid \text{<length of M in bits>}]]$$

The inclusion of the length calculation makes the job of the opponent more difficult. Either the opponent must find two messages of equal length that hash to the same value or two messages of differing lengths that, together with their length values, hash to the same value.

It remains to define the function E512, which is done in Figure 5.11. The input consists of a 512-bit block, which may be viewed as a sequence of 16 32-bit words. These words fit conveniently into the registers of most RISC machines and many other machines, enabling rapid calculation. The essence of the algorithm is (1) to perform a number of XOR operations on words in the block, using predefined 32-bit patterns known as S-boxes, and (2) to perform 8-bit or 1-octet rotation of bits within each word. A complex combination of these operations constitutes one "pass" of the algorithm; the number of passes performed on each input block is a design parameter. The more passes that are performed, the more thoroughly the input is hashed; therefore the number of passes can be viewed as a security level.

An important auxiliary variable is a two-dimensional array of the 32-bit S-boxes. The second index defines a subarray of 256 32-bit words. The first index dictates that there are two subarrays for each pass of the algorithm. The actual content of these arrays is derived from the table of random numbers published by Rand [RAND55]. This is meant to assure the observer that there are no hidden trapdoors in the S-boxes.

If we examine the function, we see that there is a set of **for** loops nested to a depth of three. The outer loop is executed once for each pass of the algorithm; the index variable is used to select the two S-boxes used for that pass. The first two boxes are used on the first pass; the next two boxes are used on the second pass, and so on. The next loop, indexed by byteInWord, dictates that the inner algorithm be performed four times, and that the result be rotated, as discussed below.

```
function E512 (x : int512) : int512;
begin
  tempBlock, Block : array[0..15] of int32;
  StandardSBoxes : array[1..passes*2, 0..255] of int32;
  rotateSchedule : array[1..4] := [16, 8, 16, 24];
  SBoxEntry : int32;
  Block := x;
  for index := 1 to passes do
    for byteInWord := 1 to 4 do
      begin
        for i := 0 to 15 do
          begin
            next := (i + 1) mod 16;
            last := (i - 1) mod 16;
            SBoxEntry := StandardSBoxes[2*index + ((i/2) mod 2) - 1,
Block[i].bottomByte];
            Block[next] := Block[next] xor SBoxEntry;
            Block[last] := Block[last] xor SBoxEntry;
          end;
        for i := 0 to 15 do
          Block[i] := RotateRight[Block[i], rotateSchedule[byteInWord]];
      end;

  tempBlock := Block;
  for i := 0 to 15 do
    Block[i] := tempBlock[15-i];
end
```

FIGURE 5.11.   Basic Building Block of Snefru

The innermost level consists of two **for** loops executed in sequence. The first of these loops is actually the heart of the algorithm. What is done is to step through the block one 32-bit word at a time. At each iteration, a particular S-box is selected. The subarray of 256 S-boxes that is chosen follows the sequence 1, 1, 2, 2, 1, 1, and so on for the first pass; 3, 3, 4, 4, 3, 3, and so on for the second pass; and so on. A particular S-box is selected from the subarray by indexing into the subarray using the value of the rightmost byte of the current block. The resulting S-box is then XORed into the preceding block and into the next block (Figure 5.12).

Once all the XOR operations are performed, the final function of the inner loop is a right circular rotation within each of the 16 32-bit words of the block. Each word is rotated one or more octets (multiples of 8 bits) according to the schedule 16, 8, 16, 24. The result is that a different octet is in the rightmost position after each

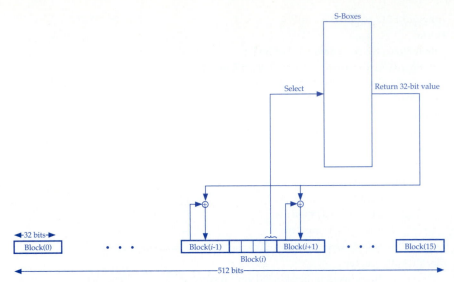

FIGURE 5.12. E512 Inner Logic

rotation. To see this, consider that a 32-bit word is in the form of four octets ABCD. Then:

- Rotate right 16 bits: CDAB
- Rotate right 8 bits: BCDA
- Rotate right 16 bits: DABC
- Rotate right 24 bits: ABCD

Finally, after all passes are completed, the words in the block are pairwise exchanged: 0 with 15, 1 with 14, and so on.

The complex nature of this hashing algorithm would make it difficult to break. Nevertheless, Merkle points out in has paper that a method for producing two messages that yield the same hash code under the 2-pass Snefru has been found. He thus suggested using 4 passes and later expanded that to 8 passes. As of this writing, no one has challenged the 8-pass algorithm.

5.5

DIGITAL SIGNATURES

We have already made reference to digital signatures earlier in this chapter and in Chapter 4. In this section, we review the requirements for and definition of the digital signature and examine some of its ramifications.

Requirements

Message authentication protects two parties who exchange messages from any third party. However, it does not protect the two parties against each other. Several forms of dispute between the two are possible.

For example, suppose that John sends an authenticated message to Mary, using one of the schemes of Figure 5.4. Consider the following disputes that could arise:

1. Mary may forge a different message and claim that it came from John. Mary would simply have to create a message and append an authentication code using the key that John and Mary share.
2. John can deny sending the message. Because it is possible for Mary to forge a message, there is no way to prove that John did in fact send the message.

Both scenarios are of legitimate concern. An example of the first scenario: An electronic funds transfer takes place, and the receiver increases the amount of funds transferred and claims that the larger amount had arrived from the sender. An example of the second scenario: An electronic mail message contains instructions to a stockbroker for a transaction that subsequently turns out badly. The sender pretends that the message was never sent.

In situations where there is not complete trust between sender and receiver, something more than authentication is needed. The most attractive solution to this problem is the digital signature. The digital signature is analogous to the handwritten signature. It must have the following properties:

- It must be able to verify the author and the date and time of the signature.
- It must be able to authenticate the contents at the time of the signature.
- The signature must be verifiable by third parties, to resolve disputes.

Thus the digital signature function includes the authentication function.

On the basis of these properties, we can formulate the following requirements for a digital signature:

- The signature must be a bit pattern that depends on the message being signed.
- The signature must use some information unique to the sender, to prevent both forgery and denial.
- It must be relatively easy to produce the digital signature.
- It must be relatively easy to recognize and verify the digital signature.
- It must be computationally infeasible to forge a digital signature, either by constructing a new message for an existing digital signature or by constructing a fraudulent digital signature for a given message.
- It must be practical to retain a copy of the digital signature in storage.

A secure hash function, embedded in a scheme such as that of Figure 5.5c or d, satisfies these requirements.

A variety of approaches has been proposed for the digital signature function. They fall into two categories: direct and arbitrated.

Direct Digital Signature

The direct digital signature involves only the communicating parties (source, destination). It is assumed that the destination knows the public key of the source. A digital signature may be formed by encrypting the entire message with the sender's private key (Figure 5.1c) or by encrypting a hash code of the message with the sender's private key (Figure 5.5c).

Confidentiality can be provided by further encrypting the entire message plus signature with either the receiver's public key (public-key encryption) or a shared secret key (conventional encryption); for example see Figure 5.1d and Figure 5.5d. Note that it is important to perform the signature function first and then an outer confidentiality function. In case of dispute, some third party must view the message and its signature. If the signature is calculated on an encrypted message, then the third party also needs access to the decryption key in order to read the original message. However, if the signature is the inner operation, then the recipient can store the plaintext message and its signature for later use in dispute resolution.

All direct schemes described so far share a common weakness. The validity of the scheme depends upon the security of the sender's private key. If a sender later wishes to deny sending a particular message, the sender can claim that the private key was lost or stolen and that someone else forged his or her signature. Administrative controls relating to the security of private keys can be employed to thwart or at least weaken this ploy, but the threat is still there, at least to some degree. One example is to require every signed message to include a timestamp (date and time) and to require prompt reporting of compromised keys to a central authority.

Another threat is that some private key might actually be stolen from X at time T. The opponent can then send a message signed with X's signature and stamped with a time before or equal to T.

Arbitrated Digital Signature

The problems associated with direct digital signatures can be addressed by using an arbiter.

As with direct signature schemes, there is a variety of arbitrated signature schemes. In general terms, they all operate as follows. Every signed message from a sender X to a receiver Y goes first to an arbiter A, who subjects the message and its signature to a number of tests to check its origin and content. The message is then dated and sent to Y with an indication that it has been verified to the satisfaction of the arbiter. The presence of A solves the problem faced by direct signature schemes: that X might disown the message.

TABLE 5.4   Arbitrated Digital Signature Techniques

(a) Conventional Encryption, Arbiter Sees Message

  (1) $X \rightarrow A$: $M || E_{K_{xa}}[ID_X || H(M)]$

  (2) $A \rightarrow Y$: $E_{K_{ay}}\left[ID_X || M || E_{K_{xa}}[ID_X || H(M)], T\right]$

(b) Conventional Encryption, Arbiter Does Not See Message

  (1) $X \rightarrow A$: $ID_X || E_{K_{xy}}[M] || E_{K_{xa}}\left[ID_X || H(E_{K_{xy}}[M])\right]$

  (2) $A \rightarrow Y$: $E_{K_{ay}}\left[ID_X || E_{K_{xy}}[M] || E_{K_{xa}}[ID_X || H(E_{K_{xy}}[M])], T\right]$

(c) Public-Key Encryption, Arbiter Does Not See Message

  (1) $X \rightarrow A$: $ID_X || E_{KR_x}\left[ID_X || E_{KU_y}(E_{KR_x}[M])\right]$

  (2) $A \rightarrow Y$: $E_{KR_a}\left[ID_X || E_{KU_y}(E_{KR_x}[M]) || T\right]$

Notation:

X = sender

Y = recipient

A = arbiter

M = message

The arbiter plays a sensitive and crucial role in this sort of scheme, and all parties must have a great deal of trust that the arbitration mechanism is working properly. The use of a trusted system, described in Chapter 6, might satisfy this requirement.

Table 5.4, based on scenarios described in [AKL83] and [MITC92], gives several examples of arbitrated digital signatures. In the first, conventional encryption is used. It is assumed that the sender X and the arbiter A share a secret key K_{xa} and that A and Y share secret key K_{ay}. X constructs a message M and computes its hash value $H(M)$. Then X transmits the message plus a signature to A. The signature consists of an identifier of X plus the hash value, all encrypted using K_{xa}. A decrypts the signature and checks the hash value to validate the message. Then A transmits a message to Y, encrypted with K_{ay}. The message includes ID_X, the original message from X, the signature, and a timestamp. Y can decrypt this to recover the message and the signature. The timestamp informs Y that this message is timely and not a replay. Y can store M and the signature. In case of dispute, Y, who claims to have received M from X, sends the following message to A:

$$E_{K_{ay}}\left[ID_X || M || E_{K_{xa}}[ID_X || H(M)]\right]$$

The arbiter uses K_{ay} to recover ID_X, M, and the signature, and then uses K_{xa} to decrypt the signature and verify the hash code. In this scheme, Y cannot directly check X's signature; the signature is there solely to settle disputes. Y considers the message from X authentic because it comes through A. In this scenario, both sides must have a high degree of trust in A:

- X must trust A not to reveal K_{xa} and not to generate false signatures of the form $E_{K_{xa}}[ID_X || H(M)]$.

- Y must trust A to send $E_{K_{ay}}\left[ID_X || M || E_{K_{xa}}[ID_X || H(M)]\right]$ only if the hash value is correct and the signature was generated by X.
- Both sides must trust A to resolve disputes fairly.

If the arbiter does live up to this trust, then X is assured that no one can forge his signature and Y is assured that X cannot disavow his signature.

The preceding scenario also implies that A is able to read messages from X to Y and, indeed, that any eavesdropper is able to do so. Table 5.4b shows a scenario that provides the arbitration as before but also assures confidentiality. In this case it is assumed that X and Y share the secret key K_{xy}. Now, X transmits an identifier, a copy of the message encrypted with K_{xy}, and a signature to A. The signature consists of the identifier plus the hash value of the encrypted message, all encrypted using K_{xa}. As before, A decrypts the signature and checks the hash value to validate the message. In this case, A is working only with the encrypted version of the message and is prevented from reading it. A then transmits everything that it received from X, plus a timestamp, all encrypted with K_{ay}, to Y.

Although unable to read the message, the arbiter is still in a position to prevent fraud on the part of either X or Y. A remaining problem, one shared with the first scenario, is that the arbiter could form an alliance with the sender to deny a signed message, or with the receiver to forge the sender's signature.

All the problems just discussed can be resolved by going to a public-key scheme, one version of which is shown in Table 5.4c. In this case, X double-encrypts a message M first with X's private key, KR_x, and then with Y's public key, KU_y. This is a signed, secret version of the message. Now, this signed message together with X's identifier is encrypted again with KR_x and, together with ID_X, is sent to A. The inner, double-encrypted message is secure from the arbiter (and everyone else except Y). However, A can decrypt to outer encryption to assure that the message must have come from X (because only X has KR_X). A checks to make sure that X's private/public key pair is still valid and, if so, verifies the message. Then A transmits a message to Y, encrypted with KR_a. The message includes ID_X, the double-encrypted message, and a timestamp.

This scheme has a number of advantages over the preceding two schemes. First, no information is shared among the parties before communication, preventing alliances to defraud. Second, no incorrectly dated message can be sent, even if KR_x is compromised, assuming that KR_a is not compromised. And finally, the content of the message from X to Y is secret from A and anyone else.

5.6

AUTHENTICATION PROTOCOLS

The basic tools described in Sections 5.1 through 5.4 are used in a variety of applications, including the digital signature discussed in Section 5.5. Other uses are numerous and growing. In this section, we focus on two general areas and examine some of the implications of authentication techniques in both.

Mutual Authentication

An important application area is that of mutual authentication protocols. Such protocols enable communicating parties to satisfy themselves mutually about each other's identity and to exchange session keys. This topic was examined in Section 3.3 (conventional techniques) and Section 4.3 (public-key techniques). There, the focus was key distribution. We return to this topic here to consider the wider implications of authentication.

Central to the problem of authenticated key exchange are two issues: confidentiality and timeliness. To prevent masquerade and to prevent compromise of session keys, essential identification and session key information must be communicated in encrypted form. This requires the prior existence of secret or public keys that can be used for this purpose. The second issue, timeliness, is important because of the threat of message replays. Such replays, at worst, can allow an opponent to compromise a session key or successfully impersonate another party. At minimum, a successful replay can disrupt operations by presenting parties with messages that appear genuine but are not.

[GONG93] lists the following examples of replay attacks:

- *Simple replay:* The opponent simply copies a message and replays it later.
- *Repetition that can be logged:* An opponent can replay a timestamped message within the valid time window.
- *Repetition that cannot be detected:* This situation could arise because the original message could have been suppressed and thus did not arrive at its destination; only the replay message arrived.
- *Backward replay without modification:* This is a replay back to the message sender. This attack is possible if conventional encryption is used and the sender cannot easily recognize the difference between messages sent and messages received on the basis of content.

One approach to coping with replay attacks is to attach a sequence number to each message used in an authentication exchange. A new message is accepted only if its sequence number is in the proper order. The difficulty with this approach is that it requires each party to keep track of the last sequence number for each claimant it has dealt with. Because of this overhead, sequence numbers are generally not used for authentication and key exchange. Instead, one of the following two general approaches is used:

- *Timestamps:* Party A accepts a message as fresh only if the message contains a timestamp that, in A's judgment, is close enough to A's knowledge of current time. This approach requires that clocks among the various participants be synchronized.

- *Challenge/Response:* Party A, expecting a fresh message from B, first sends B a nonce (challenge) to B and requires that the subsequent message (response) received from B contain the correct nonce value.

It can be argued (e.g., [LAM92a]) that the timestamp approach should not be used for connection-oriented applications because of the inherent difficulties with this technique. First, some sort of protocol is needed to maintain synchronization among the various processor clocks. This protocol must be both fault-tolerant, to cope with network errors, and secure, to cope with hostile attacks. Second, the opportunity for a successful attack will arise if there is a temporary loss of synchronization resulting from a fault in the clock mechanism of one of the parties. And finally, because of the variable and unpredictable nature of network delays, distributed clocks cannot be expected to maintain precise synchronization. Therefore, any timestamp-based procedure must allow for a window of time sufficiently large to accommodate network delays, yet sufficiently small to minimize the opportunity for attack.

On the other hand, the challenge-response approach is unsuitable for a connectionless type of application because it requires the overhead of a handshake before any connectionless transmission, effectively negating the chief characteristic of a connectionless transaction. For such applications, reliance on some sort of secure time server and a consistent attempt by each party to keep its clocks in synchronization may be the best approach (e.g., [LAM92b]).

Conventional Encryption Approaches

As was discussed in Section 3, a two-level hierarchy of conventional encryption keys can be used to provide confidentiality for communication in a distributed environment. In general, this strategy involves the use of a trusted key distribution center (KDC). Each party in the network shares a secret key, known as a master key, with the KDC. The KDC is responsible for generating keys to be used for a short time over a connection between two parties, known as session keys, and for distributing those keys using the master keys to protect the distribution. This approach is quite common. As an example, we look at the Kerberos system in Chapter 9. The discussion in this subsection is relevant to an understanding of the Kerberos mechanisms.

Figure 3.10 illustrates a proposal initially put forth by Needham and Schroeder [NEED78] for secret key distribution using a KDC, that, as was mentioned in Chapter 3, includes authentication features. The protocol[2] can be summarized as follows:

1. $A \rightarrow KDC$: $ID_A \mid\mid ID_B \mid\mid N_1$

2. $KDC \rightarrow A$: $E_{K_a}\left[K_s \mid\mid ID_B \mid\mid N_1 \mid\mid E_{K_b}[K_s \mid\mid ID_A]\right]$

3. $A \rightarrow B$: $E_{K_b}[K_s \mid\mid ID_A]$

---

[2]The following format is used. A communication step in which P sends a message M to Q is represented as $P \rightarrow Q$: M.

4. $B \rightarrow A$: $E_{K_s}[N_2]$

5. $A \rightarrow B$: $E_{K_s}\big[f(N_2)\big]$

Secret keys K_a and K_b are shared between A and the KDC and B and the KDC, respectively. The purpose of the protocol is to securely distribute a session key K_s to A and B. A securely acquires a new session key in step 2. The message in step 3 can be decrypted, and hence understood, only by B. Step 4 reflects B's knowledge of K_s, and step 5 assures B of A's knowledge of K_s and assures B that this is a fresh message, because of the use of the nonce N_2. Recall from our discussion in Chapter 3 that the purpose of steps 4 and 5 is to prevent a certain type of replay attack. In particular, if an opponent is able to capture the message in step 3 and replay it; this might in some fashion disrupt operations at B.

Despite the handshake of steps 4 and 5, the protocol is still vulnerable to a form of replay attack. Suppose that an opponent, X, has been able to compromise an old session key. Admittedly, this is a much more unlikely occurrence than that an opponent has simply observed and recorded step 3. Nevertheless, it is a potential security risk. X can impersonate A and trick B into using the old key by simply replaying step 3. Unless B remembers indefinitely all previous session keys used with A, B will be unable to determine that this is a replay. If C can intercept the handshake message, step 4, then it can impersonate A's response, step 5. From this point on, C can send bogus messages to B that appear to B to come from A using an authenticated session key.

Denning [DENN81, DENN82] proposes to overcome this weakness by a modification to the Needham/Schroeder protocol that includes the addition of a timestamp to steps 2 and 3. Her proposal assumes that the master keys, K_a and K_b, are secure, and consists of the following steps:

1. $A \rightarrow KDC$: $ID_A \mid\mid ID_B$

2. $KDC \rightarrow A$: $E_{K_a}\big[K_s \mid\mid ID_B \mid\mid T \mid\mid E_{K_b}[K_s \mid\mid ID_A \mid\mid T]\big]$

3. $A \rightarrow B$: $E_{K_b}[K_s \mid\mid ID_A \mid\mid T]$

4. $B \rightarrow A$: $E_{K_s}[N_1]$

5. $A \rightarrow B$: $E_{K_s}\big[f(N_1)\big]$

T is a timestamp that assures A and B that the session key has only just been generated. Thus, both A and B know that the key distribution is a fresh exchange. A and B can verify timeliness by checking that

$$|Clock - T| < \Delta t_1 + \Delta t_2$$

where Δt_1 is the estimated normal discrepancy between the KDC's clock and the local clock (at A or B), and Δt_2 is the expected network delay time. Each node can set its clock against some standard reference source. Because the timestamp T is encrypted using the secure master keys, an opponent, even with knowledge of an old session key, cannot succeed since a replay of step 3 will be detected by B as untimely.

A final point: Steps 4 and 5 were not included in the original presentation [DENN81] but were added later [DENN82]. These steps confirm the receipt of the session key at B.

The Denning protocol seems to provide an increased degree of security compared to the Needham/Schroeder protocol. However, a new concern is raised: namely, that this new scheme requires reliance on clocks that are synchronized throughout the network. [GONG92] points out a risk involved. The risk is based on the fact that the distributed clocks can become unsynchronized as a result of sabotage on or faults in the clocks or the synchronization mechanism.[3] The problem occurs when a sender's clock is ahead of the intended recipient's clock. In this case, an opponent can intercept a message from the sender and replay it later when the timestamp in the message becomes current at the recipient's site. This replay could cause unexpected results. Gong refers to such attacks as suppress-replay attacks.

One way to counter suppress-replay attacks is to enforce the requirement that parties regularly check their clocks against the KDC's clock. The other alternative, which avoids the need for clock synchronization altogether, is to rely on handshaking protocols using nonces. This latter alternative is not vulnerable to a suppress-replay attack because the nonces the recipient will choose in the future are unpredictable to the sender. The Needham/Schroeder protocol relies on nonces only but, as we have seen, has other vulnerabilities.

An attempt was made in [KEHN92] to respond to the concerns about suppress-replay attacks and at the same time to fix the problems in the Needham/Schroeder protocol. Subsequently, an inconsistency in this latter protocol was noted and an improved strategy was presented in [NEUM93a].[4] The protocol is as follows:

1. $A \rightarrow B$: $ID_A \mid\mid N_a$
2. $B \rightarrow KDC$: $ID_B \mid\mid N_b \mid\mid E_{K_b}[ID_A \mid\mid N_a \mid\mid T_b]$
3. $KDC \rightarrow A$: $E_{K_a}[ID_B \mid\mid N_a \mid\mid K_s \mid\mid T_b] \mid\mid E_{K_b}[ID_A \mid\mid K_s \mid\mid T_b] \mid\mid N_b$
4. $A \rightarrow B$: $E_{K_b}[ID_A \mid\mid K_s \mid\mid T_b] \mid\mid E_{K_s}[N_b]$

Let us follow this exchange step by step.

1. A initiates the authentication exchange by generating a nonce, N_a, and sending that plus its identifier to B in plaintext. This nonce will be returned to A in an encrypted message that includes the session key, assuring A of its timeliness.
2. B alerts the KDC that a session key is needed. Its message to the KDC includes its identifier and a nonce, N_b. This nonce will be returned to B in an

---

[3]Such things can and do happen. In recent years, flawed chips were used in a number of computers and other electronic systems to track the time and date. The chips had a tendency to skip forward one day [NEUM90].

[4]It really is hard to get these things right!

encrypted message that includes the session key, assuring B of its timeliness. B's message to the KDC also includes a block encrypted with the secret key shared by B and the KDC. This block is used to instruct the KDC to issue credentials to A; the block specifies the intended recipient of the credentials, a suggested expiration time for the credentials, and the nonce received from A.

3. The KDC passes on to A B's nonce and a block encrypted with the secret key that B shares with the KDC. The block serves as a "ticket" that can be used by A for subsequent authentications, as will be seen. The KDC also sends A a block encrypted with the secret key shared by A and the KDC. This block verifies that B has received A's initial message (ID_B) and that this is a timely message and not a replay (N_a), and provides A with a session key (K_s) and the time limit on its use (T_b).

4. A transmits the ticket to B, together with B's nonce, the latter encrypted with the session key. The ticket provides B with the secret key that is used to decrypt $E_{K_s}[N_b]$ to recover the nonce. The fact that B's nonce is encrypted with the session key authenticates that the message came from A and is not a replay.

This protocol provides an effective, secure means for A and B to establish a session with a secure session key. Furthermore, the protocol leaves A in possession of a ticket that can be used for subsequent authentication to B, avoiding the need to repeatedly contact the authentication server. Suppose that A and B establish a session using the above protocol and then conclude that session. Subsequently, but within the time limit established by the protocol, A desires a new session with B. The following protocol ensues:

1. $A \rightarrow B$: $E_{K_b}[ID_A || K_s || T_b], N_a'$
2. $B \rightarrow A$: $N_b', E_{K_s}[N_a']$
3. $A \rightarrow B$: $E_{K_s}[N_b']$

When B receives the message in step 1, it verifies that the ticket has not expired. The newly generated nonces N_a' and N_b' assure each party that there is no replay attack.

In all the foregoing, the time specified in T_b is a time relative to B's clock. Thus, this timestamp does not require synchronized clocks because B checks only self-generated timestamps.

Public-Key Encryption Approaches

In Chapter 4, we presented one approach to the use of public-key encryption for the purpose of session key distribution (Figure 4.16). This protocol assumes that each of the two parties is in possession of the current public key of the other. It may not be practical to require this assumption.

A protocol using timestamps is provided in [DENN81]:

1. $A \rightarrow AS$: $ID_A \mid\mid ID_B$
2. $AS \rightarrow A$: $E_{KR_{as}}[ID_A \mid\mid KU_a \mid\mid T] \mid\mid E_{KR_{as}}[ID_B \mid\mid KU_b \mid\mid T]$
3. $A \rightarrow B$: $E_{KR_{as}}[ID_A \mid\mid KU_a \mid\mid T] \mid\mid E_{KR_{as}}[ID_B \mid\mid KU_b \mid\mid T] \mid\mid E_{KU_B}\left[E_{KR_{aA}}[K_s \mid\mid T]\right]$

In this case, the central system is referred to as an authentication server (AS), because it is not actually responsible for secret key distribution. Rather, the AS provides public-key certificates. The session key is chosen and encrypted by A; hence, there is no risk of exposure by the AS. The timestamps protect against replays of compromised keys.

This protocol is compact but as before requires synchronization of clocks. Another approach, proposed by Woo and Lam [WOO92a], makes use of nonces. The protocol consists of the following steps:

1. $A \rightarrow KDC$: $ID_A \mid\mid ID_B$
2. $KDC \rightarrow A$: $E_{KR_{auth}}[ID_B \mid\mid KU_b]$
3. $A \rightarrow B$: $E_{KU_b}[N_a \mid\mid ID_A]$
4. $B \rightarrow KDC$: $ID_B \mid\mid ID_A \mid\mid E_{KU_{auth}}[N_a]$
5. $KDC \rightarrow B$: $E_{KR_{auth}}[ID_A \mid\mid KU_a] \mid\mid E_{KU_b}\left[E_{KR_{auth}}[N_a \mid\mid K_s \mid\mid ID_B]\right]$
6. $B \rightarrow A$: $E_{KU_a}\left[E_{KR_{auth}}[N_a \mid\mid K_s \mid\mid ID_B] \mid\mid N_b\right]$
7. $A \rightarrow B$: $E_{K_s}[N_b]$

In step 1, A informs the KDC of its intention to establish a secure connection with B. The KDC returns to A a copy of B's public-key certificate (step 2). Using B's public key, A informs B of its desire to communicate and sends a nonce N_a (step 3). In step 4, B asks the KDC for A's public-key certificate and requests a session key; B includes A's nonce so that the KDC can stamp the session key with that nonce. The nonce is protected using the KDC's public key. In step 5, the KDC returns to B a copy of A's public-key certificate, plus the information $\{N_a, K_s, ID_B\}$. This information basically says that K_s is a secret key generated by the KDC on behalf of B and tied to N_a; the binding of K_s and N_a will assure A that K_s is fresh. This triple is encrypted, using the KDC's private key, to allow B to verify that the triple is in fact from the KDC. It is also encrypted using B's public key, so that no other entity may use the triple in an attempt to establish a fraudulent connection with A. In step 6, the triple $\{N_a, K_s, ID_B\}$, still encrypted with the KDC's private key, is relayed to A, together with a nonce N_b generated by B. All the foregoing are encrypted using A's public key. A retrieves the session key K_s and uses it to encrypt N_b and return it to B. This last message assures B of A's knowledge of the session key.

This seems to be a secure protocol that takes into account the various attacks. However, the authors themselves spotted a flaw and submitted a revised version of the algorithm in [WOO92b]:

1. $A \rightarrow KDC$: $ID_A \,||\, ID_B$
2. $KDC \rightarrow A$: $E_{KR_{auth}}[ID_B \,||\, KU_b]$
3. $A \rightarrow B$: $E_{KU_b}[N_a \,||\, ID_A]$
4. $B \rightarrow KDC$: $ID_B \,||\, ID_A \,||\, E_{KU_{auth}}[N_a]$
5. $KDC \rightarrow B$: $E_{KR_{auth}}[ID_A \,||\, KU_a] \,||\, E_{KU_b}\!\left[E_{KR_{auth}}[N_a \,||\, K_s \,||\, ID_A \,||\, ID_B]\right]$
6. $B \rightarrow A$: $E_{KU_A}\!\left[E_{KR_{auth}}[N_a \,||\, K_s \,||\, ID_A \,||\, ID_B] \,||\, N_b\right]$
7. $A \rightarrow B$: $E_{K_s}[N_b]$

The identifier of A, ID_A, is added to the set of items encrypted with the KDC's private key in steps 5 and 6. This binds the session key K_s to the identities of the two parties that will be engaged in the session. This inclusion of ID_A accounts for the fact that the nonce value N_a is considered unique only among all nonces generated by A, not among all nonces generated by all parties. Thus, it is the pair $\{ID_A, N_a\}$ that uniquely identifies the connection request of A.

In both this example and the protocols described earlier, protocols that appeared secure were revised after additional analysis. These examples highlight the difficulty of getting things right the first time in the area of authentication.

One-Way Authentication

One application for which encryption is growing in popularity is electronic mail (e-mail). The very nature of electronic mail, and its key benefit, is that it is not necessary for the sender and receiver to be on-line at the same time. Instead, the e-mail message is forwarded to the receiver's electronic mailbox, where it is buffered until the receiver is available to read it.

The "envelope" or header of the e-mail message must be in the clear, so that the message can be handled by the store-and-forward e-mail protocol, such as X.400 or the Simple Mail Transfer Protocol (SMTP). However, it is often desirable that the mail-handling protocol not require access to the plaintext form of the message, because that would require trusting the mail-handling mechanism. Accordingly, the e-mail message should be encrypted such that the mail-handling system is not in possession of the decryption key.

A second requirement is that of authentication. Typically, the recipient wants some assurance that the message is from the alleged sender.

Conventional Encryption Approach

Using conventional encryption, the decentralized key distribution scenario illustrated in Figure 3.12 is impractical. This scheme requires the sender to issue a request to the intended recipient, await a response that includes a session key, and only then send the message.

With some refinement, the KDC strategy illustrated in Figure 3.10 is a candidate for encrypted electronic mail. Because we wish to avoid requiring that the recipient (B) be on line at the same time as the sender (A), steps 4 and 5 must be eliminated. For a message with content M, the sequence is as follows:

1. $A \rightarrow KDC$: $ID_A || ID_B || N_1$
2. $KDC \rightarrow A$: $E_{K_a}\big[K_s || ID_B || N_1 || E_{K_b}[K_s || ID_A]\big]$
3. $A \rightarrow B$: $E_{K_b}[K_s, ID_A] || E_{K_s}(M)$

This approach guarantees that only the intended recipient of a message will be able to read it. It also provides a level of authentication that the sender is A. As specified, the protocol does not protect against replays. Some measure of defense could be provided by including a timestamp with the message. However, because of the potential delays in the e-mail process, such timestamps may have limited usefulness.

Public-Key Encryption Approaches

We have already presented public-key encryption approaches that are suited to electronic mail, including the straightforward encryption of the entire message for confidentiality (Figure 5.1b), authentication (Figure 5.1c), or both (Figure 5.1d). These approaches require that either the sender know the recipient's public key (confidentiality), or that the recipient know the sender's public key (authentication), or both (confidentiality plus authentication). In addition, the public-key algorithm must be applied once or twice to what may be a long message.

If confidentiality is the primary concern, then the following may be more efficient:

$A \rightarrow B$: $E_{KU_b}(K_s) || E_{K_s}(M)$

In this case, the message is encrypted with a one-time secret key. A also encrypts this one-time key with B's public key. Only B will be able to use the corresponding private key to recover the one-time key and then use that key to decrypt the message. This scheme is more efficient than simply encrypting the entire message with B's public key.

If authentication is the primary concern, then a digital signature may suffice, as was illustrated in Figure 5.5c:

$A \rightarrow B$: $M || E_{KR_a}[H(M)]$

This method guarantees that A cannot later deny having sent the message. However, this technique is open to another kind of fraud. Bob composes a message to his boss Alice that contains an idea that will save the company money. He appends his digital signature and sends it into the e-mail system. Eventually, the message will get delivered to Alice's mailbox. But suppose that Max has heard of Bob's idea and gains access to the mail queue before delivery. He finds Bob's message, strips off his signature, appends his, and requeues the message to be delivered to Alice. Max gets credit for Bob's idea.

To counter such a scheme, both the message and signature can be encrypted with the recipient's public key:

$$A \rightarrow B: \quad E_{KU_b}\left[M \mid\mid E_{KR_a}[H(M)]\right]$$

The latter two schemes require that B know A's public key and be convinced that it is timely. An effective way to provide this assurance is the digital certificate, described in Chapter 4. Now we have:

$$A \rightarrow B: \quad M \mid\mid E_{KR_a}[H(M)] \mid\mid E_{KR_{as}}[T \mid\mid ID_A \mid\mid KU_a]$$

In addition to the message, A sends B the signature, encrypted with A's private key, and A's certificate, encrypted with the private key of the authentication server. The recipient of the message first uses the certificate to obtain the sender's public key and verify that it is authentic and then uses the public key to verify the message itself. If confidentiality is required, then the entire message can be encrypted with B's public key.

5.7

RECOMMENDED READING

[WOO92a] is an excellent survey of various aspects of authentication. [JUEN85] and [JUEN87] focus on cryptographic checksums and hash functions. [SIMM92b] provides a more abstract, mathematical treatment of authentication. [LAMP92] presents a formalism for characterizing authentication protocols, together with a number of examples of its use.

[AKL83] is the classic paper on digital signatures, and is still highly relevant. A more recent, and excellent, survey is [MITC92].

AKL83   Akl, S. "Digital Signatures: A Tutorial Survey." *Computer,* February 1983.
JUEN85   Jueneman, R.; Matyas, S.; and Meyer, C. "Message Authentication." *IEEE Communications Magazine,* September 1985.
JUEN87   Jueneman, R. "Electronic Document Authentication." *IEEE Network Magazine,* April 1987.
LAMP92   Lampson, B.; Abadi, M.; Burrows, M.; and Wobber, E. "Authentication in Distributed Systems: Theory and Practice. *ACM Transactions on Computer Systems,* November 1992.
MITC92   Mitchell, C.; Piper, F. ; and Wild, P. "Digital Signatures." in [SIMM92a].
SIMM92a   Simmons, G., editor. *Contemporary Cryptology: The Science of Information Integrity.* Piscataway, NJ: IEEE Press, 1992.
SIMM92b   Simmons, G. "A Survey of Information Authentication." in [SIMM92a].

WOO92a   Woo, T., and Lam, S. " 'Authentication for Distributed Systems." *Computer*, January 1992.

5.8

PROBLEMS

5.1 In Section 5.6, we outlined the public-key scheme proposed in [WOO92a] for the distribution of secret keys. The revised version includes ID_A in steps 5 and 6. What attack, specifically, is countered by this revision?

5.2 The protocol referred to in Problem 5.1 can be reduced from seven steps to five, having the following sequence:

$$(1) \quad A \to B:$$
$$(2) \quad B \to KDC:$$
$$(3) \quad KDC \to B:$$
$$(4) \quad B \to A:$$
$$(5) \quad A \to B:$$

Show the message transmitted at each step. Hint: the final message in this protocol is the same as the final message in the original protocol.

5.3 If F is an error-detection function, either internal or external use (Figure 5.2) will provide error-detection capability. If any bit of the transmitted message is altered, this will be reflected in a mismatch of the received FCS and the calculated FCS, whether the FCS function is performed inside or outside the encryption function. Some codes also provide an error-correction capability. Depending on the nature of the function, if one or a small number of bits is altered in transit, the error-correction code contains sufficient redundant information to determine the errored bit or bits and correct them. Clearly, an error-correction code will provide error correction capability when used external to the encryption function. Will it also provide this capability if used internal to the encryption function?

5.4 The data authentication algorithm, described in Section 5.3, can be defined as using the cipher block chaining (CBC) mode of operation of DES with an initialization vector of zero (Figure 5.6). Show that the same result can be produced using the cipher feedback mode.

5.5 The high-speed transport protocol XTP (Xpress Transfer Protocol) uses a 32-bit checksum function defined as the concatenation of two 16-bit functions: XOR, and RXOR, defined in Section 5.4 as "two simple hash functions" and illustrated in Figure 5.8.

   a. Will this checksum detect all errors caused by an odd number of error bits? Explain.

   b. Will this checksum detect all errors caused by an even number of error bits? If not, characterize the error patterns that will cause the checksum to fail.

   c. Comment on the effectiveness of this function for use as a hash function for authentication.

5.6 **a.** Consider the Davies and Price hash code scheme described in Section 5.4 and assume that DES is used as the encryption algorithm:

$$H_i = E_{M_i}[H_{i-1}] \oplus H_{i-1}$$

and recall the complementarity property of DES (Problem 2.11): If $Y = DES_K(X)$, then $Y' = DES_{K'}(X')$. Use this property to show how a message consisting of blocks $M_1, M_2, \ldots, M_N$ can be altered without altering its hash code.

   b. Show that a similar attack will succeed against the scheme proposed in [MEYE88]:

$$H_i = E_{H_{i-1}}[M_i] \oplus M_i$$

5.7 It is possible to use a hash function to construct a block cipher with a structure similar to DES. Because a hash function is one-way and a block cipher must be reversible (to decrypt), how is it possible?

5.8 Now consider the opposite problem: using an encryption algorithm to construct a one-way hash function. Consider using RSA with a known key. Then, process a message consisting of a sequence of blocks as follows: Encrypt the first block, XOR the result with the second block and encrypt again, etc. Show that this scheme is not secure by solving the following problem. Given a two-block message B1, B2, and its hash

$$RSAH(B1, B2) = RSA(RSA(B1) \oplus B2)$$

Given an arbitrary block C1, choose C2 so that RSAH(C1, C2) = RSAH(B1, B2).

5.9 In the E512 function of Snefru (Figure 5.11), the function ends with an exchange that reverses the encrypted block. What is the purpose of this exchange?

5.10 Also in E512, StandardSBoxes is declared an ARRAY [1 . . passes*2] of ARRAY [0 . . 255] of int32. This defines an array of S-boxes, where each individual S-box has 256 entries of 32 bits. Why not use a single S-box, i.e., declare StandardSBox: ARRAY [0 . . 255] of int32? This would eliminate the rather complicated subscript computations that determine which S-box to use in each table lookup.

5.11 Modify the digital signature techniques of Table 5.4a and b to enable the receiver to verify the signature.

5.12 Modify the digital signature technique of Table 5.4c to avoid triple encryption of the entire message.

5.13 In discussing Table 5.4c, it was stated that alliances to defraud were impossible. In fact, there is one possibility. Describe it and explain why it would have so little credibility that we can safely ignore it.

5.14 With reference to the suppress-replay attack described in Section 5.6:

a. Give an example of an attack when a party's clock is ahead of that of the KDC.

b. Give an example of an attack when a party's clock is ahead of that of the another party.

5.15 There are three typical ways to use nonces as challenges. Suppose N_a is a nonce generated by A, A and B share key K, and f() is a function such as increment. The three usages are:

Usage 1	**Usage 2**	**Usage 3**
1. A → B: N_a	1. A → B: $E_K[N_a]$	1. A → B: $E_K[N_a]$
2. B → A: $E_K[N_a]$	2. B → A: N_a	2. B → A: $E_K[f(N_a)]$

Describe situations for which each usage is appropriate.

5.16 Dr. Watson patiently waited until Sherlock Holmes finished his work at his workstation. "Some interesting problem to solve, Holmes?" he asked when Holmes finally logged out.

"Oh, not exactly. I merely checked my e-mail and then made a couple of network experiments instead of my usual chemical ones. I have only one client now and I have already solved his problem. If I remember correctly, you once mentioned cryptology among your other hobbies, so it may be of interest to you too."

"Well, I am only an amateur cryptologist, Holmes. But of course I am interested in the problem. What is it about?"

"My client is Mr. Hosgrave, director of a small but progressive bank. The bank is fully computerized and of course uses network communications extensively. They already use RSA to protect their data and to digitally sign documents that are communicated. Now they want to introduce some changes in their procedures; in particular they need to digitally sign some documents by two signatories so that

1. The first signatory prepares the document, forms its signature, and passes the document to the second signatory.

2. The second signatory as a first step must verify that the document was really signed by the first signatory. She then incorporates her signature into the document signature so that the recipient, as well as any member of the public, may verify that the document was indeed signed by both signatories. In addition only the second signatory has to be able to verify the document's signature after step (1); that is, the recipient (or any member of the public) should be able to verify only the complete document with signatures of both signatories, but not the document in its intermediate form where only one signatory has signed it. Moreover, they would like to make use of their existing modules that support RSA-style digital signatures."

"Hm, I understand how RSA can be used to digitally sign documents by one signatory, Holmes. I guess you have solved the problem of Mr. Hosgrave by appropriate generalization of RSA digital signatures."

"Exactly, Watson," nodded Sherlock Holmes. "Originally, the RSA digital signature was formed by encrypting the document by the signatory's private decryption key 'd', and the signature could be verified by anyone through its decryption using publicly known encryption key 'e'. One can verify that the signature S was formed by the person who knows d, which is supposed to be the only signatory. Now the problem of Mr. Hosgrave can be solved in the same way by slight generalization of the process, that is . . .

APPENDIX 5A

MATHEMATICAL BASIS OF BIRTHDAY ATTACK

In this appendix, we derive the mathematical justification for the birthday attack. We begin with a related problem and then look at the problem from which the name "birthday attack" is derived.

Related Problem

A general problem relating to hash functions is the following. Given a hash function H, with n possible outputs and a specific value $H(x)$, if H is applied to k random inputs, what must be the value of k so that the probability that at least one input y satisfies $H(y) = H(x)$ is 0.5?

For a single value of y, the probability that $H(y) = H(x)$ is just $1/n$. Conversely, the probability that $H(y) \neq H(x)$ is $[1 - (1/n)]$. If we generate k random values of y, then the probability that none of them match is just the product of the probabilities that each individual value does not match, or $[1 - (1/n)]^k$. Thus the probability that there is at least one match is $1 - [1 - (1/n)]^k$.

Now, the binomial theorem can be stated as follows:

$$(1-a)^k = 1 - ka + \frac{k(k-1)}{2!}a^2 - \frac{k(k-1)(k-2)}{3!}a^3 + \ldots$$

For very small values of a, this can be approximated as $(1 - ka)$. Thus, the probability of at least one match is approximately k/n. For a probability of 0.5, we have $k = n/2$.

In particular, for an m-bit hash code, the number of possible codes is 2^m and the value of k that produces a probability of one half is $2^{(m-1)}$.

The Birthday Paradox

The birthday paradox is often presented in elementary probability courses to demonstrate that probability results are sometimes counterintuitive. The problem can be stated as follows: What is the minimum value of k such that the probability is greater than 0.5 that at least two people in a group of k people have the same birthday? Ignore February 29th and assume that each birthday is equally likely. To answer, let us define:

P(n, k) = Pr [at least one duplicate in k items, with each item able to take on one of n equally likely values between 1 and n]

Thus, we are looking for the smallest value of k such that P(365, k) ≥ 0.5. It is easier to first derive the probability that there are no duplicates, which we designate as Q(365, k). If k > 365, then it is impossible for all values to be different. So, we assume k ≤ 365. Now, consider the number of different ways, N, that we can have k values with no duplicates. We may choose any of the 365 values for the first item, any of the remaining 364 numbers for the second item, and so on. Hence, the number of different ways is:

$$N = 365 \times 364 \times \cdots \times (365 - k + 1) = \frac{365!}{(365 - k)!} \tag{5.1}$$

If we remove the restriction that there are no duplicates, then each item can be any of 365 values, and the total number of possibilities is 365^k. So the probability of no duplicates is simply the fraction of sets of values that have no duplicates out of all possible sets of values:

$$Q(365, k) = \frac{365!/(365 - k)!}{365^k} = \frac{365!}{(365 - k)!\,365^k}$$

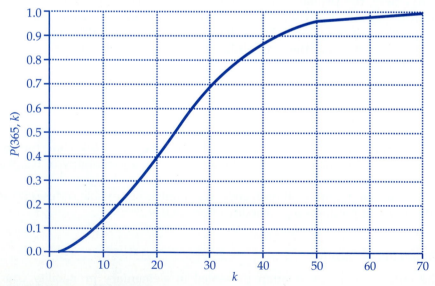

FIGURE 5.13.   The Birthday Paradox

And

$$P(365, k) = 1 - Q(365, k) = 1 - \frac{365!}{(365 - k)! \, k^{365}} \qquad (5.2)$$

This function is plotted in Figure 5.13. The probabilities may seem surprisingly large to anyone who has not considered the problem before. Many people would guess that to have a probability greater than 0.5 that there is at least one duplicate, the number of people in the group would have to be about 100. In fact, the number is 23, with $P(365, 23) = 0.5073$. For $k = 100$, the probability of at least one duplicate is 0.9999997.

Perhaps the reason that the result seems so surprising is that if you consider a particular person in a group, the probability that some other person in the group has the same birthday is small. But the probability that we are concerned with is the probability that *any* pair of people in the group has the same birthday. In a group of 23, there are $[23(23 - 1)]/2 = 253$ different pairs of people. Hence, the high probabilities.

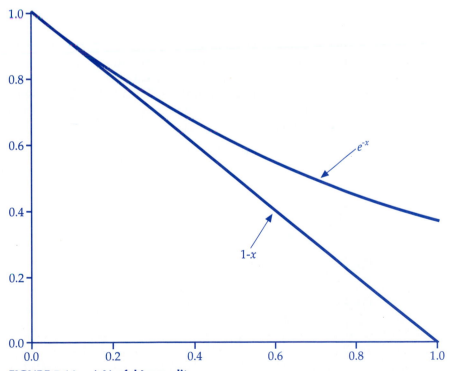

FIGURE 5.14.   A Useful Inequality

Useful Inequality

Before developing a generalization of the birthday problem, we derive an inequality that will be needed:

$$(1 - x) \leq e^{-x} \qquad \text{for all } x \geq 0 \tag{5.3}$$

Figure 5.14 demonstrates the inequality. To see that the inequality holds, note that the lower line is the tangent to e^{-x} at $x = 0$. The slope of that line is just the derivative of e^{-x} at $x = 0$:

$$f(x) = e^{-x}$$
$$f'(x) = \frac{d}{dx} e^{-x} = -e^{-x}$$
$$f'(0) = -1$$

The tangent is a straight line of the form $ax + b$, with $a = -1$, and the tangent at $x = 0$ must equal $e^{-0} = 1$. Thus, the tangent is the function $(1 - x)$, confirming the inequality of Equation (5.3).

The General Case of Duplications

The birthday problem can be generalized to the following problem: Given a random variable that is an integer with uniform distribution between 1 and n, and a selection of k instances ($k \leq n$) of the random variable, what is the probability, $P(n, k)$, that there is at least one duplicate? The birthday problem is just the special case with $n = 365$. By the same reasoning as before, we have the following generalization of Equation (5.2):

$$P(n, k) = 1 - \frac{n!}{(n - k)! n^k} \tag{5.4}$$

We can rewrite as:

$$P(n, k) = 1 - \frac{n \times (n - 1) \times \cdots \times (n - k + 1)}{n^k}$$

$$P(n, k) = 1 - \left[\frac{n - 1}{n} \times \frac{n - 2}{n} \times \cdots \times \frac{n - k + 1}{n} \right]$$

$$P(n, k) = 1 - \left[\left(1 - \frac{1}{n}\right) \times \left(1 - \frac{2}{n}\right) \times \cdots \times \left(1 - \frac{k - 1}{n}\right) \right]$$

Using the inequality of Equation (5.3):

$$P(n,k) > 1 - \left[\left(e^{-1/n}\right) \times \left(e^{-2/n}\right) \times \cdots \times \left(e^{-(k-1)/n}\right)\right]$$

$$P(n,k) > 1 - e^{-\left[1/n + 2/n + \cdots + (k-1)/n\right]}$$

$$P(n,k) > 1 - e^{-[k \times (k-1)]/2n}$$

Now, let us pose the question, what value of k is required such that $P(n, k) > 0.5$? To satisfy the requirement, we have:

$$\frac{1}{2} = 1 - e^{-[k \times (k-1)]/2n}$$

$$2 = e^{[k \times (k-1)]/2n}$$

$$\ln(2) = \frac{k \times (k - 1)}{2n}$$

For large k, we can replace $k \times (k - 1)$ by k^2, and we get:

$$k = \sqrt{2(\ln 2)n} = 1.17\sqrt{n} \approx \sqrt{n} \tag{5.5}$$

As a reality check, for $n = 365$, we get $k = 1.17 \times \sqrt{365} = 22.35$, which is very close to the correct answer of 23.

We can now state the basis of the birthday attack in the following terms. Suppose a function H, with 2^m possible outputs (i.e., an m-bit output). If H is applied to k random inputs, what must be the value of k so that there is the probability of at least one duplicate [i.e., H(x) = H(y) for some inputs x, y]? Using the approximation in (5.5):

$$k = \sqrt{2^m} = 2^{m/2}$$

Overlap Between Two Sets

There is a problem related to the general case of duplications that is also of relevance for our discussions. The problem is this: Given a random variable that is an integer with uniform distribution between 1 and n, and two sets of k instances ($k \leq n$) of the random variable, what is the probability, R(n, k), that the two sets are not disjoint; that is, what is the probability that there is at least one value found in both sets?

Let us call the two sets X and Y, with elements $\{x_1, x_2, \ldots, x_k\}$ and $\{y_1, y_2, \ldots, y_k\}$, respectively. Given the value of x_1, the probability that $y_1 = x_1$ is just $1/n$, and therefore the probability that y_1 does not match x_1 is $[1 - (1/n)]$. Now, if we generate the k random values in Y, the probability that none of these values is equal to x_1 is $[1 - (1/n)]^k$. Thus, the probability that there is at least one match to x_1 is $1 - [1 - (1/n)]^k$.

To proceed, let us make the assumption that all the elements of X are distinct. If n is large, and if k is also large (e.g., on the order of $\sqrt{n}$, then this is a good approximation. In fact, there may be a few duplications but most of the values will be distinct. With that assumption, we can make the following derivation:

$$\Pr[\text{no match in Y to } x_1] = \left(1 - \frac{1}{n}\right)^k$$

$$\Pr[\text{ no match in Y to X}] = \left[\left(1 - \frac{1}{n}\right)^k\right]^k = \left(1 - \frac{1}{n}\right)^{k^2}$$

$$R(n, k) = \Pr[\text{ at least one match in Y to X}] = 1 - \left(1 - \frac{1}{n}\right)^{k^2}$$

Using the inequality of (5.3):

$$R(n, k) > 1 - \left(e^{-1/n}\right)^{k^2}$$

$$R(n, k) > 1 - \left(e^{-k^2/n}\right)$$

Now, let us pose the questions, what value of k is required such that $R(n,k) > 0.5$? To satisfy the requirement, we have:

$$\frac{1}{2} = 1 - \left(e^{-k^2/n}\right)$$

$$2 = e^{k^2/n}$$

$$\ln(2) = \frac{k^2}{n}$$

$$k = \sqrt{(\ln 2)n} = 0.83\sqrt{n} \approx \sqrt{n} \tag{5.6}$$

We can state this in terms related to birthday attacks as follows. Suppose a function H, with 2^m possible outputs (i.e., an m-bit output). Apply H to k random inputs to produce the set X and again to k additional random inputs to produce the set Y. What must be the value of k so that there is the probability of 0.5 of at least one match between the two sets (i.e., $H(x) = H(y)$ for some inputs $x \in X, y \in Y$)? Using the approximation in (5.6):

$$k = \sqrt{2^m} = 2^{m/2}$$

CHAPTER 6

INTRUDERS, VIRUSES, AND WORMS

What is the concept of defense: The parrying of a blow. What is its characteristic feature: Awaiting the blow.

> — *On War*
> Carl Von Clausewitz

The art of war teaches us to rely not on the likelihood of the enemy's not coming, but on our own readiness to receive him; not on the chance of his not attacking, but rather on the fact that we have made our position unassailable.

> — *The Art of War*
> Sun Tzu

The developers of secure software cannot adopt the various probabilistic measures of quality that developers of other software often can. For many applications, it is quite reasonable to tolerate a flaw that is rarely exposed and to assume that its having occurred once does not increase the likelihood that it will occur again. It is also reasonable to assume that logically independent failures will be statistically independent and not happen in concert. In contrast, a security vulnerability, once discovered, will be rapidly disseminated among a community of attackers and can be expected to be exploited on a regular basis until it is fixed.

> — *Computers at Risk: Safe Computing in the Information Age*
> National Research Council, 1991

They agreed that Graham should set the test for Charles Mabledene. It was neither more nor less than that Dragon should get Stern's code. If he had the 'in' at Utting which he claimed to have this should be possible, only loyalty to Moscow Centre would prevent it. If he got the key to the code he would prove his loyalty to London Central beyond a doubt.

> — *Talking to Strange Men*
> Ruth Rendell

A significant security problem for networked systems is hostile, or at least un-wanted, trespass by users or software. User trespass can take the form of unauthorized logon to a machine or, in the case of an authorized user, acquiring privileges or performing actions beyond those that have been authorized. Software trespass can take the form of a virus, worm, or Trojan horse.

All these attacks relate to network security because entry to a system can be achieved by means of a network. However, these attacks are not confined to network-based attacks. A user with access to a local terminal may attempt trespass without using an intermediate network. A virus or Trojan horse may be introduced into a system by means of a diskette. Only the worm is a uniquely network phenomenon. Thus, system trespass is an area where the concerns of network security and computer security overlap.

Because the focus of this book is network security, we do not attempt a comprehensive analysis of either the attacks or the security countermeasures related to system trespass. Instead, a broad overview of these concerns is presented in this chapter.

The chapter begins with the subject of intruders. First, we examine the nature of the attack and then look at strategies intended for prevention and, failing that, detection. Next, the well-publicized topic of viruses is examined. Then, we discuss network worms. Finally, this chapter introduces some concepts related to access control and trusted systems.

6.1

INTRUDERS

One of the two most publicized threats to security (the other is viruses) is the intruder, generally referred to as a hacker or cracker. In an important early study of intrusion, Anderson [ANDE80] identified three classes of intruders:

- *Masquerader:* An individual who is not authorized to use the computer, and who penetrates a system's access controls to exploit a legitimate user's account.
- *Misfeasor:* A legitimate user who accesses data, programs, or resources for which such access is not authorized, or who is authorized for such access but misuses his or her privileges.
- *Clandestine user:* An individual who seizes supervisory control of the system and uses this control to evade auditing and access controls or to suppress audit collection altogether.

The masquerader is likely to be an outsider; the misfeasor generally is an insider; and the clandestine user can be either an outsider or an insider.

Intruder attacks range from the benign to the serious. At the benign end of the scale, there are many people who simply wish to explore internets and see what is out there. At the serious end are individuals who are attempting to read privileged data, perform unauthorized modifications to data, or disrupt the system.

The intruder threat has been well publicized, particularly because the famous "Wily Hacker" incident of 1986-1987, documented by Cliff Stoll [STOL88, 89].

Then, in 1990 there was a nationwide crackdown on illicit computer hackers, with arrests, criminal charges, one dramatic show trial, several guilty pleas, and confiscation of massive amounts of data and computer equipment [STER92]. Many people believed that the problem had been brought under control.

In fact, the problem has not been brought under control. To cite one recent example, a group at Bell Labs [BELL92, BELL93] has reported persistent and frequent attacks on their computer complex via the Internet over an extended period and from a variety of sources. At the time of these reports, they were experiencing the following:

- Attempts to copy the password file (discussed later) at a rate exceeding once every other day
- Suspicious remote procedure call (RPC) requests at a rate exceeding once per week
- Attempts to connect to nonexistent "bait" machines at least every two weeks

Benign intruders might be tolerable, although they do consume resources and may slow performance for legitimate users. However, there is no way in advance to know whether an intruder will be benign or malign. Consequently, even for systems with no particularly sensitive resources, there is a motivation to control this problem. Furthermore, serious attacks from intruders are a real and growing problem. [FREE93] lists the following as key reasons for this trend:

- *Globalization:* The pressures of international competition have spawned a number of recent cases of industrial espionage. There is also evidence that a number of the "hacker clubs" are beginning to sell their services for this purpose.
- *The move to client/server architecture:* Companies have traditionally kept most of their data either on mainframes, which can be guarded with sophisticated security software, or on stand-alone PCs, which usually have not been accessible remotely. But as client/server architectures become increasingly popular, both barriers are removed (e.g., see [STAL94b] for a description of such architectures). Most servers run UNIX, which is notorious for its lack of mainframe-style security features and is a particular favorite of hackers.
- *Hackers' steep learning curve:* Hackers love to share information. Underground bulletin boards are used to exchange dial-in port phone numbers, compromised passwords, security holes in systems, and intrusion techniques [HAFN91, STER92]. Because of a natural reluctance of security and systems personnel to share security-related information, especially concerning vulnerabilities, intruders are better able than their adversaries to stay abreast of the latest tricks of the trade and corporate vulnerabilities. Furthermore, when security personnel do exchange information about vulnerabilities, attackers can often eavesdrop and exploit these vulnerabilities before the holes are plugged on all affected systems.

An example that dramatically illustrates this last point occurred at Texas A&M University [SAFF93]. In August 1992, the computer center there was notified that one of their machines was being used to attack computers at another location via the Internet. By monitoring activity, the computer center personnel learned that there were several outside intruders involved who were running password-cracking routines on various computers (the site consists of a total of 12,000 inter-connected machines). The center disconnected affected machines, plugged known security holes, and resumed normal operation. A few days later, one of the local system managers detected that the intruder attack had resumed. It turned out that the attack was far more sophisticated than had been originally believed. Files were found containing hundreds of captured passwords, including some on major and supposedly secure servers. In addition, one local machine had been set up as a hacker bulletin board, which the hackers used to contact each other and to discuss techniques and progress.

An analysis of this attack revealed that there were actually two levels of hackers. The high level were sophisticated users with a thorough knowledge of the technology; the low level were the "foot soldiers" who merely used the supplied cracking programs with little understanding of how they worked. This teamwork combined the two most serious weapons in the intruder armory: sophisticated knowledge of how to intrude and a willingness to spend countless hours "turning doorknobs" to probe for weaknesses.

One of the results of the growing awareness of the intruder problem has been the establishment of a number of Computer Emergency Response Teams (CERTs). These cooperative ventures collect information about system vulnerabilities and disseminate it to systems managers. Unfortunately, hackers can also gain access to CERT reports. In the Texas A&M incident, later analysis showed that the hackers had developed programs to test the attacked machines for virtually every vulnerability that had been announced by CERT. If even one machine had failed to respond promptly to a CERT advisory, it was wide open to such attacks.

In addition to running password-cracking programs, the intruders attempted to modify log-in software to enable them to capture passwords of users logging on to systems. This made it possible for them to build up an impressive collection of compromised passwords, which was made available on the bulletin board set up on one of the victim's own machines!

We begin this section by looking at the techniques used for intrusion. Then we examine ways to prevent intrusion. Failing prevention, intrusion detection is a second line of defense and is discussed in the final section.

Intrusion Techniques

The objective of the intruder is to gain access to a system or to increase the range of privileges accessible on a system. Generally, this requires the intruder to acquire information that should have been protected. In most cases, this information is in the form of a user password. With knowledge of some other user's password, an intruder can log in to a system and exercise all the privileges accorded to the legitimate user.

Typically, a system must maintain a file that associates a password with each authorized user. If such a file is stored with no protection, then it is an easy matter to gain access to it and learn passwords. The password file can be protected in one of two ways:

- *One-way encryption:* The system stores only an encrypted form of the user's password. When the user presents a password, the system encrypts that password and compares it with the stored value. In practice, the system usually performs a one-way transformation (not reversible) in which the password is used to generate a key for the encryption function and in which a fixed-length output is produced.
- *Access control:* Access to the password file is limited to one or a very few accounts.

If one or both of these countermeasures are in place, some effort is needed for a potential intruder to learn passwords. On the basis of a survey of the literature and interviews with a number of password crackers, [ALVA90] reports the following techniques for learning passwords:

1. Try default passwords used with standard accounts that are shipped with the system. Many administrators don't bother to change these defaults.
2. Exhaustively try all short passwords (those of one to three characters).
3. Try words in the system's on-line dictionary or a list of likely passwords. Examples of the latter are readily available on hacker bulletin boards.
4. Collect information about users, such as their full names, the names of their spouse and children, pictures in their office, and books in the office that are related to hobbies.
5. Try users' phone numbers, Social Security numbers, and room numbers.
6. Try all legitimate license plate numbers for this state.
7. Use a Trojan horse (described in Section 6.2) to bypass restrictions on access.
8. Tap the line between a remote user and the host system.
9. Pretend to be a legitimate user and ask the operator or system manager to give you a new password.
10. Observe passwords written down in a temporarily unoccupied office, or observe the user typing in his or her password.

The first six methods are various ways of guessing a password. Now, if an intruder has to verify the guess by attempting to login, it is a tedious and easily countered means of attack. For example, a system can simply reject any login after three password attempts, thus requiring the intruder to reconnect to the host to try again. Under these circumstances, it is not practical to try more than a handful of passwords. However, the intruder is unlikely to try such crude methods. For example, if an intruder can gain access with a low level of privileges to an encrypted password file, then the strategy would be to capture that file and then use the encryption mechanism of that particular system at leisure until a valid password that provided greater privileges is discovered.

A similar strategy is effective if encrypted passwords are used over a network. For example, in the Kerberos protocol, discussed in Chapter 8, a key distribution center encrypts its initial response packet using a key derived from a user's password. Therefore, an opponent can observe the packet and attempt to match it by encrypting a series of guesses of the password. The opponent can readily determine if a guess is valid if the computed ciphertext matches the observed ciphertext.

Guessing attacks are feasible, and indeed highly effective, when a large number of guesses can be attempted automatically and each guess verified without the guessing process being detectable. Later in this section, we have much to say about thwarting guessing attacks.

The seventh method of attack listed earlier, the Trojan horse, can be particularly difficult to counter. An example of a program that bypasses access controls was cited in [ALVA90]. A low-privilege user produced a game program and invited the system operator to use it in his spare time. The program did indeed play a game, but in the background, it also contained code to copy the password file, which was unencrypted but access-protected, into the user's file. Because the game was running under the operator's high-privilege mode, it was able to gain access to the password file.

The eighth attack listed, line tapping, is a matter of physical security. It can be countered with link encryption techniques.

Because the last two attacks in the list are nontechnical, the response generally must also be nontechnical. It is worth elaborating on the nature of such attacks. [KAPL93] provides the following lists of methods that have been used:

- *Misrepresentation, deceit, and fraud:* This is the area commonly referred to as "social engineering" by hackers [HAFN91]. Examples include pretending to be a secretary whose boss has forgotten his or her password and needs it immediately, pretending to be a maintenance engineer and asking for access to the system, and simply chatting with a victim and trying to elicit information that can be used to guess passwords.
- *Bribes:* This would not be the method of choice for the individual hacker but is certainly within the realm of possibility for industrial espionage.
- *Forced disclosure:* Threats, blackmail, or other means of intimidation can be used to obtain the wanted information and to silence the source.
- *Intelligence-based attacks:* This refers to a variety of techniques traditionally used by intelligence operatives to gain information. The hope is either to directly obtain wanted information or to collect enough seemingly unrelated information for use as a basis for achieving the ultimate goal. Techniques include examining trash and loose paper, in the building if possible or even in the outside dumpster, eavesdropping on conversations, collecting and collating personal information on employees, and so on.

We turn now to a discussion of the two principal countermeasures: prevention and detection. Prevention is a challenging security goal and an uphill battle at all times. The difficulty stems from the fact that the defender must attempt to thwart all possible attacks, whereas the attacker is free to try to find the weakest link in the defense chain and attack at that point. Detection is concerned with learning of an attack, either before or after its success.

Defense Against Nontechnical Attacks

Determined nontechnical attacks are particularly difficult to defend against because most people are not trained to keep secrets. Thus, people are not in the habit of shredding scraps of paper that they may have used to temporarily write a password on, of guarding their conversations in case of eavesdroppers, or even refraining from keeping a permanent written record of their password near (or even on!) their terminal or personal computer.

Kaplan and Kovara recommend that, at a minimum, security policies and procedures should provide for the following [KAPL93]:

- Continued education of all employees about the security threat from nontechnical attacks, with directives on how to handle specific types of requests for information. Employees must also be taught the vulnerabilities of electronic mail, voice mail, and fax.
- Comprehensive, periodic auditing intended to detect intrusion.
- Signed agreements by all employees and contractors stating that they understand their responsibilities under the rules in company policies and procedures.

In addition, an organization needs to develop some sort of classification system that indicates the level of sensitivity of various categories of computerized data, plus policies that determine which employees have access to those data. As part of ongoing employee training, privileged users should be taught that they have special responsibilities to protect the information under their care and will be held responsible for adhering to these policies.

Password Protection

The front line of defense against intruders is the password system. Virtually all multiuser systems require that a user provide not only a name or identifier (ID) but also a password. The password serves to authenticate the ID of the individual logging on to the system. In turn, the ID provides security in the following ways:

- The ID determines whether the user is authorized to gain access to a system. In some systems, only those who already have an ID filed on the system are allowed to gain access.
- The ID determines the privileges accorded to the user. A few users may have supervisory or "superuser" status that enables them to read files and perform functions that are especially protected by the operating system. Some systems have guest or anonymous accounts, and users of these accounts have more limited privileges than others.
- The ID is used in what is referred to as discretionary access control. For example, by listing the IDs of the other users, a user may grant permission to them to read files owned by that user.

The Vulnerability of Passwords

To understand the nature of the attack, let us consider a scheme that is widely used on UNIX systems, in which passwords are never stored in the clear. Rather, the following procedure is employed (Figure 6.1a). Each user selects a password of up to 8 printable characters in length. This is converted into a 56-bit value (using 7-bit ASCII) that serves as the key input to an encryption routine. The encryption routine, known as crypt(3), is based on DES. The E table of the DES algorithm is modified using a 12-bit "salt" value. Typically, this value is related to the time at which the password is assigned to the user. The modified DES algorithm is exercised with a data input consisting of a 64-bit block of zeros. The output of the algorithm then serves as input for a second encryption. This process is repeated for a total of 25 encryptions. The resulting 64-bit output is then translated into an 11-character sequence. The ciphertext password is then stored, together with a plaintext copy of the salt, in the password file for the corresponding user ID.

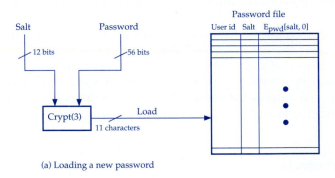

(a) Loading a new password

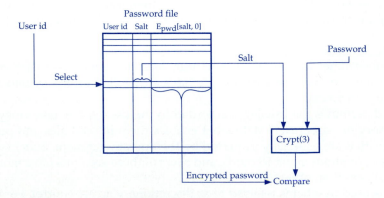

(b) Verifying a password

FIGURE 6.1.   UNIX Password Scheme

The salt serves three purposes:

- It prevents duplicate passwords from being visible in the password file. Even if two users choose the same password, those passwords will be assigned at different times. Hence, the "extended" passwords of the two users will differ.
- It effectively increases the length of the password without requiring the user to remember two additional characters. Hence, the number of possible passwords is increased by a factor of 4,096, increasing the difficulty of guessing a password.
- It prevents the use of a hardware implementation of DES, which would ease the difficulty of a brute-force guessing attack.

When a user attempts to log on to a UNIX system, the user provides an ID and a password. The operating system uses the ID to index into the password file and retrieve the plaintext salt and the encrypted password. The plaintext password and the salt are used as input to the encryption routing. If the result matches the encrypted password, the password is accepted.

The encryption routine is designed to discourage guessing attacks. Software implementations of DES are slow compared to hardware versions, and the use of 25 iterations multiplies the time required by 25. However, since the original design of this algorithm, two changes have occurred. First, newer implementations of the algorithm itself have resulted in speedups. For example, the Internet worm, discussed in Section 6.3, was able to do on-line password guessing of a few hundred passwords in a reasonably short time by using a more efficient encryption algorithm than the standard one stored on the UNIX systems that it attacked. And second, hardware performance continues to increase, so that any software algorithm executes more quickly.

Thus, there are two threats to the UNIX password scheme. First, a user can gain access on a machine using a guest account or by some other means, and then run a password guessing program, called a password cracker, on that machine. The attacker should be able to check hundreds and perhaps thousands of possible passwords with little resource consumption. In addition, if an opponent is able to obtain a copy of the password file, then a cracker program can be run on another machine at leisure. This enables the opponent to run through many thousands of possible passwords in a reasonable period.

As an example, the fastest password cracker known to the author was reported on the Internet in August 1993 [MADS93]. Using a Thinking Machines Corporation parallel computer, a performance of 1,560 encryptions per second per vector unit was achieved. With four vector units per processing node (a standard configuration), this works out to 800,000 encryptions per second on a 128-node machine (which is a modest size) and 6.4 million encryptions per second on a 1,024-node machine.

Even these stupendous guessing rates do not yet make it feasible for an attacker to use a dumb brute-force technique of trying all possible combinations of characters to discover a password. Instead, password crackers rely on the fact that some people choose easily guessable passwords.

Unfortunately, human nature gives the attacker a practical alternative. Some users, when permitted to choose their own password, pick one that is absurdly short. The results of one study at Purdue University are shown in Table 6.1. The study observed password change choices on 54 machines, representing approximately 7,000 user accounts. Almost 3% of the passwords were three characters or fewer in length! An attacker could begin the attack by exhaustively testing all possible passwords of length three or fewer. A simple remedy is for the system to reject any password choice of fewer than, say, six characters or even to require that all passwords be exactly eight characters in length. Most users would not complain about such a restriction.

Alas, password length is only part of the problem. Many people, when permitted to choose their own password, pick a password that is guessable, such as their own name, their street name, a common dictionary word, and so forth. This makes the job of password cracking straightforward. The cracker simply has to test the password file against lists of likely passwords. Because many people use guessable passwords, such a strategy should succeed on virtually all systems.

One demonstration of the effectiveness of guessing is reported in [KLEI90]. From a variety of sources, the author collected UNIX password files containing nearly 14,000 encrypted passwords. The result, which the author rightly characterizes as frightening, is shown in Table 6.2. In all, nearly one-fourth of the passwords were guessed. Following is the strategy that was used:

1. Try the user's name, initials, account name, and other relevant personal information. In all, 130 different permutations for each user were tried.
2. Try words from various dictionaries. The author compiled a dictionary of over 60,000 words, including the on-line dictionary on the system itself, and various other lists as shown.
3. Try various permutations on the words from step 2. This included making the first letter uppercase or a control character, making the entire word uppercase,

TABLE 6.1   Observed Password Lengths[a]

Length	Number	Fraction of Total
1	55	0.004
2	87	0.006
3	212	0.02
4	449	0.03
5	1260	0.09
6	3035	0.22
7	2917	0.21
8	5772	0.42
Total	13787	1.0

[a]From [SPAF92a].

TABLE 6.2   Passwords Cracked from a Sample Set of 13,797 Accounts[a]

Type of Password	Search Size	Number of Matches	Percentage of Passwords Matched	Cost/Benefit Ratio[b]
User/account name	130	368	2.7%	2.830
Character sequences	866	22	0.2%	0.025
Numbers	427	9	0.1%	0.021
Chinese	392	56	0.4%	0.143
Place names	628	82	0.6%	0.131
Common names	2239	548	4.0%	0.245
Female names	4280	161	1.2%	0.038
Male names	2866	140	1.0%	0.049
Uncommon names	4955	130	0.9%	0.026
Myths & legends	1246	66	0.5%	0.053
Shakespearean	473	11	0.1%	0.023
Sports terms	238	32	0.2%	0.134
Science fiction	691	59	0.4%	0.085
Movies and actors	99	12	0.1%	0.121
Cartoons	92	9	0.1%	0.098
Famous people	290	55	0.4%	0.190
Phrases and patterns	933	253	1.8%	0.271
Surnames	33	9	0.1%	0.273
Biology	58	1	0.0%	0.017
System dictionary	19683	1027	7.4%	0.052
Machine names	9018	132	1.0%	0.015
Mnemonics	14	2	0.0%	0.143
King James bible	7525	83	0.6%	0.011
Miscellaneous words	3212	54	0.4%	0.017
Yiddish words	56	0	0.0%	0.000
Asteroids	2407	19	0.1%	0.007
TOTAL	62727	3340	24.2%	0.053

[a]From [KLEI90].

[b]Computed as the number of matches divided by the search size. The more words that needed to be tested for a match, the lower the cost/benefit ratio.

reversing the word, changing the letter "o" to the digit "0", and so on. These permutations added another 1 million words to the list.

4. Try various capitalization permutations on the words from step 2 that were not considered in step 3. This added almost 2 million additional words to the list.

Thus, the test involved in the neighborhood of 3 million words. Using the fastest Thinking Machines implementation listed earlier, the time to encrypt all these words for all possible salt values is under an hour. Keep in mind that such a thorough search could produce a success rate of about 25%, whereas even a single hit may be enough to gain a wide range of privileges on a system.

Access Control

One way to thwart a password attack is to deny the opponent access to the password file. If the encrypted password portion of the file is accessible only by a privileged user, then the opponent cannot read it without already knowing the password of a privileged user. [SPAF92a] points out several flaws in this strategy:

- Many systems, including most UNIX systems, are susceptible to unanticipated break-ins. Once an attacker has gained access by some means, he or she may wish to obtain a collection of passwords in order to use different accounts for different logon sessions to decrease the risk of detection. Or a user with an account may desire another user's account to access privileged data or to sabotage the system.
- An accident of protection might render the password file readable, thus compromising all the accounts.
- Some of the users have accounts on other machines in other protection domains, and they use the same password. Thus, if the passwords could be read by anyone on one machine, it might compromise a machine in another location.

Thus, a more effective strategy would be to force users to select passwords that are difficult to guess.

Password Selection Strategies

The lesson from the two experiments just described (Tables 6.1 and 6.2) is that, left to their own devices, many users choose a password that is too short or too easy to guess. At the other extreme, if users are assigned passwords consisting of eight randomly selected printable characters, password cracking is effectively impossible. But it would be almost as impossible for most users to remember their passwords. Fortunately, even if we limit the password universe to strings of characters that are reasonably memorable, the size of the universe is still too large to permit practical cracking. Our goal, then, is to eliminate guessable passwords while allowing the user to select a password that is memorable. Four basic techniques are in use:

- User education
- Computer-generated passwords
- Reactive password checking
- Proactive password checking

Users can be told the importance of using hard-to-guess passwords and can be provided with guidelines for selecting strong passwords. Table 6.3 gives some suggestions. This **user education** strategy is unlikely to succeed at most installations, particularly where there is a large user population or a lot of turnover. Many users will simply ignore the guidelines. Others may not be good judges of what is a strong password. For example, many users (mistakenly) believe that reversing a word or capitalizing the last letter makes a password unguessable.

TABLE 6.3 Effective Strategies for User Selection of Easily Remembered Passwords[a]

(a) Lines of a chosen childhood verse

Verse Line	Password
One for the money	14munny
Two for the show	24show
Three to get ready	32ready
Four to go (to)	42goto

(b) Expressions inspired by name of city

City	Intermediate Expression	Password
Paris	I love Paris in the springtime	ILPITST
Rome	Three (bright) coins in the (Trevi) fountain	TBCITTF
New York	The sidewalks of New York City	TSWONYC
San Francisco	I left my heart in San Francisco	ILMHISF

(c) Foods disliked during childhood

Food	Password
Chocolate-covered peanuts	chocovpea
Pepsi-Cola (and) pretzels	pepcolpre
Pineapple-cocoanut suckers	pincocsuc
Fried (-) eggplant	frieggpla

(d) Transform Techniques

Transform	Illustrative Expression	Password
Transliteration	Photographic	fotografik
	Schizophrenic	skitsofrenik
Interweaving of characters in successive words	duke, iron	diurkoen
	tent pole	tepontle
Translation	strangers	etraniere
Replacement of letter by decimal digit (mod 10 index of letter in natural order)	cabbage	3122175
Replacement of decimal number by letter (with corresponding position in natural order)	10/12/1492	jabadib
Shift from "home" position on keyboard	zucchini	xivvjomo
Substitution of synonyms	coffee break	javarest
Substitution of antonyms	stoplight	startdark
Actuation of keyboard "shift"	6/6/1944	^?^?!($$
Substitution of abbreviations	relative humidity	relhum
Substitution of acronyms	Mothers Against Drunk Drivers National Organization of Women	maddnow
Repetition	pan	panpan
Imagistic manipulation (180 degree rotation of letters)	swimshow	smiwshom

[a]From [ALVA90].

Computer-generated passwords also have problems. If the passwords are quite random in nature, users will not be able to remember them. Even if the password is pronounceable, the user may have difficulty remembering it and so be tempted to write it down. In general, computer-generated password schemes have a history of poor acceptance by users.

FIPS PUB 181 defines one of the best-designed automated password generators. The standard includes not only a description of the approach but also a complete listing of the C source code of the algorithm. The algorithm generates words by forming pronounceable syllables and concatenating them to form a word. A random number generator produces a random stream of characters used to construct the syllables and words.

A **reactive password checking** strategy is one in which the system periodically runs its own password cracker to find guessable passwords. The system cancels any passwords that are guessed and notifies the user. This tactic has a number of drawbacks. First, it is resource-intensive if the job is done right. Because a determined opponent who is able to steal a password file can devote full CPU time to the task for hours or even days, an effective reactive password checker is at a distinct disadvantage. Furthermore, any existing passwords remain vulnerable until the reactive password checker finds them.

The most promising approach to improved password security is a **proactive password checker**. In this scheme, a user is allowed to select his or her own password. However, at the time of selection, the system checks to see if the password is allowable and, if not, rejects it. Such checkers are based on the philosophy that, with sufficient guidance from the system, users can select memorable passwords from a fairly large password space that are not likely to be guessed in a dictionary attack.

The trick with a proactive password checker is to strike a balance between user acceptability and strength. If the system rejects too many passwords, users will complain that it is too hard to select a password. If the system uses some simple algorithm to define what is acceptable, this provides guidance to password crackers to refine their guessing technique. In the remainder of this subsection, we look at possible approaches to proactive password checking.

The first approach is a simple system for rule enforcement. For example, the following rules could be enforced:

- All passwords must be at least 8 characters long
- In the first eight characters, they must include at least one each of uppercase, lowercase, numeric digits, and punctuation marks

These rules could be coupled with advice to the user. Although this approach is superior to simply educating users, it may not be sufficient to thwart password crackers. This scheme alerts crackers as to which passwords *not* to try but may still make it possible to do password cracking.

Another possible procedure is simply to compile a large dictionary of possible "bad" passwords. When a user selects a password, the system checks to make sure that it is not on the disapproved list. There are two problems with this approach:

- *Space:* The dictionary must be very large to be effective. For example, the dictionary used in the Purdue study [SPAF92a] occupies more than 30 megabytes of storage.
- *Time:* The time required to search a large dictionary may itself be large. In addition, to check for likely permutations of dictionary words, either those words must be included in the dictionary, making it truly huge, or each search must also involve considerable processing.

Two techniques for developing an effective and efficient proactive password checker that is based on rejecting words on a list show promise. One of these develops a Markov model for the generation of guessable passwords [DAVI93]. Figure 6.2 shows a simplified version of such a model. This model shows a language consisting of an alphabet of three characters. The state of the system at any time is the identity of the most recent letter. The value on the transition from one state to another represents the probability that one letter follows another. Thus, the probability that the next letter is b given that the current letter is a is 0.5.

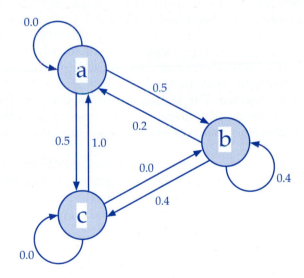

M = {3, {a, b, c} , T, 1 }   where

$$T = \begin{bmatrix} 0.0 & 0.5 & 0.5 \\ 0.2 & 0.4 & 0.4 \\ 1.0 & 0.0 & 0.0 \end{bmatrix}$$

e.g., string probably from this language: abbcacaba

e.g., string probably not from this language: aacccbaaa

FIGURE 6.2.   An Example Markov Model

In general, a Markov model is a quadruple $[m, A, T, k]$, where m is the number of states in the model, A is the state space, T is the matrix of transition probabilities, and k is the order of the model. For a kth order model, the probability of making a transition to a particular letter depends on the previous k letters that have been generated. The figure shows a simple first-order model.

The authors report on the development and use of a second-order model. To begin, a dictionary of guessable passwords is constructed. Then, the transition matrix is calculated as follows:

1. Determine the frequency matrix f, where $f(i, j, k)$ is the number of occurrences of the trigram consisting of the ith, jth, and kth character. For example, the password *parsnips* yields the trigrams par, ars, rsn, sni, nip, and ips.
2. For each bigram ij, calculate $f(i, j, \infty)$ as the total number of trigrams beginning with ij. For example, $f(a, b, \infty)$ would be the total number of trigrams of the form aba, abb, abc, and so on.
3. Compute the entries of T as follows:

$$T(i, j, k) = \frac{f(i, j, k)}{f(i, j, \infty)}$$

The result is a model that reflects the structure of the words in the dictionary. With this model, the question "Is this a bad password?" is transformed into the question "Was this string (password) generated by this Markov model?" For a given password, the transition probabilities of all its trigrams can be looked up. Some standard statistical tests can then be used to determine if the password is likely or unlikely for that model. Passwords that are likely to be generated by the model are rejected. The authors report good results for a second-order model. Their system catches virtually all the passwords in their dictionary and does not exclude so many potentially good passwords as to be user-unfriendly.

A quite different approach has been reported by Spafford [SPAF92a, SPAF92b]. It is based on the use of a Bloom filter [BLOO70]. To begin, we explain the operation of the Bloom filter. A Bloom filter of order k consists of a set of k independent hash functions $H_1(x), H_2(x), \ldots, H_k(x)$, where each function maps a password into a hash value in the range 0 to $N - 1$. That is,

$$H_i(X_j) = y \qquad 1 \le i \le k; \qquad 1 \le j \le D; \qquad 0 \le y \le N - 1$$

where

$$X_j = j\text{th word in password dictionary}$$
$$D = \text{number of words in password dictionary}$$

The following procedure is then applied to the dictionary:

1. A hash table of N bits is defined, with all bits initially set to 0.
2. For each password, its k hash values are calculated, and the corresponding bits in the hash table are set to 1. Thus, if $H_i(X_j) = 67$ for some (i, j), then the 67th bit of the hash table is set to 1; if the bit already has the value 1, it remains at 1.

When a new password is presented to the checker, its k hash values are calculated. If all the corresponding bits of the hash table are equal to 1, then the password is rejected. All passwords in the dictionary will be rejected. But there will also be some "false positives," that is, passwords that are not in the dictionary but that produce a match in the hash table. To see this, consider a scheme with two hash functions. Suppose that the passwords *undertaker* and *hulkhogan* are in the dictionary, but $xG\%\#jj98$ is not. Further suppose that:

$H_1(\text{undertaker}) = 25$	$H_1(\text{hulkhogan}) = 83$	$H_1(xG\%\#jj98) = 665$
$H_2(\text{undertaker}) = 998$	$H_2(\text{hulkhogan}) = 665$	$H_2(xG\%\#jj98) = 998$

If the password $xG\%\#jj98$ is presented to the system, it will be rejected even though it is not in the dictionary. If there are too many such false positives, it will be difficult for users to select passwords. Therefore, we would like to design the hash scheme to minimize false positives. It can be shown that the probability of a false positive can be approximated by:

$$P \approx (1 - e^{-kD/N})^k \approx (1 - e^{-k/R})^k$$

or, equivalently,

$$R \approx \frac{-k}{\ln(1 - P^{1/k})}$$

where

k = number of hash functions
N = number of bits in hash table
D = number of words in dictionary
$R = \dfrac{N}{D}$, ratio of hash table size (bits) to dictionary size (words)

Figure 6.3 plots P as a function of R for various values of k. Suppose we have a dictionary of 1 million words and we wish to have a 0.01 probability of rejecting a password not in the dictionary. If we choose six hash functions, the required ratio is $R = 9.6$. Therefore, we need a hash table of 9.6×10^6 bits or about 1.2 MBytes of storage. In contrast, storage of the entire dictionary would require on the order of 8 MBytes. Thus, we achieve a compression of almost a factor of 7. Furthermore, password checking involves the straightforward calculation of six hash functions and is independent of the size of the dictionary, whereas with the use of the full dictionary, there is a substantial searching.[1]

---

[1]Both the Markov model and the Bloom filter involve the use of probabilistic techniques. In the case of the Markov model, there is a small probability that some passwords in the dictionary will not be caught and a small probability that some passwords not in the dictionary will be rejected. In the case of the Bloom filter, there is a small probability that some passwords not in the dictionary will be rejected. We have seen this introduction of probabilistic concepts before, in Appendix 4A, for determining whether a number is prime. It is often the case in designing algorithms that the use of probabilistic techniques results in a less time-consuming or less complex solution, or both.

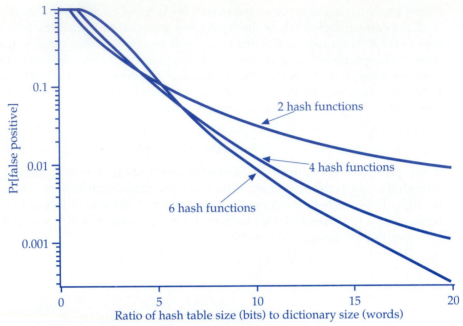

FIGURE 6.3.   Performance of Bloom Filter

Password Management

Assuring that users are assigned passwords that are difficult to guess is only one aspect of password management. Password management encompasses all the policies and procedures used to ensure the security of passwords. FIPS PUB 112 provides a useful set of guidelines for all aspects of the administration and management of passwords. Table 6.4 summarizes the guidelines.

Intrusion Detection

Inevitably, the best intrusion prevention system will fail. A system's second line of defense is intrusion detection, and this has been the focus of much research in recent years. This interest is motivated by a number of considerations, including the following:

1. If an intrusion is detected quickly enough, the intruder can be identified and ejected from the system before any damage is done or any data are compromised. Even if the detection is not sufficiently timely to preempt the intruder, the sooner that the intrusion is detected, the less the amount of damage, and the more quickly that recovery can be achieved.
2. An effective intrusion detection system can serve as a deterrent, so acting to prevent intrusions.

TABLE 6.4 Password Usage Guidelines[a]

Factor	Definition	Low Protection	Medium Protection	High Protection
Composition	The set of characters that may be used in a valid password.	Digits (0–9)	Uppercase letters (A–Z), lowercase letters (a–z), and digits (0–9)	Full 95-character set
Length	The lengths of passwords, expressed as a minimum and maximum number of characters.	4–6 characters	4–8 characters	6–8 characters
Lifetime	Maximum period of time for which a password is valid.	1 year	6 months	One month
Source	Entities that can create or select a valid password.	User	System generated and user selected	Automated password generator within the authentication system.
Ownership	Individuals authorized to use a password.	Individual (personal passwords); group (access passwords)	Individual	Individual
Distribution	Methods for providing (transporting) a new password to its owner and to all places where it will be needed in the password system.	Unmarked envelope in U.S. mail	Terminal and special mailer	Registered mail, receipt required; personal delivery, affidavit required
Storage	Methods of storing a valid password during its lifetime.	Central computer on-line storage as plaintext	Encrypted passwords	Encrypted passwords
Entry	Methods by which a password may be entered by a user for authentication or authorization purposes.	Nonprinting "PIN-PAD"	Nonprinting keyboard and masked-printing keyboard	Nonprinting keyboard
Transmission	Methods for communicating a password from its point of entry to its point of comparison with a stored, valid password.	Plaintext	Plaintext	Encrypted communication with message numbering
Authentication Period	Maximum period between any initial authentication process and subsequent reauthentication processes during a single terminal session or during the period data is being accessed.	Each transaction	Log-in and after 10 minutes of terminal activity	Log-in and after 5 minutes of terminal activity

[a]From FIPS PUB 112.

3. Intrusion detection enables the collection of information about intrusion techniques that can be used to strengthen the intrusion prevention facility.

Intrusion detection is based on the assumption that the behavior of the intruder differs from that of a legitimate user in ways that can be quantified. Of course, we cannot expect that there will be a crisp, exact distinction between an attack by an intruder and the normal use of resources by an authorized user. Rather, we must expect that there will be some overlap.

Figure 6.4 suggests, in very abstract terms, the nature of the task confronting the designer of an intrusion detection system. Although the typical behavior of an intruder differs from the typical behavior of an authorized user, there is an overlap in these behaviors. Thus, a loose interpretation of intruder behavior, which will catch more intruders, will also lead to a number of "false positives," or authorized users identified as intruders. On the other hand, an attempt to limit false positives by a tight interpretation of intruder behavior will lead to an increase in false negatives, or intruders not identified as intruders. Thus, there is an element of compromise and art in the practice of intrusion detection.

In Anderson's study [ANDE80], it was postulated that one could, with reasonable confidence, distinguish between a masquerader and a legitimate user. Patterns of legitimate user behavior can be established by observing past history, and significant deviation from such patterns can be detected. Anderson suggests that the task of detecting a misfeasor (legitimate user performing in an

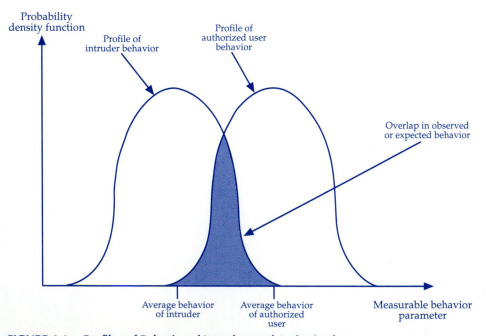

FIGURE 6.4.   Profiles of Behavior of Intruders and Authorized Users

unauthorized fashion) is more difficult, in that the distinction between abnormal and normal behavior may be small. Anderson concluded that such violations would be undetectable solely through the search for anomalous behavior. However, misfeasor behavior might nevertheless be detectable by intelligent definition of the class of conditions that suggest unauthorized use. Finally, the detection of the clandestine user was felt to be beyond the scope of purely automated techniques. These observations, which were made in 1980, remain true today.

[PORR92] identifies the following approaches to intrusion detection:

1. *Statistical Anomaly Detection:* This approach involves the collection of data relating to the behavior of legitimate users over a period of time. Then, statistical tests are applied to observed behavior to determine, with a high level of confidence, whether that behavior is not legitimate user behavior.
   a. Threshold detection: This approach involves defining thresholds, independent of user, for the frequency of occurrence of various events.
   b. Profile-based: A profile of the activity of each user is developed and used to detect changes in the behavior of individual accounts.
2. *Rule-Based Detection:* This approach involves an attempt to define a set of rules that can be used to decide that a given behavior is that of an intruder.
   a. Anomaly detection: rules are developed to detect deviation from previous usage patterns.
   b. Penetration Identification: an expert system approach that searches for suspicious behavior.

In a nutshell, statistical approaches attempt to define normal, or expected, behavior, whereas rule-based approaches attempt to define proper behavior.

In terms of the types of attackers listed earlier, statistical anomaly detection is effective against masqueraders, who are unlikely to mimic the behavior patterns of the accounts they appropriate. On the other hand, such techniques may be unable to deal with misfeasors. For such attacks, rule-based approaches may be able to recognize events and sequences that, in context, reveal penetration. In practice, a system may exploit a combination of both approaches in order to be effective against a broad range of attacks.

Audit Records

A fundamental tool for intrusion detection is the audit record. Some record of ongoing activity by user must be maintained as input to an intrusion detection system. Basically, two plans are used:

- *Native audit records:* Virtually all multiuser operating systems include accounting software that collects information on user activity. The advantage of using this information is that no additional collection software is needed. The disadvantage is that the native audit records may not contain the needed information or may not contain it in a convenient form.

- *Detection-specific audit records:* A collection facility can be implemented that generates audit records containing only that information required by the intrusion detection system. One advantage of such an approach is that it could be made vendor-independent and ported to a variety of systems. The disadvantage is the extra overhead involved in having, in effect, two accounting packages running on a machine.

A good example of detection-specific audit records is one developed by Dorothy Denning [DENN87]. Each audit record contains the following fields (Figure 6.5):

- *Subject:* initiators of actions. A subject is typically a terminal user but might also be a process acting on behalf of users or groups of users. All activity arises through commands issued by subjects. Subjects may be grouped into different access classes, and these classes may overlap.
- *Action:* Operation performed by the subject on or with an object; examples include, log in, read, perform I/O, execute.
- *Object:* receptors of actions. Examples include files, programs, messages, records, terminals, printers, and user- or program-created structures. When a subject is the recipient of an action, such as electronic mail, then that subject is considered an object. Objects may be grouped by type. Object granularity may vary by object type and by environment. For example, database actions may be audited for the database as a whole or at the record level.
- *Exception-Condition:* denotes which, if any, exception condition is raised on return.
- *Resource-Usage:* a list of quantitative elements in which each element gives the amount used of some resource (e.g., number of lines printed or displayed, number of records read or written, processor time, I/O units used, session elapsed time).
- *Time-stamp:* Unique time and datestamp identifying when the action took place.

Most user operations are made up of a number of elementary actions. For example, a file copy involves the execution of the user command, which includes doing access validation and setting up the copy, plus the read from one file, plus the write to another file. Consider the command

<code>COPY GAME.EXE TO <Library>GAME.EXE</code>

issued by Smith to copy an executable file GAME from the current directory to the <Library> directory. The following audit records may be generated:

| Smith | execute | <Library>COPY.EXE | 0 | CPU = 00002 | 11058721678 |

| Smith | read | <Smith>GAME.EXE | 0 | RECORDS = 0 | 11058721679 |

| Smith | execute | <Library>COPY.EXE | write-viol | RECORDS = 0 | 11058721680 |

Subject	Action	Object	Exception-Condition	Resource-Usage	Time-Stamp

FIGURE 6.5.   Detection-Specific Audit Record Format

In this case, the copy is aborted because Smith does not have write permission to
<Library>.

The decomposition of a user operation into elementary actions has three advantages:

1. Because objects are the protectable entities in a system, the use of elementary
   actions enables an audit of all behavior affecting an object. Thus, the system can
   detect attempted subversions of access controls (by noting an abnormality in
   the number of exception conditions returned), and can detect successful subversions by noting an abnormality in the set of objects accessible to the subject.
2. Single-object, single-action audit records simplify the model and the implementation.
3. Because of the simple, uniform structure of the detection-specific audit records,
   it may be relatively easy to obtain this information or at least part of it by a
   straightforward mapping from existing native audit records to the detection-specific audit records.

Statistical Anomaly Detection

As was mentioned, statistical anomaly detection techniques fall into two broad categories: threshold detection and profile-based systems. Threshold detection involves counting the number of occurrences of a specific event type over an interval of time. If the count surpasses what is considered a reasonable number that one might expect to occur, then intrusion is assumed.

Threshold analysis, by itself is a crude and ineffective detector of even moderately sophisticated attacks. Both the threshold and the time interval must be determined. Because of the variability across users, such thresholds are likely to generate either a lot of false positives or a lot of false negatives. However, simple threshold detectors may be useful in conjunction with more sophisticated techniques.

Profile-based anomaly detection focuses on characterizing the past behavior of individual users or related groups of users, and then detecting significant deviations. A profile may consist of a set of parameters, so that deviation on just a single parameter may not be sufficient in itself to signal an alert.

The foundation of this approach is an analysis of audit records. The audit records provide input to the intrusion detection function in two ways. First, the designer must decide on a number of quantitative metrics that can be used to measure user behavior. An analysis of audit records over a period of time can be used to determine the activity profile of the average user. Thus, the audit records serve to define typical behavior. Secondly, current audit records are the input used to detect intrusion. That is, the intrusion detection model analyzes incoming audit records to determine deviation from average behavior.

Examples of metrics that are useful for profile-based intrusion detection are the following:

- *Counter:* A nonnegative integer that may be incremented but not decremented until it is reset by management action. Typically, a count of certain event types is kept over a particular period of time. Examples include the number of logins by a single user during an hour, the number of times a given command is executed during a single user session, and the number of password failures during a minute.
- *Gauge:* A nonnegative integer that may be incremented or decremented. Typically, a gauge is used to measure the current value of some entity. Examples include the number of logical connections assigned to a user application and the number of outgoing messages queued for a user process.
- *Interval timer:* The length of time between two related events. An example is the length of time between successive logins to an account.
- *Resource utilization:* Quantity of resources consumed during a specified period. Examples include the number of pages printed during a user session and total time consumed by a program execution.

Given these general metrics, various tests can be performed to determine whether current activity fits within acceptable limits. [DENN87] lists the following approaches that may be taken:

- Mean and standard deviation
- Multivariate
- Markov process
- Time series
- Operational

The simplest statistical test is to measure the **mean and standard deviation** of a parameter over some historical period. The following equations are used:

sample mean:
$$\overline{X} = \frac{1}{n} \sum_{i=1}^{n} X_i$$

sample variance:
$$S^2 = \frac{\sum_{i=1}^{n} (X_i - \overline{X})^2}{n-1}$$

$$= \frac{n \sum_{i=1}^{n} X_i - \left(\sum_{i=1}^{n} X_i \right)^2}{n(n-1)}$$

sample standard
deviation:
$$S = \sqrt{S^2}$$

where

$$n = \text{sample size}$$
$$X_i = i\text{th sample}$$

With these estimates of the mean and standard deviation of a particular parameter, we can define statistical tolerance limits, which are defined as the two outer
values or limits that contain nearly all the parameter values.[2] These limits are conveniently defined in terms of multiples of the standard deviation, using the
Chebyshev Inequality. The probability of a value of a random variable X falling
outside the interval:

$$E[X] \pm k \times \sigma$$

where $E[X]$ is the mean and σ is the standard deviation, is given by:

$$\Pr[|X - E[X]| \geq k \times \sigma] \leq \frac{1}{k^2}$$

Thus, if $k = 4$, then the probability that any given observation will differ from the
mean by more than 4 standard deviations is less than 0.0625.

The following three reservations need to be stated:

1. The inequality holds for the actual mean and standard deviation of a random
variable. Because we have access to only a finite historical record, we can only
estimate the mean and standard deviation.
2. Even if we had an exact value for the mean and standard deviation, normal user
behavior may change over time, which may invalidate the interval used at least
to some extent.
3. A trade-off must be made between false positives, which will occur more frequently if we use a wide interval (larger value of k), and false negatives, which
will occur more frequently if we use a narrow interval.

These considerations in fact apply to all the measures we are discussing.

The use of mean and standard deviation is applicable to a wide variety of counters, timers, and resource measures. In some cases a **multivariate** model may be
more appropriate. Such a model is based on correlations between two or more
variables. Intruder behavior may be characterized with greater confidence by considering such correlations. For example, processor time and resource usage, or
login frequency and session elapsed time.

A **Markov process** model is used to establish transition probabilities among various states. As an example, this model might be used to look at transitions between
certain commands.

---

[2]The term *confidence interval* is often mistakenly used for this concept. A confidence interval is an interval
within which we estimate a particular statistical measure, such as the mean, to lie. Statistical tolerance
limits for a given random variable are limits within which we expect a stated fraction of values to lie.

A **time series** model focuses on time intervals, looking for sequences of events that happen too rapidly or too slowly. A variety of statistical tests can be applied to characterize abnormal timing.

Finally, an **operational model** is based on a judgment of what is considered abnormal, rather than an automated analysis of past audit records. Typically, fixed limits are defined and intrusion is suspected for an observation that is outside the limits. This type of approach works best where intruder behavior can be deduced from certain types of activities. For example, a large number of login attempts over a short period suggests an attempted intrusion.

As an example of the use of these various metrics and models, Table 6.5 shows various measures considered or tested for the Stanford Research Institute (SRI) intrusion detection system (IDES) [DENN87, JAVI91, LUNT88].

The main advantage of the use of statistical profiles is that a prior knowledge of security flaws is not required. The detector program learns what is "normal" behavior and then looks for deviations. The approach is not based on system-dependent characteristics and vulnerabilities. Thus, it should be readily portable among a variety of systems.

Rule-Based Intrusion Detection

Rule-based techniques detect intrusion by observing events in the system and applying a set of rules that lead to a decision whether a given pattern of activity is or is not suspicious. In very general terms, we can characterize all approaches as focusing on either anomaly detection or penetration identification, although there is some overlap in these approaches.

Rule-based anomaly detection is similar in terms of its approach and strengths to statistical anomaly detection. With the rule-based approach, historical audit records are analyzed to identify usage patterns and to automatically generate rules that describe those patterns. Rules may represent past behavior patterns of users, programs, privileges, time slots, terminals, and so on. Current behavior is then observed, and each transaction is matched against the set of rules to determine if it conforms to any historically observed pattern of behavior.

As with statistical anomaly detection, rule-based anomaly detection does not require a knowledge of security vulnerabilities within the system. Rather, the scheme is based on observing past behavior and, in effect, assuming that the future will be like the past. In order for this approach to be effective, a rather large database of rules will be needed. For example, a scheme described in [VACC89] contains anywhere from 10^4 to 10^6 rules.

Rule-based penetration identification takes a very different approach to intrusion detection, one based on expert system technology. The key feature of such systems is the use of rules for identifying known penetrations or penetrations that would exploit known weaknesses. Rules can also be defined that identify suspicious behavior, even when the behavior is within the bounds of established patterns of usage. Typically, the rules used in these systems are specific to the machine and operating system. Also, such rules

TABLE 6.5   Measures That May Be Used for Intrusion Detection

Measure	Model	Type of Intrusion Detected
Login and Session Activity		
Log in frequency by day and time	Mean and standard deviation	Intruders may be likely to log in during off-hours.
Frequency of log in at different locations	Mean and standard deviation	Intruders may log in from a location that a particular user rarely or never uses.
Time since last log in	Operational	Break-in on a "dead" account.
Elapsed time per session	Mean and standard deviation	Significant deviations might indicate masquerader.
Quantity of output to location	Mean and standard deviation	Excessive amounts of data transmitted to remote locations could signify leakage of sensitive data.
Session resource utilization	Mean and standard deviation	Unusual processor or I/O levels could signal an intruder.
Password failures at log in	Operational	Attempted break-in by password guessing.
Failures to log in from specified terminals	Operational	Attempted break-in.
Command or Program Execution Activity		
Execution frequency	Mean and standard deviation	May detect intruders, who are likely to use different commands, or a successful penetration by a legitimate user, who has gained access to privileged commands.
Program resource utilization	Mean and standard deviation	An abnormal value might suggest injection of a virus or Trojan horse, which performs side-effects that increase I/O or processor utilization.
Execution denials	Operational model	May detect penetration attempt by individual user who seeks higher privileges.
File access activity		
Read, write, create, delete frequency	Mean and standard deviation	Abnormalities for read and write access for individual users may signify masquerading or browsing.
Records read, written	Mean and standard deviation	Abnormality could signify an attempt to obtain sensitive data by inference and aggregation.
Failure count for read, write, create, delete	Operational	May detect users who persistently attempt to access unauthorized files.
File resource exhaustion counter	Operational	

are generated by "experts" rather than by means of an automated analysis of audit records. The normal procedure is to interview system administrators and security analysts to collect a suite of known penetration scenarios and key events that threaten the security of the target system.[3] Thus, the strength of the approach depends on the skill of those involved in setting up the rules.

A simple example of the type of rules that can be used is found in NIDX, an early system that used heuristic rules that can be used to assign degrees of suspicion to activities [BAUE88]. Example heuristics are the following:

1. Users should not read files in other users' personal directories.
2. Users must not write other users' files.
3. Users who log in after hours often access the same files they used earlier.
4. Users do not generally open disk devices directly but rely on higher-level operating-system utilities.
5. Users should not be logged in more than once to the same system.
6. Users do not make copies of system programs.

The penetration identification scheme used in IDES [DENN87, JAVI91, LUNT88] is representative of the strategy followed. Audit records are examined as they are generated, and they are matched against the rule base. If a match is found, then the user's *suspicion rating* is increased. If enough rules are matched, then the rating will pass a threshold that results in the reporting of an anomaly.

The IDES approach is based on an examination of audit records. A weakness of this plan is its lack of flexibility. For a given penetration scenario, there may be a number of alternative audit record sequences that could be produced, each varying from the others slightly or in subtle ways. It may be difficult to pin down all these variations in explicit rules. Another method is to develop a higher-level model independent of specific audit records. An example of this is a state-transition model known as USTAT [ILGU93, PORR92]. USTAT deals in general actions rather than the detailed specific actions recorded by the UNIX auditing mechanism. USTAT is implemented on a SunOS system that provides audit records on 239 events. Of these, only 28 are used by a preprocessor, which maps these onto 10 general actions (Table 6.6). Using just these actions and the parameters that are invoked with each action, a state-transition diagram is developed that characterizes suspicious activity. Because a number of different auditable events map into a smaller number of actions, the rule-creation process is simpler. Furthermore, the state-transition diagram model is easily modified to accommodate newly learned intrusion behaviors.

---

[3]Such interviews may even extend to reformed or unreformed crackers who will share their expertise for a fee [FREE93].

TABLE 6.6   USTAT Actions versus SunOS Event Types

USTAT Action	SunOS Event Type
Read	open_r, open_rc, open_rtc, open_rwc, open_rwtc, open_rt, open_rw, open_rwt
Write	truncate, ftruncate, creat, open_rtc, open_rwc, open_rwtc, open_rt, open_rw, open_rwt, open_w, open_wt, open_wc, open_wct
Create	mkdir, creat, open_rc, open_rtc, open_rwc, open_rwtc, open_wc, open_wtc, mknod
Delete	rmdir, unlink
Execute	exec, execve
Exit	exit
Modify_Owner	chown, fchown
Modify_Perm	chmod, fchmod
Rename	rename
Hardlink	link

Distributed Intrusion Detection

Until recently, work on intrusion detection systems focused on single-system stand-alone facilities. The typical organization, however, needs to defend a distributed collection of hosts supported by a LAN or internetwork. Although it is possible to mount a defense by using stand-alone intrusion detection systems on each host, a more effective defense can be achieved by coordination and cooperation among intrusion detection systems across the network.

Porras points out the following major issues in the design of a distributed intrusion detection system [PORR92]:

- A distributed intrusion detection system may need to deal with different audit record formats. In a heterogeneous environment, different systems will employ different native audit collection systems and, if using intrusion detection, may employ different formats for security-related audit records.
- One or more nodes in the network will serve as collection and analysis points for the data from the systems on the network. Thus, either raw audit data or summary data must be transmitted across the network. Therefore, there is a requirement to assure the integrity and confidentiality of these data. Integrity is required to prevent an intruder from masking his or her activities by altering the transmitted audit information. Confidentiality is required because the transmitted audit information could potentially be valuable.
- Either a centralized or decentralized architecture can be used. With a centralized architecture, there is a single central point of collection and analysis of all audit data. This eases the task of correlating incoming reports but creates a potential bottleneck and single point of failure. With a decentralized architecture, there are more than one analysis centers, but these must coordinate their activities and exchange information.

A good example of a distributed intrusion detection system is one developed at the University of California at Davis [HEBE92, SNAP91]. Figure 6.6 shows the overall architecture, which consists of three main components:

- *Host agent module:* An audit collection module operating as a background process on a monitored system. Its purpose is to collect data on security-related events on the host and transmit these to the central manager.
- *LAN monitor agent module:* Operates in the same fashion as a host agent module except that it analyzes LAN traffic and reports the results to the central manager.
- *Central manager module:* Receives reports from LAN monitor and host agents, and processes and correlates these reports to detect intrusion.

The scheme is designed to be independent of any operating system or system auditing implementation. Figure 6.7 [SNAP91] shows the general approach that is taken. The agent captures each audit record produced by the native audit collection system. A filter is applied that retains only those records that are of security interest. These records are then reformatted into a standardized format referred to as the host audit record (HAR). Next, a template-driven logic module analyzes the records for suspicious activity. At the lowest level, the agent scans for notable events that are of interest independent of any past events. Examples include failed file accesses, accessing system files, and changing a file's access control. At the next higher level, the agent looks for se-

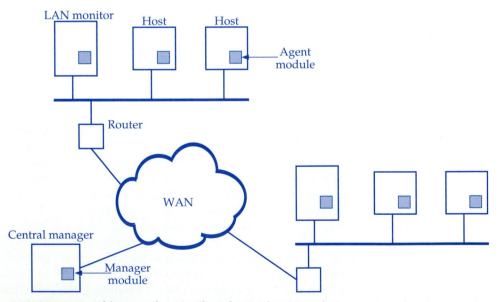

FIGURE 6.6.   Architexture for Distributed Intrusion Detection

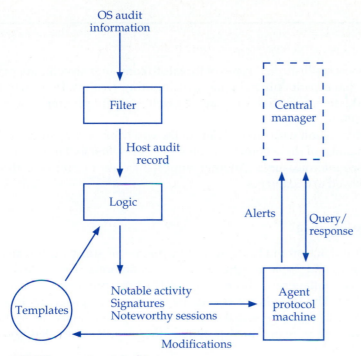

FIGURE 6.7.   Agent Architecture

quences of events, such as known attack patterns (signatures). Finally, the agent looks for anomalous behavior of an individual user based on a historical profile of that user, such as number of programs executed, number of files accessed, and the like.

When suspicious activity is detected, an alert is sent to the central manager. The central manager includes an expert system that can draw inferences from received data. The manager may also query individual systems for copies of HARs to correlate with those from other agents.

The LAN monitor agent also supplies information to the central manager. The LAN monitor agent audits host–host connections, services used, and volume of traffic. It searches for significant events, such as sudden changes in network load, the use of security-related services, and network activities such as *rlogin*.

The architecture depicted in Figures 6.6 and 6.7 is quite general and flexible. It offers a foundation for a machine-independent approach that can expand from stand-alone intrusion detection to a system that is able to correlate activity from a number of sites and networks to detect suspicious activity that would otherwise remain undetected.

VIRUSES

Perhaps the most sophisticated types of threats to computer systems are presented by programs that exploit vulnerabilities in computing systems. In this context, we are concerned with application programs as well as utility programs, such as editors and compilers.

We begin this section with an overview of the spectrum of such software threats. Then the remainder of the section is devoted to viruses, first looking at their nature and then at countermeasures. Another important class of software threat, the worm, is reviewed in Section 6.3

Malicious Programs

Figure 6.8 [BOWL92] provides an overall taxonomy of software threats, or malicious programs, and Table 6.7 provides brief definitions. These threats can be divided into two categories: those that need a host program, and those that are independent. The former are essentially fragments of programs that cannot exist independently of some actual application program, utility, or system program. The latter are self-contained programs that can be scheduled and run by the operating system.

We can also differentiate between those software threats that do not replicate and those that do. The former are fragments of programs that are to be

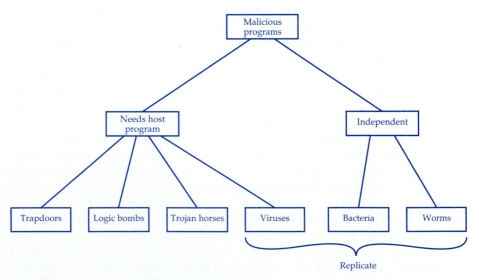

FIGURE 6.8.   Taxonomy of Malicious Programs

TABLE 6.7   Program-Related Threats

Bacteria
Program that consumes system resources by replicating itself.

Logic Bomb
Logic embedded in a computer program that checks for a certain set of conditions to be present on the system. When these conditions are met, it executes some function resulting in unauthorized actions.

Trapdoor
Secret undocumented entry point into a program, used to grant access without normal methods of access authentication.

Trojan Horse
Secret undocumented routine embedded within a useful program. Execution of the program results in execution of the secret routine.

Virus
Code embedded within a program that causes a copy of itself to be inserted in one or more other programs. In addition to propagation, the virus usually performs some unwanted function.

Worm
Program that can replicate itself and send copies from computer to computer across network connections. Upon arrival, the worm may be activated to replicate and propagate again. In addition to propagation, the worm usually performs some unwanted function.

activated when the host program is invoked to perform a specific function. The latter consist of either a program fragment (virus) or an independent program (worm, bacterium) that, when executed, may produce one or more copies of itself to be later activated on the same system or some other system.

Although the taxonomy of Figure 6.8 is useful in organizing the information we are discussing, it is not the whole picture. In particular, logic bombs or Trojan horses may be part of a virus or worm.

Trapdoors

A trapdoor is a secret entry point into a program that allows someone who is aware of the trapdoor to gain access without going through the usual security access procedures. Trapdoors have been used legitimately for many years by programmers to debug and test programs. This usually is done when the programmer is developing an application that has an authentication procedure or a long setup that requires the user to enter many different values to run the application. To debug the program, the developer may wish to gain special privileges or to avoid all the necessary setup and authentication. The programmer may also want to ensure that there is a method of activating the program should something be wrong with the authentication procedure that is being built into the application. The trapdoor is code that recognizes some special sequence of input, or that is triggered by being run from a certain user ID or by an unlikely sequence of events.

Trapdoors become threats when they are used by unscrupulous programmers to gain unauthorized access. The trapdoor was the basic idea for the vulnerability portrayed in the movie "WarGames" [COOP89]. Another example: During the development of Multics, penetration tests were conducted by an Air Force "tiger team" (simulating adversaries). One tactic employed was to send a bogus operating system update to a site running Multics. The update contained a Trojan horse (described later) that could be activated by a trapdoor and that allowed the tiger team to gain access. The threat was so well implemented that the Multics developers could not find it, even after they were informed of its presence [ENGE80].

It is difficult to implement operating-system controls for trapdoors. Security measures must focus on the program development and software update activities.

Logic Bomb

One of the oldest types of program threat, predating viruses and worms, is the logic bomb. The logic bomb is code embedded in some legitimate program that is set to "explode" when certain conditions are met. Examples of conditions that can be used as triggers for a logic bomb are the presence or absence of certain files, a particular day of the week or date, or a particular user running the application. In one famous case [SPAF89], a logic bomb checked for a certain employee ID number (that of the bomb's author) and then triggered if the ID failed to appear in two consecutive payroll calculations. Once triggered, a bomb may alter or delete data or entire files, cause a machine halt, or do some other damage. A striking example of how logic bombs can be employed was the case of the Montgomery County, Maryland, library system [TIME90]. The contractor who had developed a computerized circulation system inserted a logic bomb that would disable the system on a certain date unless the contractor had been paid. When the library withheld its final payment because the system had poor response time, the contractor revealed the existence of the bomb and threatened to allow it to go off unless payment was forthcoming.

Trojan Horses

A Trojan horse is a useful, or apparently useful, program or command procedure containing hidden code that when invoked performs some unwanted or harmful function.

Trojan horse programs can be used to accomplish functions indirectly that an unauthorized user could not accomplish directly. For example, to gain access to the files of another user on a shared system, a user could create a Trojan horse program that, when executed, changed the invoking user's file permissions so that the files are readable by any user. The author could then induce users to run the program by placing it in a common directory and naming it such that it appears to be a useful utility. An example is a program that ostensibly produces a listing of the user's files in a desirable format. After another user has run the program, the author can then access the information in the user's files. An example of a Trojan horse program that would be difficult to detect is a compiler that has been modified to insert additional code into certain programs as they are compiled, such as a system login program [THOM84]. The code creates a trapdoor in the login program that permits the author to log onto the system using a special password. This Trojan horse can never be discovered by reading the source code of the login program.

Another common motivation for the Trojan horse is data destruction. The program appears to be performing a useful function (e.g., a calculator program), but it may also be quietly deleting the user's files. For example, a CBS executive was victimized by a Trojan horse that destroyed all information contained in his computer's memory [TIME90]. The Trojan horse was implanted in a graphics routine offered on an electronic bulletin board system.

Viruses

A virus is a program that can "infect" other programs by modifying them; the modification includes a copy of the virus program, which can then go on to infect other programs.

Biological viruses are tiny scraps of genetic code—DNA or RNA—that can take over the machinery of a living cell and trick it into making thousands of flawless replicas of the original virus. Like its biological counterpart, a computer virus carries in its instructional code the recipe for making perfect copies of itself. Lodged in a host computer, the typical virus takes temporary control of the computer's disk operating system. Then, whenever the infected computer comes into contact with an uninfected piece of software, a fresh copy of the virus passes into the new program. Thus, the infection can be spread from computer to computer by unsuspecting users who either swap disks or send programs to one another over a network. In a network environment, the ability to access applications and system services on other computers provides a perfect culture for the spread of a virus.

Viruses are examined in greater detail later in this section.

Bacteria

Bacteria are programs that do not explicitly damage any files. Their sole purpose is to replicate themselves. A typical bacteria program may do nothing more than execute two copies of itself simultaneously on a multiprogramming system or perhaps create two new files, each of which is a copy of the original source file of the bacteria program. Both programs then copy themselves twice, and so on. Bacteria reproduce exponentially, eventually taking up all the processor capacity, memory, or disk space, denying users access to those resources.

Worms

Network worm programs use network connections to spread from system to system. Once active within a system, a network worm can behave as a computer virus or bacteria (see below), or it can implant Trojan horse programs or perform any number of disruptive or destructive actions.

Worms are examined in Section 6.3.

The Nature of Viruses

A virus can do anything that other programs do. The only difference is that it attaches itself to another program and executes secretly every time the host program is run. Table 6.8 shows a simple example of how a virus can be implemented in such a way as to spread. This example only indicates the mechanism by which the virus remains hidden and by which it spreads. If this were all that there were to viruses, they would not be a cause for concern. Unfortunately, once a virus is executing, it can perform any function, such as erasing files and programs. This is the threat of the virus. Table 6.9 lists some of the better-known viruses and indicates the damage that they can do.

During its lifetime, a typical virus goes through the following four stages:

1. A dormant phase, in which the virus is idle. The virus will eventually be activated by some event, such as a date, the presence of another program or file,

---

TABLE 6.8   Trail of the Virus

A very simple assembly language virus that does nothing more than infect programs might work something like this:

Find the first program instruction
Replace it with a jump to the memory location following the last instruction in the program
Insert a copy of the virus code at that location
Have the virus simulate the instruction replaced by the jump
Jump back to the second instruction of the host program
Finish executing the host program

Every time the host program is run, the virus would infect another program and then execute the host program. Except for a short delay, a user wouldn't notice anything suspicious.

TABLE 6.9 Some Common Viruses

IBM-PC Viruses

Pakistani Brain

One of the most prevalent viruses, so called because it originated in Pakistan. It infects the boot sector on a PC-DOS disk and replicates, infecting every floppy disk inserted into the system. The virus takes over the floppy disk controller interface. If it sees a read operation, it pushes the original read operation aside and attempts to read the boot track. If it determines that the boot is uninfected, it modifies the boot to contain the virus. In some versions, the virus starts to mark areas on your disk as bad even though they are good. Eventually, the disk contains nothing but bad sectors.

Jerusalem Virus

This virus infects executable programs, such as .COM or .EXE files. It resides in the memory and infects every program that is executed. It destroys file allocation tables, which makes it impossible to access files on disk, and scrambles data on the disk. This virus is spread by floppy disks but attacks hard disks as well.

LeHigh Virus

This virus infects the operating system by getting into the command processor. Whenever a disk access is made, it checks to see if the command processor on that disk is infected. If not, the virus is introduced. If so, a counter controlled by the virus is incremented. When the counter reaches four (or ten, in a more recent version), the virus destroys all the data on the hard disk.

Alemeda Virus

This virus infects the system's boot sector. It then infects any floppy disk inserted during reboot and destroys the last track on the disk.

Macintosh Viruses

Scores Virus

This virus is designed to replicate for a specified number of days, followed by several days of dormancy. Thereafter, when the user attempts to save information in a file, the virus will not let it, and crashes the system.

nVIR

This virus comes in a variety of forms, of which at least a dozen have been detected. The technique by which it spreads is especially virulent. It invades the system file; once this crucial resource is infected, every application that is subsequently launched is contaminated.

or the capacity of the disk exceeding some limit. Not all viruses have this stage.

2. A propagation phase, during which the virus places an identical copy of itself into other programs or into certain system areas on the disk. Each infected program will now contain a clone of the virus, which will itself enter a propagation phase.

3. The triggering phase, in which the virus is activated to perform the function for which it was intended. As with the dormant phase, the triggering phase can be caused by a variety of system events, including a count of the number of times that this copy of the virus has made copies of itself.

4. The execution phase, in which the function is performed. The function may be harmless, such as a message on the screen, or damaging, such as the destruction of programs and data files.

Most viruses carry out their work in a manner that is specific to a particular operating system and, in some cases, specific to a particular hardware platform. Thus, they are designed to take advantage of the details and weaknesses of particular systems.

Virus Structure

A virus can be prepended or postpended to an executable program, or it can be embedded in some other fashion. The key to its operation is that the infected program, when invoked, will first execute the virus code and then execute the original code of the program.

A very general depiction of virus structure is shown in Figure 6.9 (based on [COHE90]). In this case, the virus code, V, is prepended to infected programs, and it is assumed that the entry point to the program, when invoked, is the first line of the program.

An infected program begins with the virus code and works as follows. The first line of code is a jump to the main virus program. The second line is a special marker that is used by the virus to determine whether or not a potential victim program has already been infected with this virus. When the program is invoked, control is immediately transferred to the main virus program. The virus program first seeks out uninfected executable files and infects them. Next, the virus may perform some action, usually detrimental to the system. This action could be performed every time the program is invoked, or it could be a logic bomb that triggers only under certain conditions. Finally, the virus transfers control to the original program. If the infection phase of the program is reasonably rapid, a user is unlikely to notice any difference between the execution of an infected and uninfected program.

A virus such as the one just described is easily detected because an infected version of a program is longer than the corresponding uninfected one. A way to thwart such a simple means of detecting a virus is to compress the executable file so that both the infected and uninfected versions are of identical length. Figure 6.10 [COHE90] shows in general terms the logic required. The key lines in this virus are numbered, and Figure 6.11 [COHE90] illustrates the operation. We assume that program P_1 is infected with the virus CV. When this program is invoked, control passes to its virus, which performs the following steps:

```
        program V :=

{goto main;
      1234567;


             subroutine infect-executable :=
                  {loop:
                  file := get-random-executable-file;
                  if (first-line-of-file = 1234567)
                        then goto loop
                        else prepend V to file; }



             subroutine do-damage :=
                  {whatever damage is to be done}


             subroutine trigger-pulled :=
                  {return true if some condition holds}



main:     main-program :=
                  {infect-executable;
                  if trigger-pulled then do-damage;
                  goto next;}


next:


}
```

FIGURE 6.9.   A Simple Virus

1. For each uninfected file P_2 that is found, the virus first compresses that file to produce $P_{2'}$, which is shorter than the original program by the size of the virus.
2. A copy of the virus is prepended to the compressed program.
3. The compressed version of the original infected program, $P_{1'}$, is uncompressed.
4. The uncompressed original program is executed.

In this example, the virus does nothing other than propagate. As in the previous example, the virus may include a logic bomb.

Initial Infection

Once a virus has gained entry to a system by infecting a single program, it is in a position to infect some or all other executable files on that system when the in-

```
        program CV :=

{goto main;
    01234567;


        subroutine infect-executable :=
                {loop:
                        file := get-random-executable-file;
                        if (first-line-of-file = 01234567) then goto loop;
    (1)             compress file;
    (2)             prepend CV to file;
                }



main:  main-program :=
                {if ask-permission then infect-executable;
    (3)         uncompress rest-of-file;
    (4)         run uncompressed file;}
                }
```

FIGURE 6.10.   Logic for a Compression Virus

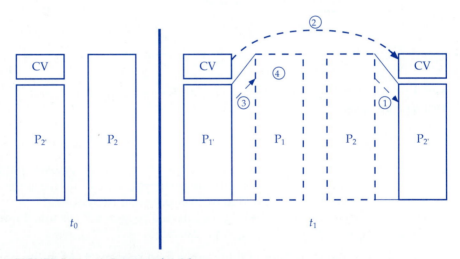

FIGURE 6.11.   A Compression Virus

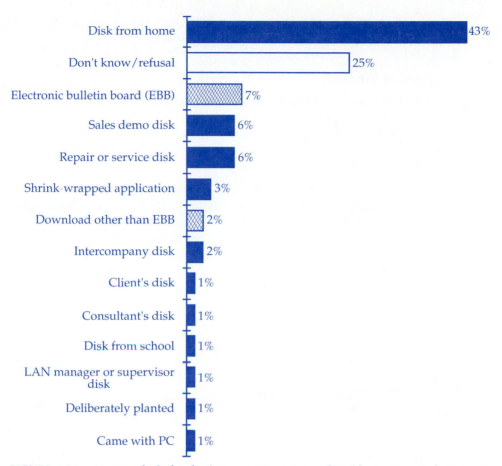

FIGURE 6.12. Means of Viral Infection as a Percentage of Incidents Reported. Source: Dataquest, Inc. 1992

fected program executes. Thus, viral infection can be completely prevented by preventing the virus from gaining entry in the first place. Unfortunately, prevention is extraordinarily difficult because a virus can be part of any program outside a system. Thus, unless one is content to take an absolutely bare piece of iron and write all one's own system and application programs, one is vulnerable.

Figure 6.12 brings this point home. Most viral infections initiate with a disk from which programs are copied onto a machine (indicated in black in the figure). Many of these are disks that have games or simple but handy utilities that employees obtain for their home computers and then bring in and put on an office machine. Some, incredibly, are present on disks that come shrink-wrapped from the manufacturer of an application.

Only a small fraction of infections begin across a network connection (indicated in gray in the figure). Most of these are obtained from an electronic bulletin board system. Again, typically, an employee will download a game or apparently useful utility only to discover later that it contains a virus.

Types of Viruses

There has been a continuous arms race between virus writers and writers of antivirus software since viruses first appeared. As effective countermeasures have been developed for existing types of viruses, new types have been developed. [STEP93] suggests the following categories as being among the most significant types of viruses:

- *Parasitic virus:* the traditional and still most common form of virus. A parasitic virus attaches itself to executable files and replicates, when the infected program is executed, by finding other executable files to infect.
- *Memory-resident virus:* lodges in main memory as part of a resident system program. From that point on, the virus infects every program that executes.
- *Boot sector virus:* infects a master boot record or boot record and spreads when a system is booted from the disk containing the virus.
- *Stealth virus:* a form of virus explicitly designed to hide itself from detection by antivirus software.
- *Polymorphic virus:* a virus that mutates with every infection, making detection by the "signature" of the virus impossible.

One example of a **stealth virus** was discussed earlier: a virus that uses compression so that the infected program is exactly the same length as an uninfected version. Far more sophisticated techniques are possible. For example, a virus can place intercept logic in disk I/O routines, so that when there is an attempt to read suspected portions of the disk using these routines, the virus will present back the original, uninfected program. Thus, stealth is not a term that applies to a virus as such but, rather, is a technique used by a virus to evade detection.

A **polymorphic virus** creates copies during replication that are functionally equivalent but have distinctly different bit patterns. As with a stealth virus, the purpose is to defeat programs that scan for viruses. In this case, the "signature" of the virus will vary with each copy. To achieve this variation, the virus may randomly insert superfluous instructions or interchange the order of independent instructions. A more effective approach is to use encryption. A portion of the virus, generally called a *mutation engine,* creates a random encryption key to encrypt the remainder of the virus. The key is stored with the virus, and the mutation engine itself is altered. When an infected program is invoked, the virus uses the stored random key to decrypt the virus. When the virus replicates, a different random key is selected.

Another weapon in the virus writers' armory is the virus-creation toolkit. Such a toolkit enables a relative novice to quickly create a number of different viruses. Although viruses created with toolkits tend to be less sophisticated than viruses designed from scratch, the sheer number of new viruses that can be generated creates a problem for antivirus schemes.

Yet another tool of the virus writer is the virus exchange bulletin board. A number of such boards have sprung up [ADAM92] in the United States and other countries. These boards offer copies of viruses that can be downloaded, as well as tips for the creation of viruses.

Antivirus Approaches

The ideal solution to the threat of viruses is prevention: Don't allow a virus to get into the system in the first place. This goal is, in general, impossible to achieve, although prevention efforts can reduce the number of successful viral attacks. The next best approach is to be able to do the following:

- *Detection:* Once the infection has occurred, determine that it has occurred and locate the virus.
- *Identification:* Once detection has been achieved, identify the specific virus that has infected a program. Remove the virus from all infected systems, so that the disease cannot spread further.
- *Removal:* Once the specific virus has been identified, remove all traces of the virus from the infected program and restore it to its original state.

If detection succeeds but either identification or removal is not possible, then the alternative is to discard the infected program and reload a clean backup version.

Advances in virus and antivirus technology go hand in hand. Early viruses were relatively simple code fragments and could be identified and purged with relatively simple antivirus software packages. As the virus arms race has evolved, both viruses and, necessarily, antivirus software have grown more complex and sophisticated.

[STEP93] identifies four generations of antivirus software:

- First generation: simple scanners
- Second generation: heuristic scanners
- Third generation: activity traps
- Fourth generation: full-featured protection

A **first-generation** scanner requires a virus signature to identify a virus. The virus may contain "wild cards" but has essentially the same structure and bit pattern in all copies. Such signature-specific scanners are limited to the detection of known viruses. Another type of first-generation scanner maintains a record of the length of programs and looks for changes in length.

A **second-generation** scanner does not rely on a specific signature. Rather, the scanner uses heuristic rules to search for probable virus infection. One class of such scanners looks for fragments of code that are often associated with viruses. For example, a scanner may look for the beginning of an encryption loop used in a polymorphic virus and discover the encryption key. Once the key is discovered, the scanner can decrypt the virus to identify it, then remove the infection and return the program to service.

Another second-generation approach is integrity checking. A checksum can be appended to each program. If a virus infects the program without changing the checksum, then an integrity check will catch the change. To counter a virus that is sophisticated enough to change the checksum when it infects a program, an encrypted hash function can be used. The encryption key is stored separately from the program so that the virus cannot generate a new hash code and encrypt that. By using a hash function rather than a simpler checksum, the virus is prevented from adjusting the program to produce the same hash code as before.

Third-generation programs are memory-resident programs that identify a virus by its actions rather than its structure in an infected program. Such programs have the advantage that it is not necessary to develop signatures and heuristics for a wide array of viruses. Rather, it is necessary only to identify the small set of actions that indicate an infection is being attempted, and to then intervene.

Fourth-generation products are packages consisting of a variety of antivirus techniques used in conjunction. These include scanning and activity trap components. In addition, such a package includes access control capability, which limits the ability of viruses to penetrate a system and then limits the ability of a virus to update files in order to pass on the infection.

The arms race continues. With fourth-generation packages, a more comprehensive defense strategy is employed, broadening the scope of defense to more general-purpose computer security measures.

6.3

WORMS

A network worm shares characteristics of both viruses and intruders. Like a virus, a worm is a self-replicating piece of code that, at minimum, produces copies of itself and may also activate malicious code each time it is executed. Like an intruder, the objective of a worm is system penetration: The worm attempts to plant replicas of itself on other computers over a network or internetwork.

Worm Propagation

A network worm goes through a series of phases that are similar to those of a computer virus: a dormant phase, a propagation phase, a triggering phase, and an execution phase. The propagation phase generally performs the following functions:

1. Searches for other systems to infect by examining host tables or similar repositories of remote system addresses.
2. Establishes a connection with a remote system.
3. Copies itself to the remote system. The new copy of the worm program is then run on the remote system where, in addition to any functions that it performs on that system, it continues to spread in the same fashion.

A network worm may also attempt to determine whether a system has previously been infected before copying itself to the system. In a multiprogramming system, it may also disguise its presence by naming itself as a system process or using some other name that may not be noticed by a system operator.

The vulnerability of a network to a worm is a function of the ability of the worm to propagate itself across the network to the various hosts on the network. This, in turn, is a function of the logical coupling among systems. The more tightly coupled systems are, the more possibilities there are for a worm to exploit. Figure 6.13, suggested by [FERB92], illustrates a spectrum of the degree of coupling. As the degree of coupling increases, the risk from worms increases.

The least flexible form of coupling is via electronic mail. A worm exploits such a facility by mailing a copy of itself to other systems. In most cases, the use of a mail system requires human intervention at some point in the cycle. For example, the Christmas tree worm, launched in December 1987 spread widely on BITNET, the European Academic Research Network (EARN), and IBM's internal network. The worm was an e-mail message that included a text message to the recipient plus code that was executable on IBM mainframes. The message indicated that if the code was executed, a Christmas tree would be drawn on the display. This was true, but in addition, the program sent a copy of itself to everyone on the user's address list. It was not a true worm as the name is usually understood, because it required user intervention. Rather, it was a Trojan horse with a chain-letter type of replicating mechanism. It is, however, possible to exploit flaws in the design of an

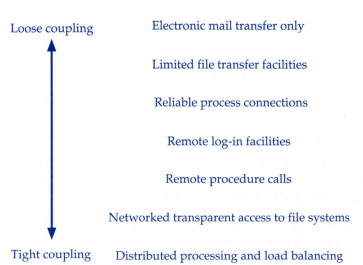

Loose coupling   Electronic mail transfer only

                        Limited file transfer facilities

                        Reliable process connections

                        Remote log-in facilities

                        Remote procedure calls

                        Networked transparent access to file systems

Tight coupling   Distributed processing and load balancing

FIGURE 6.13.   Degree of System Coupling

e-mail system to perform automated replication. This is one of the techniques used by the famous Internet worm.

Returning to Figure 6.13, as the degree of coupling increases, worm programs may be designed that exploit a wider range of vulnerabilities and that have greater opportunities for concealment.

The Internet Worm

The best-known worm was released onto the Internet by Robert Morris in 1988. It is a good example to use because it exhibits many of the characteristics that make for an effective worm.

The Internet worm was designed to spread on UNIX systems and used a number of different techniques for propagation. When a worm began execution, its first task was to discover other hosts known to this host that would allow entry from this host. It performed this task by examining a variety of lists and tables, including system tables that declared which other machines were trusted by this host, users' mail forwarding files, tables by which users gave themselves permission for access to remote accounts, and from a program that reported the status of network connections. For each discovered host, the worm tried a number of methods for gaining access:

1. It attempted to log on to a remote system as a legitimate user. In this method, the worm first attempted to crack the local password file, and then used the discovered passwords and corresponding user IDs. The assumption was that many users would use the same password on different systems. To obtained the passwords, the worm ran a password cracking program that tried:
   (a) Each user's account name and simple permutations of it.
   (b) A list of 432 built-in passwords that the author thought to be likely candidates (Table 6.10).
   (c) All the words in the local system dictionary.
2. It exploited a bug in the finger protocol, which reports the whereabouts of a remote user.
3. It exploited a trapdoor in the debug option of the remote process that receives and sends mail.

If any of these attacks succeeded, the worm achieved communication with the operating system command interpreter. It then sent this interpreter a short bootstrap program, issued a command to execute that program, and then logged off. The bootstrap program then called back the parent program and downloaded the remainder of the worm. The block transferred actually consisted of an encrypted version of the worm. The bootstrap program then decrypted the block to form a new worm and requested its execution.

The worm was designed to be difficult to locate and understand. The main worm was transmitted between systems only in encrypted form. It left no traces in the file system: All files to be used were copied into main memory and no files were written out. The worm disabled the system function that produces a memory

TABLE 6.10   Passwords Tested by the Internet Worm

aaa	carmen	engineer	herbert	minimum	rainbow	super
academia	carolina	enterprise	hiawatha	minsky	raindrop	superstage
aerobics	caroline	enzyme	hibernia	moguls	raleigh	support
airplane	cascades	ersatz	honey	moose	random	supported
albany	castle	establish	horse	morley	rascal	surfer
albatross	cat	estate	horus	mozart	really	suzanne
albert	cayuga	euclid	hutchins	nancy	rebecca	swearer
alex	celtics	evelyn	imbroglio	napoleon	remote	symmetry
alexander	cerulean	extension	imperial	nepenthe	rick	tangerine
algebra	change	fairway	include	ness	ripple	tape
aliases	charles	felicia	ingres	network	robotics	target
alphabet	charming	fender	inna	newton	rochester	tarragon
ama	charon	fermat	innocuous	next	rolex	taylor
amorphous	chester	fidelity	irishman	noxious	romano	telephone
analog	cigar	finite	isis	nutrition	ronald	temptation
anchor	classic	fishers	japan	nyquist	rosebud	thailand
andromache	clusters	flakes	jessica	oceanography	rosemary	tiger
animals	coffee	float	jester	ocelot	roses	toggle
answer	coke	flower	jixian	olivetti	ruben	tomato
anthropogenic	collins	flowers	johnny	olivia	rules	topography
anvils	comrades	foolproof	joseph	oracle	ruth	tortoise
anything	computer	football	joshua	orca	sal	toyota
aria	condo	foresight	judith	orwell	saxon	trails
ariadne	cookie	format	julia	osiris	scamper	trivial
arrow	cooper	forsythe	kathleen	outlaw	scheme	trombone
arthur	cornelius	fourier	kermit	oxford	scott	tubas
athena	couscous	fred	kernel	pacific	scotty	tuttle
atmosphere	creation	friend	kirkland	painless	secret	umesh
aztecs	creosote	frighten	knight	pakistan	sensor	unhappy
azure	cretin	fun	ladle	pam	serenity	unicorn
bacchus	daemon	fungible	lambda	papers	sharks	unknown
bailey	dancer	gabriel	lamination	password	sharon	urchin
banana	daniel	gardner	larkin	patricia	sheffield	utility
bananas	danny	garfield	larry	penguin	sheldon	vasant
bandit	dave	gauss	lazurus	peoria	shiva	vertigo
banks	december	george	lebesque	percolate	shivers	vicky
barber	defoe	gertrude	lee	persimmon	shuttle	village
baritone	deluge	ginger	leland	persona	signature	virginia
bass	desperate	glacier	leroy	pete	simon	warren
bassoon	develop	gnu	lewis	peter	simple	water
batman	dieter	golfer	light	philip	singer	weenie
beater	digital	gorgeous	lisa	phoenix	single	whatnot
beauty	discovery	gorges	louis	pierre	smile	whiting
beethoven	disney	gosling	lynne	pizza	smiles	whitney
beloved	dog	gouge	macintosh	plover	smooch	will
benz	drought	graham	mack	plymouth	smother	william
beowulf	duncan	gryphon		polynomial	snatch	williamsburg

Continued.

TABLE 6.10   Passwords Tested by the Internet Worm—cont'd

berkeley	eager	guest	maggot	pondering	snoopy	willie
berliner	easier	guitar	magic	pork	soap	winston
beryl	edges	gumption	malcolm	poster	socrates	wisconsin
beverly	edinburgh	guntis	mark	praise	sossina	wizard
bicameral	edwin	hacker	markus	precious	sparrows	wombat
bob	edwina	hamlet	marty	prelude	spit	woodwind
brenda	egghead	handily	marvin	prince	spring	wormwood
brian	eiderdown	happening	master	princeton	springer	yacov
bridget	eileen	harmony	maurice	protect	squires	yang
broadway	einstein	harold	mellon	protozoa	strangle	yellowstone
bumbling	elephant	harvey	merlin	pumpkin	stratford	yosemite
burgess	elizabeth	hebrides	mets	puneet	stuttgart	zap
campanile	ellen	heinlein	michael	puppet	subway	zimmerman
cantor	emerald	hello	michelle	rabbit	success	
cardinal	engine	help	mike	rachmaninoff	summer	

dump in case of error. Finally, the worm had an innocuous-sounding name and frequently changed its process identifier.

Countermeasures

A report by the National Institute of Standards and Technology summarizes the key characteristics of worms [BASS92]:

• Worms exploit flaws in an operating system or inadequate system management to replicate.
• Release of a worm usually results in brief but spectacular outbreaks, shutting down entire networks.

The following three approaches can be used to counter worms:

• *Access control:* proper identification and authentication of users prevents a worm from propagating onto a machine without authorization. Measures to assure proper identification and authentication include password protection techniques, as discussed in Section 6.1.
• *Intrusion detection:* the intrusion detection techniques discussed in Section 6.1 are also appropriate in worm defense.
• *Firewalls:* a single LAN or an internetwork domain consisting of a number of interconnected networks can be protected by a firewall system. Any attempt to log on to a system in the protected domain must go through the firewall and first log on to the firewall.

Fortunately, worms are relatively rare because they are difficult to write. Worms require a network environment that includes many systems that exhibit the same flaws, and a worm author who can figure out how to exploit those flaws to develop a self-propagating and self-perpetuating program.

6.4

TRUSTED SYSTEMS

One way to enhance the ability of a system to defend against intruders and malicious programs is to implement trusted system technology. This section provides a brief overview of this topic. We begin by looking at some basic concepts of data access control.

Data Access Control

Following successful log on, the user has been granted access to one or a set of hosts and applications. This is generally not sufficient for a system that includes sensitive data in its database. Through the user access control procedure, a user is identified to the system. Associated with each user, there is a profile that specifies permissible operations and file accesses. The operating system can then enforce rules based on the user profile. The file or database management system, however, must control access to specific records or even portions of records. For example, it may be permissible for anyone in administration to obtain a list of company personnel, but only selected individuals may have access to salary information. The issue is more than just one of level of detail. Whereas the operating system may grant a user permission to access a file or use an application, following which there are no further security checks, the database management system must make a decision on each individual access attempt. That decision depends not only on the user's identity but also on the specific parts of the data being accessed and even on the information already divulged to the user.

A general model of access control as exercised by a file or database management system is that of an **access matrix** (Figure 6.14a). The basic elements of the model are the following:

- *Subject:* an entity capable of accessing objects. Generally, the concept of subject equates with that of process. Any user or application actually gains access to an object by means of a process that represents that user or application.
- *Object:* Anything to which access is controlled. Examples include files, portions of files, programs, and segments of memory.
- *Access right:* The way in which an object is accessed by a subject. Examples are read, write, and execute.

One axis of the matrix consists of identified subjects that may attempt data access. Typically, this list consists of individual users or user groups, although access can be controlled for terminals, hosts, or applications instead of or in addition to users. The other axis lists the objects that may be accessed. At the greatest level of detail, objects may be individual data fields. More aggregate groupings, such as records, files, or even the entire database, may also be objects in the matrix. Each entry in the matrix indicates the access rights of that subject for that object.

	Program1	• • •	SegmentA	SegmentB
Process1	Read Execute		Read Write	
Process2				Read
•				
•				
•				

(a) Access matrix

Access Control List for Program1:
Process1 (Read, Execute)

Access Control List for SegmentA:
Process1 (Read, Write)

Access Control List for SegmentB:
Process2 (Read)

(b) Access control list

Capability List for Process1:
Program1 (Read, Execute)
SegmentA (Read, Write)

Capability List for Process2:
SegmentB (Read)

(c) Capability list

FIGURE 6.14.   Access Control Structures

In practice, an access matrix is usually sparse and is implemented by decomposition in one of two ways. The matrix may be decomposed by columns, yielding **access control lists** (Figure 6.14b). Thus, for each object, an access control list lists users and their permitted access rights. The access control list may contain a default, or public, entry. This allows users that are not explicitly listed as having special rights to have a default set of rights. Elements of the list may include individual users as well as groups of users.

Decomposition by rows yields **capability tickets** (Figure 6.14c). A capability ticket specifies authorized objects and operations for a user. Each user has a number of tickets and may be authorized to loan or give them to others. Because tickets may be dispersed around the system, they present a greater security problem than access control lists. In particular, the ticket must be unforgeable. One way to accomplish this is to have the operating system hold all tickets on behalf of users. These tickets would have to be held in a region of memory inaccessible to users.

The Concept of Trusted Systems

Much of what we have discussed so far has been concerned with protecting a given message or item from passive or active attack by a given user. A somewhat different but widely applicable requirement is to protect data or resources on the basis of levels of security. This is commonly found in the military, where information is categorized as unclassified (U), confidential (C), secret (S), top secret (TS), or beyond. This concept is equally applicable in other areas, where information can be organized into gross categories and users can be granted clearances to access certain categories of data. For example, the highest level of security might be for strategic corporate planning documents and data, accessible by only corporate officers and their staff; next might come sensitive financial and personnel data, accessible only by administration personnel, corporate officers, and so on.

When multiple categories or levels of data are defined, the requirement is referred to as **multilevel security.** This requirement was first addressed in the context of a single computer system and was subsequently extended to networks. We examine the single-system concept first.

The general statement of the requirement for multilevel security is that a subject at a high level may not convey information to a subject at a lower or noncomparable level unless that flow accurately reflects the will of an authorized user. For implementation purposes, this requirement is in two parts and is simply stated. A multilevel secure system must enforce the following two rules:

- *No read up:* A subject can read only an object of less or equal security level. This is referred to in the literature as the **Simple Security Property.**
- *No write down:* A subject can write only into an object of greater or equal security level. This is referred to in the literature as the ***-Property** (pronounced *star property*).[4]

These two rules, if properly enforced, provide multilevel security. For a data processing system, the approach that has been taken and that has been the object of much research and development is based on the *reference monitor* concept (depicted in Figure 6.15). The reference monitor is a controlling element in the hardware and operating system of a computer that regulates the access of subjects to objects on the basis of security parameters of the subject and object. The reference monitor has access to a file, known as the *security kernel database,* that lists the access privileges (security clearance) of each subject and the protection attributes (classi-

---

[4]The "*" does not stand for anything. No one could think of an appropriate name for the property during the writing of the first report on the model. The asterisk was a dummy character entered in the draft so that a text editor could rapidly find and replace all instances of its use once the property was named. No name was ever devised, and so the report was published with the "*" intact.

fication level) of each object. The reference monitor enforces the security rules (no read up, no write down) and has the following properties:

- *Complete mediation:* The security rules are enforced on every access, not just, for example, when a file is opened.
- *Isolation:* The reference monitor and database are protected from unauthorized modification.
- *Verifiability:* The reference monitor's correctness must be provable. That is, it must be possible to mathematically demonstrate that the reference monitor enforces the security rules and provides complete mediation and isolation.

These are stiff requirements. The requirement for complete mediation means that every access to data within main memory and on disk and tape must be mediated. Pure software implementations impose too high a performance penalty to be practical; the solution must be at least partly in hardware. The requirement for isolation means that it must not be possible for an attacker, no matter how clever, to change the logic of the reference monitor or the contents of the security kernel database. Finally, the requirement for mathematical proof is formidable for something as complex as a general-purpose computer. A system that can provide such verification is referred to as a **trusted system.**

A final element illustrated in Figure 6.15 is an audit file. Important security events, such as detected security violations and authorized changes to the security kernel database, are stored in the audit file.

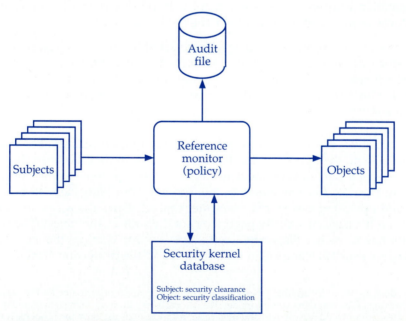

FIGURE 6.15.   Reference Monitor Concept

In an effort to meet its own needs, and also as a service to the public, the U.S. Department of Defense in 1981 established the Computer Security Center within the National Security Agency (NSA) with the goal of encouraging the widespread availability of trusted computer systems. This goal is realized through the center's Commercial Product Evaluation Program. In essence, the center attempts to evaluate commercially available products as meeting the security requirements just outlined. The center classifies evaluated products according to the range of security features that they provide. These evaluations are needed for Department of Defense procurements but are published and freely available. Hence, they can serve as guidance to commercial customers for the purchase of commercially available, off-the-shelf equipment.

Trojan Horse Defense

One way to secure against Trojan horse attacks is the use of a secure, trusted operating system. Figure 6.16 illustrates an example taken from [BOEB85]. In this case, a Trojan horse is used to get around the standard security mechanism used by most file management and operating systems: the access control list. In this example, a user named Doe interacts through a program with a data file containing the critically sensitive character string "CPE1704TKS." User Doe has created the file with read/write permission provided only to programs executing on his own behalf: that is, only processes that are owned by Doe may access the file.

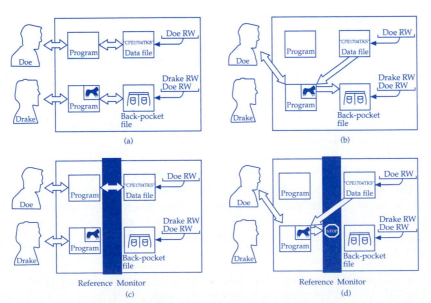

FIGURE 6.16.   Trojan Horse and Secure Operating System

The Trojan horse attack begins when a hostile user, named Drake, gains legitimate access to the system and installs both a Trojan horse program and a private file to be used in the attack as a "back pocket." Drake gives read/write permission to himself for this file and gives Doe write-only permission (Figure 6.16a). Drake now induces Doe to invoke the Trojan horse program, perhaps by advertising it as a useful utility. When the program detects that it is being executed by Doe, it copies the sensitive character string from Doe's file and copies it into Drake's back-pocket file (Figure 6.16b). Both the read and write operations satisfy the constraints imposed by access control lists. Drake then has only to access his file at a later time to learn the value of the string.

Now consider the use of a secure operating system in this scenario (Figure 6.16c). Security levels are assigned to subjects at log-on on the basis of criteria such as the terminal from which the computer is being accessed and the user involved, as identified by password/ID. In this example, there are two security levels, sensitive and public, ordered so that sensitive is higher than public. Processes owned by Doe and Doe's data file are assigned the security level sensitive. Drake's file and processes are restricted to public. Now, if Doe invokes the Trojan horse program (Figure 6.16d), that program acquires Doe's security level. It is therefore able, under the Simple Security Property, to observe the sensitive character string. When the program attempts to store the string in a public file (the back-pocket file), however, the *-Property is violated and the attempt is disallowed by the reference monitor. Thus, the attempt to write into the back-pocket file is denied even though the access control list permits it: The security policy takes precedence over the access control list mechanism.

Multilevel Network Security

The concept of a trusted system can be extended to a network environment. In this case, we wish to enforce the security policy (no read up, no write down) among a number of hosts and terminals connected to a network, such as a local area network (LAN).

One solution to this problem is to require that all hosts on the network be trusted systems. Because a trusted system is generally more expensive than an untrusted system, this might not be an attractive choice. An alternative is a product that has been announced by several vendors and is referred to as a **trusted interface unit** (TIU). A TIU attaches to a network, and terminals or hosts attach to the TIU. The TIU accepts data from attached devices and transmits the data in packets on the network. Similarly, incoming packets from the network are delivered to the attached device.

The TIU is designed to operate at an assigned security level. Two functions are required:

- The TIU will label each packet that it transmits with its security label.
- The TIU will accept only packets that are labeled with its own or a lesser security level.

Figure 6.17 depicts the architecture that can be supported by TIUs. Single-level hosts at a given security level connect to the network via a TIU of the same level. The TIU assures that the host receives data up to only the classification that it is permitted. All data transmitted by the host are labeled by the TIU with its security level, thereby ensuring that no end point of a lower classification level can receive the data.

As with hosts, terminals are also connected to the network via TIUs. All terminals connected to the same TIU must operate at the same level.

Note that unclassified devices require a TIU operating at the unclassified level, not a simple network interface unit (NIU), which performs the interfacing function but not the security function. The filtering function is most important for unclassified devices. That is, we must ensure that an unclassified terminal or computer is prevented from receiving classified data.

The TIU approach is attractive because of the relative ease of building a trusted interface unit. The performance penalty is slight: Only a small amount of additional processing per packet is required. And compared to a general-purpose trusted computer, the TIU is quite simple to verify.

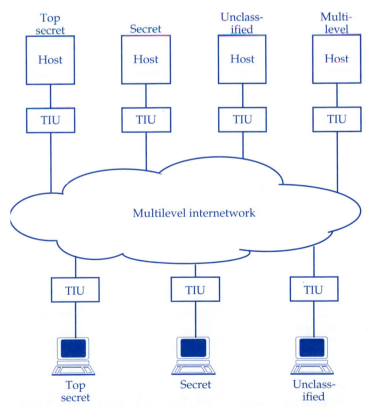

FIGURE 6.17.   Application of the Trusted Interface Unit (TIU)

The TIU is one way to apply the technology of trusted systems to network security. The technology can be applied in a number of other ways. Any critical security function can be implemented as a separate piece of trusted hardware or as an isolated piece of trusted software within a general-purpose system. For example, the front-end processors, access control center, and key distribution center of Figure 3.11 are good candidates for trusted-system technology. Any function, such as public/private key generation done within a host, is a candidate for isolation as a trusted service. Because the technology of trusted systems is relatively new, it will be some time before all the possible security applications are evident.

6.5

RECOMMENDED READING

A highly readable account of the most famous intruder incident is [STOL89]. [HAFN91] looks at some of the most famous incidents and provides useful insight into intruder techniques. [STER92] provides a useful history of intrusion and discusses the techniques and objectives of the main players: intruders, law enforcement, and civil libertarians. [DENN90] contains reprints of many key papers dealing with intruders.

[HOFF90] and [DENN90] contain reprints of many key papers dealing with viruses and worms. The following are excellent technical accounts of virus and antivirus technology: [COHE90], [FERB92], and [HRUS92]. [LUND89] provides an interesting history of viruses and discusses the techniques and objectives of both virus writers and antivirus software writers. [MUNG92] is a more up-to-date account that also covers intruders.

[GASS88] provides a comprehensive study of trusted computer systems. Reprints of some key papers on this topic are to be found in [ABRA87].

ABRA87   Abrams, M., and Podell, H. *Computer and Network Security.* Los Alamitos, CA: IEEE Computer Society Press, 1987.

COHE 90   Cohen, F. *A Short Course on Computer Viruses.* Pittsburgh, PA: ASP Press, 1990.

DENN90   Denning, P., editor. *Computers Under Attack: Intruders, Worms, and Viruses.* Reading, MA: Addison-Wesley, 1990.

FERB92   Ferbrache, D. *A Pathology of Computer Viruses.* New York: Springer-Verlag, 1992.

GASS88   Gasser, M. *Building a Secure Computer System.* New York: Van Nostrand Reinhold, 1988.

HAFN91   Hafner, K., and Markoff, J. *Cyberpunk: Outlaws and Hackers on the Computer Frontier.* New York: Simon & Schuster, 1991.

HOFF90   Hoffman, L., editor. *Rogue Programs: Viruses, Worms, and Trojan Horses.* New York: Van Nostrand Reinhold, 1990.

HRUS92   Hruska, J. *Computer Viruses and Antivirus Warfare.* New York: Ellis Horwood, 1992.

LUND89   Lundell, A. *Virus! The Secret World of Computer Invaders That Breed and Destroy.* Chicago: Contemporary Books, 1989.

MUNG92   Mungo, P., and Clough, B. *Approaching Zero: The Extraordinary Underworld of Hackers, Phreakers, Virus Writers, and Keyboard Criminals.* New York: Random House, 1992.

STER92   Sterling, B. *The Hacker Crackdown: Law and Disorder on the Electronic Frontier.* New York: Bantam, 1992.

STOL89   Stoll, C. *The Cuckoo's Egg.* New York: Doubleday, 1989.

6.6

PROBLEMS

6.1 Because of the known risks of the UNIX password system, the SunOS-4.0 documentation recommends that the password file be removed and replaced with a publicly readable file called /etc/publickey. An entry in the file for user A consists of a user's identifier ID_A, the user's public key, KU_a, and the corresponding private key KR_a. This private key is encrypted using DES with key derived from the user's login password P_a. When A logs in the system decrypts $E_{P_a}[KU_a]$ to obtain KU_a.

   a. The system then verifies that P_a was correctly supplied. How?

   b. How can an opponent attack this system?

6.2 The encryption scheme used for UNIX passwords is in fact one-way; it is not possible to reverse it. Therefore, would it be accurate to say that this is in fact a hash code rather than an encryption of the password?

6.3 It was stated that the inclusion of the salt in the UNIX password scheme increases the difficulty of guessing by a factor of 4096. But the salt is stored in plaintext in the same entry as the corresponding ciphertext password. Therefore, those two characters are known to the attacker and need not be guessed. Therefore, why is it asserted that the salt increases security?

6.4 Assuming that you have successfully answered the preceding problem and understand the significance of the salt, here is another question. Wouldn't it be possible to completely thwart all password crackers by dramatically increasing the salt size to, say, 24 or 48 bits?

6.5 Assume that passwords are limited to the use of 64 characters (A–Z, a–z, 0–9, ".", and "/"), and that all passwords are eight characters in length. Assume a password cracker with an encryption rate of 6.4 million encryptions per second.

   a. How long will it take to exhaustively test all possible passwords on a UNIX system?

   b. If a UNIX password file contains N encrypted passwords, what is the expected number of guesses to find at least one password?

   c. How long will it take to perform the expected number of guesses?

6.6 Consider the Bloom filter discussed in Section 6.1. Define k = number of hash functions; N = number of bits in hash table; and D = number of words in dictionary.

a. Show that the expected fraction of bits in the hash table that are equal to zero is expressed as:

$$\phi = \left(1 - \frac{k}{N}\right)^D$$

b. Show that the probability that an input word, not in the dictionary, will be falsely accepted as being in the dictionary is

$$P = (1 - \phi)^k$$

c. Show that the preceding expression can be approximated as:

$$P \approx (1 - e^{-kD/N})^k$$

6.7 There is a flaw in the virus program of Figure 6.9.
   a. What is it?
   b. Fix it.

6.8 Assume that passwords are selected from four-character combinations of 26 alphabetic characters. Assume that an adversary is able to attempt passwords at a rate of one per second.
   a. Assuming no feedback to the adversary until each attempt has been completed, what is the expected time to discover the correct password?
   b. Assuming feedback to the adversary flagging an error as each incorrect character is entered, what is the expected time to discover the correct password?

6.9 A phonetic password generator picks two segments randomly for each six-letter password. The form of each segment is CVC (consonant, vowel, consonant), where V = <a,e,i,o,u> and C = $\bar{V}$.
   a. What is the total password population?
   b. What is the probability of an adversary guessing a password correctly?

6.10 In Figure 6.16 one link of the Trojan horse copy-and-observe-later chain is broken. There are two other possible angles of attack by Drake: Drake logging on and attempting to read the string directly, and Drake assigning a security level of sensitive to the back-pocket file. Does the reference monitor prevent these attacks?

PART II

INTERNETWORK SECURITY PRACTICE

In practice, the effectiveness of a countermeasure often depends on how it is used; the best safe in the world is worthless if no one remembers to close the door.

— *Computers at Risk: Safe Computing in the Information Age*
National Research Council, 1991

Part II is a survey of internetwork security applications. Of necessity, the author has had to be selective in the material to include in this part. The intent is to discuss the most widely used applications as well as those that appear likely to enjoy significant popularity in the near future.

Chapter 7 discusses basic cryptographic algorithms that are found or are likely in the future to be found in a number of applications. These include both encryption algorithms and hash functions.

Chapter 8 deals with applications related to authentication. The most important such application based solely on conventional encryption is Kerberos. The X.509 specification is important in its own right and is also used in a number of other applications. The Digital Signature Standard (DSS) is a recent U.S. federal standard that appears likely to enjoy widespread use. Finally, the Diffie-Hellman key exchange is a simple algorithm that is found in a number of network security products.

Chapter 9 deals with the security of electronic mail. Two applications with similar technology but very different philosophies seem likely to dominate this area: Pretty Good Privacy (PGP) and Privacy Enhanced Mail (PEM).

Finally, Chapter 10 examines network management security. The chapter focuses on the Simple Network Management Protocol (SNMP) and version 2 of that protocol (SNMPv2). SNMP and SNMPv2 are, together, by far the most widely used means of managing multivendor networks.

CHAPTER 7

CRYPTOGRAPHIC ALGORITHMS

The increased use of computer and communications systems by industry has increased the risk of theft of proprietary information. Although these threats may require a variety of countermeasures, encryption is a primary method of protecting valuable electronic information.

> — Communications Privacy: Federal Policy and Actions
> General Accounting Office Report GAO/OSI-94-2
> November 1993

"It seems very simple."
"It is very simple. But if you don't know what the key is it's virtually indecipherable."

> — *Talking to Strange Men*
> Ruth Rendell

This chapter examines some of the key cryptographic algorithms used in confidentiality and authentication algorithms.[1] We begin with an examination of the two hash algorithms that are likely to see the most use: the MD5 message-digest algorithm and the secure hash algorithm (SHA). The remainder of the chapter deals with encryption algorithms. The international data encryption algorithm (IDEA) was developed to provide a more secure conventional encryption scheme than DES; although relatively new, it has already become quite popular. SKIPJACK is a proposed scheme designed to meet certain U.S. law enforcement objectives. Finally, LUC is a public-key encryption scheme comparable in strength and functionality to RSA.

---

[1]Two important algorithms, DES and RSA, were examined in detail in Part I and are not discussed in this chapter.

THE MD5 MESSAGE-DIGEST ALGORITHM

The MD5 message-digest algorithm (RFC 1321) was developed by Ron Rivest at MIT (the "R" in the RSA [Rivest–Shamir–Adelman] public-key encryption algorithm).

MD5 Logic

The algorithm takes as input a message of arbitrary length and produces as output a 128-bit message digest. The input is processed in 512-bit blocks.

Figure 7.1 depicts the overall processing of a message to produce a digest. The processing consists of the following steps:

•Step 1: Append Padding Bits

The message is padded so that its length in bits is congruent to 448 modulo 512 (length ≡ 448 mod 512). That is, the length of the padded message is 64 bits less than an integer multiple of 512 bits. Padding is always added, even if the message is already of the desired length. For example, if the message is 448 bits long, it is

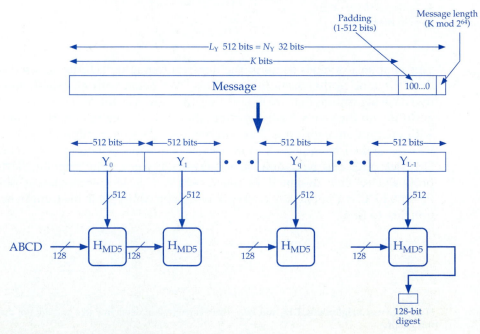

FIGURE 7.1.   Message Digest Generation Using MD5

padded by 512 bits to a length of 960 bits. Thus, the number of padding bits is in the range of 1 to 512.

The padding consists of a single 1-bit followed by the necessary number of 0-bits.

• Step 2: Append Length

A 64-bit representation of the length in bits of the original message (before the padding) is appended to the result of step 1. If the original length is greater than 2^{64}, then only the low-order 64 bits of the length are used. Thus, the field contains the length of the original message, modulo 2^{64}.

The outcome of the first two steps yields a message that is an integer multiple of 512 bits in length. In the figure, the expanded message is represented as the sequence of 512-bit blocks $Y_0, Y_1, \ldots, Y_{L-1}$, so that the total length of the expanded message is $L \times 512$ bits. Equivalently, the result is a multiple of 16 32-bit words. Let $M[0 \ldots N-1]$ denote the words of the resulting message, with N an integer multiple of 16. Thus $N = L \times 16$.

• Step 3: Initialize MD Buffer

A 128-bit buffer is used to hold intermediate and final results of the hash function. The buffer can be represented as four 32-bit registers (A, B, C, D). These registers are initialized to the following hexadecimal values (low-order octets first):

$$A = 01234567$$
$$B = 89ABCDEF$$
$$C = FEDCBA98$$
$$D = 76543210$$

• Step 4: Process Message in 512-Bit (16-Word) Blocks

The heart of the algorithm is a module that consists of four "rounds" of processing; this module is labeled H_{MD5} in Figure 7.1, and its logic is illustrated in Figure 7.2. The four rounds have a similar structure, but each uses a different primitive logical function, referred to as F, G, H, and I in the specification. In the figure, the four rounds are labeled f_F, f_G, f_H, f_I, to indicate that each round has the same general functional structure, f, but depends on a different primitive function (F, G, H, I).

Note that each round takes as input the current 512-bit block being processed (Y_q) and the 128-bit buffer value ABCD and updates the contents of the buffer. Each round also makes use of one-fourth of a 64-element table T[1 . . . 64], constructed from the sine function. The ith element of T, denoted T[i], has the value equal to the integer part of $2^{32} \times \text{abs}(\sin(i))$, where i is in radians. Since $\text{abs}(\sin(i))$ is a number between 0 and 1, each element of T is an integer that can be represented in 32 bits. The table provides a "randomized" set of 32-bit patterns, which should eliminate any regularities in the input data. Table 7.1b lists the values of T.

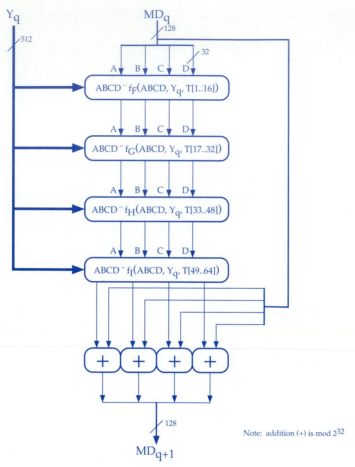

Note: addition (+) is mod 2^{32}

FIGURE 7.2.   MD5 Processing of Single 512-bit Block (HD$_{\text{MD5}}$)

Overall, for block Y_q, the algorithm takes Y_q and an intermediate digest value MD_q as inputs. MD_q is placed into buffer ABCD. The output of the fourth round is added to MD_q to produce MD_{q+1}. The addition is done independently for each of the four words in the buffer with each of the corresponding words in MDq, using addition modulo 2^{32}.

•Step 5: Output

After all L 512-bit blocks have been processed, the output from the Lth stage is the 128-bit message digest.

Let us look in more detail at the logic in each of the four rounds of the processing of one 512-bit block. Each round consists of a sequence of 16 steps operating on the buffer ABCD. Each step is of the form (Figure 7.3):

TABLE 7.1　Key Elements of MD5

(a)　Truth table of logical functions

b	c	d	F	G	H	I
0	0	0	0	0	0	1
0	0	1	1	0	1	0
0	1	0	0	1	1	0
0	1	1	1	0	0	1
1	0	0	0	0	1	1
1	0	1	0	1	0	1
1	1	0	1	1	0	0
1	1	1	1	1	1	0

(b) Table T, constructed from the sine function

T[1]　= D76AA478	T[17] = F61E2562	T[33] = FFFA3942	T[49] = F4292244
T[2]　= E8C7B756	T[18] = C040B340	T[34] = 8771F681	T[50] = 432AFF97
T[3]　= 242070DB	T[19] = 265E5A51	T[35] = 69D96122	T[51] = AB9423A7
T[4]　= C1BDCEEE	T[20] = E9B6C7AA	T[36] = FDE5380C	T[52] = FC93A039
T[5]　= F57C0FAF	T[21] = D62F105D	T[37] = A4BEEA44	T[53] = 655B59C3
T[6]　= 4787C62A	T[22] = 02441453	T[38] = 4BDECFA9	T[54] = 8F0CCC92
T[7]　= A8304613	T[23] = D8A1E681	T[39] = F6BB4B60	T[55] = FFEFF47D
T[8]　= FD469501	T[24] = E7D3FBC8	T[40] = BEBFBC70	T[56] = 85845DD1
T[9]　= 698098D8	T[25] = 21E1CDE6	T[41] = 289B7EC6	T[57] = 6FA87E4F
T[10] = 8B44F7AF	T[26] = C33707D6	T[42] = EAA127FA	T[58] = FE2CE6E0
T[11] = FFFF5BB1	T[27] = F4D50D87	T[43] = D4EF3085	T[59] = A3014314
T[12] = 895CD7BE	T[28] = 455A14ED	T[44] = 04881D05	T[60] = 4E0811A1
T[13] = 6B901122	T[29] = A9E3E905	T[45] = D9D4D039	T[61] = F7537E82
T[14] = FD987193	T[30] = FCEFA3F8	T[46] = E6DB99E5	T[62] = BD3AF235
T[15] = A679438E	T[31] = 676F02D9	T[47] = 1FA27CF8	T[63] = 2AD7D2BB
T[16] = 49B40821	T[32] = 8D2A4C8A	T[48] = C4AC5665	T[64] = EB86D391

$$a \leftarrow b + CLS_s (a + g(b, c, d) + X[k] + T[i])$$

where

a, b, c, d = the four words of the buffer, in a specified order that varies across steps

g = one of the primitive functions F, G, H, I

CLS_s = circular left shift (rotation) of the 32-bit argument by s bits

$X[k]$ = $M[q \times 16 + k]$ = the kth 32-bit word in the qth 512-bit block of the message

$T[i]$ = the ith 32-bit word in matrix T

$+$ = addition modulo 2^{32}

One of the four primitive logical functions is used for each of the four rounds of the algorithm. Each primitive function takes three 32-bit words as input and produces a 32-bit word output. Each function performs a set of bitwise logical opera-

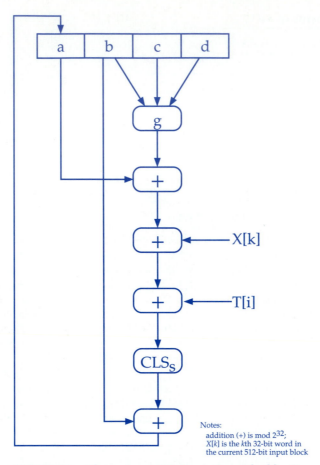

FIGURE 7.3.   Elementary MD5 Operation: [abcd k s i]

tions; that is, the nth bit of the output is a function of the nth bit of the three inputs. The functions can be summarized as follows:

Round	Primitive function g	g(b, c, d)
f_F	F(b, c, d)	$(b \cdot c) \vee (\bar{b} \cdot d)$
f_G	G(b, c, d)	$(b \cdot d) \vee (c \cdot \bar{d})$
f_H	H(b, c, d)	$b \oplus c \oplus d$
f_I	I(b, c, d)	$c \oplus (b \cdot \bar{d})$

The logical operators (AND, OR, NOT, XOR) are represented by the symbols $(\cdot, \vee, \bar{}, \oplus)$. Function F is a conditional function: If b then c else d. Similarly, G can be stated: If d then b else c. Function H produces a parity bit. Table 7.1a is a truth table of the four functions.

Figure 7.4, adapted from RFC 1321, defines the processing algorithm of step 4. The expression ($w <<< s$) denotes the 32-bit value obtained by performing a circular left shift (rotation) of w by s bit positions. The array of 32-bit words X[0..15] holds the value of the current 512-bit input block being processed. Note that each round consists of 16 steps for a total of 64 steps. Each 32-bit word of input is used four times, once per round, and each of the 64 32-bit word elements of T is used

```
/* Process each 16-word (512-bit) block. */
For q = 0 to (N/16) - 1 do
    /* Copy block i into X. */
    For j = 0 to 15 do
        Set X[j] to  M[q*16 + j].
    end /* of loop on j */

    /* Save A as AA, B as BB, C as CC, and
       D as DD. */
    AA = A
    BB = B
    CC = C
    DD = D

    /* Round 1. */
    /* Let [abcd  k  s  i] denote the operation
       a = b + ((a + F(b,c,d) + X[k] + T[i] <<<s).
    Do the following 16 operations. */
    [ABCD    0    7    1]
    [DABC    1   12    2]
    [CDAB    2   17    3]
    [BCDA    3   22    4]
    [ABCD    4    7    5]
    [DABC    5   12    6]
    [CDAB    6   17    7]
    [BCDA    7   22    8]
    [ABCD    8    7    9]
    [DABC    9   12   10]
    [CDAB   10   17   11]
    [BCDA   11   22   12]
    [ABCD   12    7   13]
    [DABC   13   12   14]
    [CDAB   14   17   15]
    [BCDA   15   22   16]

    /* Round 2. */
    /* Let [abcd  k  s  i] denote the operation
       a = b + ((a + G(b,c,d) + X[k] + T[i] <<<s).
    Do the following 16 operations. */
    [ABCD    1    5   17]
    [DABC    6    9   18]
    [CDAB   11   14   19]
    [BCDA    0   20   20]
    [ABCD    5    5   21]
    [DABC   10    9   22]
    [CDAB   15   14   23]
    [BCDA    4   20   24]
    [ABCD    9    5   25]
    [DABC   14    9   26]
    [CDAB    3   14   27]
    [BCDA    8   20   28]
    [ABCD   13    5   29]
    [DABC    2    9   30]
    [CDAB    7   14   31]
    [BCDA   12   20   32]

    /* Round 3. */
    /* Let [abcd  k  s  i] denote the operation
       a = b + ((a + H(b,c,d) + X[k] + T[i] <<<s).
    Do the following 16 operations. */
    [ABCD    5    4   33]
    [DABC    8   11   34]
    [CDAB   11   16   35]
    [BCDA   14   23   36]
    [ABCD    1    4   37]
    [DABC    4   11   38]
    [CDAB    7   16   39]
    [BCDA   10   23   40]
    [ABCD   13    4   41]
    [DABC    0   11   42]
    [CDAB    3   16   43]
    [BCDA    6   23   44]
    [ABCD    9    4   45]
    [DABC   12   11   46]
    [CDAB   15   16   47]
    [BCDA    2   23   48]

    /* Round 4. */
    /* Let [abcd  k  s  i] denote the operation
       a = b + ((a + I(b,c,d) + X[k] + T[i] <<<s).
    Do the following 16 operations. */
    [ABCD    0    6   49]
    [DABC    7   10   50]
    [CDAB   14   15   51]
    [BCDA    5   21   52]
    [ABCD   12    6   53]
    [DABC    3   10   54]
    [CDAB   10   15   55]
    [BCDA    1   21   56]
    [ABCD    8    6   57]
    [DABC   15   10   58]
    [CDAB    6   15   59]
    [BCDA   13   21   60]
    [ABCD    4    6   61]
    [DABC   11   10   62]
    [CDAB    2   15   63]
    [BCDA    9   21   64]

    /* Then increment each of the four registers by the
       value it had before this block was started. */
    A = A + AA
    B = B + BB
    C = C + CC
    D = D + DD

end /* of loop on q */
```

FIGURE 7.4.   Basic MD5 Update Algorithm (RFC 1321)

exactly once. Also, note that for each step, only one of the four bytes of the ABCD buffer is updated. Hence, each byte of the buffer is updated 16 times during the round, and then a 17th time at the end to produce the final output for this block.

We can summarize the behavior of MD5 as follows:

$$MD_0 = IV$$

$$MD_{q+1} = MD_q + f_I\left[Y_q, f_H\left[Y_q, f_G\left[Y_q, f_F[Y_q, MD_q]\right]\right]\right]$$

$$MD = MD_{L-1}$$

where

IV = initial value of the ABCD buffer, defined in step 3
Y_q = the qth 512-bit block of the message
L = the number of blocks in the message (including padding and length fields)
MD = final message digest value

MD4

MD4 is a precursor to MD5 developed by the same designer, Ron Rivest. Originally published as an RFC in October 1990, a slightly revised version was published as RFC 1320 in April 1992, the same date as MD5. It is worth briefly discussing MD4 because MD5 shares the design goals of MD4, which were documented in a paper by Rivest [RIVE90]. The following goals were listed:

- *Security:* There is the usual requirement for a hash code, namely, that it be computationally infeasible to find two messages that have the same message digest.
- *Speed:* The algorithm should lend itself to implementations in software that execute rapidly. In particular, the algorithm is intended to be fast on 32-bit architectures. Thus, the algorithm is based on a simple set of primitive operations on 32-bit words.
- *Simplicity and compactness:* The algorithm should be simple to describe and simple to program, without requiring large programs or substitution tables. These characteristics not only have obvious programming advantages but are desirable from a security point of view, because a simple algorithm is more likely to receive the necessary critical review.
- *Favor little-endian architecture:* Some processor architectures (such as the Intel 80xxx line) store the least significant byte of a word in the low-address byte position (little endian). Others (such as a SUN Sparcstation) store the most significant byte of a word in the low-address byte position (big endian). This distinction is significant when treating a message as a sequence of 32-bit words, because one of the two architectures will have to byte-reverse each word for processing. Rivest chose to use a little-endian scheme for interpreting a message as a sequence of 32-bit words. This choice was made on the basis of Rivest's observation that big-endian processors are generally faster and can therefore better afford the processing penalty.

These design goals carried over to MD5. MD5 is somewhat more complex and hence somewhat slower to execute than MD4. Rivest felt that the added complexity was justified by the increased level of security afforded. Following are the main differences between the two:

1. MD4 uses three rounds of 16 steps each, whereas MD5 uses four rounds of 16 steps each.
2. In MD4, no additive constant is used in the first round. The same additive constant is used for each of the steps of the second round. Another additive constant is used for each of the steps of the third round. In MD5, a different additive constant, T[i], is used for each of the 64 steps.
3. MD5 uses four primitive logical functions, one for each round, compared to three for MD4, again one for each round.
4. In MD5, each step adds in the result of the preceding step. For example, the step 1 result updates word A. The step 2 result, which is stored in D, is formed by adding A to the circular left shift result. Similarly, the step 3 result is stored in C and is formed by adding D to the circular left shift result. MD4 did not include this final addition. Rivest feels that the inclusion of the previous step's result promotes a greater avalanche effect.

Strength of MD5

The MD5 algorithm has the property that every bit of the hash code is a function of every bit in the input. The complex repetition of the basic functions (F, G, H, I) produces results that are well mixed; that is, it is unlikely that two messages chosen at random, even if they exhibit similar regularities, will have the same hash code. Rivest conjectures in the RFC that MD5 is as strong as possible for a 128-bit hash code; namely, the difficulty of coming up with two messages having the same message digest is on the order of 2^{64} operations, whereas the difficulty of finding a message with a given digest is on the order of 2^{128} operations.

As of this writing, no analysis has been done to disprove these conjectures. Two results are, however, noteworthy. [BERS92] showed, using differential cryptanalysis, that it is possible in reasonable time to find two messages that produce the same digest for a single-round MD5. The result was demonstrated for each of the four rounds. However, the author has not been able to show how to generalize the attack to the full four-round MD5.

[BOER93] shows how to find a message block x and two related digest values that yield the same output state. That is, execution of MD5 on a single block of 512 bits will yield the same output for two different input values in buffer ABCD. At present, there does not seem to be any way to extend this approach to a successful attack on MD5.

Finally, it is worth comparing the overall strategy of Snefru and MD5. Like MD5, Snefru is designed to execute efficiently on a 32-bit machine. A major difference is that Snefru relies on the use of S-boxes and the XOR function, whereas MD5 emphasizes addition mod 2^{32}. Thus, Snefru can be characterized as a DES-like cryptosystem, and, as discussed in Chapter 2, such systems are vulnerable to differential cryptanalysis [BIHA93]. Designers of cryptosystems (both encryption algorithms and hash codes) published since the development of differential cryptanalysis have sought to avoid this vulnerability by using alternatives to the XOR operation. MD5 is an example of this trend. [BERS92] suggests that this strategy may not make these newer systems invulnerable to cryptanalysis. The jury is still out on this point, but so far it appears that the modular arithmetic approach is stronger than the XOR approach.

7.2

THE SECURE HASH ALGORITHM

The Secure Hash Algorithm (SHA) was developed by the National Institute of Standards and Technology (NIST) and published as a federal information processing standard (FIPS PUB 180) in 1993. SHA is based on the MD4 algorithm and its design closely models MD4.

SHA Logic

The algorithm takes as input a message with a maximum length of less than 2^{64} bits and produces as output a 160-bit message digest. The input is processed in 512-bit blocks.

Figure 7.5 depicts the overall processing of a message to produce a digest. The processing consists of the following steps:

• Step 1: Append Padding Bits

The message is padded so that its length is congruent to 448 modulo 512 (length $\equiv$ 448 mod 512). Padding is always added, even if the message is already of the desired length. Thus, the number of padding bits is in the range of 1 to 512. The padding consists of a single 1-bit followed by the necessary number of 0-bits.

• Step 2: Append Length

A block of 64 bits is appended to the message. This block is treated as an unsigned 64-bit integer and contains the length of the original message (before the padding)

The outcome of the first two steps yields a message that is an integer multiple of 512 bits in length. In the figure, the expanded message is represented as the sequence of 512-bit blocks $Y_0, Y_1, \ldots, Y_{L-1}$, so that the total length of the expanded message is $L \times 512$ bits. Equivalently, the result is a multiple of 16 32-bit words. Let $M[0 \ldots N-1]$ denote the words of the resulting message, with N an integer multiple of 16. Thus $N = L \times 16$.

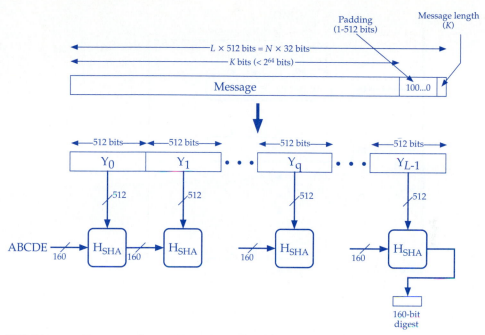

FIGURE 7.5.   Message Digest Generation Using SHA

• Step 3: Initialize MD Buffer

A 160-bit buffer is used to hold intermediate and final results of the hash function. The buffer can be represented as five 32-bit registers (A, B, C, D, E). These registers are initialized to the following hexadecimal values (high-order octets first):

$$
\begin{aligned}
A &= 67452301 \\
B &= EFCDAB89 \\
C &= 98BADCFE \\
D &= 10325476 \\
E &= C3D2E1F0
\end{aligned}
$$

Note that the first four values are the same as those used in MD5; the difference in appearance is caused by the use of a different convention for expressing the values (high-order vs. low-order octet first).

• Step 4: Process Message in 512-Bit (16-Word) Blocks

The heart of the algorithm is a module that consists of 80 steps of processing; this module is labeled H_{SHA} in Figure 7.5, and its logic is illustrated in Figure 7.6. The 80 steps have a similar structure, as explained below.

Note that each round takes as input the current 512-bit block being processed (Y_q) and the 160-bit buffer value ABCDE, and updates the contents of the buffer.

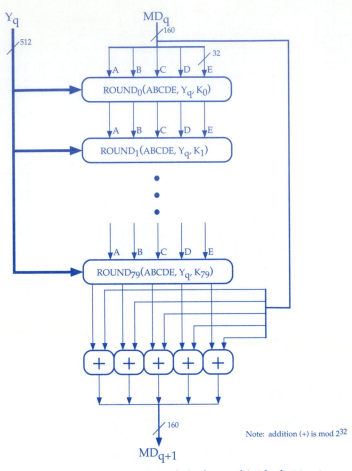

FIGURE 7.6.   SHA Processing of Single 512-bit Block (H_{SHA})

Each round also makes use of an additive constant K_t. In fact, only four distinct constants are used. The values, in hexadecimal, are as follows:

$$0 \le t \le 19 \quad K_t = 5A827999$$
$$20 \le t \le 39 \quad K_t = 6ED9EBA1$$
$$40 \le t \le 59 \quad K_t = 8F1BBCDC$$
$$60 \le t \le 79 \quad K_t = CA62C1D6$$

Overall, for block Y_q, the algorithm takes Y_q and an intermediate digest value MD_q as inputs. MD_q is placed into buffer ABCDE. The output of the 80th step is added to MD_q to produce MD_{q+1}. The addition is done independently for each of the five words in the buffer with each of the corresponding words in MD_q, using addition modulo 2^{32}.

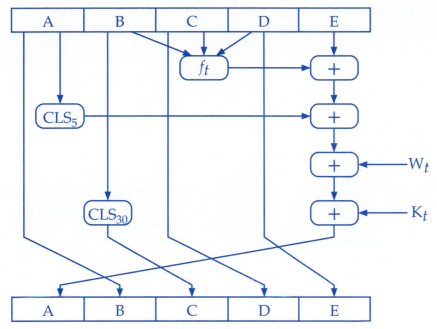

FIGURE 7.7. Elementary SHA Operation

• Step 5: Output

After all L 512-bit blocks have been processed, the output from the Lth stage is the 160-bit message digest.

Let us look in more detail at the logic in each of the 80 rounds of the processing of one 512-bit block. Each round is of the form (Figure 7.7):

$$A, B, C, D, E \leftarrow (CLS_5(A) + f_t(B, C, D) + E + W_t + K_t), A, CLS_{30}(B), C, D$$

where

A, B, C, D, E	= the five words of the buffer
t	= round, or step, number; $0 \leq t \leq 79$
f_t	= a primitive logical function
CLS_s	= circular left shift (rotation) of the 32-bit argument by s bits
W_t	= a 32-bit word derived from the current 512-bit input block
K_t	= an additive constant; four distinct values are used, as defined above
$+$	= addition modulo 2^{32}

Each primitive function takes three 32-bit words as input and produces a 32-bit word output. Each function performs a set of bitwise logical operations; that is, the *n*th bit of the output is a function of the *n*th bit of the three inputs. The functions can be summarized as follows:

Round	$f_t(B, C, D)$
$(0 \le t \le 19)$	$(B \cdot C) \vee (\bar{B} \cdot D)$
$(20 \le t \le 39)$	$B \oplus C \oplus D$
$(40 \le t \le 59)$	$(B \cdot C) \vee (B \cdot D) \vee (C \cdot D)$
$(60 \le t \le 79)$	$B \oplus C \oplus D$

As can be seen, only three different functions are used. For $0 \le t \le 19$, the function is the conditional function: If B then C else D. For $20 \le t \le 39$ and $60 \le t \le 79$, the function produces a parity bit. For $40 \le t \le 59$, the function is true if two or three of the arguments are true. Table 7.2 is a truth table of these functions.

It remains to indicate how the 32-bit word values W_t are derived from the 512-bit message. Figure 7.8 illustrates the mapping. The first 16 values of W_t are taken directly from the 16 words of the current block. The remaining values are defined as follows:

$$W_t = W_{t-16} \oplus W_{t-14} \oplus W_{t-8} \oplus W_{t-3}$$

Thus, in the first 16 rounds of processing, the input from the message block consists of a single 32-bit word from that block. For the remaining 64 rounds, the input consists of the XOR of a number of the words from the message block.

We can summarize the behavior of SHA as follows:

$$
\begin{aligned}
MD_0 &= IV \\
MD_{q+1} &= SUM_{32}(MD_q, ABCDE_q) \\
MD &= MD_{L-1}
\end{aligned}
$$

where

IV   = initial value of the ABCDE buffer, defined in step 3
$ABCDE_q$ = the output of the last round of processing of the *q*th message block

TABLE 7.2   Truth Table of Logical Functions for SHA

b	c	d	$f_{0..19}$	$f_{20..39}$	$f_{40..59}$	$f_{60..79}$
0	0	0	0	0	0	0
0	0	1	1	1	0	1
0	1	0	0	1	0	1
0	1	1	1	0	1	0
1	0	0	0	1	0	1
1	0	1	0	0	1	0
1	1	0	1	0	1	0
1	1	1	1	1	1	1

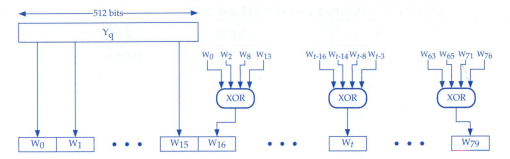

FIGURE 7.8.   Creation of 80-word Input Sequence for SHA Processing of Single Block

L = the number of blocks in the message (including padding and length
                fields)
SUM_{32} = Addition modulo 2^{32} performed separately on each word of the pair
                of inputs
MD   = final message digest value

Comparison of SHA and MD5

Because both are derived from MD4, SHA and MD5 are quite similar to one another. Accordingly, their strengths and other characteristics should be similar.

Table 7.3 summarizes key differences between the two algorithms. With this
table in mind, let us compare the two algorithms using the design goals cited earlier for MD4:

- *Security:* The most obvious, and most important, difference is that the SHA digest is 32 bits longer than the MD5 digest. If neither algorithm contains any
  structural flaws that are vulnerable to cryptanalytic attack, which is so far a reasonable assumption, then SHA is the stronger algorithm. Using a brute-force
  technique, the difficulty of producing any message having a given message digest is on the order of 2^{128} operations for MD5 and 2^{160} for SHA. Again, using a
  brute-force technique, the difficulty of producing two messages having the
  same message digest is on the order of 2^{64} operations for MD5 and 2^{80} for SHA.
- *Speed:* Because both algorithms rely heavily on addition modulo 2^{32}, both do
  well on a 32-bit architecture. SHA involves more steps (80 versus 64) and must
  process a 160-bit buffer compared to MD5's 128-bit buffer. Thus, SHA should
  execute about 25% slower than MD5 on the same hardware.
- *Simplicity and compactness:* Both algorithms are simple to describe and simple to
  implement, without requiring large programs or substitution tables. However,
  SHA uses a single-step structure, compared to the four structures used in MD5.
  Furthermore, the manipulation of the buffer words is the same for all SHA
  steps, whereas in MD5, the arrangement of words is specified individually for
  each step. Thus, in this category, SHA gets the nod.

TABLE 7.3   A Comparison of MD5 and SHA

	MD5	SHA
Digest length	128 bits	160 bits
Basic unit of processing	512 bits	512 bits
Number of steps	64 (four rounds of 16)	80
Maximum message size	∞	2^{64} bits
Primitive logical functions	4	3
Additive constants used	64	4

- *Little-endian versus big-endian architecture:* MD5 uses a little-endian scheme for interpreting a message as a sequence of 32-bit words, whereas SHA uses a big-endian scheme.[2] There is no strong advantage to either approach.

7.3

INTERNATIONAL DATA ENCRYPTION ALGORITHM (IDEA)

IDEA is a new block-oriented conventional encryption algorithm developed by Xuejia Lai and James Massey of the Swiss Federal Institute of Technology. The original version was published in [LAI90]. A revised version of the algorithm, designed to be stronger against differential cryptanalytic attacks, was presented in [LAI91] and is described in greater detail in [LAI92].

IDEA is one of a number of conventional encryption algorithms that have been proposed in recent years to replace DES, which, as was discussed in Chapter 2, many feel is approaching or has even reached the end of its useful lifetime. In terms of adoption, IDEA is by far the most successful of these proposals. For example, IDEA is included in PGP, to be discussed in Chapter 9, which alone assures widespread use of the algorithm.

Design Principles

IDEA is a block cipher that uses a 128-bit key to encrypt data in blocks of 64 bits. By contrast, DES also uses 64-bit blocks but a 56-bit key.

The design goals for IDEA can be grouped into those related to cryptographic strength and those related to ease of implementation.

Cryptographic Strength

The following characteristics of IDEA relate to its cryptographic strength:

- *Block length:* The block length should be long enough to deter statistical analysis, that is, to deny the opponent any advantage that some blocks appear

[2]Probably because the NSA designers of SHA used a Sun for the prototype implementation.

more often than others. On the other hand, the complexity of implementing an effective encryption function appears to grow exponentially with block size [WEGE87]. The use of a block size of 64 bits is generally recognized as sufficiently strong. Furthermore, the use of a cipher feedback mode of operation further strengthens this aspect of the algorithm.

- *Key length:* The key length should be long enough to effectively prevent exhaustive key searches. With a length of 128 bits, IDEA seems to be secure in this area far into the future.
- *Confusion:* The ciphertext should depend on the plaintext and key in a complicated and involved way. The objective is to complicate the determination of how the statistics of the ciphertext depend on the statistics of the plaintext. IDEA achieves this goal by using three different operations, as explained below. This is in contrast to DES, which relies principally on the XOR operation and on small nonlinear S-boxes.
- *Diffusion:* Each plaintext bit should influence every ciphertext bit, and each key bit should influence every ciphertext bit. The spreading out of a single plaintext bit over many ciphertext bits hides the statistical structure of the plaintext. IDEA is very effective in this regard.

Let us elaborate on the last two points. In IDEA, **confusion** is achieved by mixing three different operations. Each operation is performed on two 16-bit inputs to produce a single 16-bit output. The operations are

- Bit-by-bit exclusive-OR, denoted as $\oplus$.
- Addition of integers modulo 2^{16} (modulo 65536), with inputs and outputs treated as unsigned 16-bit integers. This operation is denoted as $\boxplus$.
- Multiplication of integers modulo $2^{16} + 1$ (modulo 65537), with inputs and outputs treated as unsigned 16-bit integers, except that a block of all zeros is treated as representing 2^{16}. This operation is denoted as $\odot$.

For example,

$$0000000000000000 \odot 1000000000000000 = 1000000000000001$$

because

$$2^{16} \times 2^{15} \bmod (2^{16} + 1) = 2^{15} + 1$$

Table 7.4 shows values for the three operations operating on 2-bit numbers (rather than 16-bit numbers). These three operations are incompatible in the sense that:

1. No pair of the three operations satisfies a distributive law. For example:

$$a \boxplus (b \odot c) \neq (a \boxplus b) \odot (a \boxplus c)$$

2. No pair of the three operations satisfies an associative law. For example,

$$a \boxplus (b \oplus c) \neq (a \boxplus b) \oplus c$$

TABLE 7.4   Functions Used in IDEA (for operand length of 2 bits)

X		Y		X $\boxplus$ Y		X $\odot$ Y		X $\oplus$ Y	
0	00	0	00	0	00	1	01	0	00
0	00	1	01	1	01	0	00	1	01
0	00	2	10	2	10	3	11	2	10
0	00	3	11	3	11	2	10	3	11
1	01	0	00	1	01	0	00	1	01
1	01	1	01	2	10	1	01	0	00
1	01	2	10	3	11	2	10	3	11
1	01	3	11	0	00	3	11	2	10
2	10	0	00	2	10	3	11	2	10
2	10	1	01	3	11	2	10	3	11
2	10	2	10	0	00	0	00	0	00
2	10	3	11	1	01	1	01	1	01
3	11	0	00	3	11	2	10	3	11
3	11	1	01	0	00	3	11	2	10
3	11	2	10	1	01	1	01	1	01
3	11	3	11	2	10	0	00	0	00

The use of these three separate operations in combination provides for a complex transformation of the input, making cryptanalysis much more difficult than with an algorithm such as DES, which relies solely on the XOR function.

In IDEA, **diffusion** is provided by the basic building block of the algorithm, known as the multiplication/addition (MA) structure (Figure 7.9). This structure takes as inputs two 16-bit values derived from the plaintext and two 16-bit subkeys derived from the key and produces two 16-bit outputs. An exhaustive computer check has determined that each output bit of the first round depends on every bit of the plaintext-derived inputs and on every bit of the subkeys [LAI90]. This particular structure is repeated eight times in the algorithm, providing very effective diffusion. Furthermore, it can be shown that this structure uses the least number of operations (four) required to achieve complete diffusion [LAI90].

Implementation Considerations

IDEA is designed to facilitate both software and hardware implementation. Hardware implementation, typically in VLSI, is designed to achieve high speed.

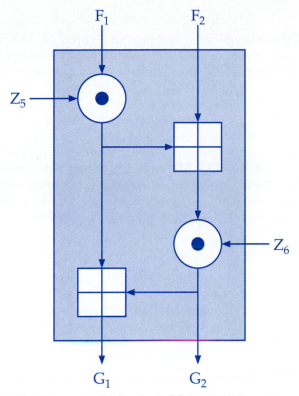

FIGURE 7.9.   Multiplication/addition (MA) Structure

Software implementation has the advantage of flexibility and low cost. [LAI90] cites the following design principles:

- Design principles for software implementation:
  —Use subblocks: Cipher operations should operate on subblocks that are "natural" for software, such as 8, 16, or 32 bits. IDEA uses 16-bit subblocks.
  —Use simple operations: Cipher operations should be easily programmed using addition, shifting, and so on. The three basic elements of IDEA meet this requirement. The most difficult of the three, multiplication modulo $(2^{16} + 1)$ can be readily constructed from simple primitive operations (see Problem 7.4).
- Design principles for hardware implementation:
  —Similarity of encryption and decryption: Encryption and decryption should differ only in the way of using the key so that the same device can be used for both encryption and decryption. Like DES, IDEA has a structure that satisfies this requirement.
  —Regular structure: The cipher should have a regular modular structure to facilitate VLSI implementation. IDEA is constructed from two basic modular building blocks repeated multiple times.

IDEA Encryption

The overall scheme for IDEA encryption is illustrated in Figure 7.10. As with any encryption scheme, there are two inputs to the encryption function: the plaintext to be encrypted and the key. In this case, the plaintext is 64 bits in length and the key is 128 bits in length.

Looking at the left-hand side of the figure, we see that the IDEA algorithm consists of eight rounds, or iterations, followed by a final transformation function. The algorithm breaks the input up into four 16-bit subblocks. Each of the iteration rounds takes four 16-bit subblocks as input and produces four 16-bit output blocks. The final transformation also produces four 16-bit blocks, which are concatenated to form the 64-bit ciphertext. Each of the iterations also makes use of six 16-bit subkeys, whereas the final transformation uses four subkeys, for a total of 52 subkeys. The right-hand portion of the figure indicates that these 52 subkeys are all generated from the original 128-bit key.

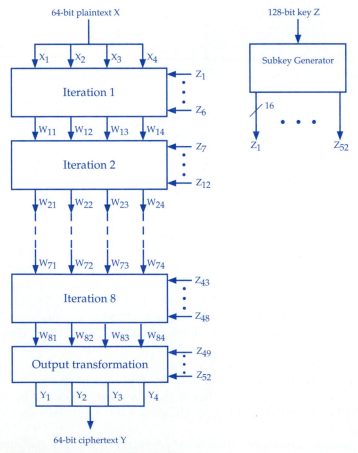

FIGURE 7.10.   Overall IDEA Structure

Details of a Single Iteration

Now let us look more closely at the algorithm for a single iteration, as illustrated in Figure 7.11. In fact, this figure shows the first iteration. Subsequent iterations have the same structure but with different subkey and plaintext-derived inputs. The iteration begins with a transformation that combines the four input subblocks with four subkeys, using the addition and multiplication operations. This transformation is highlighted as the upper shaded rectangle. The four output blocks of this transformation are then combined using the XOR operation to form two 16-bit blocks that are input to the MA structure (see Figure 7.9), which is shown as the lower shaded rectangle. The MA structure also takes two subkeys as input and combines these inputs to produce two 16-bit outputs.

Finally, the four output blocks from the upper transformation are combined with the two output blocks of the MA structure using XOR to produce the four output blocks for this iteration. Note that the two outputs that are partially

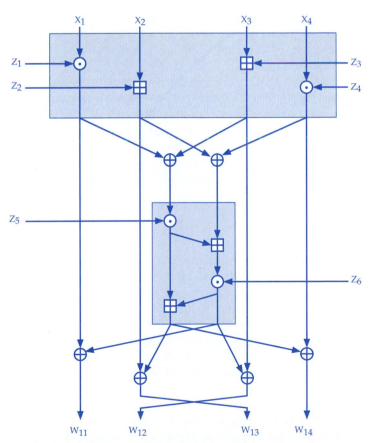

FIGURE 7.11.   Single Iteration of IDEA (first iteration)

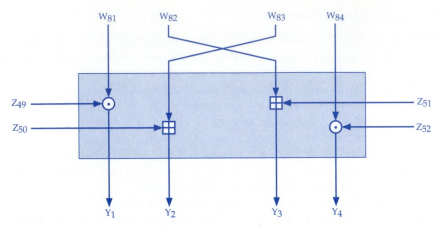

FIGURE 7.12.   Output Transformation Stage of IDEA

generated by the second and third inputs (X_2 and X_3) are interchanged to produce the second and third outputs (W_{12} and W_{13}). This increases the mixing of the bits being processed and makes the algorithm more resistant to differential crypt-analysis.

The ninth stage of the algorithm, labeled the output transformation stage in Figure 7.10, is shown in Figure 7.12. Note that it has the same structure as the upper, shaded portion of the preceding iterations (Figure 7.11). The only difference is that the second and third inputs are interchanged before being applied to the operational units. In fact, this has the effect of undoing the interchange at the end of the eighth iteration. The reason for this extra interchange is so that decryption has the same structure as encryption, as will be seen. Note also that this ninth stage requires only four subkey inputs, compared to six subkey inputs for each of the first eight stages.

Subkey Generation

Returning to Figure 7.10, we see that 52 16-bit subkeys are generated from the 128-bit encryption key. The scheme for generation is as follows. The first eight subkeys, labeled $Z_1, Z_2, \ldots, Z_8$, are taken directly from the key, with Z_1 being equal to the first (most significant) 16 bits, Z_2 corresponding to the next 16 bits, and so on. Then, a circular left shift of 25 bit positions is applied to the key, and the next eight subkeys are extracted. This procedure is repeated until all 52 subkeys are generated. Figure 7.13 indicates the bit assignments for all subkeys with respect to the original key.

This scheme provides an effective technique for varying the key bits used for subkeys in the eight iterations. Note that the first subkey used in each round uses a different set of bits from the key. If the key as a whole is labeled $Z[1..128]$, then the first key of the eight iterations has the following bit assignments:

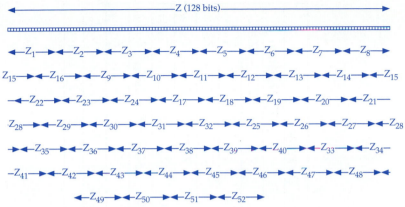

FIGURE 7.13. IDEA Subkeys

$$Z_1 = Z[1..16] \qquad Z_{25} = Z[76..91]$$
$$Z_7 = Z[97..112] \qquad Z_{31} = Z[44..59]$$
$$Z_{13} = Z[90..105] \qquad Z_{37} = Z[37..52]$$
$$Z_{19} = Z[83..98] \qquad Z_{43} = Z[30..45]$$

Also, the 96 subkey bits used for an iteration are, with the exception of the first and eighth iterations, not contiguous, so that there is not even a simple shift relationship between the subkeys of one round and those of another. The reason for this phenomenon is that only six subkeys are used in each iteration, whereas eight subkeys are extracted with each rotation of the key.

IDEA Decryption

The process of decryption is essentially the same as the encryption process. Decryption is achieved by using the ciphertext as input to the same overall IDEA structure, as shown in Figure 7.10, but with a different selection of subkeys. The decryption subkeys $U_1, \ldots, U_{52}$ are derived from the encryption subkeys as follows:

1. The first four subkeys of decryption iteration i are derived from the first four subkeys of encryption iteration $(10 - i)$, where the transformation stage is counted as iteration 9. The first and fourth decryption subkeys are equal to the multiplicative inverse modulo $(2^{16} + 1)$ of the corresponding first and fourth encryption subkeys. For iterations 2 through 8, the second and third decryption subkeys are equal to the additive inverse modulo (2^{16}) of the corresponding third and second encryption subkeys. For iterations 1 and 9, the second and third decryption subkeys are equal to the additive inverse modulo (2^{16}) of the corresponding second and third encryption subkeys.
2. For the first eight iterations, the last two subkeys of decryption iteration i are equal to the last two subkeys of encryption iteration $(9 - i)$.

TABLE 7.5　Encryption and Decryption Subkeys

Stage	Encryption		Decryption	
	Designation	Equivalent to	Designation	Equivalent to
Iteration 1	$Z_1Z_2Z_3Z_4Z_5Z_6$	$Z[1..96]$	$U_1U_2U_3U_4U_5U_6$	$Z_{49}^{-1}\,{-}Z_{50}\,{-}Z_{51}\,Z_{52}^{-1}\,Z_{47}\,Z_{48}$
Iteration 2	$Z_7Z_8Z_9Z_{10}Z_{11}Z_{12}$	$Z[97..128;\ 26..89]$	$U_7U_8U_9U_{10}U_{11}U_{12}$	$Z_{43}^{-1}\,{-}Z_{45}\,{-}Z_{44}\,Z_{46}^{-1}\,Z_{41}\,Z_{42}$
Iteration 3	$Z_{13}Z_{14}Z_{15}Z_{16}Z_{17}Z_{18}$	$Z[90..128;\ 1..25;\ 51..82]$	$U_{13}U_{14}U_{15}U_{16}U_{17}U_{18}$	$Z_{37}^{-1}\,{-}Z_{39}\,{-}Z_{38}\,Z_{40}^{-1}\,Z_{35}\,Z_{36}$
Iteration 4	$Z_{19}Z_{20}Z_{21}Z_{22}Z_{23}Z_{24}$	$Z[83..128;\ 1..50]$	$U_{19}U_{20}U_{21}U_{22}U_{23}U_{24}$	$Z_{31}^{-1}\,{-}Z_{33}\,{-}Z_{32}\,Z_{34}^{-1}\,Z_{29}\,Z_{30}$
Iteration 5	$Z_{25}Z_{26}Z_{27}Z_{28}Z_{29}Z_{30}$	$Z[76..128;\ 1..43]$	$U_{25}U_{26}U_{27}U_{28}U_{29}U_{30}$	$Z_{25}^{-1}\,{-}Z_{27}\,{-}Z_{26}\,Z_{28}^{-1}\,Z_{23}\,Z_{24}$
Iteration 6	$Z_{31}Z_{32}Z_{33}Z_{34}Z_{35}Z_{36}$	$Z[44..75;\ 101..128;\ 1..36]$	$U_{31}U_{32}U_{33}U_{34}U_{35}U_{36}$	$Z_{19}^{-1}\,{-}Z_{21}\,{-}Z_{20}\,Z_{22}^{-1}\,Z_{17}\,Z_{18}$
Iteration 7	$Z_{37}Z_{38}Z_{39}Z_{40}Z_{41}Z_{42}$	$Z[37..100;\ 126..128;\ 1..29]$	$U_{37}U_{38}U_{39}U_{40}U_{41}U_{42}$	$Z_{13}^{-1}\,{-}Z_{15}\,{-}Z_{14}\,Z_{16}^{-1}\,Z_{11}\,Z_{12}$
Iteration 8	$Z_{43}Z_{44}Z_{45}Z_{46}Z_{47}Z_{48}$	$Z[30..125]$	$U_{43}U_{44}U_{45}U_{46}U_{47}U_{48}$	$Z_7^{-1}\,{-}Z_9\,{-}Z_8\,Z_{10}^{-1}\,Z_5\,Z_6$
transformation	$Z_{49}Z_{50}Z_{51}Z_{52}$	$Z[23..86]$	$U_{49}U_{50}U_{51}U_{52}$	$Z_1^{-1}\,{-}Z_2\,{-}Z_3\,Z_4^{-1}$

Table 7.5 summarizes these relationships. For the multiplicative inverse, the notation Z_j^{-1} is used, so that we have:

$$Z_j \odot Z_j^{-1} = 1$$

Because $2^{16} + 1$ is a prime number, each nonzero integer $Z_j \leq 2^{16}$ has a unique multiplicative inverse modulo $(2^{16} + 1)$; see Appendix 4A. For the additive inverse modulo 2^{16}, the notation $-Z_j$ is used, so that we have:

$$-Z_j \boxplus Z_j = 0$$

To verify that the same algorithm with the decryption subkeys produces the correct result, consider Figure 7.14, which shows the encryption process going down the left-hand side and the decryption process going up the right-hand side. Each of the eight iterations is further shown broken up into the two substages of transformation and what is referred to as subencryption; the transformation substage

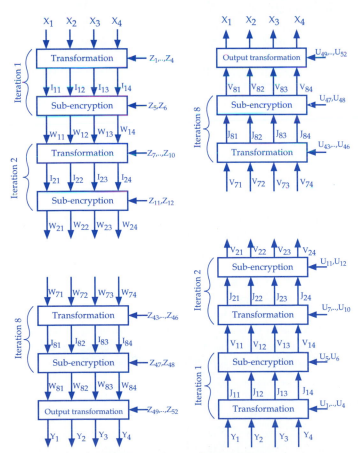

FIGURE 7.14. IDEA Encryption and Decryption

corresponds to the upper, shaded rectangle in Figure 7.11, and the sub-encryption stage refers to the remainder of the processing of that iteration.

Consider the bottom box in both diagrams. On the encryption side, the following relationships hold for the output transformation:

$$Y_1 = W_{81} \odot Z_{49} \qquad Y_3 = W_{82} \boxplus Z_{51}$$
$$Y_2 = W_{83} \boxplus Z_{50} \qquad Y_4 = W_{84} \odot Z_{52}$$

The first substage of the first iteration of the decryption process yields the following relationships:

$$J_{11} = Y_1 \odot U_1 \qquad J_{13} = Y_3 \boxplus U_3$$
$$J_{12} = Y_2 \boxplus U_2 \qquad J_{14} = Y_4 \odot U_4$$

Substituting:

$$J_{11} = Y_1 \odot Z_{49}{}^{-1} = W_{81} \odot Z_{49} \odot Z_{49}{}^{-1} = W_{81}$$
$$J_{12} = Y_2 \boxplus -Z_{50} = W_{83} \boxplus Z_{50} \boxplus -Z_{50} = W_{83}$$
$$J_{13} = Y_3 \boxplus -Z_{51} = W_{82} \boxplus Z_{51} \boxplus -Z_{51} = W_{82}$$
$$J_{14} = Y_4 \odot Z_{52}{}^{-1} = W_{84} \odot Z_{52} \odot Z_{52}{}^{-1} = W_{84}$$

Thus, the output of the first substage of the decryption process is equal to the input to the last stage of the encryption process except for an interchange of the second and third blocks. Now, consider the following relationships, which can be derived from Figure 7.11:

$$W_{81} = I_{81} \oplus MA_R(I_{81} \oplus I_{83}, I_{82} \oplus I_{84})$$
$$W_{82} = I_{83} \oplus MA_R(I_{81} \oplus I_{83}, I_{82} \oplus I_{84})$$
$$W_{83} = I_{82} \oplus MA_L(I_{81} \oplus I_{83}, I_{82} \oplus I_{84})$$
$$W_{84} = I_{84} \oplus MA_L(I_{81} \oplus I_{83}, I_{82} \oplus I_{84})$$

where $MA_R(X, Y)$ is the right-hand output of the MA structure (Figure 7.9) with inputs X and Y, and $MA_L(X, Y)$ is the left-hand output of the MA structure with inputs X and Y. Now,

$$\begin{aligned}
V_{11} &= J_{11} \oplus MA_R(J_{11} \oplus J_{13}, J_{12} \oplus J_{14}) \\
&= W_{81} \oplus MA_R(W_{81} \oplus W_{82}, W_{83} \oplus W_{84}) \\
&= I_{81} \oplus MA_R(I_{81} \oplus I_{83}, I_{82} \oplus I_{84}) \oplus \\
&\quad MA_R[I_{81} \oplus MA_R(I_{81} \oplus I_{83}, I_{82} \oplus I_{84}) \oplus I_{83} \oplus MA_R(I_{81} \oplus I_{83}, I_{82} \oplus I_{84}), \\
&\quad\quad I_{82} \oplus MA_L(I_{81} \oplus I_{83}, I_{82} \oplus I_{84}) \oplus I_{84} \oplus MA_L(I_{81} \oplus I_{83}, I_{82} \oplus I_{84})] \\
&= I_{81} \oplus MA_R(I_{81} \oplus I_{83}, I_{82} \oplus I_{84}) \oplus MA_R(I_{81} \oplus I_{83}, I_{82} \oplus I_{84}) \\
&= I_{81}
\end{aligned}$$

Similarly, we have

$$V_{12} = I_{83}$$
$$V_{13} = I_{82}$$
$$V_{14} = I_{84}$$

So the output of the second substage of the decryption process is equal to the input to the next-to-last substage of the encryption process except for an interchange of the second and third blocks. Using the same derivation, this relationship can be shown to hold at each corresponding point in Figure 7.14, until we have:

$$V_{81} = I_{11}$$
$$V_{82} = I_{13}$$
$$V_{83} = I_{12}$$
$$V_{84} = I_{14}$$

Finally, because the output transformation of the decryption process is equal to the first substage of the encryption process except for an interchange of the second and third blocks, we have the output of the entire encryption process is equal to the input to the encryption process.

IDEA Modes of Operation

As with DES, four modes of operation can be used for IDEA:

- *Electronic codebook (ECB) mode:* Each block of 64 plaintext bits is encoded independently using the same key. This technique is useful for encrypting small blocks of data. For example, it could be used for encrypting 128-bit IDEA keys.
- *Cipher block chaining (CBC) mode:* The input to the encryption algorithm is the XOR of the next 64 bits of plaintext and the preceding 64 bits of ciphertext. The result is that if the same block of 64-bit plaintext appears more than once in the input stream, it will produce a different 64-bit ciphertext block each time.
- *Cipher feedback (CFB) mode:* Input is processed J bits at a time. Preceding ciphertext is used as input to the encryption algorithm to produce pseudorandom output, which is XORed with plaintext to produce the next unit of ciphertext. Again, this is useful for encoding long blocks of input.
- *Output feedback (OFB) mode:* Similar to CFB, except that the input to the encryption algorithm is the preceding IDEA output. As was discussed in Chapter 2, this mode is useful for stream-oriented transmission over a noisy channel.

7.4

SKIPJACK

In April 1993, the Clinton administration announced a proposed encryption technology that, according to the announcement "will bring the Federal Government together with industry in a voluntary program to improve the security and privacy of telephone communication while meeting the legitimate needs of law enforcement." Subsequently, in July 1993, a more formal announcement appeared in the Federal Register as a request for comments on a proposed Federal

Information Processing Standard. The overall approach was initially referred to as Clipper, whereas the specific encryption algorithm is known as SKIPJACK.[3]

The following important points are made in these two documents:

1. A major objective of this initiative is to enable law enforcement agencies to continue, when lawfully authorized, to monitor and wiretap private communications in the face of increasing sophistication and prevalence of commercial encryption technology.

2. The other principal objective is to provide the public with access to a sophisticated and powerful encryption technology to meet private needs, especially those of business, for maintaining confidentiality. This and the preceding objective are considered equally important by the government.

3. The initiative is limited to telephone-based conversations, including voice, facsimile, and computer information communicated in a telephone system. Specifically, the intent is to cover telephone communications facilities up to 14.4 kbps. However, there is nothing inherent in the technology to prevent its being used for electronic mail, terminal-to-host sessions, and other data communications applications over higher-speed links.

4. The SKIPJACK algorithm is substantially stronger than DES and should therefore be a welcome improvement to business users. However, the algorithm itself is now and is intended to remain classified. Thus, the opportunity for critical peer review of the algorithm is limited.

5. Law enforcement agencies are not in a position to directly decrypt encrypted communications. Instead, it is necessary to obtain a pair of keys from two separate "escrow agencies" that when combined provide a key that can be used for decryption. The details of the escrow system and how it is used to create key pairs have not yet been made public and at this writing are still evolving.

6. The FIPS standard, when published, may be used by federal agencies when procuring communications products and services, when the responsible manager feels that encryption protection is justified.

7. The federal government encourages the use of SKIPJACK when it provides the desired security. Its use is voluntary.

The rationale for this dual system (provision of confidentiality with mechanism for disclosure) is that it will (1) help government agencies and the private sector develop and use cost-effective products to protect information, and (2) at the same time preserve the ability of federal, state, and local law enforcement agencies to intercept lawfully the phone conversations of criminals, such as terrorists, drug dealers, and child pornographers.

There have been widespread and vociferous negative reactions to this proposed program, together with supportive responses from a much smaller and less vocal number of individuals. Given the thrust of this text, we will not get into the merits of this debate. Instead, this section summarizes the unclassified technical information that is available.

---

[3]Because of a conflict with an existing trademark, the term *Clipper* is no longer used by the government.

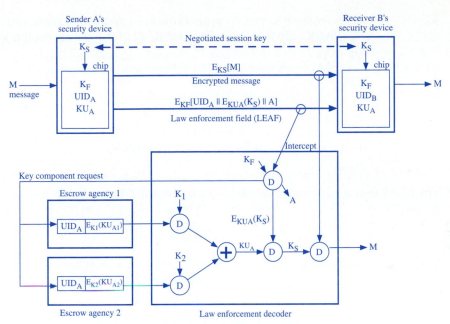

FIGURE 7.15.   Secure Communications with Law Enforcement Access

Operational Description

The overall scheme for SKIPJACK is summarized in Figure 7.15 (based on figure in [DENN93]). Any device, telephone, terminal, modem, and so on that uses the SKIPJACK scheme is equipped with a tamper-proof chip responsible for encryption and decryption. The chip does not provide any key distribution service. Key distribution must be achieved manually or by using a mutually acceptable scheme, such as Diffie-Hellman key exchange.

Once a key K_s has been agreed for a session, two parties may exchange messages encrypted using the SKIPJACK encryption/decryption algorithm. Thus, a message from user A to user B would be encrypted as follows:

$$E_{Ks}[M]$$

where M is the message and K_s is the session key.

In addition, at least once during information exchange, A must transmit a law enforcement field (LEAF) that will enable law enforcement agencies to recover the message. Before describing the content and use of the LEAF, let us define some parameters:

K_F = 80-bit family key. Stored in all devices designated as a family, it is used to create the LEAF.

UID   = an identifier unique to a particular SKIPJACK chip.

KU   = device-unique key. A cryptographic key unique to a particular SKIPJACK chip that is used to unlock all messages encrypted with the chip.

KU_1, KU_2 = a pair of key components. The following identity holds: $KU = KU_1 \oplus KU_2$

K_1, K_2 = secret key-encrypting keys

K_s = session key

P   = authentication code. A field in the LEAF that is used to ensure that the LEAF has not been modified or replaced in an unauthorized manner.

The LEAF that is transmitted as part of a communication has the following general format:

$$E_{KF}(UID_A \mid\mid E_{KUA}(K_s) \mid\mid P_A)$$

The LEAF consists of the UID of the sending chip, the session key encrypted using the device-unique key, and an authentication code, all encrypted using the family key.

The general procedure is as follows. If a law enforcement agency intends to eavesdrop on a conversation, it applies for a court order that grants the authorization to eavesdrop and to obtain the necessary keys. The law enforcement agency can then intercept the LEAF in one direction for that conversation. The law enforcement device is equipped with the family key for this family of chips and can therefore recover the UID of the sending device, the session key encrypted using the device-unique key, and the authentication code for this LEAF. Once the LEAF is authenticated, the agency can apply to two separate escrow agencies. Each agency maintains a database that contains the UID and one of the two key components for each chip, the latter in encrypted form. When both encrypted key components are returned, the agency can perform the following:

1. Recover key components:

$$KU_{A_1} = D_{K_1}\left[E_{K_1}(KU_{A_1})\right]; KU_{A_2} = D_{K_2}\left[E_{K_2}(KU_{A_2})\right]$$

   where K_1 and K_2 are secret keys known only to the requesting agency.

2. Generate device-unique key:

$$KU_A = KU_{A_1} \oplus KU_{A_2}$$

3. Recover session key:

$$K_s = D_{KU_A}\left[E_{KU_A}(K_s)\right]$$

4. Recover message:

$$M = D_{K_s}\left[E_{K_s}(M)\right]$$

In this scheme, dual control over the device-unique key is maintained by splitting knowledge of the key between two parties rather than keeping it in a single escrow agency. This form of key storage is recommended in ANSI X9.17.

Note that, because SKIPJACK is a conventional symmetric algorithm, the law enforcement agency need only obtain access through the LEAF transmitted in one direction. Once the session key is recovered, the surveillance agency can read transmissions in both directions.

Chip Programming

For the scheme described in Figure 7.15 to work, the end-user chips must be programmed with the appropriate parameters in read-only memory. Figure 7.16 (based on a figure in [DENN93]) illustrates the procedure.

End-user devices that participate in the SKIPJACK scheme are equipped with a tamper-resistant encryption chip that includes the following elements:

- The SKIPJACK encryption/decryption algorithm
- A chip-unique user ID, UID
- A device-unique key KU
- A family key KF
- Specialized control software

These elements are incorporated into the chip at a secure facility with the participation of the two escrow agencies. For each chip to be programmed, the two agen-

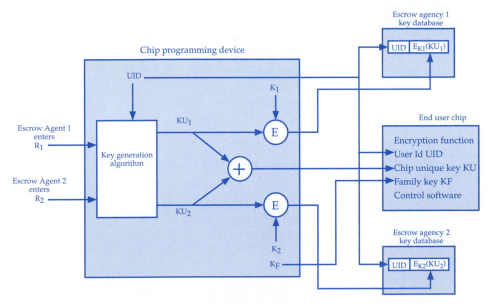

FIGURE 7.16. Chip Programming and Key Escrow

cies enter one or more random numbers. These random numbers, together with the unique UID assigned to a chip, are used to generate two key components, KU_1 and KU_2. The device-unique key KU is then generated as the bitwise XOR of the two key components. This KU, together with the UID and K_F, are programmed onto the end-user chip. Meanwhile, the two key components are encrypted using secret keys K_1 and K_2 respectively, and the results are provided to the two escrow agencies. Each agency maintains a database that lists a UID and one encrypted key component for each end-user chip. The key components are stored in encrypted form to reduce vulnerability to theft or unauthorized release. To successfully compromise this scheme, an attacker would have to gain access to two escrow agency databases, access to the two secret key-encrypting keys, and access to the family key.

SKIPJACK

The SKIPJACK algorithm itself is classified by the U.S. government as SECRET. Accordingly, it is not possible to describe the algorithm in an unclassified document such as this book. It is important to note, however, that the reason for classifying the algorithm is not related to its cryptographic strength. That is, it is asserted that knowledge of the algorithm does not make the system more vulnerable to cryptanalysis. Rather, the motivation for classifying the algorithm is to prevent the construction of devices that fail to properly implement the LEAF but that interoperate with legitimate SKIPJACK devices.

It is the desire of the government to promote the use of SKIPJACK. Understandably, potential users would be reluctant to adopt an encryption scheme whose cryptographic security is unknown. To address this problem, the government invited a panel of five outside experts to evaluate SKIPJACK. The reviewers were given access to the classified documentation as well as to the designers of the algorithm. The panel has issued an interim report that details their findings to date [BROC93]. Table 7.6 summarizes the conclusions of the panel.

This subsection provides an overview of the report.

TABLE 7.6   Conclusions of the SKIPJACK Review Panel

1. Under an assumption that the cost of processing power is halved every 18 months, it will be 36 years before the cost of breaking SKIPJACK by exhaustive search will be equal to the cost of breaking the Data Encryption Standard today. Thus, there is no significant risk that SKIPJACK will be broken by exhaustive search in the next 30 to 40 years.
2. There is no significant risk that SKIPJACK can be broken through a shortcut method of attack.
3. Although the internal structure of SKIPJACK must be classified in order to protect law enforcement and national security objectives, the strength of SKIPJACK against a cryptanalytic attack does not depend on the secrecy of the algorithm.

The SKIPJACK Algorithm

SKIPJACK is a block cipher that uses an 80-bit key to encrypt data in blocks of 64 bits. The algorithm involves 32 rounds of processing for a single encryption or decryption, using a complex nonlinear function for each round. As with DES, four modes of operation can be used for SKIPJACK: electronic codebook (ECB) mode, cipher block chaining (CBC) mode, cipher feedback (CFB) mode, and output feedback (OFB) mode.

SKIPJACK was designed and evaluated by the National Security Agency (NSA), using building blocks and techniques that date back more than 40 years. The actual design effort began in 1987.

Exhaustive Key Search Attacks

At 80 bits, the SKIPJACK key size appears to offer excellent protection against exhaustive key search attacks for the foreseeable future. The panel pointed out two ways of looking at the issue that give confidence in the 80-bit key length. First, taking into account the hardware performance available now and in the foreseeable future, the panel postulated the following SKIPJACK cracking machines:

- A currently available 8-processor Cray YMP could perform about 89,000 encryptions per processor. An optimized implementation of the encryption algorithm would require about 1 billion years to try all keys.
- A future, hypothetical, parallel machine consisting of 100,000 RISC processors, each processor capable of 100,000 encryptions per second. This device would require about 4 million years for an exhaustive search and would cost perhaps $50 million.
- A more speculative attack consisting of a special-purpose machine using 1.2 billion $1 chips with a 1 GHz clock. If the algorithm could be pipelined to permit one encryption per clock cycle, then the key space could be exhausted in 1 year by a machine costing $1.2 billion.

Another way of looking at the problem is to postulate that, despite the controversy surrounding the issue, DES remains secure today against exhaustive key search. Now, consider that the SKIPJACK key is 24 bits longer. Accordingly, the amount of time to break SKIPJACK is 2^{24} times that for DES, using the same hardware. If we assume that historical trends continue and that hardware speed doubles approximately once every 18 months, then the time required for SKIPJACK to become as vulnerable as DES is today is $24 \times 1.5 = 36$ years.[4] This leads to the first conclusion cited in Table 7.6.

---

[4]Using the same line of reasoning, IDEA, with a 128-bit key, will remain unassailable via exhaustive key search for over a century ($72 \times 1.5 = 108$ years).

Cryptanalytic Attacks

The alternative to a brute-force attack is a cryptanalytic attack that exploits some structural or mathematical property of the algorithm to enable either a key to be determined or a ciphertext to be decrypted with less effort than an exhaustive key search. Given the limited time and resources available to the panel, it was not possible for them to adequately assess SKIPJACK's vulnerability to such attacks. Instead, the panel attempted to test the reasonableness of the assumption that SKIPJACK is a strong algorithm.

It is instructive to describe the approach taken by the panel. They started with the observation that a strong encryption algorithm will behave like a random function of the key and plaintext so that it is impossible to determine any of the key bits or plaintext bits from the ciphertext bits. The result is that for a given key, a sequence of plaintext inputs should produce a pseudorandom output, and for a given plaintext, a sequence of different keys should produce a pseudorandom output.

One set of tests that were run were statistical tests of the randomness of the output and of the correlation between the input and output or between the key and the output. To briefly summarize: The randomness tests looked at the pattern of outputs produced given a sequence of inputs and applied statistical tests of the hypothesis that the output numbers were drawn (with replacement) from a uniform distribution on all possible outputs. The correlation tests were standard statistical tests of the correlation between a sequence of inputs and outputs and between a sequence of keys and outputs.

Other tests were performed that, again, were geared toward determining if the algorithm behaved as a strong encryption algorithm should behave. Although this sort of "black box" approach is not definitive, it does tend to either reinforce or cast doubt on the assumption that SKIPJACK is strong. In this case, the results of the various tests uniformly supported the assertion that SKIPJACK is a strong cryptographic algorithm and therefore resistant to cryptanalysis.

7.5

LUC PUBLIC-KEY ENCRYPTION

LUC is a public-key system developed by a group of researchers based in New Zealand [SMIT93a, SMIT93b]; a similar scheme had previously been reported in [MULL81]. Like RSA, it can be used for encryption, signature, and key exchange. It is similar to RSA, but because it was developed outside the United States, it is not subject to U. S. export controls.

LUC is based on large integers in a Lucas sequence. We begin with an overview of Lucas sequences, then show how these can be used to develop a public-key system, and finally compare this approach to RSA. Some of the more tedious mathematics is relegated to Appendix 7A.

Lucas Sequences

Lucas sequences are two series of integers U_n and V_n generated by two integers P and Q. The general theory of these series was first developed by Edouard Lucas in 1878. The main focus of interest in Lucas sequences has been for testing for prime numbers. We provide the bare minimum of detail on these sequences here; a detailed treatment can be found in [RIBE91].

Definition of Lucas Sequences

Select two nonnegative integers, P and Q, and consider the quadratic equation:

$$X^2 - PX + Q = 0$$

The roots of this equation are $\left(P \pm \sqrt{P^2 - 4Q}\right)/2$. The expression $(P^2 - 4Q)$ is called the discriminant D. Let us label the two roots as α and β. Then

$$\left.\begin{matrix} \alpha \\ \beta \end{matrix}\right\} = \frac{P \pm \sqrt{D}}{2}$$

The following relationships between α and β are readily seen:

$$\alpha + \beta = P \qquad \alpha\beta = Q \qquad \alpha - \beta = \sqrt{D}$$

Now, assume that we have chosen P and Q so that $D \neq 0$. Then the Lucas sequences of numbers are defined as follows:

$$U_n(P,Q) = \frac{\alpha^n - \beta^n}{\alpha - \beta} \qquad \text{and} \qquad V_n(P,Q) = \alpha^n + \beta^n, \qquad \text{for } n \geq 0$$

It is easy to see that

$$U_0(P,Q) = 0 \qquad U_1(P,Q) = 1$$
$$V_0(P,Q) = 2 \qquad V_1(P,Q) = P$$

We can rewrite the sequences to show that each member depends only on the preceding two members. Consider:

$$P(\alpha^{n-1} + \beta^{n-1}) - Q(\alpha^{n-2} + \beta^{n-2}) = \alpha^{n-2}(P\alpha - Q) + \beta^{n-2}(P\beta - Q)$$
$$= \alpha^{n-2}[(\alpha + \beta)\alpha - \alpha\beta] + \beta^{n-2}[(\alpha + \beta)\beta - \alpha\beta]$$
$$= \alpha^{n-2}(\alpha^2) + \beta^{n-2}(\beta^2)$$
$$= \alpha^n + \beta^n$$

Therefore, we have, for $n \geq 2$:

$$V_n(P,Q) = PV_{n-1}(P,Q) - QV_{n-2}(P,Q) \tag{7.1}$$

TABLE 7.7   Lucas Sequences for P = 3, Q = 1

n	$V_n(3,1)$	$U_n(3,1)$
0	2	0
1	3	1
2	7	3
3	18	8
4	47	21
5	123	55
6	322	144
7	843	377
8	2,207	987
9	5,778	2,584
10	15,127	6,765
11	39,603	17,711
12	103,682	46,368
13	271,443	121,393
14	710,647	317,811
15	1,860,498	832,040
16	4,870,847	2,178,309
17	12,752,043	5,702,887
18	33,385,282	14,930,352
19	87,403,803	39,088,169
20	228,826,127	102,334,155
21	599,074,578	267,914,296
22	1,568,397,607	701,408,733
23	4,106,118,243	1,836,311,903
24	10,749,957,122	4,807,526,976

Similarly, we can show that

$$U_n(P,Q) = PU_{n-1}(P,Q) - QU_{n-2}(P,Q) \qquad (7.2)$$

Table 7.7 shows the first 25 Lucas numbers for $P = 3, Q = 1$.

Properties of $V_n(P,Q)$

In developing the LUC scheme, our interest is in only the Lucas sequence $V_n(P, Q)$, so we will concentrate on that. Similar properties can be shown to hold for $U_n(P,Q)$.

Let us consider the development of the sequence modulo some integer $N > 2$. From Table 7.7, it is clear that the Lucas numbers grow very rapidly. So we would like to answer the following question: If we calculate the Lucas sequence $V_n(P,Q)$ out to some point n and then take the result modulo N, do we get the same result as if we had applied the modulo operation at each step in the sequence? That is, we would like to know if the following is true:

$$V_n(P \bmod N,\ Q \bmod N) = V_n(P,Q) \bmod N \qquad (7.3)$$

The answer is yes. To see this, consider:

$$V_0(P \bmod N,\ Q \bmod N) = 2$$
$$(V_0(P,Q)) \bmod N = (2) \bmod N = 2$$
$$V_1(P \bmod N,\ Q \bmod N) = P \bmod N$$
$$(V_1(P,Q)) \bmod N = (P) \bmod N$$

We can now prove the result by induction on n. Suppose that Equation 7.3 holds for all values up to $n - 1$. Then,

$$V_n(P,\ Q) \bmod N = (PV_{n-1}(P,\ Q) - QV_{n-2}(P,\ Q)) \bmod N$$

by definition of the Lucas sequence. Then by the rules of modular arithmetic:

$$V_n(P,\ Q) \bmod N = (P \bmod N)(V_{n-1}(P,\ Q) \bmod N) - (Q \bmod N)(V_{n-2}(P,\ Q) \bmod N)$$

And by our inductive assumption:

$$V_n(P,\ Q) \bmod N = (P \bmod N)V_{n-1}(P \bmod N,\ Q \bmod N)$$
$$- (Q \bmod N)V_{n-2}(P \bmod N,\ Q \bmod N)$$

Then, by our definition of the Lucas sequence, we can rewrite the right-hand side:

$$V_n(P,Q) \bmod N = V_n(P \bmod N,\ Q \bmod N)$$

Thus Equation 7.3 is validated.

Let us leave this result for a moment and consider another result. Recall that the Lucas sequences were defined in terms of the roots of the equation:

$$X^2 - PX + Q = 0$$

where P and Q are arbitrary integers. Consider choosing in place of the values of P and Q, the values $V_k(P,\ Q)$ for P and Q^k for Q, for some positive integer k. These two values are nonnegative integers and therefore are legitimate choices. Our quadratic equation is now:

$$X^2 - V_k(P,Q)X + Q^k = 0$$

The roots of this equation, α' and β' must satisfy:

$$\alpha' + \beta' = V_k(P,Q) \qquad \alpha'\beta' = Q^k$$

just as we saw before for the original quadratic equation. The Lucas sequence based on these two integers can then be written:

$$V_n(V_k(P,Q),\ Q^k) = (\alpha')^n + (\beta')^n$$

But then we can see the following equivalences:

$$\alpha' + \beta' = V_k(P,Q) = \alpha^k + \beta^k \qquad \text{by the definition of } V_k$$
$$\alpha'\beta' = Q^k = (\alpha\beta)^k = \alpha^k\beta^k$$

So we must have $\alpha' = \alpha^k$ and $\beta' = \beta^k$ (or vice versa). This means that we can write:

$$\begin{aligned} V_n(V_k(P,Q), Q^k) &= (\alpha')^n + (\beta')^n \\ &= (\alpha^k)^n + (\beta^k)^n \\ &= \alpha^{nk} + \beta^{nk} \\ &= V_{nk}(P,Q) \end{aligned}$$

If we set $Q = 1$, then we get the simple relationship:

$$V_{nk}(P,1) = V_n[V_k(P,1), 1] \tag{7.4}$$

Application to Public-Key Cryptography

The two results, Equations (7.3) and (7.4), taken together, yield a tantalizing prospect, namely, the prospect of a scheme for public-key cryptography. Suppose that we could find two integers, e and d, such that the following were true:

$$V_{de}(X,1) \equiv X \bmod N$$

Then, by Equation (7.3),

$$V_{de}(X \bmod N, 1) = V_{de}(X, 1) \bmod N = X \bmod N$$

And by Equation (7.4),

$$V_{de}(X \bmod N, 1) = V_d(V_e(X \bmod N, 1), 1) = X \bmod N$$

So, we could take a plaintext in the form of an integer X less than N, encrypt that message as $V_e(X \bmod N, 1) = Y$, and subsequently decrypt that ciphertext by $V_d(Y \bmod N, 1) = X \bmod N$.

It turns out that such integers exist. Before exhibiting such integers, we need to define two more quantities.

Two Important Quantities

The first quantity that we need is the Legendre symbol, (D/p), which is defined as:

$$\left(\frac{D}{p}\right) = \begin{cases} 0 & \text{if } p \text{ divides } D \\ 1 & \text{if there is a number } x \text{ such that } D \equiv x^2 \bmod p \\ -1 & \text{if no such number exists} \end{cases}$$

With any Lucas sequence defined by two different prime numbers P and Q, there is a generalization of the Euler totient function called the Lehmer totient function. For the integer $N = pq$ with p and q different odd primes, the Lehmer totient function of N is:

$$T(N) = \left[p - \left(\frac{D}{p} \right) \right]\left[q - \left(\frac{D}{q} \right) \right]$$

For our later purposes, the full product is not needed but only the least common multiple of the factors. This is expressed as:

$$S(N) = \text{lcm}\left[\left(p - \left(\frac{D}{p} \right) \right), \left(q - \left(\frac{D}{q} \right) \right) \right]$$

Now, if $N = pq$ is a product of two different odd primes, and we select e as any number relatively prime to $S(N)$, then we can determine d so that:

$$ed = kS(N) + 1 \qquad \text{for some integer } k$$

or, equivalently,

$$ed \equiv 1 \bmod S(N)$$

Then, given any number $X < N$, we have:

$$V_e(V_d(X, 1), 1) = V_d(V_e(X, 1), 1) = X$$

And thus we have the basis for a public-key scheme. A partial derivation of the foregoing result is in Appendix 7A.

The LUC Public-Key Algorithm

The overall structure of LUC is similar to RSA. Plaintext is encrypted in blocks, with each block having a binary value less than some number N. Encryption and decryption are of the following form, for some plaintext block P and ciphertext clock C:

$$C = V_e(P, 1) \bmod N$$
$$M = V_d(C, 1) \bmod N$$

Both sender and receiver must know the value of N, the sender knows the value of e and only the receiver knows the value of d. Thus, this is a public-key encryption algorithm with a public key of KU = $\{e, N\}$ and a private key of KR = $\{d, N\}$. For this algorithm to be satisfactory for public-key encryption, the following requirements must be met:

1. Is must be possible to find values of e, d, N such that

$$V_d(V_e(P, 1) \bmod N, 1) \bmod N = P \bmod N$$

2. It is relatively easy to calculate $V_e(P, 1) \bmod N$ and $V_d(C, 1) \bmod N$ for all values of $P < N$.
3. It is infeasible to determine d given e and N, and infeasible to determine P given C, e, and N.

We consider each of these points in turn.

Validity of LUC

The validity of LUC depends on being able to select appropriate values of e and d. We can use our earlier results to make the selection. We are looking for an e and d that satisfy

$$ed \equiv 1 \bmod S(N) \tag{7.5}$$

Key Generation

Select p, q	p and q both prime
Calculate N	$N = p \times q$
Select integer e	$\gcd\big[(p-1)(q-1)(p+1)(q+1),\ e\big] = 1$
Calculate D	$D = P^2 - 4$
Calculate $S(N)$	$S(N) = \operatorname{lcm}\left[\left(p - \left(\dfrac{D}{p}\right)\right),\ \left(q - \left(\dfrac{D}{q}\right)\right)\right]$
Calculate d	$d = e^{-1} \bmod S(N)$
Public key	KU = {e, N}
Private key	KR = {d, N}

Encryption

Plaintext: $P < N$

Ciphertext: $C = V_e(P, 1) \pmod{N}$

Decryption

Ciphertext: C

Plaintext: $P = V_d(C, 1) \pmod{N}$

FIGURE 7.17. The LUC Algorithm

If e is relatively prime to S(N), then there is a unique multiplicative inverse of e, modulo S(N). This is a basic requirement of number theory, and was discussed in Appendix 4A.

We begin by selecting two prime numbers, p and q, and setting $N = p \times q$. By our previous definitions:

$$D = P^2 - 4$$

$$S(N) = \text{lcm}\left[\left(p - \left(\frac{D}{p}\right)\right), \left(q - \left(\frac{D}{q}\right)\right)\right]$$

But now we see a problem. S(N) is a function of P, the plaintext message, and yet we need to find a public key e that is relatively prime to S(N). To get around this problem, if we choose e to be relatively prime to $(p - 1)(q - 1)(p + 1)(q + 1)$, then e is also relatively prime to S(N); see Appendix 7a for details. Having chosen e, we can find its multiplicative inverse mod N and use that value for d. Thus, the ingredients of LUC are:

p, q, two prime numbers	(private, chosen)
$N = pq$	(public, calculated)
e, relatively prime to $[(p - 1)(q - 1)(p + 1)(q + 1)]$	(public, chosen)
$d \equiv e^{-1} \bmod S(N)$	(private, calculated)

The private key consists of $\{d, N\}$ and the public key consists of $\{e, N\}$. Suppose that user A has published its public key and that user B wishes to send the message M to A. Then B calculates $C = V_e(P,1) \bmod N$ and transmits C. On receipt of this ciphertext, user A decrypts by calculating $P = V_d(C,1) \bmod N$.

Figure 7.17 summarizes the LUC algorithm. The following is an example:

1. Choose primes $p = 1949, q = 2089$
2. $N = p \times q = 4071461$
3. $e = 1103$, which is relatively prime to $1948 \times 2088 \times 1950 \times 2090$
4. Choose plaintext $P = 11111$
5. $D = (11111)^2 - 4 = 123454317$; S(N) = lcm $[(1949 + 1), (2089 + 1)] = 407550$
6. $d = e^{-1} \bmod 407550 = 24017$
7. $C = V_{1103}{}^{(11111,1)} \bmod 4071461 = 3975392$
8. $P = V_{24017}{}^{(3975392,1)} = 11111$

Calculation of Lucas Numbers

There are two apparent difficulties with the LUC approach. The first is that the calculation of V_e and V_d looks to be extremely lengthy. The second apparent difficulty is that the private key, d, appears to depend on the message to be sent, which would require the sender to generate a new private key for every use of the algorithm! We now show that both difficulties are not serious.

First, consider the computation of V_k for large values of k. We need the following equality:

$$V_{2n}(P,Q) = [V_n(P,Q)]^2 - 2Q^n$$

which is easily proved:

$$
\begin{aligned}
V_n^2(P,Q) - 2Q^n &= (\alpha^n + \beta^n)^2 - 2(\alpha\beta)^n \\
&= \alpha^{2n} + 2\alpha^n\beta^n + \beta^{2n} - 2(\alpha\beta)^n \\
&= \alpha^{2n} + \beta^{2n} \\
&= V_{2n}(P,Q)
\end{aligned}
$$

Therefore, we have

$$V_{2n}(P,1) \bmod N = [(V_n(P, 1) \bmod N)]^2 - 2) \bmod N$$

Thus, if we wish to calculate V_{16}, it is not necessary to perform 16 individual iterations. Instead, we can achieve the same final result with only four iterations if we repeatedly take the square of each partial result, successively forming V_2, V_4, V_8, V_{16}. This is essentially the same level of difficulty as is encountered in RSA.

The second problem is that d is a function of the message P. However, for a given value of e, there are only four possible values of $S(N)$:

$$\text{lcm} [(p + 1), (q + 1)]$$
$$\text{lcm} [(p + 1), (q - 1)]$$
$$\text{lcm} [(p - 1), (q + 1)]$$
$$\text{lcm} [(p - 1), (q - 1)]$$

And therefore there are only four possible values of d:

$$d = e^{-1} \bmod (\text{lcm} [(p + 1), (q + 1)])$$
$$d = e^{-1} \bmod (\text{lcm} [(p + 1), (q - 1)])$$
$$d = e^{-1} \bmod (\text{lcm} [(p - 1), (q + 1)])$$
$$d = e^{-1} \bmod (\text{lcm} [(p - 1), (q - 1)])$$

These can be calculated at the time that e is chosen. Then, given a message P to which to apply the private key process, it is necessary to calculate the two quantities:

$$\left(\frac{P^2 - 4}{p}\right)\left(\frac{P^2 - 4}{q}\right)$$

This calculation is referred to in number theory as determining if $(P^2 - 4)$ is a quadratic residue of p and q, respectively. This can be done by an algorithm analogous to the Euclidean algorithm (see [LEVE90] or [RIBE91] for details) and does not add significantly to the computational load.

Cryptographic Strength of LUC

The cryptographic strength of LUC depends on two considerations:

1. Is it infeasible to determine d given e and N?
2. Is it infeasible to determine P given C, e, and N?

Both of these questions yield answers that are essentially the same as for RSA. To determine d given e and N would appear to require determining the two prime factors of N. As was discussed in Chapter 4, this appears to be computationally infeasible for large values of N. Furthermore, in the case of LUC, there are four different values of d for each e and N, only one of which will work for a given P. Thus, the LUC version of the problem seems to be harder than the RSA version.

The second problem can be tackled in a brute-force fashion of trying all possible values of d. As we have seen, the computational load for LUC is similar to that of RSA. Therefore, for a given key size, LUC is as resistant to brute-force methods as RSA.

7.5

PROBLEMS

7.1 Comment on the differences between MD4 and MD5. Specifically, to what extent do you think that MD5 is stronger than MD4, and why?

7.2 In the first 16 steps of SHA, each word of the 512-bit message block is used as input once. For the total 80 steps, how many times is each word used as input?

7.3 In Figure 7.8, it is assumed that an array of 80 32-bit words is available to store the values of W_t, so that they can be precomputed at the beginning of the processing of a block. Now assume that space is at a premium.

    a. As an alternative, consider the use of a 16-word circular buffer that is initially loaded with W_0 through W_{15}. Design an algorithm that, for each step t, computes the required input value W_t.

    b. Now consider the use of a 16-word static buffer that is loaded with W_0 through W_{15}. Design a table lookup scheme that specifies which words are to be used to compute the input value W_t at each step.

7.4 The most difficult part of the implementation of IDEA is multiplication modulo $(2^{16} + 1)$. The following equality suggests a way in which an efficient implementation can be achieved. Let a, b be two n-bit nonzero integers. Then,

$$ab \bmod (2^n + 1) = \begin{cases} (ab \bmod 2^n) - (ab \operatorname{div} 2^n) & \text{if } (ab \bmod 2^n) \geq (ab \operatorname{div} 2^n) \\ (ab \bmod 2^n) - (ab \operatorname{div} 2^n) + 2^n + 1 & \text{if } (ab \bmod 2^n) \leq (ab \operatorname{div} 2^n) \end{cases}$$

Note that $(ab \bmod 2^n)$ corresponds to the n least significant bits of ab, and $(ab \operatorname{div} 2^n)$ is just the right shift of ab by n bits. The purpose of this problem is to prove that the foregoing equation is true.

a. Show that there exist unique nonnegative integers q and r such that $ab = q(2^n + 1) + r$.

b. What are the upper and lower bounds on q and r?

c. Prove that $q + r < 2^{n+1}$

d. Derive an expression for (ab div 2^n) in terms of q.

e. Derive an expression for (ab mod 2^n) in terms of q and r.

f. Derive an expression for r using the results of (d) and (e).

g. Demonstrate the r is equal to the right-hand side of the equation at the beginning of this problem.

7.5 IDEA uses four operations to provide complete diffusion (Figure 7.9). Prove that this is the minimum number of required operations. To do this, consider a function of the form

$$(Y_1, Y_2) = E(X_1, X_2, Z_1, Z_2) \qquad 0 \le X_i, Y_i \le 2^m; 0 \le Z_i \le 2^k$$

such that for every choice of (Z_1, Z_2), $E(\cdot, \cdot, Z_1, Z_2)$ is invertible. Such a function may be called a cipher function. A cipher function is said to have *complete diffusion* if each of its output variables depends on every input variable. We would like to prove that, if a cipher function is of the above form and has complete diffusion, then the algorithm contains at least four operations.

a. Show that the function must contain at least three operations.

b. Now suppose that E has exactly three operations and demonstrate that such a function cannot be invertible.

c. Demonstrate that the MA structure shown in Figure 7.9, which has four operations, is a cipher function with complete diffusion.

7.6 a. Why is the multiplication operation of IDEA modulo $(2^{16} + 1)$ instead of simply 2^{16}?

b. Why is the addition operation of IDEA modulo 2^{16} instead of $(2^{16} + 1)$?

7.7 The original proposal for an encryption algorithm by Lai and Massey, referred to as PES, differs from IDEA as follows:

1. The four functions in the upper gray box of Figure 7.11 are in the order $\odot$, $\boxplus$, $\boxplus$, $\odot$ for IDEA and in the order $\odot$, $\odot$, $\boxplus$, $\boxplus$ for PES.

2. In IDEA, after each iteration, the second and third blocks are interchanged. In PES, after each iteration, the first and second blocks are interchanged with the third and fourth blocks.

a. Demonstrate that the first change makes no difference in cryptographic strength. Hint: Can you do some pre- and post-processing that provides the same effect?

b. Argue that the second change increases resistance to differential cryptanalysis. Hint: Use the concept of symmetry.

7.8 One of the methods used by the SKIPJACK review panel to determine if SKIPJACK behaves like a good pseudorandom number generator is the following. Select a set of 80-bit keys, S, and an arbitrary 64-bit plaintext block, m, and a function h that maps 64-bit inputs into the set S. That is, h: M → S, where M is the set of all 64-bit blocks. Now define the function f: S → S to be $f(k) = h(ES_k[m])$, where ES denotes encryption using the SKIPJACK algorithm. Now, pick an arbitrary k_0 in S and consider the following sequence:

$$k_1 = f(k_0)$$
$$k_2 = f(k_1)$$
$$k_3 = f(k_2)$$

and so on. The cycle length of f is defined to be the number of iterations required for the same key to appear twice. Finally, define N to be the number of keys in S. The test consists of determining the cycle length for various values of N and comparing this result with the expected cycle length.

    a. What is the expected cycle length of f as a function of N?

    b. Justify the relevance of this test.

7.9 In what sense is it the case that the SKIPJACK escrow scheme uses the principle of the one-time pad?

7.10 Show that Equation 7.2 holds. That is, given the definition of the Lucas sequence U_n, show that $U_n(P,Q) = PU_{n-1}(P,Q) - QU_{n-2}(P,Q)$.

7.11 Demonstrate the converse of Equations 7.1 and 7.2. That is, given nonnegative integers P and Q and two sequences Y and Z defined as follows:

$$Y_0 = 0 \qquad Y_1 = 1 \qquad Y_n = PY_{n-1} - QY_{n-2}$$
$$Z_0 = 2 \qquad Z_1 = P \qquad Z_n = PZ_{n-1} - QZ_{n-2}$$

show that Y_n and Z_n are the Lucas sequences $U_n(P,Q)$ and $V_n(P,Q)$, respectively.

7.12 Evaluate the Legendre symbols $\left(\dfrac{5}{17}\right)$, $\left(\dfrac{6}{31}\right)$, $\left(\dfrac{8}{11}\right)$.

APPENDIX 7A

MATHEMATICAL DETAILS OF THE LUC ALGORITHM

This appendix fills in some of the mathematical details referred to in Section 7.5.

7A.1 The Basic LUC Equality

We would like to prove that

$$V_d[V_e(P, 1), 1] = P$$

for values of e and d selected as in Figure 7.17.

LEMMA 1. $2Q^m V_{n-m}(P,Q) = V_n(P,Q)V_m(P,Q) - DU_n(P,Q)U_m(P,Q)$

Proof:

$$V_n(P,Q)V_m(P,Q) - DU_n(P,Q)U_m(P,Q)$$

$$= (\alpha^n + \beta^n)(\alpha^m + \beta^m) - (\alpha - \beta)^2 \frac{\alpha^n - \beta^n}{\alpha - \beta} \frac{\alpha^m - \beta^m}{\alpha - \beta}$$

$$= (\alpha^n + \beta^n)(\alpha^m + \beta^m) - (\alpha^n - \beta^n)(\alpha^m - \beta^m)$$

$$= (\alpha^{n+m} + \alpha^n\beta^m + \alpha^m\beta^n + \beta^{n+m}) - (\alpha^{n+m} - \alpha^n\beta^m - \alpha^m\beta^n + \beta^{n+m})$$

$$= 2\alpha^n\beta^m + 2\alpha^m\beta^n$$

$$= 2\alpha^m\beta^m(\alpha^{n-m} + \beta^{n-m})$$

$$= 2Q^m V_{n-m}(P, Q)$$

Q.E.D.

LEMMA 2. Using the definition of $S(N)$ in Figure 7.17, when $N = pq$, p and q different odd primes not dividing $D = (P^2 - 4)$, the following hold:

$$U_{kS(N)}(P,1) \equiv 0 \bmod N \qquad \text{for any integer } k$$
$$V_{kS(N)}(P,1) \equiv 2 \bmod N \qquad \text{for any integer } k$$

The proof is lengthy and is not included here. The interested reader may refer to [RIBE91] or [WILL82].

THEOREM: Using the definitions of Figure 7.17, $V_d(V_e(P, 1), 1) = P$.

$$
\begin{aligned}
V_d(V_e(P, 1), 1) &= V_{de}(P, 1) &&\text{by Equation (7.4)}\\
&= V_{kS(N) + 1}(P, 1) &&\text{by definition of } d, e\\
&= PV_{kS(N)}(P, 1) - V_{kS(N)-1}(P, 1) &&\text{by Equation (7.1)}\\
&= PV_{kS(N)}(P, 1) \\
&\quad - \frac{1}{2}\Big[V_{kS(N)}(P,1)V_1(P,1) - DU_{kS(N)}(P,1)U_1(P,1)\Big] &&\text{by Lemma 1}\\
&= PV_{kS(N)}(P,1) - \frac{1}{2}\Big[PV_{kS(N)}(P,1) - DU_{kS(N)}(P,1)\Big] \\
&\equiv 2P - \frac{1}{2}\,[2P - 0] \bmod N &&\text{by Lemma 2}\\
&= P
\end{aligned}
$$

Q.E.D.

7A.2 Selection of e

In Section 7.5 we made the statement that if we choose e to be relatively prime to $(p - 1)(q - 1)(p + 1)(q + 1)$, then e is also relatively prime to $S(N)$. Recall that

$$S(N) = \text{lcm}\left[\left(p - \left(\frac{D}{p}\right)\right), \left(q - \left(\frac{D}{q}\right)\right)\right]$$

and that

$$\left(\frac{D}{p}\right) = \begin{cases} 0 & \text{if } p \text{ divides } D \\ 1 & \text{if there is a number } x \text{ such that } D \equiv x^2 \bmod p \\ -1 & \text{if no such number exists} \end{cases}$$

And $D = P^2 - 4$

It should be clear that if $\left(\frac{D}{p}\right)$ and $\left(\frac{D}{q}\right)$ each take on only the values of 1 or -1 regardless of the value of the plaintext message P, then e is also relatively prime to $S(N)$. So, the desired condition is achieved if p does not divide D and q does not devide D. Looking at the definition of D, we can say that the desired condition is achieved if p does not divide P and q does not divide P. Since p and q are both prime numbers, the only values of P that are divided by either p or q are p, 2_p, 3_p, ... $(q-1)p$, q, 2_q, 3_q, ... $(p-1)q$. This is an infinitesimally small fraction of the total number of possible values of P, so that for all practical purposes, we can say that p does not divide P and q does not divide P.

CHAPTER 8

AUTHENTICATION AND KEY EXCHANGE

The interaction of threat and countermeasure poses distinctive problems for security specialists: the attacker must find but one of possible multiple vulnerabilities in order to succeed; the security specialist must develop countermeasures for all. The advantage is therefore heavily to the attacker until very late in the mutual evolution of threat and countermeasure.

> — *Computers at Risk: Safe Computing in the Information Age*
> National Research Council, 1991

We cannot enter into alliance with neighboring princes until we are acquainted with their designs.

> — *The Art of War*
> Sun Tzu

This chapter examines some of the authentication functions that have been developed to support application-level authentication and digital signatures.

We begin by looking at one of the earliest and also one of the most widely used services, which is known as Kerberos. Next, the X.509 directory authentication service is examined. This standard is important as part of the directory service that it supports but is also a basic building block used in other standards, such as Privacy Enhanced Mail, discussed in Chapter 9. Then we describe Diffie–Hellman key exchange, which is a widely used public-key technique. Finally, we examine the Digital Signature Standard developed by the National Institute of Standards and Technology (NIST).

8.1

KERBEROS

Kerberos[1] is an authentication service developed as part of Project Athena at MIT. The problem that Kerberos is intended to solve is this: Assume an open distributed environment in which users at workstations wish to access services on servers distributed throughout the network. We would like for servers to be able to restrict access to authorized users and to be able to authenticate requests for service. In this environment, a workstation cannot be trusted to identify its users correctly to network services. In particular, the following three threats exist:

- A user may gain access to a particular workstation and pretend to be another user operating from that workstation.
- A user may alter the network address of a workstation so that the requests sent from the altered workstation appear to come from the impersonated workstation.
- A user may eavesdrop on exchanges and use a replay attack to gain entrance to a server or to disrupt operations.

In any of these cases, an unauthorized user may be able to gain access to services and data that he or she is not authorized to access. Rather than building in elaborate authentication protocols at each server, Kerberos provides a centralized authentication server whose function is to authenticate users to servers and servers to users. Unlike most other authentication schemes described in this book, Kerberos relies exclusively on conventional encryption, making no use of public-key encryption.

Two versions of Kerberos are in common use. Version 4 [MILL88, STEI88] is the most widely used version. Version 5 [KOHL94] corrects some of the security deficiencies of version 4 and has been issued as a draft Internet Standard (RFC 1510).[2]

We begin this section with a brief discussion of the motivation for the Kerberos approach. Then because of the complexity of Kerberos, it is best to start with a description of the authentication protocol used in version 4. This enables us to see the essence of the Kerberos strategy without considering some of the details required to handle subtle security threats. Then, we examine version 5.

Motivation

If a set of users is provided with dedicated personal computers that have no network connections, then a user's resources and files can be protected by physically

---

[1]In Greek mythology, Kerberos was "a many headed dog, commonly three, perhaps with a serpent's tail, the guardian of the entrance of Hades." From *Dictionary of Subjects and Symbols in Art*, by James Hall, Harper & Row, 1979. Just as the Greek Kerberos has three heads, the modern Kerberos was intended to have three components to guard a network's gate: authentication, accounting, and audit. The last two heads were never implemented.

[2]Versions 1 through 3 were internal development versions. Version 4 is the "original" Kerberos.

securing each personal computer. When these users instead are served by a centralized time-sharing system, the time-sharing operating system must provide the security. The operating system can enforce access control policies based on user identity and use the logon procedure to identify users.

Today, neither of these scenarios is typical. More common is a distributed architecture consisting of dedicated user workstations (clients) and distributed or centralized servers. In this environment, three approaches to security can be envisioned:

1. Rely on each individual client workstation to assure the identity of its user or users and rely on each server to enforce a security policy based on user identification (ID).
2. Require that client systems authenticate themselves to servers, but trust the client system concerning the identity of its user.
3. Require the user to prove identity for each service invoked. Also require that servers prove their identity to clients.

In a small, closed environment, in which all systems are owned and operated by a single organization, the first or perhaps the second strategy may suffice.[3] But in a more open environment, in which network connections to other machines are supported, the third approach is needed in order to protect user information and resources housed at the server. This third approach is supported by Kerberos. Kerberos assumes a distributed client/server architecture and employs one or more Kerberos servers to provide an authentication service.

The first published report on Kerberos [STEI88] listed the following requirements for Kerberos:

- *Secure:* A network eavesdropper should not be able to obtain the necessary information to impersonate a user. More generally, Kerberos should be strong enough that a potential opponent does not find it to be the weak link.
- *Reliable:* For all services that rely on Kerberos for access control, lack of availability of the Kerberos service means lack of availability of the supported services. Hence, Kerberos should be highly reliable and should employ a distributed server architecture, with one system able to back up another.
- *Transparent:* Ideally, the user should not be aware that authentication is taking place, beyond the requirement to enter a password.
- *Scalable:* The system should be capable of supporting large numbers of clients and servers. Again, this suggests a modular, distributed architecture.

To support these requirements, the overall scheme of Kerberos is that of a trusted third-party authentication service that uses a protocol based on that proposed by Needham and Schroeder [NEED78], which was discussed in Chapter 3. It is trusted in the sense that clients and servers trust Kerberos to mediate their mutual

---

[3]However, even a closed environment faces the threat of attack by a disgruntled employee.

authentication. Assuming the Kerberos protocol is well designed, then the authentication service is secure if the Kerberos server itself is secure.[4]

Kerberos Version 4

Version 4 of Kerberos makes use of DES, in a rather elaborate protocol, to provide the authentication service. Viewing the protocol as a whole, it is difficult to see the need for the many elements contained therein. Therefore, we adopt a strategy used by Bill Bryant of Project Athena [BRYA88] and build up to the full protocol by looking first at several hypothetical dialogues. Each successive dialogue adds additional complexity to counter security vulnerabilities revealed in the preceding dialogue.

After examining the protocol, we look at some other aspects of version 4.

A Simple Authentication Dialogue

In an unprotected network environment, any client can apply to any server for service. The obvious security risk is that of impersonation. An opponent can pretend to be another client and obtain unauthorized privileges on server machines. To counter this threat, servers must be able to confirm the identities of clients who request service. Each server can be required to undertake this task for each client/server interaction, but in an open environment, this places a substantial burden on each server.

An alternative is to use an authentication server (AS) that knows the passwords of all users and stores these in a centralized database. In addition, the AS shares a unique secret key with each server. These keys have been distributed physically or in some other secure manner. Now consider the following hypothetical dialogue:

$$
\begin{aligned}
&(1)\ C \rightarrow AS: \qquad ID_C, P_C, ID_V \\
&(2)\ AS \rightarrow C: \qquad Ticket \\
&(3)\ C \rightarrow V: \qquad ID_C, Ticket \\
&\qquad Ticket = E_{K_v}[ID_C, AD_C, ID_V]
\end{aligned}
$$

where

$$
\begin{aligned}
C\ &= client \\
AS\ &= authentication\ server \\
V\ &= server
\end{aligned}
$$

[4]Remember that the security of the Kerberos server should not automatically be assumed but must be guarded carefully (in a locked room). It is well to remember the fate of the Greek Kerberos, whom Hercules was ordered by Eurystheus to capture as his Eleventh Labor: "Hercules found the great dog on its chain and seized it by the throat. At once the three heads tried to attack, and Kerberos lashed about with his powerful tail. Hercules hung on grimly, and Kerberos relaxed into unconsciousness. Eurystheus may have been surprised to see Hercules alive—when he saw the three slavering heads and the huge dog they belonged to he was frightened out of his wits, and leapt back into the safety of his great bronze jar." From *The Hamlyn Concise Dictionary of Greek and Roman Mythology* by Michael Stapleton, Hamlyn, 1982.

ID_C = identifier of user on C
ID_V = identifier of V
P_C = password of user on C
AD_C = network address of C
K_v = secret encryption key shared by AS and V

In this scenario, the user logs on to a workstation and requests access to server V. The client module C in the user's workstation requests the user's password and then sends a message to the AS that includes the user's ID, the server's ID, and the user's password. The AS checks its database to see if the user has supplied the proper password for this user ID and whether this user is permitted access to server V. If both tests are passed, the AS accepts the user as authentic and must now convince the server that this user is authentic. To do so, the AS creates a ticket that contains the user's ID and network address and the server's ID. This ticket is encrypted using the secret key shared by the AS and this server. This ticket is then sent back to C. Because the ticket is encrypted, it cannot be altered by C or by an opponent.

With this ticket, C can now apply to V for service. C sends a message to V containing C's ID and the ticket. V decrypts the ticket and verifies that the user ID in the ticket is the same as the unencrypted user ID in the message. If these two match, the server considers the user authenticated and grants the requested service.

Each of the ingredients of message (3), above, is significant. The ticket is encrypted to prevent alteration or forgery. The server's ID (ID_V) is included in the ticket so that the server can verify that it has decrypted the ticket properly. ID_C is included in the ticket to indicate that this ticket has been issued on behalf of C. Finally, AD_C serves to counter the following threat. An opponent could capture the ticket transmitted in message (2), then use the name ID_C and transmit a message of form (3) from another workstation. The server would receive a valid ticket that matches the user ID and grant access to the user on that other workstation. To prevent this attack, the AS includes in the ticket the network address from which the original request came. Now the ticket is valid only if it is transmitted from the same workstation that initially requested the ticket.

A More Secure Authentication Dialogue

Although the foregoing scenario solves some of the problems of authentication in an open network environment, problems remain. Two in particular stand out. First, we would like to minimize the number of times that a user has to enter a password. Suppose each ticket can be used only once. If user C logs on to a workstation in the morning and wishes to check his or her mail at a mail server, C must supply a password to get a ticket for the mail server. If C wishes to check the mail several times during the day, each attempt requires re-entering the password. We can improve matters by saying that tickets are reusable. For a single logon session, the workstation can store the mail server ticket after it is received and use it on behalf of the user for multiple accesses to the mail server.

However, under this scheme it remains the case that a user would need a new ticket for every different service. If a user wished to access a print server, a mail server, a file server, and so on, the first instance of each access would require a new ticket and hence require the user to enter the password.

The second problem is that the earlier scenario involved a plaintext transmission of the password (message 1). An eavesdropper could capture the password and use any service accessible to the victim.

To solve these additional problems, we introduce a scheme for avoiding plaintext passwords and a new server, known as the ticket-granting server (TGS). The new but still hypothetical scenario is as follows:

Once per user logon session:
(1) $C \rightarrow AS$: ID_C, ID_{tgs}
(2) $AS \rightarrow C$: $E_{K_c}[Ticket_{tgs}]$

Once per type of service:
(3) $C \rightarrow TGS$: $ID_C, ID_V, Ticket_{tgs}$
(4) $TGS \rightarrow C$: $Ticket_v$

Once per service session:
(5) $C \rightarrow V$: $ID_C, Ticket_v$

$Ticket_{tgs} = E_{K_{tgs}}[ID_C, AD_C, ID_{tgs}, TS_1, Lifetime_1]$
$Ticket_v = E_{K_v}[ID_C, AD_C, ID_V, TS_2, Lifetime_2]$

The new service, TGS, issues tickets to users who have been authenticated to AS. Thus, the user first requests a ticket-granting ticket ($Ticket_{tgs}$) from the AS. This ticket is saved by the client module in the user workstation. Each time the user requires access to a new service, the client applies to the TGS, using the ticket to authenticate itself. The TGS then grants a ticket for the particular service. The client saves each service-granting ticket and uses it to authenticate its user to a server each time a particular service is requested. Now, let us look at the details of this scheme:

1. The client requests a ticket-granting ticket on behalf of the user by sending its user's ID to the AS, together with the TGS ID, indicating a request to use the TGS service.
2. The AS responds with a ticket that is encrypted with a key that is derived from the user's password. When this response arrives at the client, the client prompts the user for his or her password, generates the key, and attempts to decrypt the incoming message. If the correct password is supplied, the ticket is successfully recovered.

Because only the correct user should know the password, only the correct user can recover the ticket. Thus, we have used the password to obtain credentials from Kerberos without having to transmit the password in plaintext. The ticket itself includes the ID and network address of the user, and the ID of the TGS. This corresponds to the first scenario. Now, the idea is that this ticket can be used by the client to request multiple service-granting tickets. So the ticket-granting ticket is to be reusable. However, we do not wish an opponent to be able to capture the ticket and use it. Consider the following scenario: An opponent captures the ticket and waits until the user has logged off his or her workstation. Then the opponent either gains access to that workstation or configures his or her workstation with the same network address as that of the victim. Then, the opponent would be able to reuse the ticket to spoof the TGS. To counter this, the ticket includes a timestamp, indicating the date and time at which the ticket was issued, and a lifetime, indicating the length of time for which the ticket is valid (e.g., 8 hours). Thus, the client now has a reusable ticket and need not bother the user for a password for each new service request. Finally, note that the ticket-granting ticket is encrypted with a secret key known only to the AS and the TGS. This prevents alteration of the ticket. The ticket is re-encrypted with a key based on the user's password. This assures that the ticket can be recovered only by the correct user providing the authentication.

Now that the client has a ticket-granting ticket, access to any server can be obtained with steps (3) and (4):

3. The client requests a service-granting ticket on behalf of the user. For this purpose, the client transmits a message to the TGS containing the user's ID, the ID of the desired service, and the ticket-granting ticket.
4. The TGS decrypts the incoming ticket and verifies the success of the decryption by the presence of its ID. It checks to make sure that the lifetime has not expired. Then it compares the user ID and network address with the incoming information to authenticate the user. Finally, it issues a ticket to grant access to the requested service.

The service-granting ticket has the same structure as the ticket-granting ticket. Indeed, because the TGS is a server, we would expect that the same elements are needed to authenticate a client to the TGS and to authenticate a client to an application server. Again, the ticket contains a timestamp and lifetime. If the user wants access to the same service at a later time, the client can simply use the previously acquired service-granting ticket and need not bother the user for a password. Note that the ticket is encrypted with a secret key (E_{Kv}) known only to the TGS and the server, preventing alteration.

Finally, with a particular service-granting ticket, the client can gain access to the corresponding service with step 5:

5. The client requests access to a service on behalf of the user. For this purpose, the client transmits a message to the server containing the user's ID and the service-granting ticket. The server authenticates by using the contents of the ticket.

This new scenario satisfies the two requirements of only one password query per user session and protection of the user password.

The Version 4 Authentication Dialogue

Although the foregoing scenario enhances security compared to the first attempt, two additional problems remain. The heart of the first problem is the lifetime associated with the ticket-granting ticket. If this lifetime is very short (e.g., minutes), then the user will be repeatedly asked for a password. If the lifetime is long (e.g., hours), then an opponent has a greater opportunity for replay. An opponent could eavesdrop on the network and capture a copy of the ticket-granting ticket and then wait for the legitimate user to log out. Then, the opponent could forge the legitimate user's network address and send the message of step (3) to the TGS. This would give the opponent unlimited access to the resources and files available to the legitimate user.

Similarly, if an opponent captures a service-granting ticket and uses it before it expires, the opponent has access to the corresponding service.

Thus, we arrive at an additional requirement. A network service (the TGS or an application service) must be able to prove that the person using a ticket is the same person to whom that ticket was issued.

The second problem is that there may be a requirement for servers to authenticate themselves to users. Without such authentication, an opponent could sabotage the configuration so that messages to a server were directed to another location. The false server would then be in a position to act as a real server and capture any information from the user and deny the true service to the user.

We examine these problems in turn and refer to Table 8.1, which shows the actual Kerberos protocol.

First, consider the problem of captured ticket-granting tickets and the need to determine that the ticket presenter is the same as the client for whom the ticket was issued. The threat is that an opponent will steal the ticket and use it before it expires. To get around this problem, let us have the AS provide both the client and the TGS with a secret piece of information in a secure manner. Then, the client can prove its identity to the TGS by revealing the secret information, again in a secure manner. An efficient way of accomplishing this is to use an encryption key as the secure information; this is referred to as a session key in Kerberos.

Table 8.1a shows the technique for distributing the key, known as a session key. As before, the client sends a message to the AS requesting access to the TGS. The AS responds with a message, encrypted with a key derived from the user's password (K_c), that contains the ticket. The encrypted message also contains a copy of the session key, $K_{c,tgs}$, where the subscripts indicate that this is a session key for C and TGS. Because this session key is inside the message encrypted with K_c, only the user's client can read it. The same session key is included in the ticket, which can be read only by the TGS. Thus, the session key has been securely delivered to both C and TGS.

Before proceeding, note that several additional pieces of information have been added to this first phase of the dialogue. Message (1) includes a timestamp, so that

TABLE 8.1   Summary of Kerberos Version 4 Message Exchanges

(a) Authentication Service Exchange: to obtain ticket-granting ticket

(1) $C \rightarrow AS: ID_c \mid\mid ID_{tgs} \mid\mid TS_1$

(2) $AS \rightarrow C: E_{K_c}[K_{c,tgs} \mid\mid ID_{tgs} \mid\mid TS_2 \mid\mid Lifetime_2 \mid\mid Ticket_{tgs}]$

$Ticket_{tgs} = E_{K_{tgs}}[K_{c,tgs} \mid\mid ID_c \mid\mid AD_c \mid\mid ID_{tgs} \mid\mid TS_2 \mid\mid Lifetime_2]$

(b) Ticket-Granting Service Exchange: to obtain service-granting ticket

(3) $C \rightarrow TGS: ID_v \mid\mid Ticket_{tgs} \mid\mid Authenticator_c$

(4) $TGS \rightarrow C: E_{K_{c,tgs}}[K_{c,v} \mid\mid ID_v \mid\mid TS_4 \mid\mid Ticket_v]$

$Ticket_{tgs} = E_{K_{tgs}}[K_{c,tgs} \mid\mid ID_c \mid\mid AD_c \mid\mid ID_{tgs} \mid\mid TS_2 \mid\mid Lifetime_2]$

$Ticket_v = E_{K_v}[K_{c,v} \mid\mid ID_c \mid\mid AD_c \mid\mid ID_v \mid\mid TS_4 \mid\mid Lifetime_4]$

$Authenticator_c = E_{K_{c,tgs}}[ID_c \mid\mid AD_c \mid\mid TS_3]$

(c) Client/Server Authentication Exchange: to obtain service

(5) $C \rightarrow TGS: Ticket_v \mid\mid Authenticator_c$

(6) $K \rightarrow C: E_{K_{c,v}}[TS_5 + 1]$ (for mutual authentication)

$Ticket_v = E_{K_v}[K_{c,v} \mid\mid ID_c \mid\mid AD_c \mid\mid ID_v \mid\mid TS_4 \mid\mid Lifetime_4]$

$Authenticator_c = E_{K_{c,v}}[ID_c \mid\mid AD_c \mid\mid TS_5]$

the AS knows that the message is timely. Message (2) includes several elements of the ticket in a form accessible to C. This enables C to confirm that this ticket is for the TGS and to learn its expiration time.

Now, armed with the ticket and the session key, C is ready to approach the TGS. As before, C sends TGS a message that includes the ticket plus the ID of the requested service (message 3 in Table 8.1b). In addition, C transmits an authenticator, which includes the ID and address of C's user and a timestamp. Unlike the ticket, which is reusable, the authenticator is intended for use only once and has a very short lifetime. Now, the TGS can decrypt the ticket with the key that it shares with the AS. This ticket indicates that user C has been provided with the session key $K_{c,tgs}$. In effect, the ticket says, "anyone who uses $K_{c,tgs}$ must be C." The TGS uses the session key to decrypt the authenticator. The TGS can then check the name and address from the authenticator with that of the ticket and with the network address of the incoming message. If all match, then the TGS is assured that the sender of the ticket is indeed the ticket's real owner. In effect, the authenticator says "At time TS_3, I hereby use $K_{c,tgs}$." Note that the ticket doesn't prove anyone's identity but is a way to distribute keys securely. It is the authenticator that proves the client's identity. Because the authenticator can be used only once and has a short lifetime, the threat of an opponent stealing both the ticket and the authenticator for presentation later is countered.

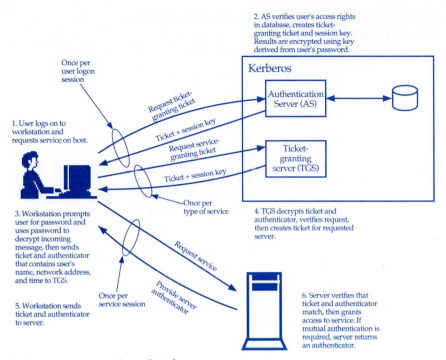

FIGURE 8.1. Overview of Kerberos

The reply from the TGS, in message (4), follows the form of message (2). The message is encrypted with the message key shared by TGS and C and includes a session key to be shared between C and the server V, the ID of V, and the time-stamp of the ticket. The ticket itself includes the same session key.

C now has a reusable service-granting ticket for V. When C presents this ticket, as shown in message (5), it also sends an authenticator. The server can decrypt the ticket, recover the session key, and decrypt the authenticator.

If mutual authentication is required, the server can reply as shown in message (6). The server returns the value of the timestamp from the authenticator, incremented by 1, and encrypted in the session key. C can decrypt this message to recover the incremented timestamp. Because the message was encrypted by the session key, C is assured that it could have been created only by V. The contents of the message assures C that this is not a replay of an old reply.

Finally, at the conclusion of this process, the client and server share a secret key. This key can be used to encrypt future messages between the two or to exchange a new random session key for that purpose.

Table 8.2 summarizes the justification for each of the elements in the Kerberos protocol, and Figure 8.1 provides a simplified overview of the action.

TABLE 8.2   Rationale for the Elements of the Kerberos Version 4 Protocol

(a) Authentication Service Exchange

Message (1)	Client requests ticket-granting ticket
ID_C:	Tells AS identity of user from this client
ID_{tgs}:	Tells AS that user requests access to TGS
TS_1:	Allows AS to verify that client's clock is synchronized with that of AS
Message (2)	AS returns ticket-granting ticket
E_{K_c}:	Encryption is based on user's password, enabling AS and client to verify password, and protecting contents of message (2)
$K_{c,tgs}$:	Copy of session key accessible to client; created by AS to permit secure exchange between client and TGS without requiring them to share a permanent key
ID_{tgs}:	Confirms that this ticket is for the TGS
TS_2:	Informs client of time this ticket was issued
$Lifetime_2$:	Informs client of the lifetime of this ticket
$Ticket_{tgs}$:	Ticket to be used by client to access TGS

(b) Ticket-Granting Service Exchange

Message (3)	Client requests service-granting ticket
ID_V:	Tells TGS that user requests access to server V
$Ticket_{tgs}$:	Assures TGS that this user has been authenticated by AS
$Authenticator_c$:	Generated by client to validate ticket
Message (4)	TGS returns service-granting ticket
$E_{K_{c,tgs}}$:	Key shared only by C and TGS; protects contents of message (2)
$K_{c,tgs}$:	Copy of session key accessible to client; created by TGS to permit secure exchange between client and server without requiring them to share a permanent key
ID_V:	Confirms that this ticket is for server V
TS_4:	Informs client of time this ticket was issued
$Ticket_V$:	Ticket to be used by client to access server V
$Ticket_{tgs}$	Reusable so that user does not have to reenter password
$E_{K_{tgs}}$:	Ticket is encrypted with key known only to AS and TGS, to prevent tampering
$K_{c,tgs}$:	Copy of session key accessible to TGS; used to decrypt authenticator, thereby authenticating ticket
ID_c:	Indicates the rightful owner of this ticket
AD_c:	Prevents use of ticket from workstation other than one that initially requested the ticket
ID_{tgs}:	Assures server that it has decrypted ticket properly
TS_2:	Informs TGS of time this ticket was issued
$Lifetime_2$:	Prevents replay after ticket has expired
$Authenticator_c$:	Assures TGS that the ticket presenter is the same as the client for whom the ticket was issued; has very short lifetime to prevent replay

TABLE 8.2   Rationale for the Elements of the Kerberos Version 4 Protocol   (continued)

$E_{K_{c,tgs}}$:	Authenticator is encrypted with key known only to client and TGS, to prevent tampering
ID_c:	Must match ID in ticket to authenticate ticket
AD_c:	Must match address in ticket to authenticate ticket
TS_2:	Informs TGS of time this authenticator was generated

(c) Client/Server Authentication Exchange

Message (5)	Client requests service
$Ticket_v$:	Assures server that this user has been authenticated by AS
$Authenticator_c$:	Generated by client to validate ticket
Message (6)	Optional authentication of server to client
$E_{K_{c,v}}$:	Assures C that this message is from V
$TS_5 + 1$:	Assures C that this is not a replay of an old reply.
$Ticket_v$	Reusable so that client does not need to request a new ticket from TGS for each access to the same server
E_{K_v}:	Ticket is encrypted with key known only to TGS and server, to prevent tampering
$K_{c,v}$:	Copy of session key accessible to client; used to decrypt authenticator, thereby authenticating ticket
ID_c:	Indicates the rightful owner of this ticket
AD_c:	Prevents use of ticket from workstation other than one that initially requested the ticket
ID_v:	Assures server that it has decrypted ticket properly
TS_4:	Informs server of time this ticket was issued
$Lifetime_4$:	Prevents replay after ticket has expired
$Authenticator_c$:	Assures server that the ticket presenter is the same as the client for whom the ticket was issued; has very short lifetime to prevent replay
$E_{K_{c,v}}$:	Authenticator is encrypted with key known only to client and server, to prevent tampering
ID_c:	Must match ID in ticket to authenticate ticket
AD_c:	Must match address in ticket to authenticate ticket
TS_5:	Informs server of time this authenticator was generated

Kerberos Realms and Multiple Kerberi

A full-service Kerberos environment consisting of a Kerberos server, a number of clients, and a number of application servers, requires the following:

1. The Kerberos server must have the UID and hashed password of all participating users in its database. All users are registered with the Kerberos server.
2. The Kerberos server must share a secret key with each server. All servers are registered with the Kerberos server.

Such an environment is referred to as a **realm.** Networks of clients and servers under different administrative organizations generally constitute different realms. That is, it generally is not practical, or does not conform to administrative policy, to have users and servers in one administrative domain registered with a Kerberos server elsewhere. However, users in one realm may need access to servers in other realms, and some servers may be willing to provide service to users from other realms, provided that those users are authenticated.

Kerberos provides a mechanism for supporting such inter-realm authentication. For two realms to support inter-realm authentication, a third requirement is added:

3. The Kerberos server in each interoperating realm shares a secret key with the server in the other realm. The two Kerberos servers are registered with each other.

The scheme requires that the Kerberos server in one realm trust the Kerberos server in the other realm to authenticate its users. Furthermore, the participating servers in the second realm must also be willing to trust the Kerberos server in the first realm.

With these ground rules in place, we can describe the mechanism as follows (Figure 8.2): A user wishing service on a server in another realm needs a ticket for that server. The user's client follows the usual procedures to gain access to the local TGS and then requests a ticket-granting ticket for a remote TGS (TGS in another realm). The client can then apply to the remote TGS for a service-granting ticket for the desired server in the realm of the remote TGS.

The details of the exchanges illustrated in Figure 8.2 are as follows (compare Table 8.1):

(1) $C \rightarrow AS$: $ID_c \ || \ ID_{tgs} \ || \ TS_1$

(2) $AS \rightarrow C$: $E_{K_c}[K_{c,tgs} \ || \ ID_{tgs} \ || \ TS_2 \ || \ Lifetime_2 \ || \ Ticket_{tgs}]$

(3) $C \rightarrow TGS$: $ID_{tgsrem} \ || \ Ticket_{tgs} \ || \ Authenticator_c$

(4) $TGS \rightarrow C$: $E_{K_{c,tgs}}[K_{c,tgsrem} \ || \ ID_{tgsrem} \ || \ TS_4 \ || \ Ticket_{tgsrem}]$

(5) $C \rightarrow TGS_{rem}$: $ID_{vrem} \ || \ Ticket_{tgsrem} \ || \ Authenticator_c$

(6) $TGS \rightarrow C$: $E_{K_{c,tgsrem}}[K_{c,vrem} \ || \ ID_{vrem} \ || \ TS_6 \ || \ Ticket_{vrem}]$

(7) $C \rightarrow V_{rem}$: $Ticket_{vrem} \ || \ Authenticator_c$

The ticket presented to the remote server (V_{rem}) indicates the realm in which the user was originally authenticated. The server chooses whether to honor the remote request.

One problem presented by the foregoing approach is that it does not scale well to many realms. If there are N realms, then there must be $[N(N-1)]/2$ secure key

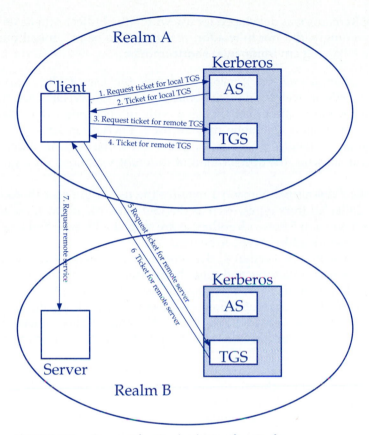

FIGURE 8.2.   Request for Service in Another Realm

exchanges so that each Kerberos realm can interoperate with all other Kerberos realms.

Kerberos Version 5

Version 5 of Kerberos is specified in RFC 1510 and provides a number of improvements over version 4 [KOHL93]. To begin, we provide an overview of the changes from version 4 to version 5 and then look at the version 5 protocol.

Differences Between Versions 4 and 5

Version 5 is intended to address the limitations of version 4 in two areas: environmental shortcomings and technical deficiencies. Let us briefly summarize the improvements in each area.[5]

---

[5]The following discussion follows the presentation in [KOHL94].

Version 4 of Kerberos was developed for use within the Project Athena environment and, accordingly, did not fully address the need to be of general purpose. This led to the following **environmental shortcomings:**

1. *Encryption system dependence:* Version 4 requires the use of DES. Export restriction on DES as well as doubts about the strength of DES are thus of concern. In version 5, ciphertext is tagged with an encryption type identifier so that any encryption technique may be used. Encryption keys are tagged with a type and a length, allowing the same key to be used in different algorithms and allowing the specification of different variations on a given algorithm.
2. *Internet protocol dependence:* Version 4 requires the use of Internet Protocol (IP) addresses. Other address types, such as the ISO network address, are not accommodated. Version 5 network addresses are tagged with type and length, allowing any network address type to be used.
3. *Message byte ordering:* In version 4, the sender of a message employs a byte ordering of its own choosing and tags the message to indicate least significant byte in lowest address or most significant byte in lowest address. This technique works but does not follow established conventions. In version 5, all message structures are defined using Abstract Syntax Notation One (ASN.1) and Basic Encoding Rules (BER), which provide an unambiguous byte ordering.
4. *Ticket lifetime:* Lifetime values in version 4 are encoded in an 8-bit quantity in units of 5 minutes. Thus, the maximum lifetime that can be expressed is $2^8 \times 5 = 1280$ minutes, or a little over 21 hours. This may be inadequate for some applications (e.g., a long-running simulation that requires valid Kerberos credentials throughout execution). In version 5, tickets include an explicit start time and end time, allowing tickets with arbitrary lifetimes.
5. *Authentication forwarding:* Version 4 does not allow credentials issued to one client to be forwarded to some other host and used by some other client. This capability would enable a client to access a server and have that server access another server on behalf of the client. For example, a client issues a request to a print server that then accesses the client's file from a file server, using the client's credentials for access. Version 5 provides this capability.
6. *Inter-realm authentication:* In version 4, interoperability among N realms requires on the order of N^2 Kerberos-to-Kerberos relationships, as described earlier. Version 5 supports a method that requires fewer relationships, as described shortly.

Apart from these environmental limitations, there are **technical deficiencies** in the version 4 protocol itself. Most of these deficiencies were documented in [BELL90], and version 5 attempts to address these. The deficiencies are the following:

1. *Double encryption:* Note in Table 8.1 (messages 2 and 4) that tickets provided to clients are encrypted twice, once with the secret key of the target server and

then again with a secret key known to the client. The second encryption is not necessary and is computationally wasteful.

2. *PCBC encryption:* Encryption in version 4 makes use of a nonstandard mode of DES known as plain-and-cipher block chaining (PCBC).[6] It has been demonstrated that this mode is vulnerable to an attack involving the interchange of ciphertext blocks [KOHL89]. PCBC was intended to provide an integrity check as part of the encryption operation. Version 5 provides explicit integrity mechanisms, allowing the standard CBC mode to be used for encryption.

3. *Session keys:* Each ticket includes a session key that is used by the client to encrypt the authenticator sent to the service associated with that ticket. In addition, the session key may subsequently be used by the client and the server to protect messages passed during that session. However, because the same ticket may be used repeatedly to gain service from a particular server, there is the risk that an opponent will replay messages from an old session to the client or the server. In version 5, it is possible for a client and server to negotiate a subsession key, which is to be used for only that one connection. A new access by the client would result in the use of a new subsession key.

4. *Password attacks:* One vulnerability shared by both versions is to a password attack. The message from the AS to the client includes material encrypted with a key based on the client's password.[7] An opponent can capture this message and attempt to decrypt it by trying various passwords. If the result of a test decryption is of the proper form, then the opponent has discovered the client's password and may subsequently use it to gain authentication credentials from Kerberos. This is the same type of password attack described in Chapter 6, with the same kinds of countermeasures being applicable. Version 5 does provide a mechanism known as preauthentication, which should make password attacks more difficult, but it does not prevent them altogether.

The Version 5 Authentication Dialogue

Table 8.3 summarizes the basic version 5 dialogue. This is best explained by comparison with version 4 (Table 8.1).

First, consider the **authentication service exchange.** Message (1) is a client request for a ticket-granting ticket. As before, it includes the ID of the user and the TGS. The following new elements are added:

- *Realm:* indicates realm of user.
- *Options:* used to request that certain flags be set in the returned ticket, as explained below.

---

[6]Described in Appendix 8A.

[7]Appendix 8A describes the mapping of passwords to encryption keys.

TABLE 8.3   Summary of Kerberos Version 5 Message Exchanges

(a) Authentication Service Exchange: to obtain ticket-granting ticket

(1) C → AS : Options $||$ ID_c $||$ $Realm_c$ $||$ ID_{tgs} $||$ Times $||$ $Nonce_1$

(2) K → C : $Realm_c$ $||$ ID_c $||$ $Ticket_{tgs}$ $||$ $E_{Kc}[K_{c,tgs}$ $||$ Times $||$ $Nonce_1$ $||$ $Realm_{tgs}$ $||$ $ID_{tgs}]$

$Ticket_{tgs}$ = $E_{K_{tgs}}$ [Flags $||$ $K_{c,tgs}$ $||$ $Realm_c$ $||$ ID_c $||$ AD_c $||$ Times]

(b) Ticket-Granting Service Exchange: to obtain service-granting ticket

(3) C → TGS : Options $||$ ID_v $||$ Times $||$ $||$ $Nonce_2$ $||$ $Ticket_{tgs}$ $||$ $Authenticator_c$

(4) TGS → C : $Realm_c$ $||$ ID_c $||$ $Ticket_v$ $||$ $E_{K_{c,tgs}}$ $[K_{c,v}$Times $||$ $||$ $Nonce_2$ $||$ $Realm_v$ $||$ $ID_v]$

$Ticket_{tgs}$ = $E_{K_{tgs}}$ [Flags $||$ $K_{c,tgs}$ $||$ $Realm_c$ $||$ ID_c $||$ AD_c $||$ Times]

$Ticket_v$ = E_{K_v} [Flags $||$ $K_{c,v}$ $||$ $Realm_c$ $||$ ID_c $||$ AD_c $||$ Times]

$Authenticator_c$ = $E_{K_{c,tgs}}$ $[ID_c$ $||$ $Realm_c$ $||$ $TS_1]$

(c) Client/Server Authentication Exchange: to obtain service

(5) C → TGS : Options $||$ $Ticket_v$ $||$ $Authenticator_c$

(6) TGS → C : $E_{K_{c,v}}$ $[TS_2$ $||$ Subkey $||$ Seq#]

$Ticket_v$ = E_{K_v} [Flags $||$ $K_{c,v}$ $||$ $Realm_c$ $||$ ID_c $||$ AD_c $||$ Times]

$Authenticator_c$ = $E_{K_{c,v}}$ $[ID_c$ $||$ $Realm_c$ $||$ TS_2 $||$ Subkey $||$ Seq#]

- *Times:* used by the client to request the following time settings in the ticket:
  —from: the desired start time for the requested ticket
  —till: the requested expiration time for the requested ticket
  —rtime: requested renew-till time
- *Nonce:* a random value to be repeated in message 2 to assure that the response is fresh and has not been replayed by an opponent.

Message (2) returns a ticket-granting ticket, identifying information for the client, and a block encrypted using the encryption key based on the user's password. This block includes the session key to be used between the client and TGS, times specified in message 1, the nonce from message 1, and TGS identifying information. The ticket itself includes the session key, identifying information for the client, the requested time values, and flags that reflect the status of this ticket and the requested options. These flags introduce significant new functionality to version 5. For now, we defer a discussion of these flags and concentrate on the overall structure of the version 5 protocol.

Let us now compare the **ticket-granting service exchange** for versions 4 and 5. We see that message (3) for both versions includes an authenticator, a ticket, and the name of the requested service. In addition, version 5 includes requested times and options for the ticket and a nonce, all with functions similar to those of message (1). The authenticator is essentially the same as the one used in version 4.

Message (4) has the same structure as message (2), returning a ticket plus information needed by the client, the latter encrypted with the session key now shared by the client and the TGS.

Finally, for the **client/server authentication exchange,** several new features appear in version 5. In message (5), the client may request as an option that mutual authentication is required. The authenticator includes several new fields as follows:

- *Subkey:* the client's choice for an encryption key to be used to protect this specific application session. If this field is omitted, the session key from the ticket ($K_{c,v}$) is used.
- *Sequence number:* an optional field that specifies the starting sequence number to be used by the server for messages sent to the client during this session. Messages may be sequence numbered to detect replays.

If mutual authentication is required, the server responds with message (6). This message includes the timestamp from the authenticator. Note that in version 4, the timestamp was incremented by one. This is not necessary in version 5 because the nature of the format of messages is such that it is not possible for an opponent to create message (6) without knowledge of the appropriate encryption keys. The subkey field, if present, overrides the subkey field, if present, in message (5). The optional sequence number field specifies the starting sequence number to be used by the client.

Ticket Flags

The flags field included in tickets in version 5 supports expanded functionality compared to that available in version 4. Table 8.4 summarizes the flags that may be included in a ticket.

The INITIAL flag indicates that this ticket was issued by the AS, not by the TGS. Now, when a client requests a service-granting ticket from the TGS, it presents a ticket-granting ticket obtained from the AS. In version 4, this was the only way to ultimately obtain a service-granting ticket. Version 5 provides the additional capability that the client can get a service-granting ticket directly from the AS. The utility of this is as follows: A server, such as a password-changing server, may wish to know that the client's password was recently tested.

The PRE-AUTHENT flag, if set, indicates that when the AS received the initial request (message 1), it authenticated the client before issuing a ticket. The exact form of this preauthentication is left unspecified. As an example, the MIT implementation of version 5 has encrypted timestamp preauthentication, enabled by default. When a user wants to get a ticket, it has to send to the AS a preauthentication block containing a random confounder, a version number, and a timestamp, encrypted in the client's password-based key. The AS decrypts the block and will not send a ticket-granting ticket back unless the timestamp in the preauthentication block is within the allowable time skew (time interval to account for clock drift and network delays). Another possibility is the use of a smart card that generates continually changing passwords that are included in the preauthenticated messages. The passwords generated by the card can be based on a user's password but be transformed by the card so that, in effect, arbitrary passwords are used. This

TABLE 8.4   Kerberos Version 5 Flags

INITIAL	This ticket was issued using the AS protocol, and not issued based on a ticket-granting ticket.
PRE-AUTHENT	During initial authentication, the client was authenticated by the KDC before a ticket was issued.
HW-AUTHENT	The protocol employed for initial authentication required the use of hardware expected to be possessed solely by the named client.
RENEWABLE	Tells TGS that this ticket can be used to obtain a replacement ticket that expires at a later date.
MAY-POSTDATE	Tells TGS that a post-dated ticket may be issued based on the this ticket-granting ticket.
POSTDATED	Indicates that this ticket has been postdated; the end-server can check the authtime field to see when the original authentication occurred.
INVALID	This ticket is invalid and must be validated by the KDC before use.
PROXIABLE	Tells TGS that a new service-granting ticket with a different network address may be issued based on the presented ticket.
PROXY	Indicates that this ticket is a proxy.
FORWARDABLE	Tells TGS that a new ticket-granting ticket with a different network address may be issued based on this ticket-granting ticket.
FORWARDED	Indicates that this ticket has either been forwarded or was issued based on authentication involving a forwarded ticket-granting ticket

prevents an attack based on easily guessed passwords. If a smart card or similar device was used, this is indicated by the HW-AUTHENT flag.

When a ticket has a long lifetime, there is the potential for it to be stolen and used by an opponent for a considerable period. If a short lifetime is used to lessen the threat, then overhead is involved in acquiring new tickets. In the case of a ticket-granting ticket, the client would either have to store the user's secret key, which is clearly risky, or repeatedly ask the user for a password. A compromise scheme is the use of renewable tickets. A ticket with the RENEWABLE flag set includes two expiration times: one for this specific ticket and one that is the latest permissible value for an expiration time. A client can have the ticket renewed by presenting it to the TGS with a requested new expiration time. If the new time is within the limit of the latest permissible value, the TGS can issue a new ticket with a new session time and a later specific expiration time. The advantage of this mechanism is that the TGS may refuse to renew a ticket reported as stolen.

A client may request that the AS provide a ticket-granting ticket with the MAY-POSTDATE flag set. The client can then use this ticket to request a ticket that is flagged as POSTDATED and INVALID from the TGS. Subsequently, the client may submit the postdated ticket for validation. This scheme can be useful for running a long batch job on a server that requires a ticket periodically. The client can obtain a number of tickets for this session at once, with spread-out time values. All but the first ticket are initially invalid. When the execution reaches a point in time when a new ticket is required, the client can get the appropriate ticket validated.

With this approach, the client does not have to repeatedly use its ticket-granting ticket to obtain a service-granting ticket.

In version 5 it is possible for a server to act as a proxy on behalf of a client, in effect adopting the credentials and privileges of the client to request a service from another server. If a client wishes to use this mechanism, it requests a ticket-granting ticket with the PROXIABLE flag set. When this ticket is presented to the TGS, the TGS is permitted to issue a service-granting ticket with a different network address; this latter ticket will have its PROXY flag set. An application receiving such a ticket may accept it or require additional authentication in order to provide an audit trail.[8]

The proxy concept is a limited case of the more powerful forwarding procedure. If a ticket is set with the FORWARDABLE flag, a TGS can issue to the requestor a ticket-granting ticket with a different network address and the FORWARDED flag set. This ticket can then be presented to a remote TGS. This capability allows a client to gain access to a server on another realm without requiring that each Kerberos maintain a secret key with Kerberos servers in every other realm. For example, realms could be structured hierarchically. Then, a client could walk up the tree to a common node and then back down to reach a target realm. Each step of the walk would involve forwarding a ticket-granting ticket to the next TGS in the path.

8.2

X.509 DIRECTORY AUTHENTICATION SERVICE

CCITT recommendation X.509 is part of the X.500 series of recommendations that define a directory service. The directory is, in effect, a server or distributed set of servers that maintains a database of information about users. The information includes a mapping from user name to network address, as well as other attributes and information about the users.

X.509 defines a framework for the provision of authentication services by the X.500 directory to its users. The directory may serve as a repository of public-key certificates of the type discussed in Chapter 4. Each certificate contains the public key of a user and is signed with the private key of a trusted certification authority. In addition, X.509 defines alternative authentication protocols based on the use of public-key certificates.

X.509 is an important standard because it is expected that the X.500 directory service will become widely used. In addition, the certificate structure and authentication protocols defined in X.509 can be used in other contexts. For example, we will see in Chapter 9 that the X.509 certificate format is used in Privacy Enhanced Mail (PEM).

---

[8]For a discussion of some of the possible uses of the proxy capability, see [NEUM93b].

X.509 was initially issued in 1988. The standard was subsequently revised to address some of the security concerns documented in [IANS90, MITC89]; a revised recommendation was issued in 1993.

X.509 is based on the use of public-key cryptography and digital signatures. The standard does not dictate the use of a specific algorithm but recommends RSA. The digital signature scheme is assumed to require the use of a hash function. Again, the standard does not dictate a specific hash algorithm. The 1988 recommendation included the description of a recommended hash algorithm; this algorithm has since been shown to be insecure and has been dropped from the 1993 recommendation.

Certificates

The heart of the X.509 scheme is the public-key certificate associated with each user. These user certificates are assumed to be created by some trusted certification authority (CA) and placed in the directory by the CA or by the user. The directory server itself is not responsible for the creation of public keys or for the certification function; it merely provides an easily accessible location for users to obtain certificates.

Figure 8.3 shows the general format of a certificate, which includes the following elements:

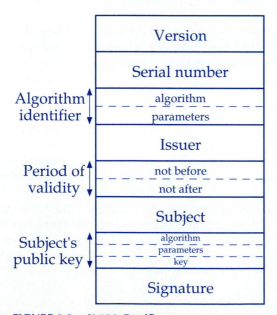

FIGURE 8.3.   X.509 Certificate

- *Version:* differentiates among successive versions of the certificate format; the default is 1988.
- *Serial number:* an integer value, unique within the issuing CA, which is unambiguously associated with this certificate.
- *Algorithm identifier:* the algorithm used to sign the certificate, together with any associated parameters.
- *Issuer:* the CA that created and signed this certificate.
- *Period of validity:* consisting of two dates: the first and last on which the certificate is valid.
- *Subject:* the user to whom this certificate refers.
- *Public-key information:* the public key of the subject, plus an identifier of the algorithm for which this key is to be used.
- *Signature:* covers all of the other fields of the certificate, and consists of a hash code of the other fields, encrypted with the CA's private key.

The standard uses the following notation to define a certificate:

$$CA<<A>> = CA\ \{V, SN, AI, CA, T_A, A, Ap\}$$

where

$$Y<<X>> = \text{the certificate of user X issued by certification authority Y}$$
$$Y\ \{I\} = \text{the signing of I by Y. It consists of I with an enciphered hash code appended}$$

The CA signs the certificate with its secret key. If the corresponding public key is known to a user, then that user can verify that a certificate signed by the CA is valid. This is the typical digital signature approach illustrated in Figure 5.5c.

Obtaining a User's Certificate

User certificates generated by a CA have the following characteristics:

- Any user with access to the public key of the CA can recover the user public key that was certified
- No party other than the certification authority can modify the certificate without this being detected

Because certificates are unforgeable, they can be placed in a directory without the need for the directory to make special efforts to protect them.

If all users subscribe to the same CA, then there is a common trust of that CA. All user certificates can be placed in the directory for access by all users. In addition, a user can transmit his or her certificate directly to other users. In either case, once B is in possession of A's certificate, B has confidence that messages it encrypts with A's public key will be secure from eavesdropping and that messages signed with A's private key are unforgeable.

If there is a large community of users, it may not be practical for all users to subscribe to the same CA. Because it is the CA that signs certificates, each participating user must have a copy of the CA's own public key in order to verify signatures. This public key must be provided to each user in an absolutely secure (with respect to integrity and authenticity) way so that the user has confidence in the associated certificates. Thus, with many users, it may be more practical for there to be a number of CAs, each of which securely provides its public key to some fraction of the users.

Now suppose that A has obtained a certificate from certification authority X_1 and B has obtained a certificate from CA X_2. If A does not securely know the public key of X_2, then B's certificate, issued by X_2, is useless to A. A can read B's certificate, but A cannot verify the signature. However, if the two CAs have securely exchanged their own public keys, the following procedure will enable A to obtain B's public key.

1. A obtains, from the directory, the certificate of X_2 signed by X_1. Because A securely knows X_1's public key, A can obtain X_2's public key from its certificate and verify it by means of X_1's signature on the certificate.
2. A then goes back to the directory and obtains the certificate of B signed by X_2. Because A now has a trusted copy of X_2's public key, A can verify the signature and securely obtain B's public key.

A has used a chain of certificates to obtain B's public key. In the notation of X.509, this chain is expressed as:

$$X_1<<X_2>> X_2<<B>>$$

In the same fashion, B can obtain A's public key with the reverse chain:

$$X_2<<X_1>> X_1<<A>>$$

This scheme need not be limited to a chain of two certificates. An arbitrarily long path of CAs can be followed to produce a chain. A chain with N elements would be expressed as:

$$X_1<<X_2>> X_2<<X_3>> \ldots X_N<<B>>$$

In this case, each pair of CAs in the chain (X_i, X_{i+1}) must have created certificates for each other.

All these certificates of CAs by CAs need to appear in the directory, and the user needs to know how they are linked in order to follow a path to another user's public-key certificate. X.509 suggests that CAs be arranged in a hierarchy, so that navigation is straightforward.

Figure 8.4, taken from X.509, is an example of such a hierarchy. The connected circles indicate the hierarchical relationship among the CAs; the associated boxes indicate certificates maintained in the directory for each CA entry. The directory entry for CA X includes two types of certificates:

- Forward certificates: certificates of X generated by other CAs
- Reverse certificates: certificates generated by X that are the certificates of other CAs

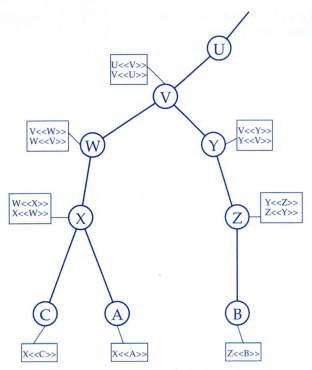

FIGURE 8.4.   X.509 CA Hierarchy: A Hypothetical Example

In this example, user A can acquire the following certificates from the directory to establish a certification path to B:

$$X<<W>> \ W<<V>> \ V<<Y>> \ Y<<Z>> \ Z<<B>>$$

When A has obtained these certificates, it can unwrap the certification path in sequence to recover a trusted copy of B's public key. Using this public key, A can send encrypted messages to B. If A wishes to receive encrypted messages back from B, or to sign messages sent to B, then B will require A's public key, which can be obtained from the following certification path:

$$Z<<Y>> \ Y<<V>> \ V<<W>> \ W<<X>> \ X<<A>>$$

B can obtain this set of certificates from the directory, or A can provide them as part of its initial message to B.

Revocation of Certificates

Recall from Figure 8.3 that each certificate includes a period of validity, much like a credit card. Typically, a new certificate is issued just before the expiration of the old one. In addition, it may be desirable on occasion to revoke a certificate before it expires for one of the following reasons:

1. The user's secret key is assumed to be compromised.
2. The user is no longer certified by this CA.
3. The CA's secret key is assumed to be compromised.

   Each CA must maintain a list consisting of all revoked but not expired certificates issued by that CA, including both those issued to users and to other CAs. These lists should also be posted on the directory.

   Each certificate revocation list posted to the directory is signed by the issuer and consists of the issuer's name, the date the list was created, and an entry for each revoked certificate. Each entry consists of the serial number of a certificate and revocation date for that certificate.

   When a user receives a certificate in a message, the user must determine whether the certificate has been revoked. The user could check the directory each time a certificate is received. To avoid the delays (and possible costs) associated with directory searches, it is likely that the user would maintain a local cache of certificates and lists of revoked certificates.

Authentication Procedures

X.509 also includes three alternative authentication procedures that are intended for use across a variety of applications. All these procedures make use of public-key signatures. It is assumed that the two parties know each other's public key, either by obtaining each other's certificates from the directory or because the certificate is included in the initial message from each side.

   Figure 8.5 illustrates the three procedures.

One-Way Authentication

One-way authentication involves a single transfer of information from one user (A) to another (B), and establishes the following:

1. The identity of A, and that the message was generated by A
2. That the message was intended for B
3. The integrity and originality (it has not been sent multiple times) of the message

Note that only the identity of the initiating entity is verified in this process, not that of the responding entity.

   At a minimum, the message includes a timestamp t_A, a nonce r_A, and the identity of B, and is signed with A's public key. The timestamp consists of an optional generation time and an expiration time. This prevents delayed delivery of messages. The nonce can be used to detect replay attacks. The nonce value must be unique within the expiration time of the message. Thus, B can store the nonce until it expires and reject any new messages with the same nonce.

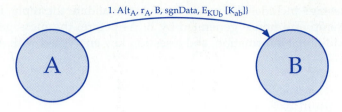

(a) One-way authentication

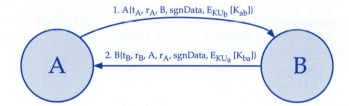

(b) Two-way authentication

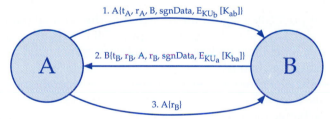

(c) Three-way authentication

FIGURE 8.5. X.509 Strong Authentication Procedures

For pure authentication, the message is used simply to present credentials to B. The message may also include information to be conveyed. This information, sgnData, is included within the scope of the signature, guaranteeing its authenticity and integrity. The message may also be used to convey a session key to B, encrypted with B's public key.

Two-Way Authentication

In addition to the three elements just listed, two-way authentication establishes the following elements:

4. the identity of B and that the reply message was generated by B
5. that the message was intended for A
6. the integrity and originality of the reply

Two-way authentication thus permits both parties in a communication to verify the identity of the other.

The reply message includes the nonce from A, to validate the reply. It also includes a timestamp and nonce generated by B. As before, the message may include signed additional information, and a session key encrypted with A's public key.

Three-Way Authentication

In three-way authentication, a final message from A to B is included, which contains a signed copy of the nonce r_B. The intent of this design is that timestamps need not be checked: Because each nonce is echoed back by the other side, each side can check the returned nonce to detect replay attacks. This approach is needed when synchronized clocks are not available.

8.3

DIFFIE-HELLMAN KEY EXCHANGE

The first published public-key algorithm appeared in the seminal paper by Diffie and Hellman that defined public-key cryptography [DIFF76b] and is generally referred to as Diffie-Hellman key exchange. A number of commercial products employ this key exchange technique.

The purpose of the algorithm is to enable two users to securely exchange a key that can then be used for subsequent encryption of messages. The algorithm itself is limited to the exchange of the keys (see Table 4.3).

The Diffie-Hellman algorithm depends for its effectiveness on the difficulty of computing discrete logarithms. Briefly, we can define the discrete logarithm in the following way. First, we define a primitive root of a prime number p as one whose powers generate all the integers from 1 to $p - 1$. That is, if a is a primitive root of the prime number p, then the numbers

$$a \bmod p, a^2 \bmod p, \ldots, a^{p-1} \bmod p$$

are distinct and consist of the integers from 1 through $p - 1$ in some permutation.

For any integer b and a primitive root a of prime number p, one can find a unique exponent i such that

$$b = a^i \bmod p \qquad \text{where } 0 \leq i \leq (p - 1)$$

The exponent i is referred to as the discrete logarithm, or index, of b for the base a, mod p. This value is denoted as $\text{ind}_{a,p}(b)$. See Appendix 8B for an extended discussion of discrete logarithms.

With this background we can define the Diffie-Hellman key exchange, which is summarized in Figure 8.6 For this scheme, there are two publicly known numbers: a prime number q and an integer α that is a primitive root of q. Now, suppose the

---

Global public elements

q prime number

α $\alpha < q$ and α a primitive root of q

User i key generation

Select private X_i $X_i < q$

Calculate public Y_i $Y_i = \alpha^{X_i} \bmod q$

User j key generation

Select private X_j $X_j < q$

Calculate public Y_j $Y_j = \alpha^{X_j} \bmod q$

Generation of secret key by user i

$K = (Y_j)^{X_i} \bmod q$

Generation of secret key by user j

$K = (Y_i)^{X_j} \bmod q$

FIGURE 8.6.   The Diffie–Hellman Key Exchange Algorithm

users i and j wish to exchange a key. User i selects a random integer $X_i < q$, and computes $Y_i = \alpha^{X_i} \bmod q$. Similarly, user j independently selects a random integer $X_j < q$, and computes $Y_j = \alpha^{X_j} \bmod q$. Each side keeps the X value private and makes the Y value available publicly to the other side. Now, user i computes the key as $K = (Y_j)^{X_i} \bmod q$ and user i computes the key as $K = (Y_i)^{X_j} \bmod q$.

These two calculations produce identical results:

$$
\begin{aligned}
K &= (Y_j)^{X_i} \bmod q \\
&= (\alpha^{X_j} \bmod q)^{X_i} \bmod q \\
&= (\alpha^{X_j})^{X_i} \bmod q \qquad \text{by the rules of modular arithmetic} \\
&= \alpha^{X_j X_i} \bmod q \\
&= (\alpha^{X_i})^{X_j} \bmod q \\
&= (\alpha^{X_i} \bmod q)^{X_j} \bmod q \\
&= (Y_i)^{X_j} \bmod q
\end{aligned}
$$

Thus, the two sides have exchanged a secret key. Furthermore, because X_i and X_j are private, an opponent only has the following ingredients to work with: q, α, Y_i, and Y_j. Thus, the opponent is forced to take a discrete logarithm to determine the key. For example, attacking the secret key of user j, the opponent must compute

$$
X_j = \mathrm{ind}_{\alpha,q}(Y_j)
$$

The opponent can then calculate the key K in the same manner as user j calculates it.

The security of the Diffie-Hellman key exchange lies in the fact that, while it is relatively easy to calculate exponentials modulo a prime, it is very difficult to calculate discrete logarithms. For large primes, the latter task is considered infeasible.

Figure 8.7 shows a simple protocol that makes use of the Diffie-Hellman calculation. Suppose that user i wishes to set up a connection with user j and use a secret key to encrypt messages on that connection. User i can generate a one-time private key X_i, calculate Y_i, and send that to user j. User j responds by generating a private value X_j, calculating Y_j, and sending Y_j to user i. Both users can now calculate the key. The necessary public values q and α would need to be known ahead of time. Alternatively, user i could pick values for q and α and include those in the first message.

As an example of another use of the Diffie-Hellman algorithm, suppose that a group of users (e.g., all users on a LAN) each generate a long-lasting private value X_i and calculate a public value Y_i. These public values, together with global public values for q and α, are stored in some central directory. At any time, user j can access user i's public value, calculate a secret key, and use that to send an encrypted message to user i. If the central directory is trusted, then this form of communication provides both confidentiality and a degree of authentication. Because only i and j can determine the key, no other user can read the message (confidentiality). Recipient i knows that only user j could have created a message using this key (authentication). However, the technique does not protect against replay attacks.

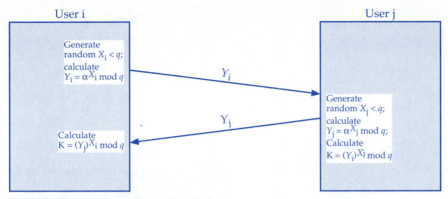

FIGURE 8.7. Diffie–Hellman Key Exchange

8.4

DIGITAL SIGNATURE STANDARD

The National Institute of Standards and Technology (NIST) has published a draft Federal Information Processing Standard known as the Digital Signature Standard (DSS). The DSS makes use of the Secure Hash Algorithm (SHA) described in Chapter 7 and presents a new digital signature technique, the Digital Signature Algorithm (DSA). The DSS was originally proposed in 1991 and revised in 1993 in response to public feedback concerning the security of the scheme.

The DSS Approach

The DSS uses an algorithm that is designed to provide only the digital signature function. Unlike RSA, it cannot be used for encryption or key exchange. Nevertheless, it is a public-key technique.

Figure 8.8 contrasts the DSS approach for generating digital signatures to that used with algorithms such as RSA or LUC. In the RSA approach, the message to be signed is input to a hash function that produces a secure hash code of fixed length. This hash code is then encrypted using the sender's private key to form the signature. Both the message and the signature are then transmitted. The recipient takes the message and produces a hash code. The recipient also decrypts the signature using the sender's public key. If the calculated hash code matches the decrypted signature, the signature is accepted as valid. Because only the sender knows the private key, only the sender could have produced a valid signature.

The DSS approach also makes use of a hash function. The hash code is provided as input to a signature function along with a random number k generated for this particular signature. The signature function also depends on the sender's private key (KR_a) and a set of parameters known to a group of communicating principals.

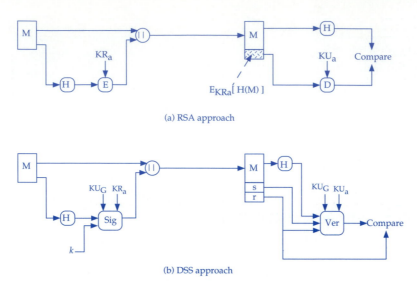

(a) RSA approach

(b) DSS approach

FIGURE 8.8.   Two Approaches to Digital SIgnatures

We can consider this set to constitute a global public key (KU_G).[9] The result is a signature consisting of two components, labeled s and r.

At the receiving end, the hash code of the incoming message is generated. This plus the signature is input to a verification function. The verification function also depends on the global public key as well as the sender's public key (KU_a), which is paired with the sender's private key. The output of the verification function is a value that is equal to the signature component r if the signature is valid. The signature function is such that only the sender, with knowledge of the private key, could have produced the valid signature.

We turn now to the details of the algorithm.

The Digital Signature Algorithm

The DSA is based on the difficulty of computing discrete logarithms (see Appendix 8B) and is based on schemes originally presented by ElGamal [ELGA85] and Schnorr [SCHN91].

Figure 8.9 summarizes the algorithm. There are three parameters that are public and can be common to a group of users. A 160-bit prime number q is chosen. Next, a prime number p is selected with a length between 512 and 1024 bits such that q divides $(p-1)$. Finally g is chosen to be of the form $h^{(p-1)/q} \bmod p$ where h is an integer between 1 and $(p-1)$ with the restriction that g must be greater than 1.[10]

---

[9]It is also possible to allow these additional parameters to vary with each user, so that they are a part of a user's public key. In practice, it is more likely that a global public key will be used that is separate from each user's public key.

[10]In number-theoretic terms, g is of order $q \bmod p$; see Appendix 8B.

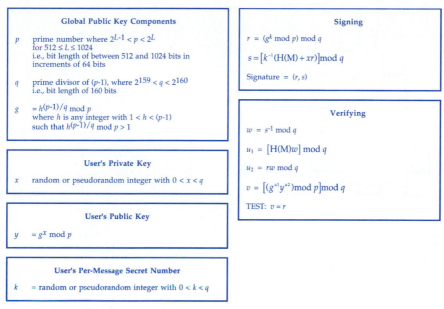

FIGURE 8.9. The DSS Algorithm

With these numbers in hand, each user selects a private key and generates a public key. The private key x must be a number from 1 to $(q-1)$ and should be chosen randomly or pseudorandomly. The public key is calculated from the private key as $y = g^x \bmod p$. The calculation of y given x is relatively straightforward. However, given the public key y, it is believed to be computationally infeasible to determine x, which is the discrete logarithm of y to the base g, mod p (see Appendix 8B).

To create a signature, a user calculates two quantities, r and s, which are functions of the public key components (p, q, g), the user's private key (x), the hash code of the message, H(M), and an additional integer k that should be generated randomly or pseudorandomly and be unique for each signing.

At the receiving end, verification is performed using the formulas shown in Figure 8.9. The receiver generates a quantity v that is a function of the public key components, the sender's public key, and the hash code of the incoming message. If this quantity matches the r component of the signature, then the signature is validated.

Figure 8.10 depicts the functions of signing and verifying.

The structure of the algorithm, as revealed in Figure 8.10, is quite interesting. Note that the test at the end is on the value r, which does not depend on the message at all! Instead, r is a function of k and the three global public-key components. The multiplicative inverse of k (mod p) is passed to a function that also has as inputs the message hash code and the user's private key. The structure of this function is such that the receiver can recover r using the incoming message and signa-

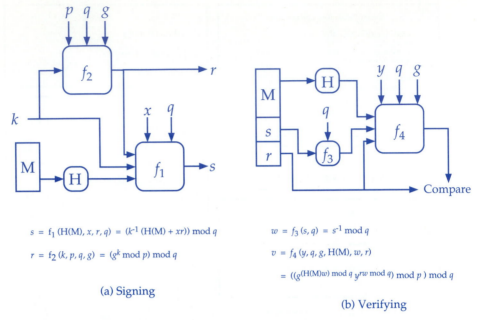

$$s = f_1 (H(M), x, r, q) = (k^{-1} (H(M) + xr)) \bmod q$$

$$r = f_2 (k, p, q, g) = (g^k \bmod p) \bmod q$$

(a) Signing

$$w = f_3 (s, q) = s^{-1} \bmod q$$

$$v = f_4 (y, q, g, H(M), w, r)$$

$$= ((g^{(H(M)w) \bmod q} \, y^{rw \bmod q}) \bmod p) \bmod q$$

(b) Verifying

FIGURE 8.10.   DSS Signing and Verifying

ture, the public key of the user, and the global public key. It is certainly not obvious from Figure 8.9 or Figure 8.10 that such a scheme would work. A proof is provided in Appendix 8C.

Given the difficulty of taking discrete logarithms, it is infeasible for an opponent to recover k from r or to recover x from s.

Another point worth noting is that the only computationally demanding task in signature generation is the exponential calculation g^k mod p. Because this value does not depend on the message to be signed, it can be computed ahead of time. Indeed, a user could precalculate a number of values of r to be used to sign documents as needed. The only other somewhat demanding task is the determination of a multiplicative inverse, k^{-1}. Again, a number of these values can be precalculated.

8.5

PROBLEMS

8.1 Show that a random error in one block of ciphertext is propagated to all subsequent blocks of plaintext in PCBC mode (Figure 8.12).

8.2 Suppose that, in PCBC mode, blocks C_i and C_{i+1} are interchanged during transmission. Show that this affects only the decrypted blocks P_i and P_{i+1} but not subsequent blocks.

8.3 The three-way authentication procedure for X.509 illustrated in Figure 8.5c contains a security flaw. The essence of the protocol is as follows:

$$A \rightarrow B: \quad A\,\{t_A, r_A, B\}$$
$$B \rightarrow A: \quad B\,\{t_B, r_B, A, r_A\}$$
$$A \rightarrow B: \quad A\,\{r_B\}$$

The text of X.509 states that checking timestamps t_A and t_B is optional for three-way authentication. But consider the following example. Suppose A and B have used the above protocol on some previous occasion, and that opponent C has intercepted the above three messages. In addition suppose that timestamps are not used and are all set to 0. Finally, suppose C wishes to impersonate A to B. C initially sends the first captured message to B:

$$C \rightarrow B: \quad A\,\{0, r_A, B\}$$

B responds, thinking it is talking to A but is actually talking to C:

$$B \rightarrow C: \quad B\,\{0, r_B', A, r_A\}$$

C meanwhile causes A to initiate authentication with C, by some means. As a result A sends C the following:

$$A \rightarrow C: \quad A\,\{0, r_A', C\}$$

C responds to A, using the same nonce provided to C by B.

$$C \rightarrow A: \quad C\,\{0, r_B', A, r_A'\}$$

A responds with:

$$A \rightarrow C: \quad A\,\{r_B'\}$$

This is exactly what C needs to convince B that it is talking to A, so C now repeats the incoming message back out to B.

$$C \rightarrow B: \quad A\,\{r_B'\}$$

So B will believe it is talking to A whereas it is actually talking to C. Suggest a simple solution to this problem that does not involve the use of timestamps.

8.4 The 1988 version of X.509 lists properties that RSA keys must satisfy in order to be secure, given current knowledge about the difficulty of factoring large numbers. The discussion concludes with a constraint on the public exponent and the modulus n:

> It must be ensured that $e > \log_2(n)$ in order to prevent attack by taking the eth root mod n to disclose the plaintext.

Although the constraint is correct, the reason given for requiring it is incorrect. What is wrong with the reason given and what is the correct reason?

8.5 Demonstrate that in DSA, g is of order q mod p.

8.6 DSA specifies that if the signature generation process results in a value of $s = 0$, a new value of k should be generated and the signature should be recalculated. Why?

8.7 What happens if a k value used in creating a DSA signature is compromised?

8.8 "But," said Dr. Watson, "your clients use Diffie-Hellman key exchange protocol in their network. It is based on a discrete logarithm, and this is known to be a hard problem, isn't it?"

"Yes, Watson," nodded Holmes, "for appropriate choice of parameters the discrete logarithm problem is really hard. My clients know that and that's why they opted for this method of key distribution. Unfortunately, their security consultants didn't realize that an active adversary might often be more successful than the passive one. An adversary also knows that he can't solve a discrete logarithm problem in a reasonable time, thus he has to try something else. And because I am sure Moriarty himself is interested in my clients' communications, I must suppose some kind of active attack on their network. Moriarty would never stay passive, Watson."

"Do you think, Holmes," Dr. Watson was really surprised, "that Moriarty could find a way to break the Diffie–Hellman key exchange scheme?"

"Oh, it is not so hard, Watson," smiled Holmes. All that Moriarty needs is to place himself somewhere in the communication path to be able not only to intercept but also to change all the messages. I am sure this is completely within Moriarty's abilities. Now in this position he will . . .

8.9 The DSS document includes a recommended algorithm for testing a number for primality, as follows:

(1) [Choose w] Let w be a random odd integer. Then $(w - 1)$ is even and can be expressed in the form $2^a m$ with m odd. That is, 2^a is the largest power of 2 that divides $(w - 1)$.

(2) [Generate b] Let b be a random integer in the range $1 < b < w$.

(3) [Exponentiate] Set $j = 0$ and $z = b^m \bmod w$.

(4) [Done?] If $j = 0$ and $z = 1$, or if $z = w - 1$, then w passes the test and may be prime; go to step 8.

(5) [Terminate?] If $j > 0$ and $z = 1$, then w is not prime; terminate algorithm for this w.

(6) [Increase j] Set $j = j + 1$. If $j < a$, set $z = z^2 \bmod w$ and go to step 4.

(7) [Terminate] w is not prime; terminate algorithm for this w.

(8) [Test again?] If enough random values of b have been tested, then accept w as prime and terminate algorithm; otherwise, go to step 2.

Describe the algorithm and show that it is equivalent to the Miller–Rabin test described in Appendix 4A.

8.10 It is tempting to try to develop a variation on Diffie–Hellman that could be used as a digital signature. Here is one that is simpler than DSA and that does not require a secret random number in addition to the private key.

Public elements:

q prime number

α $\alpha < q$ and α is a primitive root of q

Private key

X $X < q$

Public key

$Y = \alpha^X \bmod q$

To sign a message M, compute $h = H(M)$, the hash code of the message. We require that gcd $(h, p - 1) = 1$. If not, append the hash to the message and calculate a new hash. Continue this process until a hash code is produced that is relatively prime to $(p - 1)$. Then calculate Z to satisfy $Z \times h \equiv X \bmod (q-1)$. The signature of the message is α^Z. To verify the signature, a user verifies that $(\alpha^Z)^h = \alpha^X \bmod q$.

a. Show that this scheme works. That is, show that the verification process produces an equality if the signature is valid.

b. Show that the scheme is unacceptable by describing a simple technique for forging a user's signature on an arbitrary message.

8.11 With DSS, because the value of k is generated for each signature, even if the same message is signed twice on different occasions, the signatures will differ. This is not true of RSA signatures. What is the practical implication of this difference?

8.12 Find all primitive roots of 25.

8.13 Given 2 as a primitive root of 29, construct a table of indices, and use it to solve the following congruences:

(a) $17x^2 \equiv 10 \bmod 29$

(b) $x^2 - 4x - 16 \equiv 0 \bmod 29$

(c) $x_7 \equiv 17 \bmod 29$

APPENDIX 8A

KERBEROS ENCRYPTION TECHNIQUES

Kerberos includes an encryption library that supports various encryption-related operations.

Password-to-Key Transformation

In Kerberos, passwords are limited to the use of the characters that can be represented in a 7-bit ASCII format. This password, of arbitrary length, is converted into an encryption key that is stored in the Kerberos database. Figure 8.11 illustrates the procedure.

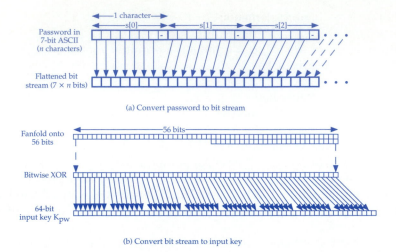

(a) Convert password to bit stream

(b) Convert bit stream to input key

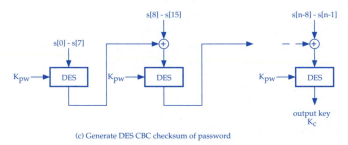

(c) Generate DES CBC checksum of password

FIGURE 8.11.   Generation of Encryption Key from Password

First, the character string, s, is packed into a bit string, b, such that the first character is stored in the first 7 bits, the second character in the second 7 bits, and so on. This can be expressed as:

$$b[0] = \text{bit } 0 \text{ of } s[0]$$

. . .

$$b[6] = \text{bit } 6 \text{ of } s[0]$$
$$b[7] = \text{bit } 0 \text{ of } s[1]$$

. . .

$$b[7i + m] = \text{bit } m \text{ of } s[i] \qquad 0 \le m \le 6$$

Next, the bit string is compacted to 56 bits by aligning the bits in "fanfold" fashion and performing a bitwise XOR. For example, if the bit string is of length 59, then

$$b[55] = b[55] \oplus b[56]$$
$$b[54] = b[54] \oplus b[57]$$
$$b[53] = b[53] \oplus b[58]$$

This creates a 56-bit DES key. To conform to the expected 64-bit key format, the string is treated as a sequence of eight 7-bit blocks and is mapped into eight 8-bit blocks to form an input key K_{pw}.

Finally, the original password is encrypted using the cipher block chaining (CBC) mode of DES with key K_{pw}. The last 64-bit block returned from this process, known as the CBC checksum, is the output key associated with this password.

The entire algorithm can be viewed as a hash function that maps an arbitrary password into a 64-bit hash code.

Plain-and-Cipher Block Chaining Mode (PCBC)

Recall from Chapter 2 that, in the CBC mode of DES, the input to the DES algorithm at each stage consists of the XOR of the current plaintext block and the preceding ciphertext block, with the same key used for each block (Figure 2.14). The advantage of this mode over the electronic codebook (ECB) mode, in which each plaintext block is independently encrypted, is this: With CBC, the same plaintext block, if repeated, produces different ciphertext blocks.

CBC has the property that if an error occurs in transmission of ciphertext block C_I, then this error propagates to the recovered plaintext blocks P_I and P_{I+1}.

Version 4 of Kerberos uses an extension to CBC, called the PCBC mode [MEYE82]. This mode has the property that an error in one ciphertext block is

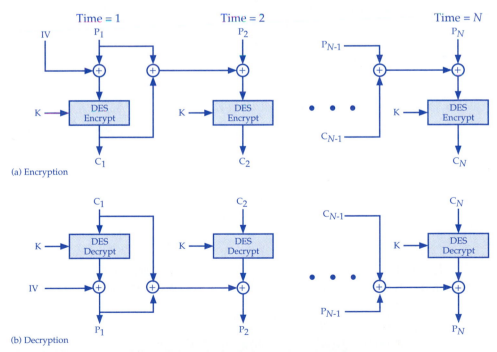

(a) Encryption

(b) Decryption

FIGURE 8.12. Propagating Cipher Block Chaining (PCBC) Mode

propagated to all subsequent decrypted blocks of the message, rendering each block useless. Thus, data encryption and integrity are combined in one operation.

PCBC is illustrated in Figure 8.12. In this scheme, the input to the encryption algorithm is the XOR of the current plaintext block, the preceding cipher text block, and the preceding plaintext block:

$$C_n = E_K[C_{n-1} \oplus P_{n-1} \oplus P_n]$$

On decryption, each ciphertext block is passed through the decryption algorithm. Then the output is XORed with the preceding ciphertext block and the preceding plaintext block. We can demonstrate that this scheme works, as follows:

$$D_K[C_n] = D_K\left[E_K[C_{n-1} \oplus P_{n-1} \oplus P_n]\right]$$
$$= C_{n-1} \oplus P_{n-1} \oplus P_n$$
$$C_{n-1} \oplus P_{n-1} \oplus D_K[C_n] = P_n$$

APPENDIX 8B

DISCRETE LOGARITHMS

Discrete logarithms are fundamental to a number of public-key algorithms, including the digital signature algorithm (DSA). This appendix provides a brief overview of discrete logarithms. For the interested reader, clear developments of this topic can be found in [ORE76] and [LEVE90].

The Powers of an Integer, Modulo n

Recall from Euler's theorem (Appendix 4A.3) that, for every a and n that are relatively prime:

$$a^{\phi(n)} \equiv 1 \bmod n$$

where $\phi(n)$, Euler's totient function, is the number of positive integers less than n and relatively prime to n. Now consider the more general expression:

$$a^m \equiv 1 \bmod n \tag{8.1}$$

If a and n are relatively prime, then there is at least one integer m that satisfies equation (8.1) namely $m = \phi(n)$. The least positive exponent m for which equation (8.1) holds is referred to in several ways:

- the order of a (mod n)
- the exponent to which a belongs (mod n)
- the length of the period generated by a

To see this last point consider the powers of 7, modulo 19:

$$
\begin{aligned}
7^1 &= && 7 \bmod 19 \\
7^2 &= 49 = 2 \times 19 + 11 = && 11 \bmod 19 \\
7^3 &= 343 = 18 \times 19 + 1 = && 1 \bmod 19 \\
7^4 &= 2401 = 126 \times 19 + 7 = && 7 \bmod 19 \\
7^5 &= 16807 = 884 \times 19 + 11 = && 11 \bmod 19
\end{aligned}
$$

There is no point in continuing because the sequence is repeating. This can be proven by noting that $7^3 = 1$ (mod 19) and therefore $7^{3+j} = 7^3 7^j = 7^j$ (mod 19), and hence any two powers of 7 whose exponents differ by 3 (or a multiple of 3) are congruent to each other (mod 19). In other words, the sequence is periodic, and the length of the period is the smallest positive exponent m such that $7^m = 1$ (mod 19).

Table 8.5 shows all the powers of a, modulo 19 for all positive $a < 19$. The length of the sequence for each base value is indicated by outlining. Note the following:

1. All sequences end in 1. This is consistent with the reasoning of the preceding few paragraphs.
2. The length of a sequence divides $\phi(19) = 18$. That is, an integral number of sequences occur in each row of the table.
3. Some of the sequences are of length 18. In this case, it is said that the base integer a generates (via powers) the set of nonzero integers modulo 19. Each such integer is called a primitive root of the modulus 19.

More generally, we can say that the highest possible exponent to which a number can belong (mod n) is $\phi(n)$. If a number is of this order, it is referred to as a primitive root of n. The importance of this notion is that if a is a primitive root of n, then its powers

$$ a, a^2, \ldots, a^{\phi(n)} $$

are distinct (mod n) and are all relatively prime to n. In particular, for a prime number p, if a is a primitive root of p, then

$$ a, a^2, \ldots, a^{p-1} $$

are distinct (mod p). For the prime number 19, its primitive roots are 2, 3, 10, 13, 14, and 15.

Not all integers have primitive roots. In fact, the only integers with primitive roots are those of the form 2, 4, p^α, and $2p^\alpha$, where p is any odd prime.

Indices

With ordinary positive real numbers, the logarithm function is the inverse of exponentiation. An analogous function exists for modular arithmetic.

TABLE 8.5 Powers of Integers, Modulo 19

a	a^2	a^3	a^4	a^5	a^6	a^7	a^8	a^9	a^{10}	a^{11}	a^{12}	a^{13}	a^{14}	a^{15}	a^{16}	a^{17}	a^{18}
1	1	1	1	1	1	1	1	1	1	1	1	1	1	1	1	1	1
2	4	8	16	13	7	14	9	18	17	15	11	3	6	12	5	10	1
3	9	8	5	15	7	2	6	18	16	10	11	14	4	12	17	13	1
4	16	7	9	17	11	6	5	1	4	16	7	9	17	11	6	5	1
5	6	11	17	9	7	16	4	1	5	6	11	17	9	7	16	4	1
6	17	7	4	5	11	9	16	1	6	17	7	4	5	11	9	16	1
7	11	1	7	11	1	7	11	1	7	11	1	7	11	1	7	11	1
8	7	18	11	12	1	8	7	18	11	12	1	8	7	18	11	12	1
9	5	7	6	16	11	4	17	1	9	5	7	6	16	11	4	17	1
10	5	12	6	3	11	15	17	18	9	14	7	13	16	8	4	2	1
11	7	1	11	7	1	11	7	1	11	7	1	11	7	1	11	7	1
12	11	18	7	8	1	12	11	18	7	8	1	12	11	18	7	8	1
13	17	12	4	14	11	10	16	18	6	2	7	15	5	8	9	3	1
14	6	8	17	10	7	3	4	18	5	13	11	2	9	12	16	15	1
15	16	12	9	2	11	13	5	18	4	3	7	10	17	8	6	14	1
16	9	11	5	4	7	17	6	1	16	9	11	5	4	7	17	6	1
17	4	11	16	6	7	5	9	1	17	4	11	16	6	7	5	9	1
18	1	18	1	18	1	18	1	18	1	18	1	18	1	18	1	18	1

Let us briefly review the properties of ordinary logarithms. The logarithm of a number is defined to be the power to which some positive base (except 1) must be raised in order to equal the number. That is, for base x and for a value y:

$$y = x^{\log_x(y)}$$

Properties of logarithms:

$$\log_x(1) = 0 \tag{8.2}$$
$$\log_x(x) = 1 \tag{8.3}$$
$$\log_x(yz) = \log_x(y) + \log_x(z) \tag{8.4}$$
$$\log_x(y^r) = r \times \log_x(y) \tag{8.5}$$

Now, consider a primitive root a for some prime number p (the argument can be developed for nonprimes as well). Then we know that the powers of a from 1 through $(p - 1)$ produce each integer from 1 through $(p - 1)$ exactly once. We also know that any integer b can be expressed in the form:

$$b = r \bmod p \qquad \text{where } 0 \leq r \leq (p - 1)$$

by the very definition of modular arithmetic. It follows that for any integer b and a primitive root a of prime number p, one can find a unique exponent i such that

$$b = a^i \bmod p \qquad \text{where } 0 \leq i \leq (p - 1)$$

This exponent i is referred to as the index of the number b for the base a (mod p). We denote this value as $\text{ind}_{a,p}(b)$.

Note the following:

$$\text{ind}_{a,p}(1) = 0, \text{ because } a^0 \bmod p = 1 \bmod p = 1 \tag{8.6}$$
$$\text{ind}_{a,p}(a) = 1, \text{ because } a^1 \bmod p = a \tag{8.7}$$

Now, consider

$$x = a^{\text{ind}_{a,p}(x)} \bmod p \qquad y = a^{\text{ind}_{a,p}(y)} \bmod p$$
$$xy = a^{\text{ind}_{a,p}(xy)} \bmod p$$

Using the rules of modular multiplication,

$$a^{\text{ind}_{a,p}(xy)} \bmod p = (a^{\text{ind}_{a,p}(x)} \bmod p)(a^{\text{ind}_{a,p}(y)} \bmod p)$$
$$= (a^{\text{ind}_{a,p}(x) + \text{ind}_{a,p}(y)}) \bmod p$$

But now consider Euler's theorem which states that for every a and n that are relatively prime:

$$a^{\phi(n)} \equiv 1 \bmod n$$

Now, any positive integer z can be expressed in the form $z = q + k\phi(n)$. Therefore, by Euler's theorem,

$$a^z = a^q \bmod n \quad \text{if } z = q \bmod \phi(n)$$

TABLE 8.6   Tables of Discrete Logarithms, Modulo 19

(a) Discrete logarithms to the base 2, modulo 19

a	1	2	3	4	5	6	7	8	9	10	11	12	13	14	15	16	17	18
$\text{Ind}_{2,19}(a)$	18	1	13	2	16	14	6	3	8	17	12	15	5	7	11	4	10	9

(b) Discrete logarithms to the base 3, modulo 19

a	1	2	3	4	5	6	7	8	9	10	11	12	13	14	15	16	17	18
$\text{Ind}_{3,19}(a)$	18	7	1	14	4	8	6	3	2	11	12	15	17	13	5	10	16	9

(c) Discrete logarithms to the base 10, modulo 19

a	1	2	3	4	5	6	7	8	9	10	11	12	13	14	15	16	17	18
$\text{Ind}_{10,19}(a)$	18	17	5	16	2	4	12	15	10	1	6	3	13	11	7	14	8	9

(d) Discrete logarithms to the base 13, modulo 19

a	1	2	3	4	5	6	7	8	9	10	11	12	13	14	15	16	17	18
$\text{Ind}_{13,19}(a)$	18	11	17	4	14	10	12	15	16	7	6	3	1	5	13	8	2	9

(e) Discrete logarithms to the base 14, modulo 19

a	1	2	3	4	5	6	7	8	9	10	11	12	13	14	15	16	17	18
$\text{Ind}_{14,19}(a)$	18	13	7	8	10	2	6	3	14	5	12	15	11	1	17	16	4	9

(f) Discrete logarithms to the base 15, modulo 19

a	1	2	3	4	5	6	7	8	9	10	11	12	13	14	15	16	17	18
$\text{Ind}_{15,19}(a)$	18	5	11	10	8	16	12	15	4	13	6	3	7	17	1	2	14	9

Applying this to the foregoing equality, we have

$$\text{ind}_{a,p}(xy) = [\text{ind}_{a,p}(x) + \text{ind}_{a,p}(y)] \bmod \phi(p) \tag{8.8}$$

and generalizing,

$$\text{ind}_{a,p}(y^r) = [r \times \text{ind}_{a,p}(y)] \bmod \phi(p) \tag{8.9}$$

This demonstrates the analogy between true logarithms and indices. For this reason, the latter are now commonly referred to as discrete logarithms.

Keep in mind that unique discrete logarithms mod m to some base a exist only if a is a primitive root of m. Table 8.6, which is directly derived from Table 8.5, shows the sets of discrete logarithms that can be defined for modulus 19.

Calculation of Discrete Logarithms

Consider the equation

$$y = g^x \bmod p$$

Given g, x, and p, it is a straightforward matter to calculate y. At the worst, one must perform x repeated multiplications, and algorithms exist for achieving greater efficiency.

However, given y, g, and p, it is in general very difficult to calculate x (take the discrete logarithm). The difficulty seems to be on the same order of magnitude as that of factoring primes required for RSA. At the time of this writing, the asymptotically fastest known algorithm for taking discrete logarithms modulo a prime number is on the order of [BETH91]:

$$e^{((\ln p)^{1/3} \ln(\ln p))^{2/3}}$$

which is not feasible for large primes.

APPENDIX 8C
_____

PROOF OF THE DSS ALGORITHM

The purpose of this appendix is to provide a proof that in the signature verification we have $v = r$ if the signature is valid. The following proof is based on that which appears in the FIPS standard but includes additional details to make the derivation clearer.

LEMMA 1. For any integer t, if

$$g = h^{(p-1)/q} \bmod p$$
$$\text{then } g^t \bmod p = g^{t \bmod q} \bmod p$$

Proof: By Fermat's theorem (Appendix 4A), because h is relatively prime to p, we have $h^{p-1} \bmod p = 1$. Hence for any nonnegative integer n,

$$g^{nq} \bmod p = \left(h^{(p-1)/q} \bmod p \right)^{nq} \bmod$$

$$= h^{((p-1)/q)nq} \bmod p \qquad\qquad \text{by the rules of modular arithmetic}$$

$$= h^{(p-1)n} \bmod p$$

$$= \left((h^{(p-1)} \bmod p)^n \right) \bmod p \qquad \text{by the rules of modular arithmetic}$$

$$= 1^n \bmod p = 1$$

So, for nonnegative integers n and z, we have

$$g^{nq+z} \bmod p = (g^{nq} g^z) \bmod p$$

$$= \left((g^{nq} \bmod p)(g^z \bmod p) \right) \bmod p$$

$$= g^z \bmod p$$

Any nonnegative integer t can be represented uniquely as $t = nq + z$ where n and z are nonnegative integers and $0 < z < q$. So $z = t \bmod q$. The result follows. **QED.**

LEMMA 2. For nonnegative integers a and b: $g^{(a \bmod q + b \bmod q)} \bmod p = g^{(a+b) \bmod q} \bmod p$

Proof: By Lemma 1, we have

$$g^{(a \bmod q + b \bmod q)} \bmod p = g^{(a \bmod q + b \bmod q) \bmod q} \bmod p$$

$$= g^{(a+b) \bmod q} \bmod p$$

Q.E.D.

LEMMA 3. $y^{(rw) \bmod q} \bmod p = g^{(xrw) \bmod q} \bmod p$

Proof: By definition (Figure 8.9), $y = g^x \bmod p$. Then:

$$y^{(rw) \bmod q} \bmod p = (g^x \bmod p)^{(rw) \bmod q} \bmod p$$

$$= g^{x((rw) \bmod q)} \bmod p \qquad \text{by the rules of modular arithmetic}$$

$$= g^{(x((rw) \bmod q)) \bmod q} \bmod p \qquad \text{by Lemma 1}$$

$$= g^{(xrw) \bmod q} \bmod p$$

Q.E.D.

LEMMA 4. $((H(M) + xr)w) \bmod q = k$

Proof: By definition (Figure 8.9), $s = \left(k^{-1}(H(M) + xr) \right) \bmod q$. Also, because q is prime, any nonnegative integer less than q has a multiplicative inverse (Appendix 4A.2). So $(k\,k^{-1}) \bmod q = 1$. Then:

$$(ks) \bmod q = \left(k\left(\left(k^{-1}(H(M) + xr) \right) \bmod q \right) \right) \bmod q$$

$$= \left(\left(k\left(k^{-1}(H(M) + xr) \right) \right) \right) \bmod q$$

$$= \left(\left((kk^{-1}) \bmod q \right)\left((H(M) + xr) \bmod q \right) \right) \bmod q$$

$$= ((H(M) + xr) \bmod q$$

By definition, $w = s^{-1} \bmod q$ and therefore $(ws) \bmod q = 1$. Therefore,

$$
\begin{aligned}
((H(M) + xr)w) \bmod q &= (((H(M) + xr) \bmod q)\,(w \bmod q)) \bmod q \\
&= (((ks) \bmod q)\,(w \bmod q)) \bmod q \\
&= (kws) \bmod q \\
&= ((k \bmod q)\,((ws) \bmod q)) \bmod q \\
&= k \bmod q
\end{aligned}
$$

Because $0 < k < q$, we have $k \bmod q = k$.

Q.E.D.

THEOREM: Using the definitions of Figure 8.9, $v = r$.

$$
\begin{aligned}
v &= \left((g^{u1}y^{u2}) \bmod p\right) \bmod q && \text{by definition} \\[4pt]
&= \left((g^{(H(M)w)\bmod q}\, y^{(rw)\bmod q}) \bmod p\right) \bmod q \\[4pt]
&= \left((g^{(H(M)w)\bmod q}\, g^{(xrw)\bmod q}) \bmod p\right) \bmod q && \text{by Lemma 3} \\[4pt]
&= \left((g^{(H(M)w)\bmod q + (xrw)\bmod q}) \bmod p\right) \bmod q \\[4pt]
&= \left((g^{(H(M)w)\bmod q + (xrw)\bmod q}) \bmod p\right) \bmod q \\[4pt]
&= \left((g^{(H(M)w + xrw)\bmod q}) \bmod p\right) \bmod q && \text{by Lemma 2} \\[4pt]
&= \left((g^{(H(M) + xrw)\bmod q}) \bmod p\right) \bmod q \\[4pt]
&= \left(g^{k} \bmod p\right) \bmod q && \text{by Lemma 4} \\[4pt]
&= r && \text{by definition}
\end{aligned}
$$

Q.E.D.

CHAPTER 9

ELECTRONIC MAIL SECURITY

Despite the refusal of VADM Poindexter and LtCol North to appear, the Board's access to other sources of information filled much of this gap. The FBI provided documents taken from the files of the National Security Advisor and relevant NSC staff members, including messages from the PROF system between VADM Poindexter and LtCol North. The PROF messages were conversations by computer, written at the time events occurred and presumed by the writers to be protected from disclosure. In this sense, they provide a first-hand, contemporaneous account of events.

> — *The Tower Commission Report*
> *to President Reagan on the Iran-Contra Affair*
> 1987

While nonelectronic proprietary information can be compromised through the theft of marketing reports or photos of prototypes, the theft of electronic proprietary information can be accomplished through breaking into a computer system. Individuals can compromise information, for example, by guessing passwords or exploiting system weaknesses. Additionally, message and voice monitoring during data and voice transmission can occur at a number of locations throughout the communications flow.

> — *Communications Privacy: Federal Policy and Actions*
> General Accounting Office Report GAO/OSI-94-2
> November 1993

Bless the man who made it,
And pray that he ain't dead.
He could've made a million
If he'd sold it to the feds,
But he was hot for freedom;
He gave it out for free.
Now every common citizen's got PGP.

> — *from the song, P.G.P.*
> by Leslie Fish

Each of the messages, like each one he had ever read of Stern's commands, began with a number and ended with a number or row of numbers. No efforts on the part of Mungo or any of his experts had been able to break Stern's code, nor was there any clue as to what the preliminary number and those ultimate numbers signified.

— *Talking to Strange Men*
  Ruth Rendell

In virtually all distributed environments, electronic mail is the most heavily used network-based application. It is also the only distributed application that is widely used across all architectures and vendor platforms. Users expect to be able to, and do, send mail to others who are connected directly or indirectly to the Internet, regardless of host operating system or communications suite.

With the explosively growing reliance on electronic mail for every conceivable purpose, there grows a demand for authentication and confidentiality services. Two schemes stand out as approaches that are likely to enjoy widespread use in the next few years: Pretty Good Privacy (PGP) and Privacy-Enhanced Mail (PEM). Both are examined in this chapter.

9.1

PRETTY GOOD PRIVACY (PGP)

PGP is a remarkable phenomenon. Largely the effort of a single person, Phil Zimmermann, PGP provides a confidentiality and authentication service that can be used for electronic mail and file storage applications. In essence what Zimmermann has done is the following:

1. Selected the best available cryptographic algorithms as building blocks.
2. Integrated these algorithms into a general-purpose application that is independent of operating system and processor and that is based on a small set of easy-to-use commands.
3. Made the package and its documentation, including the source code, freely available via the Internet, bulletin boards, and commercial networks such as Compuserve.
4. Entered into an agreement with a company (Viacrypt) to provide a fully compatible, low-cost commercial version of PGP.

From its beginnings just a few years ago, PGP has grown explosively and is now widely used. A number of reasons can be cited for this growth:

1. It is available free worldwide in versions that run on a variety of platforms including DOS/Windows, UNIX, Macintosh, and many more. In addition, the commercial version satisfies users who want a product that comes with vendor support.

2. It is based on algorithms that have survived extensive public review and are considered extremely secure. Specifically, the package includes RSA for public-key encryption, IDEA for conventional encryption, and MD5 for hash coding.
3. It has a wide range of applicability, from corporations that wish to select and enforce a standardized scheme for encrypting files and messages to individuals who wish to communicate securely with others worldwide over the Internet and other networks.
4. It was not developed by, nor is it controlled by, any governmental or standards organization. For those with an instinctive distrust of "the establishment," this makes PGP attractive.

Some have hesitated to use the product, for several reasons. First, the developer lives and works in the United States. Because PGP is a cryptographic product, there may be a concern about export controls for organizations that wish to interoperate between U.S. and non-U.S. sites. However, the most recent versions of PGP (2.3a at the time of this writing) have initially seen the light of day outside the United States, which would seem to make U.S. export controls irrelevant. Second, the freeware version of PGP was developed and disseminated without bothering to obtain a license for the use of RSA, which is required within the United States, but not outside. For those concerned with this issue, the commercial version of PGP has such a license.

Much could be said about the political and social ramifications of PGP, but that is not our purpose here. For the reader interested in such topics, a good starting point is [LEVY93]. For a user's guide, see [STAL95].

We begin with an overall look at the operation of PGP. Next, we examine how cryptographic keys are created and stored. Then, the vital issue of public-key management is addressed. Finally, we examine the formats of the key data structures in PGP. Our strategy is to start with a general approach, leaving out some of the details, then gradually elaborate on the scheme until a detailed description of all PGP parameters is possible in the final subsection.

Notation

Most of the notation used in this chapter has been used before, but a few terms are new. It is perhaps best to summarize those at the beginning. The following symbols are used:

K_s = session key used in conventional encryption scheme
KR_a = private key of user A, used in public-key encryption scheme
KU_a = public key of user A, used in public-key encryption scheme
ER = public-key encryption, using the RSA algorithm
DR = public-key decryption, using the RSA algorithm
EI = conventional encryption, using IDEA
DI = conventional decryption, using IDEA
H = hash function (e.g., using MD5)
|| = concatenation

Z   = compression using ZIP algorithm
R64 = conversion to radix 64 ASCII format

The PGP documentation often uses the term *secret key* to refer to a key paired with a public key in a public-key encryption scheme. As was mentioned earlier, this practice risks confusion with a secret key used for conventional encryption. Hence, we will stick consistently to the term *private key* instead.

Operational Description

The actual operation of PGP, as opposed to the management of keys, consists of five services: authentication, confidentiality, compression, e-mail compatibility, and segmentation (Table 9.1). We examine each of these in turn.

Authentication

Figure 9.1a illustrates the digital signature service provided by PGP. This is the digital signature scheme discussed in Chapter 5 and illustrated in Figure 5.5c. The sequence is as follows:

1. The sender creates a message.
2. MD5 is used to generate a 128-bit hash code of the message.

TABLE 9.1   Summary of PGP Services

Function	Algorithms Used	Description
Message encryption	IDEA, RSA	A message is encrypted using IDEA with a one time session key generated by the sender. The session key is encrypted using RSA with the recipient's public key, and included with the message.
Digital signature	RSA, MD5	A hash code of a message is created using MD5. This message digest is encrypted using RSA with the sender's private key, and included with the message.
Compression	ZIP	A message may be compressed, for storage or transmission, using ZIP.
E-mail compatibility	Radix 64 conversion	To provide transparency for e-mail applications, an encrypted message may be converted to an ASCII string using radix-64 conversion.
Segmentation	—	To accommodate maximum message size limitations, PGP performs segmentation and reassembly.

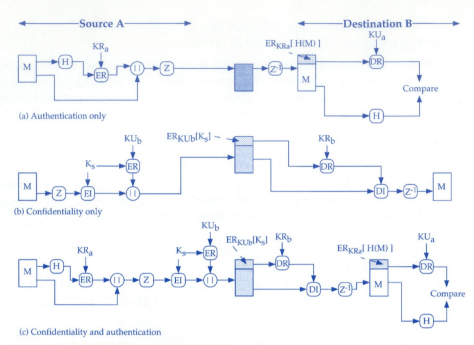

(a) Authentication only

(b) Confidentiality only

(c) Confidentiality and authentication

FIGURE 9.1.   PGP Cryptographic Functions

3. The hash code is encrypted with RSA using the sender's private key, and the result is prepended to the message.
4. The receiver uses RSA with the sender's public key to decrypt and recover the hash code.
5. The receiver generates a new hash code for the message and compares it with the decrypted hash code. If the two match, the message is accepted as authentic.

The combination of MD5 and RSA provides an effective digital signature scheme. Because of the strength of RSA, the recipient is assured that only the possessor of the matching private key can generate the signature. Because of the strength of MD5, the recipient is assured that no one else could generate a new message that matches the hash code and, hence, the signature of the original message.

Although signatures normally are found attached to the message or file that they sign, this is not always the case: Detached signatures are supported. A detached signature may be stored and transmitted separately from the message it signs. This is useful in several contexts. A user may wish to maintain a separate signature log of all messages sent or received. A detached signature of an executable program can detect subsequent virus infection. Finally, detached signatures can be used when more than one party must sign a document, such as a legal contract. Each person's signature is independent and therefore is applied only to the document. Otherwise, signatures would have to be nested, with the second signer signing both the document and the first signature, and so on.

Confidentiality

Another basic service provided by PGP is confidentiality, which is provided by encrypting messages to be transmitted or to be stored locally as files. In both cases, the conventional encryption algorithm IDEA is used. Recall that IDEA makes use of a 128-bit key. The 64-bit cipher feedback (CFB) mode of IDEA is used, with a null (all zeros) initialization vector (IV).

As always, one must address the problem of key distribution. In PGP, each conventional key is used only once. That is, a new key is generated as a random 128-bit number for each message. Thus, although this is referred to in the documentation as a session key, it is in reality a one-time key. Because it is to be used only once, the session key is bound to the message and transmitted with it. To protect the key, it is encrypted with the receiver's public key. Figure 9.1b illustrates the sequence, which can be described as follows:

1. The sender generates a message and a random 128-bit number to be used as a session key for this message only.
2. The message is encrypted, using IDEA with the session key.
3. The session key is encrypted with RSA, using the recipient's public key, and is prepended to the message.
4. The receiver uses RSA with its private key to decrypt and recover the session key.
5. The session key is used to decrypt the message.

Several observations may be made. First, to reduce encryption time the IDEA/RSA combination is used in preference to simply using RSA to directly encrypt the message: IDEA is substantially faster than RSA. Also, the use of RSA solves the session key distribution problem, because only the recipient is able to recover the session key that is bound to the message. Note that we do not need a session key exchange protocol of the type discussed in Chapter 5, because we are not beginning an ongoing session. Rather, each message is a one-time independent event with its own key. Furthermore, given the store-and-forward nature of electronic mail, the use of handshaking to assure that both sides have the same session key is not practical. Finally, the use of one-time conventional keys strengthens what is already a strong conventional encryption approach. Only a small amount of plaintext is encrypted with each key, and there is no relationship among the keys. Thus, to the extent that RSA is secure, the entire scheme is secure. To this end, PGP provides the user with several RSA key size options:

- Casual (384 bits): known to be breakable, but with much effort
- Commercial (512 bits): possibly breakable by three-letter organizations
- Military (1024 bits): generally believed unbreakable

Confidentiality and Authentication

As Figure 9.1c illustrates, both services may be used for the same message. First, a signature is generated for the plaintext message and prepended to the message.

Then, the plaintext message plus signature is encrypted using IDEA, and the session key is encrypted using RSA. As was discussed in Chapter 5, this sequence is preferable to the opposite: encrypting the message and then generating a signature for the encrypted message. It is generally more convenient to store a signature with a plaintext version of a message. Furthermore, for purposes of third-party verification, if the signature is performed first, a third party need not be concerned with the conventional key when verifying the signature.

In summary, when both services are used, the sender first signs the message with its own private key, then encrypts the message with a session key, and then encrypts the session key with the recipient's public key.

Compression

As a default, PGP compresses the message after applying the signature but before encryption. This has the benefit of saving space both for e-mail transmission and for file storage.

The placement of the compression algorithm, indicated by Z for compression and Z^{-1} for decompression in Figure 9.1, is critical:

1. The signature is generated before compression for two reasons:
   (a) It is preferable to sign an uncompressed message so that one can store only the uncompressed message together with the signature for future verification. If one signed a compressed document, then it would be necessary either to store a compressed version of the message for later verification or to re-compress the message when verification is required.
   (b) Even if one were willing to dynamically generate a re-compressed message for verification, PGP's compression algorithm presents a difficulty. The algorithm is not deterministic; various implementations of the algorithm achieve different trade-offs in running speed versus compression ratio, and as a result produce different compressed forms. However, these different compression algorithms are interoperable because any version of the algorithm can correctly decompress the output of any other version. Applying the hash function and signature after compression would constrain all PGP implementations to the same compression algorithm.
2. Message encryption is applied after compression to strengthen cryptographic security. Because the compressed message has less redundancy than the original plaintext, cryptanalysis is more difficult.

The compression algorithm used is ZIP, which is described in Appendix 9A.

E-mail Compatibility

When PGP is used, at least part of the block to be transmitted is encrypted. If only the signature service is used, then the message digest is encrypted (with the sender's private RSA key). If the confidentiality service is used, the message plus signature (if present) are encrypted (with a one-time IDEA key). Thus, part or all of the resulting block consists of a stream of arbitrary 8-bit octets. However, many electronic mail systems only permit the use of blocks consisting of ASCII text. To accommodate this restriction, PGP provides the service of converting the raw 8-bit binary stream to a stream of printable ASCII characters.

The scheme used for this purpose is radix-64 conversion. Each group of three octets of binary data is mapped into four ASCII characters. This format also appends a CRC to detect transmission errors. See Appendix 9B for a description.

The use of radix 64 expands a message by 33%. Fortunately, the session key and signature portions of the message are relatively compact, and the plaintext message has been compressed. In fact, the compression should be more than enough to compensate for the radix-64 expansion. For example, [HELD91] reports an average compression ratio of about 2.0 using ZIP. If we ignore the relatively small signature and key components, the typical overall effect of compression and expansion of a file of length X would be $1.33 \times 0.5 \times X = 0.665 \times X$. Thus, there is still an overall compression of about one-third.

One noteworthy aspect of the radix-64 algorithm is that it blindly converts the input stream to radix-64 format regardless of content, even if the input happens to be ASCII text. Thus, if a message is signed but not encrypted, and the conversion is applied to the entire block, the output will be unreadable to the casual observer, which provides a certain level of confidentiality. As an option, PGP can be configured to convert to radix-64 format only the signature portion of signed plaintext messages. This enables the human recipient to read the message without using PGP. PGP would still have to be used to verify the signature.

Figure 9.2 shows the relationship among the four services so far discussed. On transmission, if it is required, a signature is generated using a hash code of the compressed plaintext. Then, the plaintext plus signature, if present, are compressed. Next, if confidentiality is required, the block (compressed plaintext or compressed signature plus plaintext) is encrypted and prepended with the RSA-encrypted conventional encryption key. Finally, the entire block is converted to radix-64 format.

On reception, the incoming block is first converted back from radix-64 format to binary. Then, if the message is encrypted, the recipient recovers the session key and decrypts the message. The resulting block is then decompressed. If the message is signed, the recipient recovers the transmitted hash code and compares it to its own calculation of the hash code.

Segmentation and Reassembly

E-mail facilities often are restricted to a maximum message length. For example, many of the facilities accessible through the Internet impose a maximum length of 50,000 octets. Any message longer than that must be broken up into smaller segments, each of which is mailed separately.

To accommodate this restriction, PGP automatically subdivides a message that is too large into segments that are small enough to send via e-mail. The segmentation is done after all of the other processing, including the radix-64 conversion. Thus, the session key component and signature component appear only once, at the be-

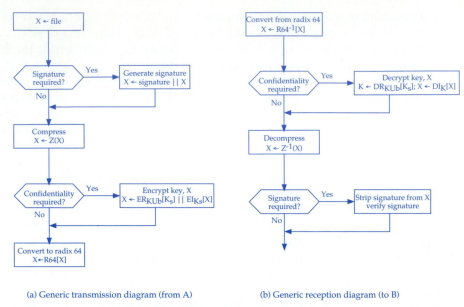

(a) Generic transmission diagram (from A)   (b) Generic reception diagram (to B)

FIGURE 9.2.   Transmission and Reception of PGP Messages

ginning of the first segment. At the receiving end, PGP must strip off all e-mail headers and reassemble the entire original block before performing the steps illustrated in Figure 9.2b.

Cryptographic Keys and Key Rings

PGP makes use of four types of keys: one-time session conventional keys, public keys, private keys, and passphrase-based conventional keys (Table 9.2). Three separate requirements can be identified with respect to these keys:

1. A means of generating unpredictable session keys is needed.
2. We would like to allow a user to have multiple public-key/private-key pairs. One reason is that the user may wish to change his or her key pair from time to time. When this happens, any messages in the pipeline will be constructed with an obsolete key. Furthermore, recipients will know only the old public key until an update reaches them. In addition to the need to change keys over time, a user may wish to have multiple key pairs at a given time to interact with different groups of correspondents or simply to enhance security by limiting the amount of material encrypted with any one key. The upshot of all this is that there is not a one-to-one correspondence between users and their public keys. Thus, some means is needed for identifying particular keys.
3. Each PGP entity must maintain a file of its own public/private key pairs as well as a file of public keys of correspondents.

We examine each of these requirements in turn.

TABLE 9.2   Encryption Keys Used in PGP

Name	Encryption Algorithm	Use
Session key	IDEA	Used to encrypt messages for transmission. Each session key is used only once and is generated randomly.
Public key	RSA	Used to encrypt session keys for transmission with messages. Both senders and recipients must maintain a copy of each public key.
Private key	RSA	Used to encrypt message digests to form a digital signature. Only a sender needs to maintain a copy of its private key.
Passphrase-based key	IDEA	Used to encrypt private keys for storage at key sender.

Session Key Generation

Each session key is associated with a single message and is used only for the purpose of encrypting and decrypting that message. Recall that message encryption/decryption is done with the symmetric encryption algorithm IDEA, which uses 128-bit keys.

Random 128-bit numbers are generated using IDEA itself. The input to the random number generator consists of a 128-bit key and two 64-bit blocks that are treated as plaintext to be encrypted. Using cipher feedback mode, the IDEA encrypter produces two 64-bit ciphertext blocks, which are concatenated to form the 128-bit session key. The algorithm that is used is based on the one specified in ANSI X9.17.

The "plaintext" input to the random number generator, consisting of two 64-bit blocks, is itself derived from a stream of 128-bit randomized numbers. These numbers are based on keystroke input from the user. Both the keystroke timing and the actual keys struck are used to generate the randomized stream. Thus, if the user hits arbitrary keys at his or her normal pace, a reasonably "random" input will be generated. This random input is also combined with previous session key output from IDEA to form the key input to the generator. The result, given the effective scrambling of IDEA, is to produce a sequence of session keys that is in practice unpredictable.

Appendix 9-C discusses PGP random number generation techniques in more detail.

Key Identifiers

As we have discussed, an encrypted message is accompanied by an encrypted form of the session key that was used. The session key itself is encrypted with the recipient's public key. Hence, only the recipient will be able to recover the session key and therefore recover the message. Now, if each user employed a single public/private key pair, then the recipient would automatically know which key to use to decrypt the session key: the recipient's unique private key. However, we have stated a requirement that any given user may have multiple public/private key pairs.

How, then, does the recipient know which of its public keys was used to encrypt the session key? One simple solution would be to transmit the public key with the message. The recipient could then verify that this is indeed one of its public keys, and proceed. This scheme would work, but it is unnecessarily wasteful of space. An RSA public key may be hundreds of decimal digits in length. Another solution would be to associate an identifier with each public key that is unique at least within one user. That is, the combination of user ID and key ID would be sufficient to uniquely identify a key. Then, only the much shorter key ID would need to be transmitted. This solution, however, raises a management and overhead problem. Key IDs must be assigned and stored so that both sender and recipient could map from key ID to public key. This seems unnecessarily burdensome.

The solution adopted by PGP is to assign a key ID to each public key that is, with very high probability, unique within a user ID.[1] The key ID associated with each public key consists of its least significant 64 bits. That is, the key ID of public key KU_a is (KU_a mod 2^{64}). This is a sufficient length so that the probability of duplicate key IDs is very small.

A key ID is also required for the PGP digital signature. Because a sender may use one of a number of private keys to encrypt the message digest, the recipient must know which public key is intended for use. Accordingly, the digital signature component of a message includes the 64-bit key ID of the required public key. When the message is received, the recipient verifies that the key ID is for a public key that it knows for that sender and then proceeds to verify the signature.

Now that the concept of key ID has been introduced, we can take a more detailed (but still incomplete) look at the format of a transmitted message, which is shown in Figure 9.3. A message consists of three components: the message component, a signature (optional), and a session key component (optional).

The **message component** includes the actual data to be stored or transmitted, as well as a filename and a timestamp that specifies the time of creation.

The **signature component** includes the following components:

- *Timestamp:* The time at which the signature was made.
- *Message digest:* The 128-bit MD5 digest. The digest is calculated over the signature timestamp concatenated with the data portion of the message component. The inclusion of the signature timestamp in the digest assures against replay types of attacks. The exclusion of the filename and timestamp portions of the message component ensures that detached signatures are exactly the same as attached signatures prefixed to the message. Detached signatures are

---

[1]Again we see that taking a probabilistic approach simplifies the solution (e.g., see footnote 1 in Chapter 6).

Content   Operation

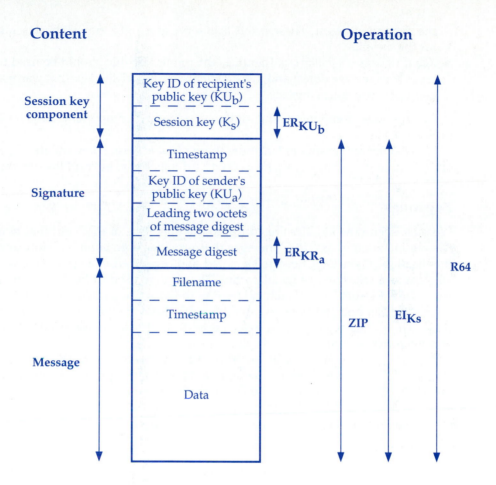

Notation:
    KU_b = public key, user b
    KR_a = private key, user a
    K_s = session key
    ER   = RSA encryption function
    EI   = IDEA encryption function
    ZIP   = PKZIP compression function
    R64   = radix-64 conversion function

FIGURE 9.3.   General Format of PGP Message (from A to B)

calculated on a separate file that has none of the message component header fields.

- *Leading two octets of message digest:* To enable the recipient to determine if the correct RSA key was used to decrypt the message digest for authentication, by comparing this plaintext copy of the first two octets with the first two octets of the decrypted digest. These octets also serve as a 16-bit frame check sequence for the message.

- *Key ID of sender's public key:* Identifies the public key that should be used to decrypt the message digest and, hence, identifies the private key that was used to encrypt the message digest.

The message component and optional signature component may be compressed.

The **session key component** includes the encrypted session key and the identifier of the recipient's public key that was used by the sender to encrypt the session key.

Key Rings

We have seen how key IDs are critical to the operation of PGP and that two key IDs are included in any PGP message that provides both confidentiality and authentication. These keys need to be stored and organized in a systematic way for efficient and effective use by all parties. The scheme used in PGP is to provide a pair of data structures at each node, one to store the public/private key pairs owned by that node and one to store the public keys of other users known at this node. These data structures are referred to, respectively, as the private-key ring and the public-key ring.

Figure 9.4 shows the general structure of a **private-key ring.**[2] We can view the ring as a table, in which each row represents one of the public/private key pairs owned by this user. Each row contains the following entries:

[2]Again, for clarity in the discussion, some details are omitted at this point and provided in the next subsection.

Private Key Ring

Timestamp	Key ID*	Public Key	Encrypted Private Key	User ID*
• • •	• • •	• • •	• • •	• • •
T_i	$KU_i \bmod 2^{64}$	KU_i	$E_{IH(P_i)}[KR_i]$	User i
• • •	• • •	• • •	• • •	• • •

Public Key Ring

Timestamp	Key ID*	Public Key	Owner Trust	User ID*	Key Legitimacy	Signature(s)	Signature Trust(s)
• • •	• • •	• • •	•	• • •	• • •	• • •	• • •
T_i	$KU_i \bmod 2^{64}$	KU_i	trust_flag$_i$	User i	trust_flag$_i$		
• • •	• • •	• • •	•	• • •	• • •	• • •	• • •

* = field used to index table

FIGURE 9.4.   General Structure of Private- and Public-Key Rings

- *Timestamp:* the date/time when this key pair was generated.
- *Key ID:* the least significant 64 bits of the public key for this entry.
- *Public key:* the public-key portion of the pair.
- *Private key:* the private-key portion of the pair; this field is encrypted.
- *User ID:* Typically, this will be the user's e-mail address (e.g., stallings @acm.org). However, the user may choose to associate a different name with each pair (e.g., Stallings, WStallings, WilliamStallings, etc.) or to reuse the same User ID more than once.

The private-key ring can be indexed by either User ID or Key ID; we will see later the need for both means of indexing.

Although it is intended that the private-key ring be stored only on the machine of the user that created and owns the key pairs and that it be accessible only to that user, it makes sense to make the value of the private key as secure as possible. Accordingly, the private key itself is not stored in the key ring. Rather, this key is encrypted using IDEA. The procedure is as follows:

1. The user selects a passphrase to be used for encrypting private keys.
2. When the system generates a new public/private key pair using RSA, it asks the user for the passphrase. Using MD5, a 128-bit hash code is generated from the passphrase, and the passphrase is discarded.
3 The system encrypts the private key using IDEA with the hash code as the key. The hash code is then discarded, and the encrypted private key is stored in the private-key ring.

Subsequently, when a user accesses the private-key ring to retrieve a private key, he or she must supply the passphrase. PGP will retrieve the encrypted private key, generate the hash code of the passphrase, and decrypt the encrypted private key using IDEA with the hash code.

This is a very compact and effective scheme. As in any system based on pass-words, the security of this system depends on the security of the password. To avoid the temptation to write it down, the user should use a passphrase that is not easily guessed but that is easily remembered.

Figure 9.4 also shows the general structure of a **public-key ring.** This data structure is used to store public keys of other users that are known to this user. For the moment, let us ignore some fields shown in the table and describe the following fields:

- *Timestamp:* the date/time when this entry was generated.
- *Key ID:* the least significant 64 bits of the public key for this entry.
- *Public key:* the public key for this entry.
- *User ID:* identifies the owner of this key. Multiple user IDs may be associated with a single public key.

The public-key ring can be indexed by either User ID or Key ID; we will see the need for both means of indexing later.

We are now in a position to show how these key rings are used in message transmission and reception. For simplicity, we ignore compression and radix-64 conversion in the following discussion. First consider message transmission (Figure 9.5) and assume that the message is to be both signed and encrypted. The sending user initiates the action by entering the appropriate command, which is of the form:

```
pgp -es textfile her_userid [-u your_userid]
```

The parameter "-es" indicates that the message is to be both encrypted and signed.

The sending PGP entity performs the following steps:

1. Signing the Message
   (a) PGP retrieves the sender's private key from the private-key ring using your_userid as an index. If your_userid was not provided in the command, the first private key on the ring is retrieved.
   (b) PGP prompts the user for the passphrase in order to recover the unencrypted private key.
   (c) The signature component of the message is constructed.
2. Encrypting the Message
   (a) PGP generates a session key and encrypts the message.
   (b) PGP retrieves the recipient's public key from the public-key ring using her_userid as an index.
   (c) The session key component of the message is constructed.

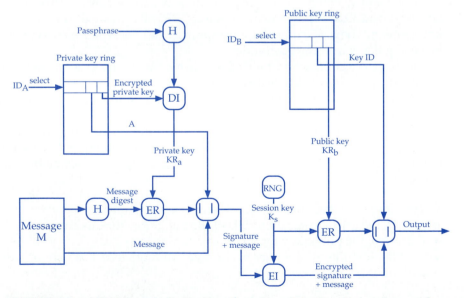

FIGURE 9.5.   PGP Message Generation (from User A to User B; no compression or radix-64 conversion)

The receiving PGP entity performs the following steps (Figure 9.6):

1. Decrypting the Message
   (a) PGP retrieves the receiver's private key from the private-key ring, using the Key ID field in the session key component of the message as an index.
   (b) PGP prompts the user for the passphrase in order to recover the unencrypted private key.
   (c) PGP then recovers the session key and decrypts the message.
2. Authenticating the Message
   (a) PGP retrieves the sender's public key from the public-key ring, using the Key ID field in the signature key component of the message as an index.
   (b) PGP recovers the transmitted message digest.
   (c) PGP computes the message digest for the received message and compares it to the transmitted message digest to authenticate.

Public-Key Management

As can be seen from the discussion so far, PGP contains a clever, efficient, interlocking set of functions and formats to provide an effective confidentiality and authentication service. To complete the system, one final area needs to be addressed,

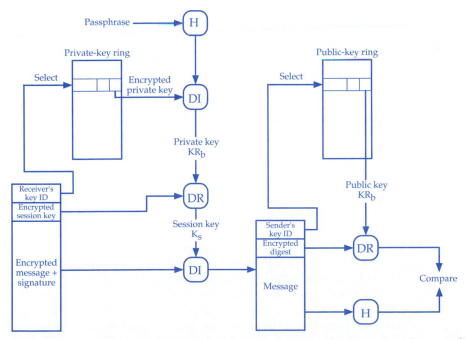

FIGURE 9.6. PGP Message Reception (from User A to User B; no compression or radix-64 conversion)

that of public-key management. The PGP documentation captures the importance of this area:

> This whole business of protecting public keys from tampering is the single most diffi-
> cult problem in practical public key applications. It is the "Achilles heel" of public key
> cryptography, and a lot of software complexity is tied up in solving this one problem.

In this area, PGP provides a structure for solving this problem, with several suggested options that may be used. Because PGP is intended for use in a variety of formal and informal environments, no rigid public-key management scheme is set up, such as we will see in Privacy Enhanced Mail (PEM) later in this chapter.

Approaches to Public-Key Management

The essence of the problem is this: User A must build up a public-key ring containing the public keys of other users in order to interoperate with them using PGP. Suppose that A's key ring contains a public key attributed to B but that it is in actual fact owned by C. This could happen if, for example, A got the key from a bulletin board system (BBS) that was used by B to post the public key but that has been compromised by C. The result is that two threats now exist. First, C can send messages to A and forge B's signature, so that A will accept the message as coming from B. Second, any encrypted message from A to B can be read by C.

A number of approaches are possible for minimizing the risk that a user's public-key ring contains false public keys. Suppose that A wishes to obtain a reliable public key for B. The following are some approaches that could be used:

1. Physically get the key from B. B could store her public key (KU_b) on a floppy disk and hand it to A. A could then load the key into his system from the floppy disk. This is a very secure method but has obvious practical limitations.
2. Verify a key by telephone. If A can recognize B on the phone, A could call B and ask her to dictate the key, in radix-64 format, over the phone. As a more practical alternative, B could transmit her key in an e-mail message to A. A could have PGP generate a 128-bit MD5 digest of the key and display it in radix-64 format; this is referred to as the "fingerprint" of the key. A could then call B and ask her to dictate the fingerprint over the phone. If the two fingerprints match, the key is verified.
3. Obtain B's public key from a mutual trusted individual D. For this purpose, the introducer, D, creates a signed certificate. The certificate includes B's public key, the time of creation of the key, and a validity period for the key. D generates an MD5 digest of this certificate, encrypts it with her private key, and attaches the signature to the certificate. Because only D could have created the signature, no one else can create a false public key and pretend that it is signed by D. The signed certificate could be sent directly to A by B or D, or could be posted on a bulletin board.

4. Obtain B's public key from a trusted certifying authority. Again, a public key certificate is created and signed by the authority. A could then access the authority, providing a user name and receiving a signed certificate.

For cases 3 and 4, A would have to already have a copy of the introducer's public key and trust that this key is valid. Ultimately, it is up to A to assign a level of trust to anyone who is to act as an introducer.

The Use of Trust

Although PGP does not include any specification for establishing certifying authorities or for establishing trust, it does provide a convenient means of using trust, associating trust with public keys, and exploiting trust information.

The basic structure is as follows. Each entry in the public-key ring is in fact a public-key certificate, as described in the preceding subsection. Associated with each such entry is a **key legitimacy field** that indicates the extent to which PGP will trust that in fact this is a valid public key for this user; the higher the level of trust, the stronger is the binding of this user ID to this key. This field is computed by PGP. Also associated with the entry are zero or more signatures that the key ring owner has collected that sign this certificate. In turn, each signature has associated with it a **signature trust field** that indicates the degree to which this PGP user trusts the signer to certify public keys. The key legitimacy field is in fact derived from the collection of signature trust fields in the entry. Finally, each entry defines a public key associated with a particular owner, and an **owner trust field** is included that indicates the degree to which this public key is trusted to sign other public-key certificates; this level of trust is assigned by the user. We can think of the signature trust fields as cached copies of the owner trust field from another entry.

The three fields mentioned in the previous paragraph are each contained in a structure referred to as a trust flag byte. The content of this trust flag for each of these three uses is shown in Table 9.3. Suppose that we are dealing with the public-key ring of user A. We can describe the operation of the trust processing as follows:

1. When A inserts a new public key on the public-key ring, PGP must assign a value to the trust flag that is associated with the owner of this public key. If the owner is in fact A, and therefore this public key also appears in the private-key ring, then a value of *ultimate trust* is automatically assigned to the trust field. Otherwise, PGP asks A for his assessment of the trust to be assigned to the owner of this key, and A must enter the desired level. The user can specify that this owner is unknown, untrusted, marginally trusted, or completely trusted.

2. When the new public key is entered, one or more signatures may be attached to it. More signatures may be added later on. When a signature is inserted into the entry, PGP searches the public-key ring to see if the author of this signature is among the known public-key owners. If so, the OWNERTRUST value for this

TABLE 9.3   Contents of Trust Flag Byte

(a) Trust Assigned to Public-Key Owner (appears after key packet; user-defined)	(b) Trust Assigned to Public Key/User ID Pair (appears after User ID packet; computed by PGP)	(c) Trust Assigned to Signature (appears after signature packet;cached copy of OWNERTRUST for this signatory)
OWNERTRUST Field —undefined trust —unknown user —usually not trusted to sign other keys —usually trusted to sign other keys —always trusted to sign other keys —this key is present in secret key ring (ultimate trust) BUCKSTOP bit —set if this key appears in secret key ring	KEYLEGIT Field —unknown or undefined trust —key ownership not trusted —marginal trust in key ownership —complete trust in key ownership WARNONLY bit —set if user wants only to be warned when key that is not fully validated is used for encryption	SIGTRUST Field —undefined trust —unknown user —usually not trusted to sign other keys —usually trusted to sign other keys —always trusted to sign other keys —this key is present in secret key ring (ultimate trust) CONTIG bit —set if signature leads up a contiguous trusted certification path back to the ultimately trusted keyring owner

owner is assigned to the SIGTRUST field for this signature. If not, an *unknown user* value is assigned.

3. The value of the key legitimacy field is calculated on the basis of the signature trust fields present in this entry. If at least one signature has a signature trust value of *ultimate,* then the key legitimacy value is set to complete. Otherwise, PGP computes a weighted sum of the trust values. A weight of 1/X is given to signatures that are always trusted and 1/Y to signatures that are usually trusted, where X and Y are user-configurable parameters. When the total of weights of the introducers of a key/UserID combination reaches 1, the binding is considered to be trustworthy, and the key legitimacy value is set to complete. Thus, in the absence of ultimate trust, at least X signatures that are always trusted or Y signatures that are usually trusted or some combination is needed.

Periodically, PGP processes the public-key ring to achieve consistency. In essence, this is a top-down process. For each OWNERTRUST field, PGP scans the ring for all signatures authored by that owner and updates the SIGTRUST field to equal the OWNERTRUST field. This process starts with keys for which there is ultimate trust. Then, all KEYLEGIT fields are computed on the basis of the attached signatures.

Figure 9.7 provides an example of the way in which signature trust and key legitimacy are related.[3] The figure shows the structure of a public-key ring. The user

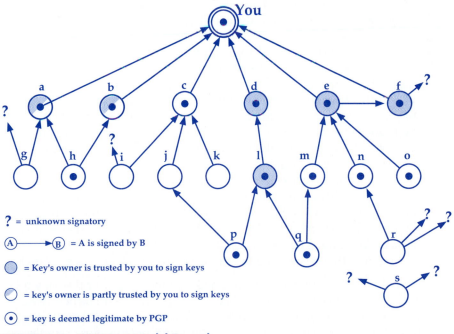

? = unknown signatory

(A) ——▶ (B) = A is signed by B

◯ = Key's owner is trusted by you to sign keys

◐ = key's owner is partly trusted by you to sign keys

⊙ = key is deemed legitimate by PGP

FIGURE 9.7.   PGP Trust Model Example

[3]Figure provided by Phil Zimmermann.

has acquired a number of public keys, some directly from their owners and some from a third party such as a key server.

The node labeled "You" refers to the entry in the public-key ring corresponding to this user. This key is legitimate and the OWNERTRUST value is ultimate trust. Each other node in the key ring has an OWNERTRUST value of undefined unless some other value is assigned by the user. In this example, this user has specified that it always trusts the following users to sign other keys: d, e, f, l. This user partially trusts users a and b to sign other keys.

So, the shading, or lack thereof, of the nodes in the figure indicate the level of trust assigned by this user. The tree structure indicates which keys have been signed by which other users. If a key is signed by a user whose key is also in this key ring, the arrow joins the signed key to the signatory. If the key is signed by a user whose key is not present in this key ring, the arrow joins the signed key to a question mark, indicating that the signatory is unknown to this user.

Several points are illustrated in this figure:

1. Note that all keys whose owners are fully or partially trusted by this user have been signed by this user, with the exception of node l. Such a user signature is not always necessary, as the presence of node l indicates, but in practice, most users are likely to sign the keys for most owners that they trust. So, for example, even though e's key is already signed by trusted introducer f, the user chose to sign e's key directly.

2   We assume that two partially trusted signatures are sufficient to certify a key. Hence, the key for user h is deemed legitimate by PGP because it is signed by a and b, both of whom are partially trusted.

3. A key may be determined to be legitimate, because it is signed by one fully trusted or two partially trusted signatories, but its user may not be trusted to sign other keys. For example, n's key is legitimate because it is signed by e, whom this user trusts, but n is not trusted to sign other keys because this user has not assigned n that trust value. Therefore, although r's key is signed by n, PGP does not consider r's key legitimate. This situation makes perfect sense. If you wish to send a private message to some individual, it is not necessary that you trust that individual in any respect. It is only necessary that you are sure that you have the correct public key for that individual.

4. The diagram also shows an example of a detached "orphan" node s, with two unknown signatures. Such a key may have been acquired from a key server. PGP cannot assume that this key is legitimate simply because it came from a reputable server. The user must declare the key legitimate by signing it or by telling PGP that it is willing to fully trust one of the key's signatories.

A final point: Earlier it was mentioned that multiple user IDs may be associated with a single public key on the public-key ring. This could be because a person has changed names or has been introduced via signature under multiple names, indicating different e-mail addresses for the same person, for example. So, we can think of a public key as the root of a tree. A public key has a number of user IDs depending from it, with a number of signatures below each user ID. The binding of a particular user ID to a key depends on the signatures associated with that user ID and that key, whereas the level of trust in this key (for use in signing other keys) is a function of all the dependent signatures.

Revoking Public Keys

A user may wish to revoke his or her current public key either because compromise is suspected or simply to avoid the use of the same key for an extended period. Note that a compromise would require that an opponent somehow had obtained a copy of your unencrypted private key or that the opponent had obtained both the private key from your private-key ring and your passphrase.

The convention for revoking a public key is for the owner to issue a key revocation certificate, signed by the owner. This certificate has the same form as a normal signature certificate but includes an indicator that the purpose of this certificate is to revoke the use of this public key. Note that the corresponding private key must be used to sign a certificate that revokes a public key. The owner should then attempt to disseminate this certificate as widely and as quickly as possible to enable potential correspondents to update their public-key rings.

Note that an opponent who has compromised the private key of an owner can also issue such a certificate. However, this would deny the opponent as well as the legitimate owner the use of the public key, and therefore it seems a much less likely threat than the malicious use of a stolen private key.

PGP Formats

The PGP specification includes the definition of a number of formats that are used to create key ring entries, certificates, and messages. These formats, referred to as packets, are building blocks from which entries, certificates, and messages are formed. Figure 9.8 illustrates the PGP packet formats.

All packets begin with the same two fields. The cipher type field indicates which type of packet this is, and the length of the next field. The packet length field indicates the length of the packet in octets. Many of the packets also include a version field specifying the version number of PGP.

Let us briefly summarize the contents of each packet. The **public-key-encrypted packet** is the format for the session key component of a message (Figure 9.3). It includes the key ID of the intended recipient's public key and the session key encrypted with that public key. The public-key algorithm used is also specified; the default is RSA.

A **signature packet** is used for a variety of purposes, including messages and certificates; the classification field indicates the nature of this signature. Most of the remaining fields were defined in our discussion of Figure 9.3. The field preceding the signature field indicates how many of the following fields are to be included in the hash calculation.

A **conventional-key-encrypted data packet** contains a literal data packet or a compressed data packet encrypted with a conventional algorithm. The plaintext or

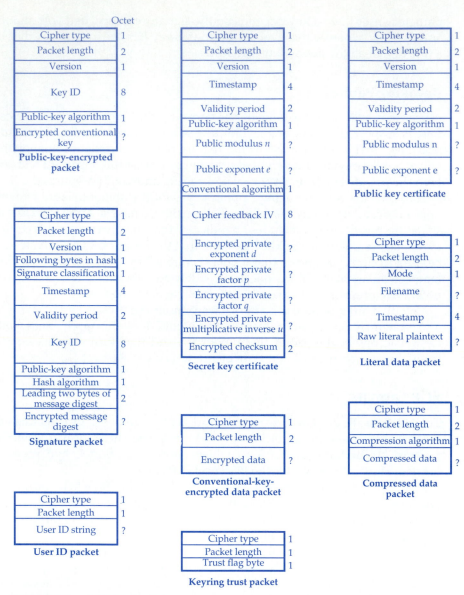

FIGURE 9.8.   PGP Packet Formats

compressed plaintext is prepended with 64 bits of random data plus 16 "key check" bits. The random prefix serves to start off the cipher feedback chaining process with 64 bits of random material; this serves the same function as an initialization vector (IV), and it is generated by the pseudorandom number generator at the same time as the session key. The key check prefix is equal to the last 16 bits of the random prefix. During decryption, a comparison is made to see if the 7th and

8th octet of the decrypted material match the 9th and 10th octets. If so, then the conventional session key is assumed to be correct.

A **compressed data packet** includes a specification of the compression algorithm used (default: ZIP), and a compressed literal data packet.

A **literal data packet** includes a mode field indicating whether this is a binary or text file, together with a filename and timestamp.

A **secret key certificate** defines the format used for an entry in a private-key ring. Note that the format assumes the use of RSA, so that both public and private keys have two parts.

A **public-key certificate** is a basic element of a public-key ring entry. Note that this certificate does not indicate the owner of the public key. On a public-key ring, a public-key certificate must always be followed by a user ID packet.

A **user ID packet** follows a public key on a public-key ring and a private key on a private-key ring. When a public-key certificate is certified by a signature, the signature covers both the public key and the user ID.

A **keyring trust packet** specifies a level of trust. The interpretation of the trust flag byte depends on context, as indicated in Table 9.3.

9.2

PRIVACY ENHANCED MAIL (PEM)

Privacy Enhanced Mail is a draft Internet standard that provides security-related services for electronic mail applications. Its most common use is in conjunction with the Internet-standard Simple Mail Transfer Protocol (SMTP), but it can be used with any electronic mail scheme, including X.400. The PEM specification consists of the following four RFCs:

- RFC 1421: Privacy Enhancement for Internet Electronic Mail: Part I: Message Encryption and Authentication Procedures
- RFC 1422: Privacy Enhancement for Internet Electronic Mail: Part II: Certificate-Based Key Management
- RFC 1423: Privacy Enhancement for Internet Electronic Mail: Part III: Algorithms, Modes, and Identifiers
- RFC 1424: Privacy Enhancement for Internet Electronic Mail: Part IV: Key Certification and Related Services

Overview

PEM is intended for use in a wide variety of contexts. RFC 1421 lists the following attributes of the design:

- Interoperability: PEM is implemented at the application layer and is independent of lower protocol layers, operating system, or host.

- Compatibility with nonenhanced components: PEM is an end-to-end service that is transparent to intermediate mail-forwarding elements. The underlying mail system need not be altered to accommodate PEM.
- Compatibility with multiple mail transport facilities: PEM provides protection not only within the SMTP environment but other mail transport environments.
- Compatibility with various user interfaces: PEM can be implemented as a separate module that works with the existing electronic mail interface seen by the user.
- Support for PC users: In many environments, a user agent (UA) module on a central system supports electronic mail for a number of distributed users. PEM enables the user to create messages with PEM protection off-line at the user's personal computer and then to submit the protected message to the UA for processing. Thus, the user is not required to trust a remote UA.
- Mailing list support: PEM includes an efficient mechanism for supporting security services for electronic mail addressed to mailing lists.
- Compatibility with various key management approaches. PEM supports the use of manual predistribution of keys, centralized key distribution based on symmetric encryption, and the use of public-key certificates. Communicating end systems must share the same key distribution mechanism.

A fundamental design principle of PEM is to limit its capability to the most critical set of services rather than addressing a wide range of security risks. The intent is to maximize the added security value that can be provided with a modest level of implementation effort. Specifically, PEM provides the following capabilities:

- Disclosure protection
- Originator authenticity
- Message integrity
- Nonrepudiation of origin (if asymmetric key management is used)

The following security-related concerns are not addressed:

- Access control
- Traffic flow confidentiality
- Routing control
- Issues relating to the serial reuse of PCs by multiple users
- Assurance of message receipt and non-deniability of receipt
- Automatic association of acknowledgments with the messages to which they refer
- Message duplicate detection, replay prevention, or other stream-oriented services

Cryptographic Algorithms and Keys

Table 9.4 summarizes the services provided by PEM and the basic algorithms that support these services. Before describing the operation of PEM, it will be useful to summarize the cryptographic algorithms and keys used.

TABLE 9.4   Summary of PEM Algorithms

Function	Algorithms Used	Description
Message encryption	DES-CBC	A message is encrypted using DES-CBC with a one-time session key. The session key is encrypted using RSA with the recipient's public key, and included with the message.
Authentication and Digital signature (asymmetric encryption)	RSA with MD2 or MD5	A hash code of a message is created using MD2 or MD5. This message digest is encrypted using RSA with the sender's private key, and included with the message.
Authentication (symmetric encryption)	DES-ECB or DES-EDE with MD2 or MD5	A hash code of a message is created using MD2 or MD5. This message digest is encrypted using either DES-ECB or DES-EDE (triple DES) using a symmetric key shared by sender and receiver, and included with the message.
Symmetric Key Management	DES-ECB or DES-EDE	The session key is encrypted using either DES-ECB or DES-EDE (triple DES) using a symmetric key shared by sender and receiver, and included with the message.
Asymmetric Key Management	RSA, MD2	Public-key certificates are created and signed using MD2 to hash the certificate and RSA to encrypt the hash code. The session key is encrypted using RSA with the recipient's public key, and included with the message.
E-mail compatibility	Radix 64 conversion	To provide transparency for e-mail applications, an encrypted message may be converted to an ASCII string using radix-64 conversion.

PEM is designed to function with a variety of cryptographic algorithms. To support this generality, every PEM message includes identifiers of the algorithms used. For some services, only one type of algorithm is currently supported. However, by providing the format to allow different algorithms to be used, PEM provides flexibility for future evolution.

The cryptographic functions performed by PEM fall into three categories: authentication, message confidentiality, and key exchange. The **authentication** function is performed as follows:

1. A hash code, called a message integrity code (MIC) is calculated for each message. Either MD2 or MD5 may be used.
2. The hash code is encrypted and attached to the message. If asymmetric (public-key) encryption is used, the algorithm is RSA, and the encrypted hash code con-

stitutes a digital signature. The key size may vary from 508 to 1024 bits. If symmetric encryption is used, then either the electronic codebook (ECB) mode of DES or triple DES is used.

Using either MD2 or MD5, the hash code is 128 bits long. The rules for the two algorithms are the following:

- DES-ECB: The 128-bit MD2 or MD5 hash code is split into two 64-bit blocks, and each is independently encrypted; the resulting two 64-blocks of ciphertext are concatenated to form the 128-bit encryption of the MIC.
- DES-EDE: This is the triple DES specified in ANSI X9.17. Two 56-bit keys are used. The plaintext is encrypted with the first key; then the result is decrypted with the second key; and then that result is encrypted with the first key.

Message confidentiality is always performed using symmetric encryption. The only algorithm approved for PEM is the cipher-block chaining (CBC) mode of DES.

PEM makes a distinction between data encryption keys (DEKs) and interchange keys (IKs). An IK can be either a symmetric key shared by a message originator and a message recipient or a public/private symmetric key pair. In the former case, all parties that wish to communicate must agree on a secret key to be used. In the latter case, there must be some means of reliably providing each party with the public key of other parties. This may involve the use of public-key certificates, which are signed by a certificate-issuing authority. A DEK is a one-time session key used to encrypt message text. It is also sometimes used to encrypt digital signatures, as explained later. These functions are summarized in Table 9.5.

Thus there is the **key management** problem of distributing DEKs. The approach taken in PEM is to include a copy of the DEK with the message and to encrypt the DEK with an IK known to the recipient. If asymmetric encryption is supported, then the DEK is encrypted using the RSA public key of the recipient. If only symmetric encryption is supported, then the DEK is encrypted with the

TABLE 9.5   Key Usage in PEM

	Asymmetric Key Management	Symmetric Key Management
Data Encryption Keys (DEKs) used to encrypt	Message text, signed representation of MIC	Message text
Interchange Keys (IKs) used to encrypt	DEK	DEK, MIC
Issuer assymetric key used to encrypt	Public-key certificate hash code	—

shared IK of originator and recipient; either the DES-CBC or DES-EDE algorithm may be used.

With this background, let us look at the operation of PEM in more detail.

Operational Description

When a message is presented to PEM for preparation for transmission, it goes through four steps of processing:

1. Convert message to canonical form
2. Generate message integrity and authentication information
3. Encrypt message (optional)
4. Convert to printable encoding form (optional)

These four stages are applied in reverse order at the destination (Figure 9.9). The user determines whether the optional steps are performed by choosing one of three message types:

- ENCRYPTED: steps 1 through 4 are performed
- MIC-ONLY: steps 1, 2, and 4 are performed
- MIC-CLEAR: steps 1 and 2 are performed

We examine each of these steps in turn.

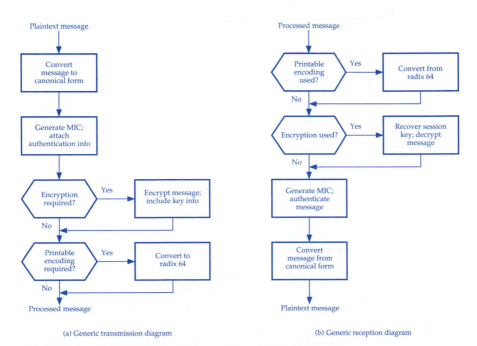

(a) Generic transmission diagram

(b) Generic reception diagram

FIGURE 9.9.   Transmission and Reception of PEM Messages

The discussion that follows refers to PEM messages other than those that carry a certificate revocation list (CRL). The rules for these messages are somewhat different and are treated later in this section.

Canonical Form

Electronic mail transport and electronic mail delivery systems generally make the assumption that messages consist of printable characters only. Although these systems are designed to deliver a message that corresponds to the message that was originally submitted, liberties are sometimes taken. For example, the carriage-return, line feed (<CR><LF>) sequences delimiting lines in mail inbound to UNIX systems are transformed to single <LF>s as mail is written into local mailbox files. It is also possible that conversion between tabs and spaces may be performed in the course of mapping between the format used for SMTP transmission and a local format. These possibilities present two problems:

1. All PEM messages include authentication information based on a hash code, called the message integrity check (MIC). If any modifications are made to the message by the intermediate mail-handling systems, then the MIC will fail to compare with that computed at the destination.
2. If a message is encrypted (an optional service), the ciphertext may, by chance, contain one or more of the bit patterns that trigger processing, such as <CR><LF> or a tab. Any modification to the ciphertext would prevent recovery of the plaintext by decryption.

The second of these problems is handled by radix-64 conversion, described later. The first problem is addressed by step 1, which converts the user's message input into a canonical form. On transmission, the PEM module converts the message from a local format to the canonical form expected by the local mail handler, in effect preempting its function. The hash code is calculated on the canonical-format message, and the mail handler has no need to modify the message in that format. On the receiving end, the PEM module converts the message from the canonical form to the local format. Note that this scenario requires that, at the destination, decryption and MIC validation must be performed before any conversions that may be necessary to transform the message into a destination-specific form.

The canonical form that is used in a PEM message is indicated by a field in the PEM message header, the Content-Domain field. Currently the only domain specified for PEM is that defined in RFC 822 for use with SMTP. In this domain, conversion to canonical form consists of the following rules:

1. The message may contain any of the characters representable in 7-bit ASCII code. All input characters are converted to ASCII. Each 7-bit code is placed in the least significant seven bits of an octet, with the most significant bit set to zero.
2. The ASCII <CR><LF> sequence is used to delimit the end of lines.

3. The maximum total length of a text line including the <CR><LF> is 1000 characters. Longer lines are broken up by inserting additional <CR><LF>s.

Message Integrity and Authentication

Message integrity and authentication processing depend on the use of a hash code, referred to in the PEM documents as a message integrity code (MIC). The MIC is calculated over the entire message in canonical form. The algorithm used to calculate the MIC is specified in a field of the PEM message header.

The PEM specification allows the use of either asymmetric or symmetric encryption techniques to provide the message integrity and authentication service. It is likely that the asymmetric approach will be by far the one more commonly used. Figures 9.10 and 9.11 show the general format of a PEM message for the two approaches.

Using **asymmetric-encryption authentication,** the MIC is encrypted with the originator's private key, forming a digital signature. Again, the encryption algorithm is specified in the message header, but in this case the only algorithm currently permitted is RSA. The recipient verifies the signature, using the originator's public key. The recipient can be provided with the originator's public key in one of two ways:

1. The PEM message header may include an originator ID field. This field identifies the authority that issued the originator's public key and includes an identifier of that public key, such as a version number or expiration date. The recipient must already know the originator's public key or must be able to access it in a public directory, such as an X.509 directory.
2. The header may include a public-key certificate, which contains the originator's public key, signed by a certifying authority. In addition, there may be one or more issuer certificates tacked onto the header. The first issuer certificate is the public-key certificate of the issuer of the originator's certificate. The second issuer certificate is that of the issuer of the first issuer certificate, and so on. Thus, a certification path, such as was described in our discussion of X.509, may be included in the header.

The asymmetric authentication information (encrypted MIC, originator ID or certificate(s)) normally appears only once in the PEM message header.

When **symmetric-encryption authentication** is used, the authentication-related contents of the header are slightly different. Again, a MIC generated by MD2 or MD5 is included. In this case, the MIC is encrypted with a secret symmetric key shared by the originator and recipient. As before, the encryption algorithm used is specified in the PEM header. In this case there are two options: DES-ECB or DES-EDE.

The message includes an entity ID field that identifies either the originator or the recipient. The field may also include an issuing authority identifier, a ver-

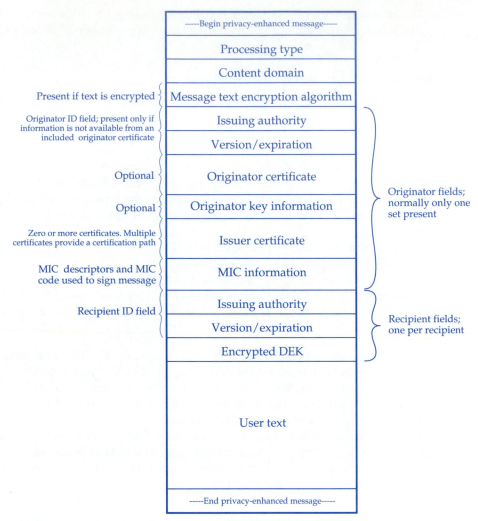

FIGURE 9.10.   PEM Format (asymmetric case)

sion/expiration subfield, or both if these are needed for the recipient to identify the shared secret key.

If a symmetric-encryption authentication is used, and if there is more than one recipient for a given message, we must take into account the fact that the originator shares a different secret key with each recipient. Accordingly, one copy of the MIC must be attached to the message for each recipient, each such copy encrypted using the shared secret key of the originator and that recipient. Also, the recipient key identification information must be included once for each recipient.

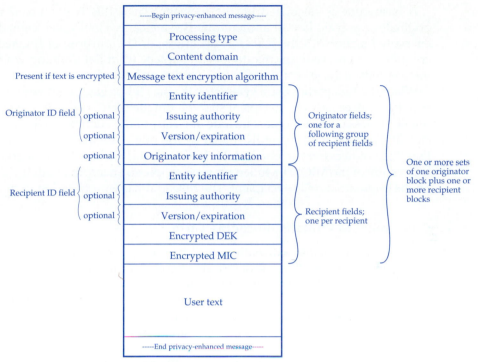

FIGURE 9.11. PEM Format (symmetric case)

Message Encryption

Message encryption is an optional service for PEM messages. If a message is encrypted, the PEM message header includes a field that indicates the encryption algorithm used. PEM encrypts a message with a one-time DEK that is created by the originator for this message only. Currently, the only allowable choice is the cipher-block-chaining (CBC) mode of DES.

Message encryption is handled somewhat differently depending on whether the IK is asymmetric or symmetric. When the two parties use an asymmetric IK, the DEK is carried in the message, encrypted with the recipient's public key. Because every recipient shares a unique private key with the originator, the PEM message header must include one copy of the encrypted DEK for each recipient, encoded with that recipient's public key. Note however that it is the same DEK that is encrypted with various IKs. In this way the message text need be encrypted only once, with the same DEK that will be revealed to each recipient.

When a message is encrypted and when the IK is asymmetric, PEM dictates that the originator must also encrypt the signed MIC with the DEK. Thus, this quantity in a message from user A has the following form:

$$E_{K_{DEK}}\left(E_{KR_a}[H(M)]\right)$$

A hash code is calculated on the message. Then this is encrypted with the originator's private key to authenticate the message. Finally, the signed MIC is encrypted again with the DEK for this message. The purpose of this second encryption is to prevent an unauthorized recipient from determining whether the intercepted message corresponds to a predetermined plaintext value.

When the two parties use a symmetric IK, the DEK is encrypted with the shared secret key. Because every recipient shares a unique secret key with the originator, the PEM message header must include one copy of the encrypted DEK for each recipient, encoded with secret IK shared by the originator and that recipient. Note that it is not necessary to encrypt the MIC with this DEK. As was mentioned earlier, a copy of the MIC is included for each recipient, encrypted with the IK shared by the originator and the recipient. The MIC is already protected from disclosure.

Conversion to Printable Encoding Form

To ensure compatibility with various mail-handling systems, a final step of processing is employed for PEM messages: the conversion of the message to printable encoding form. PEM uses radix-64 conversion (see Appendix 9B). The intent is to transform the message into a form that can be transferred by SMTP and other message-handling systems without alteration. This is essential for encrypted text, because any change to the ciphertext will render it undecipherable. It is also essential for unencrypted text, because any change to the plaintext will render the MIC invalid. In the latter case, there is much less likelihood of such modification taking place, especially because the message is in canonical form. However, it is still possible and therefore this final step applies to both encrypted and unencrypted messages.

The only exception to the use of this rule is if a user specifies that a message is to be of type MIC-CLEAR. This type may be chosen if a message is to be delivered to both PEM-enabled recipients and recipients lacking PEM capability. Such recipients would be able to easily read the message, although they would not be able to validate the message's authenticator.

Finally, for all message types, radix-64 conversion must be performed on all noncharacter fields, such as the MIC and the encrypted DEK fields.

Encapsulation

A PEM message consists of the user's message, in either plaintext or ciphertext, and associated PEM headers, as indicated in Figures 9.10 and 9.11. The entire PEM message is delimited by two boundaries. The beginning boundary is the string

```
——BEGIN PRIVACY-ENHANCED MESSAGE——
```

The ending boundary is either identical to the beginning boundary, indicating that another PEM message follows, or it is the string

```
——END PRIVACY-ENHANCED MESSAGE——
```

These boundaries encapsulate the PEM message so that the entire message can be treated as the text portion of an electronic mail message. The overall e-mail message will consist of the header used by the mail transport service (e.g., that defined in RFC 822) and the body of the e-mail message, which is the encapsulated PEM message. Furthermore, this technique enables mail systems to assemble multiple messages in a single envelope without fear of disturbing the contents of the messages.

Figure 9.12 illustrates the encapsulation process for messages sent using SMTP with RFC 822 headers.

Mailing Lists

PEM provides two methods for processing mail addressed to mailing lists: the IK-per-recipient method and the IK-per-list method.

IK-Per-Recipient Method

This technique is the most straightforward and does not introduce any new elements into PEM. If a message's originator is equipped to expand a destination mailing list into its individual constituents and knows the IK associated with each recipient for this originator, the message will be processed as follows:

1. For each asymmetric IK, the message's DEK is encrypted with the recipient's public key and included in the message header in the corresponding recipient field.

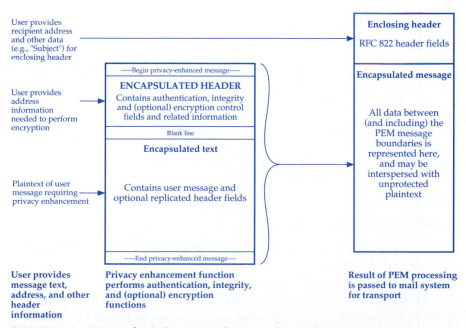

FIGURE 9.12.   PEM Submission Processing Overview [KENT93]

2. For each symmetric IK, the message's DEK and the message's MIC are encrypted and included in the message header in the corresponding recipient field.

The format of the message header allows for a mixture of both asymmetric and symmetric recipients.

This method requires per-recipient encryption but only of the relatively small DEK and MIC quantities. The message text, which is potentially much larger, is encrypted only once, with the DEK.

IK-Per-List Method

If a message's originator addresses the message to a mailing list or alias, then only one recipient field appears in the PEM message header, and the IK that is used must be shared by the originator and all recipients.

In the case of symmetric key management, a single secret IK must be shared by a number of parties. This implies an undesirable level of exposure of the shared IK and a daunting key distribution problem for all but the smallest groups of parties.

In the case of asymmetric key management, both the private and public components of an IK must be known to all parties. Again, there is a key distribution challenge to be faced, and the security of the IK is reduced. Furthermore, any party in the group can use the shared private key to impersonate any other party in the group.

Public Key Management

As we have mentioned several times in this book, the most challenging aspect of public-key protocols is the secure distribution of public keys. If an opponent can create a public key and have it accepted by a community as belonging to another party, then the opponent can impersonate the other party by signing with the private key and the opponent can read encrypted messages intended for the other party that have been encrypted with the public key.

The PEM approach is based on the certificate scheme defined in X.509. We begin by reviewing the X.509 certificate format, then look at the way in which certificates are managed, and finally discuss certificate revocation.

Public-Key Certificates

PEM uses the format for public-key certificates defined in X.509 (Figure 8.3). The fields in this format are the following:

• *Version:* Differentiates among successive versions of the certificate format; the default is a value of zero, indicating the 1988 version. PEM implementations are encouraged to accept later versions as they are endorsed by CCITT.

- *Serial number:* An integer value, unique within the issuing certifying authority (CA), which is unambiguously associated with this certificate. All PEM implementations must be capable of processing serial numbers of at least 128 bits in length.
- *Algorithm identifier:* The algorithm used to sign the certificate, together with any associated parameters.
- *Issuer:* The CA that created and signed this certificate.
- *Period of validity:* Consisting of two dates: the first and last on which the certificate is valid.
- *Subject:* The user to whom this certificate refers.
- *Public-key information:* The public key of the subject, plus an identifier of the algorithm for which this key is to be used.
- *Signature:* Covers all the other fields of the certificate and consists of a hash code of the other fields, encrypted with the CA's private key.

Internet Certification Hierarchy

The PEM specification describes an infrastructure for certification consisting of a hierarchy of certification authorities. Specifically, the following three levels are defined:

- Internet Policy Registration Authority (IPRA)
- Policy Certification Authority (PCA)
- Certification Authority (CA)

At the root of the hierarchy is the **Internet Policy Registration Authority.** The IPRA establishes global policies that apply to all certification in the PEM environment. The IPRA does not yet exist, but it is envisioned that this entity will be operated as an Internet service under the auspices of the Internet Society. Among the functions of the IPRA are the following:

- *PCA registration:* Each PCA must register with the IPRA and file a document describing its policies. The IPRA will issue a copy of the document, signed by itself, in the form of a PEM MIC-ONLY message. This enables PEM users to have access to an authenticated statement of PCA policy.
- *Ensuring uniqueness and accuracy of names:* The IPRA ensures that all PCA and CA names are unique and accurate.
- *CRL management:* The IPRA is ultimately responsible for the management of all certificate revocation lists. The IPRA maintains a CRL for all the PCAs that it certifies and ensures that each PCA maintains a CRL for all the CAs that it certifies.

Beneath the IPRA root are **Policy Certification Authorities.** Each PCA establishes and publishes its policy for registration of users. The PEM document indicates that there should be a relatively small number of PCAs, each with a substantively different policy. This will make it easier for users to readily assess the "strength" of the certification of CAs and other users.

Below PCAs, **Certification Authorities** are responsible for certifying users and other lower-level CAs. The PEM specification identifies three types of CAs:

- *Organizational:* Initially, it is expected that the majority of users will be registered via organizational affiliation, consistent with current practices for how most user mailboxes are provided. For example, a company might issue signed certificates for all its employees. Organizational CAs will include commercial, governmental, educational, nonprofit, and professional societies.
- *Residential:* Users who wish to register independently of any organizational affiliation could make use of a residential CA. Such CAs might be associated with local government organizations that for a fee would certify users in a particular geographic area.
- *PERSONA:* A PERSONA CA would enable users to obtain a certificate but remain anonymous. A user registered anonymously could make use of PEM security features while concealing his or her identity. Presumably, such a person would also need an anonymous mailbox facility. The CA, in this case, would not be vouching for the identity of the individual. Rather, the CA would have to guarantee that a PERSONA identifier is unique among all PERSONA identifiers certified by this CA.

Figure 9.13 suggests the structure of the Internet certification hierarchy. At the top is the IPRA, which certifies a number of PCAs. Each PCA certifies a number of CAs, each of which certifies users and possibly other CAs. The figure indicates the possibility that a single CA could be certified by more than one PCA. The implica-

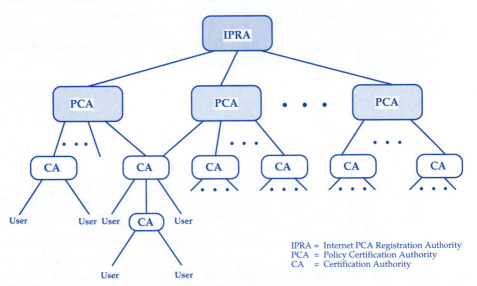

IPRA = Internet PCA Registration Authority
PCA = Policy Certification Authority
CA = Certification Authority

FIGURE 9.13. Internet Certification Hierarchy

tion is that this CA would be prepared to issue certificates under multiple disjoint policies. For example, some users might be certified under a very strong certification policy that would provide high assurance, whereas others might be certified under less stringent policies.

There can be multiple tiers of CAs but only one tier of PCAs and only one IPRA.

Certificate Revocation

In the discussion of X.509, we introduced the concept of certificate revocation. Although every certificate includes an expiration date, there may be occasions when before expiration a user might wish to revoke the certificate and hence the public key in the certificate. Some reasons for this are the following:

1. The user's secret key is assumed to be compromised.
2. The user is no longer certified by this CA.
3. The CA's certificate is assumed to be compromised.

X.509 dictates that each CA must maintain a list of the certificates that it issued that have been revoked, as well as a list of revoked certificates of all other CA's known to the CA. These lists are signed by the CA.

PEM makes use of the same strategy as X.509. The certificate revocation list (CRL) defined in PEM is based on that in X.509, and is illustrated in Figure 9.14. The CRL includes a header with the following fields:

- *Algorithm Identifier:* identifies the algorithm used to sign this list, plus any parameters associated with the algorithm.
- *Issuer:* the CA that signed this list.
- *Last Update:* when this CRL was issued.
- *Next Update:* when the next CRL is scheduled to be issued.

The body of the CRL consists of a sequence of revoked certificates. In fact, each revoked certificate consists simply of the serial number of the certificate and the revocation date. Because serial numbers are unique within a CA, the serial number is sufficient to identify the certificate.

For purposes of PEM, it cannot be assumed that an X.500 Directory will be available to store the CRLs. As an interim approach, the PEM specification calls for the IPRA to provide a robust database facility to hold the CRLs issued by the IPRA, the PCAs, and the CAs. Users may request copies of CRLs by use of a PEM message of type CRL. In addition, the issuing authority may periodically broadcast its CRL via a CRL message to its registered users.

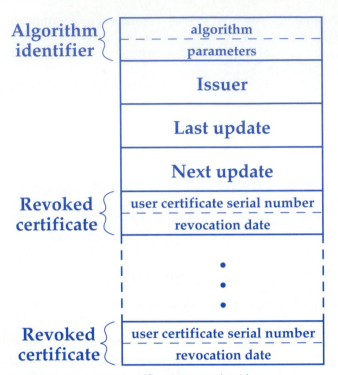

FIGURE 9.14.   PEM Certificate Revocation List

PEM Formats

The PEM specification includes a formal definition of message format using an enhanced version of Backus-Naur Form (BNF), which is defined in RFC 822. Table 9.6 summarizes the key aspects of this notation.

Figure 9.15 shows a top-level definition of message format, and Figure 9.16 provides the detail. Every message begins with a beginning encapsulation boundary and ends with either another beginning encapsulation boundary or an ending encapsulation boundary. In between are the PEM header and the text of the message.

All headers begin with a Proc-Type field, which identifies the type of PEM processing performed on the transmitted message. The first subfield is in effect a version number; the current PEM version is identified as 4. The second subfield identifies the specific processing for this message; options are ENCRYPTED, MIC-ONLY, MIC-CLEAR, and CRL.

For CRL messages, the remainder of the header consists of one or more CRL blocks. Each block includes a CRL and, optionally, the public-key certificate of the issuing CA. Each block also optionally includes a set of additional

TABLE 9.6   Augmented BNF Notation Used in Figures 9.15 and 9.16 (from RFC 822)

- Words in lower case represent variables or rules.
- DIGIT is any decimal digit; CRLF is carriage return, line feed.
- Quotation marks enclose literal text.
- Elements separated by slash ("/") are alternatives.
- Ordinary parentheses are used simply for grouping.
- The character "*" preceding an element indicates repetition. The full form is:

<I>*<J>element

indicating at least I and at most J occurrences of element. *element allows any number, including 0; 1*element requires at least one element; and 1*2element allows 1 or 2 elements; <N>element means exactly N elements.
- Square brackets, "[" "]", enclose optional elements.
- The construct "#" is used to define, with the following form:

<I>#<J>element

indicating at least I and at most J elements, each separated by a comma.
- A semicolon at the right of a rule starts a comment that continues to the end of the line.

```
<pemmsg>  ::=    <preeb>
                 <pemhdr>
                 [CRLF <pemtext>]   ; absent for CRL message
                 <posteb>

<preeb>   ::= "-----BEGIN PRIVACY-ENHANCED MESSAGE-----" CRLF
<posteb>  ::= "-----END PRIVACY-ENHANCED MESSAGE-----" CRLF / <preeb>

<pemtext> ::= <encbinbody>     ; for ENCRYPTED or MIC-ONLY messages
              / *(<text> CRLF)   ; for MIC-CLEAR

<pemhdr>  ::= <normalhdr> / <crlhdr>

<normalhdr> ::=
    <proctype>
    <contentdomain>
    [<dekinfo>]      ; needed if ENCRYPTED
    (1*(<origflds> *<recipflds>))      ; symmetric case; recipflds included for all proc types
    / ((1*<origflds>) *(<recipflds>))   ; asymmetric case; recipflds included for ENCRYPTED proc type

<crlhdr> ::= <proctype>
             1*(<crl> [<cert>] *(<issuercert>))

<origflds> ::= <asymmorig> [<keyinfo>] *(<issuercert>) <micinfo>      ; asymmetric
             / <origid-symm> [<keyinfo>]                             ; symmetric

<recipflds> ::= <recipid> <keyinfo>

<asymmorig> ::= <origid-asymm> / <cert>
```

FIGURE 9.15.   PEM BNF Definition: Top Lever (RFC 1421)

```
<proctype> ::=           "Proc-Type" ":" "4" "," <pemtypes> CRLF
<contentdomain> ::=      "Content-Domain" ":" <contentdescrip> CRLF
<dekinfo> ::=            "DEK-Info" ":" <dekalgid> [ "," <dekparameters> ] CRLF
<symmid> ::=             <IKsubfld> "," [<IKsubfld>] "," [<IKsubfld>]
<asymmid> ::=            <IKsubfld> "," <IKsubfld>
<origid-asymm> ::=       "Originator-ID-Asymmetric" ":" <asymmid> CRLF
<origid-symm> ::=        "Originator-ID-Symmetric" ":" <symmid> CRLF
<recipid> ::=            <recipid-asymm> / <recipid-symm>
<recipid-asymm> ::=      "Recipient-ID-Asymmetric" ":" <asymmid> CRLF
<recipid-symm> ::=       "Recipient-ID-Symmetric" ":" <symmid> CRLF
<cert> ::=               "Originator-Certificate" ":" <encbin> CRLF
<issuercert> ::=         "Issuer-Certificate" ":" <encbin> CRLF
<micinfo> ::=            "MIC-Info" ":" <micalgid> "," <ikalgid> "," <asymsignmic> CRLF
<keyinfo> ::=            "Key-Info" ":" <ikalgid> "," <micalgid> "," <symencdek> ","
                             <symencmic> CRLF                              ; symmetric case
                         / "Key-Info" ":" <ikalgid> "," <asymencdek> CRLF    ; asymmetric case
<crl> ::=                "CRL" ":" <encbin> CRLF


<pemtypes> ::=           "ENCRYPTED" / "MIC-ONLY" / "MIC-CLEAR" / "CRL"


<encbinchar> ::=         ALPHA / DIGIT / "+" / "/" / "="
<encbingrp> ::=          4*4<encbinchar>
<encbin> ::=             1*<encbingrp>
<encbinbody> ::=         *(16*16<encbingrp> CRLF) [1*16<encbingrp> CRLF]
<IKsubfld> ::=           1*<ia-char>
; Note: "," removed from <ia-char> set so that Orig-ID and Recip-ID
; fields can be delimited with commas (not colons) like all other fields
<ia-char> ::=            DIGIT / ALPHA / "'" / "+" / "(" / ")" / "." / "/" / "=" / "?" / "-" / "@" /
                             "%" / "!" / """ / "_" / "<" / ">"
<hexchar> ::=            DIGIT / "A" / "B" / "C" / "D" / "E" / "F"
```

FIGURE 9.16.   PEM BNF Definition: PEM Header Fields (RFC 1421)

certificates that form a certification path. For CRL messages, there is no text body.

The remainder of the message types do carry a text body, and all have the same overall header structure. Following the Proc-Type field is the Content-Domain field, which currently can take on only the value RFC 822. Then, if the message is encrypted, the next header field is the DEK-Info field, which identifies the text encryption algorithm and any necessary associated parameters.

The remainder of the header consists of originator-field blocks and recipient-field blocks. The content and arrangement of these blocks depends on whether the IK is asymmetric or symmetric.

Asymmetric IK

If the IK is asymmetric, then the remainder of the header consists of the following:

- One or more originator-field blocks. Generally, there is only one block per message. An originator may include multiple originator-field blocks if it uses more than one IK to accommodate various recipients. This is followed by:
- Zero or more recipient-field blocks. If the message is not encrypted, then no recipient blocks are needed; the identities of the intended recipients will be carried in the outer mail transport header (e.g., an RFC 822 header for an SMTP mail system). If the message is encrypted, then there is one recipient block per recipient, or mailing list, or both.

An originator-field block is constructed from the following fields:

- *Originator ID:* Consists of an Issuing Authority subfield and a Version/Expiration subfield. This field is present if the Originator Certificate field is absent.
- *Originator Certificate:* Public-key certificate of the originator. This field is present if the Originator Certificate field is absent.
- *Key Information:* Identifies the algorithm used to encrypt the DEK and includes the encrypted DEK. This field is optional and may be included for the originator's own use—for example, to decrypt an error bounce from the mail system or a local copy, effectively allowing the originator to act as a successful individual recipient.
- *Issuer Certificate:* This field is optional; zero or more instances may be present. Each field may contain issuer certificates such that the sequence of fields forms a certification path. Typically, this path ends with the originator certificate present in this block. However, one or more Issuer Certificate fields may be present even if the Originator Certificate field is not present; providing Issuer Certificates helps the recipient get current certificates, and this can be done even if the originator's certificate is not present.
- *MIC-Info:* This field is mandatory and contains the identity of the hash algorithm and the algorithm used to sign the MIC. It also includes the MIC, encrypted with the originator's private key.

A recipient-field block is constructed from the following fields:

- *Recipient ID:* Consists of an Issuing Authority subfield and a Version/Expiration subfield.
- *Key Information:* Identifies the algorithm used to encrypt the DEK and includes the encrypted DEK.

Figure 9.17 shows an example of a PEM message with an asymmetric IK.

```
-----BEGIN PRIVACY-ENHANCED MESSAGE-----
Proc-Type: 4,ENCRYPTED
Content-Domain: RFC822
DEK-Info: DES-CBC,BFF968AA74691AC1
Originator-Certificate:
 MIIB1TCCAScCAWUwDQYJKoZIhvcNAQECBQAwUTELMAkGA1UEBhMCVVMxIDAeBgNV
 BAoTF1JTQSBEYXRhIFNlY3VyaXR5LCBJbmMuMQ8wDQYDVQQLEwZCZXRhIDExDzAN
 BgNVBAsTBk5PVEFSWTAeFw05MTA5MDQxODM4MTdaFw05MzA5MDMxODM4MTZaMEUx
 CzAJBgNVBAYTAlVTMSAwHgYDVQQKExdSU0EgRGF0YSBTZWN1cml0eSwgSW5jLjEU
 MBIGA1UEAxMLVGVzdCBVc2VyIDEwWTAKBgRVCAEBAgICAANLADBIAkEAwHZHl7i+
 yJcqDtjJCowzTdBJrdAiLAnSC+CnnjOJELyuQiBgkGrgIh3j8/x0fM+YrsyF1u3F
 LZPVtzlndhYFJQIDAQABMA0GCSqGSIb3DQEBAgUAA1kACKr0PqphJYw1j+YPtcIq
 iWlFPuN5jJ79Khfg7ASFxskYkEMjRNZV/HZDZQEhtVaU7Jxfzs2wfX5byMp2X3U/
 5XUXGx7qusDgHQGs7Jk9W8CW1fuSWUgN4w==
Key-Info: RSA,
 I3rRIGXUGWAF8js5wCzRTkdhO34PTHdRZY9Tuvm03M+NM7fx6qc5udixps2Lng0+
 wGrtiUm/ovtKdinz6ZQ/aQ==
Issuer-Certificate:
 MIIB3DCCAUgCAQowDQYJKoZIhvcNAQECBQAwTzELMAkGA1UEBhMCVVMxIDAeBgNV
 BAoTF1JTQSBEYXRhIFNlY3VyaXR5LCBJbmMuMQ8wDQYDVQQLEwZCZXRhIDExDTAL
 BgNVBAsTBFRMQ0EwHhcNOTEwOTAxMDgwMDAwWhcNOTIwOTAxMDc1OTU5WjBRMQsw
 CQYDVQQGEwJVUzEgMB4GA1UEChMXUlNBIERhdGEgU2VjdXJpdHksIEluYy4xDzAN
 BgNVBAsTBkJldGEgMTEPMA0GA1UECxMGTk9UQVJZMHAwCgYEVQgBAQICArwDYgAw
 XwJYCsnp6lQCxYykNlODwutF/jMJ3kL+3PjYyHOwk+/9rLg6X65B/LD4bJHtO5XW
 cqAz/7R7XhjYCm0PcqbdzoACZtIlETrKrcJiDYoP+DkZ8k1gCk7hQHpbIwIDAQAB
 MA0GCSqGSIb3DQEBAgUAA38AAICPv4f9Gx/tY4+p+4DB7MV+tKZnvBoy8zgoMGOx
 dD2jMZ/3HsyWKWgSF0eH/AJB3qr9zosG47pyMnTf3aSy2nBO7CMxpUWRBcXUpE+x
 EREZd9++32ofGBIXaialnOgVUn0OzSYgugiQ077nJLDUj0hQehCizEs5wUJ35a5h
MIC-Info: RSA-MD5,RSA,
 UdFJR8u/TIGhfH65ieewe2lOW4tooa3vZCvVNGBZirf/7nrgzWDABz8w9NsXSexv
 AjRFbHoNPzBuxwmOAFeA0HJszL4yBvhG
Recipient-ID-Asymmetric:
 MFExCzAJBgNVBAYTAlVTMSAwHgYDVQQKExdSU0EgRGF0YSBTZWN1cml0eSwgSW5j
 LjEPMA0GA1UECxMGQmV0YSAxMQ8wDQYDVQQLEwZOT1RBUlk=,
 66
Key-Info: RSA,
 O6BS1ww9CTyHPtS3bMLD+L0hejdvX6Qv1HK2ds2sQPEaXhX8EhvVphHYTjwekdWv
 7x0Z3Jx2vTAhOYHMcqqCjA==

 qeWlj/YJ2Uf5ng9yznPbtD0mYloSwIuV9FRYx+gzY+8iXd/NQrXHfi6/MhPfPF3d
 jIqCJAxvld2xgqQimUzoS1a4r7kQQ5c/Iua4LqKeq3ciFzEv/MbZhA==
-----END PRIVACY-ENHANCED MESSAGE-----
```

FIGURE 9.17.   Example of Encapsulated ENCRYPTED Message (Asymmetric Case)

Symmetric IK

If the IK is asymmetric, then the remainder of the header consists of one or more combined blocks, where each combined block consists of one originator-field block followed by zero or more recipient-field blocks. The BNF/822 notation for this structure is:

$$1*(\text{<origflds> }*\text{<recipflds>})$$

An originator-field block is constructed from the following fields:

- *Originator ID:* Consists of an Entity Identifier subfield, an optional Issuing Authority subfield, and an optional Version/Expiration subfield.
- *Key Information:* Identifies the algorithm used to encrypt the DEK and includes the encrypted DEK. This field is optional and may be included for the originator's own use—for example, to decrypt an error bounce from the mail system or a local copy, effectively allowing the originator to act as a successful individual recipient.

A recipient-field block is constructed from the following fields:

- *Recipient ID:* Consists of an Entity Identifier subfield, an optional Issuing Authority subfield, and an optional Version/Expiration subfield.
- *Key Information:* Identifies the algorithm used to encrypt the DEK and includes the encrypted DEK.

The use of multiple combined blocks supports a scenario in which an originator may have multiple identifiers and have set up symmetric IKs with users under these different identifiers.

9.3

PROBLEMS

9.1 PGP makes use of the cipher feedback (CFB) mode of IDEA, whereas most conventional encryption applications (other than key encryption) use the cipher block chaining (CBC) mode. We have

CBC: $C_i = E_K [C_{i-1} \oplus P_i]$; $P_i = C_{i-1} \oplus D_K [C_i]$
CFB: $C_i = P_i \oplus E_K [C_{i-1}]$; $P_i = C_i \oplus E_K [C_{i-1}]$

These two appear to provide equal security. Suggest a reason why PGP uses the CFB mode.

9.2 In the PGP scheme, what is the expected number of session keys generated before a previously created session key is produced?

9.3 In PGP, what is the probability that a user with N public keys will have at least one duplicate key ID?

9.4 The first 16 bits of the 128-bit message digest in a PGP signature are transmitted in the clear.

(a) To what extent does this compromise the security of MD5?

(b) To what extent does it in fact perform its intended function, namely, to help determine if the correct RSA key was used to decrypt the digest?

9.5 In Figure 9.4, each entry in the public-key ring contains an owner trust field that indicates the degree of trust associated with this public-key owner. Why is that not enough? That is, if this owner is trusted and this is supposed to be the owner's public key, why is not that trust enough to permit PGP to use this public key?

9.6 Consider radix-64 conversion as a form of encryption. In this case, there is no key. But suppose that an opponent knew only that some form of substitution algorithm was being used to encrypt English text. How effective would this algorithm be against cryptanalysis?

APPENDIX 9A

DATA COMPRESSION USING ZIP

The current (2.3) version of PGP makes use of a compression package called ZIP, written by Jean-lup Gailly, Mark Adler, and Richard Wales. ZIP is a freeware package written in C that runs as a utility on Unix and some other systems. ZIP is functionally equivalent to PKZIP, a widely available shareware package for MSDOS systems developed by PKWARE, Inc. The ZIP algorithm is perhaps the most commonly used cross-platform compression technique; freeware and shareware versions are available for Macintosh and other systems as well as MSDOS and UNIX systems.

The core of all the ZIP packages is a compression algorithm known as the Lempel-Ziv (LZ) algorithm [ZIV77]. This algorithm is also used in the CCITT modem standard V.42 *bis.*

Whereas the familiar Huffman code makes use of a variable-length code to encode fixed-length input, the LZ algorithm uses a fixed-length code to represent variable-length input. Furthermore, the LZ code is adaptable, with the code assignments changing in response to the changing characteristics of the input. The LZ algorithm is well suited for use in transmitting text via modem.

The LZ algorithm is used to encode character strings. For this purpose, a dictionary of strings, with their codes, is maintained by both transmitter and receiver. When any of the strings in the dictionary appears in the input to the transmitter, the code for that string is substituted; the receiver, when it receives such a code, replaces it with the corresponding string from the dictionary. As transmission occurs, new strings are added to the dictionaries of the transmitter and receiver, and older strings are deleted.

Before describing the algorithm, we define the following quantities, using the notation in the standard:

C_1 = Next available unused codeword
C_2 = Codeword size; the default is 9 bits
N_2 = Maximum size of the dictionary = number of codewords = 2^{C_2}
N_3 = Character size; the default is 8 bits
N_5 = First codeword used to represent a string of more than one character
N_7 = Maximum string length that can be encoded

At any time, the dictionary contains all one-character strings plus some multiple-character strings. By the mechanism by which strings are added to the dictionary, for any multiple-character string in the dictionary, all its leading substrings are also in the dictionary. Thus, if the string MEOW is in the dictionary, with a unique codeword, then the strings MEO and ME are also in the dictionary, each with its own unique codeword.

The dictionary can logically be represented as a set of trees, with each tree having a root corresponding to a character in the alphabet. So, in the default case, there are 256 trees (N_3 = 8 bits). The general representation and a specific example are shown in Figure 9.18. Each tree represents the set of strings in the dictionary that begin with a specific character, and each node represents a particular string, consisting of the characters defined by the path from the root. The trees in Figure 9.18 indicate that the following strings are in the dictionary: A, B, BA, BAG, BAR, BAT, BI, BIN, C, D, DE, DO, and DOG.

The number in parentheses is the codeword for the corresponding string. The codes for the one-character strings are just the ASCII codes for the characters. The first code available for assignment to a multiple-character string is N_5, which in this example is 256. Thus, with a 9-bit code, a total of 256 multiple-character strings can be represented, in addition to the 256 single-character strings.

The LZ algorithm consists of three main ingredients:

- String matching and encoding
- Addition of new strings to the dictionary
- Deletion of old strings from the dictionary

The LZ algorithm will always match the input to the longest matching string in the dictionary. The transmitter partitions the input into strings that are in the dictionary and converts each string into its corresponding codeword. Because all one-character strings are always in the dictionary, all the input can be partitioned into

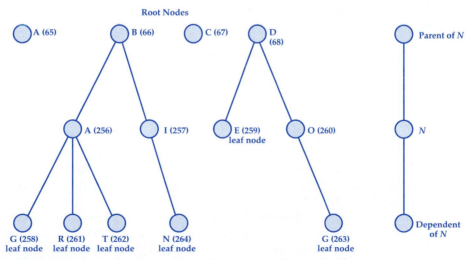

FIGURE 9.18.   Tree-Based Representation of Compression Dictionary

strings in the dictionary. The receiver accepts a stream of codewords and converts each codeword to its corresponding character string.

The algorithm is always seeking to add new strings to the dictionary, replacing older strings, which may not be as likely to appear in the future. The procedure is as follows:

1. Process incoming characters to produce the longest matching string.
2. If the matched string is of maximum length (N_7 characters), then go to step one.
3. Otherwise, append the next character to the matched string and add this string to the dictionary and assign a code to it. However, because this new string does not yet exist in the receiver's dictionary, transmit the code for the original matched string and use the remaining character to begin again at step 1.

The procedure for adding a new string to the dictionary depends on whether the dictionary is full or not. In either case, the transmitter maintains a variable C_1, which is the value of the next available codeword. When the system is initialized, C_1 is initialized to have the value N_5, which is the first value after all one-character strings are assigned values. Thus, in the default, C_1 begins with a value of 256. As long as the dictionary remains empty, as each new string is defined, it is assigned the code value of C_1, and C_1 is incremented by 1.

When the dictionary is full, the following procedure is adopted. As each new string is defined, it is assigned the code value of C_1. Then:

1. C_1 is incremented by 1.
2. If C_1 equals N_2, it is set equal to N_5. That is, once C_1 reaches its maximum value, it cycles back to its minimum value.
3. If the node identified by the value of C_1 is not a leaf node, then go to step 1.
4. If the node is a leaf node, then delete it from the dictionary.

At the end of this procedure, there is room for one new entry in the dictionary, and C_1 is the unused code to be assigned to that entry. The system is now ready to define the next new string for the dictionary.

As an example, assume that the dictionary is in the state of Figure 9.18 and that the next three input characters are BAY. The first character B is read, and the dictionary searched. Because this character is present, the next character A is read and appended, forming the string BA. The dictionary is searched and the string is found. Then Y is appended forming BAY. The dictionary search fails for this string. Y is removed and the string-matching procedure exits with BA as the matched string and Y as the unmatched character.

BA is encoded with the 9-bit binary value of 256 and passed to the control function for transmission. The string BAY is added to the dictionary by appending Y to BA under the B tree. The next available code (265) is assigned to this new string. C_1 is incremented to the value 266.

The character Y is then used to start a new string search.

APPENDIX 9B

RADIX-64 CONVERSION

Both PGP and PEM make use of an encoding technique referred to as radix-64 conversion. This technique maps arbitrary binary input into printable character output. The form of encoding has the following relevant characteristics:

1. The range of the function is a character set that is universally representable at all sites, not a specific binary encoding of that character set. Thus, the characters themselves can be encoded into whatever form is needed by a specific system. For example, the character "E" is represented in an ASCII-based system as hexadecimal 45 and in an EBCDIC-based system as hexadecimal C5.
2. The character set consists of 65 printable characters, one of which is used for padding. With $2^6 = 64$ available characters, each character can be used to represent 6 bits of input.
3. No control characters are included in the set. Thus, a message encoded in radix 64 can traverse mail-handling systems that scan the data stream for control characters.
4. The hyphen character ("-") is not used. This character has significance in the RFC 822 format and should therefore be avoided.

Table 9.7 shows the mapping of 6-bit input values to characters. The character set consists of the alphanumeric characters plus "+" and "/". The "=" character is used as the padding character.

TABLE 9.7   Radix-64 Encoding

6-bit value	Character encoding	6-bit value	Character encoding	6-bit value	Character encoding	6-bit value	Character encoding
0	A	16	Q	32	g	48	w
1	B	17	R	33	h	49	x
2	C	18	S	34	i	50	y
3	D	19	T	35	j	51	z
4	E	20	U	36	k	52	0
5	F	21	V	37	l	53	1
6	G	22	W	38	m	54	2
7	H	23	X	39	n	55	3
8	I	24	Y	40	o	56	4
9	J	25	Z	41	p	57	5
10	K	26	a	42	q	58	6
11	L	27	b	43	r	59	7
12	M	28	c	44	d	60	8
13	N	29	d	45	t	61	9
14	O	30	e	46	u	62	+
15	P	31	f	47	v	63	/
						(pad)	=

Figure 9.19 illustrates the simple mapping scheme. Binary input is processed in blocks of 3 octets, or 24 bits. Each set of 6 bits in the 24-bit block is mapped into a character. In the figure, the characters are shown encoded as 8-bit quantities. In this typical case, each 24-bit input is expanded to 32 bits of output.

One important feature of this mapping is that the least significant 6 bits of the representation of these 65 characters is the same in all commonly used character sets. For example, as was mentioned, "E" in 7-bit ASCII is 0100 0101 and in 8-bit EBCDIC is 1100 0101. The rightmost 6 bits are the same in both cases. Thus, the reverse mapping from radix 64 to binary is simply a matter of extracting the least significant 6 bits of each character.

For example, the sequence "H52Q" in ASCII is:

$$1001000 \quad 0110101 \quad 0110010 \quad 1010001$$

The extracted 6-bit values are 8, 53, 50, 17:

$$001000 \quad 110101 \quad 110010 \quad 010001$$

The resulting 24-bit value can be expressed in hexadecimal as 235CA1.

APPENDIX 9C

PGP RANDOM NUMBER GENERATION

PGP uses a complex and powerful scheme for generating random numbers and pseudorandom numbers for a variety of purposes. PGP generates random numbers from the content and timing of user keystrokes, and pseudorandom numbers using an algorithm based on the one in ANSI X9.17. PGP uses these numbers for the following purposes:

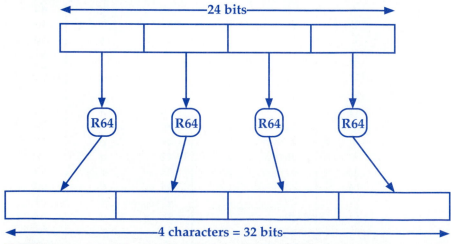

FIGURE 9.19.   Printable Encoding of Binary Data into Radix-64 Format

- True random numbers:
    used to generate RSA key pairs
    provides the initial seed for the pseudorandom number generator
    provides additional input during pseudorandom number generation
- Pseudorandom numbers:
    used to generate session keys
    used to generate initialization vectors (IVs) for use with the session key in
    CFB mode encryption

True Random Numbers

PGP maintains a 256-byte buffer or random bits. Each time PGP expects a key-stroke, it records the time, in 32-bit format, at which it starts waiting. When it receives the keystroke, it records the time the key was pressed and the 8-bit value of the keystroke. The time and keystroke information are used as to generate a key, which is in turn used to encrypt the current value of the random-bit buffe0r.

Pseudorandom Numbers

Pseudorandom numbers use a 24-octet seed and produces a 16-octet session key, an 8-octet initialization vector, and a new seed to be used for the next pseudorandom number generation. The algorithm is based on the X9.17 algorithm described in Chapter 3 (see Figure 3.15) but uses IDEA instead of triple DES for encryption. The algorithm uses the following data structures:

1. Input
    —randseed.bin (24 octets): If this file is empty, it is filled with 24 true random octets.
    —message: The session key and IV that will be used to encrypt a message are themselves a function of that message. This further contributes to the randomness of the key and IV, and if an opponent already knows the plaintext content of the message, there is no apparent need for capturing the one-time session key.
2. Output
    —K (24 octets): The first sixteen octets, K[0..15], contain a session key and the last eight octets, K[16..23], contain an IV.
    —randseed.bin (24 octets): A new seed value is placed in this file.
3. Internal data structures
    —dtbuf (8 octets): The first 4 octets, dtbuf[0..3], are initialized with the current date/time value. This buffer is equivalent to the DT variable in the X9.17 algorithm.
    —rkey (16 octets): IDEA encryption key used at all stages of the algorithm.
    —rseed (8 octets): Equivalent to the X9.17 V_i variable.

—rbuf (8 octets): A pseudorandom number generated by the algorithm. This buffer is equivalent to the X9.17 R_i variable.

—K′ (24 octets): Temporary buffer for the new value of randseed.bin.

The algorithm consists of nine steps, G1 through G9. The first and last steps are obfuscation steps, intended to reduce the value of a captured randseed.bin file to an opponent. The remaining steps are essentially equivalent to three iterations of the X9.17 algorithm and are illustrated in Figure 9.20 (compare Figure 3.15).

The following stepwise description of the algorithm is based on one provided by Stephan Neuhaus {[NEUH93]:

G1. [Prewash previous seed]
    (a) Copy randseed.bin to K[0..23].
    (b) Take the MD5 hash of the message (this has already been generated if the message is being signed; otherwise the first 4K octets of the message are used). Use the result as a key, use a null IV, and encrypt K in CFB mode; store result back in K.

G2. [Set initial seed]
    (a) Set dtbuf[0..3] to the 32-bit local time. Set dtbuf[4..7] to all zeros. Copy rkey ← K[0..15]. Copy rseed ← K[16..23].
    (b) Encrypt the 64-bit dtbuf using the 128-bit rkey in ECB mode; store the result back in dtbuf.

G3. [Prepare to generate random octets] Set rcount ← 0 and k ← 23. The loop of steps G4-G7 will be executed 24 times (k = 23...0), once for each random octet produced and placed in K. The variable rcount is the number of unused random octets in rbuf. It will count down from 8 to 0 three times to generate the 24 octets.

G4. [Bytes available?] If rcount = 0 goto G5 else goto G7. Steps G5 and G6 perform one instance of the X9.17 algorithm to generate a new batch of eight random octets.

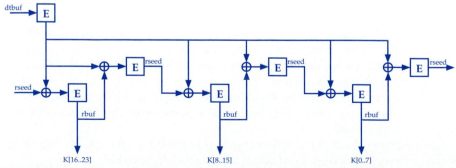

FIGURE 9.20.   PGP Session Key and IV Generation (steps G2 through G8)

G5. [Generate new random octets]
    (a) rseed ← rseed ⊕ dtbuf
    (b) rbuf ← E_{rkey}[rseed]   in ECB mode
G6. [Generate next seed]
    (a) rseed ← rbuf ≈ dtbuf
    (b) rseed ← E_{rkey}[rseed]   in ECB mode
    (c) Set rcount ← 8
G7. [Transfer one byte at a time from rbuf to K]
    (a) Set rcount ← rcount - 1
    (b) Generate a true random byte b, and set K[k] ←
        rbuf[rcount] ⊕ b
G8. [Done?] If k = 0 goto G9 else set k ← k - 1 and goto G4
G9. [Postwash seed and return result]
    (a) Generate 24 more bytes by the method of steps G4–G7,
        except do not XOR in a random byte in G7. Place the
        result in buffer K'
    (b) Encrypt K' with key K[0..15] and IV K[16..23] in CFB
        mode; store result in randseed.bin
    (c) Return K

It should not be possible to determine the session key from the 24 new octets generated in step G9.a. However, to make sure that the stored randseed.bin file provides no information about the most recent session key, the 24 new octets are encrypted and the result is stored as the new seed.

This elaborate algorithm should provide cryptographically strong pseudorandom numbers. A preliminary analysis of the algorithm indicates that there are not internal dependencies among the bits of a single session key and that successive session keys are independent [NEUH93].

CHAPTER 10

NETWORK MANAGEMENT SECURITY

*There is reason to believe that we are at a discontinuity: with respect to computer
security, the past is not a good predictor of the future.*

> — *Computers at Risk: Safe Computing in the Information Age*
> National Research Council, 1991

*Fighting with a large army under your command is nowise different from fighting with
a small one; it is merely a question of instituting signs and signals.*

> — *The Art of War*
> Sun Tzu

Networks and distributed processing systems are of critical and growing importance in business, government, and other organizations. Within a given organization, the trend is toward larger, more complex networks supporting more applications and more users. As these networks grow in scale, two facts become painfully evident:

- The network and its associated resources and distributed applications become indispensable to the organization.
- More things can go wrong, disabling the network or a portion of the network or degrading performance to an unacceptable level.

A large network cannot be put together and managed by human effort alone. The complexity of such a system dictates the use of automated network management tools. If the network includes equipment from multiple vendors, the need for such tools is increased, and the difficulty of supplying such tools is also increased. In response to this need, standards that deal with network management have been developed, covering services, protocols, and management information bases. By far, the most widely used such standard is the Simple Network Management Protocol (SNMP).

Since its publication in 1988, SNMP has found use in a growing number of networks and in increasingly complex environments. As the use of SNMP spread, the importance of providing a security capability as part of network management became increasingly apparent. To provide such capability was one of the principal motivations for the development of version 2 of SNMP in 1993.[1]

This chapter describes the rudimentary security facility available in SNMPv1 and the much more extensive set of security features provided by SNMPv2.

10.1

BASIC CONCEPTS OF SNMP

This section provides an overview of the basic framework for SNMP. For a detailed overall description of SNMPv1 and SNMPv2, see [STAL93].

Network Management Architecture

The model of network management that is used for SNMP includes the following key elements:

- Management station
- Management agent
- Management information base
- Network management protocol

The **management station** is typically a stand-alone device but may be a capability implemented on a shared system. In either case, the management station serves as the interface for the human network manager into the network management system. The management station will have the following, at minimum:

- A set of management applications for data analysis, fault recovery, and so on
- An interface by which the network manager may monitor and control the network
- The capability of translating the network manager's requirements into the actual monitoring and control of remote elements in the network
- A database of information extracted from the MIBs of all the managed entities in the network

Only the last two elements are the subject of SNMP standardization.

The other active element in the network management system is the **management agent.** Key platforms, such as hosts, bridges, routers, and hubs, may be equipped with SNMP so that they may be managed from a management station. The management agent responds to requests for information from a management

---

[1]Version 2 is denoted as SNMPv2. To distinguish the original version from the new version, the original version is now generally referred to as SNMPv1.

station, responds to requests for actions from the management station, and may asynchronously provide the management station with important but unsolicited information.

The means by which resources in the network may be managed is to represent these resources as objects. Each object is essentially a data variable that represents one aspect of the managed agent. The collection of objects is referred to as a **management information base** (MIB). The MIB functions as a collection of access points at the agent for the management station. These objects are standardized across systems of a particular class (e.g., bridges all support the same management objects). A management station performs the monitoring function by retrieving the value of MIB objects. A management station can cause an action to take place at an agent or can change the configuration settings of an agent by modifying the value of specific variables.

The management station and agents are linked by a **network management protocol.** The protocol used for the management of TCP/IP networks is the simple network management protocol (SNMP). This protocol includes the following key capabilities:

- Get: enables the management station to retrieve the value of objects at the agent.
- Set: enables the management station to set the value of objects at the agent.
- Trap: enables an agent to notify the management station of significant events.

There are no specific guidelines in the standards as to the number of management stations or the ratio of management stations to agents. In general, it is prudent to have at least two systems capable of performing the management station function, to provide redundancy in case of failure. The other issue is the practical one of how many agents a single management station can handle. As long as SNMP remains relatively "simple," that number can be quite high, certainly in the hundreds.

Network Management Protocol Architecture

SNMP was designed to be an application-level protocol that is part of the TCP/IP protocol suite. It is intended to operate over the user datagram protocol (UDP). For a stand-alone management station, a manager process controls access to the central MIB at the management station and provides an interface to the network manager. The manager process achieves network management by using SNMP, which is implemented on top of UDP, IP, and the relevant network-dependent protocols (e.g., Ethernet, FDDI, X.25).

Each agent must also implement SNMP, UDP, and IP. In addition, there is an agent process that interprets the SNMP messages and controls the agent's MIB. For an agent device that supports other applications, such as FTP, TCP as well as UDP are required.

Figure 10.1 [BENA90] illustrates the protocol context of SNMP. From a management station, three types of SNMP messages are issued on behalf of a management

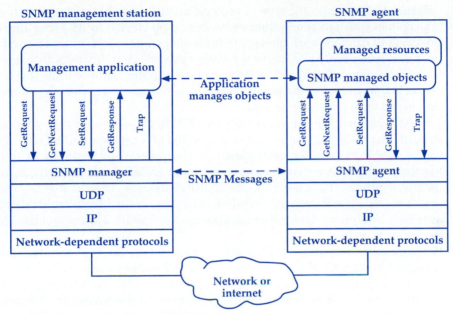

FIGURE 10.1.   The Role of SNMP

application: GetRequest, GetNextRequest, and SetRequest. The first two are variations of the Get function. All three messages are acknowledged by the agent in the form of a GetResponse message, which is passed up to the management application. In addition, an agent may issue a trap message in response to an event that affects the MIB and the underlying managed resources.

Because SNMP relies on UDP, which is a connectionless protocol, SNMP is itself connectionless. No ongoing connections are maintained between a management station and its agents. Instead, each exchange is a separate transaction between a management station and an agent.

Proxies

In SNMPv1 all agents, as well as management stations, must support UDP and IP. This limits direct management to some devices and excludes other devices, such as some bridges and modems, that do not support any part of the TCP/IP protocol suite. Furthermore, there may be numerous small systems (personal computers, workstations, programmable controllers) that do implement TCP/IP to support their applications but for which it is not desirable to add the additional burden of SNMP, agent logic, and MIB maintenance.

To accommodate devices that do not implement SNMPv1, the concept of proxy was developed. In this scheme an SNMP agent acts as a proxy for one or more other devices; that is, the SNMP agent acts on behalf of the proxied devices.

Figure 10.2 indicates the type of protocol architecture that is often involved. The management station sends queries concerning a device to its proxy agent. The proxy agent converts each query into the management protocol that is used by the device. When a reply to a query is received by the agent, it passes that reply back to the management station. Similarly, if an event notification of some sort from the device is transmitted to the proxy, the proxy sends that on to the management station in the form of a trap message.

SNMPv2 allows the use of not only the TCP/IP protocol suite but others as well. In particular SNMPv2 is intended to run on the OSI protocol suite. Thus, SNMPv2 can be used to manage a greater variety of networked configurations. With respect to proxies, any device that does not implement SNMPv2 can be managed only by means of proxy. This even includes SNMPv1 devices. That is, if a device implements the agent software for SNMPv1, it can be reached from an SNMPv2 manager only by a proxy device that implements the SNMPv2 agent and the SNMPv1 manager software.

The cases described in the preceding paragraph are referred to as foreign proxy relationships in SNMPv2. In addition, SNMPv2 supports a native proxy relationship in which the proxied device does support SNMPv2. In this case, an SNMPv2 manager communicates with an SNMPv2 node acting as an agent. This node then turns around and acts as a manager to reach the proxied device, which acts as an SNMPv2 agent. The reason for supporting this type of indirection is to enable users to configure hierarchical, decentralized network management systems, as discussed shortly.

SNMPv2

The strength of SNMP is its simplicity. SNMP provides a basic set of network management tools in a package that is easy to implement and easy to configure. But, as users have come to rely more and more on SNMP to manage ever-expanding net-

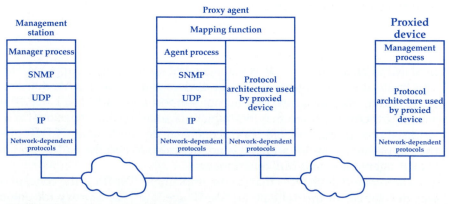

FIGURE 10.2.   Proxy Configuration

works with ever-growing workloads, its deficiencies have become all too apparent. These deficiencies fall into three categories:

- Lack of support for distributed network management
- Functional deficiencies
- Security deficiencies

SNMPv2 was issued in 1993 to correct these deficiencies. In the remainder of this subsection, we briefly summarize the new features provided by SNMPv2 in these three areas. The security features of SNMPv1 and SNMPv2 are examined in detail in Sections 10.2 and 10.3, respectively.

Distributed Network Management

Many users are content, at least for now, with a centralized management model. It is only when the scale of the network becomes truly large that a centralized architecture can introduce performance problems. With a large network and a single management station, there is a great deal of traffic to and from the manager, and there is a tremendous processing burden on that manager.

SNMPv2 readily supports both a highly centralized network management strategy and a distributed one. In the latter case there are multiple managers in the configuration. Figure 10.3 illustrates a hierarchical strategy. A number of "element" managers are responsible for logical or geographical subsets of the total configuration. Each element manager is responsible for the detailed management of its particular area. Above this level are one or more "manager servers," which take a more strategic view of operations. Typically, a manager server will receive summarized information from element managers. In this way, subordinate managers can deal with the fine detail of network management, and superior network managers can take an overall, aggregated approach.

Two features that are new to SNMPv2 provide the support for a decentralized approach. First, SNMPv2 enables one manager to send a confirmed notification to another. Second, SNMPv2 includes a manager-to-manager (M2M) MIB, whose use is described next.

As the name implies, the M2M MIB is intended to support communication between two managers, typically a superior and a subordinate manager. The MIB consists of two groups of objects:

- *Alarm group:* A collection of objects that allows the description and configuration of alarms based on thresholds.
- *Event group:* A collection of objects that allows the description and configuration of events.

These two groups provide a simple but powerful general-purpose tool for working with events. Using the alarm group, it is possible to configure a manager or an agent to monitor any object in any MIB and to generate a notification to a manager when the value of that object crosses a threshold. The event group defines the format and timing of notifications to be sent to a manager. A notification may be trig-

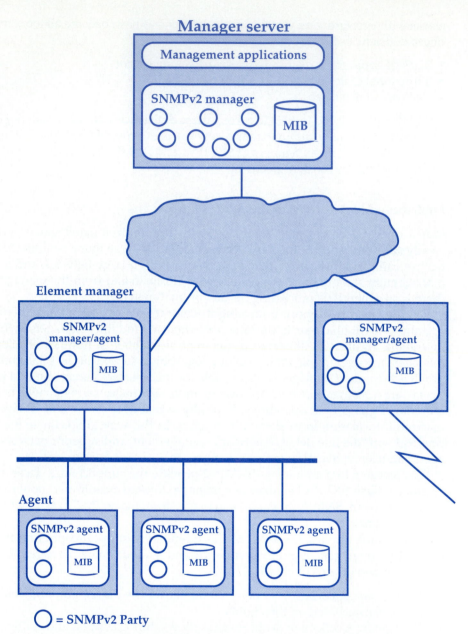

FIGURE 10.3.   Distributed Network Management Architecture

gered by a threshold crossing in the alarm group or by some other defined event, such as a line failure.

The combination of the event and alarm groups provides a useful tool for network management. For example, if the rate of packets with errors on a line crosses a threshold, this may indicate a fault on that line. If the volume of traffic on a LAN exceeds a threshold, this alerts the management station that response time may degrade unless the load is stabilized.

Functional Enhancements

Table 10.1 suggests the functional enhancements that have been made in SNMPv2. Both protocols are defined in terms of a set of commands. In the case of SNMPv1, there are five commands. The Get command is issued by a manager to an agent to retrieve values of objects in the MIB. The GetNext command exploits the fact that objects in a MIB are arranged in a tree structure. When an object is named in a GetNext command, the agent finds the next object in the tree and returns its value. GetNext is useful because it allows a manager to "walk" a tree at an agent when it does not know the exact set of objects supported by that agent. The Set command enables a manager to update values at an agent; it is also used for creating and deleting rows in tables. The Response command is used by an agent to respond to a manager command. Finally, the Trap command enables an agent to send information to a manager without waiting for a management request. For example, an agent could be configured to send a Trap when a link fails or when traffic exceeds a threshold.

SNMPv2 includes all the commands found in SNMPv1, plus two new ones. The most important of these is the Inform command. This command is sent by one management station to another and like the trap includes information relating to conditions or events at the sender. The advantage of the Inform command is that

TABLE 10.1   Simple Network Management Commands

Command	Description	Direction	SNMPv1	SNMPv2
Get	For each object listed in command, return value of that object.	Manager to agent	✔	✔
GetNext	For each object listed in command, return value of next object in MIB.	Manager to agent	✔	✔
GetBulk	For each object listed in command, return value of next N objects in MIB.	Manager to agent		✔
Set	For each object listed in command, assign corresponding value listed in command.	Manager to agent	✔	✔
Trap	Transmit unsolicited information.	Agent to manager	✔	✔
Inform	Transmit unsolicited information.	Manager to manager		✔
Response	Respond to manager request.	Agent to manager	✔	✔

it can be used to construct a configuration in which multiple managers cooperate to share management responsibility in a large network.

The other new command, GetBulk, allows a manager to retrieve a large block of data at one time. In particular, the GetBulk command is designed for the transmission of entire tables with one command.

A final significant difference: the Get command is atomic in the case of SNMPv1 but not in the case of SNMPv2. If an SNMPv1 command contains a list of objects for which values are requested, and at least one of the objects does not exist at the agent, then the entire command is rejected. For SNMPv2, partial results may be returned. The nonatomic Get command allows for more efficient use of network capacity by the manager.

Security Enhancements

Perhaps the most glaring deficiency in SNMPv1 is the lack of security. SNMPv1 provides no effective way to prevent a third party from observing the traffic between a manager and an agent. Worse, no effective way exists to prevent an unauthorized third party from acting as a manager and performing Get and Set operations at an agent. As a result, many SNMPv1 users simply disable the Set function. This reduces SNMP to a network monitoring facility, with no capability to fine-tune the system, set parameters, or alter configurations.

To overcome these threats, SNMPv2 adds the security features listed in Table 10.2. Security is based on the concept of "party." Each manager and each agent has at least one party and may have multiple parties in order to establish multiple security relationships. Between any given pair of parties, an authentication code may be used to assure the receiver of the identity of the sender. Also, between any given pair of parties, encryption may be used to protect transmissions from eavesdropping.

TABLE 10.2   Simple Network Management Security Features

Feature	Description	SNMPv1	SNMPv2
Authentication	A procedure that allows receiving party to verify that a message is from the alleged source and that the message is timely. Authentication is achieved by appending a secret code to the message.		✔
Privacy	The protection of transmitted data from eavesdropping. Privacy is achieved by encrypting SNMP messages.		✔
Access Control	Restricts manager's access to a specified portion of a MIB and to a specified subset of commands.	✔	✔

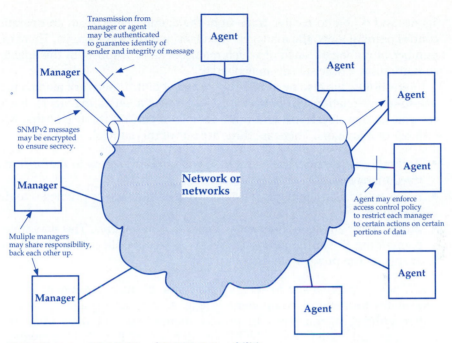

FIGURE 10.4. Highlights of SNMPv2 Capabilities

Finally, as with SNMPv1, SNMPv2 includes access control mechanisms that can be used to restrict access by a manager party to certain portions of an MIB and to certain commands.

Figure 10.4 illustrates the key capabilities of SNMPv2.

10.2

SNMPv1 COMMUNITY FACILITY

SNMPv1, as defined in RFC 1157, provides only a rudimentary security facility based on the concept of community.

Communities and Community Names

Like other distributed applications, network management involves the interaction of a number of application entities supported by an application protocol. In the case of SNMP network management, the application entities are the manager applications and the agent applications that use SNMP.

SNMP network management has several characteristics not typical of all distributed applications. The application involves a one-to-many relationship between a manager and a set of agents: The manager is able to Get and Set objects in the agents and is able to receive traps from the agents. Thus, from an operational or control point of view, the manager "manages" a number of agents. There may be a number of managers, each of which manages all or a subset of the agents in the configuration. These subsets may overlap.

Interestingly, we also need to be able to view SNMP network management as a one-to-many relationship between an agent and a set of managers. Each agent controls its own local MIB and must be able to control the use of that MIB by a number of managers. There are three aspects of this control:

- *Authentication service:* The agent may wish to limit access to the MIB to authorized managers.
- *Access policy:* The agent may wish to give different access privileges to different managers.
- *Proxy service:* An agent may act as proxy to other agents. This may involve implementing the authentication service, or access policy, or both for the other agents on the proxy system.

All these aspects relate to security concerns. In an environment in which responsibility for network components is split, such as among a number of administrative entities, agents need to protect themselves and their MIBs from unwanted/unauthorized access. SNMP, as defined in RFC 1157, provides only a primitive and limited capability for such security, namely, the concept of a community.

An **SNMP community** is a relationship between an SNMP agent and a set of SNMP managers that defines authentication, access control, and proxy characteristics. The community concept is a local one, defined at the agent. The agent establishes one community for each desired combination of authentication, access control, and proxy characteristics. Each community is given a unique (within this agent) community name, and the managers within that community are provided with and must employ the community name in all Get and Set operations. The agent may establish a number of communities, with overlapping manager membership.

Because communities are defined locally at the agent, the same name may be used by different agents. This identity of names is irrelevant and does not indicate any similarity between the defined communities. Thus, a manager must keep track of the community name or names that are associated with each of the agents that it wishes to access.

Authentication Service

The purpose of the SNMPv1 authentication service is to assure the recipient that an SNMPv1 message is from the source that it claims to be from. SNMPv1 provides for only a trivial scheme for authentication. Every message (Get or Set request) from a manager to an agent includes a community name. This name functions as a password, and the message is assumed to be authentic if the sender knows the password.

With this limited form of authentication, many network managers will be reluctant to allow anything other than network monitoring—that is, get and trap operations. Network control, via a Set operation, is clearly a more sensitive area. The community name could be used to trigger an authentication procedure, with the name functioning simply as an initial password screening device. The authentication procedure could involve the use of encryption/decryption for more secure authentication functions. This is beyond the scope of RFC 1157.

Access Policy

By defining a community, an agent limits access to its MIB to a selected set of managers. By the use of more than one community, the agent can provide different categories of MIB access to different managers. There are two aspects to this access control:

- *SNMP MIB View:* A subset of the objects within an MIB. Different MIB views may be defined for each community. The set of objects in a view need not belong to a single subtree of the MIB.
- *SNMP Access Mode:* An element of the set {READ-ONLY, READ-WRITE}. An access mode is defined for each community.

The combination of an MIB view and an access mode is referred to as an **SNMP community profile.** Thus, a community profile consists of a defined subset of the MIB at the agent, plus an access mode for those objects. The SNMP access mode is applied uniformly to all the objects in the MIB view. Thus, if the access mode READ-ONLY is selected, it applies to all the objects in the view and limits managers' access to this view to read-only operations.

A community profile is associated with each community defined by an agent; the combination of an SNMP community and an SNMP community profile is referred to as an **SNMP access policy.** Figure 10.5 illustrates the various concepts just introduced.

Proxy Service

The community concept is also useful in supporting the proxy service. Recall that a proxy is an SNMP agent that acts on behalf of other devices. Typically, the other devices are foreign, in the sense that they do not support TCP/IP and SNMP. In some cases, the proxied system may support SNMP, but the proxy is used to minimize the interaction between the proxied device and network management systems.

For each device that the proxy system represents, it maintains an SNMP access policy. Thus, the proxy knows which MIB objects can be used to manage the proxied system (the MIB view) and their access mode.

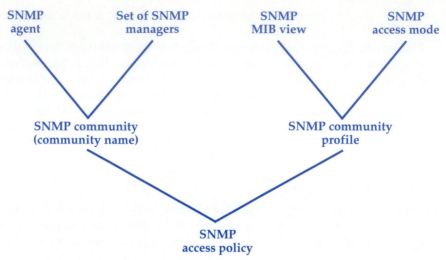

FIGURE 10.5.   Administrative Concepts

10.3

SNMPv2 SECURITY FACILITY

The SNMPv2 security facility is defined in the following documents:

- RFC 1445: Administrative Model for version 2 of the Simple Network Management Protocol (SNMPv2). Presents an elaboration of the SNMP administrative model. This model provides a unified conceptual basis for administering SNMP protocol entities to support authentication and integrity, privacy, access control, and the cooperation of multiple protocol entities.
- RFC 1446: Security Protocols for version 2 of the Simple Network Management Protocol (SNMPv2). Defines protocols to support three data security services: (1) data integrity, (2) data origin authentication, and (3) data confidentiality.
- RFC 1447: Party MIB for version 2 of the Simple Network Management Protocol (SNMPv2). Defines a portion of the Management Information Base (MIB) for use with network management protocols in TCP/IP-based internets. It describes a representation of the SNMP parties as objects, consistent with the SNMP security protocols.

Threats Addressed by SNMPv2

The SNMPv2 security facility is designed to secure SNMPv2 exchanges against the following threats:

- *Disclosure:* An opponent may observe exchanges between a manager and an agent and thereby learn the values of managed objects and learn of notifiable events. For example, the observation of a set command that changes passwords would enable an opponent to learn the new passwords.

- *Masquerade:* Management operations that are not authorized for some entity may be attempted by that entity by assuming the identity of an authorized entity.
- *Message content modification:* An opponent may alter an in-transit message generated by an authorized entity in such a way as to effect unauthorized management operations, including the setting of object values. The essence of this threat is that an unauthorized entity could change any management parameter, including those related to configuration, operations, and accounting.
- *Message sequence and timing modification:* SNMP messages could be reordered, delayed, or replayed (duplicated) to effect unauthorized management operations. For example, a message to reboot a device could be copied and replayed later.

SNMPv2 does not address the following threats:

- *Denial of service:* An opponent may prevent exchanges between a manager and an agent.
- *Traffic analysis:* An opponent may observe the general pattern of traffic between managers and agents.

The lack of a counter to the denial-of-service threat may be justified on two grounds: First, denial-of-service attacks are in many cases indistinguishable from the type of network failures with which any viable network management application must cope as a matter of course; and second, a denial-of-service attack is likely to disrupt all types of exchanges and is a matter for an overall security facility, not one embedded in a network management protocol. Finally, it was simply felt not to be worth the effort to guard against traffic-analysis attacks.

SNMPv2 Services

With the foregoing threats in mind, we begin with a brief overview of the services offered by SNMPv2. SNMPv2 is designed to provide, in essence, three security-related services: privacy, authentication, and access control.

Privacy is the protection of transmitted data from eavesdropping or wiretapping. Privacy requires that the contents of any message be disguised in such a way that only the intended recipient can recover the original message.

A message, file, document, or other collection of data is said to be authentic when it is genuine and came from its alleged source. Message **authentication** is a procedure that allows communicating parties to verify that received messages are authentic. The two important aspects are to verify that the contents of the message have not been altered and that the source is authentic. We also wish to verify a message's timeliness (it has not been artificially delayed and replayed) and sequence relative to other messages flowing between two parties.

In the context of network management, the purpose of **access control** is to ensure that only authorized users have access to a particular management information base and that access to and modification of a particular portion of data are limited to authorized individuals and programs.

Before examining these three services, we need to introduce the concept of party and look at the message structure for SNMPv2.

SNMPv2 Parties

For secure communication, it is essential to identify specifically a source and a destination for any exchange. Authentication depends on the source: It is the responsibility of the source to include information in any message that assures that the origin is authentic, and it is the responsibility of the source to perform the required functions to ensure message integrity. However, message privacy, which is achieved by encryption, depends on the destination. That is, encryption must be done in such a way that only the intended destination can perform the decryption. Finally, access control depends on both source and destination. That is, each destination may have a distinct access policy for each potential source.

Thus, each message must identify both the source and destination. Furthermore, it is insufficient to equate the source with a sending SNMPv2 entity and the destination with a receiving SNMPv2 entity. Each SNMPv2 entity may behave differently from a security point of view, depending not only on the identity of the other SNMPv2 entity involved in an exchange but also on the network management application being carried out. Put another way, the role of a SNMPv2 entity depends on the context of its operation. The concept of role is captured in SNMPv2 as the SNMPv2 **party.** Any protocol entity may include multiple party identities.

The way in which parties are handled is as follows. Each SNMPv2 entity maintains a database with information that represents all SNMPv2 parties known to it, including the following:

- *Local parties:* The set of parties whose operation is realized by the local SNMPv2 entity; that is, the set of "roles" for this SNMPv2 entity.
- *Proxied parties:* The set of parties for proxied entities that this SNMPv2 entity represents.
- *Remote parties:* The set of parties whose operation is realized by other SNMPv2 entities with which this SNMPv2 entity is capable of interacting.

The way in which parties are used to support security services should become clear as the discussion proceeds.

Message Format

In SNMPv2, information is exchanged between a manager and an agent or between two managers in the form of a message. Each message includes a message header, which contains security-related information, and one of a number of types of protocol data units. The message structure is depicted in Figure 10.6 [STAL 93].

The header consists of five fields. The **srcParty** identifies the party at a manager or agent that is sending this message. The **dstParty** identifies the party at an agent or manager to whom the message is sent. The **context** may indicate that this exchange relates to an access to a MIB local to the agent; in this case, the context value serves to identify a subset of the agent's MIB, known as an MIB view. Otherwise, the context value indicates that this exchange involves access to a third system by means of a proxy relationship; in this case, the context value serves to identify the proxied device and the access control privileges associated with accessing that proxied device. In either case, the combination of source party, destination party, and context value are used to determine the access control privileges for this exchange. The **authInfo** field contains information relevant to the authentication protocol. The **privDst** field repeats the identifier of the destination party, as will be explained.

The PDU field contains one of the commands listed in Table 10.1, together with the appropriate parameters for that command.

If the message is nonsecure (not authenticated and not private) then the authInfo field consists of an ASN.1 (Abstract Syntax Notation One) encoding of an octet string of zero length. If the message is authenticated but not private, then the authInfo field contains information needed for authentication.

When privacy is provided, the entire message, including header and PDU but excluding the privDst field, is encrypted. The privDst field must remain unen-

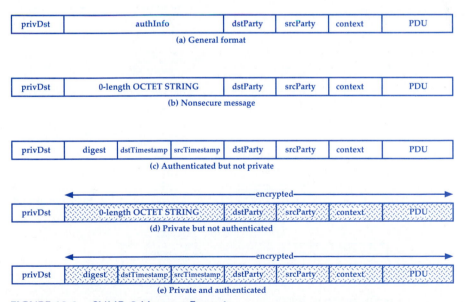

FIGURE 10.6.   SNMPv2 Message Formats

crypted so that the destination SNMPv2 entity can determine the destination party and therefore determine the privacy characteristics of the message.

Figure 10.7a shows the general procedure for message transmission: Authentication is performed first, if needed, followed by encryption, if needed. Figure 10.7b shows the general procedure for message reception. If the message is encrypted, decryption is performed first. Then, if the message is authenticated, the receiver performs the appropriate authentication algorithm. Finally, access control is performed to determine if the source party is authorized to perform the requested management operation for this context and destination party.

Privacy

For each party known to an SNMPv2 entity, the party database contains three variables whose significance is specific to the privacy protocol:

- *partyPrivProtocol:* Indicates the privacy protocol and mechanism by which all messages received by this party are protected from disclosure. The value noPriv indicates that messages received by this party are not protected from disclosure.
- *partyPrivPrivate:* A secret value needed to support the privacy protocol. It may be a conventional-encryption key or the private key in a public-key encryption scheme.

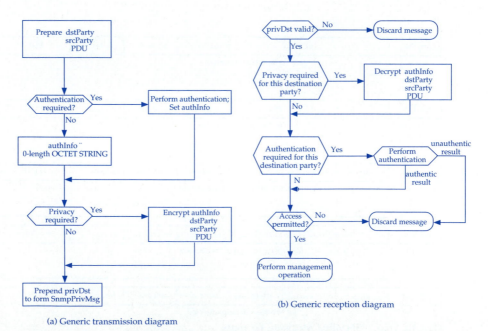

(a) Generic transmission diagram

(b) Generic reception diagram

FIGURE 10.7.   Transmission and Reception of SNMPv2 Messages

- *partyPrivPublic:* Represents any public value that may be needed to support the privacy protocol. It may be a public key in a public-key encryption scheme.

The specific privacy mechanism chosen for the current version of SNMPv2 is conventional encryption using DES, which requires that the source and destination parties share the same encryption key. It provides for protection from disclosure of a received message (i.e., only the intended recipient, and the sender, are able to read the message). The database structure, however, allows for the use of other conventional encryption schemes as well as public-key encryption schemes.

Authentication

For each party known to an SNMPv2 entity, the party database contains five variables whose significance is specific to the authentication protocol:

- *partyAuthProtocol:* Indicates the authentication protocol and mechanism used by this party to authenticate the origin and integrity of its outgoing messages. The value noAuth indicates that messages generated by this party are not authenticated.
- *partyAuthClock:* Represents a current time as kept locally for this party.
- *partyAuthPrivate:* A secret value needed to support the authentication protocol. It may be a secret value used in a message digest, a conventional-encryption key, or the private key in a public-key encryption scheme.
- *partyAuthPublic:* Represents any public value that may be needed to support the authentication protocol. It may be a public key in a public-key encryption scheme.
- *partyAuthLifetime:* An administrative upper bound on acceptable delivery delay for messages generated by this party.

The specific authentication mechanism chosen for the current version of SNMPv2 is the MD5 digest authentication protocol. It provides for the verification of the integrity of a received message (i.e., the message received is the message sent), for authentication of the origin of the message and for the timeliness of message delivery.

In essence, the authentication procedure is as follows. A message digest is computed over the message to be sent prefixed by a secret value, using the MD5 message algorithm described in Chapter 7. The message, plus the message digest (but not the secret value), is transmitted. On reception, the message digest is recomputed using the incoming message and a local copy of the secret value. If the incoming message digest matches the calculated message digest, the received message is declared authentic. The use of the message digest guarantees integrity, and the use of a secret value guarantees origin authentication.

Message Transmission

We now turn to the details of the authentication protocol, considering first transmission. To support authentication, the message header in a transmitted SNMPv2 message includes an authentication-information field, which consists of three components:

- *authDigest:* The digest computed over an appropriate portion of the message, plus the secret value (partyAuthPrivate).
- *authSrcTimestamp:* The time of generation of this message according to the partyAuthClock of the SNMPv2 party that is the source party. The granularity of the clock and therefore of this timestamp is one second.
- *authDstTimestamp:* The time of generation of this message according to the partyAuthClock of the SNMPv2 party that is the destination party. Note that this is the value of the destination party clock stored at the source SNMPv2 entity.

Now suppose that a message is to be sent from party a on one system to party b on another, using a specific context. The message carries a protocol data unit (PDU) representing one of the SNMPv2 commands. Assume that both authentication and privacy are called for. The message is prepared for transmission in the following way (Figure 10.8):

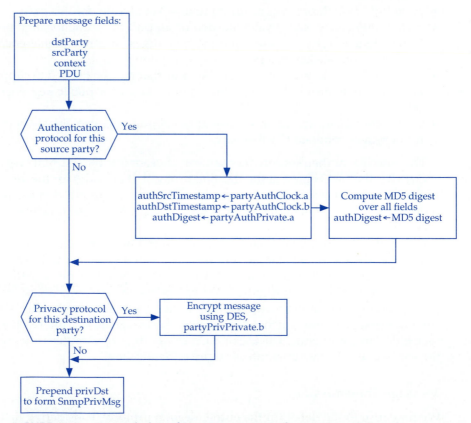

FIGURE 10.8.   **Transmission of SNMPv2 Message (from Party a to Party b)**

1. The fields dstParty, srcParty, context, and PDU are assigned the appropriate values.
2. The three subfields of the authInfo field are assigned values as follows: The srcTimestamp field is assigned the current value of party a's clock (as stored locally); the dstTimestamp field is assigned the current value of party b's clock (as stored locally); and the digest field is temporarily assigned the secret authentication value of party a.
3. The MD5 digest is calculated over authInfo, dstParty, srcParty, context, and PDU, and it is then placed in the digest field. Because the digest is calculated over a block that includes a secret value, and that secret value is not transmitted, the message is secure against modification.
4. The entire block (authInfo, dstParty, srcParty, context, PDU) is encrypted using DES and the secret encryption key shared with party b.
5. The field privDst is assigned the same value as the unencrypted dstParty and prepended to the encrypted block to form the entire message. The field privDst must be sent in the clear so that the receiving manager or agent can determine the destination party and therefore be able to decrypt the remainder of the message.

Message Reception

The procedure followed at the receiving end is more complex because various error-checking functions must be performed. Figure 10.9 summarizes the steps taken for a message from party a intended for party b. Again, we assume that both authentication and privacy are called for.

1. The recipient checks the incoming value of privDst to determine if this is a known local party. If not, the message is discarded.
2. The remainder of the message is decrypted using the secret key associated with this destination party.
3. Next some basic error checks are performed. The message must be in the proper syntactic format. The decrypted value of dstParty must match privDst. And srcParty must refer to a known nonlocal party. If any test is failed, the message is discarded.
4. If the authSrcTimestamp value does not satisfy the criterion for timeliness, the message is rejected. The timeliness criterion states that the message must be received within a reasonable period of time—that is, that it does not exceed an administratively set value. This criterion can be expressed as follows. A message is timely if:

$$\text{partyAuthClock.a} - \text{authSrcTimestamp} \leq \text{partyAuthLifetime.a}$$

Put another way, the age of the message at the time of receipt must be less than the maximum allowable lifetime.

5. The authDigest value is extracted and temporarily stored. The authDigest value is temporarily set to the secret value. The message digest is computed over the

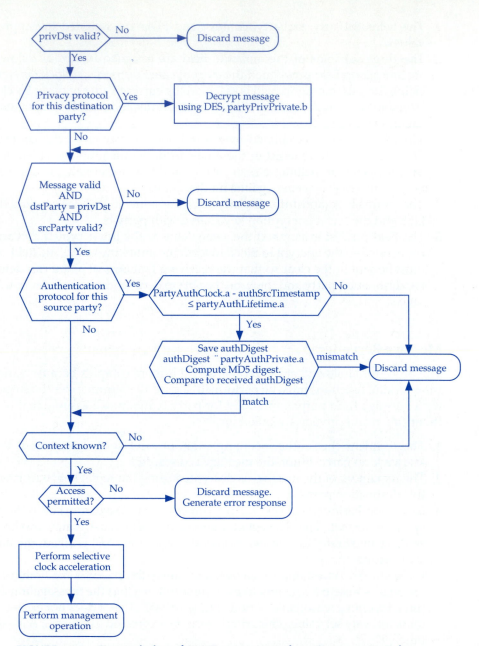

FIGURE 10.9.   Transmission of SNMPv2 Message (from Party a to Party b)

entire message (except privDst), plus the secret value (partyAuthPrivate) and compared to the value that was stored (the value that arrived in the incoming message). If the two values match, the message is accepted as authentic.

6. If the context referenced in the message header is unknown, the message is discarded.

7. The local database is consulted to determine if access privileges permit the requested operation. If not, the message is discarded and an error response is generated and sent to party a. If access is permitted, a clock synchronization function is performed (as described below) and the command specified in the PDU is executed.

Authentication Timeliness Requirement

It is important to realize that the generation of a message depends on the values associated with the source party that are stored by the sending SNMPv2 entity, where the source party resides, whereas the authentication of the message at the destination depends on the party values *for the source party* that are stored at the receiving SNMPv2 entity, where the destination party resides. The values in the two instances may therefore differ. In particular, there may be a discrepancy between the clock value associated with the sending party at the sending entity and the clock value associated with the sending party at the receiving entity. This discrepancy complicates the task of determining message timeliness.

The relationship among partyAuthClock, partyAuthLifetime, and authSrcTime stamp is illustrated in Figure 10.10. Part (a) of the figure shows the relationship that exists for a message that is authentic in terms of timeliness. When the message is sent, it is stamped with the time from the sending party's clock. To be timely, the message must arrive within a time equal to partyAuthLifetime.a (the value of partyAuthLifetime associated with party a). When the message is received, the receiving entity compares its current value of partyAuthClock.a with the outer time limit for this message (authTimestamp + partyAuthLifetime.a) and accepts the message as being timely if the clock value is less than the time limit.

Figure 10.10b shows the case of an unauthentic message. In this case, according to the value of partyAuthClock.a stored at the receiving end, the message has arrived after the time limit.

Figure 10.10c illustrates the fact that the timestamp of the incoming message may actually exceed the current value of partyAuthClock for the sending party as maintained at the destination. From a logical point of view this indicates that a message arrives "before" it is sent. Of course, this logical impossibility is due to a mismatch in clocks.

The lifetime value for a party should be chosen to be as small as possible given the accuracy of the clocks involved, round-trip communication delays, and the frequency with which clocks are synchronized. If the lifetime value is set too small, authentic messages will be rejected as unauthentic. On the other hand, a large lifetime increases the vulnerability to malicious delays of messages.

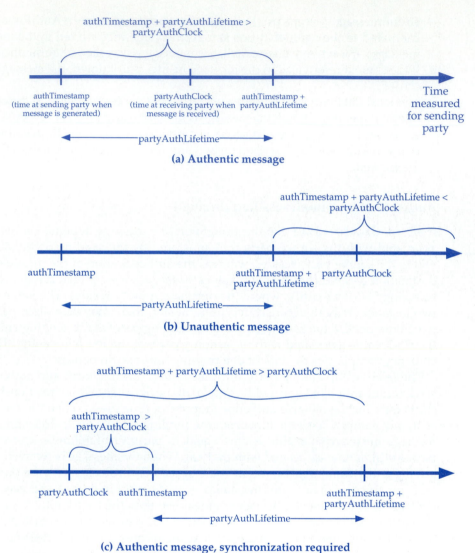

(a) Authentic message

(b) Unauthentic message

(c) Authentic message, synchronization required

FIGURE 10.10.   Authentication Timeliness Requirement

Clock Synchronization

When a message is transmitted, it includes the value of both the sending and receiving party clocks. Upon message reception, authentication depends on the timeliness of the message with reference to the source timestamp.

When a party is first configured, its clock is set to zero. The clock then increments once per second. There are, however, two versions of a party's clock: one stored with the party information at the management station and one stored with the party information at the agent. Thus, there is the potential for drift between the two versions, which could adversely affect authentication.

To compensate for clock drift, a clock synchronization function is performed every time a message is received. The general strategy is to advance a locally held clock if it is behind. Because each message includes two timestamps, the receiver synchronizes its version of both the source and destination party clocks (Figure 10.11).

For any pair of parties, four possible conditions can occur that require correction:

1. The manager's version of the agent's clock is greater than the agent's version of the agent's clock. This creates the risk of a false rejection of a message from the agent to the manager.
2. The manager's version of the manager's clock is greater than the agent's version of the manager's clock. This creates the risk of a false acceptance of a message from the manager to the agent.
3. The agent's version of the agent's clock is greater than the manager's version of the agent's clock. This creates the risk of a false acceptance of a message from the agent to the manager.
4. The agent's version of the manager's clock is greater than the manager's version of the manager's clock. This creates the risk of a false rejection of a message from the manager to the agent.

Now, let us consider the case in which an agent receives a message from a manager. If the authSrcTimestamp in the message exceeds the agent's value of partyAuthClock for the sending manager party, that clock is advanced and condition 2 is corrected. If the authDstTimestamp in the message exceeds the agent's value of partyAuthClock for the receiving agent party, the clock is advanced and

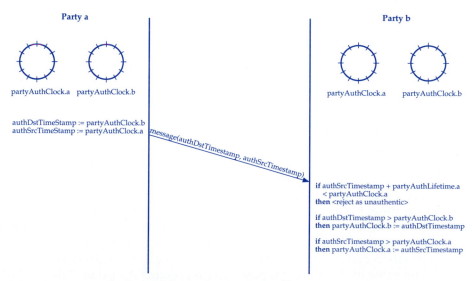

FIGURE 10.11.   Selective Clock Acceleration in SNMPv2

condition 1 is corrected. To complete this line of reasoning, consider the case in which a manager receives a message from an agent. If the authSrcTimestamp in the message exceeds the agent's value of partyAuthClock for the sending agent party, the clock is advanced and condition 3 is corrected. If the authDstTimestamp in the message exceeds the agent's value of partyAuthClock for the receiving manager party, the clock is advanced and condition 4 is corrected.

At first glance, the effects of these clock updates appear to eliminate the need for explicit, manager-directed clock synchronization, because all four clock skew conditions are corrected when messages are exchanged. However, in most cases of manager/agent interaction, the interaction is in the form of a manager request and an agent response. It is intended that a trap message, which originates at the agent, is to be used sparingly. If there has been a considerable lapse of time between requests from a particular manager party to a particular agent party, then clock drift may have created condition 4 with a substantial difference in the two clock values. The result is that any request by the manager will be rejected. Accordingly, it remains necessary for the manager to perform clock synchronization on all manager party clocks, but it is not necessary to synchronize agent party clocks. For this purpose, the manager periodically retrieves the manager party clock values from agents and advances its own clocks as necessary.

Access Control

An access control policy has four elements:

- *Destination party:* An SNMP party performing management operations as requested by the source party.
- *Source party:* An SNMP party that requests that management operations be performed by the destination party.
- *Resources:* The management information on which requested management operations may be performed, expressed as a local MIB view or a proxy relationship; this entry is referred to as a context.
- *Privileges:* The allowable operations, defined in terms of allowable protocol data units (PDUs), that pertain to a particular context and that the target is authorized to perform on behalf of the subject.

Thus, the access control policy is determined by three parameters. A source party requests a management operation of a destination party and identifies the context of the request. The context may specify an MIB view local to the destination party or may specify a remote proxied entity. For a given pair of source/destination parties, there may be multiple access control policies, one for each context. The context is communicated by the source to the destination in the SNMPv2 message header. This approach eliminates the necessity of defining a unique source/destination party pair for every access control policy, and it enables a single destination party to perform in a variety of contexts for a given source party.

The value of the privileges parameter represents the list of SNMPv2 PDUs that may be sent from the source to the destination. The parameter is encoded by assigning an integer value that is a power of 2 to each PDU. The assignments are:

Get	1
GetNext	2
Response	4
Set	8
— unused	16
Get-Bulk:	32
Inform	64
SNMPv2-Trap	128

Access control is determined by information in the Party MIB. This MIB consists of four tables: party table, context table, access control table, and MIB view table (Table 10.3). The best way to describe the function of these tables for access control is to consider their use during message transmission.

Consider that a message is sent from a manager to an agent. The message header includes the fields srcParty, dstParty, and context. The party table at the agent contains information about each local and remote party known to the agent.

TABLE 10.3   SNMPv2 Party MIB

(a) Party Table

Object	Description
partyIdentity	Unique identifier of a party.
partyIndex	A unique integer value associated with a party.
partyTDomain	The transport service used to support SNMPv2.
partyTAddr	The transport address of this party.
partyMaxMessageSize	The maximum message length in octets that this party will accept.
partyLocal	A Boolean value that indicates whether this party is local to this agent or manager.
partyAuthProtocol	Indicates the mechanism used by this party to authenticate the origin and integrity of its outgoing messages. The value noAuth signifies that messages generated by this party are not authenticated.
partyAuthClock	The local notion of the current time for this party.
partyAuthPrivate	A secret value used to support the authentication protocol.
partyAuthPublic	A public value, if needed, used to support the authentication protocol.
partyAuthLifetime	The upper bound on the acceptable delivery delay for messages generated by this party.
partyPrivProtocol	Indicates the mechanism by which messages received by this party are protected from disclosure. The value noPriv signifies that messages received by this party are not protected from disclosure.
partyPrivPrivate	A secret value used to support the privacy protocol.
partyPrivPublic	A public value, if needed, used to support the privacy protocol.
partyCloneFrom	Identity of a party from which authentication and privacy parameters are to be copied in creating this entry.

TABLE 10.3 SNMPV2 PARTY MIB (Continued)

(b) Context Table

Object	Description
contextIdentity	Unique identifier of a context.
contextIndex	A unique integer value associated with a context.
contextLocal	A Boolean value that specifies whether this context is realized by this manager or agent.
contextViewIndex	If zero, this row refers to a context which identifies a proxy relationship; otherwise, this row refers to a context that identifies an MIB view of a locally accessible entity, and the value of this object is an index into the View Table.
contextLocalEntity	If contextViewIndex is greater than 0, this value identifies the local entity whose management information is in the context's MIB view. The empty string indicates that the MIB view contains the entity's own local management information.
contextProxyDstParty	If contextViewIndex is equal to 0, this value identifies a party that is the proxy destination of a proxy relationship.
contextProxySrcParty	If contextViewIndex is equal to 0, this value identifies a party that is the proxy source of a proxy relationship.
contextProxyContext	If contextViewIndex is equal to 0, this value identifies the context of a proxy relationship.

(c) Access Control Table

Object	Description
aclTarget	The target SNMP party whose performance of management operations is constrained by this set of access privileges.
aclSubject	The subject SNMP party whose requests for management operations to be performed are constrained by this set of access privileges.
aclResources	A context in an access control policy.
aclPrivileges	An integer in the range 0 to 255 that encodes the access privileges for this (target, subject, context) triple.

(d) MIB View Table

Object	Description
viewIndex	A unique value for each MIB view.
viewSubtree	An MIB subtree.
viewMask	The bit mask which, in combination with the corresponding instance of viewSubtree, defines a family of view subtrees.
viewType	Takes on the values included(1), excluded(2). Indicates whether the corresponding family of view subtrees defined by viewSubtree and viewMask is included or excluded from the MIB view.

The party information includes authentication parameters that need to be applied to srcParty and privacy parameters that need to be applied to dstParty. The context table contains one entry for each context known to the agent. Each entry specifies whether the context is local, in which case the appropriate MIB view must be used, or remote, in which case the proxied device is indicated. The MIB view table is referenced by the contexts table. The appropriate entry defines a subset of the local MIB that is accessible through this context. Finally, each entry in the access control table has a unique combination of srcParty, dstParty, and context and indicates which management operations (which PDUs) are allowed for this combination.

Party MIB

The preceding discussion on access control gives an indication of the function of each of the four tables in the party MIB. In this section, we take a closer look at each table.

Party Table

The party table contains one entry for each party known to the local manager or agent. Each entry includes the authentication parameters (authProtocol, authClock, authPrivate, authPublic, authLifetime) and the privacy parameters (privProtocol, privPrivate, PrivPublic) that have been discussed earlier in this section. In particular, note that the clock value for this party is stored in this table. Once per second, the local manager or agent must increment the clock value of every entry in this table.

Most of the other fields indicated in Table 10.3a are self-explanatory. The cloneFrom field makes it possible for a manager to create new parties at an agent without needing to communicate all the parameters for that new party. Instead, the new party adopts the party table values of an existing party.

Context Table

The context table accommodates two kinds of entries: those that involve only local information and those that involve a proxy relationship. The kind of entry is determined by viewIndex:

- If viewIndex has a nonzero value, then the row refers to local information and the value is an index into the view table, thereby specifying the relevant MIB view. In this case, localEntity identifies the local entity whose management information is in the relevant MIB view; the local entity could be the SNMPv2 entity itself (empty string) or some other locally controlled entity (e.g., "Repeater 1"). The value of localTime identifies the temporal context.
- If contextViewIndex has a zero value, then the row refers to a proxy relationship. In this case, srcPartyIndex and dstPartyIndex are indexes into the party table for the source and destination parties for this proxy relationship, and proxyContext is the identifier of the context.

The relationships defined by the second item are illustrated in Figure 10.12 and can be explained as follows:

1. If a manager wishes to obtain management information from a remote entity by means of a proxy agent, it must issue its request to the proxy agent via SNMPv2. This requires the use a manager party, a proxy agent party, and a context. The context is sufficient to identify the proxied entity to be accessed.
2. The proxy agent assumes an SNMPv2 manager role in order to access the proxied agent on behalf of the original manager. For this purpose, a party at the proxy agent must interact with a party at the proxied agent, using some context.

Thus, four parties are involved in a native proxy relationship. The context invoked between manager and proxy agent must enable the proxy agent to determine the two parties and the context to be used between the proxy agent and a proxied agent. The access privileges available for the interaction between the parties at the proxy agent and proxied agent must also be known.

Access Control Table

The access control table is indexed by source party, destination party, and context. Thus, there is one entry for each combination of the three values for which access control privileges are defined. Each entry includes a field that defines the set of PDUs that the recipient will accept.

MIB View Table

In any manager or agent, management information is stored as a collection of objects that represent manageable resources. These objects are arranged in a tree structure to form the management information base (MIB) at the system.

For purposes of access control, the concepts of MIB view and view subtree are used. A view subtree consists of a node in the MIB tree plus all its subordinate elements. Each view subtree in the MIB view is specified as being included or ex-

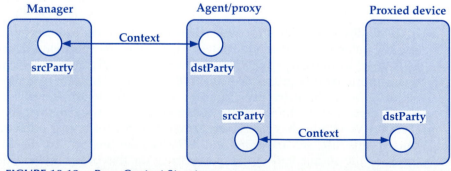

FIGURE 10.12. ProxyContext Structure

cluded. That is, the MIB view either includes or excludes all objects contained in that subtree. This specification technique provides a flexible but concise means of defining an MIB view.

The MIB view table consists of a collection of MIB views. Each MIB view is defined by a set of one or more rows in the table, all assigned the same index value. Each row corresponds to a subset of the local MIB, defined as follows:

- *Subtree:* Identifier of a specific node in the MIB. The subtree consists of that node plus all nodes below it in the MIB hierarchy.
- *Mask:* A bit mask that is used to further refine the subtree definition. In effect, the mask defines the subset of the subtree that is relevant.
- *Type:* Indicates whether the relevant portions of this subtree are to be included or excluded from the MIB view.

10.4

PROBLEMS

10.1 The selective clock acceleration algorithm requires that the slower clock be advanced to match the faster one. Would it also be acceptable to decrease the value of the clock that is ahead?

10.2 Figure 10.12 and the discussion in the book assume that the proxied device implements SNMPv2. This is known as a native proxy relationship. The SNMPv2 scheme also supports foreign proxy relationships, in which the proxy and proxied device communicate using some management protocol other than SNMPv2 native to the proxied device. In this case, it is not possible to define a context and to define parties at the proxied devices. Explain how such devices can be supported from the point of view of access control.

10.3 The following table summarizes the information that must be available in local tables to support the SNMPv2 protocol when the context is local:

	Local SNMPv2 Context	
	SNMPv2 Entity	Other Local Entity
SNMPv2 protocol information required	Party information (SNMPv2 protocol between manager party and agent party)	Party information (SNMPv2 protocol between manager party and agent party)
MIB information required	MIB View	MIB View
Access control information required	aclPrivileges (manager party, agent party, this context)	aclPrivileges (manager party, agent party, this context)

Now fill in the following table:

	Remove SNMPv2 Context	
	Foreign Proxy Relationship	Native Proxy Relationship
SNMPv2 protocol information required		
MIB information required		
Access control information required		

GLOSSARY

*In studying the Imperium, Arrakis, and the whole culture which produced Maud'Dib,
many unfamiliar terms occur. To increase understanding is a laudable goal, hence the
definitions and explanations given below.*

—*Dune*
Frank Herbert

Some of the terms in this glossary are from the *Glossary of Computer Security
Terminology* [NIST91]. These are indicated in the glossary by an asterisk.

Asymmetric Encryption.   A form of cryptosystem in which encryption and decryption are performed using two different keys, one of which is referred to as
the public key and one of which is referred to as the private key. Also known
as public-key encryption.

Authentication*.   A process used to verify the integrity of transmitted data, especially a message.

Authenticator.   Additional information appended to a message to enable the receiver to verify that the message should be accepted as authentic. The authenticator may be functionally independent of the content of the message itself
(e.g., a nonce or a source identifier), or it may be a function of the message
contents (e.g., a hash value or a cryptographic checksum).

Avalanche Effect.   A characteristic of an encryption algorithm in which a
small change in the plaintext or key gives rise to a large change in the ciphertext. For a hash code, the avalanche effect is a characteristic in which
a small change in the message gives rise to a large change in the message
digest.

Bacteria.   Program that consumes system resources by replicating itself.

Block Chaining.   A procedure used during block encryption that makes an output block dependent not only on the current plaintext input block and key
but also on earlier input, or output, or both. The effect of block chaining is that
two instances of the same plaintext input block will produce different ciphertext blocks, making cryptanalysis more difficult.

443

Cipher.   An algorithm for encryption and decryption. A cipher replaces a piece of information (an element in plaintext) with another object, with the intent to conceal meaning. Typically, the replacement rule is governed by a secret key.

Ciphertext.   The output of an encryption algorithm; the encrypted form of a message or data.

Code.   An unvarying rule for replacing a piece of information (e.g., letter, word, phrase) with another object, not necessarily of the same sort. Generally, there is no intent to conceal meaning. Examples include the ASCII character code (each character is represented by 7 bits) and frequency-shift keying (each binary value is represented by a particular frequency).

Computationally Secure.   Secure because the time or the cost or both of defeating the security is too high to be feasible.

Conventional Encryption.   Symmetric encryption.

Covert Channel.   A communications channel that enables the transfer of information in a way unintended by the designers of the communications facility.

Cryptanalysis.   The branch of cryptology dealing with the breaking of a cipher to recover information, or forging encrypted information that will be accepted as authentic.

Cryptographic Checksum.   An authenticator that is a cryptographic function of both the data to be authenticated and a secret key. Also referred to as a message authentication code (MAC).

Cryptography.   The branch of cryptology dealing with the design of algorithms for encryption and decryption, intended to ensure the secrecy and/or authenticity of messages.

Cryptology.   The study of secure communications, which encompasses both cryptography and cryptanalysis.

Decryption.   The translation of encrypted text or data (called ciphertext) into original text or data (called plaintext). Also called deciphering.

Differential Cryptanalysis.   A technique in which chosen plaintexts with particular XOR difference patterns are encrypted. The difference patterns of the resulting ciphertext provide information that can be used to determine the encryption key.

Digital Signature.   An authentication mechanism which enables the creator of a message to attach a code that acts as a signature. The signature guarantees the source and integrity of the message.

Discretionary Access Control*.   A means of restricting access to objects based on the identity of subjects and/or groups to which they belong. The controls are discretionary in the sense that a subject with a certain access permission is capable of passing that permission (perhaps indirectly) on to any other subject (unless restrained by mandatory access control).

Encryption.   The conversion of plaintext or data into unintelligible form by means of a reversible translation that is based on a translation table or algorithm. Also called enciphering.

Hash Function. A function that maps a variable-length data block or message into a fixed-length value called a hash code. The function is designed in such a way that, when protected, it provides an authenticator to the data or message. Also referred to as a message digest.

Initialization Vector. A random block of data that is used to begin the encryption of multiple blocks of plaintext when a block-chaining encryption technique is used. The IV serves to foil known-plaintext attacks.

Intruder. An individual who gains, or attempts to gain, unauthorized access to a computer system or to gain unauthorized privileges on that system.

Kerberos. The name given to Project Athena's code authentication service.

Key Distribution Center. A system that is authorized to transmit temporary session keys to principals. Each session key is transmitted in encrypted form, using a master key that the key distribution center shares with the target principal.

Logic Bomb. Logic embedded in a computer program that checks for a certain set of conditions to be present on the system. When these conditions are met, the logic bomb executes some function that results in unauthorized actions.

Mandatory Access Control. A means of restricting access to objects that is based on fixed security attributes assigned to users and to files and other objects. The controls are mandatory in the sense that they cannot be modified by users or their programs.

Master Key. A long-lasting key that is used between a key distribution center and a principal for the purpose of encoding the transmission of session keys. Typically, the master keys are distributed by noncryptographic means. Also referred to as a key-encrypting key.

Message Authentication Code (MAC). Cryptographic checksum.

Message Digest. Hash function.

Multilevel Security. A capability that enforces access control across multiple levels of classification of data.

Multiple Encryption. Repeated use of an encryption function, with different keys, to produce a more complex mapping from plaintext to ciphertext.

Nonce. An identifier or number that is used only once.

One-Way Function. A function that is easily computed, but the calculation of its inverse is infeasible.

Password*.   A character string used to authenticate an identity. Knowledge of the password and its associated user ID is considered proof of authorization to use the capabilities associated with that user ID.

Plaintext.   The input to an encryption function or the output of a decryption function.

Private Key.   One of the two keys used in a symmetric encryption system. For secure communication, the private key should be known only to its creator.

Pseudorandom Number Generator.   A function that deterministically produces a sequence of numbers that are apparently statistically random.

Public Key.   One of the two keys used in a symmetric encryption system. The public key is made public, to be used in conjunction with a corresponding private key.

Public-Key Encryption.   Asymmetric encryption.

Replay Attacks.   An attack in which a service already authorized and completed is forged by another "duplicate request" in an attempt to repeat authorized commands.

RSA Algorithm.   A public-key encryption algorithm based on exponentiation in modular arithmetic. It is the only algorithm generally accepted as practical and secure for public-key encryption.

Secret Key.   The key used in a symmetric encryption system. Both participants must share the same key, and this key must remain secret to protect the communication.

Session Key.   A temporary encryption key used between two principals.

Symmetric Encryption.   A form of cryptosystem in which encryption and decryption are performed using the same key. Also known as conventional encryption.

Trapdoor.   Secret undocumented entry point into a program, used to grant access without normal methods of access authentication.

Trapdoor One-Way Function.   A function that is easily computed, and the calculation of its inverse is infeasible unless certain privileged information is known.

Trojan Horse*.   A computer program with an apparently or actually useful function that contains additional (hidden) functions that surreptitiously exploit the legitimate authorizations of the invoking process to the detriment of security.

Trusted System.   A computer and operating system that can be verified to implement a given security policy.

Unconditionally Secure.   Secure even against an opponent with unlimited time and unlimited computing resources.

Virus. Code embedded within a program that causes a copy of itself to be inserted in one or more other programs. In addition to propagation, the virus usually performs some unwanted function.

Worm. Program that can replicate itself and send copies from computer to computer across network connections. Upon arrival, the worm may be activated to replicate and propagate again. In addition to propagation, the worm usually performs some unwanted function.

STANDARDS AND SPECIFICATIONS CITED IN THIS BOOK

ANSI Standards

Standard Number	Title	Date
ANSI X9.17	Financial Institution Key Management (Wholesale)	1985

CCITT Recommendations

Recommendation Number	Title	Date
X.509	The Directory - Authentication Framework	1988; revised 1993

Federal Information Processing Standards

FIPS PUB Number	Title	Date
46-2	Data Encryption Standard	June 1994
74	Guidelines for Implementing and Using the NBS Data Encryption Standard	April 1981
81	DES Modes of Operation	December 1980
112	Password Usage	May 1985
113	Computer Data Authentication	May 1985
180	Secure Hash Standard	May 1993
181	Automated Password Generator	December 1993
XX	Digital Signature Standard (draft)	February 1993

STANDARDS AND SPECIFICATIONS CITED IN THIS BOOK Continued

Internet RFCs

RFC Number	Title	Date
1157	A Simple Network Management Protocol	May 1990
1320	The MD4 Message-Digest Algorithm	April 1992
1321	The MD5 Message-Digest Algorithm	April 1992
1421	Privacy Enhancement for Internet Electronic Mail: Part I: Message Encryption and Authentication Procedures	February 1993
1422	Privacy Enhancement for Internet Electronic Mail: Part II: Certificate-Based Key Management	February 1993
1423	Privacy Enhancement for Internet Electronic Mail: Part III: Algorithms, Modes, and Identifiers	February 1993
1424	Privacy Enhancement for Internet Electronic Mail: Part IV: Key Certification and Related Services	February 1993
1445	Administrative Model for version 2 of the Simple Network Management Protocol (SNMPv2)	April 1993
1446	Security Protocols for version 2 of the Simple Network Management Protocol (SNMPv2)	April 1993
1447	Party MIB for version 2 of the Simple Network Management Protocol (SNMPv2)	April 1993
1510	The Kerberos Network Authentication Service	September 1993

ISO Standards

Standard Number	Title	Date
ISO 8732	Banking - Key Management (Wholesale)	1988

References

In matters of this kind everyone feels he is justified in writing and publishing the first thing that comes into his head when he picks up a pen, and thinks his own idea as axiomatic as the fact that two and two make four. If critics would go to the trouble of thinking about the subject for years on end and testing each conclusion against the actual history of war, as I have done, they would undoubtedly be more careful of what they wrote.

— *On War*
Carl von Clausewitz

ABRA87   Abrams, M., and Podell, H. *Computer and Network Security*. Los Alamitos, CA: IEEE Computer Society Press, 1987.

ADAM92   Adam, J. "Virus Threats and Countermeasures." *IEEE Spectrum*, August 1992.

AKL83   Akl, S. "Digital Signatures: A Tutorial Survey." *Computer*, February 1983.

ALVA90   Alvare, A. "How Crackers Crack Passwords or What Passwords to Avoid." *Proceedings, UNIX Security Workshop II*, August 1990.

ANDE80   Anderson, J. *Computer Security Threat Monitoring and Surveillance*. Fort Washington, PA: James P. Anderson Co., April 1980.

BARK91   Barker, W. *Introduction to the Analysis of the Data Encryption Standard (DES)*. Laguna Hills, CA: Aegean Park Press, 1991.

BASS92   Bassham, L., and Polk, W. *Threat Assessment of Malicious Code and External Attacks*. NISTIR 4939, National Institute of Standards and Technology, October 1992.

BAUE88   Bauer, D., and Koblentz, M. "NIDX—An Expert System for Real-Time Network Intrusion Detection." *Proceedings, Computer Networking Symposium*, April 1988.

BELL90   Bellovin, S., and Merritt, M. "Limitations of the Kerberos Authentication System." *Computer Communications Review*, October 1990.

BELL92   Bellovin, S. "There Be Dragons." *Proceedings, UNIX Security Symposium III*, September 1992.

BELL93   Bellovin, S. "Packets Found on an Internet." *Computer Communications Review*, July 1993.

BENA90   Ben-Artzi, A.; Chandna, A.; and Warrier, U. "Network Management of TCP/IP Networks: Present and Future." *IEEE Network Magazine*, July 1990.

BERS92   Berson, T. "Differential Cryptanalysis Mod 2^{32} with Applications to MD5." *Proceedings, EUROCRYPT '92*, May 1992; published by Springer-Verlag.

BETH91   Beth, T.; Frisch, M.; and Simmons, G., eds. *Public-Key Cryptography: State of the Art and Future Directions*. New York: Springer-Verlag, 1991.

449

BIHA93   Biham, E., and Shamir, A. *Differential Cryptanalysis of the Data Encryption Standard.* New York: Springer-Verlag, 1993.

BLOO70   Bloom, B. "Space/time Trade-offs in Hash Coding with Allowable Errors." *Communications of the ACM,* July 1970.

BOEB85   Boebert, W.; Kain, R.; and Young, W. "Secure Computing: The Secure Ada Target Approach." *Scientific Honeyweller,* July 1985. Reprinted in [ABRA87].

BOER93   Boer, B., and Bosselaers, A. "Collisions for the Compression Function of MD5." *Proceedings, EUROCRYPT '93,* 1993; published by Springer-Verlag.

BOWL92   Bowles, J., and Pelaez, C. "Bad Code." *IEEE Spectrum,* August 1992.

BRAZ94   Brazier, F., and Johansen, D. *Distributed Open Systems.* Los Alamitor, CA: IEEE Computer Society Press, 1994.

BRIC84   Brickell, E. "Breaking Iterated Knapsacks." *Proceedings, Crypto '84,* August 1984; published by Springer-Verlag.

BRIC93   Brickell, E.; Denning, D.; Kent, S.', and Maher, D. *SKIPJACK Review Interim Report: The SKIPJACK Algorithm.* July 28, 1993 report to the public; available from Georgetown University, Office of Public Affairs, Washington, DC.

BRIG79   Bright, H., and Enison, R. "Quasi-Random Number Sequences from Long-Period TLP Generator with Remarks on Application to Cryptography." *Computing Surveys,* December 1979.

BRYA88   Bryant, W. *Designing an Authentication System: A Dialogue in Four Scenes.* Project Athena document, February 1988. Reprinted in [CURR92].

CAMP92   Campbell, K, and Wiener, M. "Proof that DES is not a Group." *Proceedings, Crypto '92,* 1992; published by Springer-Verlag.

COHE90   Cohen, F. *A Short Course on Computer Viruses.* Pittsburgh, PA: ASP Press, 1990.

COOP89   Cooper, J. *Computer and Communications Security: Strategies for the 1990s.* New York: McGraw-Hill, 1989.

COPP92   Coppersmith, D. *The Data Encryption Standard (DES) and its Strength Against Attacks.* IBM Research Report RC 18613 (81421), T. J. Watson Research Center, December 1992.

CORM90   Cormen, T.; Leiserson, C.; and Rivest, R. *Introduction to Algorithms.* Cambridge, MA: MIT Press, 1990.

CURR92   Curry, D. *UNIX System Security.* Reading, MA: Addison-Wesley, 1992.

DAVI89   Davies, D., and Price, W. *Security for Computer Networks.* New York: Wiley, 1989.

DAVI93   Davies, C., and Ganesan, R. "BApasswd: A New Proactive Password Checker." *Proceedings, 16th National Computer Security Conference,* September 1993.

DENN81   Denning, D. "Timestamps in Key Distribution Protocols." *Communications of the ACM,* August 1981.

DENN82   Denning, D. *Cryptography and Data Security.* Reading, MA: Addison-Wesley, 1982.

DENN83   Denning, D. "Protecting Public Keys and Signature Keys." *Computer,* February 1983.

DENN87   Denning, D. "An Intrusion-Detection Model." *IEEE Transactions on Software Engineering,* February 1987.

DENN90   Denning, P. *Computers Under Attack: Intruders, Worms, and Viruses.* Reading, MA: Addison-Wesley, 1990.

DENN93   Denning, D. "The U. S. Key Escrow Encryption Technology." *Computer Communications,* to be published.

DIFF76a   Diffie, W., and Hellman, M. "Multiuser Cryptographic Techniques." *Proceedings of the AFIPS National Computer Conference,* June 1976.

DIFF76b Diffie, W., and Hellman, M. "New Directions in Cryptography." *IEEE Transactions on Information Theory,* November 1976.

DIFF77 Diffie, W., and Hellman, M. "Exhaustive Cryptanalysis of the NBS Data Encryption Standard." *Computer,* June 1977.

DIFF79 Diffie, W., and Hellman, M. "Privacy and Authentication: An Introduction to Cryptography." *Proceedings of the IEEE,* March 1979.

DIFF88 Diffie, W. "The First Ten Years of Public-Key Cryptography." *Proceedings of the IEEE,* May 1988. Reprinted in [SIMM92a].

ELGA85 ElGamal, T. "A Public-Key Cryptosystem and a Signature Scheme Based on Discrete Logarithms." *IEEE Transactions on Information Theory,* July 1985.

ENGE80 Enger, N., and Howerton, P. *Computer Security.* New York: Amacom, 1980.

FEIS73 Feistel, H. "Cryptography and Computer Privacy." *Scientific American,* May 1973.

FERB92 Ferbrache, D. *A Pathology of Computer Viruses.* New York: Springer-Verlag, 1992.

FREE93 Freedman, D. "The Goods on Hacker Hoods." *Forbes ASAP,* September 13, 1993.

FUMY93 Fumy, S., and Landrock, P. "Principles of Key Management." *IEEE Journal on Selected Areas in Communications,* June 1993.

GARD77 Gardner, M. "A New Kind of Cipher That Would Take Millions of Years to Break." *Scientific American,* August 1977.

GASS88 Gasser, M. *Building a Secure Computer System.* New York: Van Nostrand Reinhold, 1988.

GONG92 Gong, L. "A Security Risk of Depending on Synchronized Clocks." *Operating Systems Review,* January 1992.

GONG93 Gong, L. "Variations on the Themes of Message Freshness and Replay." *Proceedings, IEEE Computer Security Foundations Workshop,* June 1993.

GRAH89 Graham, R.; Knuth, D.; and Patashnik, O. *Concrete Mathematics: A Foundation for Computer Science.* Reading, MA: Addison-Wesley, 1989.

HAFN91 Hafner, K., and Markoff, J. *Cyberpunk: Outlaws and Hackers on the Computer Frontier.* New York: Simon & Schuster, 1991.

HAMM91 Hamming, R. *The Art of Probability for Scientists and Engineers.* Reading, MA: Addison-Wesley, 1991.

HEBE92 Heberlein, L.; Mukherjee, B.; and Levitt, K. "Internetwork Security Monitor: An Intrusion-Detection System for Large-Scale Networks." *Proceedings, 15th National Computer Security Conference,* October 1992.

HELD91 Held, G. *Data Compression.* New York: Wiley, 1991.

HELL78 Hellman, M. "An Overview of Public Key Cryptography." *IEEE Communications Magazine,* November 1978.

HOFF90 Hoffman, L., editor. *Rogue Programs: Viruses, Worms, and Trojan Horses.* New York: Van Nostrand Reinhold, 1990.

HRUS92 Hruska, J. *Computer Viruses and Anti-Virus Warfare.* New York: Ellis Horwood, 1992.

IANS90 I'Anson, C., and Mitchell, C. "Security Defects in CCITT Recommendation X.509 - The Directory Authentication Framework." *Computer Communications Review,* April 1990.

ILGU93 Ilgun, K. "USTAT: A Real-Time Intrusion Detection System for UNIX." *Proceedings, 1993 IEEE Computer Society Symposium on Research in Security and Privacy,* May 1993.

JAVI91 Javitz, H., and Valdes, A. "The SRI IDES Statistical Anomaly Detector." *Proceedings, 1991 IEEE Computer Society Symposium on Research in Security and Privacy,* May 1991.

JONE82 Jones, R. "Some Techniques for Handling Encipherment Keys." *ICL Technical Journal,* November 1982.

JUEN85   Jueneman, R.; Matyas, S.; and Meyer, C. "Message Authentication." *IEEE Communications Magazine,* September 1985.

JUEN87   Jueneman, R. "Electronic Document Authentication." *IEEE Network Magazine,* April 1987.

KAHN67   Kahn, D. *The Codebreakers: The Story of Secret Writing.* New York: Macmillan, 1967 (abridged edition, New York: New American Library, 1974).

KAPL93   Kaplan, R., and Kovara, J. "Psychological Subversion of Information Systems." *Information Systems Security,* Fall 1993.

KEHN92   Kehne, A.; Schonwalder, J.; and Langendorfer, H. "A Nonce-Based Protocol for Multiple Authentications" *Operating Systems Review,* October 1992.

KENT77   Kent, S. "Encryption-Based Protection for Interactive User/Computer Communication." *Proceedings of the Fifth Data Communications Symposium,* September 1977.

KENT93a   Kent, S. "Architectural Security," in [LYNC93].

KENT93b   Kent, S. "Internet Privacy Enhanced Mail." *Communications of the ACM,* August 1993.

KLEI90   Klein, D. "Foiling the Cracker: A Survey of, and Improvements to, Password Security." *Proceedings, UNIX Security Workshop II,* August 1990.

KNUT73   Knuth, D. *The Art of Computer Programming, Volume 1: Fundamental Algorithms.* Reading, MA: Addison-Wesley, 1973.

KNUT81   Knuth, D. *The Art of Computer Programming, Volume 2: Seminumerical Algorithms.* Reading, MA: Addison-Wesley, 1981.

KOBA78   Kobayashi, H. *Modeling and Analysis: An Introduction to Systems Performance Evaluation Methodology.* Reading, MA: Addison-Wesley, 1978.

KOBL87   Koblitz, N. *A Course in Number Theory and Cryptography.* New York: Springer-Verlag, 1987.

KOHL89   Kohl, J. "The Use of Encryption in Kerberos for Network Authentication." *Proceedings, Crypto '89,* 1989; published by Springer-Verlag.

KOHL94   Kohl, J.; Neuman, B.; and Ts'o, T. "The Evolution of the Kerberos Authentication Service," in [BRAZ94].

KOHN78   Kohnfelder, L. *Towards a Practical Public-Key Cryptosystem.* Bachelor's Thesis, M.I.T., May 1978.

KONH81   Konheim, A. *Cryptography: A Primer.* New York: Wiley, 1981.

LAI90   Lai, X., and Massey, J. "A Proposal for a New Block Encryption Standard." *Proceedings, EUROCRYPT '90,* 1990; published by Springer-Verlag.

LAI91   Lai, X., and Massey, J. "Markov Ciphers and Differential Cryptanalysis." *Proceedings, EUROCRYPT '91,* 1991; published by Springer-Verlag.

LAI92   Lai, X. *On the Design and Security of Block Ciphers.* Konstanz, Germany: Hartung-Gorre, 1992.

LAM92a   Lam, K., and Gollmann, D. "Freshness Assurance of Authentication Protocols" *Proceedings, ESORICS 92,* 1992; published by Springer-Verlag.

LAM92b   Lam, K., and Beth, T. "Timely Authentication in Distributed Systems" *Proceedings, ESORICS 92,* 1992; published by Springer-Verlag.

LAMP92   Lampson, B.; Abadi, M.; Burrows, M.; and Wobber, E. "Authentication in Distributed Systems: Theory and Practice. *ACM Transactions on Computer Systems,* November 1992.

LE93   Le, A.; Matyas. S.; Johnson, D.; and Wilkins, J. "A Public Key Extension to the Common Cryptographic Architecture." *IBM Systems Journal,* No. 3, 1993.

LEHM51   Lehmer, D. "Mathematical Methods in Large-Scale Computing." *Proceedings, 2nd Symposium on Large-Scale Digital Calculating Machinery,* Cambridge: Harvard University Press, 1951.

LEVE90   Leveque, W. *Elementary Theory of Numbers.* New York: Dover, 1990.

LEVY93   Levy, S. "Crypto Rebels." *Wired,* May/June 1993.

LEWI69   Lewis, P.; Goodman, A.; and Miller, J. "A Pseudo-Random Number Generator for the System/360" *IBM Systems Journal,* No. 2, 1969.

LUND89   Lundell, A. *Virus! The Secret World of Computer Invaders That Breed and Destroy.* Chicago: Contemporary Books, 1989.

LUNT88   Lunt, T., and Jagannathan, R. "A Prototype Real-Time Intrusion-Detection Expert System." *Proceedings, 1988 IEEE Computer Society Symposium on Research in Security and Privacy,* April 1988.

LYNC93   Lynch, D., and Rose, M. editors. *Internet System Handbook.* Reading, MA: Addison-Wesley, 1993.

MADR92   Madron, T. *Network Security in the '90s: Issues and Solutions for Managers.* New York: Wiley, 1992.

MADS93   Madsen, J. "World Record in Password Checking." Usenet, comp.security.misc newsgroup, August 18, 1993.

MATS93   Matsui, M. "Linear Cryptanalysis Method for DES Cipher." *Proceedings, EURO-CRYPT '93,* 1993; published by Springer-Verlag.

MATY91a   Matyas, S. "Key Handling with Control Vectors." *IBM Systems Journal,* No.2, 1991.

MATY91b   Matyas, S.; Le, A.; and Abraham, D. "A Key-Management Scheme Based on Control Vectors." *IBM Systems Journal,* No.2, 1991.

MERK78   Merkle, R., and Hellman, M. "Hiding Information and Signatures in Trap Door Knapsacks." *IEEE Transactions on Information Theory,* September 1978.

MERK79   Merkle, R. *Secrecy, Authentication, and Public Key Systems.* PhD Thesis, Stanford University, June 1979.

MERK81   Merkle, R., and Hellman, M. "On the Security of Multiple Encryption." *Communications of the ACM,* July 1981.

MERK90   Merkle, R. "A Fast Software One-Way Hash Function." *Journal of Cryptology,* Number 3, 1990.

MEYE82   Meyer, C., and Matyas, S. *Cryptography: A New Dimension in Computer Data Security.* New York: Wiley, 1982.

MEYE88   Meyer, C., and Schilling, M. "Secure Program Load with Modification Detection Code." *Proceedings, SECURICOM 88,* 1988.

MILL75   Miller, G. "Riemann's Hypothesis and Tests for Primality." *Proceedings of the Seventh Annual ACM Symposium on the Theory of Computing,* May 1975.

MILL88   Miller, S.; Neuman, B.; Schiller, J.; and Saltzer, J. "Kerberos Authentication and Authorization System." *Section E.2.1, Project Athena Technical Plan,* M.I.T. Project Athena, Cambridge, MA. 27 October 1988.

MITC89   Mitchell, C.; Walker, M.; and Rush, D. "CCITT/ISO Standards for Secure Message Handling." *IEEE Journal on Selected Areas in Communications,* May 1989.

MITC92   Mitchell, C.; Piper, F. ; and Wild, P. "Digital Signatures," in [SIMM92a].

MIYA90   Miyaguchi, S.; Ohta, K.; and Iwata, M. "Confirmation that Some Hash Functions Are Not Collision Free." *Proceedings, EUROCRYPT '90,* 1990; published by Springer-Verlag.

MULL81   Muller, W., and Nobauer, W. "Some Remarks on Public-Key Cryptography." *Studia Scientiarum Mathematicarum Hungarica,* v. 16, 1981.

MUNG92   Mungo, P., and Clough, B. *Approaching Zero: The Extraordinary Underworld of Hackers, Phreakers, Virus Writers, and Keyboard Criminals.* New York: Random House, 1992.

MURP90   Murphy, S. "The Cryptanalysis of FEAL-4 with 20 Chosen Plaintexts." *Journal of Cryptology,* No. 3, 1990.

MYER91   Myers, L. *Spycomm: Covert Communication Techniques of the Underground.* Boulder, CO: Paladin Press, 1991.

NECH92   Nechvatal, J. "Public Key Cryptography," in [SIMM92a].

NEED78   Needham, R., and Schroeder, M. "Using Encryption for Authentication in Large Networks of Computers." *Communications of the ACM,* December 1978.

NEUH93   Neuhaus, S. *Statistical Properties of IDEA Session Keys in PGP.* Unpublished report, available from author neuhaus@informatik.uni-kl.de, 13 June 1993.

NEUM90   Neumann, P. "Flawed Computer Chip Sold for Years." *RISKS-FORUM Digest,* Vol.10, No.54, October 18, 1990.

NEUM93a   Neuman, B., and Stubblebine, S. "A Note on the Use of Timestamps as Nonces." *Operating Systems Review,* April 1993.

NEUM93b   Neuman, B. "Proxy-Based Authorization and Accounting for Distributed Systems." *Proceedings of the 13th International Conference on Distributed Computing Systems,* May 1993.

NIST91   National Institute of Standards and Technology. *Glossary of Computer Security Terminology.* NISTIR 4659, 1991.

OORS90   Oorschot, P, and Wiener, M. "A Known-Plaintext Attack on Two-Key Triple Encryption." *Proceedings, EUROCRYPT '90,* 1990; published by Springer-Verlag.

ORE67   Ore, O. *Invitation to Number Theory.* Washington, DC: The Mathematical Association of America, 1967.

ORE76   Ore, O. *Number Theory and Its History.* New York: Dover 1976.

PARK88   Park, S., and Miller, K. "Random Number Generators: Good Ones are Hard to Find." *Communications of the ACM,* October 1988.

PATT87   Patterson, W. *Mathematical Cryptology for Computer Scientists and Mathematicians.* Totowa, NJ: Rowman & Littlefield, 1987.

PFLE89   Pfleeger, C. *Security in Computing.* Englewood Cliffs, NJ: Prentice-Hall, 1989.

POHL81   Pohl., I., and Shaw, A. *The Nature of Computation: An Introduction to Computer Science.* Rockville, MD: Computer Science Press, 1981.

POPE79   Popek, G., and Kline, C. "Encryption and Secure Computer Networks." *ACM Computing Surveys,* December 1979.

PORR92   Porras, P. *STAT: A State Transition Analysis Tool for Intrusion Detection.* Master's Thesis, University of California at Santa Barbara, July 1992.

PURS93   Purser, M. *Secure Data Networking.* Boston: Artech House, 1993.

RABI78   Rabin, M. "Digitalized Signatures," in *Foundations of Secure Computation,* DeMillo, R.; Dobkin, D.; Jones, A.; and Lipton, R., eds. New York: Academic Press, 1978.

RABI80   Rabin, M. "Probabilistic Algorithms for Primality Testing." *Journal of Number Theory,* December 1980.

RAND55   Rand Corporation. *A Million Random Digits.* New York: The Free Press, 1955.

RHEE94   Rhee, M. *Cryptography and Secure Communications.* New York: McGraw-Hill, 1994.

RIBE91   Ribenboim, P. *The Little Book of Big Primes.* New York: Springer-Verlag, 1991.

RIVE78   Rivest, R.; Shamir, A.; and Adleman, L. "A Method for Obtaining Digital Signatures and Public Key Cryptosystems." *Communications of the ACM,* February 1978.

RIVE90   Rivest, R. "The MD4 Message Digest Algorithm." *Proceedings, Crypto '90,* August 1990; published by Springer-Verlag.

RUSS91   Russel, D., and Gangemi, G. *Computer Security Basics.* Sebastopol, CA: O'Reilly & Associates, 1991.

SAFF93   Safford, D.; Schales, D.; and Hess, D. "The TAMU Security Package: An Ongoing Response to Internet Intruders in an Academic Environment." *Proceedings, UNIX Security Symposium IV,* October 1993.

SAUE81   Sauer, C., and Chandy, K. *Computer Systems Performance Modeling.* Englewood Cliffs, NJ: Prentice-Hall, 1981.

SCHN91   Schnorr, C. "Efficient Signatures for Smart Card." *Journal of Cryptology,* No. 3, 1991.

SCHN94   Schneier, B. *Applied Cryptography.* New York: Wiley, 1994.

SEBE89   Seberry, J., and Pieprzyk, J. *Cryptography: An Introduction to Computer Security.* Englewood Cliffs, NJ: Prentice-Hall, 1989.

SHAM82   Shamir, A. "A Polynomial Time Algorithm for Breaking the Basic Merkle-Hellman Cryptosystem." *Proceedings, Crypto '82,* August 1982; published by Springer-Verlag.

SIMM92a   Simmons, G., ed. *Contemporary Cryptology: The Science of Information Integrity.* Piscataway, NJ: IEEE Press, 1992.

SIMM92b   Simmons, G. "A Survey of Information Authentication." in [SIMM92a].

SIMM93   Simmons, G. "Cryptology." *Encyclopaedia Britannica,* 1993.

SINK66   Sinkov, A. *Elementary Cryptanalysis: A Mathematical Approach.* Washington, DC: The Mathematical Association of America, 1966.

SMIT93a   Smith, P. "LUC Public-Key Encryption: A Secure Alternative to RSA." *Dr. Dobb's Journal,* January 1993.

SMIT93b   Smith, P., and Lennon, M. "LUC: A New Public Key System." *Proceedings, Ninth International Conference on Information Security, IFIP/Sec,* 1993.

SNAP91   Snapp, S., et al., "A System for Distributed Intrusion Detection." *Proceedings, COMPCON Spring '91,* 1991.

SPAF89   Spafford, E.; Heaphy, K.; and Ferbrache, D. *Computer Viruses.* Arlington, VA: ADAPSO, 1989.

SPAF92a   Spafford, E. "Observing Reusable Password Choices." *Proceedings, UNIX Security Symposium III,* September 1992.

SPAF92b   Spafford, E. "OPUS: Preventing Weak Password Choices." *Computers and Security,* No. 3, 1992.

STAL93   Stallings, W. *SNMP, SNMPv2, and CMIP: The Practical Guide to Network Management Standards.* Reading, MA: Addison-Wesley, 1993.

STAL94a   Stallings, W. *Data and Computer Communications, Fourth Edition.* New York: Macmillan, 1994.

STAL94b   Stallings, W., and van Slyke, R. *Business Data Communications, Second Edition.* New York: Macmillan, 1994.

STAL95   Stallings, W. *Protect Your Privacy: the PGP User's Guide.* Englewood Cliffs, NJ: Prentice-Hall, 1995.

STEI88   Steiner, J.; Neuman, C.; and Schiller, J. "Kerberos: An Authentication Service for Open Networked Systems." *Proceedings of the Winter 1988 USENIX Conference,* February 1988.

STEP93   Stephenson, P. "Preventive Medicine." *LAN Magazine,* November 1993.

STER92   Sterling, B. *The Hacker Crackdown: Law and Disorder on the Electronic Frontier.* New York: Bantam, 1992.

STOL88   Stoll, C. "Stalking the Wily Hacker." *Communications of the ACM,* May 1988. Reprinted in [DENN90].

STOL89   Stoll, C. *The Cuckoo's Egg.* New York: Doubleday, 1989.

THOM84   Thompson, K. "Reflections on Trusting Trust (Deliberate Software Bugs)." Communications of the ACM, August 1984.

TIME90   Time, Inc. *Computer Security, Understanding Computers Series.* Alexandria, VA: Time-Life Books, 1990.

TIPP27   Tippett, L. *Random Sampling Numbers.* Cambridge, England: Cambridge University Press, 1927.

TSUD92   Tsudik, G. . "Message Authentication with One-Way Hash Functions." *Proceedings, INFOCOM '92,* May 1992.

TUCH79   Tuchman, W. "Hellman Presents No Shortcut Solutions to DES." *IEEE Spectrum,* July 1979.

VACC89   Vaccaro, H., and Liepins, G. "Detection of Anomalous Computer Session Activity." *Proceedings of the IEEE Symposium on Research in Security and Privacy,* May 1989.

VOYD83   Voydock, V., and Kent., S. "Security Mechanisms in High-Level Network Protocols." *Computing Surveys,* June 1983.

WAYN93   Wayner, P. "Should Encryption Be Regulated?" *Byte,* May 1993.

WEGE87   Wegenerm, I. *The Complexity of Boolean Functions.* New York: Wiley, 1987.

WIEN90   Wiener, M. "Cryptanalysis of Short RSA Secret Exponents." *IEEE Transactions on Information Theory,* vol IT-36, 1990.

WIEN93   Wiener, M. "Efficient DES Key Search." *Proceedings, Crypto '93,* 1993; published by Springer-Verlag.

WILL82   Williams, H. "A p+1 Method of Factoring." *Mathematics of Computation,* 39 (1982).

WOO92a   Woo, T., and Lam, S. "Authentication for Distributed Systems." *Computer,* January 1992.

WOO92b   Woo, T., and Lam, S. " 'Authentication' Revisited." *Computer,* April 1992.

YUVA79   Yuval, G. "How to Swindle Rabin." *Cryptologia,* July 1979.

ZENG91   Zeng, K.; Yang, C.; Wei, D.; and Rao, T. "Pseudorandom Bit Generators in Stream-Cipher Cryptography." *Computer,* February 1991.

ZIV77   Ziv, J., and Lempel, A. "A Universal Algorithm for Sequential Data Compression." *IEEE Transactions on Information Theory,* May 1977.

Index

Prentice Hall/Neodata
Order Processing Center
P.O. Box 11071
Des Moines, IA 50336-1071

ORDER FORM

Ship To:
(Please print or type)

Name _____

Co. _____

Address _____

_____

City _____ St _____ Zip _____

Bill To:
(If different from shipping address)

Name _____

Co. _____

Address _____

_____

City _____ St _____ Zip _____

Mail your order to the above address or call 800-374-1200 (in Iowa call 515-284-6751) or Fax 515-284-2607

Shipping Method (select one)
_____ UPS Ground
_____ 2nd Day Air
_____ Book Rate

Payment Method (select one)	
_____ Check	_____ Visa
_____ Bill Me	_____ MasterCard
_____	
Authorized Signature	
_____	_____
Card Number	Exp Date

(continued)

TEAR OUT THIS PAGE TO ORDER OTHER TITLES BY WILLIAM STALLINGS:

SEQ.	QTY.	ISBN	TITLE	PRICE	TOTAL
1	____	002-415495-4	Computer Organization and Architecture: Principles of Structure and Function, 3/E	$69.00	_____
2	____	002-415441-5	Data and Computer Communications, 4/E	$69.00	_____
3	____	002-415475-X	ISDN and Broadbased ISDN, 2/E	$62.00	_____
4	____	002-415465-2	Local and Metropolitan Area Networks, 4/E	$65.00	_____
5	____	002-415481-4	Operating Systems: Concepts and Examples	$63.00	_____
6	____	002-415433-4	Business Data Communications, 2/E	$54.00	_____